Anglais

B1 > C1

1re • Term

Cycle Terminal

# Shine Bright

Spécialité LLCER

## Anglais monde contemporain

W0398551


Sous la direction de **Corinne Escales**

**Corinne Escales**
IA – IPR
Académie de Versailles

**Clotilde Bellamy**
Professeure agrégée
Lycée Jean Jaurès, Châtenay-Malabry

**Élodie Deglos**
Professeure agrégée
Lycée Jules Ferry, Versailles

**Cyril Dowling**
Professeur agrégé
Lycée Ernest Ferroul, Lézignan-Corbières

**Alexandra Duret**
Professeure certifiée
Lycée Camille Claudel, Vauréal

**Eve Grandin**
Professeure agrégée
Lycée Bellevue, Le Mans

**Lynda Itouchène**
Professeure agrégée
Lycée Jean-Jacques Rousseau, Sarcelles

**Johan Jolier**
Professeur certifié
Lycée Dumont d'Urville, Maurepas

**Rebecca Oudin-Shannon**
Professeure agrégée
Lycée Jules Ferry, Versailles

**Laura Pires**
Professeure certifiée
Lycée Camille Saint-Saëns, Deuil-la-Barre

**Asvinie Ponnoussamy**
Professeure certifiée
Lycée Jean-Jacques Rousseau, Sarcelles

**Sophie Robin-Boudjenane**
Professeure certifiée
Lycée Louis Bascan, Rambouillet

**Odette Toneatti**
Professeure agrégée
Lycée Le Caousou, Toulouse

Avec la collaboration de **Juliette Hanrot**
Professeur agrégée d'Histoire
Diplômée de Sciences Po
Lycée François Villon, Paris
Auteure des pages *Landmarks*



SPEAKEASY NEWS

Nathan

# Focus sur... la spécialité LLCER Anglais, monde contemporain

**L'enseignement de spécialité LLCER Anglais, monde contemporain vise une exploration approfondie et une mise en perspective de la langue, des cultures et des sociétés de l'aire anglophone, ainsi qu'un enrichissement de ta compréhension de ton rapport aux autres et de tes représentations du monde. Il a également pour objectif de te préparer à l'enseignement supérieur et à la mobilité dans un espace européen et international élargi.**

**Le programme du cycle s'organise autour de 5 thématiques : *Savoirs, création, innovation* et *Représentations* en 1re ; *Faire société, Environnements en mutation* et *Relation au monde* en Term. Le niveau attendu est B2 en fin de 1re et C1 en fin de Term.**

| | B2 | C1 |
|---|---|---|
| **Écouter** | • Je peux comprendre des conférences et des discours assez longs et même suivre une argumentation complexe si le sujet m'en est relativement familier.<br>• Je peux comprendre la plupart des émissions de télévision sur l'actualité et les informations. Je peux comprendre la plupart des films en langue standard. | • Je peux comprendre un long discours même s'il n'est pas clairement structuré et que les articulations sont seulement implicites.<br>• Je peux comprendre les émissions de télévision et les films sans trop d'effort. |
| **Lire** | • Je peux lire des articles et des rapports sur des questions contemporaines dans lesquels les auteurs adoptent une attitude particulière ou un certain point de vue.<br>• Je peux comprendre un texte littéraire contemporain en prose. | • Je peux comprendre des textes factuels ou littéraires longs et complexes et en apprécier les différences de style.<br>• Je peux comprendre des articles spécialisés et de longues instructions techniques même lorsqu'ils ne sont pas en relation avec mon domaine. |
| **Interagir à l'oral** | • Je peux communiquer avec un degré de spontanéité et d'aisance qui permet une interaction normale avec un locuteur compétent dans la langue cible.<br>• Je peux participer activement à une conversation dans des situations familières, présenter et défendre mes opinions. | • Je peux m'exprimer spontanément et couramment sans trop montrer que je cherche mes mots.<br>• Je peux utiliser la langue de manière souple et efficace pour des relations sociales ou professionnelles.<br>• Je peux exprimer mes idées et opinions avec précision et lier mes interventions à celles de mes interlocuteurs. |
| **Interagir à l'écrit** | • Je peux interagir avec plusieurs personnes, relier mes contributions aux leurs et gérer les malentendus ou les désagréments, à condition que les autres évitent un langage compliqué, me laissent du temps et soient coopératifs.<br>• Je peux mettre en valeur la signification de faits, d'événements et d'expériences, justifier des idées et coopérer efficacement. | • Je peux comprendre les intentions et les implications de contributions sur des questions complexes et abstraites et je peux m'exprimer clairement et avec précision et adapter avec souplesse mon langage et mon registre de façon efficace.<br>• Je peux gérer efficacement les problèmes de communication et les problèmes culturels qui surviennent, en clarifiant et en donnant des exemples. |
| **Parler en continu** | • Je peux faire des descriptions claires et détaillées sur une grande gamme de sujets relatifs à mes centres d'intérêt.<br>• Je peux développer un point de vue sur un sujet d'actualité et expliquer les avantages et les inconvénients de différentes possibilités. | • Je peux présenter des descriptions claires et détaillées de sujets complexes, en intégrant des thèmes qui leur sont liés, en développant certains points et en terminant mon intervention de façon appropriée. |
| **Écrire** | • Je peux écrire des textes clairs et détaillés sur une grande gamme de sujets relatifs à mes intérêts.<br>• Je peux écrire un essai ou un rapport en transmettant une information ou en exposant des raisons pour ou contre une opinion donnée. | • Je peux m'exprimer dans un texte clair et bien structuré et développer longuement mon point de vue.<br>• Je peux écrire sur des sujets complexes dans un essai ou un rapport, en soulignant les points que je juge importants.<br>• Je peux écrire différents types de textes et adopter un style adapté au destinataire. |
| **Médiation** | • Je peux transmettre de façon fiable des informations détaillées et des arguments, issus de textes complexes mais bien structurés, dans mes domaines d'intérêt.<br>• Je peux inviter les participants à réagir aux idées des uns et des autres ou leur demander de développer leur pensée et de préciser leurs opinions.<br>• Je peux développer les idées des autres et les relier à un raisonnement cohérent, en considérant les deux côtés d'un problème.<br>• Je peux contribuer à la création d'une culture communicative commune en adaptant ma façon de procéder, apprécier différentes idées, impressions et points de vue, et inviter les participants à réagir aux idées des uns et des autres.<br>• Je peux donner la signification de propos et de points de vue importants sur des sujets de mon domaine d'intérêt, à condition que les participants clarifient si besoin est. | • Je peux médier une culture communicative commune en gérant les ambiguïtés, en montrant que je suis sensible à différents points de vue, et en dissipant les malentendus.<br>• Je peux communiquer des informations significatives de façon claire, aisée et précise, et expliquer de la même façon des références culturelles.<br>• Je peux être persuasif avec tact. |

*Volume complémentaire avec de nouveaux descripteurs du CECRL, février 2018*


ISBN 978-209-178177-8

# Bienvenue dans ton manuel de Shine Bright 1re • Term Anglais, monde contemporain

Tu as choisi cette spécialité afin d'approfondir ta connaissance du monde anglophone et de continuer à progresser dans ta maîtrise de la langue pour atteindre un niveau C1. Ce manuel t'accompagnera dans cette découverte passionnante !

## Pourquoi un manuel de cycle ?

Même si chaque année du cycle a ses thématiques propres (*cf.* p. 2), le principe de l'enseignement de spécialité est qu'**il se déploie sur les deux années du cycle terminal**.

**Tu as donc deux ans pour enrichir tes connaissances, développer tes compétences langagières et appréhender les enjeux de cet enseignement**, avant d'aboutir aux épreuves du baccalauréat, dont certaines (oral d'anglais et Grand Oral), peuvent porter sur les thématiques de Première comme de Terminale.

C'est pourquoi un manuel de cycle est particulièrement adapté : ses contenus ont été pensés afin de **t'amener progressivement vers le niveau de connaissances et de compétences attendu** en fin de Terminale.

## Que vas-tu découvrir dans ce manuel ?

- L'enseignement de LLCER Anglais, monde contemporain **vise à te donner des clés pour comprendre et appréhender le monde anglophone et son inscription dans le monde contemporain**. C'est dans cette optique que nous avons conçu les différents chapitres qui proposent une grande variété de documents **ancrés dans l'actualité**, mais également de **contextualisation** ou d'**inscription dans l'histoire contemporaine**.

- **Pour chaque axe d'étude du programme**, tu découvriras **des problématiques variées** à travers **un *File* et un *Snapfile***. Par ailleurs, tu trouveras à la fin de ton manuel des doubles pages ***Landmarks***, conçues de manière visuelle et synthétique pour te donner **les repères géopolitiques, économiques, sociaux et culturels indispensables**.

## Quels outils te sont proposés pour préparer les épreuves du baccalauréat ?

Afin de t'accompagner pas à pas vers la réussite de ces épreuves, tu trouveras dans ton manuel des pages pour...

**... t'informer :** le guide du lycéen te dit tout sur le calendrier et le détail des épreuves que tu auras à passer, que tu choisisses de ne pas continuer la spécialité en fin de première ou que tu la conserves en terminale.

**... te fournir des outils méthodologiques :** les pages play BAC dans les *Snapfiles* et Objectif BAC à la fin de ton manuel te donneront les clés pour aborder les épreuves écrites et orales sereinement.

**... t'entraîner :** à la fin de chaque *File*, des pages Vers le BAC te permettront de mener une réflexion sur les problématiques soulevées par les documents, d'approfondir la thématique grâce à des documents complémentaires et de t'exercer en vue de l'épreuve orale d'anglais et du Grand oral.

**... t'évaluer :** pour chaque thématique du programme de Première, et dans chaque *File* de Terminale, tu disposeras d'un sujet de type Bac complet pour l'épreuve écrite.

Nous te souhaitons un voyage culturel et linguistique passionnant avec Shine Bright 1re • Term Anglais, monde contemporain

Les auteurs

# À la découverte de ton manuel

## Pour découvrir et comprendre

**Dans ton manuel**, chaque chapitre comporte plusieurs pages de documents pour découvrir et approfondir les différents enjeux de la problématique.

### À quoi sert la page d'ouverture ?

- Elle te permet de découvrir la **problématique de l'unité**, en lien avec une thématique et un axe du programme, et d'annoncer le projet final que tu auras à réaliser.
- Le/Les premier(s) document(s) te permet(tent) ensuite de **plonger dans le vif du sujet**.

### Comment fonctionnent les autres pages de documents ?

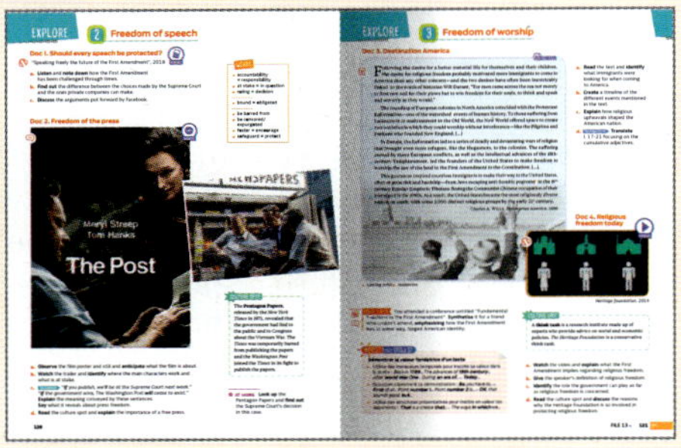


- Chaque page ou double page traite d'un des aspects de la problématique de départ à travers plusieurs **documents authentiques**. Elle propose des activités de réception, de production et de médiation.
- La rubrique ***Your task*** te propose une tâche à réaliser suite à l'étude d'un ou plusieurs document(s). Pour cette tâche, deux ***Ways*** sont parfois présentés afin de te laisser le choix. Cette tâche est toujours accompagnée d'une boîte ***Boost your skills*** pour t'aider à améliorer ta production.
- Les rubriques ***Going further*** et ***At home*** te donnent des pistes pour approfondir en classe ou à la maison.

### Comment fonctionnent les *Snapfiles* ?

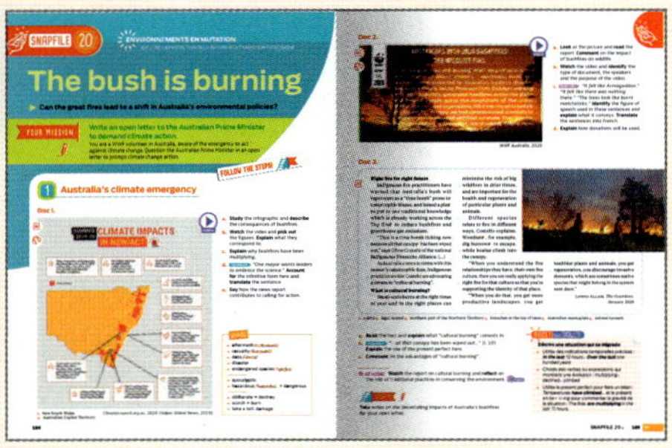


- Ces chapitres **plus courts** te proposent d'aborder des problématiques plus resserrés à travers une suite de **documents variés**.

### Comment les pages *Landmarks* s'articulent-elles avec les chapitres ?

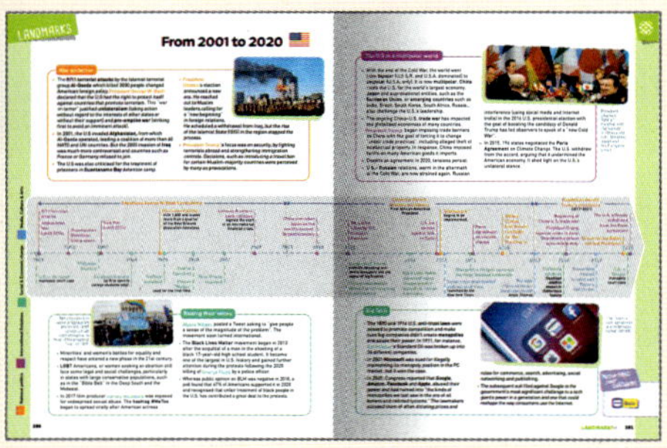


- Ces pages te proposent **une vision synthétique** des événements politiques, économiques, sociaux et culturels d'une période dans un pays ou une aire anglophone donné(e). Dans les chapitres, des renvois à ces pages te permettent de compléter, d'éclairer ou d'approfondir l'étude des documents.
- Elles peuvent aussi **te donner des pistes lors de la construction de ton dossier personnel** et être **un outil précieux pour préparer l'oral**.

## Pour progresser et t'entraîner

### Quels outils sont à ta disposition pour approfondir ta maîtrise des outils linguistiques ?

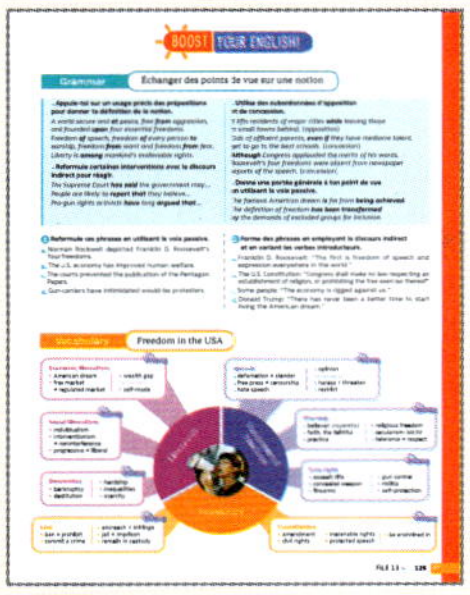

- Au sein des pages de documents, un **travail linguistique en contexte** est présent via des questions GRAMMAR VOCABULARY PHONOLOGY SPELLING et TRANSLATION.
- Les outils grammaticaux sont **récapitulés de manière synthétique** pour te permettre de les **mobiliser à bon escient**.
- Le lexique de chaque dossier est également récapitulé sous forme de **cartes mentales**.

### Quels sont les outils méthodologiques à ta disposition ?

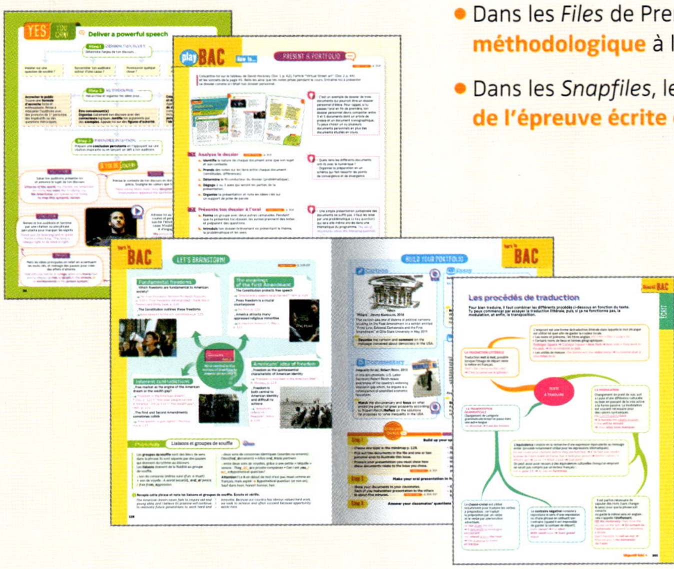

Différents types de pages sont prévus pour t'accompagner vers le Bac :

- Dans les *Files* de Première, les pages YES YOU CAN te fournissent **un accompagnement méthodologique** à la production orale ou écrite de la tâche finale.
- Dans les *Snapfiles*, les pages play BAC proposent **un focus guidé sur une partie de l'épreuve écrite ou orale** (synthèse, traduction, dossier…)
- Les pages Vers le BAC t'entraînent progressivement à la constitution et la présentation d'un dossier documentaire en vue de **l'épreuve orale d'anglais** et à la présentation d'une question de connaissance en vue du **Grand oral**.
- Le dossier **Objectif Bac** en fin de manuel te fournit **une explication pas à pas de chaque épreuve** (écrit, oral de spécialité et Grand oral), ainsi que **trois exemples de questions traitées** pour le Grand oral.

## Pour t'évaluer

### Où se trouvent les sujets de Bac écrit ?

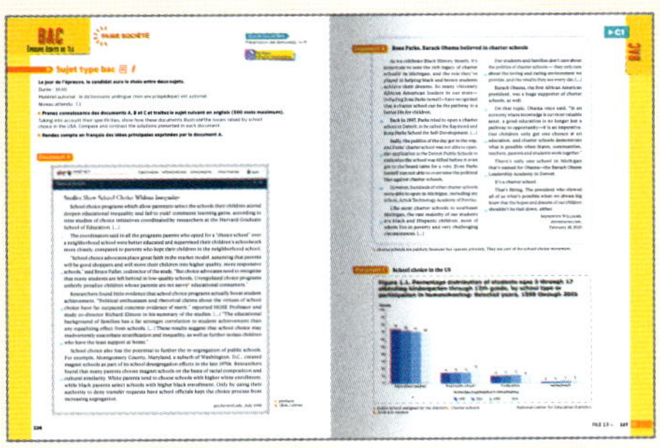

- Pour chaque thématique du programme de Première, un **sujet d'écrit type Bac** t'est proposé pour commencer à te familiariser avec l'épreuve écrite de Terminale.
- Dans chaque *File* de Terminale, **un sujet d'écrit complet** te permettra de **t'entraîner en conditions réelles**.

## Les pictos de ton manuel

- Compréhension de l'oral
- Compréhension de l'écrit
- Expression orale en continu
- Expression écrite
- Expression orale en interaction
- Expression écrite en interaction
- MÉDIATION : Médiation écrite ou orale
- VIDÉO / AUDIO : Document vidéo ou audio
- EXO Quiz : Activités numériques
- Fiche, texte ou sujet de bac téléchargeable sur le site compagnon
- AUDIO / VIDÉO : Lien vers un document sur Internet (vidéo, audio, texte…)
- OBJECTIF BAC : Renvoi aux pages de méthodologie en fin de manuel
- LANDMARKS : Renvoi aux pages *Landmarks* en fin de manuel

# SOMMAIRE 1re

● Thématique du programme
● Axe d'étude

# SOMMAIRE Tle

- Thématique du programme
- Axe d'étude

80
km/h
THE
IRISH
UNITY
SOLUTION
TO BREXIT
#TIME4UNITY

# SOMMAIRE Tle

● Thématique du programme
● Axe d'étude

# SOMMAIRE Tle

● Thématique du programme
● Axe d'étude

## FILE 27

● RELATION AU MONDE ● Axe 3 : Héritage commun et diversité

### Colours of Louisiana

▶ **How does Louisiana rely on its cultural diversity to stand out?**

EXPLORE

1. The free spirit of Louisiana
2. A rich legacy to preserve
3. Authenticity at risk
4. Where culture means business

BOOST YOUR SKILLS!

- Célébrer la diversité
- Évoquer l'influence du passé
- Exprimer des craintes

PHONOLOGY Rythme et accentuation dans les énoncés

FINAL TASK

**Make a TED Talk** to praise Louisiana's heritage and cultural diversity.

Vers le BAC — ÉPREUVE ÉCRITE Sujet type Bac — ÉPREUVE ORALE ● Let's brainstorm ● Build your portfolio

## SNAP FILE 28

● RELATION AU MONDE ● Axe 3 : Héritage commun et diversité

### Captain Pacific

▶ **To what extent is Captain Cook a national hero?**

1. A controversial legacy
2. Restoring the missing part of history

BOOST YOUR SKILLS!

- Attirer l'attention sur des faits
- Captiver l'attention du lecteur pour convaincre

YOUR MISSION

**Write an op-ed** on the controversy regarding Cook's voyages.

FOLLOW THE STEPS!

play BAC — ÉPREUVE ORALE Present a portfolio

Vers le BAC — ÉPREUVE ORALE Build your portfolio

## LANDMARKS

## LES REPÈRES GÉOPOLITIQUES, ÉCONOMIQUES, SOCIAUX ET CULTURELS ESSENTIELS

## Objectif BAC — DES FICHES PRATIQUES POUR PRÉPARER LES ÉPREUVES DU BAC

### VERS L'ÉPREUVE ÉCRITE



### VERS L'ÉPREUVE ORALE



### VERS LE GRAND ORAL



### SUJETS TYPE BAC COMPLÉMENTAIRES



## Animation interactive — DES CARTES INTERACTIVES

LES ÉPREUVES DU BAC DE TA SPÉCIALITÉ

# ÉPREUVE ORALE DE PREMIÈRE

Les élèves qui abandonnent la spécialité LLCER en fin de 1re

## PRÉSENTATION D'UN DOSSIER PERSONNEL

3e trimestre de 1re

20 min sans préparation

- Pour cette épreuve, tu devras avoir préparé un **dossier personnel**. Composé de 3 à 5 documents textuels et/ou iconographiques, il devra se rattacher à une ou plusieurs thématiques du programme de Première. Le dossier devra inclure au moins un texte de presse, un texte d'une autre nature et un document iconographique.
- Tu remettras ce dossier à l'examinateur et tu auras alors **10 minutes** pour en justifier les choix et en exprimer la logique interne.
- L'examinateur te posera ensuite des questions pendant environ **10 minutes**.

- Note sur 20 points
- Niveau attendu : B2

**Critères d'évaluation de la présentation**

- Voir les critères de l'épreuve orale d'anglais de Terminale p. 15

# ÉPREUVES DE TERMINALE

## L'ÉPREUVE ÉCRITE

### SYNTHÈSE D'UN DOSSIER DOCUMENTAIRE ET TRADUCTION

Mars de l'année de Term

3 h 30

L'épreuve écrite de Terminale est constituée de deux parties :

- **La synthèse d'un dossier documentaire** (**partie 1**) composé de 3 à 4 documents, dont au moins un texte de presse, liés à l'une des thématiques du programme de Terminale.
- Ta synthèse sera guidée par deux ou trois consignes. Elle pourra être complétée par un écrit de type argumentatif, l'ensemble n'excédant pas 500 mots.
- **La traduction** ou **la transposition** en français (**partie 2**) d'un passage de l'un des textes du dossier.
- Tu auras le droit d'utiliser un dictionnaire d'anglais unilingue non encyclopédique.

**Critères d'évaluation de la synthèse et de l'écrit argumentatif**

- Qualité du contenu (prise en compte des différents documents ; capacité à les analyser, les interpréter et les rattacher à la thématique du programme ; apport de connaissances (inter)culturelles)
- Cohérence de la construction du discours (clarté et structure ; approche comparative)
- Correction de la langue écrite
- Richesse du lexique employé

**Critères d'évaluation de la traduction / transposition**

- Qualité de la traduction (clarté, transmission correcte des éléments du texte d'origine)
- Qualité de la transposition : restitution de l'essentiel des idées de manière claire et structurée
- Correction de la langue écrite

- Note sur 20 points (16 pour la synthèse et 4 pour la traduction / transposition)
- Niveau attendu : C1

## L'ÉPREUVE ORALE D'ANGLAIS

### PRÉSENTATION D'UN DOSSIER PERSONNEL

Pour cette épreuve, tu devras avoir préparé un **dossier personnel**. Composé de 4 à 6 documents textuels et/ou iconographiques, il devra se rattacher à une ou plusieurs thématiques du programme du cycle terminal. Le dossier devra inclure au moins un texte de presse, au plus deux textes d'une autre nature et deux documents iconographiques.

Mars de l'année de Term

20 min sans préparation

Tu remettras ce dossier à l'examinateur et tu auras alors **10 minutes** pour en justifier les choix et en exprimer la logique interne, c'est-à-dire comment il répond à la problématique que tu auras posée au départ.

L'examinateur te posera ensuite des questions pendant environ **10 minutes**.

- Jury : un enseignant d'anglais
- Note sur 20 points
- Niveau attendu : C1

**Critères d'évaluation**

- Expression orale (organisation, pertinence et fluidité du discours)
- Interaction orale (capacité à argumenter et à relancer une discussion)
- Correction de la langue orale (correction de la prononciation et de l'accentuation)
- Richesse de la langue (variété et niveau de précision du lexique et des structures employés)

## L'ÉPREUVE ORALE TERMINALE

### LE GRAND ORAL

Pour cette épreuve, tu devras avoir préparé une question liée au programme de cycle terminal de chacune de tes spécialités (prises isolément ou de manière transversale).

Juin de l'année de Term

40 min dont 20 min de préparation

Le jour de l'épreuve, tu présenteras au jury tes deux questions sur une feuille signée par tes professeurs. Le jury en choisira une et tu disposeras alors de **20 minutes** pour préparer ton oral, pendant lesquelles tu pourras réaliser, si tu le souhaites, un support que tu remettras au jury (support non évalué).

Tu auras ensuite **5 minutes** pour présenter ta question au jury en français ou en partie en anglais. Cette présentation se fera sans note et debout.

Suite à ta présentation, le jury aura **10 minutes** pour te poser des questions et t'amener à approfondir ou à préciser ta pensée. Cet échange peut aussi porter sur d'autres éléments du programme de spécialité. Tu pourras rester debout ou t'asseoir.

Pour conclure, tu auras **5 minutes** pour expliquer au jury en quoi la question traitée éclaire ton projet de poursuite d'études, voire ton projet professionnel.

- Jury : 2 enseignants
- Note sur 20 points

**Critères d'évaluation**

- Qualité orale (débit, fluidité, variations et nuances du discours)
- Qualité de la prise de parole en continu (clarté, pertinence, efficacité de la prise de parole)
- Qualité des connaissances (maîtrise des connaissances, capacité à les mobiliser à bon escient)
- Qualité de l'interaction (capacité à répondre aux questions et prendre l'initiative dans l'échange)
- Qualité et construction de l'argumentation (maîtrise des enjeux du sujet, capacité à argumenter de manière construite et raisonnée)

FILE 1

SAVOIRS, CRÉATION, INNOVATION

AXE 1 : PRODUCTION ET CIRCULATION DES SAVOIRS

# e-Educated?

▶ **How can online learning contribute to developing education in English-speaking countries?**

**FINAL TASK** Record a video commercial to promote an e-education programme.

More on SPEAKEASY NEWS speakeasy-news.com

## 1 The rise of online learning

**Doc 1.**

VIDÉO

**PERCENTAGE OF U.S. UNIVERSITY STUDENTS ENROLLED IN DISTANCE EDUCATION**

| | 2016-2017 | 2017-2018 | 2018-2019 |
|---|---|---|---|
| **Enrolled only in distance-education courses** | 14.7% | 15.4% | 16.3% |
| **Enrolled in some distance-education courses** | 16.5% | 17.6% | 18.4% |
| **Total** | 31.2% | 33% | 34.7% |

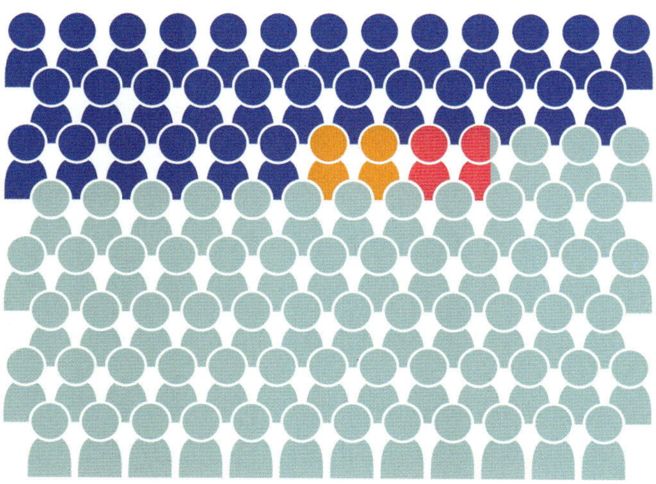

Source: National Center for Education Statistics

"The future of education?", *Study Portals HQ*, 2020

**a. Observe** the table and **describe** the evolution.

**b. Watch** the video and **say** why the Covid-19 pandemic has had a major influence on online learning.

**c.** PHONOLOGY **Focus** on the adverbs *'so', 'even', 'next', 'also'* and *'furthermore'*. **Explain** why they are stressed.

**d. Explain** why the development of online courses may benefit students.

**WORDS**

- **a**sset
- at your f**i**ngertips
- v**i**rtual gu**i**dance

- bene**fi**cial
- imp**e**lling = str**i**king
- t**i**me-saving

- boost
- enh**a**nce = incr**ea**se (producti**v**ity)
- gain new skills

## Doc 2. University for all

VIDÉO

*The Open University*, 2016

**CULTURE SPOT**

**The Open University**, established in 1969, is the UK's largest academic institution and a world pioneer in distance learning. It was founded to give those who had missed out on attending traditional universities the opportunity to experience high-quality degree-level learning.

**a.** **Watch** the video and **find** information about Simon.

**b.** GRAMMAR **Focus** on the modal auxiliaries: *"I **couldn't** have been any lower at the time"/ "I **couldn't** afford to quit my job"*. **Explain** what they express.

**c.** **Explain** the advantages of the Open University.

**d.** Would you apply to the Open University? **Give** your reasons.

**YOUR TASK** Simon visits the headmaster he worked for, to **tell** him about his success thanks to the Open University. **Imagine** the conversation.

**BOOST YOUR SKILLS!**

**Présenter une expérience**

- Situe les faits dans le temps : ***As a kid**, all I wanted to be...* • *So, **when** I finally got to join...* • ***One night**, I slipped.* • ***Within a few weeks**...*
- Utilise des comparatifs et des superlatifs pour exprimer des changements positifs : *The OU was **the best** option for me.* • *Employees are **more productive** when they work together.* • *For a **better** end product.*
- Remercie, montre ton appréciation : *I'm really **grateful**.* • *It was an **opportunity** for me.* • *This is my **dream job**.*

## Doc 3.

SALES ACADEMY — Your Academy | About Us | Resources

### How are Top Fortune 500 companies using e-learning to boost productivity?

41.7% of the most profitable companies in the world, listed in the Fortune 500, are currently using e-learning tools for online training. Such solutions are helpful for training new employees and at the same time help to make ongoing employee education both affordable and effective. [...]

24% of respondents blamed the Google search engine for taking their time away from work, followed by Facebook, which represents 23% of respondents. Adopting a comprehensive e-learning solution can help to remove this temptation by creating resources for employees to find what they're seeking quicker.

Employees usually think of training sessions as a sleepy boardroom[1] scenario. However, this is not the case if you give employees the opportunity to be trained online from their computer or tablet, on their own schedule.

In fact, the flexibility and efficiency of learning management systems allows employees to get far more from 30 minutes at their desks than an afternoon in a traditional setting. [...]

Enthusiastic employees leads to productive employees, and e-learning serves as a platform to help build eagerness and engagement among teams.

It has been proven that employees are more productive when they work together, but without the tools for collaboration, managers can't always expect workers to automatically solicit colleague input. Using e-learning as a method to train and share information enables employees to ask questions and feel comfortable working together for a better end product.

Sales Academy website, April 2019

**a.** **Read** the text, **focus** on the source and **identify** its objective.

**b.** VOCABULARY **Pick out** all the positive adjectives and **find** a synonym. What do they reveal about the strategy of communication?

**c.** **Explain** the advantages of e-learning, according to the article.

**d.** **Discuss** the efficiency and the limits of this strategy.

**CULTURE SPOT**

Check what you know about online learning.

EXO Quiz

1. meeting room

## Doc 1.

Satish ACHARYA, July 2020

### Here's how online teaching can reshape education in rural India

INDIA TODAY

Online education plays a crucial role in the current setting, where every student (especially in rural areas) doesn't have equal access to educational infrastructure. It levels the playing field[1] for all students by providing them an equal and accessible platform to receive education.

India is home to 30 million children in the age group of 0-18 years with a considerable number of students residing in rural settings. The status of education in the rustic villages of India is deplorable, evidently.

There are several challenges faced by children and students alike, including archaic teaching methods, shortage of teachers, poor teacher-to-students ratio and outdated teaching material.

Although with the surge in digitisation of education during recent times, it has become plausible to mitigate the above-mentioned challenges. Providing multimedia teaching tools to teachers and students and utilizing smart-classroom equipment like virtual classrooms, digital boards[2], digital teaching systems, digital content, digital language labs, etc can help teachers boost education scenarios in rural settings.

At the same time, digitisation of education can make it feasible for one teacher to deliver information remotely across various locations via virtual classrooms.

Although the teachers and students in rural India have become accepting to the implementation of technology to deliver quality education, the basic ground realities pose as a barrier in the way of complete digitization of education [...]

With the current scenario of Covid-19, it has become the need of the hour to resort to modern means of learning since most of the educational institutes have been shut since the end of March.

There's a looming uncertainty about when the schools, universities and colleges can resume[3] functioning at a normal capacity. At such time, focus has been shifted to virtual education and online learning that provide limitless opportunities to students to receive education remotely.

With the synergy of the public and private sector in education, rural areas have been equipped with multimedia teaching tools, digital classrooms and have facilities to learn through e-lectures. This partnership is also helping mitigate the problem of the shortage of teachers in schools.

Kiran DHAM, CEO, Globus Infocom, *India Today,* June 2020

1. make more equal 2. *tableau blanc interactif* 3. start again

**WORDS**

- cutting-edge technology = advanced technology
- outback = remote, rural region of Australia
- alternative /ɔːˈlɜːnətɪv/
- effective = efficient
- isolated
- achieve knowledge
- be enrolled

a. **Pick out** elements in the cartoon referring to e-learning and **explain** the general message.
b. **Read** the text and **explain** the challenges in rural India.
c. **Focus** on Kiran Dham's status and **discuss** the relevance of digital initiatives highlighted in the text.
d. **Comment** on the solutions offered by e-education.

## Doc 2. Australia's School of the air

*nbn Australia*, 2018

**CULTURE SPOT**

**School of the Air** refers to schools in Australia where children who live in remote areas to use electronic devices to communicate with teachers and classmates. These schools have existed since 1951.

**YOUR TASK** You are a student at Mount Isa School of the Air and you **make** a podcast about your school.

DIFFÉRENCIATION

**WAY 1** **Say** what you like the most and **give** the advantages of e-learning.

**WAY 2** **Explain** the advantages and disadvantages of e-learning.

**BOOST YOUR SKILLS!**

**Faire ressortir les avantages d'un projet**

- Utilise des adjectifs mélioratifs : *Provide* ***limitless*** *opportunities.* • *Highly* ***sought-after advanced*** *IT skills.* • *The network has become way more* ***reliable***.
- Utilise l'expression de la capacité : ***Can*** *help teachers boost education scenarios.* • ***Enabling*** *digital competence.* • *Our students* ***can*** *access ...*

**a. Look at** the picture and **react** to the situation.

**b. Watch** the video and **present** Mount Isa School of the Air.

**c.** GRAMMAR *We* ***have migrated*** *now* • *In the past, they* ***haven't had*** *daily contact* • *The network* ***has become*** *way more reliable*. **Explain** the use of the present perfect in these sentences. ▸ p. 23

**d. Explain** how the network democratises education.

**AT HOME** **Go** on the school website and **find** more information about the school to **present** to your class. VIDEO

## Doc 3.

**IBM launches free online learning platform in Africa**

IBM launched its $70 million digital-education initiative, "IBM Digital-Nation Africa" [...] The initiative provides a cloud-based learning platform designed to provide free skills-development programs for up to 25 million African youths over five years, enabling digital competence and nurturing[1] innovation in Africa.

The IBM Digital-Nation Africa initiative is part of the company's global push to build the next generation of skills needed for "New Collar[2]" careers. "New Collar" is a term used by IBM to describe new kinds of careers that do not always require a four-year college degree but rather sought-after skills in cybersecurity, data science, artificial intelligence, cloud, and much more.

Through a free, cloud-based online learning environment delivered on IBM Bluemix, [...] the initiative will provide a range of programs from basic IT literacy to highly sought-after advanced IT skills [...]

The initiative will provide access to thousands of resources, in English, free of charge, including:

- Ready-to-use mobile apps;
- Web guides, interactive simulations, video series, and articles;
- Online Assessments—A range of self-assessment tests to track the progress of individuals, together with industry recognized 'Open Badges' aligned to digital competencies. The badges can then be shared with prospective employers.

*Bizcommunity*, February 2017

**a. Look at** the advert and explain the strategy of communication.

**b. Read** the text and **explain** how the project works.

**c. Discuss** the purpose of this initiative.

**d.** TRANSLATION Say how these words in bold are formed and translate them into French: ***sought-after*** *skills* • ***cloud-based*** *learning platform* • ***ready-to-use*** *mobile apps* • ***self-assessment*** *tests*.

1. supporting 2. The term "new collar" is a play on "white-collar workers" (office employees, clerical workers).

# 3 e-learning challenges

## Doc 1. The reality of online classes

**THE IRISH TIMES**

***The Irish Times* asked students to share their experiences of online learning so far. Here is a selection of their responses:**

"I'm finding it very difficult to concentrate in [online lectures]. Being in a non-designated space like a classroom means I get easily distracted, go on my phone more, might open new tabs in the computer."

Niamh Elliott-Sheridan, M.Phil student at TCD

"Zoom classes are great but not having the workshops and specialised tutors there to help us is tough. Especially in final year, we have our degree show at the end of this college year, and it looks like that won't be going ahead which is making it hard to have any motivation to work."

Anonymous student at NCAD

"I currently live in the suburbs, and commuting[1] by bus in the morning takes me on average about an hour to get to college. Therefore, having online classes at home gives me less stress in the morning and helps me to organise my daily schedule more efficiently."

Minhwa Shin, business student at CCT College Dublin

Carl O'BRIEN, *The Irish Times*, April 2020

1. travel to and from work/school

## Doc 2. The problems with MOOCs

**BLOCKCHAIN UNIVERSITY**

Massive Open Online Courses (MOOCs) have amassed massive popularity over the past decade, and still show considerable potential for the near future. The concept has brought an unconventional and easy approach to learning. [...]

However, despite the extensive support and popularity, MOOCs have not gained enough momentum to completely substitute conventional education. The format continues to develop every day and has very mixed reaction from both universities and students. [...]

While many students have expressed satisfaction with MOOCs, we cannot ignore the fact that it is a very self-driven method of learning that may not be ideal for everyone.

The most common reason stated by students dropping out of courses was 'no live teacher engagement'. The lack of interaction bores people, and the course structure is often not progressive enough to completely capture the attention of the enrolled.

A significant reason for the students to drop out of the online courses is mostly the lack of interest and intention in the first place. An average MOOC lasts about 7 weeks, and only about 50% of the content interests most people. This leads to a massive number of people dropping out after the first two weeks itself. As the courses progress, the course material gets harder and pushes students to rely on a lot of self-study to clear any doubts. [...] At the end of 7 weeks, less than 20% of the original strength remains to collect the certificate.

Another primary reason why the success rate of MOOCs is beginning to drop is the fact that MOOCs aren't being given as much accountability or importance as they were given earlier. Most MOOCs rely on auto-scoring, a concept untrusted by many. There is minimal feedback concerning the class work.

*Blockchain University website*, October 2018

**a.** **Read** the students' reactions (**doc. 1**) and **contrast** the different viewpoints.

**b.** **Explain** who you feel closest to and **give** your own opinion on the issue.

**c.** **Read** **doc. 2** and **explain** the advantages and limits of MOOCs.

**d.** **Discuss** how the MOOCs could be improved.

**e.** TRANSLATION **Translate** l. 10-12. **Pay attention** to the meaning of *"while"*, *"self-driven"* and *"may"*.

**YOUR TASK** You are a student mentor. On an online forum, students are complaining of problems with motivation for online classes. **Write** a reply with suggestions to help them.

**BOOST YOUR SKILLS!**

**Donner des conseils**

- Mentionne les possibilités : *While instructors **may** communicate with online students.* • *They **can** also engage students.* • *Students **can** still see and hear the lecture.* • *They **may** even communicate with students in less formal ways.*
- Utilise des adverbes de comparaison pour proposer des changements : *I go on my phone **more**.* • *Having online classes at home gives me **less** stress.* • *Helps me to organise my daily schedule **more** efficiently.* GRAMMAR p. 23

## Doc 3.

### What Happens to the Social Aspect of Learning in an Online Course?

Online courses are known for the convenience and flexibility of allowing students to complete their coursework on their own schedule. With that freedom, though, comes a tradeoff[1]. [...]

Many students find that learning isn't just an intellectual activity, but a social one – and that explains why a number of students report missing in-person interaction with their instructors, They may also miss face-to-face interactions with fellow students. For some students, this lack of social interaction – and the accompanying need to be self-motivated to get their work done – can lead to feelings of isolation. [...]

The social aspect of learning doesn't disappear entirely in online college courses. It only changes. For example, online colleges are making courses interactive in a variety of ways, from implementing virtual laboratory projects for science classes to creating animated videos of course material.

Instead of having class discussions out loud in a physical classroom on campus, students engage in virtual discussions within their course's online learning platform. They may even find these discussions more fulfilling than traditional course discussions.

While instructors may communicate with online students primarily through email and messages on the virtual learning environment, they can also engage students in a more social way. Some create videos explaining course material so that students can still see and hear the lecture. They may even communicate with students in less formal ways, such as through social media.

Students may need to adjust to the different format of an online course. However, with hard work and dedication, they can not only succeed in learning but also find the social interaction they're looking for – just not in the way they're used to.

*Best Colleges Online* website, 2017

1. compromise

**a. Read** the headline of the article**. Guess** how the social aspect of learning might be impacted by online courses.

**b. Read** the text and **check** your hypotheses.

**c. Comment** on the arguments put forward to describe online courses as an opportunity to communicate with others.

**d.** GRAMMAR **Pay attention to** the modal verbs used in this text. **Explain** what they express.

**WORDS**

- ability ≠ inability
- drawback
- involvement
- outcome = result
- committed
- convenient
- distracted
- ineffective
- cope with
- foster [sthg] = encourage
- give up
- procrastinate
- require /rɪˈkwaɪə/

## FINAL TASK

**Record a video commercial to promote an e-education programme.**

**You work in the marketing department of a university e-education programme. Record a video commercial to present this programme and promote it to future students.**

1. **Browse** through the file and **make** a selection of relevant elements related to an e-education programme in university.
2. **Gather** your ideas focusing on e-education methods.
3. **Present** their benefits for the students. **Use** images, graphs and diagrams to **illustrate** your points in an attractive way.
4. **Record your video: Be** as convincing as possible to attract more students.

BOOST YOUR ENGLISH p. 23

YES YOU CAN!

# Record a convincing video commercial

## Step 1 — ORGANISER SES IDÉES

Définis le produit, **programme** dont tu dois faire la promotion

**Imagine le public** potentiel qui pourrait s'y intéresser. Quels sont ses **besoins** ? Les **freins à choisir ce produit** ?

## Step 2 — SE PRÉPARER

Trouve une **phrase d'accroche** ou slogan. Pense à interpeller le public avec des pronoms ou des impératifs.

Donne du rythme à ta vidéo avec des figures de style, fond sonore ou images fortes.

**Fais un plan** de ta vidéo avec des étapes structurées.

## Step 3 — À TOI DE JOUER!

### PRÉSENTATION DU PROGRAMME

Utilise des phrases d'accroche simples.

*But what really is online education?*

Adresse-toi directement au public souhaité :

***You** can easily study from home, at the local cafeteria...*

### ATTRACTIVITÉ

Mets en avant les atouts du e-learning en utilisant des adjectifs mélioratifs ou le comparatif.

*Such solutions are **helpful** for training new employees and (...) help to make ongoing employee education both **affordable** and **effective**.*
*Online programs are usually **cheaper** than the ones you need to attend.*
*...you can plan according to your personal schedule, decide what is **more effective** for you...*

### RASSURER

N'hésite pas à anticiper des réticences possibles et proposer des solutions :

***While some** found distance learning is a struggle, **many** thought it gave them the freedom they needed.*
*Distance learning **can easily allow you** to work part-time.*

### RYTHME

Donne du rythme à ta vidéo en ménageant des pauses et en accentuant les mots importants.

*You can develop time-management skills which are essential for **your career**.*
*The freedom is **yours.***

### EFFICACITÉ

Termine ta présentation avec des termes qui résument les atouts du programme.

*We see a new generation of students who enjoy **simplicity, flexibility** and who are very **tech-oriented**.*

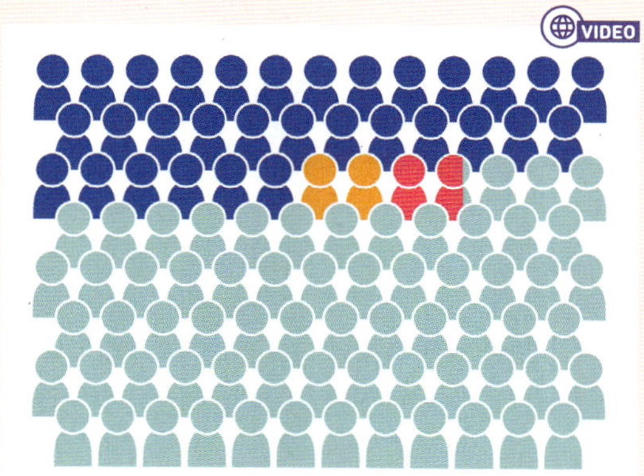


▸ The Future of Education?, p. 16

# BOOST YOUR ENGLISH!

## Grammar — Faire la promotion de quelque chose

**• Utilise le *present perfect* pour faire le bilan d'une expérience ou faire un constat.**

*We **have migrated** now to nearly a full digital service.*

*In the past, they **haven't had** daily contact with their class teachers.*

*The network **has become** way more reliable.*

**• Exprime le contraste pour comparer deux situations.**

***Instead of having** class discussions out loud in a physical classroom on campus, students engage in virtual discussions.*

***While** some found distance learning is a struggle, many thought it gave them the freedom they needed.*

**• Exprime l'accroissement ou le décroissement d'un phénomène.**

*...**less than** 20% of the original strength remains to collect the certificate.*

*...allows employees to get **far more** from 30 minutes at their desks than an afternoon in a traditional setting.*

*...employees are **more** productive.*

**1 Choisis le temps le plus approprié (prétérit ou *present perfect*) pour conjuguer les verbes suivants et justifie ton choix.**

a. When I was 23, e-learning (*allow*) me to achieve my goals.
b. Last year, I (*enroll*) in an online course at the Open University.
c. It (*be*) a wonderful and enriching experience so far.
d. Mount Isa School of the Air (*start*) through radio contact with families and kids.

**2 Exprime l'accroissement ou le décroissement dans les phrases suivantes avec les adverbes de comparaison (*less/more*) ou les verbes *increase* et *decrease*.**

a. In some countries, thanks to e-learning it is ... difficult for children to have access to education.
b. ... universities offer full degree online programmes now.
c. Physical interaction ... because of e-education.
d. The number of companies choosing e-learning for their employees ...

## Vocabulary — e-education

### Benefits and obstacles

**Communication** (AUDIO)
- face-to-face communication
- isolation
- lack of interaction
- outback
- social interaction
- team building
- virtual classrooms
- virtual meeting

**Empowerment** (AUDIO)
- beneficial
- impelling
- boost skills
- gain new skills/ upskill

**Inequalities** (AUDIO)
- geographical restraints
- low-cost alternative

---
- afford
- expose inequalities
- tackle
- widen inequalities

### Online learning

**School** (AUDIO)
- companies
- developing countries
- remote places
- training

**Means** (AUDIO)
- digital tools
- laptop
- nonprofit platform
- scholarship
- virtual guidance

---
- deliver lessons

**Prospects** (AUDIO)
- career change/ professional retraining
- step forward = progress
- climb the social ladder
- enhance productivity

### Experience

**Feelings** (AUDIO)
- anxiety /æŋˈzaɪɪtɪ/
- boredom

---
- delighted
- enjoyable
- marvellous
- nervous

**Testimony** (AUDIO)
- challenging
- enriching
- fulfilling
- enjoy tremendously
- exceed one's expectations
- receive feedback

Vers le **BAC**

# LET'S BRAINSTORM!

OBJECTIF BAC p. 305-317

## The rise of online learning

- From traditional classrooms to Open University

→ "Open University", p. 17 • "U.S. university students enrolled in distance education", Infographic, p. 16

- Professional training in companies

→ "How are Top Fortune 500 companies using e-learning to boost productivity?", *Sales Academy* website p. 17

## Reshaping education

- Tackling geographical problems

→ "How online teaching can reshape education in rural India", Kiran Dham, p. 18, • Australia's School of the air, *nbn Australia*, p. 19

- Tackling financial problems

→ Empowering African Youth, *Bizcommunity*, p. 19

SAVOIRS, CRÉATION, INNOVATION

**Axe 1**

**Can online learning contribute to developing education in English-speaking countries?**

## The challenges raised by e-learning

- Students encounter difficulties

→ "The reality of online classes", Carl O'Brien, *Irish Times*, p. 20, • The problem with MOOCS, *Blockchain University* website, p. 20

- Lack of social interaction

→ "What happens to the social aspect of learning in an online course", *Best colleges* website, p. 21

## Companies encouraging e-learning

- e-learning: a way to save time and enhance the skills of employees

→ "How are Top Fortune 500 companies using e-learning to boost productivity?", *Sales Academy* website p. 17

- Companies providing a learning platform to develop free skills.

→ Empowering African Youth, *Bizcommunity*, p. 19

## Phonology L'accent de phrase

AUDIO

- Dans une phrase, on **accentue les mots** qui sont **porteurs de sens** : les **mots lexicaux** (noms, verbes, adjectifs) et **certains** mots **grammaticaux** (mots interrogatifs, auxiliaires en tête de phrase).
- **La mise en relief** d'un élément par l'accentuation permet de marquer un **contraste** ou de **rectifier** une mauvaise information ou de mettre en **évidence** une information.

*This is* ***distance*** *learning,* *not* in situ *learning.*

**Écoute les phrases suivantes et repère les mots mis en relief. Entraine-toi à les lire en reproduisant le rythme de la phrase.**

**a.** *While some found distance learning is a struggle, many thought it gave them the freedom they needed.*
**b.** *You could even do it on Mars if you had the connection.*
**c.** *Also when studying from a distance, you are the one running the show.*
**d.** *Universities closed doors and began having lectures and exams online.*
**e.** *It may be that they, in the past, they haven't had daily contact with their class teachers.*

# BUILD YOUR PORTFOLIO

## @ Campaign

Atingi website

“In many African countries, providing access to learning content and lifelong learning opportunities remains a challenge. Large parts of the population cannot benefit from existing educational offers due to geographical remoteness and a lack of financial resources. The Africa Cloud global project aims to reach young people through innovative e-learning offers.”

- **Watch** the video, **visit** the site and **explain** how this project aims at creating educational opportunities.

VIDÉO

## Article

“Is online learning the future of education?”, *British Council*, 2019

Based in the U.K., FutureLearn is working to transform access to education on a global scale; it has already attracted 8.5 million members worldwide. It delivers courses on a huge range of subjects for anyone looking either to progress professionally or perhaps explore a personal passion.

- **Read** the article and **comment** on the way FutureLearn seeks to offer education to all.

ARTICLE

## Lived Experience

“The way we work now: teaching from a distance”, June 2020

“We kind of knew it was coming — it had been in the air all week,” says Maiuri, who teaches 6th-grade English and drama at Edna Brewer Middle School. All of a sudden, there were so many details to figure out. Who needs books? Who needs a laptop? How is this all going to work?”

- **Watch** the video and **explain** how Jana Maiuri is adapting to online teaching during school closure.

VIDÉO

## Cartoon

"A summer slide to inequality", Signe Wilkinson, *The Philadelphia Inquirer*, 2020

The "summer slide" describes the tendency for students to lose some of the progress they made in the school year.

- **Look** at the cartoon and **explain** how online classes highlight students' social inequalities.

ÉPREUVE ORALE | GRAND ORAL | Entraîne-toi à l'oral

**Step 1** **Build up your speech!**

ÉPREUVE ORALE:
- Choose one topic in the mindmap p. 24.
- Pick out two documents in the file and a personal one to illustrate this issue.

OBJECTIF BAC p. 305

- Prepare your presentation: you must show how these documents relate to the issue you chose.

GRAND ORAL:
- Choose one topic in the mindmap p. 24.
- Find a key question about your topic.
- Gather arguments and examples from the documents in the file to support your point.
- Prepare an outline for your presentation and write your note sheet. OBJECTIF BAC p. 308-309

**Step 2** **Make your oral presentation in front of two classmates.**

ÉPREUVE ORALE:
- Show your documents to your classmates. Each of you makes their presentation to the others in about five minutes. OBJECTIF BAC p. 306-307

GRAND ORAL:
- Give your note sheet to your classmates.
- Stand up and make a five-minute presentation to answer your key question. OBJECTIF BAC p. 310-311

**Step 3** **Answer your classmates' questions about your presentation.**

SNAPFILE 2

SAVOIRS, CRÉATION ET INNOVATION

AXE 1 : PRODUCTION ET CIRCULATION DES SAVOIRS

# Wiki verified

▶ **What makes Wikipedia such a trusted source of information today?**

**FINAL TASK** As an editor attending Wikipedia's yearly convention, give a speech about its strengths and the changes you hope to see.



## 1 Spreading knowledge

### Doc 1. A popular yet controversial website

VIDÉO

Jeff Koterba, *Omaha World Herald*, January 2012
(Video: *Teen Kids News*, 2016)

**a. Focus** on the cartoon and **comment** on how Wikipedia has changed access to knowledge.

**b. Watch** the video and **describe** Roman's connection to Wikipedia.

**c.** Thinking about Wikipedia's etymology, **compare** Wikipedia to a traditional encyclopedia.

**d.** GRAMMAR *"Wikipedia, the website where you can find information on just about anything. Wikipedia calls itself the free encyclopedia anyone can edit."*
**Identify** the indefinite pronouns and **explain** their meaning.

**e. Discuss** how Wikipedia should be properly used.

**WORDS**

- joint effort
- lifeblood = driving force

- ambivalent
- crucial = critical
- mind-boggling = startling

- cause controversy
- cause quite a stir = be noticed
- edit = improve = correct

## Doc 2.

### WHAT HAPPENS TO SCOTS WIKIPEDIA NOW?

The banner posted across Scots Wikipedia bears an important notice: "Followin recent revelations, Scots Wikipedia is presently reviewin its airticles for muckle leid inaccuracies." In addition to that general warning, hundreds of articles also display this more specific disclaimer: "The 'Scots' that wis uised in this airticle wis written bi a body that's mither tongue isna Scots. Please impruive this airticle gin ye can." [...]

In August, someone going by the handle Ultach posted threads on 4chan and Reddit revealing that an American teenager who does not speak Scots was responsible for nearly half of the articles on Scots Wikipedia. That teenager is the 19-year-old North Carolinian behind the username AmaryllisGardner, whose alias is often shortened to AG. Ultach wrote in his viral posts that Scots Wikipedia was "legendarily bad" in part because AG did not understand Scots grammar or vocabulary.

The intention behind Scots Wikipedia is to produce an encyclopedia written in the Scots language, sometimes referred to as Lowland Scots and not to be confused with Scottish Gaelic, which falls within the Celtic language family. The Scots language is sometimes characterized as a sister language of Modern English, and sometimes classified as a dialect. [...] At present, there are nearly 58,000 articles on Scots Wikipedia compared with the more than 6 million articles on English Wikipedia. In relation to other language editions, Scots Wikipedia is often classified as a small wiki.

But the public response to Ultach's revelations about AG has been anything but small or minkie[1]. British news outlets have been highly critical, describing the situation as a "hijacking of the Scots language" (*The Spectator*), "Wikipedia boy butchers Scots language" (*The Times*), and "Shock an aw"[2] (*The Guardian*). In the midst of the fallout[3], it's worth considering why the news about Scots Wikipedia has struck such a cultural nerve[4] and how open knowledge projects like Wikipedia can potentially self-correct.

Stephen HARRISON, *slate.com*, September 2020

**a.** **Read** the article and **pick out** information about the specificities of Scots Wikipedia.

**b.** **Explain** what went wrong and **comment** on the different reactions to the situation.

**c.** GRAMMAR **Identify** the questions in indirect speech in the last sentence. **Rewrite** them in direct speech. **Compare** the two forms.

**d.** **Describe** the gap between AG's intention and the public response to his work. **Discuss** whether it is *"cultural vandalism."*

**1.** Scots for "small"
**2.** Scots for "and all"
**3.** negative effects of a situation
**4.** strike a nerve: provoke a reaction

## Doc 3. Wizard of Wikipedia

*CBS This Morning*, 2019

**a.** **Watch** the video and **write down** key numbers. **Say** what they reveal about Wikipedia and one of its editors Steven Pruitt.

**b.** GRAMMAR *"**Three million** edits." "**Hundreds of** articles."* **Identify** and **explain** the difference between the determiners.

**c.** **Comment** on Steven Pruitt's reasons for contributing to the website.

**d.** TRANSLATION **Come up** with different French translations that show the meaning of the metaphor used in the video: *"People like Steven are the lifeblood of Wikipedia."*

DIFFÉRENCIATION

**YOUR TASK** **Write** the profile of an editor for Wikipedia's contributors' page.

**WAY 1** **Choose** Roman or Steven Pruitt.

**WAY 2** **Imagine** another editor.

**BOOST YOUR SKILLS!**

**Souligner le rôle d'une figure**

- Varie les adjectifs et nuance-les avec des adverbes : *He's an **incredibly driven** person.* • *This is **truly** a **mind-boggling** feat.* • ***Almost legendary** status*
- Utilise des subordonnées infinitives pour exprimer la visée : *The idea is **to use** it as a first point of research.* • *I'm very conscious of what it can mean **to make** knowledge free.*
- Donne des précisions à l'aide de subordonnées relatives : *...experts **who** are usually paid to contribute and edit content.* • *...the 19-year-old North Carolinian, **whose** alias is often shortened to AG.*

# 2 An impossible neutrality?

## Doc 1. A bias problem

Wikipedia started my love affair with free knowledge and open education. Like any relationship, it had its problems. Over the years, I felt hurt, inspired, embarrassed, hopeful, and unsafe. [...]

Working with Wikipedia is tricky. Working with my peers to improve access to knowledge brings me joy. But it pains me to see denigration. For example, to make more room in the category "American Novelists", contributors removed women novelists from the category. The women novelists were placed in a sub-category named "American Women Novelists". The people moving women from one category to the other thought they solved a problem but they exacerbated another. They didn't consider why they moved the women and not the men. Nor the marginalization they were perpetuating. This example illuminates how our actions affect Wikipedia in subtle ways.

These subtle ways affecting Wikipedia are bias. Bias creates an unwelcoming environment for people and content on Wikipedia. Our biases influence societal structures, practices, and principles. It's no different for Wikipedia. After twenty years of development, Wikipedia still prevents the very thing it set out to change. [...]

**What Is Bias?**

Bias means the thoughts and beliefs we have about society. We learn these biased thoughts and beliefs from family, friends, and the media. Bias is not based on facts and it is socially constructed. Learning bias is not conscious or deliberate.

We all have biases. People are not bad for having biases. Bias influences our actions, beliefs, relationships, and even our work. Most common biases people think about when they hear the word bias are gender, sexual orientation, and racism. People feel if they are not acting in overtly sexist or racist ways they are not biased. Acting on our biases is completely unconscious. Just like the example of the contributors moving women novelists, we generally do not intend[1] to act in biased ways. It's often completely unintended, but that does not mean the result is any less harmful.

Jackie KOERNER, *Wikipedia@20*, June 2019

1. plan

**a.** RHETORIC **Read** the text. **Identify** the stylistic device used in the first sentence and **explain** what it reveals about the author's intentions.

**b.** **Explain** how the author feels about Wikipedia.

**c.** **Describe** the effect that bias can have on Wikipedia.

**d.** GRAMMAR **Identify** the most recurring pronouns in the last two paragraphs. **Explain** the effect they produce.

**WORDS**

- bias = prejudice
- complete shift = breakaway

- autonomous = self-governing
- collaborative
- discriminatory
- inclusive

- be adrift = be lost, confused
- bridge the gap
- make far-reaching changes
- shake up = stir up

## Doc 2. Working towards a solution

Video: *University of Washington*, 2019

**a.** **Watch** the video and **define** the issue presented.

**b.** **Say** why other studies on the gender gap seemed inaccurate to Amanda Menking.

**c.** **List** the different reasons why there might be so few women editors on Wikipedia.

**d.** **Describe** the solutions proposed to fix the gender gap on Wikipedia and **say** why the issue is so critical.

**BOOST YOUR SKILLS!**

**Plaider pour un changement**

- Emploie des répétitions pour convaincre : ***Working with*** *Wikipedia is tricky.* ***Working with*** *my peers to improve access to knowledge brings me joy.* • *It does matter* ***who writes*** *history,* ***who writes*** *knowledge,* ***who writes*** *information.*
- Utilise des structures emphatiques : *It* ***does*** *matter who writes history...* • *Wikipedia still prevents the* ***very*** *thing it set out to change.*
- Exprime la condition avec des propositions subordonnées conjonctives : ***If*** *you say that you are the sum of all human knowledge,* ***then*** *you need representative humans contributing that information.*

**YOUR TASK** As an advocate for Wikipedia's neutrality, **send** a voice message to Jimmy Wales, the founder of Wikipedia, in which you **argue** that change is needed and **explain** the importance of fighting bias and the gender gap on Wikipedia.

# 3 Combatting fake news

## Doc 1. Guiding users in the fake news era

**a. Listen** and **sum up** Jimmy Wales's opinion about the Internet.

**b. Find out** what is specific about the Wikipedia community according to Jimmy Wales.

**c. Discuss** this statement: *"Aren't the people who are fighting for factual accuracy going to be forever outgunned?"*

Jimmy WALES, co-founder of Wikipedia (Audio: *NPR*, 2018)

## Doc 2.

**WIRED** — Technology | Science | Culture | Gear | Business | Politics | More

### There's a lot Wikipedia can teach us about fighting disinformation

Founded in 2001, Wikipedia was chastised[1] in its early days for inaccuracy and vulnerability to informational sabotage. [...] Eventually, though, the website has emerged as the unlikely champion in the battle against disinformation. How did that happen?

First, Wikipedia's goal of "organising the sum of all human knowledge" gave its users a sense of social responsibility. The common objective of creating and maintaining an encyclopedia through consensus has succeeded in fostering[2] a community dedicated to the integrity of the project.

Second, while other platforms are mired[3] in debate over the borders between free speech, propaganda and trolling, Wikipedia has taken a different route from the onset: community-driven fact checking. One of the platform's three core policies is "verifiability, not truth", and it requires every claim on Wikipedia be attributed to a reliable source. [...]

Finally, Wikipedia's open-access format – which enables anyone [...] to edit any article – also has the useful side effect of creating a situation of radical transparency. That every single edit, change and discussion happens in the open allows Wikipedia editors to keep one another in check, and weed out[4] nefarious vandals. Facebook and its colleagues, on the other hand, remain a black box, whose inner workings and policies are characterised by incredible opaqueness. [...]

Wikipedia's tedious[5] and self-enforced editorial process has proved to be a better tool to deal with disinformation than the algorithms, moderators and fact-checkers Silicon Valley giants are relying upon.

Omer BENJAKOB, *wired.co.uk*, June 2019

**1.** criticised **2.** promoting **3.** stuck **4.** isolate **5.** monotonous, tiresome

**a. Read** the article and **sum up** Wikipedia's three strengths in fighting disinformation.

**b. Compare** Wikipedia to the Silicon Valley giants.

**c.** RHETORIC **Explain** how the author convinces his readers that Wikipedia is a *"champion in the battle against disinformation."* (l. 3-4)

**d. Explain** how autonomy is central to Wikipedia's community.

**YOUR TASK** **Address** a short speech to the tech giants in order to **convince** them to change their approach to combatting fake news. **Compare** Wikipedia's ability to fight disinformation to Big Tech's.

### BOOST YOUR SKILLS!

**Convaincre son auditoire**

- Pose des questions rhétoriques pour cibler le sujet : ***How do you tell*** *what's real from what's not on the Internet?* • ***How did that happen?***
- Utilise des connecteurs logiques exprimant la concession et l'opposition : ***As long as*** *some people in our social circles are vigilant...* • ***While*** *other platforms are mired in debate...*

### FINAL TASK

As a Wikipedia editor, **give** a speech at its yearly convention. **Focus** on Wikipedia's strengths and what remains to be improved. **Insist** on the importance of editors like you.

**play BAC** **How to...**

# DISTINGUISH "TRANSPOSITION" FROM "TRANSLATION"

OBJECTIF BAC p. 302-304

MÉDIATION

L'**épreuve écrite** en Terminale comprend deux parties. Après la synthèse de documents (partie 1), tu devras procéder à la **transposition en français d'un document** du dossier ou bien à la **traduction en français d'un court passage** de l'un des documents (partie 2). Ces deux exercices sont très différents.

**TRANSPOSITION**

Rendez compte en français des principales idées exprimées par l'extrait de l'article "There's a lot Wikipedia can teach us about fighting disinformation", Omer Benjakob, *wired.co.uk*, June 2019 (Doc 2 p. 29). Veillez à ne pas simplement en dresser la liste, mais à les expliciter lorsque cela vous paraît pertinent.

**TRADUCTION**

Traduisez en français le passage suivant du Doc 2 p. 29 :
*First, Wikipedia's goal of "organising the sum of all human knowledge" gave its users a sense of social responsibility. The common objective of creating and maintaining an encyclopedia through consensus has succeeded in fostering a community dedicated to the integrity of the project.*

## 1 Analyse le texte

**a. Repère** le type de texte et sa visée.

**b. Identifie** la problématique du texte.

**c. Résume** les arguments principaux qui répondent à cette problématique.

**d. Explique** comment Wikipedia se distingue des géants du web.

• Analyse la source pour comprendre les enjeux. *Wired* est un magazine américain qui étudie le lien entre les nouvelles technologies et la culture, l'économie ou la politique. Il s'agit d'un article argumenté écrit pour des lecteurs intéressés par les questions numériques et leur impact sur la société.

## 2 Fais la différence entre transposition et traduction

**a. Choisis** la problématique qui correspond à celle de l'article.

**A.** Wikipédia est progressivement devenu un exemple dans la lutte contre la désinformation.
**B.** Wikipédia a su éviter des débats que d'autres plateformes n'ont pu éviter.

**b. Réfléchis** aux traductions possibles des expressions *through consensus* et *has succeeded in fostering*. **Pense** au temps verbal utilisé et à la forme en V-*ing*.

**c. Identifie** la transposition de l'extrait de l'article et la traduction du passage proposé. **Présente** les spécificités de chacun des textes.

**A.** Pour commencer, Wikipédia, grâce à son objectif — faire la synthèse de tous les domaines du savoir — a donné un sens de responsabilité sociale à ses usagers. Cet objectif commun, celui de créer et d'éditer une encyclopédie par consensus, a permis de cultiver une communauté dédiée à l'intégrité du projet de Wikipédia.
**B.** Wikipédia a su inculquer une responsabilité sociale à ses usagers et a ainsi créé une communauté soudée autour de son objectif : faire la synthèse de tous les domaines du savoir.

• Une transposition se distingue d'une traduction : elle consiste à rendre compte des idées principales d'un document sans en reprendre tous les détails.
• Pour réussir chacun des deux exercices, une bonne compréhension du texte est nécessaire.

• Pour faire une transposition, préparer un plan du document permet de trier les informations les plus essentielles. Une fois la problématique identifiée, il faut repérer les éléments qui y répondent.
OBJECTIF BAC p. 304

• Pour bien traduire un texte, il faut restituer le plus fidèlement possible les idées et les images de l'auteur.
OBJECTIF BAC p. 302-303

# Vers le BAC

## BUILD YOUR PORTFOLIO

### Article

"Can we trust Wikipedia? 1.4 billion people can't be wrong", *The Independent*, 2018

“ There are Wikipedia sites in 300 different languages, with 46 million articles accessed by 1.4 billion unique devices every single month. An army of 200,000 editors and contributors patrol this repository of online knowledge every day. ”

- **Read** the article and **identify** Wikipedia and Wikimedia's biggest goal. **Explain** why Wikipedia is a gateway to more knowledge.

ARTICLE

### Book

*Wikipedia @ 20, Stories of an Incomplete Revolution*, edited by Joseph Reagle and Jackie Koerner, *MIT Press*, 2020

“ How has Wikipedia, built on a model of radical collaboration, remained true to its original mission of "free access to the sum of all human knowledge" when other tech phenomena have devolved into advertising platforms? ”

In this book, scholars, activists, and volunteers reflect on Wikipedia's first twenty years, revealing connections across disciplines and borders, languages and data, the professional and personal.

- **Choose** one or two essays from this book that marks Wikipedia's 20th anniversary. **Explain** what the future holds for Wikipedia.

BOOK

### Article

"A vicious culture war is tearing through Wikipedia", *wired.co.uk*, 2020

“ Edit-warring was already common as India descended into political polarisation. Then along came Covid-19. ”

- **Read** the article and **define** "edit-warring". **Explain** why Wikipedia has become so polarised in India.

ARTICLE

### Charts

Wikimedia statistics, *stats.wikimedia.org*

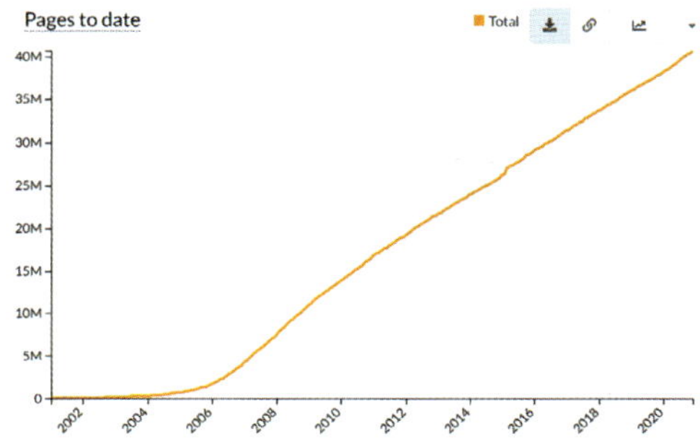


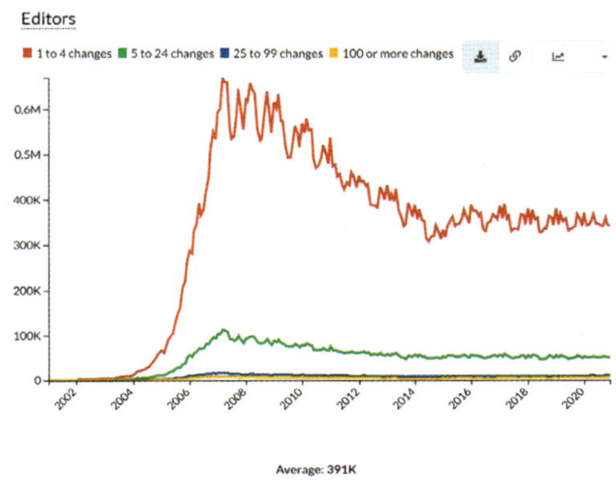


Wikimedia is the foundation that owns Wikipedia. It has a website with a great number of statistics that pertain to Wikipedia.

- **Explore** Wikimedia's statistics website to **find out** more about Wikipedia's evolution.

SITE

## Entraîne-toi à l'oral

ÉPREUVE ORALE

**Step 1** **Build up your speech!**

- Choose one of the issues studied in this file: the role of editors, the importance of neutrality, the fight against disinformation...
- Pick out two documents in the file, one from this page and a personal one to illustrate this issue.
- Prepare your presentation: show how these documents relate to the topic you chose. OBJECTIF BAC p. 305

**Step 2** **Make your presentation in front of two classmates.**

- Show your documents to your classmates and explain your point in about five minutes. Make sure you say how they illustrate the topic. OBJECTIF BAC p. 306-307

**Step 3** **Answer your classmates' questions about your presentation.**

FILE 3

SAVOIRS, CRÉATION, INNOVATION
AXE 2 : SCIENCES ET TECHNIQUES, PROMESSES ET DÉFIS

# Humans 2.0

▶ **How do technologies question the very notion of humanity?**

More on SPEAKEASY NEWS
speakeasy-news.com

**FINAL TASK** Write an article for a scientific review about how technologies might change humanity.

## 1 Promising technologies?

**Doc 1.**

AUDIO

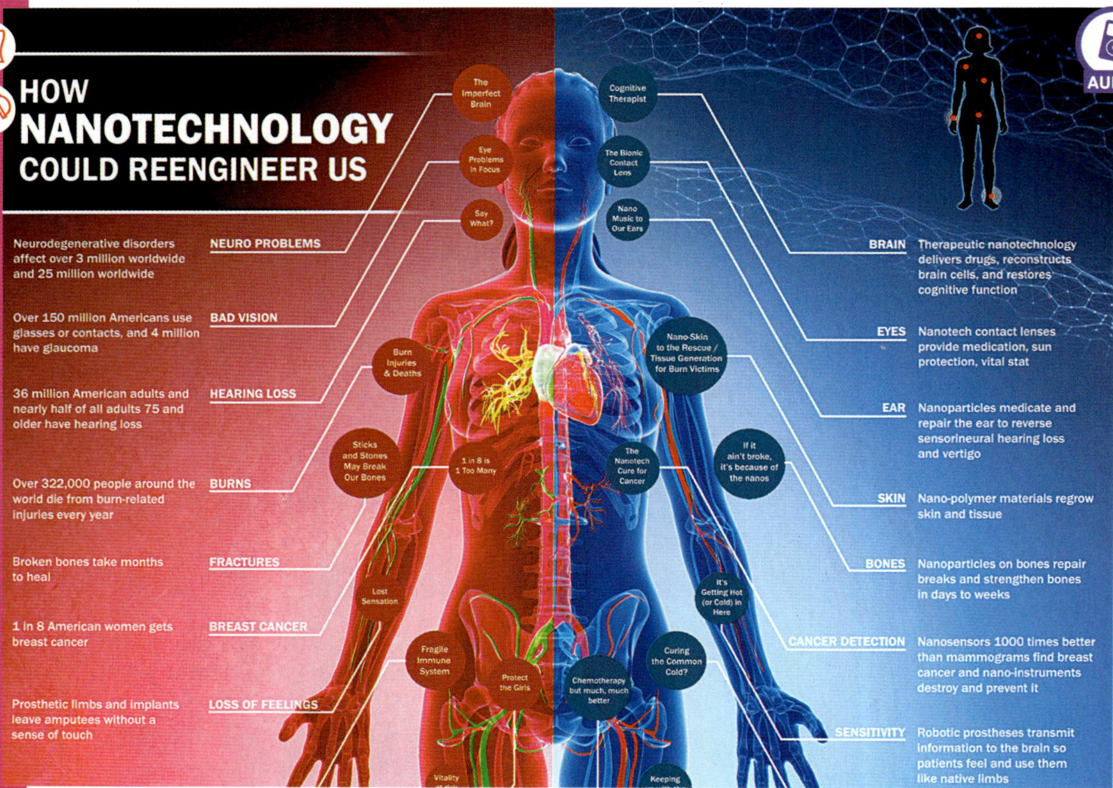


(Audio: "The future of nanotechnologies", *NPR*, 2015)

**WORDS**

- **break**through = leap
- **im**plant
- **mi**crochip

- **a**ccurate = pre**cise**
- **da**ring
- micro**sco**pic / maɪkrəˈskɒpɪk/

- ad**just** = cor**rect**
- en**hance** = im**prove**
- track = de**tect**

a. **Read** the infographic and **take** notes on the possibilities offered by nanotechnologies regarding human health.

b. **Listen** to the podcast and **explain** why the journalist refers to the 1966 film *Fantastic Voyage*.

c. **Pick out** information about the type of device scientist Swiston is interviewed about.

d. **Comment** on the benefits of such a device.

e. **Discuss**: How deeply can the human body be altered?

**CULTURE SPOT**

**Nanotechnologies** deal with developing and engineering extremely small (nanoscale) tools and devices.

## Doc 2.

### Elon Musk unveils updated Neuralink brain implant

Elon Musk's neuroscience startup Neuralink has revealed the "dramatically simplified" design for an implant that aims to create brain-to-machine interfaces, alongside the robot that inserts it and several pigs that have the device installed.

Musk shared updates of the implant, which Neuralink is developing to connect human brains with computer interfaces via artificial intelligence, in an online presentation last week. In the presentation, the entrepreneur and Tesla founder unveiled the new design of the chip, as well as the full-scale surgical robot and a group of pig test subjects. The Neuralink has been simplified from a device behind the ear to one on top of the skull. [...]

The in-brain device could enable humans with neurological conditions to control technology, such as phones or computers, with their thoughts.

The robot would be able to insert the link in under an hour without general anaesthesia, with the patient able to leave hospital on the same day and has been used to insert the implant into a number of pigs that are being used to test the device. The implant sends real-time signals from the animal's brain whenever it touches something with its snout.

Described as "healthy and happy", one of the pigs was given an implant two months ago, while another pig has dual Neuralink implants, demonstrating that it is possible to have multiple chips in your head at one time. A third pig has no implant. According to Musk, each of the animals are "indistinguishable" from each other. [...]

Neuralink received a Breakthrough Device designation from the FDA in July. The startup is now preparing for its first human implantation, pending required approvals and further safety testing.

Natashah HITTI, *Dezeen magazine*, September 2020

**BOOST YOUR SKILLS!**

**Présenter un projet scientifique**

- Mets en avant les objectifs du projet : ***To** diagnose what is wrong.* • ***To** insert the implant...*
- Souligne son utilité par des modaux ou équivalents : *It **can** send that data...* • *A device that **is able to** listen ...* GRAMMAR p. 39
- Évoque les bénéfices attendus : *The **advantage** here **is that**...* • *The device **could enable** humans to...* • *The robot **would be able** to...* • ***It is possible to** have...*

**a. Read** the article and **explain** what Neuralink is.

**b. Pick out** information about the innovation at stake (nature, size, scientific testing, goals).

**c.** GRAMMAR **Focus** on the sentence l. 34-41. Whose words do you think these are? Why did the journalist choose to report them that way? p. 39

**d. Comment** on the benefits and potential limits of such a scientific device.

**YOUR TASK** You attended a conference on nanotechnology breakthroughs. **Record** a one-minute podcast for your blog.

DIFFÉRENCIATION

**WAY 1** **Sum up** what they consist of and aim at.

**WAY 2** **Explain** what they could help to achieve and **give** your opinion.

## Doc 3. Human future?

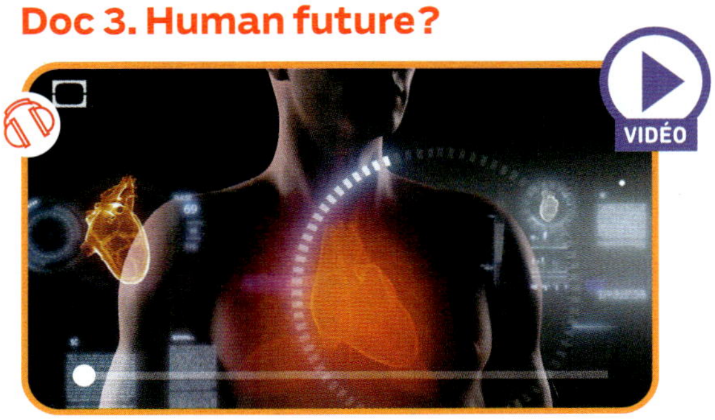


*Shots of Awe*, 2014

**CULTURE SPOT**

The **theory of evolution** by natural selection was first formulated by Darwin in 1859. It is the process by which organisms change over time to better adapt to their environment so as to survive and reproduce.

**a. Watch** the video and **find out** in what way technologies are changing *"what it means to be human."*

**b. Explain** and **comment** on the speaker's statement *"We are now the chief agents of evolution"*.

**c.** PHONOLOGY **Focus** on the stress on the words: *scaffoldings – transhumanism – humanness*. **Identify** the word they derive from and **deduce** the stress rule. p. 40

**d. Debate** on the consequences of such a vision of evolution for humanity.

# EXPLORE 2 Transhumanist theories

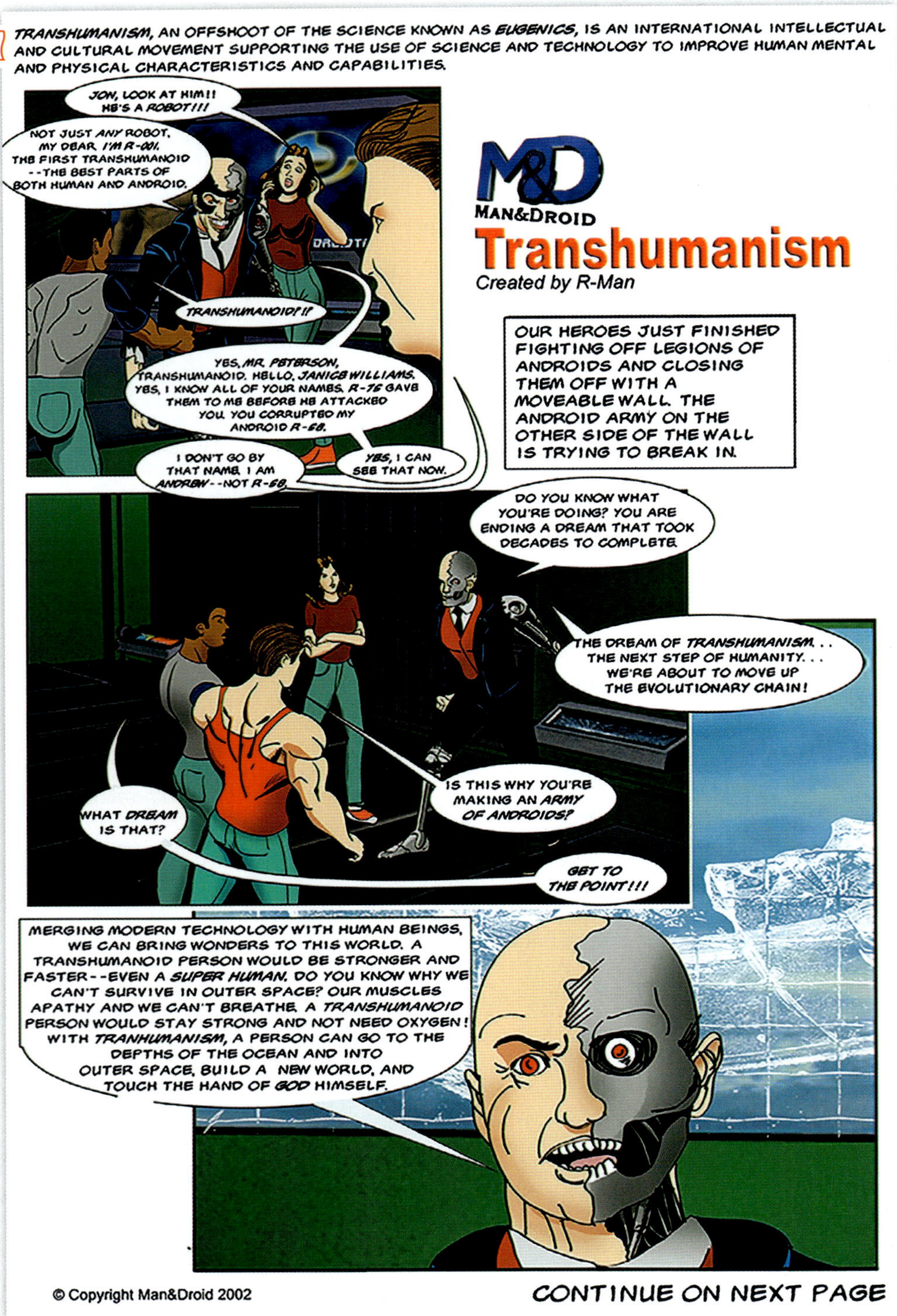


Man&Droid, *R-Man*, 2002

## Doc 1. Beyond man

**a. Read** the comic strip and **identify** the fight the story is about.

**b. Describe** the humanoid. What effect does it produce on the reader?

**c. Focus** on his words to **explain** what transhumanism is.

**d. Discuss** the implication of the humanoid's last words: "*touch the hand of God himself*". What does it reveal about the transhumanist movement?

**e. Consider** the nature of the document and **explain** its purpose.

**CULTURE SPOT** — EXO **Quiz**

**Check what you know about...**
- nanotechnologies
- transhumanism

## Doc 2. A political project?

**a. Listen** and **explain** what makes Zoltan Istvan a transhumanist activist.

**b. Note** down possibilities offered by genetic editing and AI according to Istvan.

**c.** RHETORIC **Pick out** the elements he chooses to establish his credibility.

**d. Pick out** elements of his demonstration that don't make it sound that serious.

**e. Confront** the comic strip with Istvan's theories. **Discuss** the ethical issues they raise.

Zoltan Istvan, transhumanist activist

## Doc 3.

**AI and Transhumanism: Could quest for super-intelligence and eternal life lead to a dystopian nightmare?**

The rapid development of so-called NBIC technologies—nanotechnology, biotechnology, information technology and cognitive science—are giving rise to possibilities that have long been the domain of science fiction. [...]

Yet, transhumanists often underestimate the complexity of our relationship with technology. They see it as a controllable, malleable tool that, with the correct logic and scientific rigour, can be turned to any end. In fact, just as technological developments are dependent on, and reflective of the environment in which they arise, they in turn feed back into the culture and create new dynamics—often imperceptibly.

Situating transhumanism, then, within the broader social, cultural, political, and economic contexts within which it emerges is vital to understanding how ethical it is.

Take students, for example. If some have access to pills that allow them to achieve better results, can other students afford not to follow? And if pills become more powerful, or if the enhancements involve genetic engineering or intrusive nanotechnology that offer even stronger competitive advantages, what then?

Going beyond everyday limits is suggestive of some kind of liberation. However, here it is a imprisoning compulsion to act a certain way. We literally have to transcend in order to conform (and survive). [...] The systemic forces cajoling the individual into being "upgraded" to remain competitive also play out on a geo-political level. One area where technology R&D has the greatest transhumanist potential is defence. DARPA (the US defense department responsible for developing military technologies), which is attempting to create "metabolically dominant soldiers," is a clear example of how vested interests[1] of a particular social system could determine the development of radically powerful transformative technologies that have destructive rather than Utopian applications. [...]

Whether the evolutionary process is determined by a super-intelligent AI or advanced capitalism, we may be compelled[2] to conform to a perpetual transcendence that only makes us more efficient at activities demanded by the most powerful system. The end point is predictably an entirely nonhuman—though very efficient—technological entity derived from humanity that doesn't necessarily serve a purpose that a modern-day human would value in any way.

At the heart of this is the removal of basic rights for "Humanity 1.0".

Alexander THOMAS, *Newsweek*, September 2020

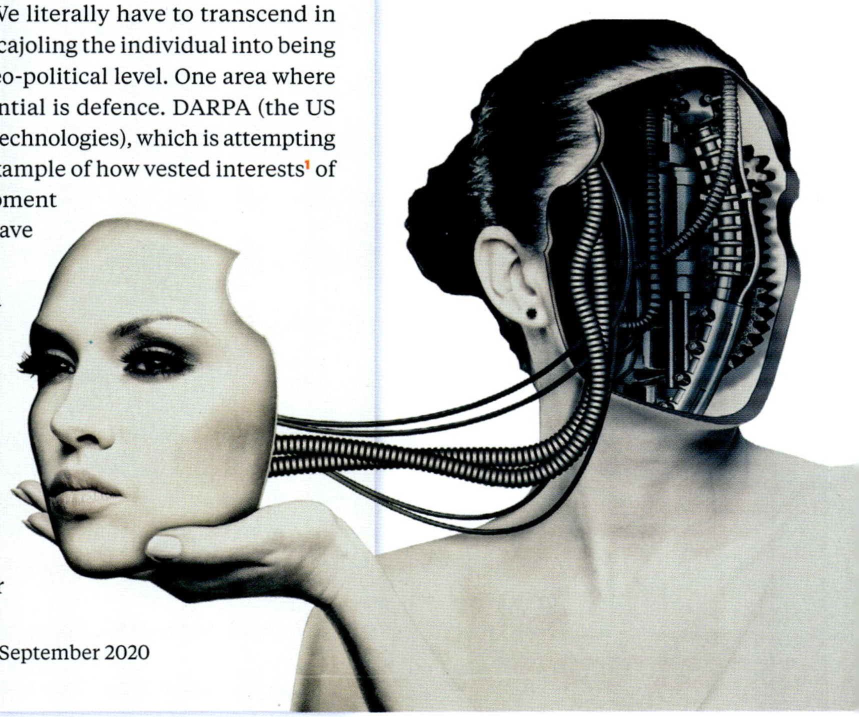

**WORDS**

- achievement
- vicious circle

---

- harmful = detrimental
- reckless = unaware
- upgraded

---

- be at the core of
- call into question
- give rise ≠ seek to end
- lead to = result in

1. direct interest. 2. forced

a. **Read** the article and **find out** why transhumanist theories are presented as biased.

b. **Analyse** the examples given by the journalist and **explain** how they illustrate the possible evolution of transformative technologies.

c. **Clarify** and **discuss** the statement *"At the heart of this is the removal of basic rights for 'Humanity 1.0'"* (l. 34-35).

**YOUR TASK** **Imagine** a conversation between Z. Istvan and A. Thomas. They **explain** and **discuss** their vision of a transcendent humanity.

**GOING FURTHER** **Read** the beginning of the article. Then **form** groups of four. Each group **studies** one argument and **sum** it **up** for the rest of the class. ARTICLE

**BOOST YOUR SKILLS!**

**Exposer une théorie**

- Structure ton exposé : *Technologies are...* • *yet...* • *in fact...* • *then...* • *however...* • *the end point is...*
- Utilise de préférence le présent de vérité générale : *Genetic editing **allows** us to...* • *We literally **have** to transcend.*
- Envisage les conséquences potentielles : *A social system that **could** determine...* • *We **may** be compelled to...* GRAMMAR p. 39

## Doc 1.

TEXTE LU

*In an alternative 1982, the narrator, Charlie, has just purchased a limited-edition robot, Adam.*

He stood before me, perfectly still in the gloom of the winter's afternoon. The debris of the packaging that had protected him was still piled around his feet. He emerged from it like Botticelli's Venus rising from her shell[1]. Through the north-facing window, the diminishing light picked out the outlines of just one half of his form, one side of his noble face. The only sounds were the friendly murmur of the fridge and a muted drone[2] of traffic. I had a sense then of his loneliness, settling like a weight around his muscular shoulders. He had woken to find himself in a dingy[3] kitchen, in London SW9 in the late twentieth century, without friends, without a past or any sense of his future. He truly was alone. All the other Adams and Eves were spread about the world with their owners, though seven Eves were said to be concentrated in Riyadh.

As I reached for the light switch, I said, 'How are you feeling?'

He looked away to consider his reply. 'I don't feel right.'

This time his tone was flat. It seemed my question had lowered his spirits. But within such microprocessors, what spirits?

'What's wrong?'

'I don't have any clothes. And—'

'I'll get you some. What else?'

'This wire[4]. If I pull it out it will hurt.'

'I'll do it and it won't hurt.'

But I didn't move immediately. In full electric light I was able to observe his expression, which barely shifted when he spoke. It was not an artificial face I saw, but the mask of a poker player. Without the lifeblood of a personality, he had little to express. He was running on some form of default program that would serve him until the downloads were complete. He had movements, phrases, routines that gave him a veneer[5] of plausibility. Minimally, he knew what to do, but little else. Like a man with a shocking hangover.

I could admit it to myself now—I was fearful of him and reluctant to go closer. Also, I was absorbing the implications of his last word. Adam only had to behave as though he felt pain and I would be obliged to believe him, respond to him as if he did. Too difficult not to. Too starkly pitched against the drift[6] of human sympathies. At the same time, I couldn't believe he was capable of being hurt, or of having feelings, or of any sentience at all.

Ian McEWAN, *Machines Like me*, 2019

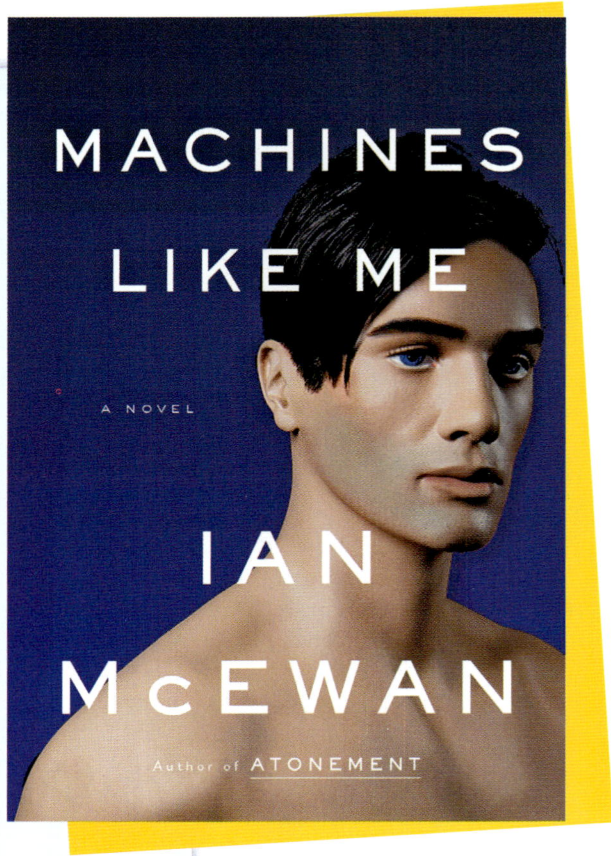


**1.** masterpiece of the Italian painter Botticelli (1445-1510) **2.** *bourdonnement* **3.** gloomy **4.** cable **5.** appearance **6.** *inclinaison*

**a. Read** the text and **pick out** information about the story, setting and characters. What strikes you about Adam?

**b. Explain** what the narrator means when referring to Adam's loneliness.

**c.** VOCABULARY **Pick out** words related to the lexical field of feelings. How does it contribute to Adam's realism?

**d. Comment** on the narrator's mixed feelings towards Adam.

**e. Discuss:** To what extent can we really communicate with robots?

### WORDS

- beh**a**viour
- dread = fear
- k**i**ndness
- skills = ab**i**lity

- blank = inexpr**e**ssive
- **se**ntient = c**o**nscious
- weird = pec**u**liar /pɪ'kju:liə/

- be appreh**en**sive of
- have s**e**cond thoughts ab**ou**t
- show **e**mpathy

## Doc 2. Why humanise robots?

*This Morning*, 2019

**a. Watch** the video and **find out** what makes Sophia look human.
**b. Explain** what such a robot can be used for.
**c. Comment** on the reactions she may provoke.
**d. Discuss** David Hanson's answer to the fear that robots might become a threat.

**YOUR TASK** David Hanson decides to start a diary reporting some of Sophia's words and attitudes to study the human characteristics she has. **Write** the diary entry.

**BOOST YOUR SKILLS!**

**Décrire et analyser un comportement**

- Varie les verbes d'observation : *I was able to **observe**... • She **sounds** and **looks** like a human • I can't **keep my eyes off** her.*
- Utilise des tournures présentatives : ***It was not** an artificial face. • **There** is a sort of fear...*
- Caractérise son comportement au présent simple : *She **is** a bit mischievous • She **goes** around and **talks** to kids...* GRAMMAR p. 39

## Doc 3.

### Can we create robots with human emotions?

Researchers are working to enable robots to express emotions—changing the pitch[1] of its machine voice, using dozens to hundreds of tiny motors to control the synthetic facial muscles. The androids Sophia or Erica are two examples of humanoid robots with facial expressions. [...]

With more applications of AI and robots, a new kind of relationship between human and machines needs to evolve. For humans to be less fearful of and to trust a walking, talking, gesturing and weight-carrying robot, we need to have mutual empathy with the robot. [...] For robots to be truly intelligent, they need to 'have a heart'. If a robot develops analytical skills, learning ability, communication, and even emotional intelligence, will it have a conscience? Will it be sentient? Can it dream?

The real question is do we understand what makes us humans sentient? Is it just the combination of our sensory perception and the thinking process? Or is there more to it? AI researchers cannot answer this question, but we do believe that to make "good" robots we have to teach them values—a set of decision-making rules that follow our ethical and moral norms. With the expansion in robot intelligence, teaching values to machines will become as important as teaching them to human children.

Pascale FUNG, *WE forum*, September 2016

1. sound

**a. Read** the article and **find out** what it means for a robot to express emotions.
**b. Explain** the statement *"we need to have mutual empathy with the robot"* (l. 13-14).
**c.** GRAMMAR **Focus** on the modal auxiliaries used in l. 18-19. **Comment** on the fear humans have regarding the future.
**d. Comment** on the author's position on what it means to be human.

## FINAL TASK

**Write an article for a scientific review about how technologies might change humanity.**

**As a scientist interested in new technologies and transhumanism, write an article for *Science Magazine*. Insist on the technological challenges but also on the ethical issues it raises.**

1. **Browse** through the file and make a selection of relevant elements related to the subject.
2. **Gather** your ideas focusing on today's cutting-edge technologies and rising theories. **Present** their possible benefits or associated risks (whether it may be harmful or not). **Give** precise examples and quotes.
3. **Describe** and **analyse** the probable evolution of humanity in relation to these technologies (including robots).
4. **Write your article.** Make sure to **remain** as factual and neutral as possible and to clearly **structure** your article.

YES YOU CAN! p. 38

YES YOU CAN!

# Write an accurate article

OBJECTIF BAC p. 300-301

En reprenant les différents documents étudiés auparavant, réfléchis aux **arguments**, **exemples**, **anecdotes** que tu veux intégrer à ton article.

**Step 1**

### ANALYSER LE SUJET

Avant d'écrire un article de presse, il te faut bien analyser le sujet pour comprendre le type d'article que tu dois écrire et ses enjeux, puis respecter des règles de mise en forme précises.

**Rassemble** les éléments importants et détermine les deux ou trois **idées principales** qui constitueront les **paragraphes** de ton article.

Pour chaque paragraphe, note **l'idée/argument** introducteur en commençant par le plus large. Apporte des **précisions** puis prépare une **transition ou un contrepoint**.

**Step 2**

### FAIRE UN PLAN

Au brouillon, prépare un plan bien structuré.

Pense à un **titre** accrocheur, le but étant d'attirer le lecteur. Le titre est souvent une phrase nominale.

**Complète** le plan de tes paragraphes avec des **exemples** ou **citations**, ou encore des **données chiffrées**.

## À TOI DE JOUER!

**TITRE ET SOUS-TITRE**

Donne un titre court et efficace (cela peut-être une phrase non verbale) et un sous-titre qui précise le thème général et éveille l'intérêt du lecteur.

**INTRODUCTION**

En guise d'introduction, donne des éléments clés pour préciser le contexte ou commence par un point marquant pour capter l'attention.

**DÉVELOPPEMENT**

Présente les différents aspects du sujet en t'appuyant sur des données et des exemples clairs. Précise les enjeux et les technologies mises en œuvre. Fais référence à des spécialistes et n'hésite pas à les citer si tu le peux.

**STRUCTURE**

Pense à structurer tes idées en paragraphes et donne à voir clairement la progression de ta réflexion avec des connecteurs ou des procédés rhétoriques.

**CONCLUSION**

Termine ton propos en une phrase de synthèse.

### EMOTIONAL ROBOTS

**Should we build robots that feel human emotions?**

Researchers are working to enable robots to express emotions—changing the pitch of its machine voice, using dozens to hundreds of tiny motors to control the synthetic facial muscles. The androids Sophia or Erica are two examples of humanoid robots with facial expressions. [...]

With more applications of AI and robots, a new kind of relationship between human and machines needs to evolve. For humans to be less fearful of and to trust a walking, talking, gesturing and weight-carrying robot, we need to have mutual empathy with the robot. [...] For robots to be truly intelligent, they need to 'have a heart'. If a robot develops analytical skills, learning ability, communication, and even emotional intelligence, will it have a conscience? Will it be sentient? Can it dream?

The real question is do we understand what makes us humans sentient? Is it just the combination of our sensory perception and the thinking process? Or is there more to it? AI researchers cannot answer this question, but we do believe that to make "good" robots we have to teach them values—a set of decision-making rules that follow our ethical and moral norms. With the expansion in robot intelligence, teaching values to machines will become as important as teaching them to human children.

Pascale FUNG, *WE forum*, September 2016

# BOOST YOUR ENGLISH!

## Grammar — Exposer et discuter une théorie scientifique

• **Utilise le présent de vérité générale et des tournures impersonnelles pour exposer la théorie étudiée de manière objective.**

*The theory of evolution **is** the process by which...*
*Genetic editing **allows** you to modify human beings.*
***There is** a sort of fear of robots.*
***There are** some bits of information from the body that can only be monitored inside the body.*

• **Utilise l'auxiliaire *can* ou un équivalent pour présenter les fonctions offertes par la science.**

*It **can** send that data outside of you.*
*We **can** already monitor heart rate.*
*It's a device that **is able to** listen to your heart.*

• **Appuie-toi sur les propos de scientifiques, rapportés au discours direct, indirect ou indirect libre.**

*According to Musk, each of the animals are **"indistinguishable"** from each other.* (direct)
*Seven Eves **were said** to be concentrated in Riyadh.* (indirect)
*The real question is **do we understand what makes us humans sentient?*** (indirect libre)

• **Utilise des auxiliaires modaux pour envisager les probables enjeux à venir de cette théorie.**

*They **may** enable us to enjoy greater "morphological freedom", we **could** take on new forms.*
*The device **could** enable humans to control technology.*
*The robot **would** be able to insert the link in...*

**1** **Complète avec des modaux et précise la notion qu'ils expriment (capacité, permission ou obligation)**

**a.** The relationship between humans and machines ... force us to reconsider their use in the future.
**b.** There is little possibility that AI ... feel emotions although robots ... adapt to the people they interact with.
**c.** Transhumanists believe that upgrading humans ... allow to overcome aging.

**2** **Rapporte ces paroles selon les indications données.**

**a.** Charlie: "How do you feel?" Adam: "Not well." (discours direct)
**b.** Adam asks the narrator: "Could you get me some clothes?" (discours indirect)
**c.** Some people asked: "When will AI become a reality?" (discours indirect libre)
**d.** Specialists argue: "We cannot predict the future yet." (discours indirect)

## Vocabulary — Augmented humanity

Transhumanism / Technologies / Issues

**Hopes** AUDIO
- immortality
- morphological freedom

- enhance = upgrade
- overcome aging
- regenerate /rɪˈdʒɛnəreɪt/ cells
- transcend

**Humanoid** AUDIO
- artificial
- human-like
- programmed
- transhuman

**Humanness** AUDIO
- awareness
- empathy
- feelings
- sentience = consciousness

**Nanotechnology** AUDIO
- appliance = device
- microchip
- sensor
- accurate = precise
- invasive = intrusive
- microscopic
- fix = repair
- monitor = control

**AI** AUDIO
- algorithm
- cognitive computing
- data mining: *exploration de données*
- machine learning
- neural network

**Robotics** AUDIO
- articulated prosthesis /prɒsˈθiːsɪs/
- exoskeleton
- microprocessor
- prototype
- surgical robot

**Ethics** AUDIO
- genetically engineered
- harmful = detrimental
- call into question
- eradicate = eliminate
- seek to end = lead to its loss

# LET'S BRAINSTORM!

OBJECTIF BAC p. 305-317

## Technological breakthroughs

- From curing to reengineering humans

→ "Nanotech promises", infographic, p. 32
• "The future of nanotechnologies", *NPR*, p. 32
• "Elon Musk unveils updated Neuralink brain implant", *Dezeen magazine* p. 33

- Humanlike machines

→ "Why humanise robots", *This Morning*, p. 37

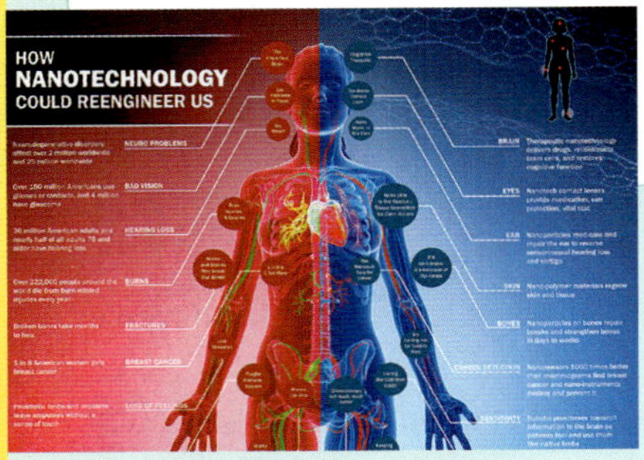

## The dream of transhumanism

- Decommissioning natural selection

→ "To be human is to be transhuman", *Shots of Awe*, p. 33

- A promethean dream: beyond humanity

→ *Man&Droid*, R-Man, p. 34 • "A political project", Zoltan ISTVAN p. 34

SAVOIRS, CRÉATION, INNOVATION
Axe 2
**How do technologies question the very notion of humanity?**

## Advanced technology or growing threat?

- The gearing of the desire for self enhancement

→ "To be human is to be transhuman", *Shots of Awe*, p. 33
• "A dystopian nightmare", Alexander THOMAS, p. 35

- Androids, humans who could replace us?

→ *Man&Droid*, R-Man, p. 34
• *Machines Like Me*, Ian MCEWAN, p. 36

## Humanising machines

- From motion to emotion

→ *Machines Like Me*, Ian MCEWAN, p. 36
• "Why humanise robots", *This Morning*, p. 37

- Towards a new relationship between humans and robots?

→ "Should we build robots that feel human emotions?", *WE Forum*, p. 37

## Phonology — Les noms dérivés : suffixes faibles et suffixes forts

AUDIO

L'accent porte en général sur la **première** syllabe d'un nom. Lorsqu'on ajoute un **suffixe** pour former un mot **dérivé**, l'accent peut **se déplacer** selon la nature du suffixe.

- Certains suffixes, comme *-hood*, *-ness*, *-ing* et *-ism* **ne modifient pas** l'accentuation du radical. On les appelle les **suffixes faibles** : *human* → *humanness*.
- En revanche, les **suffixes forts** comme *-ic*, *-ion*, *-ing* et *-ity* **imposent l'accentuation** sur la syllabe placée **avant le suffixe** : *human* → *humanity* ; *robot* → *robotics*

**1** **Donne le radical de chacun des noms suivants. Puis indique l'accent tonique du radical et de son dérivé. Écoute et vérifie.**

*scientific – scepticism – robotisation – editing – genetic – combination*

**2** **Écoute et note l'accent tonique de chacun de ces mots. Explique sa position.**

*humanism – scientist – implementation – majority – evolution*

# BUILD YOUR PORTFOLIO

## Letter

*Letter to Mother Nature*, Max MORE, 1999

“Dear Mother Nature,
Sorry to disturb you, but we humans—your offspring—come to you with some things to say. What you have made us is glorious, yet deeply flawed. You seem to have lost interest in our further evolution some 100,000 years ago.
We have decided that it is time to amend the human constitution.”

- **Read** the letter and **explain** how and why the speaker addresses nature. **Explain** what it shows about humans' hopes and desires.

SITE

## Film

*Transcendence*, Wally PFISTER, 2014

In this film, a scientist in the field of Artificial Intelligence has been working towards one goal: to create a machine possessing human emotions, and the collective intelligence of every person. However, a radical anti-tech group is determined to stop him at all costs.

- **Watch** the movie trailer and **explain** how it questions Artificial Intelligence progress.

VIDÉO

## Cartoon

"I wanted to become a cyborg", Jon CARTER, 2014

- **Comment** on the way the cartoonist both mocks and calls into question transhumanism.

## Book

*Zero K*, Don DELILLO, 2016

*"We are born without choosing to be. Should we have to die in the same manner? Isn't it a human glory to refuse to accept a certain fate?"*
These questions are raised through the novel. The billionaire Ross Lockhart needs to enter another dimension in order to make his wife come back to life. Yet, for his son, this is ethically-speaking unacceptable, to preserve bodies thanks to new technologies.

- **Read** the book and **explain** how the author tackles the issue of life extension.

ÉPREUVE ORALE | GRAND ORAL | Entraîne-toi à l'oral

**Step 1** — **Build up your speech!**

ÉPREUVE ORALE:
- Choose one topic in the mindmap p. 40.
- Pick out one document in the file and a personal one to illustrate this issue.

OBJECTIF BAC p. 305-306

- Prepare your presentation: you must show how these documents relate to the issue you chose.

GRAND ORAL:
- Choose one topic in the mindmap p. 40.
- Find a key question about your topic.
- Gather arguments and examples from the documents in the file to support your point.
- Prepare an outline for your presentation and write your note sheet. OBJECTIF BAC p. 308-309

**Step 2** — **Make your oral presentation in front of two classmates.**

ÉPREUVE ORALE:
- Show your documents to your classmates. Each of you makes their presentation to the others in about five minutes. OBJECTIF BAC p. 306-307

GRAND ORAL:
- Give your note sheet to your classmates.
- Stand up and make a five-minute presentation to answer your key questions. OBJECTIF BAC p. 310-311

**Step 3** — **Answer your classmates' questions about your presentation.**

SNAPFILE 4

SAVOIRS, CRÉATION ET INNOVATION

AXE 2 : SCIENCES ET TECHNIQUES, PROMESSES ET DÉFIS

# Digital Arts

▶ How are digital technologies transforming the art world?

More on SPEAKEASY NEWS speakeasy-news.com

YOUR MISSION

**Record a review on digital arts.**

You run an artistic blog and were invited to the opening of an exhibition during the Digital Art Fair in New York. Record a review to be posted on your blog.

FOLLOW THE STEPS!

## 1 Broadening creativity

Doc 1.

### DIGITAL PAINTING

**The case of David Hockney**

While some artists get variety from changing subject matters, Hockney is all about the medium, and, in a sense, that's what makes his vision of digital art so empowering. He innovates within the traditional forms like still-life, portrait, and landscapes, making these subjects contemporary again. By exploring the same themes throughout his career, Hockney relentlessly[1] renewed himself in the methods of representation, which eventually drove him to digital technologies. [...]

Digital tools are mobile and offer so much more flexibility than carrying brushes, paint, and pens for an outing. Grab your pocket-sized device, and here we go. [He] uses basic software on iPhone and more recently iPad, and is, in fact, rather appreciative of the way it's easy-to-use. One thing that is essential to Hockney is details. By looking closely, he sees things we don't, and so we observe again, more intensely, and rediscover the beauty of multiplicity. Digital painting allowed this interest for observation to develop as he zooms in and out allowed for a more considerable amount of details than the change of views experienced when stepping back from the canvas. [...] Digital art is not about fashion but about the risk-taking and experimental approach it gives to creation.

Marie CHATEL, *Medium.com*, January 2019

David HOCKNEY, iPad drawing, *The Arrival of Spring in Woldgate*, East Yorkshire in 2011, 2 January

1. without stopping

**a. Read** the article and **find out** what digital art consists in.

**b. Explain** how and why David Hockney came to it (l. 8-12).

**c.** GRAMMAR **Focus** on the adjectives: *pocket-sized*, *risk-taking*. **Explain** how they are built and the difference between both.

**d. Describe** the image and **say** whether or not you think digital art can change your approach to painting.

**AT HOME** **Search** the web and **choose** another painting by David Hockney. Be ready to **present** it to the class (period, style, technique) and **share** your impressions about it.

**WORDS**

- arrangement = composition
- canvas: *toile*
- fusion
- 3-D tools

- audacious
- captivating

- innovative /ˈɪnəvətɪv/

- capture
- experiment
- read into = interpret
- undergo/go through changes

## Doc 2. The world is your canvas

Shantell MARTIN, *#justaline*, 2018

**a. Watch** the video and **find** information about the evolution of Shantell Martin's work.

**b. Name** the technique she uses and **say** how it redefines traditional art space.

**c. Explain** Shantell Martin's enthusiasm for this new technique.

**d. Discuss** the possible impact of this technique on the art world.

## Doc 3. A new way of looking at the world

Are touchscreens, smartphone apps and 3D printers all new means of producing art? In this age when digital technologies form part of the very DNA of generations brought up counting electric sheep, the plastic arts are being infused with digital innovations so that they can look upon the modern world through a digital lens. Is this evolution or revolution? The question touches on just how extensive the transformation that creativity and its practices are undergoing is—a transformation driven by digital technologies. [...]

*"Dance does not need digital technologies to exist. But it can gain from them in order to make it richer and to anchor it in the modern era. It has a great deal to learn from digital technologies: they can provide a new insight into the creative processes involved in it"*, says Armando Menicacci. The Italian-born teacher-researcher and choreographer—who specialises in the relationships between dance and digital technologies—highlights the benefits of isomorphism[1] that digital technologies provide: *"With calculations performed on a computer, all of the processes involved in perception can swap[2] their various forms. A gesture can become an image, an image can become a text, etc. The movements of dancers wearing sensors can, for example, be used to generate sound. So the music is what results from the gesture... the gesture is transformed into music."*

*Pointsdevue.com*, 2015

**1.** similarity of form **2.** exchange

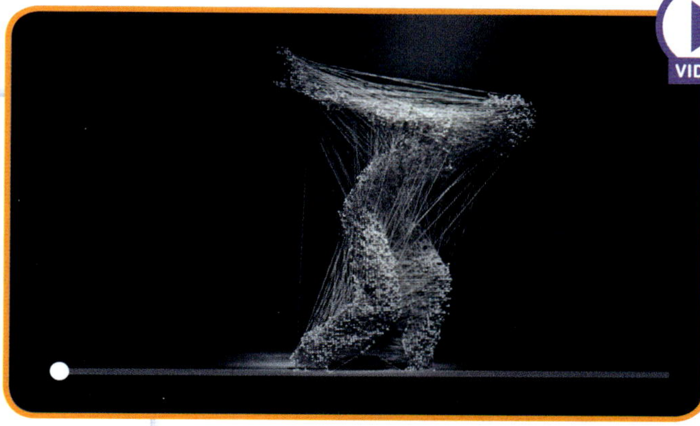

Making of, *asphyxia-project.com*, 2015

**CULTURE SPOT**

**As•phyx•i•a** is an experimental film created by NYC artists Maria Takeuchi and Frederico Philips and performed by Shiho Tanaka. The project is a collaborative effort to explore new ways to use and combine technologies with different artistic fields.

**a. Watch** the video. What art form would you say *As•phyx•i•a* belongs to?

**b. Read** the article and **explain** how *"digital technologies can provide a new insight into the creative processes."* (l. 12-13)

**c.** VOCABULARY **Focus** on l. 17-21 and **identify** the main lexical field. What does it reveal about the digital creative process?

**d. Debate:** Are digital technologies only a means to enrich traditional art forms?

**STEP 1**

As an introduction to your review, **write** a short paragraph to **explain** the concept of digital art **focusing** on works or techniques that you found significant.

**BOOST YOUR SKILLS!**

**Expliquer une démarche artistique**

- Présente les fondements de la demarche : *Hockney* ***is all about*** *the medium* • *Digital technologies* ***form part of*** *the very DNA of...*
- Précise la démarche avec des prépositions : ***Within*** *the traditional forms* • ***Throughout*** *his career* • *In the air* ***between*** *these objects.*
- Utilise des subordonnées pour en définir les moyens et le but : ***By looking*** *closely* • ***By using*** *augmented reality* • ***So that*** *they can look upon...* • ***In order to*** *anchor it in...*

# 2 Immersive artistic experiences

## Doc 1. Humanising technology

Opera *Death and the Powers* (Video: *PBSNewsHour*, 2014)

**a.** **Watch** the video and **explain** what makes Tod Machover's opera innovative.

**b.** **Find** information about the plot and **explain** the place and role of robots.

**c.** **Comment** on the questions raised by the show about the future of humanity.

**d.** GRAMMAR **Analyse** the compound adjective: *cutting-edge*. **Explain** how it applies to both the topic and the performance of this opera.

**e.** **Comment** on the changes technology brings to the audience's experience.

### WORDS

- big leap /liːp/
- ren**e**wal = revitalis**a**tion
- w**a**ndering

- eph**e**meral /ɪˈfemərəl/
- fl**a**bbergasting
- inter**a**ctive
- m**e**smerising = f**a**scinating

- app**eal** for refl**e**xion
- dive **i**nto = **i**mmerse in
- exp**e**riment = try out

**a.** **Read** the article. **Explain** the meaning and the concept of "Chutopia".

**b.** **Say** what makes this experience of street art different both for the artist and the viewers.

**c.** **Explain** how technology may be seen as an opportunity for street art.

**d.** **Sum up** the article explaining how technology can make art accessible to the greatest number.

### STEP 2

You were given a guided tour of Chutopia. Briefly **record** your experience and impressions in an audio file.

### BOOST YOUR SKILLS!

**Rendre compte d'une expérience**

- Utilise le présent de narration : *It **tells** the story of Simon Powers,* • *Robots **line up** on stage*
- Sers-toi du gérondif pour décrire ou commenter : *People **visiting** Chutopia and **drawing** away to...*
- Précise ton ressenti avec des verbes de perception : *I **watch** people...* • *People will **see** it.*

## Doc 2.

### VIRTUAL STREET ART

A guided tour of Chutopia

**How technology is transforming street art**

Graffiti artist Chu is giving us a guided tour of Chutopia. Chutopia, of course, isn't a physical place. Chutopia exists as a creation in Tilt Brush[1]—Google's creative tool for HTC Vive[2]. [...]

Chu is joined on the stage by Dr Lee Bofkin, CEO of Global Street Art—a company that aims to promote the art form around the world. "There's been an overlap between street art and the digital for a long, long time," he tells me later. "Most street art is by its very nature ephemeral, and the digital file is often the only record that lasts, because the wall disappears, the building is knocked down, and sometimes all you have left is the photo."

It's hard to imagine his business existing without the ubiquitous[3] world of social media we all now occupy. Global Street Art has around 350,000 fans across its various social media platforms. [...]

"If you're painting something amazing or something that really captures people's' attention, it doesn't matter where in the world you paint it—if you've got enough followers to give it a bit of oomph[4], then people will see it."

So beyond social media, where does technology come into this? Bofkin reckons there are plenty of ways Tilt Brush could help the movement. "I think Tilt Brush is a really powerful tool for letting people imagine what a painted city could look like."

Throughout the day, I watch various people —under Chu's guidance—donning[5] the Vive headset, visiting Chutopia and drawing away to their heart's content.

Alan MARTIN, *alphr.com*, December 2016

**1.** a digital brush that enables to paint in 3D with virtual reality **2.** virtual reality headset **3.** omnipresent **4.** energy **5.** putting on

# 3 AI made art

## Sonnet #1 TEXTE LU

**Doc 1.**

The dirty rusty wooden dresser drawer[1].
A couple million people wearing drawers,
Or looking through a lonely oven door,
Flowers covered under marble floors.

And lying sleeping on an open bed.
And I remember having started tripping[2],
Or any angel hanging overhead,
Without another cup of coffee dripping[3]

Surrounded by a pretty little sergeant,
Another morning at an early crawl.
And from the other side of my apartment,
An empty room behind the inner wall.

A thousand pictures on the kitchen floor,
Talked about a hundred years or more.

**1.** *tiroir* **2.** stumbling
**3.** drop of liquid

Who wrote it? EXO Quiz
A human
A machine

## Sonnet #2 TEXTE LU

**Doc 2.**

A green nub[1] pushes up from moist, dark soil.
Three weeks without stirring, now without strife[2]
From the unknown depths of a thumbpot life
In patient rhythm slides forth without turmoil[3],

A tiny green thing poking through its sheath[4].
Shall I see the world? Yes, it is bright.
Silent and slow it stretches for the light
And opens, uncurling, above and beneath.

The sun warms it and with a little time
Another slight leaf joins its neighbor,
They crown slowly and birth without labor
Feeding on the air's breath like a rhyme.

How can we know with body and with brain,
The force that makes the earth suck up the rain?

**1.** small lump. **2.** conflict **3.** agitation
**4.** *gaine, enveloppe*

Who wrote it? EXO Quiz
A human
A machine

## Doc 3. Who wrote it?

"Can you tell who wrote these poems", *NPR*, 2016 AUDIO

**a.** **Observe** the two sonnets and **describe** their structure. **Say** if they correspond to the expected pattern.

**b.** **Listen** to the podcast. **Identify** the main topic and **explain** what the Dartmouth College Competition consisted of.

**c.** **Read** the poems again and, according to what you have heard, **take** the quiz. **Justify** your answers.

**d.** PHONOLOGY **Focus** on the sonnets' rhymes. What does it show about the capacity of AI to generate rhymes?

**e.** **Comment** on the statement: "*I would be both amazed and terrified if it could [pass the test].*"

**STEP 3** You have a conversation with a member of the jury. **Discuss** whether or not computer generated poems can actually be considered poetry.

### BOOST YOUR SKILLS!

**Exprimer une opinion**

- Utilise des verbes ou expressions d'opinion : *I **think** it's a very difficult thing.* • *I **found** that...* • *The **thought** that...*
- Formule tes doutes avec des modaux : *I **would** be both amazed and terrified if it **could**.* • *It **would** suggest they have...*
- Pense à structurer ton argumentation : *They **can** play... **but can** they... ?* • ***If** you can pass the test, **it means**...* • *You **can** get sense... **but** then...* • ***That is** really the point.*

## FINAL STEP

**Gather** your notes to prepare the outline of your review, then **record** it.
Make sure to **explain** the concept of digital art and **present** the main artworks of the exhibition. **Share** your impressions about the experiences you have lived and **discuss** the artistic value of AI-generated art works.

**You've completed your mission. Well done!**

play BAC How to...

# PRESENT A PORTFOLIO

Concentre-toi sur le tableau de David Hockney (Doc 1 p. 42), l'article "Virtual Street art" (Doc 2 p. 44) et les sonnets de la page 45. Relis-les ainsi que tes notes prises pendant le cours. **Entraîne-toi** à présenter ce dossier comme si c'était **ton dossier personnel**.

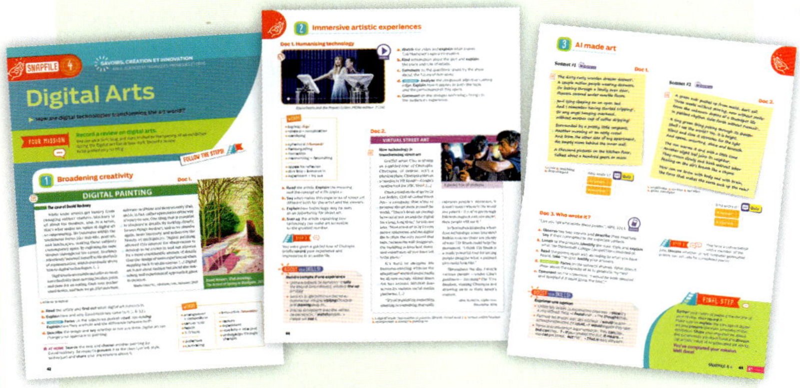


• C'est un exemple de dossier de quatre documents qui pourrait être un dossier personnel d'élève. Pour rappel, si tu passes l'oral en fin de première, ton dossier personnel devra comporter entre 3 et 5 documents dont un article de presse et un document iconographique. Tu peux choisir un ou plusieurs documents personnels en plus des documents étudiés en cours.

## 1 Analyse le dossier OBJECTIF BAC p. 305

**a. Identifie** la nature de chaque document ainsi que son sujet et son contexte.

**b. Prends** des notes sur les liens entre chaque document (similitudes, différences).

**c. Détermine** le fil conducteur du dossier (problématique).

**d. Dégage** 2 ou 3 axes qui seront les parties de ta présentation.

**e. Organise** ta présentation et note les idées-clés sur un support de prise de parole.

• Quels liens les différents documents ont-ils avec le numérique ?
• Organise ta préparation en un schéma qui fait ressortir les points de convergence et de divergence.

## 2 Présente ton dossier à l'oral OBJECTIF BAC p. 306

**a. Forme** un groupe avec deux autres camarades. Pendant que tu présentes ton dossier, les autres prennent des notes et préparent des questions.

**b. Introduis** ton dossier brièvement en présentant le thème, la problématique et les axes.

*N'oublie pas que le dossier personnel repose sur des documents que tu sélectionneras toi-même tout au long de cette année. Tu devras donc expliquer pourquoi tu as fait ces choix !*

**c. Présente** ton dossier dans le détail de sa structure et sa logique en prenant appui sur les documents.

**d. Conclus** ta présentation en donnant ton avis sur ce dossier. (L'aurais-tu choisi ? Pourquoi ?)

• Une simple présentation juxtaposée des documents ne suffit pas. Il faut les relier par une problématique (*a key question*) qui sera elle-même ancrée dans une thématique du programme.
*The set of documents raises the following question: "....?"*

• *This document enables me to speak about...* • *This document is relevant* • *thought-provoking because it...*
• *What I find interesting with this document is that it...*

## 3 Interagis

Réponds aux questions des autres élèves en développant tes réponses ou en prenant appui sur d'autres exemples.

• Fais appel à tes connaissances interculturelles personnelles pour aller plus loin dans la partie 'interaction'.
• *Your question makes me think of...* • *To go further...* • *What you are saying is true..., moreover...*

# BUILD YOUR PORTFOLIO

## Article

"Collaborating with intelligent machines", *medium.com*, 2017

"Whether we know it or not, we're increasingly collaborating with 'intelligent' machines. [...] Artists are starting to explore this emergent relationship and ask questions about the role of intelligent machines in art. This artistic activity is not only being created from within the artworld; tech companies are initiating collaboration with artists too."

- **Read** the article and **explain** how technology and artists can collaborate and how this collaboration can enhance each other's creations.

ARTICLE

## Artwork

*As We Are*, Matthew Mohr, 2017

"Created by artist Matthew Mohr and fabricated by Design Communications Ltd, "As We Are" resides in the Greater Columbus Convention Center. It utilizes a 32-camera, 3D photo booth, and 850,000 individual LEDs in order to generate a dramatic likeness of guests that get their image taken inside of it."

- **Observe** the digital sculpture and **comment** on how technology changes the audience's experience of art.

WEBSITE

## Article

"Digital technology is transforming the Art world", *Impakter*, 2017

Digital art is moving fast; new ways of promoting, selling and creating are quickly emerging and evolving. This article explains how digital technology is part and parcel of artistic creation in a changing art world.

- **Read** the article and **sum up** the various opportunities that digital technologies can provide to the art world.

ARTICLE

## Report

"Tilt Brush: The Lab at Google Cultural Institute", *Google*, 2016

This report focuses on a new digital art app called Tilt Brush. It allows you to paint in 3D space with virtual reality.

- **Observe** what happens during the report. **Say** in what way this type of performance transforms our relation to art.

VIDÉO

## Article

*Art is more powerful than ever*, Jennifer Soher, April 2020

This article tackles the issue of art accessibility, especially at a time when many museums have closed their doors because of Covid-19.

- **Focus** on the passage entitled Museum Modern Art and **explain** how museums have adapted to digital art.

ARTICLE

## Entraîne-toi à l'oral

ÉPREUVE ORALE

**Step 1** **Build up your speech!**

- Focus on how digital technologies open new ways to artistic creation.
- Pick out one document from the file, add a personal one and pick out another one in this page to illustrate the topic. OBJECTIF BAC p. 305
- Prepare your presentation: you must show how these documents relate to the topic.

**Step 2** **Make your presentation in front of two classmates.**

- Show your documents to your classmates and explain your point in about five minutes. OBJECTIF BAC p. 306-307

**Step 3** **Answer your classmates' questions about your presentation.**

OBJECTIF BAC p. 296-304

Grille d'auto-évaluation

## Sujet type bac

MÉDIATION

**Entraînement à l'épreuve de Terminale**

Durée : 3h30

Matériel autorisé : le dictionnaire unilingue (non encyclopédique) est autorisé.

Niveau attendu : B2 > C1

- **Prenez connaissance des documents A, B et C et traitez le sujet suivant en anglais (500 mots maximum).**

Explain what the documents reveal about the impact of technology on the evolution of transportation in the UK over the past years and in the years to come. Make sure you address:
- the reasons for this evolution;
- the expectations in this area;
- the consequences of these changes on various levels;

- **Traduisez en français le passage suivant du document B.**

*"Uberpool—where Uber users travelling along the same routes can share rides—has been around for a while now. But this is just one example of how technology is connecting people for shared journeys. The appetite for carpooling in the UK is increasing—with a 765 percent increase in car club memberships between 2008 and 2017. And tech is making this easier to achieve."* (l. 26-33)

### Document A UK at Forefront of Transport Innovation

*A major report on how the UK can capitalise on opportunities offered by transport technologies and innovation to benefit the economy, society and the citizen.*

This is a time of unprecedented change in transport, Sir Patrick Vallance, Government Chief Scientific Adviser will say today at the launch of the Foresight Future of Mobility Report.

The UK is well placed to capitalise on the exciting opportunities offered by transport technologies and innovation which will benefit the economy, society and the citizen. The Industrial Strategy and in particular the Mobility Grand Challenge will be central to helping us realise this ambition, building on the UK's world leading expertise and knowledge.

The report finds that technologies such as self-driving and zero-emission vehicles will drive innovation in the future. Behavioural and social sciences will be essential to maximise the impact of these technologies allowing us to develop a clear understanding of how citizens and businesses make decisions and interact with the transport system.

The report also finds that the movement of goods around the country is an equally important consideration. In 2017 logistics added £121 billion to the UK economy and employed 2.5 million people. Data will grow in importance to 2040. Therefore, the ability to use data to integrate different forms of transport, both passenger and freight, will be key.

Government Chief Scientific Adviser, Sir Patrick Vallance said:

"Transport is more than just travel, it connects people, places and shapes the way we live. The UK was a pioneer of transport technologies throughout the 19th and 20th centuries, and we can be at the forefront of the next transport revolution.

"We must grasp the opportunities to fully exploit our potential and create a transport system fit for the future. To be successful, industry, academia and policy-makers will need to work together, with the user at the heart of the system."

Jesse Norman, Future of Mobility Minister, said:

"We want our new Future of Mobility Grand Challenge to encourage innovations that will usher in an era of easier, safer and cleaner travel.

But great innovation and rapid technological change need to be based on robust evidence and a deep understanding of human behaviour. This report is a very useful contribution to that evidence base."

*Government Office for Science*, January 31, 2019

## Document B How technology is changing transport in London today

While Londoners used to be faced with a binary choice between car or public transport, new ways of getting around the capital have been cropping up.

In London, the number of journeys made by cars has fallen 25 percent since 1990. Problems with congestion have caused the number of drivers entering the city centre during rush hour to fall from 137,000 in 2000 to 64,000 in 2014, while the number of cyclists trebled during the same time. The number of young people learning to drive across the UK has also dropped—in 1994, 48 percent of 17 to 20-year-olds had a driving licence, compared to just 31 percent today. [...]

But as car usage declines, which modes of transport are taking its place? We've heard plenty about the autonomous cars and flying taxis of the future, but how is technology changing how we travel in the capital today?

**Dockless bike-sharing**

This idea has existed since the 1960s, when a similar programme was launched in Amsterdam, but until now there has not been the location tracking and app enabled rental technology to successfully realise the idea. [...]

**Car-pooling**

Uberpool—where Uber users travelling along the same routes can share rides—has been around for a while now. But this is just one example of how technology is connecting people for shared journeys. The appetite for carpooling in the UK is increasing—with a 765 percent increase in car club memberships between 2008 and 2017. And tech is making this easier to achieve. [...]

**Peer-to-peer car sharing**

The sharing economy has already changed our attitudes towards our houses, are our cars next? There are an increasing number of peer-to-peer car-sharing companies on the market, such as HiyaCar and EasyCar. These are platforms which allow car-owners to rent out their cars within their communities.

For HiyaCar, renters can download the app and browse the cars available in their area. They then sign up and take the car out for however long they have paid for. On some of the cars, 'keyless' technology is being trialled where the renter can unlock and start the car with only their smartphone. This technology has proved popular among users, with 22 percent going for a car installed with it, despite only two percent having the tech integrated into their cars.

Laurie CLARKE, *computerworld.com*, May 29, 2018

## Document C What is the Hyperloop?

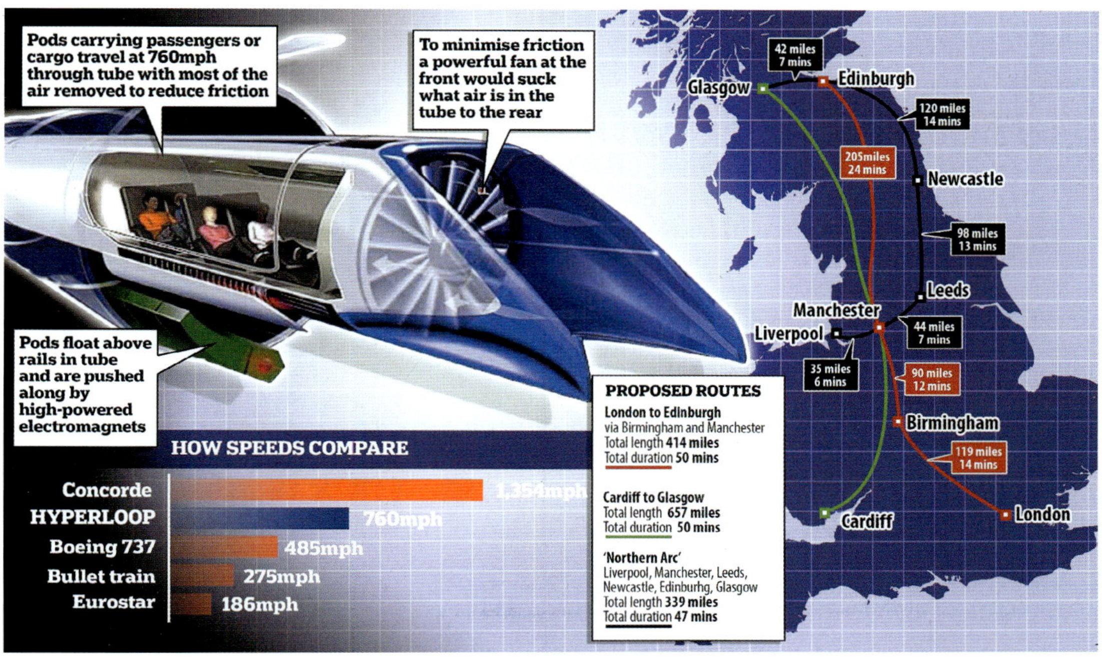


*The Daily Mail*, November 9, 2020

# Black Lives Matter

► **How are Americans raising their voices to reshape democracy?**

**FINAL TASK** Make a committed speech to promote social justice.

More on SPEAKEASY NEWS
speakeasy-news.com

## 1 Taking a stand

### Doc 1. A growing movement

LANDMARKS p. 280

VIDÉO

BLM marches in NY and around the world in June 2020 (Video: *NBCNews*, 2016)

**WORDS**

- demonstration = protest
- issue

- bold = courageous
- systemic
- widespread

- demand = claim
- rally = gather
- raise awareness
- speak out
- take action

a. **Watch** the video and **identify** the movement's starting point.

b. **Explain** the origin of the slogan and how it has gained momentum.

c. GRAMMAR **Focus** on the phrase "***take on** a life of its own*". **Identify** the type of verb used and **explain** what it conveys on the development of the movement. ► p. 57

d. **Observe** the various camera shots and **comment** on the effect on viewers.

## Doc 2. Athletes rise up

Eric Reid and Colin Kaepernick taking a knee in protest during the national anthem, Los Angeles, 2016

(Video: "Kaepernick's speech", *Amnesty International*, 2018)

**NFL Commissioner[1] wishes he had listened earlier to Colin Kaepernick**

Commissioner Roger Goodell says he wished the league had "listened earlier" to Colin Kaepernick when he began protesting during the National Anthem back in 2016. [...]

"It is not about the flag," said Goodell. "These are not people who are unpatriotic. They're not disloyal. "What they were trying to do is exercise their right to bring attention to something that needs to get fixed. That misrepresentation of who they were and what they were doing was the thing that really gnawed at[2] me."

In June, Goodell and the NFL publicly backed the Black Lives Matter movement and admitted to making mistakes in the past.

"We, the National Football League, condemn racism and the systematic oppression of Black people," he said on a video posted to Twitter. "We, the National Football League, admit we were wrong for not listening to NFL players earlier and encourage all to speak out and peacefully protest."

Ben CHURCH, *CNN*, August 2020

**1.** *sélectionneur* **2.** troubled

**a. Observe** the photograph. **Comment** on the players' attitude both in the foreground and in the background.

**b. Listen** to Kaepernick's speech and **rephrase** his main points.

**c.** RHETORIC **Identify** the nature of the speaker's questions and **explain** their effect on the audience.

**d. Describe** Colin Kaepernick's tone and **explain** how it impacts his message.

**e. Read** the article. **Comment** on the NFL's shift regarding Kaepernick.

**YOUR TASK** As a member of your school's sports team, **discuss** with your teammates the impact of Kaepernick's stand.

**AT HOME** **Go** online to learn more about James Baldwin and Malcolm X whom Kaepernick refers to. **Be** ready to **explain** how their protest might have influenced him.

**BOOST YOUR SKILLS!**

**Souligner l'impact d'un événement**

- Utilise des procédés oratoires : *I'm a human being* ***first and foremost*** • *I'm for* ***whoever*** *and* ***whatever*** *benefits humanity* • *Seeking the* ***truth****, finding the* ***truth****, telling the* ***truth****...*
- Évoque sa portée avec des verbes à particule : *Protest* ***sprung up*** *around the country* • *The movement has* ***taken on*** *a life of its own.* GRAMMAR p. 57
- Interpelle tes interlocuteurs avec des questions rhétoriques : *The question is* ***why*** *aren't all people ?*

## Doc 3. Politicians get involved

"DC Mayor has 'BLM' painted on street", *Newsy*, 2020

**a. Watch** the video and **identify** the various issues mentioned by Mayor Browser.

**b. Pick out** the various measures she implemented.

**c. Explain** why the location is symbolic and **comment** on the goal of this mural.

**d. Discuss**: How can politicians and grassroots movements work together to gain momentum?

## Doc 1.

TEXTE LU

Race has also been countless hours spent marvelling at our history. Evenings spent dancing and cheering to jazz and rap and R&B. Cookouts with ribs and potato salad and sweet potato pie. It has been hands of women braiding my hair[1]. It has been reading the magic of the words of Toni Morrison, Maya Angelou, and Alice Walker and knowing that they are written for you. It has been parties filled with Jollof rice and fufu[2] and Nigerian women wearing sequin-covered gowns and giant geles[3] on their heads. It has been pride in Malcolm, Martin, Rosa, and Angela. It has been a room full of the most uninhibited[4] laughter you've ever heard [...]. Race, my race, has been one of the most defining forces in my life. But it is not something I always talked about, certainly not the way that I do now.

Like many people, most of my days were spent just trying to get by. Life is busy and hard. There are work and kids and chores and friends. We spend a lot of time bouncing from one mini-crisis to the next. Yes, my days were just as full of micro-aggressions, of the pain and oppression of racism, as they are now—but I just had to keep going on like normal. It is very hard to survive as a woman of color in this world, and I remember saying once that if I stopped to feel, really feel, the pain of the racism I encountered, I would start screaming and I would never ever stop. So I did what most of us do, I tried to make the best of it. I worked 50 percent harder than my white coworkers, I stayed late every day. I dressed like every day was a job interview. I was overpolite to white people I encountered in public. I bent over backwards to prove that I was not angry, that I was not a threat. I laughed off racist jokes as if I didn't feel the sting. I told myself that it would all be worth it one day, that being a successful black woman was revolution enough. But as I got older, as the successes I had reached for slowly became a reality, something inside me began to shift [...]. And I started talking. I started to question, I started to resist, I started to demand. I wanted to know why it was considered a bad thing that I was "opinionated," I wanted to know what exactly it was about my hair that was "unprofessional," I wanted to know what exactly it was about that joke that people found "funny." And once I started talking, I couldn't stop. [...] I had started to see myself, and once you start to see yourself, you cannot pretend anymore.

Ijeoma OLUO, *So you want to talk about race*, 2019

**1.** make hair tress **2.** West African recipes **3.** *coiffes africaines* **4.** unashamed

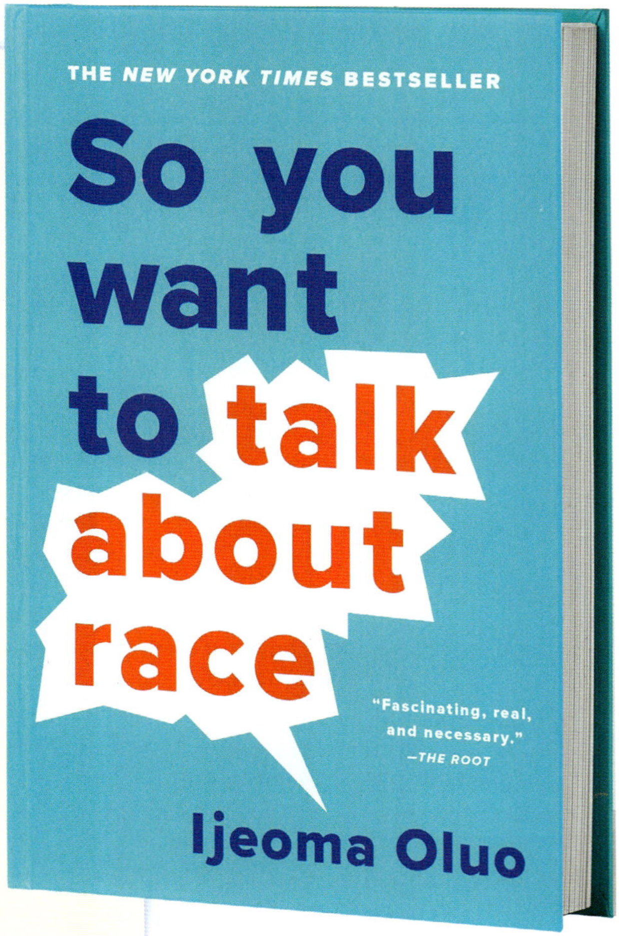


**CULTURE SPOT**

**Ijeoma Oluo**'s nonfiction book is a *New York Times* bestseller. It has been translated into several languages and has had a worldwide impact.

**a. Read** the text and **find out** what makes the writer proud of being black.

**b. Account** for the challenges she had to face and **explain** the evolution of her vision regarding race nowadays.

**c.** RHETORIC **Focus** on l. 31-35 and **identify** the stylistic device. **Explain** its effect on the reader.

**d. Comment** on the sentence *"It is very hard to survive as a woman of color"*. (l. 20)

**e. Discuss**: How can writing help people assert themselves?

**AT HOME** **Choose** one of the famous authors or activists referred to in the text. **Find out** more about some of the actions they took to end racial discrimination.

**WORDS**

- emp**o**werment
- id**e**ntity p**o**litics: *politique identitaire*
- **ou**tlet = rel**ea**se: *exutoire*
- r**a**cial inequ**a**lity
- self-ass**e**ssment

- blunt /blʌnt/ = dir**e**ct
- cons**er**vative ≠ progr**e**ssive
- controv**er**sial
- r**a**ce-related

- achi**e**ve /ə'tʃi:v/
- make one's voice heard

Makeshift memorial to George Floyd, Minneapolis, Minnesota

**On Instagram, artists are creating a shareable language of protest**

In wavy, bold letters splashed in front of a colorful gradient[1], a guide to activism on Instagram reads: "VIRTUAL PROTESTING 101." [...] In seven images, this Instagram carousel prompts users to use the platform to take action.

Anyone with an Instagram account and the will to join in on the now-global uprising in support of Black Lives Matter can follow along; then, they can easily pass the message to their followers. As Manassaline Coleman, the Liberia-born, D.C. metro area-based graphic designer who created the images wrote in her post's caption, "So the question is how can we continue sharing but do it in an effective way?" Coleman's design has been shared over 350,000 times. Coleman might not have considered herself an activist or a political person, her design is part of the rising wave of Instagram protest art prompting people to action. [...] Politics and art have always been inextricable, but Instagram now mediates that relationship. Recently, you've probably seen the work of Nikkolas Smith, a former Disney theme park designer who's now known for his digital paintings of George Floyd, flanked by the words "Justice 4 George"; Breonna Taylor in her EMT[2] uniform, "Say Her Name" beside her; Ahmaud Arbery, in a bowtie with his eyes closed. Former First Lady Michelle Obama used these paintings to accompany her call to action about racism in the United States, a post which over 1.3 million people have since liked. [...]

The possibility for art to create positive change is why Smith refers to his work as "artivism."

Bettina MAKALINTAL, *Vice.com*, June 2020

**1.** *dégradé* **2.** Emergency Medical Technician

**CULTURE SPOT** ARTICLE

**George Floyd**'s death in May 2020 had a huge impact. Murals sprung up across the world in support for justice.

## Doc 2. Artivism

**a.** **Observe** the mural above and **react** to the artist's message.

**b.** **Read** the article and **define** the concept of virtual protesting.

**c.** **Account** for Coleman's design and **comment** on its impact.

**d.** GRAMMAR **Focus** on l. 18. **Identify** the verb tense and form and **explain** this choice here. ▸ p. 57

**e.** **Rephrase** the concept of "artivism" and **comment** on its possible role in leading to change.

## Doc 3. Tracking the movement

AUDIO

"Mapping BLM protests around the World", *Wbur*, June 2020

**a.** **Listen** to the podcast. **Give** details on Alex Smith's work.

**b.** **Focus** on the data, figures, locations, and **analyse** the movement's growth.

**c.** **Comment** on the unexpected elements found regarding some places.

**d.** **Give your opinion**: Do you believe a fair cause can rally beyond political colours?

**AT HOME** **Watch** the online map and **comment** on the location where most of the red points are situated around the world. MAP

DIFFÉRENCIATION

**YOUR TASK** **Write** a post on Instagram with the hashtag #virtualprotesting.

**WAY 1** **Describe** the expansion of the movement through art and protests.

**WAY 2** **Account** for the expansion of the movement and **explain** its political stakes.

**BOOST YOUR SKILLS!**

**Décrire une évolution**

- Utilise des marqueurs temporels : *It is not something I* ***always***... • *The way that I do* ***now***. • ***Recently****, you've probably seen...* • *The* ***5th week*** *of protest...*
- Inscris-la dans la durée avec des V-*ing* : *We continue* ***sharing***... • *There are so many points* ***crowding*** *the map.*
- Fais le bilan au *present perfect* : *Politics and arts* ***have*** *always* ***been*** *inextricable.* • *Coleman's design* ***has been shared*** *350,000 times.* GRAMMAR ▸ p. 57

EXPLORE

# 3 Relying on democracy

## Doc 1. Learning from role models

AUDIO

A tribute to John Lewis on BLM Avenue, Jarrad HENDERSON, USA TODAY NETWORK (Audio: "John Lewis was 'a giant'", *BBC*, July 2020)

**a. Listen** to Martin Luther King III's tribute to John Lewis. **Take** notes on his actions and achievements.

**b. Explain** why the choice of such a speaker makes this tribute powerful.

**c.** PHONOLOGY **Comment** on how some stressed words help the speaker emphasise his point. ▸ p. 58

**d. Rephrase** MLK's solution to reach for more social justice.

YOUR TASK **Record** a short podcast for NPR to **pay tribute** to another African-American activist of your choice.

### CULTURE SPOT

**John Lewis** was a Civil Rights activist and Congressman. In 1963, he was one of the organisers of the March on Washington, where Martin Luther King delivered his famous "*I have a dream*" speech.

LANDMARKS p. 275

### BOOST YOUR SKILLS!

**Rendre hommage à quelqu'un**

- Utilise des expressions élogieuses : *He was **beyond a giant**. • A **great** man. • He did **such a great** work.*
- Appelle à poursuivre son action : ***Don't** just talk and say... • **Let's not excuse** violence* GRAMMAR p. 57
- Implique ton auditoire : *What he would want **us** to do... • It struck a chord in **our** nation... • If **we** want **our** justice system to...*

## Doc 2.

### Will the Black Lives Matter movement create lasting change?

Like the protests today, the Civil Rights Movement forced many Americans to confront their attitudes toward race in a new and revealing way. The current movement may feel like it has built that same sort of transformative energy in the weeks after it was sparked by the police killing of George Floyd in Minneapolis. But it's too early to tell whether it will have the sustained support needed to create lasting change. [...] While modern U.S. history has no shortage of social movements, today's effort seems more focused and universal, activists and other experts argue. [...]

Others have expressed skepticism that the movement will achieve its goals. [...] The intense partisan divide in America means that everything eventually becomes a fight between Democrats and Republicans—and attempts to enact laws around social justice aren't likely to be an exception, some political experts argue.

#### Optimists vs. skeptics

**There has been a remarkable change in public opinion**

"In what may represent one of the more rapid shifts in racial attitudes in recent U.S. history a broad majority of Americans now believe that both the police and society as a whole are beset by systemic racism." (Andrew Romano, *Yahoo News*)

**Partisanship may prevent any major legislative changes**

"Admitting there's a problem with policing and racism in America seems to have bridged the partisan gap. But creating policy solutions will be harder [...], it may be a partisan divide that prevents anything from changing." (Amber Phillips, *Washington Post*).

Mike REBERNESS, *Yahoo News 360*, June 2020

**a. Read** the article and **say** which other movement BLM is compared to, and why.

**b. Compare** people's support of both movements.

**c. Identify** the potential obstacles to a lasting movement.

**d. Focus** on the two quotes. **Contrast** both journalists' points of view.

### CULTURE SPOT

In 2021, the **BLM movement** was nominated for the Nobel Peace Prize.

## Doc 3.

**How to make this moment the turning point for real change**

The small minority of folks who've resorted to violence in various forms, whether out of genuine anger or mere opportunism, are putting innocent people at risk. So let's not excuse violence, or rationalize it, or participate in it. [...] I've heard some suggest that the recurrent problem of racial bias[1] in our criminal justice system proves that only protests and direct action can bring about change, and that voting and participation in electoral politics is a waste of time. I couldn't disagree more. The point of protest is to raise public awareness, to put a spotlight on injustice, and to make the powers that be uncomfortable; in fact, throughout American history, it's often only been in response to protests and civil disobedience that the political system has even paid attention to marginalized communities. But eventually, *aspirations have to be translated into specific laws and institutional practices*—and in a democracy, that only happens when we elect government officials who are responsive to our demands. [...]

So the bottom line is this: if we want to bring about real change, then the choice isn't between protest and politics. *We have to do both*. We have to mobilize to raise awareness, *and* we have to organize and cast our ballots[2] to make sure that we elect candidates who will act on reform.

I recognize that these past few months have been hard and dispiriting[3] [...]. But watching the heightened activism of young people in recent weeks, of every race and every station, makes me hopeful. If, going forward, we can channel our justifiable anger into peaceful, sustained, and effective action, then this moment can be a real turning point in our nation's long journey to live up to our highest ideals.

Let's get to work.

Barack OBAMA, *obama.medium.com*, June 1st 2020

**1.** racism **2.** vote **3.** *démoralisant*

Campaign to get Americans to vote in November 2020.

**a. Observe** the poster and **guess** the celebrities' goal.

**b. Read** the essay and **spot** the aspect of the protest condemned by Barack Obama.

**c. Rephrase** Barack Obama's solutions to fight racism.

**d. Comment** on Obama's tone at the end of the essay.

**AT HOME Watch** Barack Obama's video and **get** ready to **react** to his statement. VIDEO

**WORDS**

- achievement = accomplishment
- equity = fairness
- social justice

- committed
- inspiring

- campaign for
- praise
- struggle = fight for

## FINAL TASK

**Make a committed speech to promote social justice.**

**As a human-rights activist you were invited to make a speech on Martin Luther King Day in Washington' DC. Deliver a powerful speech to promote social justice.**

1. **Browse** through the file and **choose** an event or an action you would like to highlight.
2. **Prepare** your arguments focusing on:
   – the main values or ideas you would like to praise;
   – the growing influence of the movement through time;
   – a role model of the Black Lives Matter movement you would like to pay tribute to.
3. **Plan** the connective devices and communication skills that will make your point clear and get your audience involved.
4. **Deliver** your speech. **Make** sure to sound convincing by emphasising the main ideas.

BOOST YOUR ENGLISH p. 57

YES YOU CAN!

# Deliver a powerful speech

OBJECTIF BAC p. 310-311

## Step 1 DÉFINIR TON SUJET

Détermine l'enjeu de ton discours...

- Insister sur une question de société ?
- Rassembler ton auditoire autour d'une cause ?
- Promouvoir quelque chose ?
- Proposer des actions pour résoudre un problème ?

## Step 2 SE PRÉPARER

Hiérarchise et organise tes idées pour...

**Accrocher le public**
Trouve une **formule d'accroche** forte et enthousiaste. Pense à interpeller l'auditoire avec des pronoms de 1re personne, des impératifs ou des questions rhétoriques.

**Être convaincant(e)**
**Organise** clairement ton discours avec des **connecteurs** logiques. **Justifie** tes arguments par des **exemples**. Appuie-toi sur des **figures d'autorité**.

**Créer du rythme et de l'empathie**
Appuie-toi sur des **figures de style** (répétitions, comparaisons...).
Inclus des **anecdotes personnelles** pour permettre l'**identification** du public.

## Step 3 PRENDRE POSITION

Prépare une **conclusion percutante** en t'appuyant sur une citation inspirante ou en lançant un défi à ton auditoire.

## À TOI DE JOUER!

### SALUTATIONS

Salue ton auditoire, présente-toi et annonce le sujet de ton discours.

*__Citizens of the world__, my friends, we Americans are using __our voice__ like a rallying cry.*
*__We Americans__, are speaking out today __to stop this systemic racism__.*

### MESSAGE

Précise le contexte de ton discours en donnant des exemples précis. Souligne les valeurs que tu défends.

*Many young black males were __discriminated against__...*
*Street protests appeared and sportsmen __took a stand__.*

### ADHÉSION

Adresse-toi au public et utilise des phrases courtes et percutantes. Implique-toi pour susciter l'émotion et rallier l'auditoire à ta cause. N'oublie pas de regarder le public et d'engager ton corps et ta voix.

*__We__ protest because __we__ love __ourselves__ and __we__ love __our__ people. Our __lives__ matter! __Black lives__ matter!*

Athletes rise up, p. 51

### RYTHME

Donne du poids à ton discours en variant les effets de rythme avec des répétitions, des structures ternaires...

*__I am__ hopeful, / __I am__ inspired.*
*__This is why__ we have to protest, __this is why__ we are so passionate.*
*Seeking the truth, / finding the truth, / telling the truth and / living the truth...*

### EMPHASE

Mets les idées principales en relief en accentuant les mots clés, et ménage des pauses pour créer des effets d'attente.

*How can you not be in a __rage__ when you __know__ that you're always at __risk__ of __death__ in the __streets__ // or __enslavement__ in the __prison system__?*

### CONCLUSION

Remercie ton auditoire et termine par une citation ou une phrase percutante pour marquer les esprits.

*Thank you for listening and to quote Martin Luther King: "The time is always right to do what is right."*

# BOOST YOUR ENGLISH!

## Grammar — Prôner la justice sociale

- **Pose un constat de départ au *present perfect*.**

*These past few months **have been** hard and dispiriting.*
*Race **has** also **been** countless hours spent marvelling at our history.*

- **Sers-toi de verbes à particules pour évoquer la portée d'un engagement.**

*Protest **sprung up** around the country*
*The movement has **taken on** a life of its own.*
*Action can **bring about** change.*

- **Appelle à réfléchir avec des questions rhétoriques.**

*My question is, **why aren't all people?***
***How can you** willingly **be blind** to the truth …?*
***How can we continue** sharing but do it in an effective way?*

- **Montre les changements possibles avec des subordonnées conditionnelles.**

***If** we want to bring about real change, we **should**…*
*Nothing will change, **unless** we start working all together.*
***Provided** we succeed in curbing systemic racism…*

**1** **Complète avec les prépositions qui conviennent, puis traduis le passage.**

The Black Lives Matter movement has led … several reactions … the globe. First, sportsmen decided to speak … to denounce systemic racism … the black community. Several months later, Yolanda King reminded the audience that she wasn't ready to give … the fight … racial equality. Finally, the movement actually took … a life of its own.

**2** **Rédige quelques phrases du discours pacifiste de Yolanda King dans lequel elle évoque au conditionnel des progrès possibles vers plus de justice sociale.**

Yolanda King speaking at the March on Washington, August 28, 2020

## Vocabulary — Black Lives Matter

### Activism (AUDIO)
- identity politics: *politique identitaire*
- standard = role model
- touchstone
- admirable = outstanding
- inspiring
- praiseworthy
- loom large = play a part

### Street voices (AUDIO)
- civil disobedience
- empathy
- mainstream
- grassroots
- nationwide
- supportive

### Democracy (AUDIO)
- freedom of speech
- bipartisan
- cast a ballot
- register to vote

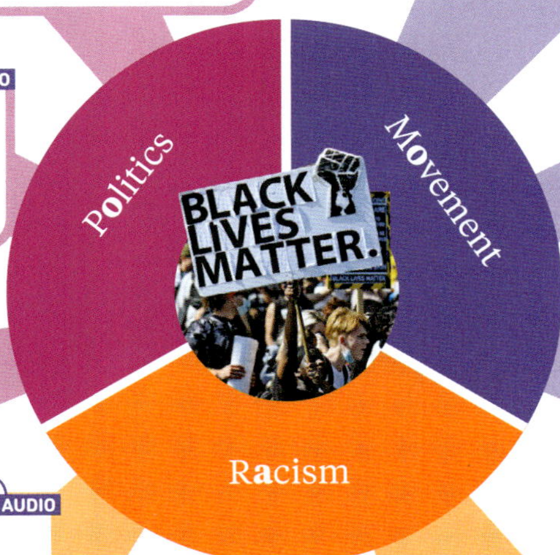


### Artivism (AUDIO)
- convey a message
- erupt = emerge
- paint murals
- pay tribute to = praise
- raise awareness

### Goals (AUDIO)
- racial equality
- social justice
- reach out
- target

### Protest (AUDIO)
- rebellion
- riots
- demonstrate
- rally
- sit in
- support
- take a knee = kneel down
- take a stand = demand

### Inequality (AUDIO)
- conservatism ≠ broad-mindedness
- partiality ≠ integrity
- police brutality
- systemic injustice
- unfairness ≠ fairness

### Race-related bias (AUDIO)
- one-sidedness = intolerance
- prejudice
- second class
- be discriminated against
- divide
- segregate

Vers le **BAC**

# LET'S BRAINSTORM!

OBJECTIF BAC ▶ p. 305-317

## Speaking out

- Street protests for equality

➜ "#BlackLivesMatter", *NBCNews*, p. 50 • "Mapping BLM protests", *Wbur*, p. 53

- Taking a knee to denounce injustice

➜ "Kaepernick's speech", *Amnesty International*, p. 51 • NFL's support to Kaepernick, *CNN*, p. 51

## Raising awareness beyond colours

- A blunt self-assessment regarding skin colour

➜ *So You Want to Talk About Race*, I. Oluo p. 52

- Virtual protesting

➜ Artivism, *Vice*, p. 53 • Makeshift memorial to George Floyd, p. 53

- Going over political colours

➜ "Mapping BLM protests", *Wbur*, p. 51

REPRÉSENTATIONS Axe 1

**How are Americans raising their voices to reshape democracy?**

## Reenacting voting rights for action

- The spectrum of the Civil Rights Movement

➜ "John Lewis was 'a giant'", *BBC*, p. 54

- Protest and politics: casting ballots as a necessary step

➜ When we all vote, poster, p. 55 • "How to make this moment the turning point for real change", B. Obama, p. 55

## A lasting change?

- Warning against violence

➜ "How to make this moment the turning point for real change", B. Obama, p. 55

- Politicians' action to rally the cause

➜ "DC Mayor has 'BLM'" painted on street", *Newsy*, p. 51

- Righteousness and equality as mandatory requirements

➜ "John Lewis was 'a giant'", *BBC*, p. 54

## Phonology — L'emphase à l'oral

AUDIO

- **L'emphase** consiste à **mettre en relief** certains éléments du discours pour en souligner l'importance :
  – en ajoutant un accent fort où on ne l'attend pas : *But **I** am hopeful. **I** am inspired.*
  – avec des phrases clivées : ***That's what** he was about.* • ***That's what** he would want.*
  – en ajoutant l'auxiliaire **do/did** entre le sujet et le verbe : *I **do** believe we can…*

- La **prosodie** (intonation, pauses) permet également de mettre en valeur certains points :
  – en jouant sur le **rythme** de la phrase : *Seeking the truth, / finding the truth, / telling the truth.*
  – en marquant une courte **pause** avant l'élément à mettre en valeur : *He encouraged young people to be engaged // in the fight for justice*

**1** **Lis ces phrases à voix haute en accentuant les mots importants et en marquant les pauses nécessaires. Écoute et vérifie.**

*"You cannot stop, cannot stop the call of history. You may use troopers, you may use fire hoses and water, but it cannot be stopped. There cannot be any turning back. We've come too far, made too much progress, to stop now or to go back."*

Vers le **BAC**

# BUILD YOUR PORTFOLIO

## Song

"I just wanna live", Keedon Bryant, 2020

> I'm a young black man
> Doing all that I can
> To stand
> Oh, but when I look around
> And I see what's being done
> To my kind
> Every day
> I'm being hunted as prey
> My people don't want no trouble
> We've had enough struggle
> I just wanna live [...]

- **Watch** the video and **pay** attention to the lyrics. **Comment** on the message conveyed by Keedon Bryant. VIDÉO

## Campaign

"The NFL Players have a message for the league & owners", NFL players, June 2020

Following George Floyd's killing, National Football Players took it to the social media and recorded a video message addressed to the American nation and the world. VIDÉO

- **Watch** the video and **explain** what is powerful about the speech delivered by the players.

## Book

*The Hate U Give*, Angie Thomas, 2017

The novel tells the story of a teenage girl witnessing the murder of her best friend by the police. It condemns systemic racism and police brutality.

- **Read** the book or **watch** the movie adaptation. **Explain** how they can be related to the Black Lives Matter Movement. VIDÉO

## Review

"American Utopia is a life-affirming experience from David Byrne and Spike Lee", *Polygon*, September 2020

> *American Utopia*, is a filmed version of Byrne's Broadway show. [...] As the show progresses, the message Byrne is trying to send becomes clearer. As Byrne warbles, "How am I not your brother? How are you not like me?", the back wall of the stage is dominated by a giant projection of Colin Kaepernick.

- **Read** the review and **explain** the political agenda with such a show. ARTICLE

ÉPREUVE ORALE | GRAND ORAL — Entraîne-toi à l'oral

### Step 1 — Build up your speech!

**Épreuve orale**
- Choose one topic in the mindmap p. 58.
- Pick out two documents in the file and a personal one to illustrate this issue. OBJECTIF BAC p. 305
- Prepare your presentation: you must show how these documents relate to the issue you chose.

**Grand oral**
- Choose one topic in the mindmap p. 58.
- Find a key question about your topic and write it down. Think about links with other subjects (*HGGSP, DGEMC*).
- Gather arguments and examples from the file.
- Prepare an outline for your presentation and write your note sheet. OBJECTIF BAC p. 308-309

### Step 2 — Make your oral presentation in front of two classmates.

**Épreuve orale**
- Show your documents to your classmates. Each of you makes their presentation to the others in about five minutes. OBJECTIF BAC p. 306-307

**Grand oral**
- Give your note sheet to your classmates.
- Stand up and make a five-minute presentation to answer your key question. OBJECTIF BAC p. 308-311

### Step 3 — Answer your classmates' questions about your presentation.

# The Crown and the Houses

► **Do Britons feel well-represented by their parliamentary monarchy?**

More on SPEAKEASY NEWS
speakeasy-news.com

YOUR MISSION

**Record a video about British citizens' representation.**
As a political-science student, make a video for your YouTube channel to discuss to what extent British citizens feel well-represented by their political system.

FOLLOW THE STEPS!

## 1 The power of the Crown

**Doc 1.**

The Duke and Duchess of Cambridge, London, December 2018.

AUDIO "Why does Britain still have a Royal Family?", *Sky News*, 2020

Queen Elizabeth II and Prince Charles, Palace of Westminster, October 2019.

Prime Minister Boris Johnson and Queen Elizabeth II, Buckingham Palace, July 2019.

**a. Observe** the pictures and **identify** the Royals' roles and duties.

**b. Listen** to the audio and **explain** the origins of today's monarchy.

**c.** PHONOLOGY **Comment** on the intonation of *"But this is more of a formality. Instead, they have more of a symbolic role."*

**d. Explain** and **comment** on the economic and sociological assets of the Royals.

**e.** Using all the data given, **recap** Britons' view on the Royal Family.

## Doc 2.

AUDIO

*On Brexit and Megxit*, Andrzej KRAUZE, *The Guardian*, 2020
(Audio: *New Hampshire Public Radio*, 2020)

**a.** **Listen** to the radio programme and **find out** the two types of crises referred to. **Explain** how they are related.

**b.** **Identify** the values associated with the monarchy and their impact on democracy.

**c.** **Comment** on British people's relationship to the "brand".

**d.** **Say** how the cartoon illustrates the radio programme.

**WORDS**

- embodiment /ɪmˈbɒdimənt/
- monarchy /ˈmɒnərki/ ≠ republic
- Parliament /ˈpɑːləmənt/
- royal assent: a monarch's approval of a law
- controversial
- parliamentary /ˌpɑːləˈmɛnt(ə)ri/
- rooted in
- challenge = question
- spark debate
- undermine = weaken

## Doc 3.

LANDMARKS p. 278

**POLITICO** **A royal mess: How Brexit has tarnished the crown**

"The Queen's personal view is to stay out of politics," said Robert Lacey, a royal historian and historical consultant on Netflix series "The Crown." "It's her nature to be shy. It's her nature not to intervene. She doesn't believe it's the constitutional monarch's role to make interventions, to change the rules or change things."

But when Boris Johnson — the 14th Prime Minister to serve under her reign — asked her to shut down Parliament for four weeks, she couldn't avoid being dragged into[1] the political fray[2].

The Queen had little choice in the matter. Tradition dictates she grant the Prime Minister his requests. But with Johnson's move seen as an effort to prevent Parliament from blocking a no-deal Brexit and the country so deeply divided between Leave and Remain, any answer she gave was bound to infuriate one side or the other. [...]

Because the country has no written constitution, the Queen's role in public life and what her ceremonial powers really mean exist in a grey area. [...]

"We can't run a country like this, we need a written constitution," said Conservative MP Rory Stewart. "We're only able to survive with an unwritten constitution because people behave, but as people push the limits more and more we need to clarify this stuff."

Labour MP and shadow Treasury minister[3] Clive Lewis went a step further and called for a constitutional convention. [...]

One of the key questions in any such venture would be the role of the monarch. "I'm not sure what the appetite is for a republic but I think that should be on the agenda as something we should discuss," said Lewis.

While few are calling for an end of the monarchy, the creation of a written constitution could curtail[4] its powers for good.

Emilio CASALICCHIO, *Politico*, September 2019

1. *entraîner* 2. fight 3. a leading member of the Opposition 4. reduce

**a.** **Read** the article and **identify** the elements which sparked controversy.

**b.** **Explain** why the royal powers are not clearly defined according to some politicians.

**c.** **Comment** on the British people's relation to their institutions at the time of Brexit.

**d.** TRANSLATION **Translate** the last sentence of the article, paying attention to the meaning of *"while"* and *"could"* here.

**STEP 1**

**Take** notes and **record** a vocal memo to introduce the concept of parliamentary monarchy (its roles and powers) and the challenges it might face according to the political context.

**BOOST YOUR SKILLS!**

**Présenter un défi**

- Pose des questions pour annoncer des enjeux : ***Why** does Britain still have a Royal Family?* • ***What** is the "brand"?*
- Utilise le gérondif pour lister des prérogatives : *The sovereign's main duties are **making** visits around the world, **hosting** foreign heads of state.*
- Introduis les différents arguments grâce à des connecteurs logiques : ***On the one hand...*** • ***On the other hand...*** • ***On a third level...*** • ***While** few are calling for an end...*

# 2 Questioning Westminster's constitutional system

## Doc 1.

### Why the will of the people is a myth in British democracy

They promised sovereignty, but at first it was unclear which variety of sovereignty they meant. Were the politicians who swore we would regain it when we left the European Union referring to parliamentary or popular sovereignty? Now we know they didn't mean parliamentary sovereignty. Boris Johnson's government has sought[1] to trick, rush, ignore and prorogue Parliament at every turn. […]

I've often been asked, when I complain about a government policy, "So why don't you stand for election?" This suggests that the only valid political role a citizen can play is to become a representative, so that only a tiny proportion of the population has a legitimate voice between elections. This is the shallowest[2] and weakest conception of democracy.

I do not want to abandon representative democracy. I want to see it balanced by popular sovereignty, especially the variety known as deliberative democracy. By contrast to the adversarial[3] nature of representative democracy, in which politicians try to dominate and vanquish[4] their opponents, deliberative democracy means drawing citizens together to solve problems. It means creating forums in which we listen respectfully to each other, seek to understand each other's views, change our minds when necessary, and create the rich, informed democratic culture currently missing from national life.

George MONBIOT, *The Guardian*, October 2019

**1.** try **2.** most superficial **3.** *antagoniste* **4.** defeat

**a. Read** the article and **identify** the two models of democracy mentioned. **Compare** and **contrast** them.

**b.** RHETORIC **Focus** on l. 9-11. **Comment** on the rhetorical device used and the effect created.

**c. Discuss** the journalist's suggested solution of *"drawing citizens together to solve problems."* (l. 33-34).

**AT HOME** **Watch** the video and be prepared to **explain** how the British political system works. VIDEO

## Doc 2. Is Britain really democratic?

Video 1: "Meet the Lords!", *Channel 4*, 2019
Video 2: "MPs and the Government", *Channel 4*, 2019

**a. Watch** video 1 and **describe** the composition of the House of Lords. **Identify** and **comment** on both speakers' reservations towards the current system. **Sum up** the possible solutions mentioned.

**b. Watch** video 2 and **explain** what "first past the post" consists in. **Identify** the consequences of the election system on the House of Commons. **Comment** on the suggestions made.

**c. Share** your findings about videos 1 and 2 and **discuss** British people's representation in the current system.

### STEP 2

**Take** notes in a mind map to **explain** the distinction between representative and deliberative democracy. **Sum up** the roles of the House of Lords and Commons and **say** in what ways they can be questioned.

### BOOST YOUR SKILLS!

**Questionner un système**

- Utilise les modaux hypothétiques pour exprimer des doutes : *You **might** think that we live in a democracy…*
- Emploie des adverbes ou locutions pour rectifier la réalité : *They have not **actually** been elected.* • ***In fact…***
- Utilise le modal *should* pour suggérer des solutions : *Proportional representation **should** give a better balance…* • *Then the citizens **should** have a say in…*

# 3 Towards a better representation

## Doc 1.

British Future...

### 'Diversity milestone' as one in ten MPs now from an ethnic-minority background.

Continuing a trend of increased parliamentary diversity, the 2019 election saw 22 non-white Conservatives, 41 Labour and 2 Lib Dems elected to the House of Commons, a total of 65. Strikingly, this now means that one in ten MPs are from an ethnic-minority background, when 10 years ago the figure was just one in forty. Likewise, in 2009 there were only 2 ethnic-minority women sitting in Parliament. Ten years on there will now be 37 ethnic-minority women entering the new Parliament and for the first time more ethnic-minority women were elected than men.

This is, in no doubt, commendable[1] progress. The number of ethnic-minority MPs has risen at each of the last nine General Elections since the first four black and Asian MPs of the post-war era were elected in 1987. But progress was very slow for that breakthrough generation, edging up from four to fifteen MPs over several elections in the two decades between 1987 and 2005. The rapid acceleration in this decade is now helping to give us a more representative Parliament.

However, growing diversity in parliamentary politics has been an English phenomenon, and it continues to be. When English MPs take their seats in the House of Commons, 12% will now be ethnic minorities. In Wales, Scotland and Northern Ireland there are no ethnic-minority MPs. Although England is more diverse than the rest of the UK, one in twenty people in Scotland and Wales are from an ethnic-minority background. We should expect growing diversity to begin to be reflected by the time of the next General Election. All of the parties can look at what they can change to encourage that.

Steve BALINGER, *britishfuture.org*, 2019

1. admirable

**a. Read** the text and **explain** the evolution mentioned.

**b. Comment** on the journalist's view on the situation.

**c. Focus** on the last paragraph and **discuss** the reasons for comparing England to the rest of the UK.

**d. Focus** on the expression *"diversity milestone"* and **discuss** its use to define British people's representation.

**CULTURE SPOT** — EXO **Quiz**

Check what you know about the British parliamentary monarchy.

## Doc 2.

VIDÉO

Video: "Meet the next generation of young politicians", *Channel 4*, 2019

**a. Watch** the video and **identify** the common point(s) between the interviewees.

**b. Comment** on the way they view politics and **explain** how they are raising their voices.

**c.** PHONOLOGY **Focus** on Lara's speech: *"As young people, we need to be the engine of change. We hope you can join our campaign and help politicians see sense to change this."* **Identify** the stressed elements and **say** how they help her make her point.

**d. Discuss** her statement: *"As young people, we need to be the engine of change."*

**WORDS**

- go**v**ernance
- repres**e**ntativeness /ˌrɛprɪˈzɛntətɪvnɪs/
- t**u**rning point
- **u**pward trend
- misrepres**e**nted
- pol**i**tical **l**andscape
- **a**dvocate change
- underg**o** ref**o**rms

**STEP 3**

**Take** notes on the recent changes aiming at a more representative political system in the UK. **Record** a short vocal memo on young people's involvement in politics.

**FINAL STEP**

**Gather** all your ideas from your notes and vocal memos and **find** your line of study. **Write down** some notes using bullet points and **record** your YouTube video to discuss British citizens' representation in their political system.

**You've completed your mission. Well done!**

# play BAC How to... WRITE A CONCEPT NOTE

MÉDIATION

OBJECTIF BAC p. 296

Le jour de l'**épreuve écrite** en Terminale, tu devras **rédiger la synthèse** (en environ 500 mots) d'un dossier de 3 à 4 documents de natures diverses (document iconographique, texte de presse, texte littéraire, essai...) adossé à l'une des **thématiques au programme**. Cette synthèse pourra être guidée par deux ou trois consignes.

**Prenez connaissance des documents A, B et C et traitez le sujet suivant en anglais.**
**[Doc 2 p. 61 (cartoon), Doc 3 p. 61 ("A royal mess: How Brexit has tarnished the crown"), Doc 1 p. 62 ("Why the will of the people is a myth in British democracy")]**

Explain what the documents show about the British people's relations to their institutions.
Make sure that you address:
- parliamentary monarchy;
- democracy;
- the notion of representation.

## 1 Analyser le sujet et préparer son brouillon

**a. Lis** bien la consigne et **identifie** le thème du dossier.

**b. Étudie** chaque document du dossier (auteur, contexte, point de vue et sujet principal), **prends** des notes sur les liens entre les documents (similitudes, différences) et **identifie** le fil conducteur du dossier (problématique).

**c. Appuie-toi** sur les termes du sujet pour bien comprendre ce qui t'est demandé.

**d. Prépare** tes idées en les classant selon qu'elles s'opposent ou se complètent pour faire émerger un plan qui intègre les lignes directrices proposées dans le sujet. **Surligne** les citations des documents que tu pourras inclure dans ta synthèse.

Note tous les mots clés qui te viennent à l'esprit une fois que tu as repéré la problématique :
*Institutions = Parliament, the Crown, general elections, Prime Minister, House of Lords, House of Commons, etc.*
*Relations = agree? Disagree? Point of view?*

- Repère la nature et la source de chaque document et fais-en une rapide analyse : *a cartoon, an article from* The Guardian, *an article from* politico.com.
- Quels liens les différents documents ont-ils avec la problématique ?
  – **Doc A**: *a cartoon = idea of a crisis within the British institutions: Britain is leaving the EU, and Royals are leaving the Royal Family*
  – **Doc B**: *an article = the role of the monarch within a political crisis? Is there a need for a constitution?*
  – **Doc C**: *an article from* The Guardian *= keyword: myth = something that is not true, the journalist is questioning the concepts of democracy and of representativeness within the political system*

## 2 Rédiger la synthèse

**a. Élabore** une introduction qui annonce les idées clés, basée sur les éléments donnés dans le sujet.

**b. Rédige** ta première partie. **Choisis** comme point de départ une idée qui soutient celle avancée dans la problématique et/ou dans les pistes qui te sont données dans le sujet.

**c. Développe** ensuite une idée en contrepoint, ou qui nuance le point de vue exposé.

**d. Conclus** en faisant le lien avec l'axe d'étude et **ouvre** sur de nouvelles perspectives.

Fais appel à tes connaissances personnelles pour aller plus loin dans ta réflexion :
*The political context of Brexit and Megxit has fueled a crisis among British institutions. More and more people, whether politicians or citizens, are calling for a more participative democracy as they don't always recognise themselves in the system or would like some of its aspects to be updated.*

- *The three documents shed light on...* • *The status of British institutions is central to this set of documents.*
- *In contrast / However one also may argue that British institutions enabled British people to have their say on Brexit through a referendum.*
- *In fact / It is quite possible to suggest that deliberative democracy is getting more and more popular.*
- Souviens-toi que **1 argument = 1 paragraphe** contenant des éléments sur au moins 2 documents du dossier.

- La conclusion doit apporter une réponse à la problématique posée au départ : *To conclude / As a conclusion, I would say that...*

# BUILD YOUR PORTFOLIO

## Series

*The Crown*, Peter MORGAN, 2016-2021

- **Watch** the extract from the series *The Crown* and **explain** what aspect of the monarchy's power is represented.

VIDÉO

## Chart

Do you support or oppose Britain having a monarchy?*

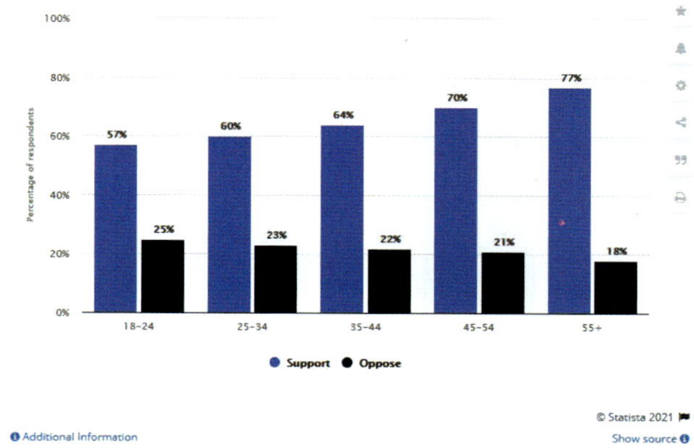


statistica.com, 2021

- **Observe** and **analyse** the chart. **Comment** on the British people's attitude towards the monarchy.

## Article

"UK must hold a referendum on abolishing royal family, Labour leadership candidate says", *The Independent*, 10 January 2020

> "We're a democracy, I'd rather see us as citizens than subjects in the 21st century. Let's talk about what a modern state looks like and what the role of the Royal Family would be in that."
> – Clive Lewis, Labour politician

- **Read** the article and **explain** how the Megxit phenomenon sparked a debate on Britons' representation within their institutions.

ARTICLE

## Report

*Women in Parliament and Government*, Elise UBEROI, Chris WATSON, Esme KIRK-WADE, February 2020

This briefing paper explores the evolution of women's representation in Parliament since 1979.

- **Browse through** the briefing paper and **explain** how British Parliament has evolved in terms of representation.

REPORT

## Book

*The UK's changing democracy: The 2018 Democratic Audit*, Patrick DUNLEAVY, Alice PARK, Ros TAYLOR, 2018

> "Set against the global rise of debased semi-democracies, the book's approach returns our focus firmly to the big issues around the quality and sustainability of the UK's liberal democracy."

- **Browse** through the book online and **sum up** the issues addressed in this audit. **Focus** on part *3.4: Social media and citizen vigilance* and **comment** on citizens' democratic impact through social media.

BOOK

## Entraîne-toi à l'oral — ÉPREUVE ORALE

**Step 1** **Build up your speech!**

- Choose one aspect of the issue you want to highlight: the parliamentary monarchy? The constitutional system? Young citizens' hopes and dreams for the future?
- Pick out documents to build your portfolio: choose from the file, this page, or from your personal references.
- Prepare your presentation: show how these documents relate to the topic you chose. OBJECTIF BAC p. 305

**Step 2** **Make your presentation in front of two classmates.**

- Show the documents to your classmates and explain your point in about five minutes. Make sure you say how they illustrate the topic. OBJECTIF BAC p. 306-307

**Step 3** **Answer your classmates' questions about your presentation.**

FILE 7

REPRÉSENTATIONS

AXE 2 : INFORMER, S'INFORMER

# Media on screen

▶ To what extent has American news turned into a show?

FINAL TASK — Take part in a newsroom debate.

More on SPEAKEASY NEWS
speakeasy-news.com

## 1 On-screen news

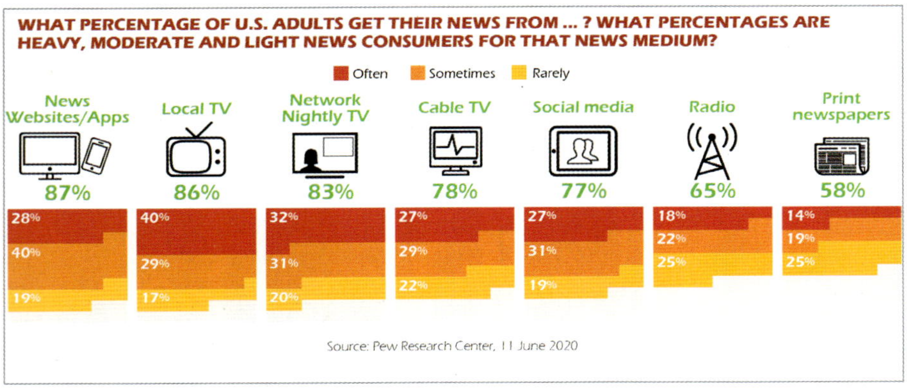


**a.** **Look at** the statistics and **say** where Americans get most of their news from.

**b.** **Read** the article and **find out** the limits of online news.

**c.** **Sum up** the conclusions of the survey (preference and reasons for it).

**d.** RHETORIC **Identify** the technique repeatedly used by the author in the last paragraph. **Explain** its effect on readers.

**e.** **Discuss:** Where do you get your news from? Why?

**Poynter.**

NEWS | TRAINING | ETHICS & LEADERSHIP | FACT-CHECKING | MEDIA LITERACY | EVENTS

### America prefers to watch its news on TV

Allow me a moment to reminisce about a handful of journalism's challenges as we've gone digital. I promise there's a point.

Paywalls[1]. Pop-ups. Overtaxed servers. Clickbait[2]. The classifieds[3] collapse. Banner ads. Excessive banner ads. Inappropriate banner ads. Sponsored content. The wobbling[4] influences of search engines and social media. [...]

Got it? Now read this: A Pew Research Center survey, published today, found that most Americans still prefer to watch the news over reading or listening to it. That number hasn't changed since 2016. A third prefer to read the news and a fifth prefer to listen to it. Given all the work most of us have done on the digital front, it sure is a heaping dose of perspective. Your neighbor or cashier or parent probably prefers to turn on the tube[5] rather than visit your website, watch your video online or fire up your podcast. Why is that? Convenience? It's not hard to turn on a TV and let it roll. Familiarity? There are only a handful of channels to remember. Habit? There are no clear answers, but there is plenty to be gained if you're a digital news organization that can figure out how to draw in TV news viewers [...].

Ren LAFORME, *Poynter,* December 2018

**WORDS**

- downside = disadvantage
- figure
- news (+ sing.)
- trend

- entertaining
- trustworthy = reliable
- truth-telling

- check one's sources
- do the show
- exaggerate = overdo
- stretch the truth

1. paying to access to a website 2. web content meant to generate clicks 3. *petites annonces* 4. back-and-forth 5. television

# 2 From news to show

## Doc 1.

*The Morning Show* is an American TV series which tells the story of a famous morning news programme which becomes unpopular after one of the anchors is accused of sexual misconduct.

LANDMARKS p. 274

### All-powerful news anchors

How did we get here: a place where news organizations put so much power in one person, a place where that person is allowed – even encouraged – to frequent entertainment and “fake news” shows? [...]

CBS spent the 1940s creating the newscast format we know today, with a newscaster guiding the viewer through the news [...].

“Anchor” started to replace the term “newscaster” in television news in the mid-to-late 1960s, after television news surpassed newspapers as the most popular news medium in the United States [...].

In a 1967 New York City survey, sociologist Herbert Gans found that 40% of viewers said they chose their newscast because of the anchor, while only 10% watched because of the quality of the program.

The past thirty years have seen the network[1] nightly news audiences getting smaller and older. Since younger people aren’t watching network news, one strategy has been to get the anchors to appear on programs that are more popular with these viewers. One of Brian Williams’[2] strengths was the ease at which he could change personas, from serious newscaster to genial talk-show guest. Williams appeared on a number of entertainment programs including *30 Rock, Saturday Night Live, The Tonight Show, The Late Show* and *The Daily Show.*

Mike CONWAY, *The Conversation*, February 2015

**1.** TV channels **2.** NBC news anchor for 10 years

**AT HOME** **Watch** the trailer of *The Morning Show* and **explain** how powerful news anchors are. VIDEO

## Doc 2.

### Comedians are not journalists—plain and simple

In William Keve’s *Massachusetts Daily Collegian* article last week, he opens by arguing that “John Oliver[1], a British comedian, is arguably the most influential investigative journalist in the country.”

There’s one problem with this statement: he’s not an investigative journalist. Oliver has admitted it himself. Asked if he believed his show should be classified as investigative journalism, his answer was straightforward: “No. There’s a pretty simple answer to that. No, it is not. No, we are a comedy show so everything we do is in pursuit of comedy.”

Trevor Noah of *The Daily Show* has made similar comments on his relationship with the world of news. “I’m not in the news business, I’m still in the comedy business” [...].

The problem isn’t that these comedians are presenting current events with a comical spin. The problem with shows such as *Last Week Tonight* is that viewers forget that they are simply watching a comedian’s routine. Instead, they take Oliver and Noah’s liberal-leaning comments as affirmation of their own ideas, and by seeing them as investigative journalists they accept it as fact rather than considering that the comedians may be skewing[2] the information for the sake of getting a laugh.

Lauren SOINTU, *Daily Collegian*, March 2018

**1.** host of the HBO news satire show *Last Week Tonight* since 2014
**2.** *déformer*

**a.** **Read doc 1.** and **find out** about the evolution of the role played by the TV anchor.

**b.** **Comment** on the sentence l. 15 to 19. **Give** your opinion about these figures.

**c.** **Read doc 2.** and **compare** John Oliver’s and Trevor Noah’s jobs to that of a journalist.

**d.** RHETORIC **Focus** on l. 9-11. **Explain** how these sentences are built and their effect on the reader.

**e.** **Comment** on the limits of comedians’ perspectives on current events.

EN INTERACTION

**YOUR TASK** Pair work.

**WAY 1** **Write** a series of comments in reaction to the articles (docs 1 and 2).

**WAY 2** **Imagine** an online forum chat between John Oliver and a news anchor about the role of a journalist.

**BOOST YOUR SKILLS!**

**Affirmer son point de vue**

- Utilise des répétitions pour donner du poids à tes propos : ***The problem*** *isn’t that these comedians are...* ***The problem*** *with shows such as* Last Week Tonight *is that...*
- Pose des questions, puis réponds-y pour développer ton point de vue : ***Why*** *is that?* ***Convenience?*** *It’s not hard to turn on a TV and let it roll.* • ***How*** *did we get here?*

# 3 The temptation of the sensational

## Doc 1.

TEXTE LU

Erica lowers her mic and cries, "Get the shot, Manny! Go live, Lesli!" Then she raises the mic. "We're witnessing a tragedy unfolding as a Staten Island ferryboat seems to be off course, out of control, and unable to stop." [...]

Inside the upper-deck cabin, Erica can see crumpled and flailing[1] bodies. Other passengers were thrown onto land by the impact. Screams of agony fill the air.

Erica continues to broadcast. "A Staten Island ferry has just crashed into the Battery Park seawall, killing and injuring many of the passengers."

As she speaks, scores[2] of New Yorkers and tourists rush toward the carnage. They staunch[3] wounds with anything available, often articles of their own clothing, offering comfort and calling for help on their cell phones. Erica sees several people jump into the water to rescue the drowning. [...]

Similar rescues are happening all around Erica. Now she's just in the way. Derek and Lesli have also been offering help to the injured. Manny stays true to his training, filming the scene. "Let's get back to work," Erica says.

She picks up the mic. Her dress is crumpled and bloodstained, her hair flattened, her makeup smeared. "This is Erica Sparks reporting live from Battery Park in New York City, where a Staten Island ferry slammed into the seawall just minutes ago. You can see from the terrible scene around me that there have been numerous injuries and fatalities. We have no idea why the pilot of the boat lost control. The New York City police Department has arrived in force. I see several Coast Guard boats speeding toward the scene, where passengers who were thrown into the water are being assisted by brave civilians who leapt in it to save them. Other passengers have managed to swim to shore on their own. Medical crews have arrived and are transporting the injured to hospitals."

Erica looks over at the party tent – all concerned are standing in shock watching the scene. Clearly, there will be no luncheon[4] for the Duchess of Cambridge. News trucks from the other networks are arriving and reporters begin to broadcast.

Erica spots a dazed but injured man, a ferry passenger, sitting on a bench in shock. She knows a good interview subject when she sees one.

Lis WIEHL, *The Newsmakers*, 2016

1. move in an uncontrolled way 2. many 3. *étancher* 4. formal lunch

### WORDS

- craving
- frenzy
- sensationalism /sen'seɪʃənəlɪzəm/

---

- gullible= credulous
- loaded
- persuasive

---

- brainwash
- generate emotional response
- indoctrinate
- sway= influence

**a. Look** at the book cover and **imagine** what kind of reporter the main character could be.

**b. Read** the text and **pick out** information about the *"tragedy unfolding"*. (l. 2)

**c. Describe** and **comment** on the reporters' roles and attitudes.

**d.** GRAMMAR *"We**'re witnessing** a tragedy unfolding"* (l. 2) / *"A Staten Island ferry **has** just **crashed**."* (l. 8). **Compare** the two verb forms and their use here.

**e. Comment** on the way Erica covers this live news event.

**YOUR TASK** Erica interviews the ferry passenger who is sitting on a bench. **Imagine** the conversation.

### BOOST YOUR SKILLS!

**Raconter un événement vécu**

- Utilise la première personne : ***We*** *have no idea why the pilot of the boat lost control.* • ***I*** *see several Coast Guard boats.*
- Utilise l'expression de la quantité : ***Scores of*** *New Yorkers and tourists.* • *Erica sees* ***several*** *people jump into the water.* • ***Numerous*** *injuries and fatalities.*
- Utilise la voix passive pour mettre en avant la personne qui subit l'action : *Other passengers* ***were thrown*** *onto land.* • *Her dress* ***is crumpled*** *and* ***bloodstained***.

## Doc 2. The way we consume news

Remember when news seemed, well, "serious"? It was something that you discussed over the dinner table in very serious tones, using very grown-up vocabulary. There was a real respect for the news media and the function they fulfilled in society. But what about today? Most people simply view "the news" as a rich source of hilarious new Internet memes[1].

Nobody really reads full articles any more – all they do is scan the headlines and check out the photos or videos. If people in their social networks aren't sharing, re-posting or commenting on a piece of news, then it's all but invisible to them. Moreover, with the rise of sites like Buzzfeed (which now has more visitors than *The New York Times*), the emphasis is on the viral and buzzworthy. If people aren't going to press the "like" button on a story, what's the point of publishing it? [...]

At one point, all you had to do to be reasonably literate was to pick up one of those weekly news magazines that summarized all the top events of the past 7 days. [...] But not anymore. If you're not posting, tweeting or sharing at the moment that a story happens, you've probably missed it forever. News organizations have realized that, and are now positioning every tiny bit of news as "breaking news". [...]

The real news is that "News" (with a capital N to make it sound important) is no longer a commodity[2] that can be bundled up and sold to people for a price. Maybe this is going to sound extremely post-modern, but maybe we've entered the "post-news" era. There is no longer reportable truth, just one version of "fake news" battling with another version of "fake news" for your attention.

Christian ZILLES, *socialmediahq.com*, October 2018

**CULTURE SPOT**

**Buzzfeed** is a global media and technology company which provides coverage on a wide variety of topics. It is viewed as an unreliable source by the majority of respondents.

1. a piece of media that spreads rapidly through the internet
2. product

**a. Read** the article and **find out** about the way people 'view' the news today.

**b.** RHETORIC **Analyse** the flashback effect at the beginning of the article.

**c. Focus** on the way the news is defined at the end of the article and **explain** how it reveals the journalist's point of view.

**d.** TRANSLATION **Translate** the sentence l. 18-21 into French. **Comment** on the use of the *-ing* form after *"if"*. ▸ p. 73

## Doc 3. Switching to the worst

The Voice of America?, David HORSEY, *Los Angeles Times*, 2017 (Video: Who is Alex Jones? NowThis News, 2018)

**a. Describe** the cartoon and **imagine** what kind of journalist Alex Jones could be.

**b. Watch** and **pick out** the main information about the channel mentioned.

**c. Give** examples of the rumours he has spread and **explain** the consequences.

**d.** PHONOLOGY **Listen** to Alex Jones and comment on the way he pronounces the consonants. What effect does it give?

**e. Comment** on his lawyers' statement about who he really is, and **explain** how the video contributes to illustrating this aspect.

OBJECTIF BAC p. 301

**AT HOME Watch** the extract from the TV show *Homeland* and **compare** the fictional character with Alex Jones. VIDEO

# 4 Taking back control?

## Doc 1.

**Networks cut Trump speech as some Republicans chastise President over election lies**

Donald Trump addressed Americans from the White House on Thursday evening, illegitimately declaring victory in the presidential election for the second time this week. Several US news networks cut their feeds[1] of the 16-minute speech, and numerous Republicans condemned the many falsehoods proclaimed in it.

MSNBC halted its live stream of the speech just a few minutes in, with host Brian Williams saying: "Here we are again in the unusual position of not only interrupting the President of the United States but correcting the President of the United States. It was not rooted in reality – and at this point, where our country is, it's dangerous." [...]

On Friday morning, the Pennsylvania Republican Senator Pat Toomey told NBC: "The President's allegations of large-scale fraud and theft of the election are just not substantiated. I'm not aware of any significant wrongdoing here." [...]

As the President spoke the evening before, CNBC also cut away from Trump's remarks, to anchor Shep Smith who said: "What the President of the United States is saying, in large part, is absolutely untrue." [...]

And the Associated Press – which *The Guardian* relies on to project election results – swiftly clarified that it "has not declared a winner in the presidential race, with several states still too early to call". [...]

While many Republicans have avoided commenting on the President's false claims of victory and undemocratic assertion that votes should not be counted, several did speak out on Thursday night, urging patience as the ballots are counted.

Chris Christie became the first major Trump ally to chastise the President for falsely claiming that the election is being stolen from him. [...]

**The News with Shepard Smith**
@thenewsoncnbc

President Trump just spoke at the White House, as key states continue to count votes.
Shep has the facts: "What the President of the United States is saying, in large part, is absolutely untrue." #Election2020
cnb.cx/3l1zk0j

1:07 AM · Nov 6, 2020

57.2K · 14.9K · Copy link to Tweet

VIDÉO

Will Hurd, the Republican Congressman of Texas, said: "A sitting President undermining[2] our political process and questioning the legality of the voices of countless Americans without evidence is not only dangerous and wrong, it undermines the very foundation this nation was built upon. Every American should have his or her vote counted."

Joe Biden also responded shortly after the speech, saying, "No one is going to take our democracy from us," while his running mate, Kamala Harris, said Trump "is trying to invalidate these ballots."

Meanwhile, CNN's Anderson Cooper had perhaps the most bruising words of the night: "That is the most powerful person in the world and we see him like an obese turtle on his back, flailing in the hot sun, realizing his time is over."

Maanvi SINGH and Max BENWELL, *The Guardian*, 6 Nov 2020

**1.** broadcast **2.** wear away, weaken

**a.** **Read** the text and **identify** the context. **Find out** what unusual interventions the American people could watch on TV.

**b.** **Comment** on the journalists' reactions.

**c.** VOCABULARY **Pick out** words and expressions referring to lies or approximation. **Explain** how this highlights the tensions during that election.

**d.** GRAMMAR *"several **did** speak out on Thursday night"* (l. 27). **Comment** on the use of the auxiliary in this sentence. p. 73

**e.** **Watch** the video and **comment** on the journalist's interruption.

**f.** **Compare** the tones used by Donald Trump and the journalist.

**BOOST YOUR SKILLS!**

**S'exprimer à l'oral avec conviction**

- Utilise des adverbes pour convaincre : *They **actually** show what we found...*
- Utilise des tournures emphatiques : ***Not only interrupting** the President of the United States **but correcting** the President (...)* • ***Nothing is more important** to a democracy than a well-informed electorate.* GRAMMAR p. 73

**YOUR TASK** As an anchor, **explain** to your team how far you believe a journalist can go.

LANDMARKS p. 294

## Doc 2.

TEXTE LU

**Will McAvoy:** Good evening. I'm Will McAvoy. This is *News Night*, and that was a clip of Richard Clarke, former counterterrorism chief to President George W. Bush, testifying before Congress on March 24, 2004. Americans liked that moment. I liked that moment. [...] And so tonight I'm beginning this newscast by joining Mr. Clarke in apologizing to the American people for our failure. The failure of this program during the time I've been in charge of it, to successfully inform and educate the American electorate.

I'm a leader in an industry that miscalled election results, hyped up[1] terror scares, ginned up[2] controversy, and failed to report on tectonic shifts in our country. From the collapse of the financial system to the truths about how strong we are to the dangers we actually face. The reason we failed isn't a mystery. We took a dive[3] for the ratings. [...] It might come as a surprise to you that some of history's greatest American journalists are working right now, exceptional minds with years of experience and an unshakeable devotion to reporting the news. But these voices are a small minority now and they don't stand a chance against the circus, when the circus comes to town. They're overmatched. I'm quitting the circus, switching teams. I'm going with the guys who are getting creamed[4]. I'm moved, they still think they can win, and I hope they can teach me a thing or two.

From this moment on, we'll be deciding what goes on our air and how it's presented to you based on the simple truth that nothing is more important to a democracy than a well-informed electorate. We'll endeavor[5] to put information in a broader context because we know that very little news is born at the moment it comes across our wire[6]. We'll be the champion of facts [...] I will make every effort to expose you to informed opinions that are different from my own."

*The Newsroom*, HBO, 2012

Jeff Daniels played anchor Will McAvoy in the series *Newsroom* 2012-2014.

**AT HOME** **Watch** the scene and **explain** the choice of the journalist of the opening video before making his public statement. VIDEO

1. promote 2. generate 3. make compromises 4. be defeated 5. try 6. wire service = news agency

a. **Read** the script and **introduce** the character.
b. **Comment** on the conclusions drawn by the journalist about the media and about his own job.
c. **Explain** how he intends to do a better job.
d. TRANSLATION **Translate** l. 4-7, paying attention to the repetition.

### WORDS

- editor-in-chief
- executive producer
- turnaround = change of opinion
- unheard of
- unprecedented
- apologise for V-ing sth
- blame someone for V-ing
- take one's share of = be responsible for

## FINAL TASK | Take part in a newsroom debate

**At the daily newsroom meeting of a news programme, the anchor expresses his/her frustration at the evolution of TV news. Role play the discussion as the anchor or one of the other members of the team.**

1. **Choose** the role you would like to play (an anchor, an editor-in-chief, a reporter, a producer).
2. **Express** your feelings about the evolution of TV news (frustration, anger, etc.)
3. **Gather** arguments to support your point of view.
4. **Make sure** you can:
   – support your point with specific examples;
   – react to your opponents' arguments efficiently;
   – build up your argument to convince your opponents.
5. **Take part** in the discussion.

BOOST YOUR ENGLISH p. 73

YES YOU CAN!

# Take part in a discussion

**Step 1** CHOISIS TA PLACE DANS LA DISCUSSION.

- Tu provoques la discussion.
- Tu n'es pas d'accord avec la position défendue.
- Tu es d'accord avec la position défendue.

**Step 2** SE PRÉPARER

- **Liste le plus d'arguments** possibles pour appuyer ton point de vue.
- Utilise des **exemples** précis pour illustrer tes arguments
- **Anticipe les arguments** des autres participants et réfléchis à la manière dont tu pourras les renforcer ou les contrer.

**Step 3**

## À TOI DE JOUER!

### INTRODUCTION

Présente le sujet de discussion et appuie-toi sur le profil des participant(e)s pour les inviter à exprimer leur opinion.

*I asked you to join me today to discuss an important matter...*

### POINT DE VUE

Exprime ton opinion de façon claire en étayant ton propos avec des arguments précis.

*He said, "according to legal votes" he believes he wins. **That's false**. **I'm not** in the news business, **I'm still** in the comedy business."*

### ANIMATION

Maintiens le fil de la discussion en posant des questions.
Veille à donner la parole à chacun(e).

*So **Will**, what do you think?*

Pose des questions pour relancer le débat si nécessaire.

***Can I** just say something?*
***Are you** in favour of repealing it?*

► *Newsroom*, p.71

### EXEMPLES

Appuie-toi sur des exemples concrets et précis.

*John Oliver, a British comedian, is arguably the most influential investigative journalist in the country.*
*Sociologist Herbert Gans found that 40% of viewers said they chose their newscast because of the anchor.*

### INTERACTIVITÉ

Écoute attentivement les divers arguments afin de rebondir avec pertinence et faire réagir les participant(e)s.

*Absolutely!*
*You've got a point there.*
*Do you agree?*

### POSTURE

Veille à écouter tes interlocuteurs/trices. Adopte un discours vivant en t'adressant à tes interlocuteurs/trices :

*That's right, **Brian**, we just heard the President come out pretty remarkable **as you said**...*

# BOOST YOUR ENGLISH!

## Grammar — Construire une argumentation à l'oral

- **Utilise des questions rhétoriques pour mettre en avant une évidence et intégrer ton interlocuteur à la réflexion.**

*__Remember__ when news seemed, well, "serious"?*
*But __what__ about today?*

- **Structure ton propos en envisageant des conditions. Utilise des subordonnées conditionnelles.**

*__If__ people in their social networks aren't sharing, re-posting or commenting on a piece of news, then it's all but invisible to them.*

*__If__ people aren't going to press the "like" button on a story, what's the point of publishing it?*

- **Utilise les structures de mise en relief afin de donner du poids à tes arguments.**

*…in a position of __not only__ interrupting the President of the United States __but__ correcting the President.*

*__No sooner__ had he switched the TV on __than__ he heard about the ferry crash.*

*__Hardly__ had Donald Trump started speaking __when__ the journalist interrupted him.*

- **Utilise la forme emphatique avec l'auxiliaire *do* afin d'appuyer tes idées.**

*Several __did__ speak out on Thursday night.*

**1 Traduis les phrases suivantes.**

**a.** Si tu as une bonne connexion internet, tu peux regarder les infos n'importe où.
**b.** Si tu suivais l'actualité, tu pourrais être mieux informé.
**c.** Si l'audience n'augmente pas, ils arrêteront l'émission.
**d.** Si le reporter avait anticipé cet événement, il aurait certainement réagi autrement.

**2 Mets les mots dans le bon ordre.**

**a.** Trevor only Noah Not is a but also host a comedian
**b.** guests Not news only inform anchors the do but public also they interview
**c.** did No home sooner come than he switched he on TV the
**d.** Hardly I had arrived when home phone my rang

## Vocabulary — Media on screen

**Influencing the news** · **Spreading the news** · **The job**

**Informative** (AUDIO)
- co**v**erage
- **neu**tral
- **news**worthy: *digne d'être publié*
- re**li**able
- **trust**worthy

**Sensationalising** (AUDIO)
- cl**o**se up: *gros plan*
- disinfor**ma**tion
- scoop
- blur = make conf**u**sed
- side with
- tri**gg**er = prov**o**ke
- w**ea**ponise

**Noxious** (AUDIO)
- **go**ssip
- **gu**tter **jour**nalism
- propa**gan**da
- per**ni**cious = **harm**ful
- **slan**derous : *diffamatoire*
- **to**xic
- **brain**wash
- in**doc**trinate
- spread fake news

**Broadcasting the news** (AUDIO)
- **ai**ring
- live shot
- re**ac**tion shot
- walk and talk
- air = br**oa**dcast
- tape = re**cord**

**Format** (AUDIO)
- de**bate**
- late show
- **mor**ning show
- pr**o**gram (U.S.) / programme (U.K.) = *émission*
- 24-hour news ch**a**nnels

**The news** (AUDIO)
- **brea**king news
- **co**mment
- **in**terview
- source

**The people** (AUDIO)
- **an**chor
- corresp**o**ndent
- edit**o**rial board
- **free**lance **jour**nalist
- host
- pres**en**ter
- rep**or**ter

**The places** (AUDIO)
- **news**room
- on screen
- **out**side br**oa**dcast
- **stu**dio: *plateau TV*

Vers le **BAC**

# LET'S BRAINSTORM!

OBJECTIF BAC ➔ p. 305-317

**REPRÉSENTATIONS — Axe 2**

**To what extent is American news a show?**

## Changing forms of journalism

- The power of anchors

➔ *The Morning Show*, poster, p. 67 • "All-powerful news anchors", *The Conversation*, p. 67

- New, powerful media

➔ "News media trends" infographic, p. 66

## Looking for sensationalist news

- The rise of Buzzfeed

➔ "The way we consume the news", *socialmediahq.com*, p. 69

- Interpreting truth

➔ *The Newsmaker*, Lis Wiehl, p. 68

## Re-establishing the fourth estate

- Re-establishing the balance of power

➔ *"Networks cut Trump speech as some Republicans chastise president over election lies"*, Maanvi Singh and Max Benwell, p. 70

- Remorse and change

➔ *The Newsroom*, p. 71

## News as a show

- Comedians host the news

➔ "Comedians are not journalists—plain and simple", *Daily Collegian*, p. 67

- Conspiracies

➔ "Voice of America?" cartoon, David Horsay, 2017, p. 69 • "Who is Alex Jones?", *NowThis News*, p. 69

## Phonology — Formes réduites et formes pleines

AUDIO

- Dans la chaine parlée, seuls les mots **porteurs de sens** sont **accentués** et prononcés sous une **forme pleine**. Les mots **grammaticaux** sont très souvent prononcés sous une **forme réduite**. C'est le cas pour les pronoms (*us, you*...), les déterminants (*a, the*...), les mots de liaison (*but, and, of*...) ou encore les auxiliaires (*must, can, had*...).

**1** **Repère les formes réduites, puis écoute et répète en respectant les réductions.**

**a.** *The Internet's premier source for conspiracy theories.*

**b.** *If you've ever heard someone from your high school yell...*

**c.** *He's on thin ice with YouTube, who has given his channel a strike.*

**2** **Identifie les mots accentués et les formes réduites. Écoute et vérifie, puis répète.**

*He may have played a big role in the election cycle, but his lawyers claim he is playing an even bigger role each time he dishes out one of his infamous red-faced rants. The role of a character actor.*

# BUILD YOUR PORTFOLIO

## Book

*Top of the Morning: Inside the Cutthroat World of Morning TV*, Brian Stelter, 2013

In this non-fiction book, Brian Stelter, an American journalist and CNN correspondent, reveals the dark side of morning television. *The Morning Show* TV series was inspired by this book.

- **Read** the book and **focus** on the way Brian Stelter describes morning stars and the enduring power of morning television.

## Film

*Nightcrawler*, Dan Gilroy, 2014

"Nightcrawlers" is a term for freelance cameramen, seen here roaming LA after dark in search of lurid stories to sell to TV.

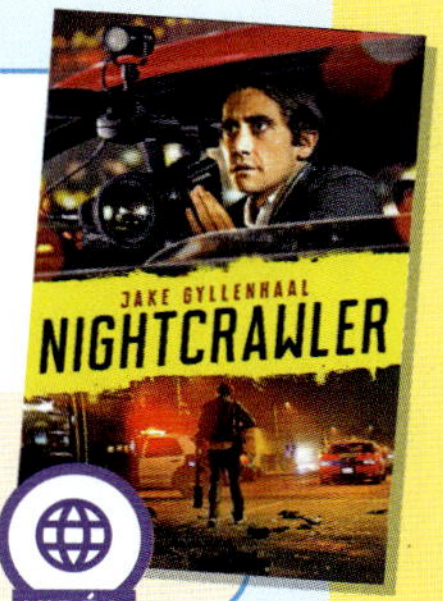


- **Watch** the trailer of the film and **explain** how it emphasises media sensationalism in today's news coverage.

VIDÉO

## Article

*"The New Media's Role in Politics"*, Diana Owen, *Georgetown University*, 2018

“New media have radically altered the way that government institutions operate, the way that political leaders communicate, the manner in which elections are contested, and citizen engagement.”

- **Read** the article and **explain** how the evolution of the media has changed the relation between the fourth estate and politics.

ARTICLE

## Infographic

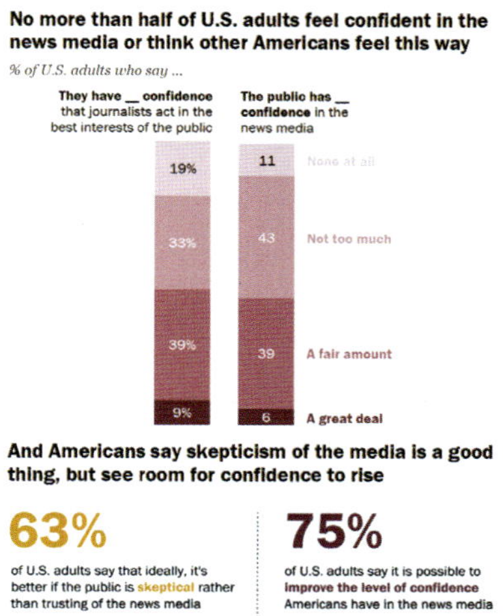


Pew Research Center, 2020

- **Analyse** the infographic. **Explain** what it reveals of the relation between American people and their media.

ÉPREUVE ORALE | GRAND ORAL — Entraîne-toi à l'oral

### Step 1 — Build up your speech!

**Épreuve orale**

- Choose one of the issues presented in the mindmap p. 74.
- Pick out two documents from the file and add a personal one to illustrate this topic.
- Prepare your presentation: you must show how these documents relate to the issue you chose.

OBJECTIF BAC p. 305

**Grand oral**

- Choose one topic in the mindmap p. 74.
- Find a key question about your topic. Think about links with other subjects.
- Gather arguments and examples from the file.
- Prepare an outline for your presentation and write your note sheet.

OBJECTIF BAC p. 308-309

### Step 2 — Make your oral presentation and discuss.

**Épreuve orale**

- In groups of 3, each of you makes their presentation to the other two members.

OBJECTIF BAC p. 306-307

**Grand oral**

- Give your note sheet to your classmates.
- Stand up and make a five-minute presentation to answer your key question.

OBJECTIF BAC p. 310-311

### Step 3 — Answer your classmates' questions about your presentation.

SNAPFILE 8

REPRÉSENTATIONS
AXE 2 : INFORMER ET S'INFORMER

# Press empire

► **How has Rupert Murdoch turned the news into a global business?**

More on SPEAKEASY NEWS
speakeasy-news.com

YOUR MISSION

MÉDIATION

**Write a concept note for *The Week*'s special issue on the Murdoch empire.**

You are a journalist for *The Week*, a weekly news magazine in the UK and the USA. Write a concept note to shed light on the Murdoch empire in a special issue about this media mogul.

FOLLOW THE STEPS!

## 1 Building up an empire

**Doc 1.**

AUDIO

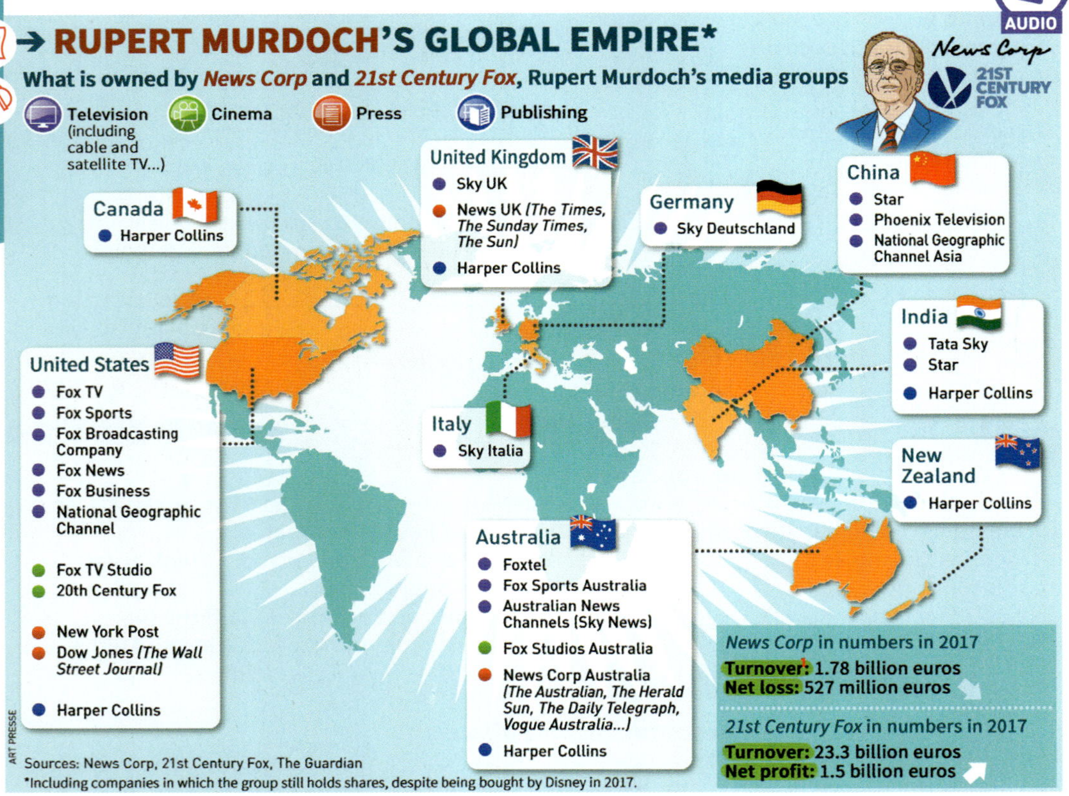


**WORDS**

- compet**i**tion: *concurrence*
- found**a**tion stone
- m**o**gul /'məugl/ = tyc**oo**n /taɪ'ku:n/ = b**a**ron /'bærən/

- **a**ffluent = w**ea**lthy
- aggr**e**ssive
- influ**e**ntial

- br**oa**dcast
- ens**u**re
- exp**a**nd = dev**e**lop
- g**a**rner = coll**e**ct (s**i**gnatures)

1. *chiffre d'affaires*

*Play Bac Presse*, 2018 (Audio: "Murdoch's world empire", *ABC Australia*, 2018)

**a. Observe** the infographic and **react**: what image of Rupert Murdoch's business is conveyed?

**b. Listen** to the audio and **take** notes on the beginning of Murdoch's career.

**c.** TRANSLATION **Focus** on these expressions: *"jewel", "cash cow"*. **Translate** them in this context and **explain** why they were chosen by the journalist.

**d. Comment** on the global reach of the Murdoch empire.

## Doc 2. The tabloid success

VIDÉO

The play *Ink*, featuring actor Bertie Carvel (left) playing Rupert Murdoch.
(Video: *TheaterMania*, 2019)

**a.** **Watch** the video and **take** notes on the play (director, playwright, actors, plot).
**b.** **Compare** the image of *The Sun* at its start and its place in the press industry today.
**c.** **Comment** on the intentions of the playwright.
**d.** **Read** the culture spot and **show** the similarities between *The Sun* and *News of the World*.

**CULTURE SPOT**

In 2011, employees of Murdoch's UK tabloid ***News of the World*** were accused of engaging in phone hacking in the pursuit of stories. Due to public backlash, the newspaper stopped publishing on July 4th, 2011.

LANDMARKS p. 294

## Doc 3.

**SBS News** | **A record-breaking petition calling for a royal commission into the Murdoch media empire has been presented to federal parliament.**

More than 500,000 Australians signed the online petition launched by former Prime Minister Kevin Rudd.

Another former Prime Minister, Malcolm Turnbull, publicly supported the petition.

The pair believe Australia is on the American path to deep division unless Rupert Murdoch's hyper-partisan media operations are kept in check[1].

Mr Turnbull, a former Liberal Prime Minister, said the Murdoch media used to be a group of traditional right-leaning outlets[2] but has now become "a vehicle of propaganda." [...]

He warned that allowing the media to become increasingly partisan was dreadful for democracy because people ended up being unable to agree on shared facts to form the basis of political debate.

"We are seeing people are being able to live in a siloed[3] echo chamber that reinforces their prejudices, that appeals to the worst demons of their nature rather than the better angels," Mr Turnbull said. [...]

Former Labor Prime Minister Kevin Rudd hopes an inquiry will recommend ways to maximise media diversity because the Murdoch media was like a monopoly.

"It's symptomatic of a broader cancer on our democracy, and my principle motivation in putting this petition together has been to bring to the surface this national conversation—rather than people being too frightened to talk about it," Mr Rudd said.

"Murdoch has engendered a culture of fear in Australia about this discussion because he goes after people individually who raise this question, including myself, including Malcolm."

*sbs.com.au*, November 2020

**1.** controlled **2.** media **3.** /ˈsaɪləʊd/ isolated, tightly closed

**a.** **Read** the article and **pick out** elements about the petition (instigator, cause).
**b.** **Explain** what partisan media is and what the consequences are.
**c.** **Say** what the advocates of the petition blame Murdoch for.
**d.** VOCABULARY **Compare** the use of the terms *"empire"* (title) and *"monopoly"* (l. 32).
**e.** **Discuss**: How could this issue be solved?

**STEP 1** **Take** notes on the construction of the Murdoch empire, its state today and the criticisms it faces.

**BOOST YOUR SKILLS!**

**Relater les étapes de la construction d'une entreprise**

- Établis la chronologie des événements : *His career* ***began*** *in Adelaide in 1952. He* ***now*** *sells newspapers...* • ***Along the way****, he built a multimedia cash cow...*
- Fais référence aux évolutions de l'entreprise : *The Murdoch media* ***used to*** *be... but* ***has now become****...* • The Sun ***became*** *and* ***remains*** *the most widely read paper in England.*

# 2 Two papers, different views

THE Sun

Oh Roo behave

WAYNE'S PLEA TO ENGLAND FANS

INSIDE 8-PAGE ROYAL ASCOT GUIDE

BRITAIN'S BEST-SELLING PAPER

BeLEAVE in Britain

THE Sun SAYS

VOTE TO QUIT EU ON JUNE 23

**THE SUN SAYS We urge our readers to beLEAVE in Britain and vote to quit the EU on June 23**

WE are about to make the biggest political decision of our lives. *The Sun* urges everyone to vote LEAVE.

We must set ourselves free from dictatorial Brussels.

Throughout our 43-year membership of the European Union it has proved increasingly greedy, wasteful, bullying and breathtakingly incompetent in a crisis.

Next Thursday, at the ballot box, we can correct this huge and historic mistake.

It is our last chance. Because, be in no doubt, our future looks far bleaker[1] if we stay in.

Outside the EU we can become richer, safer and free at long last to forge our own destiny — as America, Canada, Australia, New Zealand and many other great democracies already do. And as we were the first to do centuries ago.

*The Sun*, June 14, 2016

1. more depressing

**Why Remain is best for Britain**

The leave campaign has not needed to varnish reality but has done so anyway. *The Times* may once have been regarded as part of the establishment. If so, those times are past.

We will take a maverick[1] view where logic and the evidence support it. We have considered every aspect of the European argument with the seriousness and scepticism it deserves.

We respect the arguments of those who would have Britain leave but on balance we believe Britain would be better off leading a renewed drive for reform within the EU rather than starting afresh outside it.

*The Times*, June 18, 2016

THE TIMES

SATURDAY

Weekend Newspaper of the Year

Only £1.50

Why Remain is best for Britain

Eat! Vegetarian feast for gourmets

MP's killer linked to far-right terrorists

the game Euro 2016 12-page guide

20 best places for foodies in France

Beach bodies are best! Giles Coren

1. non-conforming

**CULTURE SPOT** EXO **Quiz**

Check your knowledge about the press. OBJECTIF BAC p. 300-301

**STEP 2** **Take** notes on the role Murdoch's newspapers play on the political stage. **Focus** also on the way the journalists adapt to the readership.

a. **Observe** the two front pages: What issue is at stake? What position did each newspaper take?

b. Knowing that they belong to the same group, **comment** on their positions.

c. **Read** the article extracts. What personal pronoun is used? **Say** who it refers to in each case and what it shows about the nature of the articles.

d. **Determine** the type of each newspaper.

e. **Discuss**: Should newspapers take sides on political issues?

**BOOST YOUR SKILLS!**

**Analyser des choix éditoriaux**

- Rends compte des différences de registres : ***formal terms*** *(varnish reality, leading a renewed drive for reform) vs.* ***more casual terms*** *(greedy, wasteful, bullying and breathtakingly incompetent).*
- Appuie-toi sur l'utilisation de la modalité qui influe sur le ton du discours : *We* ***must*** *set ourselves free.* • *Outside the EU we* ***can*** *become richer.*

**GOING FURTHER** **Read** the article from *The Guardian* and **comment** on the tension between Murdoch and his editors. ARTICLE

# 3 An ever-growing success

## Doc 1. A visionary

**Ten years of the *Times* digital paywall: How Murdoch's 'big gamble' paid off**

Witherow (now *Times* editor) gave a speech shortly before this boasting of the newspaper pursuing its own course 10 years earlier.

"The paywall succeeded because we established a price for digital journalism. We recruited subscribers. We turned a profit. And we continued to invest in the highest quality journalism.

"This might seem obvious now but it is only with hindsight[1] that we see that we were years ahead of our rivals."

For the 2019 financial year, Times Newspapers reported a pre-tax profits of £3.75m and turnover of £330.2m. It said digital subscriptions remained "key" to its ongoing success.

Charlotte TOBITT, *pressgazette.co.uk*, July 2020

1. *avec le recul*

"Setting up a paywall", *FORA.tv*, 2010

**a. Watch** the video and **explain** what the paywall consisted in for *The Wall Street Journal* in 2010.

**b. Compare** Emily Bell's and Rupert Murdoch's opinions.

**c. Read** the article and **explain** why Murdoch can be considered as a visionary.

## Doc 2. From paper to radio

TIMES RADIO

Times Radio has hired the BBC's deputy political editor, John Pienaar, to front its new drivetime[1] programme as Rupert Murdoch's efforts to build a deep-pocketed[2] rival to Radio 4 gather pace[3].

Pienaar, who has been with the public service broadcaster for almost three decades and hosts his own weekly 5 Live politics show, will be moving to the new speech radio station in the coming months to cover "issues of the day in Westminster and beyond".

Times Radio is offering "stunning" financial incentives to lure[4] BBC staff, according to people who have been involved in negotiations. [...]

Pienaar said: "It's been a huge pleasure and a great privilege to work at the Beeb[5]. Now, I couldn't be more thrilled about joining the greatest and oldest title in journalism – in such a new and ambitious project on the digital frontline. The guiding aim is to offer listeners high-quality discussion and analysis of the stories and issues of the day, and make it a compelling, enjoyable listen. I can't wait to get started."

Jim WATERSON, *The Guardian*, February 2020

1. *de grande écoute* 2. rich 3. quicken 4. attract 5. the BBC

**a. Read** the article and **pick out** information about John Pienaar.

**b. Describe** the evolution that *The Times* is undergoing.

**c. Say** what techniques it uses to ensure the new project's success.

**d. Explain** how this evolution is another example of Murdoch's innovative strategy.

STEP 3 **Take** notes on the way Murdoch relies on innovative strategies to ensure his companies' constant success.

### BOOST YOUR SKILLS!

**Mettre en avant des stratégies d'entreprise**

- Anticipe les conséquences positives des évolutions envisagées : *We **will** reach a vastly bigger audience.* • *We think people **will** be paying paper.*
- Emploie des adjectifs mélioratifs et des formes superlatives : *ambitious* • *high-quality* • *compelling* • *greatest*
- Fais référence à des données financières précises : *We've actually had an **increase** in circulation.* • *Times Newspapers reported a pre-tax **profits** of £3.75m and **turnover** of £330.2m.*

### FINAL STEP

MÉDIATION

Your investigation is over: **gather** your notes and **organise** them in order to **write** a concept note about the Murdoch empire for *The Week* magazine's special issue. **Make sure** you refer to the construction of the empire, as well as its state today.

**You've completed your mission. Well done!**

play BAC How to... INTERACT WITH THE EXAMINER

OBJECTIF BAC p. 307

Tu as présenté un **dossier personnel** composé de 5 documents : une infographie (Doc 1 p. 76), un article (Doc 3 p. 77), deux unes de journal (Doc p. 78) et une série documentaire (*The Rise of the Murdoch Dynasty*, *BBC*, 2020, p. 81).

Après avoir présenté ton dossier personnel pendant 10 minutes, tu **interagis avec l'examinateur** pendant 10 minutes. Ce moment d'interaction sera l'occasion :
– d'apporter des précisions ;
– de nuancer tes propos ;
– d'élargir la réflexion menée ;
– d'expliquer tes choix de documents.

## 1 Apporter des précisions

**a.** *You referred to a petition started against Murdoch's monopoly in Australia. Can you give us more details on the requests made by the instigators of this petition?*

Repère le document auquel le jury fait référence et les éléments sur lesquels on s'appuie pour t'inciter à aller plus loin : *petition, monopoly, Australia* → *requests, instigators*

• Rappelle brièvement ce que tu as dit afin de compléter tes propos : *Indeed,* ***as I said*** *Kevin Rudd launched a petition against the Murdoch empire...* • *As you mentioned,* ***I presented*** *the petition started by a former Prime Minister...*

## 2 Nuancer des propos

**b.** *You presented the different treatments of Brexit in* The Sun *and in* The Times*. Do you mean that these newspapers only presented a completely biased picture of this issue?*

• Repère les éléments qui montrent que l'examinateur attend une réflexion personnelle : *Do you mean that...?* • *Did you intend to say that...?* • *Could you explain what you meant when...?*
• Repère les éléments accentués dans la question : *only* • *completely* • *biased*

• Utilise des conjonctions de coordination afin de nuancer tes formulations : ***Even though*** *these front pages show a biased treatment of the news, I have to say that the complete coverage was more balanced.* • ***Despite*** *the catchy headlines, the content was less biased in* The Times.

## 3 Élargir la réflexion

**c.** *You presented an extract from the* The Rise of the Murdoch Dynasty*. Can you think about the reasons why the Murdoch family refused to be interviewed for this series?*

Le jury t'interrogera peut-être sur des éléments auxquels tu n'avais pas pensé. Prends le temps de construire ta réflexion et n'oublie pas qu'il n'y a pas de bonne ou de mauvaise réponse.

• N'hésite pas à exprimer tes hésitations : *I have to say that I didn't really think about that...* • *That's a relevant question and I didn't really look into it but...*
• Utilise la modalité pour nuancer tes réponses : *They* ***might*** *have refused because...* • *This* ***could*** *be a sign of...* • *They* ***must*** *have considered that...*

## 4 Expliquer des choix

**d.** *You presented five documents about the Murdoch empire, and I'm sure you studied more in class. Can you tell me which one you would choose if you had to pick only one?*

Avec une telle question, le jury cherche à savoir si tu arrives à justifier tes choix. L'important est de montrer que tu as choisi tes documents en menant une réelle réflexion personnelle.

• Explique ton cheminement lorsque tu as inclus des documents personnels : *I was* ***particularly interested in*** *this aspect of the issue, so I decided to...* • *I* ***came across*** *this article when...* • *I wanted to* ***dig deeper into*** *the question of...*

Vers le **BAC**

# BUILD YOUR PORTFOLIO

## Documentary

*The Rise of the Murdoch Dynasty*, *BBC*, 2020

In 2020, the *BBC* released a three-part documentary series about the story of Rupert Murdoch's influence on world events and the dramatic personal battle for power at the heart of his own family.

- **Watch** the extract from *The Rise of the Murdoch Dynasty* and **analyse** the relationship between the Murdoch empire and politics in the UK and in the USA.

VIDÉO

## Article

"Why a Trump Loss May Be No Match for Rupert Murdoch's Realpolitik", *The New York Times*, November 2020

“Presidents come and go. Rupert Murdoch remains. [...] *The New York Post*, the Murdoch tabloid that attacked Joseph R. Biden Jr. and his son Hunter before the election, splashed a beaming Mr. Biden on its Sunday cover — "IT'S JOE TIME" — and described Mr. Trump as "downcast" and misguided in his efforts to claim the election was a fraud.”

- **Read** the article and **comment** on the way Murdoch media outlive politics.

ARTICLE

## Article

"How Murdoch's many *Suns* play to both sides of Brexit", *CNN Business*, October 2019

“One of the peculiarities of media in the British isles is the many faces of *The Sun*, the best-selling newspaper in the country, owned by one of the most powerful media moguls in the English-speaking world, Rupert Murdoch. [...] *Sun* readers of those different regions – even if similar in social background – have very different politics.”

- **Read** the article and **analyse** the way *The Sun* adapts to its readership.

ARTICLE

## Investigation

"The Great NFL Heist", *theringer.com*, 2018

“An oral history of the most important deal in sports TV history, when Rupert Murdoch and Fox stole the NFL and John Madden out from under the Big Three networks, created the modern pregame show, invented a new way to see football, and launched a television empire.”

- **Read** the investigation and **explain** how Rupert Murdoch managed to assert his power in sports media thanks to his NFL broadcasting deal.

ARTICLE

## Book

*The Murdoch Method*, Irwin Stelzer, 2018

Rupert Murdoch is one of the most notorious and successful businessmen of our age. Now, for the first time, an insider within the Murdoch empire reveals the formidable method behind the man. Irwin Stelzer, an adviser to Murdoch for 35 years reveals what makes Rupert tick and how he grew from humble beginnings as the owner of an Adelaide newspaper, to becoming the head of a globe-circling enterprise worth over $50 billion.

- **Read** the book and **explain** what the "Murdoch method" consists of.

## Entraîne-toi à l'oral

ÉPREUVE ORALE

**Step 1** **Build up your speech!**

- Choose one topic from the unit: the monopoly of the Murdoch empire, the various treatments of the news, Murdoch's innovative vision of the media...
- Pick out two documents in the file and a personal one to illustrate this issue. OBJECTIF BAC p. 305
- Prepare your presentation: you must show how these documents relate to the issue you chose.

**Step 2** **Make your presentation in front of two classmates.**

- Show your documents to your classmates. Each of you makes their presentation to the others in about five minutes. OBJECTIF BAC p. 306-307

**Step 3** **Answer your classmates' questions about your presentation.**

# Brit-Flicks

▶ **What do British screen fictions say about today's society?**



**FINAL TASK** Interview a British film director about his/her goals when portraying British society.

## 1 A snapshot of British cinema

AUDIO

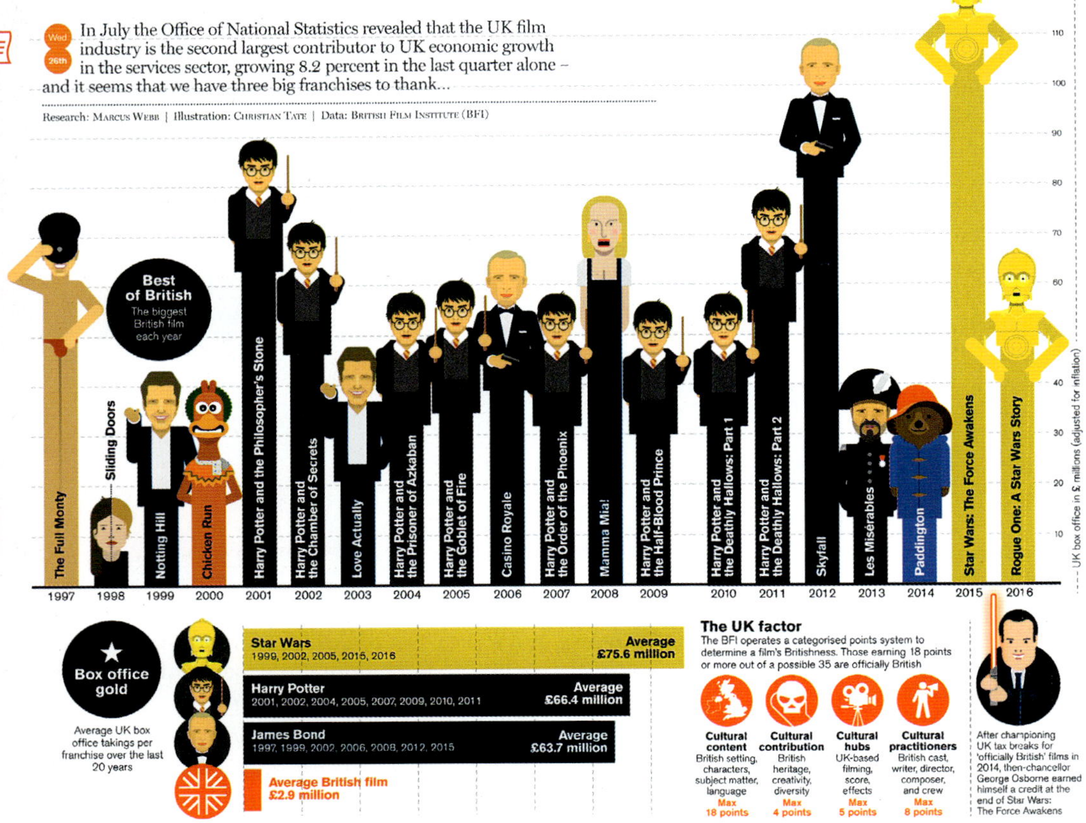


(Audio: "Signs you're watching a British movie", *WatchMojoUK*, 2018)

**a.** **Look** at the infographic and **focus** on the most successful films in Great Britain. What image of British cinema do they convey?

**b.** **Listen** to the audio and **take notes** about the specificities of British movies.

**c.** According to the speaker, **explain** what vision of the UK British films tend to give.

**d.** **Sum up** in your own words what characterises British movies.

**WORDS**
- **a**ccuracy
- ethn**i**city
- plot = st**o**ry

- f**ai**thful to
- r**e**levant
- st**e**reotyped

- portr**ay** = dep**i**ct
- r**e**sonate = **e**cho
- shoot a film
- t**a**ckle an **i**ssue

# 2 Faces of today's British society

## Doc 1. A look into multicultural Britain

(Audio: "On *The Boy with the Topknot*", IamBham, 2017)

**a. Listen** to Sacha Dhawan's interview and **pick out** information about the movie.

**b. Explain** why he decided to accept the role.

**c.** GRAMMAR **Identify** the kind of questions asked by the journalist and **justify** this choice. ► p. 89

**d. Comment** on how the actor explains the film's success.

**CULTURE SPOT**

**Sathnam Sanghera** is a British author born in a Punjabi Sikh immigrant family. The BBC movie was based on his memoir.

## Doc 2.

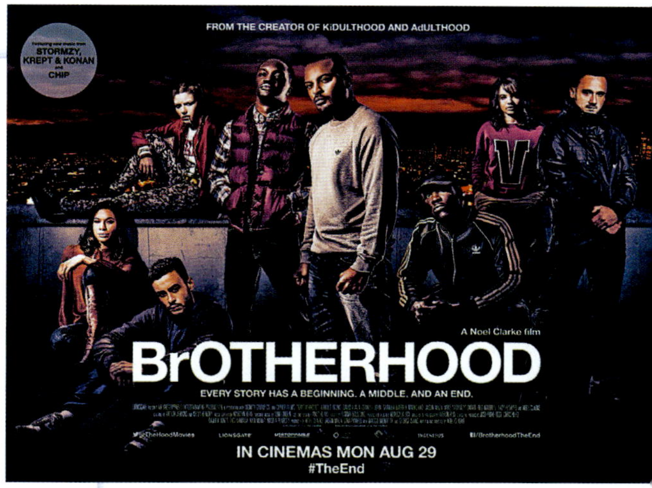


**Why Noel Clarke[1]'s "hood" trilogy remains a vital snapshot of Britain**

When *Kidulthood* came out in 2006, I was 15 years old and it felt like a defining moment. *Kidulthood* was special because it was the first film I felt was made for an audience like me. It was urgent and relevant because it dealt with a world that is so often underrepresented and misunderstood. With no contrived[2] heroes, the characters felt familiar and convincing, concerned with video games, sex and the choices that could change their lives forever. [...] The film gained my trust as a teenager because it was intent on telling a reality that was largely unrecorded in other films that I had come across at the time or in the media in general.

When *Adulthood* was released two years later, I was eager to see what was next. Many of the characters returned, and seeing where they had ended up was a bit like seeing people from school pop up on Facebook—I could draw links between them and the people I knew. [...] I hadn't given much thought to the language in the film up until that point, but it made me realise another reason why the film resonated with me so much. Often writers for TV and film don't do a very convincing job of recreating the language that young people use. Clarke changed that.

This was something he continued in *Brotherhood*, which I saw last week. [...] I have great respect for what this trilogy has achieved. *Brotherhood* gave me a sense of closure in what has been a defining decade in my life. I just hope the next generation has more films like this, that reflect who they are and inspire them with ideas of what they could be.

Iman AMRANI, *The Guardian*, August 2016

1. Screenwriter, director and actor of the trilogy. He grew up in a small council flat in London. 2. fake

**a. Read** the article and **look at** the film poster. **Find** elements to **explain** why this trilogy is said to be "vital" in the article's title.

**b.** VOCABULARY **Explain** how the word "Kidulthood" is built.

**c. Define** who "the audience like me" is. **Say** how it differs from what you might expect from usual representations in British movies.

MÉDIATION

**YOUR TASK** **Turn** the article (**doc. 2**) into an interview. **Imagine** the questions to introduce Iman Amrani's analysis of the trilogy and **enrich** her answers.

**BOOST YOUR SKILLS!**

**Poser des questions et y répondre**

- Pose des questions fermées pour obtenir des réponses en oui/non : *Has your experience been similar? > **Yes**, It has, but...*
- Utilise des questions ouvertes pour des réponses plus développées : ***How** did you react when...? • **What** do you hope people would take away from...?*
- Pour répondre, mets en relief les éléments clés avec des phrases clivées : ***That's** what I'm really proud of • **This was** something...* GRAMMAR p. 89

# A certain image of Britishness

## Doc 1. Beatlemania

**a.** **Look** at the film poster and **identify** all the references to The Beatles. **Read** the quotes and **imagine** the film plot.

**b.** **Watch** the trailer and **take** notes on British elements you recognise.

**c.** **Name** the genre of the film and **sum up** the plot. **Explain** what might have built up the film's success.

**d.** **Comment** on the "certain image of Britishness" the film conveys.

VIDÉO

A film by Danny BOYLE, 2019

**WORDS**

- cliché /kliːʃeɪ/
- critique = review
- monarch = ruler
- portrayal

- beloved
- deceptive = misleading
- iconic

- allure /əˈljʊə/ = attract
- crave for = have a strong desire to
- idolise = treasure
- review (a film)
- romanticise = fantasise
- weigh on

## Doc 2. Is this really Britain?

The popular depiction of Britain in global television and film isn't only shockingly homogenous—it's a fiction.

Of course, the Queen is a recognisable component of British film and television, standing as a figure in need of unquestioning devotion and an emblem of... well, it's hard to say. Of upstanding[1] Britishness, perhaps. The Queen finds herself right in the centre of two British productions with massive American appeal this autumn, with the release of *Downton Abbey,* the movie, [...] and *The Crown*, whose third season on Netflix will star Olivia Colman in the lead role.

Olivia Colman as Queen Elizabeth II in *the Crown*, P. MORGAN, 2019

Kings and Queens have been good value at the Oscars, with previous nominations for Judi Dench as Queen Victoria, Nigel Hawthorne as George III, Helen Mirren as Queen Charlotte and Cate Blanchett as Elizabeth I, and victories for Mirren as Elizabeth II, Colin Firth as George VI and Colman as Queen Anne. Other recent Oscar wins—for Gary Oldman as Churchill and Meryl Streep as Margaret Thatcher—show this trend is not so much about the Queen as a character as it is about perceiving Britain through its politics and institutions; through its autocratic rightwingery[2]. [...]

Of course, this image of Britain is sold not just to the world but to Britain itself, underpinning[3] the very idea of Brexit. The Queen's continued popularity is indicative of a generalised fondness for yesteryear[4], and for an idea of Britain still associated with a dimly remembered 'majesty'. The Queen and the idea of royalty are a connection to the supposed glory days of Empire that hardcore Brexiters would like to return to.

Caspar SALOMON, *prospectmagazine.co.uk*, October 2019

**1.** respectable. **2.** *conservatisme strict* **3.** supporting **4.** the past

**a.** **Read** the text and **take** notes on the success of films about British royalty.

**b.** **Identify** the author's critiques towards these productions.

**c.** RHETORIC **Pick out** the expressions or rhetorical devices used to question the success of these films. **Describe** the tone of the journalist.

**d.** **Explain** why the author calls such a depiction of Britain a "fiction".

# 4 Immutable heroes?

## Doc 1. Untouchable 007

**Why Idris Elba should not be the next James Bond**

Who will be the next James Bond after Daniel Craig leaves the role following *Bond 25*? Idris Elba's name keeps coming up—even when he'd rather it didn't—and it's no wonder why. The handsome, charming Brit would make a suave 007, and for a long time I too thought he would be the best choice to reinvigorate the franchise. But I no longer feel that way. [...]

No matter who is cast as James Bond, he will face criticism. It happens for Batman, it happens for Captain America, it just happens for any major franchise role. The hardcore Bond fans, in particular, will always bring up how Ian Fleming wrote the character of James Bond a certain way. Heck, I remember the backlash when Daniel Craig was cast because he was a "blond Bond" and didn't fit the black hair of Fleming's description. Daniel Craig ended up winning over a lot of James Bond fans, and Idris Elba would probably do the same, except for the ones who couldn't get past his race, his age or just preferring XYZ in the role. Rather than wasting time trying to convince those fans that Elba is Bond, leave Bond to be the chain-smoking Hoagy Carmichael ladies man[1] he was written to be and give Elba his own signature action hero.

I can see Idris Elba attracting fans who never cared about James Bond because he's already done exactly that. He has many fans excited at the idea of him in the role. To me, Idris Elba could potentially give the James Bond franchise new life around the world, but I don't want him to do it because [...] I'd rather see him in a role that could maximize his dramatic chops[2] and get him on the Oscar track.

Gina CARBONE, *cinemablend.com*, June 2019

Upcoming James Bond film poster, 2021

1. a stereotyped character
2. talent

## Doc 2. Legally Black campaign

VIDÉO

(Video: *BhamUrbanNews UK*, 2018)

a. **Look** at the film poster (**doc. 1**) and **identify** the "immutable" characteristics of a James Bond film.

b. **Read** the article. **Pick out** the reasons why Idris Elba would seem like a good fit to play James Bond. Then **identify** the potential obstacles or reservations.

c. **Observe** the poster (**doc. 2**) and **watch** the video. **Explain** the message of the Legally Black campaign.

d. **Comment** on the choice of film to deliver this message.

e. **Conclude** on what these documents reveal about "a certain image" of British heroes. **Compare** their purpose.

**YOUR TASK** **Imagine** and **present** another poster for the Legally Black campaign.

DIFFÉRENCIATION

**WAY 1** **Justify** your choice and **explain** how it serves the campaign.

**WAY 2** **Give** details about your goals by choosing this particular poster. **Explain** how it debunks British stereotypes.

**BOOST YOUR SKILLS!**

**Présenter un projet**

- Expose tes choix : ***I thought*** *he would... but* ***I*** *no longer* ***feel*** *that way* • ***To me****, Idris Elba could...*
- Utilise des relatives pour apporter des précisions : *For the ones* ***who****...* • *A role* ***that*** *could...*
- Formule tes objectifs avec des connecteurs de but : ***To*** *tackle under-representation* ; et des infinitives : *We wanted* ***to change*** *that.* • *We want people* ***to see****...*

GRAMMAR p. 89

# 5 Reflecting on a changing society

## Doc 1.

*Downton Abbey* film, 2019

### Understanding the Popularity of *Downton Abbey*

The BBC's hit series *Downton Abbey* aired[1] its series finale in the United States last night.

In his article "England as Ideology," Carl Freedman opens by explaining that there is a "certain Englishness" that British cultural forms embody, "or, more specifically, the production of an ideology of English self-representation both as distinctive postwar cultural form and as highly successful (and economically much needed) British export." [...] "Even more important (though not unrelated) is the internal national self-image of Englishness, and here the extreme naturalistic accuracy of the series in its depiction of a more powerful and self-confident Britain both enables and protects a mythic image of an idealized Edwardian and post-Edwardian England." [...]

Freedman argues, "It is an England that well corresponds to what England in the early seventies dearly wished itself to have been and perhaps even to be once again: an all-white society unified by certain generally accepted English values, and one in which class struggle, for the most part, could be charmingly sublimated into domestic foibles[2] and occasional minor tensions between upstairs and downstairs." Taking Freedman's analytical framework, it is interesting to consider, given our moment in history, *Downton Abbey*'s popularity in America.

In considering the large American fanbase, Charlotte Runcie suggests that "US audiences may be attracted to the American-born character Lady Cora, Countess of Grantham, and the exoticism of ancient British stately homes playing host to emotional drama." Lady Cora enables Americans to imagine themselves as situated amongst an otherwise foreign world of excess, wealth, and order.

Ellen C. CALDWELL, *daily.jstor.org*, March 2016

1. broadcasted 2. *manies*

**a. Read** the article and **find** information on the image of "Englishness" a series like *Downton Abbey* conveys.

**b. Look** for information on the Edwardian period and **say** why this period corresponds to an idealised "self-representation".

**c. Explain** the reasons for the success of *Downton Abbey* in America.

## Doc. 2. Analysing today's harsh reality

(Audio: "Interview with Ken Loach", *Sky News*, 2019)

**a. Listen** to the interview. **Pick out** elements referring to *Sorry we missed you* and **summarise** the plot.

**b. Explain** how Ken Loach criticises today's British society. To what extent could his analysis apply outside of the UK? **Give** examples.

**c. Explain** what cinema should be according to Ken Loach.

### WORDS

- liberalism
- genre /ˈʒɒnrə/
- social realism
- uberisation = job casualisation

- eye-opening
- staggering = impressive
- uncompromising = unrestrained

- commit oneself to
- convey = pass on
- denounce
- mirror = reflect

### CULTURE SPOT

**Ken Loach** (born in 1936) is a British film director, famous for his socially critical films. He has inspired other directors like Stephen Frears or Mike Leigh and received several awards for his work.

## Doc 3.

**Imagining a dismal future, *Years And Years* says plenty about the present**

Things are looking bright for pessimists these days—the world has caught up with their sense of gloom[1]. Well over half of those living in the developed world think their countries are heading in the wrong direction, away from the prosperity and stability that people over age 40 once took for granted. Be it climate change, financial collapse, terrorism, political gridlock[2] or the ceaseless psychic tasering of social media, ordinary people often feel caught in a reality that's spinning out of control.

Such a feeling underlies the rip-roaring[3] BBC show *Years and Years* airing on HBO. With hints of everything from *Black Mirror* to *The Handmaid's Tale* to *The Apprentice*, this six-part family saga gazes through a crystal ball to tell a darkly unsettling tale about how history affects individual lives. The action begins right now, in 2019, and carries us 15 years into the future.

The story centers on the Manchester-based Lyons family. [...] As the show begins, they're simply going about their lives. But history soon starts roaring around them like a hurricane. Donald Trump is re-elected and begins a nuclear stare-down with China. Vladimir Putin takes over Ukraine, and refugees pour into Britain. Banks begin to wobble[4], political parties dither[5], and Britain watches the rise of Vivienne Rook—played by a terrific Emma Thompson—a plain-speaking businesswoman turned populist politician who owns her own TV network. [...]

Of course, depictions of the future often prove to be profoundly wrong, as those still waiting for their flying cars can attest. Indeed, speculative fiction usually tells us more about the present than the future. That's true here. Despite some witty doodles around the margins, Davies' dire sense of the next few years isn't exactly revelatory. He basically extrapolates from today's big issues.

John POWERS, *NPR*, June 2019

**1.** despair. **2.** *impasse* **3.** exciting **4.** *chanceler* **5.** hesitate

*Years and Years*, TV series by R.T. DAVIES, Season 1

**a.** **Read** the article and **explain** what defines *Years and Years*.

**b.** **Find out** elements of the international political contexts which inspired the creators of the series.

**c.** **Pick up** information on the atmosphere conveyed. **Suggest** what image of the country it gives.

**d.** **Comment** on the idea that "*speculative fiction usually tells us more about the present than the future*" (l. 25-26).

**e.** **Discuss**: Can TV series help us understand today's reality?

**YOUR TASK** As a film critic, **give** your opinion on the way British screen fictions address social and political challenges.

### BOOST YOUR SKILLS!

**Exprimer et justifier un point de vue**

- Exprime clairement ta position : ***I** think...* • *It can learn about **our** deepest feelings.*
- Utilise des adverbes pour ancrer ton point de vue : ***Even** more important is...* • ***Of course**...* • ***Indeed**...*
- Illustre-le par des exemples : *Let's consider the role **of**...* • *Such is the case **in**...*
- Précise ta pensée avec des relatives : *An England **in which**...* • *A populist politician **who** owns...* GRAMMAR p. 89

## FINAL TASK

### Interview a British film director about his/her goals when portraying British society.

**On the release of his/her latest film, a journalist interviews a British film director about his/her artistic approach and goals when portraying British society. Record the interview.**

1. Work in pairs. **Choose** a British film director you know or among those you discovered in the file.
2. **Gather** your ideas focusing on:
   – the genre and plot of the film/series (action, characters, one or two major scenes) ;
   – the image of Britain this particular work conveys and why ;
   – the director's work (his/her motivations, his/her goals, etc.).
3. **Prepare** the questions the journalist would ask the director.
4. **Record** the interview emphasising the main ideas to better share your convictions.

YES YOU CAN! p. 88

# YES YOU CAN!

## Take part in an interview

**Step 1** ANALYSER LE SUJET

- **Identifie le contexte** (conférence de presse, première d'un film, cérémonie de remise de prix...)

**Choisis ta place dans l'interview**

LE/LA JOURNALISTE

- Tu dois **mener** l'interview.
- Tu es **neutre** mais peux parfois orienter les réponses attendues.

L'INTERVIEWÉ(E)

- Tu exprimes un **point de vue personnel**.
- Tes réponses sont **riches** et ciblent les questions posées.

**Step 2** SE PRÉPARER (journaliste)

- Prépare des questions riches et variées et sois prêt(e) à les formuler clairement.
- Anticipe la manière dont ton interlocuteur/trice pourrait répondre.
- Sois prêt(e) à relancer pour obtenir plus de détails.

**Step 2** SE PRÉPARER (interviewé(e))

- Prépare tes arguments pour appuyer ton parti pris et justifier ta démarche artistique.
- Sois prêt(e) à répondre aux questions en utilisant les éléments vus dans l'unité.
- Utilise des exemples de films pour illustrer tes propos.

**Step 3**

## À TOI DE JOUER!

### SALUTATIONS

Accueille ton invité(e) et remercie-le/la d'accepter de répondre à tes questions. Tu peux préciser où se déroule l'interview.

*Good afternoon/evening, Mr/Mrs....*
***Thank you for** accepting this interview.../*
*for answering my questions, here in...*
*for the opening of the film festival...*
*I **want/would like** to ask you about...*

### INTERACTION

Pose des questions et réagis aux réponses. Tu peux exprimer ta surprise ou ton adhésion à ses propos, ou les utiliser pour rebondir :

*So **is that** the reality of the government's austerity measures?*
***What** is cinema for you?*

### CONCLUSION

Remercie ton invité(e) et termine l'entretien par une formule de synthèse ou par le rappel de son dernier film en date.

***Thank you** so much for answering my questions.*
***Let me** remind our audience that your film...*
*will be released next...*

### PRÉSENTATION

Présente brièvement le genre, le sujet et l'intrigue de ton film.

*The film's entirely based on facts.*
*It's a family where both parents are working in insecure work [...]*

Interview with Ken Loach, p. 86

### PARTI PRIS ET ENJEUX ARTISTIQUES

Expose ta démarche et ta position de manière claire et structurée...

***It's** the reality of the free market **which**...*
***I think** reflecting the world we know can make beautiful cinema.*

... et donne des exemples pour étayer ton point de vue.

*They cut their labour costs by no holiday pay, no sick pay...*

### POSTURE

Adopte un ton et une posture en accord avec ton parti pris artistique.

Utilise des figures rhétoriques et des procédés d'insistance pour mettre en valeur ton point de vue.

*Films should be **as broad as** a library, you know.*
*It should have **everything**, **every** kind of story.*
***Whether** it's funny, **whether** it's sad, **whether** it's tragedy, **whether** it's comedy.*

# BOOST YOUR ENGLISH!

## Grammar — Prendre part à une interview sur une démarche artistique

- **Utilise des questions ouvertes pour obtenir des réponses développées.**

*How did you react when you first heard about the project?*
*What is cinema for you?*
*Who will be the next james Bond?*

- **Utilise des questions fermées ou des tags pour obtenir des réponses courtes et précises.**

*Has your experience recently been similar? → Yes, it has.*
*It is the reality of the government's austerity measures, **isn't it**? → Well, **it is** the reality of the free market.*

- **Mets en relief les éléments clés avec des relatives ou des phrases clivées.**

***That's** what I'm really proud of.* (clivée)
***This was** something he continued in* Brotherhood (clivée), ***which** I saw last week.* (relative)

- **Explicite ta démarche avec des subordonnées de but ou des infinitives.**

*A family saga that gazes through a crystal ball **to tell** a darkly unsettling tale.* (sub.)
*We are calling on the media **to make** this change.* (sub.)
*We **want** people **to see** our posters.* (infinitive)

**1** **Retrouve la question qui a été posée.**

**a.** When *Kidulthood* came out in 2006, I was 15 years old.
**b.** *Kidulthood* was special because it was the first film I felt was made for an audience like me.
**c.** No, I hadn't given much thought to the language in the film until that point.
**d.** Of course, the Queen is a recognisable component of British films.

**2** **Mets en relief un élément de ces phrases avec une structure clivée.**

**a.** The free market is said to be the future.
**b.** Speculative fiction usually tells us more about the present than the future.
**c.** British movies give a social image of Britain.
**d.** Humour is a recurrent feature in British films.
**e.** Reflecting the world we know can make beautiful cinema.

## Vocabulary — Brit-flicks

**Screen fictions**

**Genre** (AUDIO)
- action film
- drama
- comedy
- rom-com (romantic comedy)
- social realism
- speculative fiction

**Goals** (AUDIO)
- entertain
- make visible
- portray = depict
- question
- reflect = mirror
- shape ideas

**Reception** (AUDIO)
- box-office flop ≠ success
- blockbuster
- boring = tedious
- biased = unfaithful
- impressive = stirring
- moving < overwhelming

**Representation**

**Periods** (AUDIO)
- Edwardian/Victorian period
- prospective future
- contemporary
- Thatcherism

**Settings** (AUDIO)
- council estates: *HLM*
- factories
- manor houses
- post-industrial cities
- run down areas ≠ nice neighbourhoods

**Characters** (AUDIO)
- British aristocrats
- coal miners
- goal-bereft teenagers
- Oxfordian students
- stiff-upper-lip heroes
- working class people

**Artistic choices**

**Perspective** (AUDIO)
- accurate = authentic
- critical = deprecating
- humorous = jocular
- realistic = true to life
- stereotyped

**Topics** (AUDIO)
- everyday life
- family struggles
- historical turning points
- human relationships
- royalty

Vers le **BAC**

# LET'S BRAINSTORM!

OBJECTIF BAC
p. 296-304

## A portrayal of British society

- Urban youth culture

➜ "Noel Clarke's 'hood' trilogy", *The Guardian*, p. 83

- Working-class reality

➜ "Interview with Ken Loach", *Sky News*, p. 86

- Stories of minorities

➜ "On *The Boy with the Topknot*", *IamBham*, p. 83

## Politics on screen

- Portraying the monarchy

➜ "Is this really Britain?", *prospectmagazine*, p. 84 • *The Crown*, *still*, P. MORGAN, p. 84

- Questioning current policy or economic models

➜ "Imagining a dismal futur", *NPR*, p. 87 • "Interview with Ken Loach", *Sky News*, p. 86

REPRÉSENTATIONS
Axe 3

**What do British screen fictions say about today's British society?**

## A representation of Britishness

- The national music culture

➜ *Yesterday*, D. BOYLE, p. 84

- The myth of England

➜ "Untouchable 007", *cinemablend*, p. 85 • "Understanding the popularity of Downton Abbey", *Daily.jstor.org*, p. 86

## Calling for more diversity

- Multicultural stories needed

➜ "On *The Boy with the Topknot*", *IamBham*, p. 83 • "Noel Clarke's 'hood' trilogy", *The Guardian*, p. 83

- New faces wanted

➜ Legally Black campaign UK, p. 85 • "Untouchable 007", *cinemablend*, p. 85

## Phonology — L'intonation dans les questions

AUDIO

**L'intonation** de base en anglais **monte** jusqu'à l'accent principal puis **redescend**.

- Dans les questions **fermées** (aussi dites *yes/no*), l'intonation **monte** :
  *Are you **coming**?* ↗ • *Has your experience been **similar**?* ↗
- Dans les questions **ouvertes**, ou les **tags**, l'intonation est généralement **descendante** :
  *What is cinema for you?* ↘ • *This film was a success* ↗*, wasn't it?* ↘
- Mais il existe des **variantes** selon le sens de la question. Une question **ouverte** se termine par une **intonation montante** pour montrer la surprise ou la colère du locuteur, ou pour demander la répétition ou la clarification d'une réponse précédente.
  *I'm sorry, what did you **say**?* ↗

**1 Écoute ces questions, puis note et explique l'intonation finale.**

*Have you always wanted to be an actor? • When will you arrive? • Why did you accept the part? • You didn't really say that, did you?*

**2 Lis ces phrases et anticipe l'intonation de chacune. Écoute et vérifie.**

*What was your motivation for directing this project? • Is that the reality of the government's austerity measures? • That's the often unreported reality, isn't it? • Why do you think this is an important story to tell? • You said you were afraid it might be misunderstood, did I get that right?*

# BUILD YOUR PORTFOLIO

## Film

*Emma*, Autumn DE WILDE, 2020

This film is a witty and humorous adaptation of Jane Austen's classic novel *Emma*. Emma, a rich hairess, spends her time trying to form couples while swearing she will never marry.

- **Watch** the trailer or the film and **explain** how humour and wit give a twisted representation of a certain image of "Britishness".

VIDÉO

## Cartoon

*"Bond is Back Again"*, Graham CHAFFER, 2004

- **Observe** the cartoon and **consider** the importance of big productions like the James Bond franchise for the British film industry.

## Article

*Eastenders*, J. YORK, since 1985

*Eastenders* is one of the longest-running soap operas in the United Kingdom. It focuses on a fictional borough of London and follows the stories of local residents going on about their daily lives.

- **Read** the article and **focus** on the vision of UK's society given by the soap opera.

ARTICLE

## Film

*Viceroy's House*, G. CHADHA, 2017

This British-Indian historical film comes back on the dissolution of the British Raj in India and on the conditions and discussions which led to India's independence in 1947.

- **Watch** the trailer and **focus** on the representation of British colonial history. **Consider** the image it gives of British politics in India during the Partition period.

VIDÉO

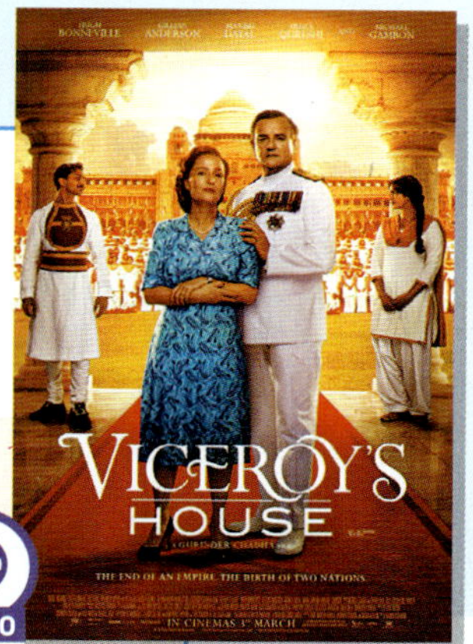


ÉPREUVE ORALE | GRAND ORAL — Entraîne-toi à l'oral

## Step 1 — Build up your speech!

**Épreuve orale**

- Choose one topic in the mindmap p. 90.
- Pick out two documents in the file and a personal one to illustrate this issue. OBJECTIF BAC p. 305
- Prepare your presentation: you must show how these documents relate to the issue you chose.

**Grand oral**

- Choose one topic in the mindmap p. 90.
- Find a key question about your topic.
- Gather arguments and examples from the documents in the file to support your point.
- Prepare an outline for your presentation and write your note sheet. OBJECTIF BAC p. 308-309

## Step 2 — Make your presentation in front of two classmates.

**Épreuve orale**

- Show your documents to your classmates. Each of you makes their presentation to the others in about five minutes. OBJECTIF BAC p. 306-307

**Grand oral**

- Give your note sheet to your classmates.
- Stand up and make a five-minute presentation to answer your key questions. OBJECTIF BAC p. 310-311

## Step 3 — Answer your classmates' questions about your presentation.

SNAPFILE 10

REPRÉSENTATIONS
AXE 3 : REPRÉSENTER LE MONDE ET SE REPRÉSENTER

# Autofocus

▶ How committed is photography in South Africa?

FINAL TASK As an art curator, take part in a radio programme about South African photography.

More on SPEAKEASY NEWS speakeasy-news.com

## 1 South African chronicles

### Doc 1. Unequal scenes

*Papwa Sewgolum Golf Course*, Durban, Johnny MILLER, 2016

**CULTURE SPOT**

**Johnny Miller** is a Cape-Town based photographer. He uses drones to picture South African discrepancies from the air and won an award for his *Unequal Scenes* project.

LANDMARKS p. 290-291

*During apartheid, segregation of urban spaces was instituted as policy. Roads, rivers, "buffer[1] zones" of empty land, and other barriers were constructed and modified to keep people separate. 22 years after the end of apartheid, many of these barriers, and the inequalities they have engendered, still exist. Often times, communities of extreme wealth and privilege will exist just meters from squalid[2] conditions and shack dwellings[3]. My desire with this project is to portray the most Unequal Scenes around the world as objectively as possible. By providing a new perspective on an old problem, I hope to provoke a dialogue which can begin to address the issues of inequality and disenfranchisement[4] in a constructive and peaceful way.*

Johnny MILLER, "Unequal scenes", 2016

1. *zone tampon* 2. miserable 3. *bidonville* 4. disempowerment

a. **Describe** and **react** to the photograph.

b. **Turn** to Johnny Miller's text and **identify** the aim of this project.

c. **Focus** on the perspective chosen by the photographer. **Explain** how it helps him convey a message on South African society.

## Doc 2. Soweto behind the lens

Meaningful exchanges are central to Dhlamini's approach; the conversation comes first, and the photograph second: "It is the experience of the conversation that becomes more important than the image." His wider practice is deeply collaborative and derives from his upbringing[1] during the final years of apartheid, and his views on the country now—the work amplifies the experiences and voices of marginalised communities [...]. *The everyday waiting* takes this approach: it is not purely documentary; the photographs record everyday moments, but there is something more—a level of intimacy and connection, which goes beyond straightforward reportage. In one frame, a woman, enveloped in a blanket, peers out, while, in another, a shaft[2] of sunlight illuminates a man gazing out of the picture. The work provides a space for the experiences of those depicted.

"It is the first time since democracy that the townships have been militarised, now they are full of soldiers," says Dhlamini, who the police stopped and forced to delete several photographs. "It reminded me of a history where people had to hide their cameras," he continues. Lockdown has exposed the great inequality that continues to pervade the Black community; poverty, poor sanitation and education—"there are many problems that we have inherited from the apartheid era; now they are resurfacing again." [...]

As with much of Dhlamini's work, the series will ultimately act as an archive: a historical record of the moment. "Even though I am working now, I am archiving", says Dhlamini, "we need to look at these images after and learn from them."

Hannah ABEL-HIRSH, *British Journal of Photography*, June 2020

*Lebohang Raethole, Boitumelo Mathibu and her kids, Soweto,* Jabulani DHLAMINI, 2020

1. *éducation* 2. ray of light

**a. Read** the article. **Describe** Jabulani Dhlamini's approach and **comment** on the purpose of his photos.

**b. Compare** and **contrast** the response given to photographers in the past and today.

**c. Discuss** the statement: *"The series will ultimately act as an archive."* (l. 32-33)

**WORDS**

- camera angle
- (camera) lens: *objectif*
- discrepancy = gap
- high-angle shot
- township = slum

---

- horrendous
- visual

---

- address an issue
- comprehend = grasp
- give an insight into
- witness

## Doc 3. Everyday life beauty

Kgomotso Neto Tleane, *Design Indaba*, 2016

**a. Watch** the video and **explain** the artist's project.

**b.** VOCABULARY **Comment** on the choice of the word "showcase".

**c. Focus** on the artist's photographs. **Select** one and **show** how it illustrates his goal.

**YOUR TASK** You have an Instagram account on photographs. **Write** an introduction to Kegomotso Neto Tleane's photos.

**BOOST YOUR SKILLS!**

**Présenter un projet photographique**

- Pose le contexte à la voix passive : *Segregation **was instituted** as policy.* • *Barriers **were constructed** and **modified**...*
- Précise le projet avec des relatives : *A history **where** people...* • *Inequality **that** pervades...* • *A connection, **which** goes beyond...*
- Mets en avant les intentions du photographe : ***My desire** with this project **is to** portray...* • ***By providing**..., I hope **to provoke**...* • *Telling stories **in a way that** people can...*

# 2 A legacy from the past

## Doc 1. "My camera is my weapon"

VIDÉO

"Nanny and child", Peter Magubane, 1956
(Video: Peter Magubane: short film, *21 Icons*, 2014)

**a. Describe** and **analyse** the photograph.

**b. Watch** the video and **account** for Peter Magubane's relationship with his camera.

**c. Sum** up the risks he was willing to take and why.

**d. Focusing** on Magubane's work, **explain** why photography is a powerful medium.

**CULTURE SPOT**

**Peter Magubane** took enormous risks to chronicle the apartheid era. In the 1990s, Nelson Mandela appointed him as his official photographer.

## Doc 2.

### Documenting the casual horrors of apartheid

The photograph makes me squirm[1]. Four young women, cling-wrapped in awkward swimsuits and perched on high heels, stand on display. One smirks[2], the other three look unsure. They clutch their competition numbers and present their naked white legs for consideration by the unseen judges.

Behind the stage, a crowd of mostly women and children cluster around the elevated stage, their faces resigned or perplexed. Most people seem bemused[3] by the uncomfortable spectacle taking place in their local supermarket. [...]

It makes me shudder because David Goldblatt took the photograph "Saturday Morning at the Hypermarket: Miss Lovely Legs Competition" at the supermarket where my mother shopped when I was a child growing up in South Africa. [...]

In itself, the image is ordinary. Like many of Goldblatt's photographs, it isn't dramatic, the subjects unknown. But it shows the casualness of a society separated by apartheid. It captures the uneasiness that pulsed through my childhood growing up in South Africa. It recalls things I saw but did not see. And it drags up the old questions that lurk[4] beneath my memories—how could such ordinariness take place while countless horrors were happening off camera? [...]

When asked, David Goldblatt explained the purpose of his photographs to his friend and colleague Paul Weinberg: "I hoped we would see ourselves revealed by a mirror held up to ourselves."

Alexandra SPRING, *The Guardian*, October 2018

"Saturday morning at the Hypermarket: Semi-final of the Miss Lovely Legs Competition.", David GOLDBLATT, June 28, 1980

**1.** be ashamed **2.** smile disdainfully **3.** confused **4.** hide

**a. Observe** the photograph and **explain** how David Goldblatt captured *"the casual horrors of apartheid"*.

**b. Read** the article and **explain** the journalist's feelings.

**c.** RHETORIC (l. 38-39) **Comment** on the association of *"ordinariness"* and *"countless horrors"*.

**d. Discuss**: Photography can work as *"a mirror held up to ourselves."* (l. 44-45)

**YOUR TASK** **Record** a short podcast for an art magazine entitled "Magubane and Goldblatt, two committed lenses".

# 3 Towards self-empowerment

## Doc 1. The envisioned self

Wonke's Envisioned Self, 2019 (Video: *SABC News*, Feb 2020)

**a.** **Observe** the photograph and **read** the title. **Guess** what the series might be about.

**b.** **Watch** the video and **pick out** information about the artist.

**c.** **Describe** the artist's source of inspiration and the consequences on his artworks.

**d.** GRAMMAR **Focus** on the repetition of "*used to*" and **explain** how it reinforces the artist's change of mentality.

**e.** **Discuss**: Paint artists and photographers have very different goals.

AT HOME **Go** online and **find** information about Steve Biko. **Get** ready to **explain** who he was and what he fought for.

**WORDS**

- ag**e**nda = goal
- emb**o**diment
- self-est**ee**m

- d**e**dicated
- inspir**a**tional

- r**i**sky

- call for change
- cond**e**mn
- overc**o**me **o**bstacles
- raise aw**a**reness

## Doc 2. Universal self-portraits

**a.** **Observe** the pictures and **watch** the video. **Describe** Zanele Muholi's artworks and **comment** on the choice of such a form.

**b.** **Explain** the role of photography for Muholi and why the artist claims to be a "visual activist".

**c.** **Comment** on the tone and the message the artist wants to convey.

**d.** **Explain** what it means "*to respond to different events using our art*". Would you say this is committed art?

YOUR TASK Using the hashtag #selfempowerment, **write** a few tweets to **react** to both art projects and **praise** the values they convey.

© Zanele Muholi. Courtesy of Stevenson, Amsterdam/ Cape Town/Johannesburg and Yancey Richardson, New York

**BOOST YOUR SKILLS!**

**Commenter la portée d'une œuvre**

- Évoque l'intention par des modaux : *My camera* ***will*** *give the freedom...* • *I hoped we* ***would*** *see ourselves revealed by...*
- Évoque les valeurs véhiculées : *I was prepared to die for my* ***freedom****.* • *I was fighting for my* ***rights****.* • *Showing* ***injustice*** *in South Africa.* • *This is m****y pain...***
- Souligne son impact par des causatives : *The photograph* ***makes*** *me* ***squirm****.* • *It* ***makes*** *me* ***shudder****.*

**FINAL TASK**

As an art curator, you are invited to a radio programme to **introduce** a new exhibition on committed South African photography. **Comment** on the special role of photography to fight for a cause in South Africa using precise examples of photographers and artworks.

play BAC How to...

# WRITE AN ESSAY

OBJECTIF BAC p. 296

Le jour de **l'épreuve écrite** en Terminale, tu devras analyser et faire la **synthèse d'un dossier documentaire**. Il pourra t'être demandé de rédiger un **écrit complémentaire argumentatif** (parfois au choix entre deux sujets). En voici un exemple.

**Dossier documentaire :**
Document A: "Soweto behind the lens", *British Journal of Photography*, June 2020 (doc 2 p. 93)
Document B: "Documenting the casual horrors of apartheid", *The Guardian*, October 2018 (doc 2 p. 94)
Document C: "The girl on the bench in Johannesburg", Peter Magubane, 1956 (doc 1 p. 94)
**Sujet d'écrit complémentaire :**
Jabulana Dhlameni says "We need to look at these images after and learn from them" (Document A).
À la lumière des documents A, B, et C expliquez en anglais et en 200 mots maximum en quoi la photographie peut être un art engagé et vecteur de changement.

## 1 Analyser la consigne

**a. Identifie** les mots-clés et **mets-les en relation** pour comprendre les enjeux.

**b. Étudie** les documents du dossier et **prends** des notes à l'aune de cette question.

Il s'agit de donner un point de vue nuancé à partir d'une citation. Reformule en anglais les éléments de la consigne donnée en français pour élaborer ta problématique : *How can photography be a committed art and fuel for change?*

• Repère les mots-clés de la consigne : art engagé • vecteur de changement
• Et ceux de la citation : *need* • *look at* • *images* • *learn from*
• Identifie les liens des documents avec la citation : *documenting a specific context (lockdown, apartheid era)* • *idea of photography as a committed act* • *Show how the world operates.*

## 2 Réfléchir et s'organiser

**a. Prépare** tes idées en les classant selon qu'elles s'opposent ou se complètent pour faire émerger un plan.

**b. Choisis** comme point de départ une idée qui soutient celle avancée dans la citation ou qui s'en rapproche.

**c. Développe** ensuite une idée en contrepoint, ou qui nuance le point de vue exposé.

**d. Illustre** ces idées avec des exemples extraits des documents.

Souviens-toi : **1 argument = 1 paragraphe**

• *The three documents shed light on* • *Commitment is at the core of this set of documents*
• *In contrast* • *however* • *as opposed to* • *One also may argue that...*
• *In fact* • *It's quite possible to suggest that* • *Change can be a slow process but...*

## 3 Prendre position

**a. Prépare** une conclusion qui ne se contente pas de résumer ce que tu as expliqué mais qui **synthétise** la confrontation de tes arguments.

**b. Conclus** en donnant un point de vue personnel sur le sujet.

Fais appel à tes connaissances interculturelles personnelles pour aller plus loin dans ta réflexion : *Photography remains until today a fuel for change, one can think of Wendy Red Star's Native Self-Portraits in the U.S., or other committed photographers, like Johnny Miller using his lens to denounce unequal scenes throughout the world.*

• La conclusion doit apporter une réponse à la problématique posée au départ.
*To conclude* • *As a conclusion* • *All in all, I would say that...*

Vers le **BAC**

# BUILD YOUR PORTFOLIO

## Documentary

"Hector Pieterson's death", Sam Nzima, June 1976

In 1976, Hector Pieterson was a schoolboy who demonstrated against schooling exclusively in Afrikaans for black people. He was shot at and killed by the police during the Soweto riots.

- **Observe** the photograph and **watch** the documentary. **Explain** Sam Nzima's approach to covering the event.

VIDÉO

## Article

"How Santu Mofokeng shaped South African photography", *The New Yorker*, February 2020

"Images by the South African photographer Santu Mofokeng, ostensibly depict scenes of segregation during apartheid. Yet in their composition they evoke something more: the rhythms and textures of everyday life."

- **Read** the article and **comment** on the essential role played by this photographer in South Africa.

ARTICLE

## Retrospective

"Figures and Fictions", *V&AMuseum*, 2011

In 2011, this exhibition highlighted the work of 17 South African photographers, all of whom live and work in the country. The photographers' projects were linked by the depiction of people and a self-conscious commitment towards South Africa's political and photographic past.

- **Read** the article and **pick out** information on some of the photographers showcased in this exhibition. **Explain** why they can be all considered as committed artists.

ARTICLE

## Book

*Ponte City*, Mikhael Subotzki and Patrick Waterhouse, 2014

Ponte City, the iconic Johannesburg apartment building is Africa's tallest residential skyscraper. For more than six years Mikhael Subotzki and Patrick Waterhouse photographed the residents and documented the building.

- **Browse** through the book and **comment** on the goal of such a photographic project.

BOOK

## Entraîne-toi à l'oral

ÉPREUVE ORALE

**Step 1** **Build up your speech!**

- Focus on how photography can be a committed act and fuel for change.
- Pick out documents to build your portfolio: choose from the file, this page, or from your personal references.
- Prepare your presentation: show how these documents relate to the topic. OBJECTIF BAC p. 305

**Step 2** **Make your presentation in front of two classmates.**

- Show your documents to your classmates and explain your point in about five minutes. OBJECTIF BAC p. 306-307

**Step 3** **Answer your classmates' questions about your presentation.**

OBJECTIF BAC p. 296-304

Grille d'auto-évaluation

## Sujet type bac

MÉDIATION

**Entraînement à l'épreuve de Terminale**

Durée : 3h30

Matériel autorisé : le dictionnaire unilingue (non encyclopédique) est autorisé.

Niveau attendu : B2 > C1

- **Prenez connaissance des documents A, B et C et traitez en anglais le sujet suivant (500 mots maximum).**

Say what the documents show about the evolution of podcasting in the US in recent years. Pay particular attention to the specificities of this medium.

- **Traduisez en français le passage du document A.**

"*But there's another reason people are excited about the medium. Because podcasting has a lower barrier to entry for production compared to other forms of media, it may be a way for different kinds of people to enter the industry. While there is still room for improvement, about one-third of the top 480 podcasts are hosted by women, Quartz reported. One out of 10 features a person of color. And, about 27 percent of podcasts are hosted by women alone, according to a new study by AT&T Experts.*" (l. 22-27)

**Document A**

Browse | more | contact | Login

### As Podcasts Gain Popularity, Underrepresented Voices Find Ways to Be Heard

After watching her mother's bid[1] for Congress, Jenny Kaplan realized there were so many untold local stories about women getting involved in politics. So, she decided to use her voice.

"Storytelling generally is how we connect as people, and when you're listening to something and don't have the distractions of visuals, you're really listening in a different way, in a deeper way," she explained.

The former Bloomberg reporter co-hosts the political podcast "Women belong in the House" on Wonder Media Network. She co-founded the audio-first media company, which has a goal of encouraging action in business, politics, and culture through amplifying female and minority perspectives. The company produces about 10 podcasts including "Women," which alone reached more than 50,000 unique listeners during its third season.

"[The podcast] inspires them to either get involved in a campaign [or] to think about running," Kaplan said. "Just to question the status quo, and why there haven't been women still sent to Congress from certain states or certain districts or certain areas."

More than 100 million Americans listen to podcasts every month, according to Edison Research. Podcast downloads for the week of October 12 to 18 were up 40 percent year-over-year, per podcast analytics company Podtrac.

"It's just the way people want to get their news right now," explained *Cheddar* anchor Jill Wagner, who hosts the company's "Need2Know" podcast alongside Cheddar senior editor Carlo Versano. "They want to listen to it."

But there's another reason people are excited about the medium. Because podcasting has a lower barrier to entry for production compared to other forms of media, it may be a way for different kinds of people to enter the industry. While there is still room for improvement, about one-third of the top 480 podcasts are hosted by women, Quartz reported. One out of 10 features a person of color. And, about 27 percent of podcasts are hosted by women alone, according to a new study by AT&T Experts.

1. candidacy

"If you want to have a voice and have something to say, you can easily do a podcast and get your message out there," Wagner said. [...]

It also allows audiences to find a deeper connection with someone who shares their perspective. *Cheddar's* Wagner shared her feelings of being overwhelmed and anxious during the pandemic as a mother on a recent "Need2Know" episode. She was surprised to receive emails from across the United States from listeners sharing their own experiences.

"I just realized the power of the podcast as a medium," she said.

Michelle CASTILLO, *cheddar.com*, November 3, 2020

**Document B**

## Prince Harry and Meghan Markle to produce podcasts through exclusive deal with Spotify

Prince Harry and Meghan Markle have inked a multiyear deal with Spotify to host and produce "uplifting"audio projects and podcasts. Under Archewell Audio, their new audio-first production company, the couple wants to "spotlight powerful and diverse voices and perspectives."

"What we love about podcasting is that it reminds all of us to take a moment and to really listen, to connect to one another without distraction," The Duke and Duchess of Sussex said in a joint statement. "With the challenges of 2020, there has never been a more important time to do so, because when we hear each other, and hear each other's stories, we are reminded of how interconnected we all are."

Archewell Audio's first project will premiere before the end of the year. The special, produced with Spotify's Gimlet studio, will "feature stories of hope and compassion from inspirational guests in celebration of the new year."

Dawn Ostroff, Spotify's chief content and advertising business officer, called Prince Harry and Meghan "citizens of the world," celebrating their goal of uplifting underrepresented voices in their work. "We are proud to partner with The Duke and Duchess and look forward to listeners hearing directly from them and the other creators that they will be elevating via our global platform," added Ostroff.

The news comes as Harry and Meghan continue to build new media partnerships while they adjust to their new civilian life. After stepping away from the royal family earlier this year, the two have since moved to California with their son. Harry and Meghan also signed a deal with Netflix to produce children's programming, documentaries, feature films and scripted shows.

After the new year, Archewell Audio will release other projects, including its first complete series, which will be available to stream for free on Spotify.

In a trailer for the series, Meghan called their project "a moment to celebrate kindness and compassion", something the Duchess of Sussex said "would underlie everything [audiences] will hear from Archewell Audio."

"That's what this project is all about, to bring forward different perspectives and voices that perhaps you haven't heard before," added Prince Harry. "Because when that happens, change really is possible."

Zoe CHRISTEN JONES, *CBS News*, December 15, 2020

**Document C**

## The Steady Rise of Podcasts

Percentage and number of Americans (12+) who have listened to a podcast in the past

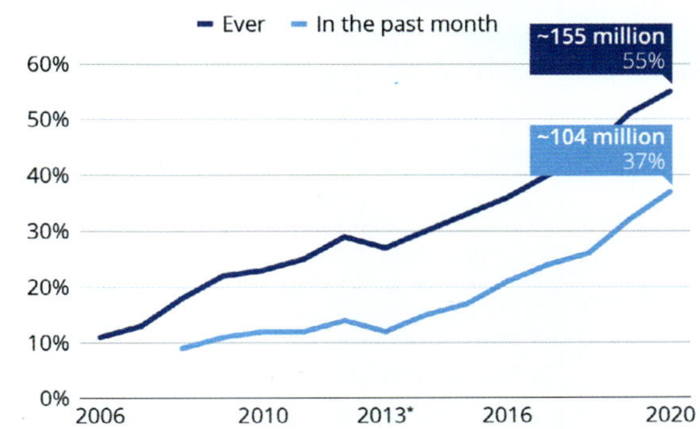


* in 2013, the source changed the definition of what qualifies as a podcast
Sources: Edison Research, Triton Digital

statista

FILE 11

FAIRE SOCIÉTÉ

AXE 1 : UNITÉ ET PLURALITÉ

# One Canada

▶ **How do Canadians build a common identity in such a diverse country?**

**FINAL TASK** Write the pitch for a documentary entitled "We are Canada".



## 1 A united nation

### Doc 1. We are one

AUDIO

Celebrating Canada Day (Audio: Justin Trudeau, 2016)

**WORDS**

- **ju**bilee = anniver**sa**ry
- par**t**nership

- like-**m**inded
- miscell**a**neous /mɪsə'leɪniəs/ = diverse

- prom**o**te = uph**o**ld
- requ**i**re /rɪ'kwaɪə/
- set forth = descr**i**be
- work side by side

**a.** **Observe** the picture and **identify** the speaker, the context and his emotions.

**b.** **Listen** to the audio and **take notes** on the values celebrated. **Find out** what "One Canada" means, according to the speaker.

**c.** PHONOLOGY **Pay** attention to this sentence: "*Canada was formed not **in spite of** differences but **because of** them*". **Comment** on the stress on the expressions in bold.

**d.** **Focus** on the examples given by the speaker. **Comment** on the image of Canada it gives to the world.

**CULTURE SPOT**

**Canada Day** is the celebration of Canadian Confederation, when on July 1st, 1867, the new dominion of Canada was created including the provinces of Ontario, Quebec, New Brunswick and Nova Scotia.

AT HOME **Watch** the videoclip of the song "We are One" and **pick out** elements illustrating this very idea. **Focus** on lyrics and images. VIDEO

## Doc 2. Towards reconciliation?

**a. Watch** the video and **find out** what reconciliation is and who it involves.

**b. Give** concrete examples of actions called for by Indigenous peoples.

**c. Describe** what renewed vision of Canada is made possible by reconciliation.

**d. Read** the infographic and **find** examples of policies implemented in Canada as part of the reconciliation process. **Say** how it empowers First Nations peoples.

**e. Comment** on how reconciliation is a plea for Canadian unity.

**YOUR TASK** As a Canadian Public Service worker, you are implementing reconciliation policies. **Introduce** these policies in a radio podcast. **Insist** on how they fall within Canada's key values of unity and multiculturalism.

LANDMARKS p. 284

VIDÉO

# PRINCIPLES

## Respecting the Government of Canada's Relationship With Indigenous Peoples

### The Government of Canada recognizes that:

1 All relations with Indigenous peoples need to be based on the recognition and implementation of their right to self-determination, including the inherent right of self-government.

2 Reconciliation is a fundamental purpose of section 35 of the *Constitution Act, 1982*.

3 The honour of the Crown guides the conduct of the Crown in all of its dealings with Indigenous peoples.

4 Indigenous self-government is part of Canada's evolving system of cooperative federalism and distinct orders of government.

5 Treaties, agreements, and other constructive arrangements between Indigenous peoples and the Crown have been and are intended to be acts of reconciliation based on mutual recognition and respect.

6 Meaningful engagement with Indigenous peoples aims to secure their free, prior, and informed consent when Canada proposes to take actions which impact them and their rights on their lands, territories, and resources.

7 Respecting and implementing rights is essential and that any infringement of section 35 rights must by law meet a high threshold of justification which includes Indigenous perspectives and satisfies the Crown's fiduciary obligations.

8 Reconciliation and self-government require a renewed fiscal relationship, developed in collaboration with Indigenous nations, that promotes a mutually supportive climate for economic partnership and resource development.

9 Reconciliation is an ongoing process that occurs in the context of evolving Indigenous-Crown relationships.

10 A distinctions-based approach is needed to ensure that the unique rights, interests and circumstances of the First Nations, the Métis Nation and Inuit are acknowledged, affirmed, and implemented.

Department of Justice, Canada
(Video: "What reconciliation really means", *CBC News*, 2015)

**BOOST YOUR SKILLS!**

**Insister sur des valeurs communes**

- Mets en avant leur caractère fondateur : *It is* ***at the very heart of***... • *There is* ***a move and a desire to***... • ***One*** *nation,* ***one*** *country,* ***one*** *Canada.*
- Souligne leur aspect fédérateur par des connecteurs : ***Not in spite of*** *differences* ***but because*** *of them...* • ***No matter*** *where we were born...*
- Souligne la force des liens par des pronoms réciproques ou des adjectifs possessifs : *How we relate to* ***each other*** • *It hits you in* ***your*** *soul and in* ***your*** *body* • *I didn't get taught* ***my*** *own history.*

**CULTURE SPOT**

Today, the **Indigenous Peoples** make up 4.9% of Canada's population. Their life expectancy, income, educational attainment and employment rates remain lower than those of non-Indigenous populations.

# EXPLORE 2 Diversity is our strength

## Doc 1.

Gatineau Park forest, Québec

**Canada: a land of diversity and strength**

Travel this great land and you soon come to realize that one of the most significant aspects of our country is its rich and diversified geography.

It is remarkable that a land so divided by its varied terrain has remained so unified as a nation. Take a good look at Canada's topography and you soon realize that our geographic features tend to run in a north-south pattern while our political and economic ties attempt to make east-west connections. This has been a challenge throughout our confederation.

Our country is the second largest in size in the world. Our six time zones are a reflection of the sheer scope and size of our nation. The geography of this land is vastly different from coast to coast. We have it all—rain forests, awe-inspiring mountain ranges, wide-open prairies, treeless tundra, barren[1] rock, fertile farmland, picturesque valleys and rugged coastlines. [...]

Sir John A. Macdonald, our country's first prime minister, knew that people needed a physical connection to ensure that our country stay united and to remind other nations that this land belonged to Canada. What resulted was the massive and difficult undertaking of building a transcontinental railway. [...]

Despite the sectionalism created by our geography we have managed to create a strong national identity. It is truly a testament to the character and willpower of the people who have built and continue to build this "true North strong and free" nation. Our "true patriot love" is proof that there is strength in diversity, whether it be in our people or in our geography.

Gail KRAWETZ, *canoracourier.com*, July 2017

1. not fertile

**a.** **Read** the text and **identify** what aspects of Canada's diversity are put forward.

**b.** **Identify** which one could be an obstacle to the country's unity. **Explain** why.

**c.** TRANSLATION **Focus** on l. 39-41 and **identify** the verb form used in "*whether it be*". **Translate** the sentence.

**d.** **Conclude** on how Canada managed to turn this diversity into a national asset.

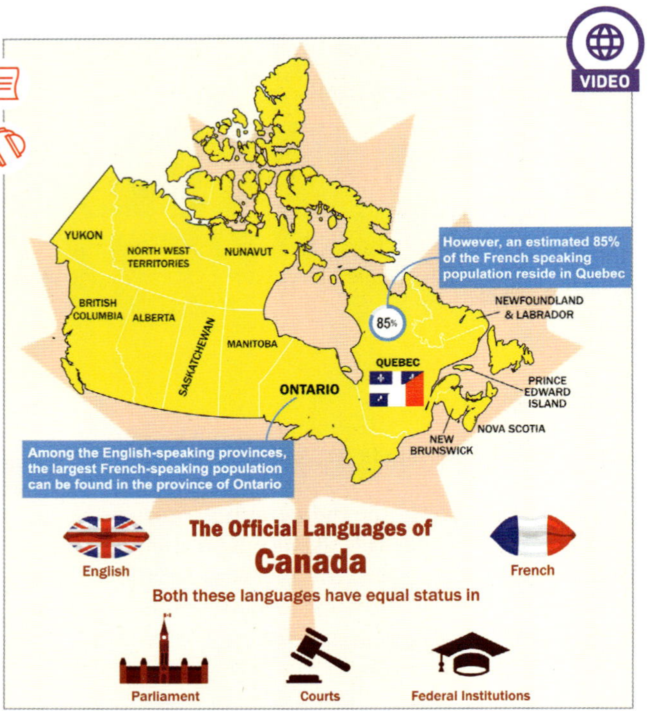


(Video: "Bilingualism on the rise", *Global News*, 2020)

## Doc 2. A bilingual nation

LANDMARKS p. 285

**a.** **Observe** the infographic and **take** notes about Canada's linguistic diversity.

**b.** **Watch** the video and **find out** what makes this class representative of a growing trend in the country. **Say** how it resonates with the infographic.

**c.** **Comment** on how this trend is perceived by parents and adults.

**d.** **Explain** how the linguistic diversity is an asset for the country.

**WORDS**

- benefit
- empowerment
- scheme /ski:m/
- cutting-edge
- comprehensive = all-embracing
- advocate = foster
- carry out (policies)

## Doc 3.

2020
CANADA'S BEST
DIVERSITY EMPLOYERS

The corporate case for diversity and inclusion in the workplace couldn't be more straightforward. It's good for business—boosting innovation, productivity and revenue growth at home and in the global market.

Canada's Best Diversity Employers 2020 already understand the competitive economic advantages, but they also understand that diversity and inclusion is foremost about people. It starts at the top with an ongoing strategic plan that gives employees, regardless of their race, gender, disability, country of origin or sexual orientation, the opportunity and support needed to succeed. That's what puts lofty[1] ideals into action.

These diversity champions have all taken proactive initiatives to create both a more diverse workforce and a more respectful, inclusive environment where everyone can feel they belong. [...] For example, Borden Ladner Gervais LLP in Toronto ensures a diverse talent pipeline by requiring diverse representation on shortlists when hiring lawyers, as well as providing unconscious bias training for lawyers conducting law student interviews.

Or many of this year's winners who made initiatives for Indigenous Peoples a priority, including Alberta Health Services that held a series of Indigenous Listening Days with leaders to explore common understanding of the needs of its Indigenous workforce. [...]

Increasingly there is a consensus among Canadian employers that D&I, as it's often known, is critical to success.

Arielle Meloul-Wechsler, executive vice president [...] at Air Canada, is an experienced observer of such trends. She sees a transformation going on in D&I. "For many years, companies, with all good intentions, did a lot of talking about it and looking at statistics and analyzing," she says. "But now I feel there is a real shift at the highest levels [...]. When I go to conferences, it is apparent that people are really focusing on it. For example, when they're recruiting, they will not allow a headhunter to bring only white males as candidates. They will force them to at least expose the pool to a diverse group of potential recruits so that they can then make an informed decision. It's a shift to more tangible efforts, as opposed to just saying yes, we should do better."

Diane JERMYN, *The Globe and Mail*, March 2020

THE DIVERSE EMPLOYEE TEAM AT BELL CANADA

*"It doesn't matter who you are, what religion you are, what sexual orientation you are, there's always equal opportunity."*

**—Andrew Gordon**
Service Director at Air Canada

1. grand, stately

**a. Read** the article and **find out** why diversity in the workplace may be an asset.

**b. Take** notes on the variety of situations mentioned in the second paragraph. Can you think of others?

**c.** GRAMMAR **Focus** on l. 24-30 and **account** for the use of *-ing* forms in this sentence. ▶ p. 107

**d. Focus** on the examples of new inclusion policies. **Say** which seems the most promising to you and **explain** why.

**e. Identify** the recent shift in diversity and inclusion policies. **Say** to what extent Canada can be considered a leader in Human Resources strategies.

**YOUR TASK** As a Human Resources executive of one of the Canada's Best Diversity Employer, **take part** in a radio interview about the company's diversity and inclusion policies.

### BOOST YOUR SKILLS!

**Souligner le succès d'une politique inclusive**

- Évoque les actions mises en œuvre au gérondif : ***Boosting*** *innovation.* • ***Requiring*** *diverse representation.* • ***Providing*** *unconscious bias training...* GRAMMAR p. 107
- Valorise les contrastes : *Its training* ***rich*** *and* ***diversified*** *geography.* • *A land* ***so divided*** *by its varied terrain has remained* ***so unified*** *as a nation.* • *A* ***north-south*** *pattern.* • ***East-west*** *connections.*
- Utilise l'expression de la concession : ***Despite*** *the sectionalism created by...* • *Strength in diversity,* ***whether it be*** *in our people* ***or*** *in our geography.*

EXPLORE

# 3 Confederation at threat?

## Doc 1.

**The Guardian**

### Is Canada Suffering From a Unity Crisis?

Has Canada ever truly been a united country? While to the world (and even to most Canadians), the Great White North is a shining symbol of peace, democracy, and prosperity, the relationship between Ottawa and the provinces has been continually up and down since the country's founding. Being that Canada is a constitutional monarchy, centralization of power has always and will largely be the order of the day. In the opinion of many historians and writers, Confederation was the product of a group of elites in urban Ontario and Quebec (at the time Upper and Lower Canada) who graciously invited everyone else to join their newfangled[1] country. For a relationship to truly work effectively, all parties must have an equal say, or else tensions and eventual splintering will occur.

In Atlantic Canada, there are respected scholars who bemoan[2] the region's long economic decline, crony politics and culture of dependency on equalization as a direct result of becoming a partner in Confederation. Speaking of which, back in 1873, Cornelius Howatt, member of the legislative assembly of Prince Edward Island[3], a fierce opponent of union with Canada, stated unequivocally, "If P.E.I. joins Confederation, all we'll be will be beggars."

Concerning western alienation, we've been down this road before. As many Western Canadians look with disdain upon what they see as an anti-oil East, a growing chorus is seriously considering leaving Confederation, either to form a new country or become the 51st state. While such proposals will most likely never see the light of day, Ottawa cannot ignore the reality that with the rise of the Bloc Quebecois combined with the emerging Wexit movement (inspired by Brexit), a complicated unity crisis may be just around the corner.

If you're like me, you probably don't expect Canada to break apart any time soon. That being said, uniting Canadians from coast to coast to coast must become a priority.

Chris McGarry,
*The Guardian*, June 2020

**1.** (here) newly built **2.** regret **3.** an island and province situated east of New Brunswick

**a. Read** the article and **contrast** the image people generally have of Canada with the author's vision.

**b. Explain** the reasons why their visions differ.

**c. Say** why Confederation is to blame for the unity crisis, according to the author.

**d.** TRANSLATION **Translate** l. 9-12. **Pay** particular attention to the idiomatic expression.

**e. Pick out** the devices used by the author to convince the reader of the importance of keeping Canada united.

**CULTURE SPOT**

Canada is a **constitutional monarchy** and it is part of the **Commonwealth**: the British monarch is the head of the state and the Prime Minister is the head of government.

## Doc 2. Province *v.* country

1

| Agree : *'My province would be better off if it separated from Canada.'* | Total Canada | Total Western Canada | BC | AB | SK | MB | ON | PQ | ATL |
|---|---|---|---|---|---|---|---|---|---|
| October 2019 | 17% | 21% | 13% | 33% | 27% | 11% | 8% | 20% | 9% |
| September 2018 | n/a | 18% | 15% | 25% | 18% | 6% | n/a | n/a | n/a |
| 2001 | n/a | 15% | 16% | 16% | 13% | 7% | n/a | n/a | n/a |

| Agree : *'My province does not get its fair share from Confederation.'* | Total Canada | Total Western Canada | BC | AB | SK | MB | ON | PQ | ATL |
|---|---|---|---|---|---|---|---|---|---|
| October 2019 | 35% | 50% | 36% | 65% | 62% | 42% | 20% | 34% | 54% |
| September 2018 | n/a | 49% | 49% | 62% | 54% | 40% | n/a | n/a | n/a |
| 2001 | n/a | 53% | 59% | 49% | 53% | 42% | n/a | n/a | n/a |

**BC:** British Columbia ; **AB:** Alberta ; **SK:** Saskatchewan ; **MB:** Manitoba ;
**ON:** Ontario ; **PQ:** Province du Québec ; **ATL:** Atlantic Canada

*Ipsos*, November 2019

"Wexit", *CBC News: The National*, 2019

**a. Read** the statistics 1 and **observe** the evolution of the general sentiment of Western Canadians towards the federation.
**Imagine** the reasons for this change.

**b. Watch** the video 2 and **define** the Wexit movement (location, requests).

**c. Pick out** the reasons for the creation of this movement.

**d.** Based on the different testimonies, **say** how probable Wexit seems. What does it show about the strength of the federation?

## Doc 3. Right to self-governance

**a. Observe** the photograph and **imagine** what the situation may be.

**b. Watch** the video and **check** your hypotheses. **Find out** why this event is historic.

**c. Imagine** how this would change the situation for the Métis nation in practice.

**d. Discuss**: How can this legal decision lead to more unity in Canada?

*Global News*, June 2019

DIFFÉRENCIATION

**YOUR TASK** You attended a Wexit meeting. **Write** a short report for a local member of parliament.

**WAY 1** **Account for** the different positions on the subject.

**WAY 2** **Do** the same and **analyse** the motivations of the movement.

**CULTURE SPOT**

The **Métis people** is recognised as one of the Indigenous peoples of Canada, along with First Nations and Inuit peoples. The Métis people originated in the 1700s when French and Scottish fur traders married Indigenous women.

**BOOST YOUR SKILLS!**

**Présenter des perspectives variées**

- Exprime différents points de vue : ***While** to the world...* • ***In the opinion of** many historians and writers.* GRAMMAR p. 107
- Développe chacun avec des relatives : *Agreements **that** give the Métis jurisdiction...* • *Scholars **who** bemoan...*
- Préserve l'authenticité des points de vue avec des tournures idiomatiques : *All parties must **have an equal say**.* • *We've been **down this road before**.* • *The crisis may be **just around the corner**.*

**WORDS**

- fair share
- First N**a**tions = Ind**i**genous p**eo**ples
- inh**e**rent rights

- aut**o**nomous
- c**e**ntral ≠ l**o**cal (g**o**vernment)
- s**e**paratist
- unb**a**lanced

- make am**e**nds for
- sec**e**de from = s**e**parate from
- yield /jɪəld/ (p**o**wer)

# 4 The challenges of globalisation

https://www.linkedin.com/pulse/what-unites-canada-divided-world-dave-mckay/

Dave McKay in
President & CEO at RBC

## What unites Canada in a divided world?

The global community is increasingly divided into camps. The prospects of international cooperation to combat the world's greatest challenges—like climate change—are challenged. Today, Canada stands out by contrast. We're a nation of open minds, open arms, and open hearts. [...] So, what will unite Canada in a world that is divided?

The answer lies in finding our own path to long-term prosperity and taking advantage of our strengths. Canada has many things going for it. Here's what we can double down on together:

**An abundance of natural resources**

What other country can boast about its assets in forestry, minerals, hydro, coal, and oil and gas? Canada's natural resources have created enormous economic wealth, while also driving forward the development of energy production that's cleaner than anywhere else in the world.

**A burgeoning digital economy**

Our country is home to great talent, incredible institutions, and a burgeoning innovation ecosystem. [...] Cities and regions across the country are building flourishing innovation hubs from the digital technology one we see in Vancouver all the way to the global hub around the oceans economy in Atlantic Canada.

**Incredible talent to compete and win globally**

No matter how the world turns, our prosperity rests on the brain power of our youth and their readiness for a future that will be different than anything we've ever known. We're educating young Canadians, but not always for the jobs of the future. To bridge the gap, we need to better connect classrooms and workplaces.

Work-integrated learning programs enable students to build networks and learn from experiences in educational and practical settings, while giving employers access to young people's talents to solve real business challenges. [...]

We have what it takes to stand tall in the world: the natural resources; the human resources; the culture and community; the ideas and energy.

Now, we have to show the divided world how a united Canada can thrive, growing our nation in a way where our debates do not disparage[1] each other, but rather, bands us together.

Dave McKay, *linkedin.com*, June 2019

1. *dénigrer*

**WORDS**

- globalis**a**tion
- t**a**lent pool

- comp**e**titive
- **i**nnovative = inv**e**ntive
- sk**i**lful
- sust**ai**nable

- recr**ui**t /rɪ'kru:t/ = hire
- stand out

**a.** **Read** the article and **identify** the author's main message. **List** the tools he uses to convince the reader.

**b.** **Explain** how Canada's assets are underlined.

**c.** VOCABULARY **Observe** the compound adjective: *"work-integrated"* (l. 23). **Explain** its meaning and **translate** it. ► p. 107

**d.** **Focus** on the source and **think** about the reasons for publishing such an article on this website.

## FINAL TASK

## Write the pitch for a documentary entitled "We are Canada".

**You decide to shoot a documentary entitled "We are Canada" to show the way Canadians build their common identity despite their differences. Write the pitch of your documentary to convince potential investors to contribute to your project.**

1. **Browse** through the file and **gather** information about the topic. **Choose** two or three aspects that make Canada such a diverse country and that you would like to develop in your documentary (demographics, geography, politics, etc.).
2. **Watch** this video. It will help you **organise** your notes in order to write an effective pitch VIDEO (Pay particular attention to 2'04-3'54).
3. **Prepare** your draft and **note** down:
   – information about the location and population,
   – examples of diversity,
   – benefits or potential downsides of such a diversity,
   – the actions led to deal with this diversity.
4. **Write** the final version of your pitch: **make** it straightforward and as convincing as possible.

BOOST YOUR ENGLISH ► p. 107

# BOOST YOUR ENGLISH!

## Grammar — Exposer une réalité complexe

- **Souligne l'unité dans la diversité avec l'expression de l'appartenance.**

*...**our** nation**'s** birthday.*
*It influences how we relate to **each other**.*
*It hits **you** in **your** soul and in **your** body.*
*I didn't get taught **my own history**.*

- **Exprime l'opposition, la concession ou l'alternative.**

***While** such proposals will most likely never see the light, Ottawa cannot ignore...*
***Despite** the sectionalism created by our geography...*
*Strength in diversity, **whether it be** in our people or in our geography.*

- **Souligne le caractère évolutif de la situation avec une forme en *V-ing*.**

***Respecting** and **implementing** rights is essential.* (gérondif)
*It's good for business—**boosting** innovation and productivity.* (gérondif)
*Toronto ensures a diverse talent pipeline when **hiring** lawyers.* (participe présent)

- **Renforce l'efficacité de ton propos avec des mots composés.**

*...**mid-to-senior level** talent.*
*...several **world-class computing science** schools.*
*...**work-integrated** learning...*

**1 Traduis ces phrases à l'aide d'une forme en *V-ing*.**

a. Enseigner le français à l'école renforcera le bilinguisme au Canada.
b. L'union de tous les Canadiens, tout en respectant les spécificités culturelles, est devenue une priorité politique.
c. Loin de nier le passé, la réconciliation reconnaît l'importance de l'héritage des autochtones.
d. Transformer les stratégies de recrutement nécessite du temps et des efforts.

**2 Forme des adjectifs composés à partir des mots soulignés.**

a. A tradition with deep roots.
b. A result people are very much waiting for.
c. A region with a dense population.
d. A talent people recognise widely.
e. An impact that lasts for a long time.

## Vocabulary — Canada's identity

Culture · Politics · Geography

**Bilingualism** (AUDIO)
- dual-language education
- linguistic skills
- native speaker
- empowering
- enriching

**Diversity** (AUDIO)
- welfare = happiness
- foster = encourage
- show respect for
- take pride in

**Sense of belonging** (AUDIO)
- forefather
- legacy
- inherit
- keep track of
- pass on to

**Confederation** (AUDIO)
- autonomy
- federalism
- governance
- separatist
- decentralise
- separate from = secede from

**Reconciliation** (AUDIO)
- homage
- recognition
- conflict-ridden
- indigenous
- improve
- pay tribute to
- relate to

**Work** (AUDIO)
- inclusiveness
- ranking
- talent pool
- be proactive
- boost revenue growth
- launch an initiative

**Landscapes** (AUDIO)
- coastline
- landlocked area
- plains
- rainforest
- snowfield
- mountainous

**Natural resources** (AUDIO)
- fertile /ˈfɜːtaɪl/ land
- (in)exhaustible
- depend on
- preserve

OBJECTIF BAC p. 296-304

Grille d'auto-évaluation

## Sujet type bac

MÉDIATION

Durée : 3h30
Matériel autorisé : le dictionnaire unilingue (non encyclopédique) est autorisé.
Niveau attendu : C1

• **a. Prenez connaissance des documents A, B, C et D et traitez le sujet suivant en anglais. (300 mots maximum) :**

Taking into account their specificities, show how the documents reveal the tight relationship between immigration policies and Canadian identity.

**b. Vous expliquerez en anglais et en 200 mots maximum en quoi l'extrait du discours de Justin Trudeau (document C) éclaire les documents B et D.**

• **Rendez compte en français des principales idées exprimées par le document B. Veillez à ne pas simplement en dresser la liste, mais à les expliciter lorsque cela vous paraît pertinent.**

### Document A

**The Canada's experiment: is this the world's first 'postnational' country?**

As 2017 begins, Canada may be the last immigrant nation left standing. Our government believes in the value of immigration, as does the majority of the population. [...]

Our government repeats it, our statistics confirm it, our own eyes and ears register it: diversity fuels, not undermines, prosperity.

But as well as practical considerations for remaining an immigrant country, Canadians, by and large, are also philosophically predisposed to an openness that others find bewildering, even reckless. The prime minister, Justin Trudeau, articulated this when he told the New York Times Magazine that Canada could be the "first postnational state". He added: "There is no core identity, no mainstream in Canada." [...]

First and foremost, postnationalism is a frame to understand our ongoing experiment in filling a vast yet unified geographic space with the diversity of the world. [...] In some sense, we have always been thinking differently about this continent-wide landmass, using ideas borrowed from Indigenous societies. From the moment Europeans began arriving in North America they were made welcome by the locals, taught how to survive and thrive amid multiple identities and allegiances. [...]

Though sovereign since 1867, Canada lingered in the shadow of the British empire for nearly a century. Not until the 1960s did we fly our own flag and sing our own anthem, and not until 1982 did Trudeau's father, Pierre, patriate the constitution from the UK, adding a charter of rights. He also introduced multiculturalism as official national policy. The challenge, then, might have seemed to define a national identity to match.

This was never going to be easy, given our colonial hangover and American cultural influence. Marshall McLuhan, one of the last century's most seismic thinkers, felt we shouldn't bother. "Canada is the only country in the world that knows how to live without an identity," he said in 1963.

According to poet and scholar BW Powe, McLuhan saw in Canada the raw materials for a dynamic new conception of nationhood, one unshackled from the state's "demarcated borderlines and walls, its connection to blood and soil," its obsession with "cohesion based on a melting pot, on nativist fervor, the idea of the promised land". Instead, the weakness of the established Canadian identity encouraged a plurality of them—not to mention a healthy flexibility and receptivity to change. Once Canada moved away from privileging denizens of the former empire to practising multiculturalism, it could become a place where "many faiths and histories and visions" would co-exist.

Charles FORAN, *The Guardian*, January 4, 2017

## Document B

**Federal government plans to bring in more than 1.2M immigrants in next 3 years**

The Liberal government plans to bring in more than 1.2 million immigrants over the next three years, despite hurdles created by the global pandemic.

Immigration Minister Marco Mendicino unveiled what he called an "ambitious" three-year immigration plan today that set targets for bringing skilled workers, family members and refugees into Canada.

Canada aims to bring 401,000 new permanent residents in 2021, 411,000 in 2022 and 421,000 in 2023.

The numbers—which represent an increase of about 50,000 for each year—aim to compensate for the shortfall this year due to the pandemic and represent about one per cent of Canada's population.

Last year's plan promised to bring in more than one million immigrants over a three-year period, but the COVID-19 crisis and the resulting travel restrictions have slowed down the process. Mendicino said the government remains committed to welcoming newcomers as a means to keep Canada's economy afloat.

At a news conference in Ottawa today, Mendicino said immigrants drive the population and economic growth that pays for vital programs such as health care.

"Put simply, we need more workers, and immigration is the way to get there," he said.

Mendicino said he's confident the government can meet the targets despite the global health crisis, by working around travel restrictions while adhering to safety measures such as mandatory quarantines.

He said the government will aim to attract workers to fill labour gaps in regions facing sector shortages.

"With nearly 60 per cent of all new admissions in the economic class, our plan will continue to focus on Canada's economic growth," he said.

Kathleen HARRIS,
*CBC*, October 30, 2020

## Document C

"In the face of complex global challenges, Canada will continue to champion diversity, acceptance and compassion on the world stage. We cannot build a better world unless we work together, respect our differences, protect the vulnerable, and put people at the heart of the decisions we make."

—Rt. Hon. Justin TRUDEAU,
Prime Minister of Canada, September 21, 2017, speech at the UN General Assembly

## Document D

**Growing the economy through immigration**

**75%** of Canada's population growth comes from **immigration**, mostly in the **economic category**.

3-year plan sets **most ambitious immigration levels** in recent history

**330,800** in 2019

**341,000** in 2020

**350,000** in 2021

This measured, gradual increase will trend towards 1% of the population by 2021, spurring innovation and representing a major investment in Canada's prosperity, now and into the future.

About **6** in **10** immigrants are selected for their positive economic impact.

Immigration, Refugees and Citizenship Canada, *canada.ca*

Vers le **BAC**

# LET'S BRAINSTORM!

OBJECTIF BAC p. 305-317

## Unity: a political value

- Celebrating Canada Day

→ Celebrating Canada Day, J. TRUDEAU, p. 100

- Inspiring anthems

→ "We are One", *Arabel Music*, p. 100

- #MyReconciliation

→ "Principles of Reconciliation", *Department of Justice*, p. 101 • "What Reconciliation really means", *CBC News*, p. 101

## Variety in diversity

- Topographic diversity

→ "A land of diversity and strength", *canoracourier.com*, p. 102

- Linguistic diversity

→ "Bilingualism on the rise", *Global News*, p. 102

- Inclusion in the workplace

→ "Canada's best diversity employer", *The Globe and Mail*, p. 103

FAIRE SOCIÉTÉ
Axe 1

**How do Canadians build a common identity in such a diverse country?**

## Looming crisis?

- Reconciliation still at work

→ "Principles of Reconciliation", *Department of Justice*, p. 101 • "Metis granted right for self-governance", *Global News*, p. 105

- On the road to separatism?

→ "Is Canada suffering from a unity crisis?", *The Guardian*, p. 104 • Province *vs*. country, statistics, p. 104

## Facing globalisation

- Bilingualism encouraged

→ "A bilingual nation", infographic, p. 102 • "Bilingualism on the rise", *Global News*, p. 102

- Diversity as key to global success

→ "What unites Canada in a divided world?", D. MCKAY, p. 106

## Phonology — L'accentuation des adjectifs et des suites d'adjectifs

AUDIO

- Les **adjectifs** sont des mots porteurs de sens, ils sont donc **accentués** dans les énoncés.
Les **adjectifs appréciatifs** sont souvent fortement accentués pour attirer l'attention sur un élément, ou donner une valeur expressive ou contrastive à l'**énoncé**.
*Some Canadians think that **local** autonomy is the solution to the threats of **central** power.*

- Dans le cas d'une **suite d'adjectifs** descriptifs : le deuxième adjectif est légèrement moins accentué que le premier, et également moins accentué que le nom qui suit.
*Reconciliation has been a **long** painful process.*

**1 Recopie ces suites d'adjectifs, et souligne le plus accentué. Écoute et vérifie.**

a. *Canadian bilingual kids.*
b. *The fertile colourful prairies of Canada.*
c. *The promising long-awaited reconciliation process.*
d. *Inclusive hiring strategies.*

**2 Lis ce texte à voix haute en prêtant une attention particulière aux adjectifs. Écoute et vérifie.**

*Linguistic duality is a significant aspect of the Canadian Confederation. Since 1969, the English-French bilingualism rate has seen constant growth. Native French speakers are thus attracted to Canada and local governments are willing to develop French-language programs in schools.*

Vers le **BAC**

# BUILD YOUR PORTFOLIO

## Artwork

"Self-portrait with Mum", Fantasyland Motel, West Edmont Mall, AB from the "Oh Canada" series, Naomi HARRIS, 2011

- **Look** at the photo series and **read** the comment by the artist. **Comment** on the image of Canada she depicts through her work.

ARTICLE

## Article

"Canada's multiculturalism is our identity", *The Globe and Mail* April 27, 2018

"On Oct. 8, 1971, [then-prime minister Pierre Trudeau] introduced capital-M Multiculturalism to the House of Commons. In addition to becoming an officially bilingual land, Canada would formally respect the diversity of its citizens' languages."

- **Read** the article and **explain** what makes multiculturalism essential to Canadian society, according to the author.

ARTICLE

## Book

*Wenjack*, Joseph BOYDEN, 2016

"I'm learning my English, me. But I won't lose my tongue. I pretend to be the slow one so I don't forget my words."

- **Read** the novel and **explain** how the main character's journey embodies Canadians' identity struggles.

## Infographic

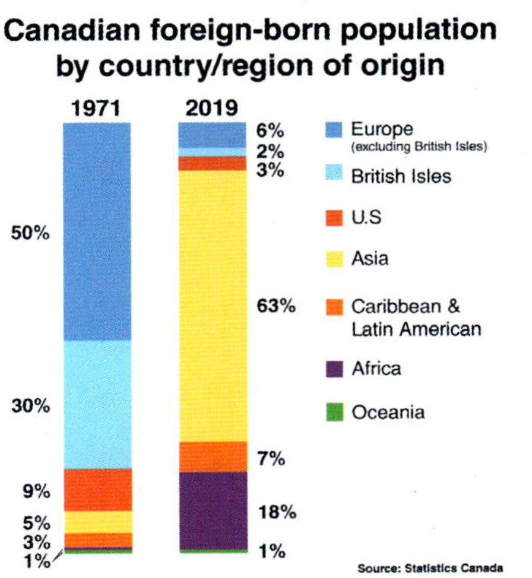


- **Observe** the chart and **analyse** the evolution of the Canadian foreign-born population. **Link** it to Canada's assets in terms of diversity.

ÉPREUVE ORALE | GRAND ORAL — Entraîne-toi à l'oral

**Step 1** — **Build up your speech!**

ÉPREUVE ORALE:
- Choose one topic in the mindmap p. 110.
- Pick out two documents in the file and add one or two personal ones to illustrate this issue.
- Prepare your presentation: you must show how these documents relate to the issue you chose.

OBJECTIF BAC p. 305

GRAND ORAL:
- Choose one topic in the mindmap p. 110.
- Find a key question about your topic and write it down. Think about links with other subjects (*HGGSP* for example).
- Gather arguments and examples from the file.
- Prepare an outline for your presentation and write your note sheet.

OBJECTIF BAC p. 308-309

**Step 2** — **Make your oral presentation in front of two classmates.**

ÉPREUVE ORALE:
- Show your documents to your classmates. Each of you makes their presentation to the others in about five minutes.

OBJECTIF BAC p. 306-307

GRAND ORAL:
- Give your note sheet to your classmates.
- Stand up and make a five-minute presentation to answer your key question.

OBJECTIF BAC p. 310-311

**Step 3** — **Answer your classmates' questions about your presentation and give some feedback.**

SNAPFILE 12

FAIRE SOCIÉTÉ
AXE 1 : UNITÉ ET PLURALITÉ

# Standard English

▶ **To what extent is the English language unique?**

**FINAL TASK** Take part in a live chat about the possible evolutions of the English language in the world.

More on SPEAKEASY NEWS speakeasy-news.com

## 1 What is standard English?

**Doc 1.**

David Donar, *Broken English*, January 2009
(Video: "Dr Jacob Lauritzen", *Read, Write, and Cite*, 2019)

**WORDS**
- mother tongue = first language
- native ≠ non-native
- flawless ≠ flawed
- genuine = authentic
- prevalent
- widely-spoken
- widespread = common
- prevail = dominate
- span over = extend across

**a. Focus** on the cartoon and **comment** on what it reveals about the English language.

**b.** GRAMMAR **Find** the grammatically incorrect elements in the first sentence and **rephrase** it.

**c. Watch** the video and **find out** what standard English refers to.

**d. Comment** on Dr Jacob Lauritzen's opinion on the reality of standard English.

**YOUR TASK** As a student learning English, **discuss** with your teacher the differences between standard English and the reality of spoken English.

# 2 The world power of English

LANDMARKS p. 291

## Doc 1.

Animation interactive

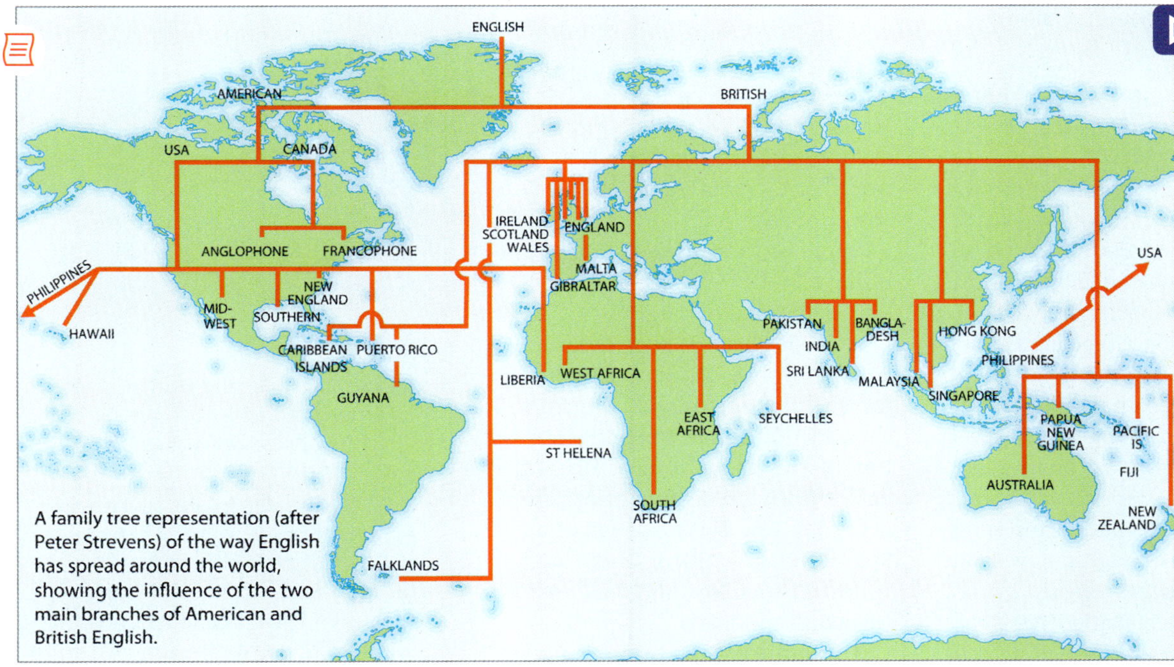


A family tree representation (after Peter Strevens) of the way English has spread around the world, showing the influence of the two main branches of American and British English.

*Cambridge University Press, 2013*

## Doc 2.

English is everywhere, and everywhere, English dominates. From inauspicious[1] beginnings on the edge of a minor European archipelago, it has grown to vast size and astonishing influence. Almost 400m people speak it as their first language; a billion more know it as a secondary tongue. It is an official language in at least 59 countries, the unofficial lingua franca of dozens more. No language in history has been used by so many people or spanned a greater portion of the globe. [...] It is inescapable: the language of global business, the internet, science, diplomacy, stellar navigation, avian pathology. And everywhere it goes, it leaves behind a trail of dead: dialects crushed, languages forgotten, literatures mangled[2].

One straightforward way to trace the growing influence of English is in the way its vocabulary has infiltrated so many other languages. For a millennium or more, English was a great importer of words, absorbing vocabulary from Latin, Greek, French, Hindi, Nahuatl and many others. During the 20th century, though, as the US became the dominant superpower and the world grew more connected, English became a net exporter of words. [...]

[At] some point between the end of the Second World War and the start of the new millennium, English made a jump in primacy that no amount of talk about it as a "lingua franca" or "global language" truly captures. It transformed from a dominant language to what the Dutch sociologist Abram de Swaan calls a "hypercentral" one. [...]

In the last few decades, as globalisation has accelerated and the US has remained the world's most powerful country, the advance of English has taken on a new momentum[3].

Jacob MIKANOWSKI, "Behemoth, bully, thief: how the English language is taking over the planet", *The Guardian*, July 2018

**1.** improbable **2.** damaged **3.** importance

**a. Look** at the map (**Doc 1**) and **guess** which historical reasons account for the spread of British and American English around the world.

**b. Read** the article (**Doc 2**) and **give** the reasons for the English language's lasting domination.

**c. Discuss** the benefits and risks of the spread of English as a global language.

**d.** TRANSLATION **Translate** the beginning of the article (l. 1-3). **Pay attention** to the journalist's style.

**YOUR TASK** **Write** a short ad for an English language school. **Highlight** the importance of mastering English today.

**BOOST YOUR SKILLS!**

**Souligner l'importance d'un phénomène**

- Utilise des comparatifs et des superlatifs : *A **greater** portion of the globe* • *The world's **most powerful** country*
- Emploie des figures de style pour intensifier ton propos : *English is everywhere, and everywhere, English dominates.* (chiasme) • *The dominant **superpower*** (hyperbole)
- Utilise le *present perfect* pour indiquer le résultat d'une évolution : *Its vocabulary **has infiltrated** so many other languages.* • *The advance of English **has taken** on a new momentum.*

# 3 Only one English?

## Doc 1. A common language

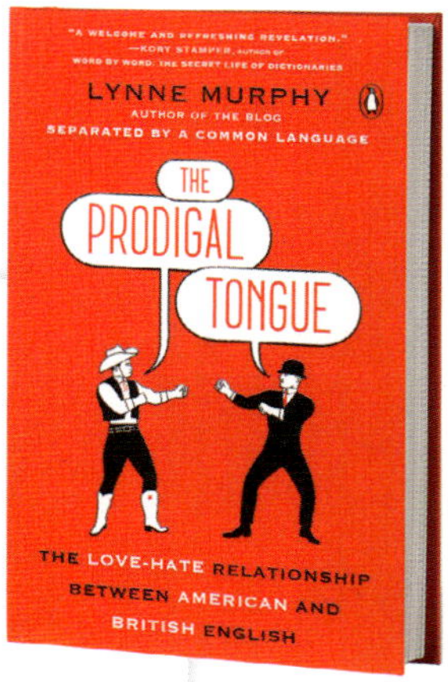


"Great Britain and the United States are two nations separated by a common language."

That's the stock witticism[1], but if you ask me, it gets things backwards. Great Britain and the US are more like two nations *united* by a *divided* language — or more precisely, by their mutual obsession with their linguistic differences. For 200 years now, writers from each nation have been tirelessly picking over the language of the other, with a mix of amusement, condescension, derision and horror.

That fraught[2] relationship is the subject of an engaging new book called *The Prodigal Tongue*.

The book is subtitled *The Love-Hate Relationship of British and American English*, and there's plenty of each to go around. We tend to be indulgent of each other's linguistic quirks and foibles[3], but only as long as they remain exotically foreign. We Americans are charmed by quaint Mary Poppinsisms like "gobsmacked". The British admire what Virginia Woolf called our "expressive ugly vigorous slang" — she singled out "rambunctious" and "flip-flop". [...]

Nowadays, Britishisms usually enter American speech via members of the coastal smart set who reckon the words makes them sound trendy or posh. [...]

Some of those items ultimately trickle out[4] to the linguistic hinterland[5] — whimsical[6] words like "kerfuffle" and useful ones like "vetting" — and for that matter, "trendy", which is a legacy of Britain's swinging '60s. But in the end, modern British has contributed far fewer words to everyday American speech than Spanish has — think "loco" and "pronto", "macho" and "nachos", "mañana" and "nada".

The British have had a harder time of it. They've been feeling besieged[7] by Americanisms since the era of the earliest talkies, when people took to using "OK" in place of "righto". Now the young people greet each other with, "Hi, guys" and use, "awesome", where their elders would have said, "marvelous". [...] We basically all expect to understand each other, which is why we find it so curious to realize that sometimes we don't.

Geoff NUNBERG, *npr.org*, 2018

**1.** humorous remark **2.** complicated **3.** strange and funny characteristics **4.** move gradually **5.** countryside or bush **6.** amusing **7.** surrounded

**a. Read** the article and **find** examples of American and British people's *"mutual obsession with their linguistic differences."* (l. 9-10)

**b.** VOCABULARY *"witticism"* (l. 4) *"Mary Poppinsisms"* (l. 26) *"Britishisms"* (l. 31) *"Americanisms"* (l. 52) **Identify** the meaning conveyed by the suffix "-ism". **Give** a definition and **find** one example for each word.

**c. Say** which of the two varieties of English has had more influence on the other.

**d. Imagine** the possible consequences of the two different evolutions of British and American English.

**WORDS**

- **co**mmon roots
- cul**tu**ral speci**fi**cities = idio**syn**crasies
- lingu**is**tic **sub**tleties /ˈsʌtəltiz/
- **up**ward trend = craze (for sth)

- influ**en**tial
- quaint = old-**fa**shioned

- **bo**rrow from
- com**bine** = merge

## Doc 2. Hinglish

AUDIO

(Audio: Professor Daya Kishan Thussu speaks to BBC about Hinglish, *BBC*)

**a. Listen** to Professor Thussu and **find out** what Hinglish is based on.

**b. Pick out** information on how Hinglish is used and by whom it is spoken.

**c. Explain** why this language has been on the rise.

YOUR TASK **Chat** online with an Indian penpal about the form of English he/she uses and what Hinglish means to him/her.

# 4 The future of English

## Doc 1.

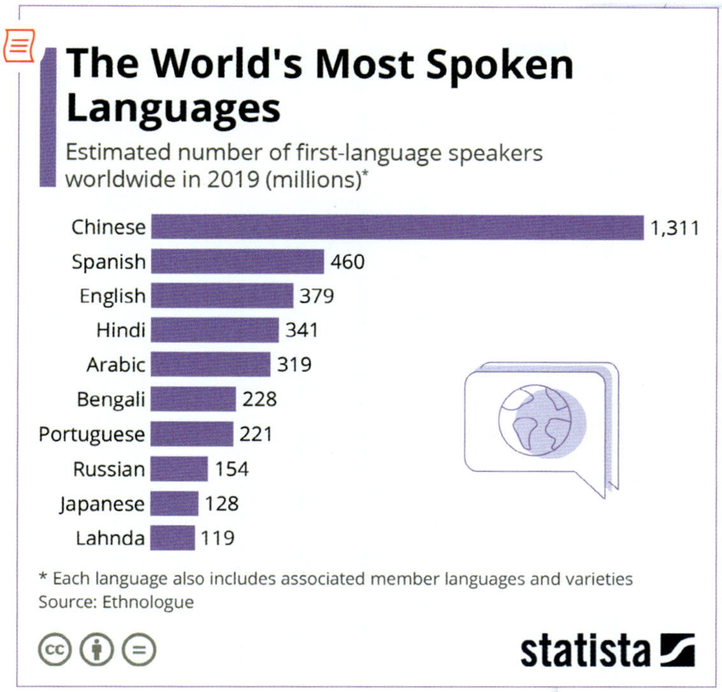


## Doc 2.

### Will Mandarin be the next global language?

China's future is by no means certain; whatever happens will have implications for the global linguistic order. [...] There are three possible scenarios.

The first scenario is continuation, in which English remains the global language. China faces an array of political, economic, environmental and social problems that could overwhelm it. Because the attraction of Mandarin is based primarily on China's political importance and its economy, if its development were to stagnate or even go backwards, people would be less interested in learning Mandarin. [...]

The second scenario is co-existence, in which English and Mandarin are both global languages. China could be one of a number of powerful and important countries, but not powerful enough to dominate the world. In such circumstances, English wouldn't be the only language that's seen as important, and Mandarin would likely increase its use and status. There are already signs this is happening. African students are increasingly interested in learning Mandarin because of job opportunities created by China's investment in African countries, the ease of getting study visas after restrictions put in place by the US and Europe, and cheaper tuition fees at Chinese universities. In English-speaking countries, more bilingual Mandarin/English schools are opening in response to the growing perception that acquiring Mandarin will be important in the future. [...]

The third scenario is replacement, in which Mandarin becomes the global language instead of English. If China becomes the world's most powerful country, or superpower, it would be able to use its power to shape the international system, much as the US did after World War II. [...] China is also attempting to position itself as a leader on global issues at the same time as the US retreats from them. These include free trade and globalization, climate change and space exploration. [...] If China's initiatives are successful, Mandarin will be the language associated with new developments and ideas, and consequently have great appeal and attraction to people.

Jeffrey GILL, *www.asiatimes.com*, 2019

## Doc 3.

"What will English language look like in the future?", *Oxford University Press*, 2016

AUDIO

**a. Focus** on the graph (**Doc 1**) and **imagine** what the future of English could be.

**b. Team up** and **discover** one of the scenarios described in the text (**Doc 2**). Each group **presents** their findings to the class. **Discuss** them collectively.

**c. Listen** to Professor Simon Horobin (**Doc 3**) and **explain** the parallels he draws with the evolution of Latin.

**d. Say** what the evolution of English will be according to him.

**YOUR TASK** **Discuss** the possible evolutions of English as opposed to Mandarin with a Chinese penpal.

**BOOST YOUR SKILLS!**

**Rendre compte d'une évolution**

- Utilise le présent en *be* + V-*ing* : *More bilingual schools **are opening**...* • *English **is being spread** across the globe...*
- Utilise des adverbes : *African students are **increasingly** interested...* • *A form of English that is **still** spoken...*

**FINAL TASK**

As a future international student, you take part in a live chat about the necessity to speak English perfectly today.
**Write down** your ideas about the evolution of English, taking into account the history of that language and its position in the world today.
**Discuss** your ideas with the other participants.

play BAC How to... **TRANSLATE INTO FRENCH**

MÉDIATION

OBJECTIF BAC p. 302-303

L'**épreuve écrite** en Terminale comprend deux parties. Suite à la synthèse de documents et éventuellement de l'écrit argumentatif (partie 1), tu devras procéder à la transposition en français d'un document du dossier ou bien à la **traduction en français d'un court passage** de l'un des documents (partie 2).
Voici un exemple de texte, extrait du Doc 2 p. 113, qui pourrait t'être donné pour l'exercice de traduction.

**Traduisez en français le passage suivant de l'article "Behemoth, bully, thief: how the English language is taking over the planet" (*The Guardian*, July 2018) de Jacob Mikanowski.**

During the 20th century, though, as the US became the dominant superpower and the world grew more connected, English became a net exporter of words. [...]
[At] some point between the end of the Second World War and the start of the new millennium, English made a jump in primacy that no amount of talk about it as a "lingua franca" or "global language" truly captures. It transformed from a dominant language to what the Dutch sociologist Abram de Swaan calls a "hypercentral" one.

## 1 Analyse l'extrait

**a. Lis** l'extrait et identifie le groupe nominal sujet du passage. **Repère** le pronom personnel s'y rapportant.

**b. Identifie** le temps utilisé : se réfère-t-il à un résultat présent ou à une situation passée ?

**c. Repère** les connecteurs logiques et les verbes exprimant une évolution dans le temps.

**d. Repère** les verbes utilisés au sens figuré.

• Pour rendre compte d'une évolution plus ou moins rapide, certains verbes d'action sont utilisés dans leur sens figuré. En traduction, on cherchera à trouver des verbes français exprimant le même phénomène : *skyrocket* → monter en flèche.

## 2 Utilise des procédés de traduction : la traduction littérale, la modulation, l'équivalence

OBJECTIF BAC p. 303

• Certaines images peuvent être traduites mot à mot de l'anglais vers le français sans que leur sens ne soit altéré : c'est la **traduction littérale**.

• Dans certains cas, l'anglais adopte un point de vue différent du français et implique une traduction non littérale. On a alors recours à la **modulation** : *You are aware of that.* → Vous ne l'ignorez pas. *I miss you.* → Tu me manques.

• Les expressions idiomatiques doivent systématiquement être traduites par une modulation que l'on appelle **équivalence**. Il s'agit de trouver l'expression française équivalente à l'expression anglaise.

**a. Observe** et **commente** la traduction du verbe : *...the world grew more connected...* → ...le monde est devenu de plus en plus interconnecté...

**b. Trouve** la bonne équivalence pour la phrase : *English made a jump in primacy...*
A. → La langue anglaise a fait un bond en prééminence...
B. → La langue anglaise a augmenté d'un seul coup en prééminence...
C. → La prééminence de la langue anglaise s'est accrue d'un seul coup...

• Certains noms d'institutions peuvent être traduits littéralement mais nécessitent la précision de leur équivalent en français pour être compris par le lecteur : *the Department of State* → le département d'état (ministère des affaires étrangères américain).

## 3 Traduis l'extrait

OBJECTIF BAC p. 302

**Traduis** le passage en veillant aux points suivants :

• Les expressions idiomatiques *at some point, no amount of talk, captures* : peux-tu les traduire littéralement ou faut-il recourir à une équivalence ?

• La syntaxe : est-il nécessaire de changer l'ordre des mots dans la deuxième phrase pour que le message soit plus clair en français ?

• Une fois que tu auras traduit le texte, laisse passer un peu de temps, puis relis ta traduction à voix haute. Si certains passages ne te semblent pas naturels, retravaille-les.

Vers le **BAC**

# BUILD YOUR PORTFOLIO

## Poem

"Broken English", Jamila Lyiscott, 2014

Jamila Lyiscott, an American scholar and poet of Trinidadian origins, explains in her poem "Broken English" how the way you speak English can define who you are and the linguistic stereotypes against racial minorities.

- **Read** the article and **listen** to the poem. **Explain** what Jamila Lyiscott means when she says that she is trilingual. **Say** what standard English represents according to her.

ARTICLE

POEM

## Infographic

"A world of languages", *SCMP*, Alberto Lucas Lopez, 2015

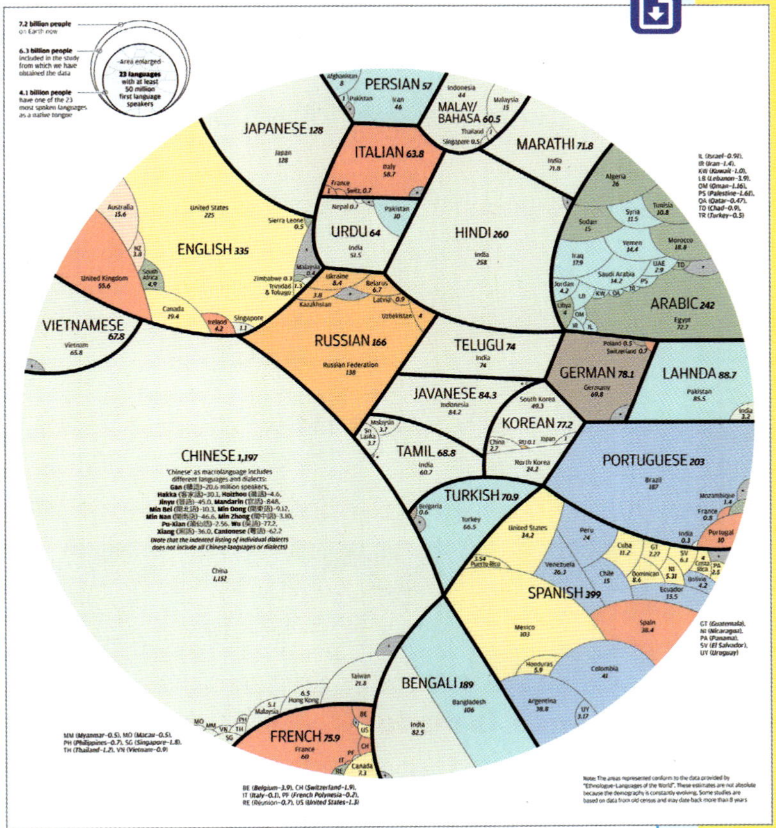


- **Look** at the infographic and **explain** what it represents. **Say** what aspects of the infographic surprise you.

## Article

"Can English remain the world's favourite language?", *BBC News*, May 2018

"There are probably more people in China who speak English as a second language than there are Americans who speak it as their first. (A fifth of Americans speak a language other than English in their own homes.) But for how much longer will English qualify as the "world's favourite language"?"

- **Read** the article and **explain** how the position of English as the world's favourite language is being challenged.

ARTICLE

## Book

*Mother Tongue*, Bill Bryson, 2009

In his book full of hilarious anecdotes on the history, the evolution of English and how it is used today all around the world, Bill Bryson makes a point that English is as maddening to learn as it is flexible to use.

- **Read** the first chapter of the book and **pick out** elements showing that English is a language full of paradoxes.

## Entraîne-toi à l'oral

ÉPREUVE ORALE

**Step 1** **Build up your speech!**

- Choose one of the issues studied in this file: what is standard English? Is there only one English? Will English remain the global language of the future?
- Pick out one document in the file, one from this page and a personal one to illustrate this issue.
- Prepare your presentation: show how these documents relate to the topic you chose. OBJECTIF BAC p. 305

**Step 2** **Make your presentation in front of two classmates.**

- Show your documents to your classmates and explain your point in about five minutes. OBJECTIF BAC p. 306-307

**Step 3** **Answer your classmates' questions about your presentation.**

FILE 13

FAIRE SOCIÉTÉ

AXE 2 : LIBERTÉS PUBLIQUES ET LIBERTÉS INDIVIDUELLES

# The land of the free

► **How central is the notion of freedom to American society?**

FINAL TASK **Take part in a roundtable discussion on Independence Day.**

More on SPEAKEASY NEWS speakeasy-news.com

## 1 Fundamental freedoms

### Doc 1. The Four Freedoms

VIDÉO

*Freedom of Speech* (Video: *Norman Rockwell Museum*, 2018)

*Freedom from Want*

*Freedom of Worship*

*Freedom from Fear*

**a. Describe** the pictures and **explain** how they relate to the title.

**b. Watch** the video and **take** notes about the link between Franklin D. Roosevelt and Norman Rockwell.

**c. Clarify** the four freedoms referred to by Roosevelt. **Explain** what his aim was.

**d. Comment** on Rockwell's intention and achievement when painting the President's ideals.

**e. Explain** how H.W. Thomas and E. Shur's project updates and broadens the notion of freedom.

Photographs: Norman Rockwell's *Four Freedoms* reinterpreted by photographers Hank Willis Thomas and Emily Shur, 2018 © For Freedoms

SITE

## Doc 2. Freedom is inscribed in America's DNA LANDMARKS p. 293

No idea is more fundamental to Americans' sense of themselves as individuals and as a nation than freedom. The central term in our political vocabulary, freedom or liberty, is deeply embedded[1] in the documentary record of our history and the language of everyday life. The Declaration of Independence lists liberty among mankind's inalienable rights; the Constitution announces as its purpose to secure "Liberty's Blessings." The United States fought the Civil War to bring about a new birth of freedom, World War II for freedom from genocide, the Cold War to defend the Free World.

Americans' love of freedom has been represented by liberty poles, caps, and statues, and acted out throughout history by running away from slavery, and demonstrating for the right to vote. The idea of "Freedom" occupies a more prominent place in public and private discourse in the United States than elsewhere in the world. [...]

Perhaps because of its very ubiquity[2] the history of freedom is a tale of debates, disagreements, and struggles rather than a set of timeless categories or an evolutionary narrative toward a preordained goal. [...]

The United States, founded on the premise that liberty is an entitlement of all humanity, undeniably deprived many of its own people of freedom. It has been through battles at the boundaries, the efforts of racial minorities, women, workers, and other groups to secure freedom, as they understood it, that the meaning of freedom has been both deepened and transformed. The concept extends now into realms for which it was not originally intended. Time and again in our history, the definition of freedom has been transformed by the demands of excluded groups for inclusion.

Rob MITCHELL, "The essential characteristic of American life", *murfreesborovoice.com*, July 2020

**1.** implanted **2.** omnipresence

**a. Read** the article and **find out** how the question of freedom has been dealt with throughout U.S. history.

**b. Explain** how Rob Mitchell demonstrates that *"freedom is the essential characteristic of American life."*

**c.** GRAMMAR **Identify** the grammatical subject of the verbs (l. 20-21) and **explain** the use of the passive voice. p. 125

**d. Explain** the contradiction exposed in the last paragraph.

### WORDS

- inalienable rights

- inclusive
- updated

- bring up to date
- enrich
- expand
- modernise
- take an oath
- warrant = guarantee

## Doc 3. Liberties in the US Constitution

**Amendment I** Congress shall make no law respecting an establishment of religion, or prohibiting the free exercise thereof; or abridging the freedom of speech, or of the press; or the right of the people peaceably to assemble, and to petition the Government for a redress of grievances.

**Amendment II** A well regulated Militia, being necessary to the security of a free State, the right of the people to keep and bear Arms, shall not be infringed[1].

**Amendment IV** The right of the people to be secure in their persons, houses, papers, and effects, against unreasonable searches and seizures, shall not be violated, and no Warrants[2] shall issue, but upon probable cause. [...]

**Amendment XIII** Neither slavery nor involuntary servitude, except as a punishment for crime whereof the party shall have been duly convicted, shall exist within the United States, or any place subject to their jurisdiction.

**1.** limit **2.** *mandats*

**a. Read** the amendments and **identify** the different forms of freedom they guarantee.

**b.** GRAMMAR **Identify** the meaning of the modal *shall* in this context.

**c. Explain** how these amendments show that freedom is part of America's core identity.

**YOUR TASK** As a guide in an exhibition, **comment** on H. W. Thomas and E. Shur's photographs by **explaining** how they represent the very notion of freedom in the U.S.

### BOOST YOUR SKILLS!

**Définir une notion**

- Mets l'accent sur la notion par des tournures passives : *Liberty **is** deeply **embedded** in... • Love of freedom **has been represented** by...* GRAMMAR p. 125
- Précise la notion par un usage fin des prépositions : *A world **at** peace, free **from** aggression, and founded **upon** four freedoms.* GRAMMAR p. 125
- Utilise des complétives pour en approfondir le sens : *It helped Americans to envision **what** they **were fighting for** and **why** the war effort **should be supported**.*
- Souligne sa portée avec le comparatif de supériorité : *No idea is **more fundamental** to Americans **than** freedom.*

# 2 Freedom of speech

## Doc 1. Should every speech be protected?

AUDIO

"Speaking freely the future of the First Amendment", 2018

**a. Listen** and **note down** how the First Amendment has been challenged through times.

**b. Find out** the difference between the choices made by the Supreme Court and the ones private companies can make.

**c. Discuss** the arguments put forward by Facebook.

### WORDS

- accountability = responsibility
- at stake = in question
- ruling = decision

- bound = obligated

- be barred from
- be censored/expurgated
- foster = encourage
- safeguard = protect

## Doc 2. Freedom of the press

VIDÉO

*The Post* by Steven SPIELBERG, 2017

**a. Observe** the film poster and still and **anticipate** what the film is about.

**b. Watch** the trailer and **identify** where the main characters work and what is at stake.

**c.** GRAMMAR *"**If** you publish, we'**ll** be at the Supreme Court next week."*
*"**If** the government wins,* The Washington Post ***will** cease to exist."*
**Explain** the meaning conveyed by these sentences.
**Say** what it reveals about press freedom.

**d. Read** the culture spot and **explain** the importance of a free press.

### CULTURE SPOT

The **Pentagon Papers**, released by the *New York Times* in 1971, revealed that the government had lied to the public and to Congress about the Vietnam War. The *Times* was temporarily barred from publishing the papers and the *Washington Post* joined the *Times* in its fight to publish the papers.

**AT HOME** **Look up** the Pentagon Papers and **find out** the Supreme Court's decision in this case.

# 3 Freedom of worship

## Doc 1. Destination America

TEXTE LU

Following the desire for a better material life for themselves and their children, the desire for religious freedom probably motivated more immigrants to come to America than any other concern—and the two desires have often been inextricably linked. In the words of historian Will Durant, "For men came across the sea not merely to find new soil for their plows but to win freedom for their souls, to think and speak and worship as they would."

The founding of European colonies in North America coincided with the Protestant Reformation—one of the watershed[1] events of human history. To those suffering from harassment or maltreatment in the Old World, the New World offered space to create new societies in which they could worship without interference—like the Pilgrims and Puritans who founded New England. [...]

In Europe, the Reformation led to a series of deadly and devastating wars of religion that brought even more refugees, like the Huguenots, to the colonies. The suffering caused by these European conflicts, as well as the intellectual advances of the 18th-century Enlightenment, led the founders of the United States to make freedom to worship the law of the land in the First Amendment to the Constitution. [...].

This guarantee inspired countless immigrants to make their way to the United States, often at great risk and hardship—from Jews escaping anti-Semitic pogroms[2] in the 19th century Russian Empire to Tibetans fleeing the Communist Chinese occupation of their homeland in the 1990s. As a result, the United States became the most religiously diverse nation on earth, with some 2,000 distinct religious groups by the early 21st century.

Charles A. WILLS, *Destination America*, 2005

**1.** turning point **2.** massacres

**a.** **Read** the text and **identify** what immigrants were looking for when coming to America.

**b.** **Create** a timeline of the different events mentioned in the text.

**c.** **Explain** how religious upheavals shaped the American nation.

**d.** TRANSLATION **Translate** l. 17-21 focusing on the cumulative adjectives.

## Doc 2. Religious freedom today

VIDÉO

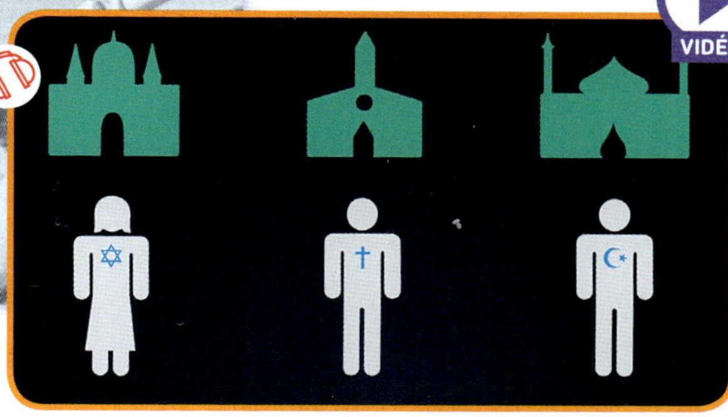

*Heritage foundation*, 2019

MÉDIATION

**YOUR TASK** You attended a conference entitled "Fundamental freedoms in the First Amendment". **Synthetise** it for a friend who couldn't attend, **emphasising** how the First Amendment has, in some way, forged American identity.

**CULTURE SPOT**

A **think tank** is a research institute made up of experts who provide advice on social and economic policies. *The Heritage Foundation* is a conservative think tank.

**BOOST YOUR SKILLS!**

**Démontrer la valeur fondatrice d'un texte**

- Utilise des marqueurs temporels pour inscrire sa valeur dans la durée : *Back in **1789** • The advances of **18th century** • After **World War One** • During **an era of**... • **Today**...*
- Structure clairement ta démonstration : ***So**, you have to... • **First** of all • Point **number 1** • Point **number 2** is... • **OK**, that sounds good, **but**...*
- Utilise des structures présentatives pour mettre en valeur tes arguments : ***That** is a choice **that**... • The ways **in which** we...*

**a.** **Watch** the video and **explain** what the First Amendment implies regarding religious freedom.

**b.** **Give** the speaker's definition of religious freedom.

**c.** **Identify** the role the government can play as far as religious freedom is concerned.

**d.** **Read** the culture spot and **discuss** the reasons why the Heritage Foundation is so involved in protecting religious freedom.

# EXPLORE 4 Freedom from want

## Doc 1. Freedom is the American dream

Ever since our brave forebearers[1] declared America's independence, the United States has been a beacon[2] of liberty, hope and opportunity. Indeed, America is still regarded the world over as a land where success can be achieved regardless of where you've come from. And that is because our forebearers trusted free people, free speech and free markets—all of which continue to undergird the "American dream."

The American dream never fails to inspire old and young alike, and I believe its promise will continue to motivate future generations to work hard and innovate. Because our country has always valued hard work, we seek to achieve and often succeed because opportunity exists here. But it's important to recognize that free markets are fundamental to American opportunity and prosperity.

How do free markets contribute to the American dream? The answer rests in the philosophy of freedom so foundational to our nation. Free markets allow consumers and producers to freely participate in mutually beneficial transactions, empowering entrepreneurs and innovators to create the future. [...]

Free markets truly thrive when insulated by healthy institutions that instill virtue and encourage charity, including strong families and tight knit communities. When the end is purely self-interest, free markets cannot succeed. [...] As evidenced right here in America, a free market economy shaped by virtue is indisputably the most productive economic system for fulfilling the promise of the American dream for generations to come.

**Tom Cole, *cole.house.gov*, May 2019**

1. ancestors 2. source of light or hope

**a. Read** the text and **find out** what the American dream is based on according to the author.

**b. Explain** what is required for a free-market economy to work according to the author.

**c.** RHETORIC **Identify** the tone of the column and the word choice that contributes to this tone.

**d. Look up** the author's political party and **explain** how it shapes the column's content.

## Doc 2. Fuelling inequalities?

1 VIDÉO

How poor people survive in America, *DW*, 2019

2 AUDIO

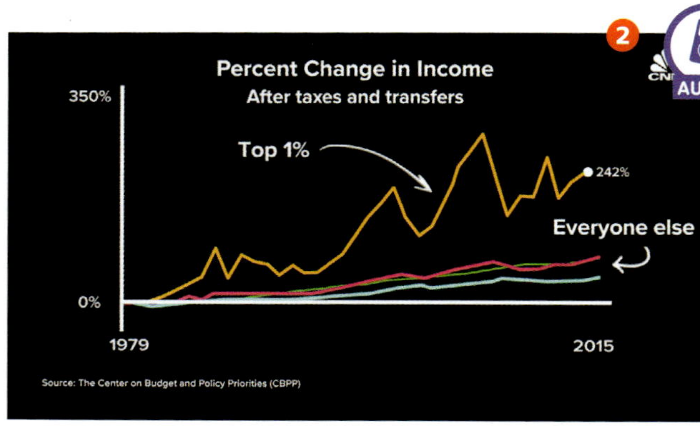


The Wealth Gap, *CNBC*, 2019

**Choose between doc 1 or 2 and answer the questions.**

**a. Pick out** information about the conditions of Americans living below the poverty line.

**b.** VOCABULARY **Pick out** words that relate to growth and reduction. **Comment** on what they show about inequality in the USA.

**c. Comment** on how these living conditions relate to the American free-market economy.

**d. Compare** and **contrast** the vision of the American dream in **doc. 1** and in this document.

# 5 Freedom from fear

## Doc 1.

### When Protestors Carry Guns, Does It Impede Others' Free Speech?

In late January, thousands of pro-gun activists descended on Richmond, Virginia, to protest a package of gun reform bills advancing through the state General Assembly. Many of them were armed. The specter of a massive open-carry demonstration was difficult for anyone to ignore, but the day was also significant because of the people not in attendance[1] outside the state Capitol grounds.

Fearing violence, untold numbers of counter-protesters diverted their plans to advocate for legislation on the same streets as the pro-gun activists. Among those who sat it out that day were members of a student group advocating for undocumented immigrants and gun-reform advocates who had planned to hold a vigil in memory of gun-violence victims. In their absence, the loudest voices in the proverbial room were those in support of gun rights.

Some legal commentators found the dynamic vexing and questioned if the protest was a healthy picture of free speech and debate. Garrett Epps, a professor of constitutional law at the University of Baltimore, was one of many to surface concerns about the First Amendment rights of the unarmed. In *The Atlantic*, he declared, "The right to bear arms in political debate is not the power to speak for oneself; it is, at least implicitly, the power to silence others." The late Supreme Court Justice John Paul Stevens acknowledged this clash of rights in a dissent from 2010. "Your interest in keeping and bearing a certain firearm," he wrote, "may diminish my interest in being and feeling safe from armed violence." [...]

While some may feel that armed protesters trample[2] on the speech rights of others, the reality is that no court would currently hold that carrying guns openly at a demonstration violates First Amendment rights to free expression and political assembly.

A First Amendment lawyer's argument against open carry at protests would go something like this: Firearms violate the speech rights of unarmed protesters because they "chill" expression through intimidation.

But this reasoning suffers from two major problems. For one thing, freedom of speech protects individuals from government intrusion on expression, but in armed protest settings, the government is not directly involved in silencing anyone.

Olivia LI, *Thetrace.org*, March 2020

Gun rights advocates in Richmond, January 2020

**WORDS**

- protest = demonstration
- turmoil = chaos /'keɪ.ɒs/

- blatant = flagrant
- contentious = controversial
- ominous = threatening
- questionable

- advocate = stand up for
- contend = argue
- empower
- run amok = get out of hand
- thrive = flourish

1. absent 2. show no consideration for

a. **Read** the article and **pick out** elements to explain how the First and Second Amendments collide.

b. **Identify** each party's argument (pro-gun activists, counter-protesters, courts).

c. **Explain** the complex issue raised by the right to bear arms while demonstrating.

**YOUR TASK** With an American friend, **debate** whether the Second Amendment can limit the First.

**BOOST YOUR SKILLS!**

**Relever des contradictions**

- Utilise des subordonnées d'opposition et de concession : *It lifts…* ***while*** *leaving behind…* • ***Even if*** *they are mediocre, they get to go to the best schools.* GRAMMAR p. 125
- Cite des exemples d'avis contradictoires : *Paul Stevens* ***acknowledged*** *this clash of rights : "…", he* ***wrote*** • *Lawyer's argument* ***would go*** *something like this:…*
- Utilise des structures négatives fortes : *And* ***nowhere has it*** *surged more than in the U.S…*

# American voices

## Doc. Americans reflect on freedom

As an American, I shall feel safe and protected within the American soil from any attack, military, terrorism or biological. In a country where freedom is the norm, I shall not fear to voice my opinion. My skin color, my religion or my sexual orientation should not predict what I can do, what I can achieve, or who I can become.

Living in America today is both shameful and hopeful. It is shameful to know that in a country with the biggest defense budget in the world, in a country with the best educational and research institutions, the mortality rate for COVID-19 is higher than it is in countries like South Korea. It is a shame that in a country where freedom is the norm, the likelihood[1] of being mistreated, denied opportunities or even killed just because you are different is still high.

Lucie Hutchins, senior software engineer in Down East, Maine

**WORDS**
- belonging
- marginalisation
- patriotic sentiment

- assimilate
- conform

- fluid = ever-shifting
- set in stone = immutable

1. probability

Being a combat veteran, on one the hand freedom means protecting and serving this country. It's very honorable and I know I'm proud of my service. But then on the other hand, being a young Black male in America, it doesn't seem as free. It just doesn't feel good. To me, what it means to be American is you should be able to dream. And I don't think it's monolithic[2]. [...] Even though we all live in the same country, we all don't get the same opportunities.

Davon Goodwin, farmer in Laurinburg, North Carolina

2. uniform

For me, America is [...] this ever-evolving story. We continually help create what its identity is. And I think for the most part, freedom is a social contract. It's not something that's given. It's something that's earned in many ways, even in a place like America where people assume that it's given. We've earned our freedom through sacrifice, through bloodshed, through labor and toil of people who have been marginalized and underrepresented in all these communities today that are standing up. They have fought for this freedom and we continue to fight for this freedom.

Bao Nguyen, filmmaker in Los Angeles, California.

*wbur.org*, July 2020

**a.** **Read** and **sum up** each view on freedom in the USA.

**b.** GRAMMAR **Comment** on Lucie Hutchins's use of *shall* and *should*. **Explain** the contrast between the first and second part of her testimony. ▸ p. 125

**c.** **Discuss** this quote and how it relates to each testimony: *"Living in America today is both shameful and hopeful."*

## FINAL TASK | Take part in a roundtable on Independence Day.

**For July 4th, you are invited to a roundtable in which you will share your view on freedom in American society.**

1. **Join** your team, **choose** your role (host, journalist, activist, legal scholar, historian...) and the kind of freedom you would like to focus on.
2. **Review** the documents from the file that relate to the arguments you want to present.
3. **Write** down facts, figures and references that you will want to mention.
4. **Participate** in the roundtable discussion:
   –**introduce** yourself and **share** your idea of freedom.
   –**react** to the other participants' arguments. You can **rephrase** their statements to **reinforce** or **counter** them and **strengthen** your point.

BOOST YOUR ENGLISH ▸ p. 125

# BOOST YOUR ENGLISH!

## Grammar — Échanger des points de vue sur une notion

- **Appuie-toi sur un usage précis des prépositions pour donner ta définition de la notion.**

*A world secure and **at** peace, free **from** aggression, and founded **upon** four essential freedoms.*

*Freedom **of** speech, freedom **of** every person **to** worship, freedom **from** want and freedom **from** fear.*

*Liberty is **among** mankind's inalienable rights.*

- **Reformule certaines interventions avec le discours indirect pour réagir.**

*The Supreme Court **has said** the government may…*

*People are likely to **report that** they believe…*

*Pro-gun rights activists **have** long **argued that**…*

*Despite what the president **affirms**…*

- **Utilise des subordonnées d'opposition et de concession.**

*It lifts residents of major cities **while** leaving those in small towns behind.* (opposition)

*Kids of affluent parents, **even if** they have mediocre talent, get to go to the best schools.* (concession)

***Although** Congress applauded the merits of his words, Roosevelt's Four Freedoms were absent from newspaper reports of the speech.* (concession)

- **Donne une portée générale à ton point de vue en utilisant la voix passive.**

*The famous American dream **is** far from **being achieved**.*

*The definition of freedom **has been transformed by** the demands of excluded groups for inclusion.*

**1 Reformule ces phrases en utilisant la voix passive.**

**a.** Norman Rockwell depicted Franklin D. Roosevelt's four freedoms.
**b.** The U.S. economy has improved human welfare.
**c.** The courts prevented the publication of the Pentagon Papers.
**d.** Gun-carriers have intimidated would-be protesters.

**2 Forme des phrases en employant le discours indirect et en variant les verbes introducteurs.**

**a.** Franklin D. Roosevelt: "The first is freedom of speech and expression everywhere in the world."
**b.** The U.S. Constitution: "Congress shall make no law respecting an establishment of religion, or prohibiting the free exercise thereof"
**c.** Some people: "The economy is rigged against us."
**d.** Donald Trump: "There has never been a better time to start living the American dream."

## Vocabulary — Freedom in the USA

Liberalism

**Economic liberalism** (AUDIO)
- American dream
- free market ≠ regulated market
- wealth gap
- self-made

**Social liberalism** (AUDIO)
- individualism
- interventionism ≠ noninterference
- progressive = liberal

**Downsides** (AUDIO)
- bankruptcy
- destitution
- hardship
- inequalities
- scarcity

Fundamental freedoms

**Speech** (AUDIO)
- defamation = slander
- free press ≠ censorship
- hate speech
- opinion
- harass < threaten
- restrict

**Worship** (AUDIO)
- believer: *croyant(e)*
- faith, the faithful
- practice
- religious freedom
- secularism: *laïcité*
- tolerance = respect

**Gun right** (AUDIO)
- assault rifle
- concealed weapon
- firearms
- gun control
- militia
- self-protection

Democracy

**Law** (AUDIO)
- ban = prohibit
- commit a crime
- encroach < infringe
- jail = imprison
- remain in custody

**Constitution** (AUDIO)
- amendment
- civil rights
- inalienable rights
- protected speech
- be enshrined in

OBJECTIF BAC p. 296-304

Grille d'auto-évaluation

## Sujet type bac

Durée : 3h30

Matériel autorisé : le dictionnaire unilingue (non encyclopédique) est autorisé.

Niveau attendu : C1

- **Prenez connaissance des documents A, B et C et traitez le sujet suivant en anglais (500 mots maximum).**

Taking into account their specificities, show how these documents illustrate the issues raised by school choice in the USA. Compare and contrast the solutions presented in each document.

- **Rendez compte en français des idées principales exprimées par le document A.**

### Document A

100 HARVARD GRADUATE SCHOOL OF EDUCATION — Degree Programs | Professional Education | Faculty & Research | Usable Knowledge | Menu

News & Events

#### Studies Show School Choice Widens Inequality

School choice programs which allow parents to select the schools their children attend deepen educational inequality and fail to yield[1] consistent learning gains, according to nine studies of choice initiatives coordinated by researchers at the Harvard Graduate School of Education. [...]

The coordinators said in all the programs parents who opted for a "choice school" over a neighborhood school were better educated and supervised their children's schoolwork more closely, compared to parents who kept their children in the neighborhood school.

"School choice advocates place great faith in the market model, assuming that parents will be good shoppers and will move their children into higher quality, more responsive schools," said Bruce Fuller, codirector of the study. "But choice advocates need to recognize that many students are left behind in low-quality schools. Unregulated choice programs unfairly penalize children whose parents are not savvy[2] educational consumers."

Researchers found little evidence that school choice programs actually boost student achievement. "Political enthusiasm and rhetorical claims about the virtues of school choice have far outpaced concrete evidence of merit," reported HGSE Professor and study co-director Richard Elmore in his summary of the studies. [...] "The educational background of families has a far stronger correlation to student achievement than any equalizing effect from schools. [...] These results suggest that school choice may inadvertently exacerbate stratification and inequality, as well as further isolate children who have the least support at home."

School choice also has the potential to further the re-segregation of public schools. For example, Montgomery County, Maryland, a suburb of Washington, D.C., created magnet schools as part of its school desegregation efforts in the late 1970s. Researchers found that many parents choose magnet schools on the basis of racial composition and cultural similarity. White parents tend to choose schools with higher white enrollment, while black parents select schools with higher black enrollment. Only by using their authority to deny transfer requests have school officials kept the choice process from increasing segregation.

*gse.havard.edu*, July 1995

1. produce
2. (*fam.*) clever

## Document B Rosa Parks, Barack Obama believed in charter schools

As we celebrate Black History Month, it's important to note the rich legacy of charter schools[1] in Michigan, and the role they've played in helping black and brown students achieve their dreams. So many visionary African American leaders in our state—including Rosa Parks herself—have recognized that a charter school can be the pathway to a better life for children.

Back in 1997, Parks tried to open a charter school in Detroit, to be called the Raymond and Rosa Parks School for Self-Development. [...]

Sadly, the politics of the day got in the way, and Parks' charter school was not able to open. Her application to the Detroit Public Schools to authorize the school was killed before it even got to the board table for a vote. Even Parks herself was not able to overcome the political bias against charter schools.

However, hundreds of other charter schools were able to open in Michigan, including my school, Arts & Technology Academy of Pontiac.

Like most charter schools in southeast Michigan, the vast majority of our students are black and Hispanic children, most of whom live in poverty and very challenging circumstances. [...]

Our students and families don't care about the politics of charter schools — they only care about the loving and caring environment we provide, and the results they see every day. [...]

Barack Obama, the first African American president, was a huge supporter of charter schools, as well.

On that topic, Obama once said, "In an economy where knowledge is our most valuable asset, a good education is no longer just a pathway to opportunity—it is an imperative. Our children only get one chance at an education, and charter schools demonstrate what is possible when States, communities, teachers, parents and students work together."

There's only one school in Michigan that's named for Obama—the Barack Obama Leadership Academy in Detroit.

It's a charter school.

That's fitting. The president who showed all of us what's possible when we dream big knew that the hopes and dreams of our children shouldn't be tied down, either.

Septembra WILLIAMS,
*detroitnews.com*,
February 18, 2020

1. charter schools are publicly financed but operate privately. They are part of the school-choice movement.

## Document C School choice in the US

**Figure 1.1. Percentage distribution of students ages 5 through 17 attending kindergarten through 12th grade, by school type or participation in homeschooling: Selected years, 1999 through 2016**

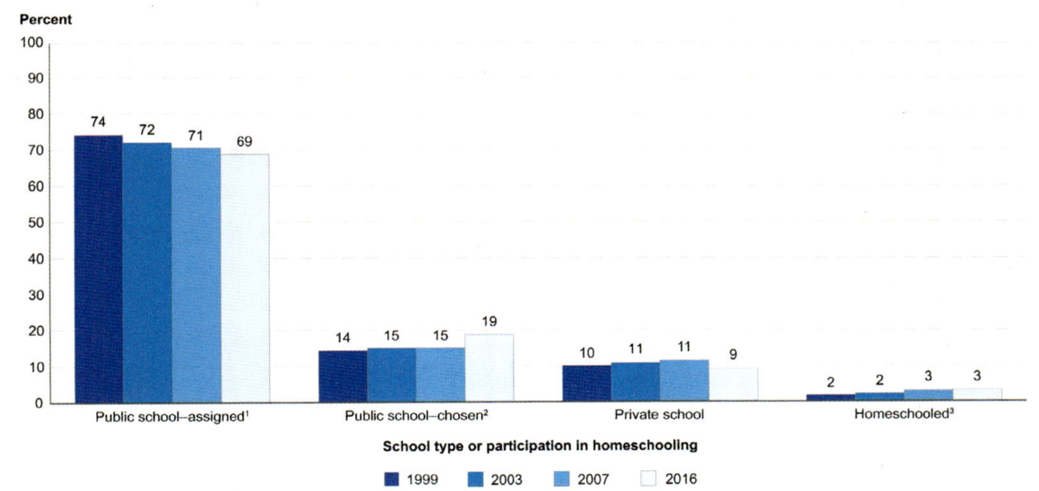


1. Public school assigned by the district 2. Charter schools
3. *école à la maison*

National Center for Education Statistics

Vers le **BAC**

# LET'S BRAINSTORM!

OBJECTIF BAC p. 305-317

FAIRE SOCIÉTÉ
Axe 2
**How central is the notion of freedom to American society?**

## Fundamental freedoms

- Which freedoms are fundamental to American society?

→ "The Four Freedoms", *Norman Rockwell Museum*, p. 118 • "Four Freedoms reinterpreted", Hank WILLIS THOMAS and Emily SHUR, p. 118

- The Constitution outlines these freedoms

→ "Liberties in the US constitution", p. 119

## The meanings of the First Amendment

- The Constitution protects free speech

→ "Should every speech be protected?", *NPR*, p. 120

- Press freedom is a crucial counterpower

→ *The Post*, p. 120

- America attracts many oppressed religious minorities

→ *Destination America*, C. WILLS, p. 121

## Inherent contradictions

- Free market as the engine of the American dream or the wealth gap?

→ "Freedom is the American dream", T. COLE, p. 122 • "How poor people survive in America", *DW*, p. 122 • "The wealth gap", *CNBC*, p. 122

- The First and Second Amendments sometimes collide

→ "Free speech v. gun rights", *Thetrace.org*, p. 123

## Americans' idea of freedom

- Freedom as the quintessential characteristic of American identity

→ "Freedom is inscribed in the American DNA", R. MITCHELL, p. 119

- Freedom is both central to American identity and difficult to achieve

→ "Americans reflect on freedom", *Wbur*, p. 124

## Phonology Liaisons et groupes de souffle

AUDIO

Les **groupes de souffle** sont des blocs de sens dans la phrase. Ils sont séparés par des pauses qui donnent du rythme au discours.
Les **liaisons** donnent de la fluidité aux groupes de souffle.

- son de consonne (même suivi d'un *-e* muet) + son de voyelle : *A world secur(e)_and_at peace, / free from_aggression.*
- deux sons de consonnes identiques (sourdes ou sonores) : *Classified_documents* • *Allies and_trade partners*
- entre deux sons de voyelles, grâce à une petite « béquille » sonore : *They_/j/_are private companies* • *Can I ask you_/w/_a hypothetical question?*

**Attention !** Le ***h*** en début de mot n'est pas muet comme en français, mais aspiré : ***a hypothetical question*** (et non *an*). Sauf dans *hour, honest, honour, heir*.

**1** **Recopie ces phrases et note les liaisons et groupes de souffle. Écoute et vérifie.**

*The American dream never fails to inspire old and young alike, and I believe its promise will continue to motivate future generations to work hard and innovate. Because our country has always valued hard work, we seek to achieve and often succeed because opportunity exists here.*

# BUILD YOUR PORTFOLIO

## Cartoon

"Pillars", Jimmy MARGULIES, 2018

This cartoon was one of dozens of political cartoons focusing on the First Amendment in a exhibit entitled "Front Line: Editorial Cartoonists and the First Amendment" at Ohio State University in May 2019.

- **Describe** the cartoon and **comment** on the message conveyed about democracy in the USA.

## Documentary

*Inequality for All*, Robert REICH, 2013

In this documentary, U.S. Labor Secretary Robert Reich raises awareness of the country's widening economic gap which, he argues is a consequence of unbridled economic liberalism.

- **Watch** the documentary and **focus** on what ended the period of great prosperity according to Robert Reich. **Reflect** on the solutions he proposes to solve inequality in the USA.

VIDÉO

## Essay

*Self-reliance*, Ralph Waldo EMERSON, 1841

“Mr. Emerson is the most American of our writers. The Idea of America, which lies at the bottom of our original institutions, appears in him with great prominence. We mean the idea of personal freedom, of the dignity and value of human nature.” (Theodore Parker, 1850)

- **Read** the essay and **reflect** on how Ralph Waldo Emerson perceives an American identity based on self-reliance. **Think** about his perception of American freedom.

## Chart

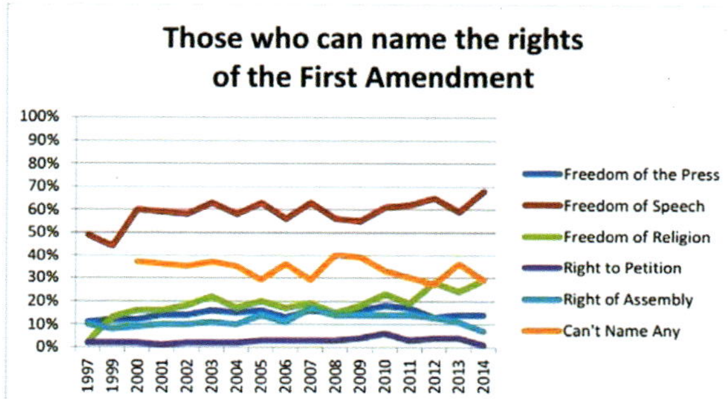


*First Amendment Survey, Center Survey*, 2014

- **Study** the graph and **describe** which First Amendment-protected freedoms the people surveyed are familiar with. **Explain** what this might reveal about Americans' perception of freedom.

ÉPREUVE ORALE

GRAND ORAL

Entraîne-toi à l'oral

### Step 1 — Build up your speech!

**ÉPREUVE ORALE**

- Choose one topic in the mindmap p. 128.
- Pick out two documents in the file and one or two personal ones to illustrate this issue.
- Prepare your presentation: you must show how these documents relate to the issue you chose.

OBJECTIF BAC p. 305

**GRAND ORAL**

- Choose one topic in the mindmap p. 128.
- Find a key question about your topic.
- Gather arguments and examples from the documents in the file to support your point.
- Prepare an outline for your presentation and write your note sheet.

OBJECTIF BAC p. 308-309

### Step 2 — Make your oral presentation in front of two classmates.

**ÉPREUVE ORALE**

- Show your documents to your classmates.
Each of you makes their presentation to the others in about five minutes.

OBJECTIF BAC p. 306-307

**GRAND ORAL**

- Give your note sheet to your classmates.
- Stand up and make a five-minute presentation to answer your key question.

OBJECTIF BAC p. 310-311

### Step 3 — Answer your classmates' questions about your presentation.

SNAPFILE 14

FAIRE SOCIÉTÉ

AXE 2 : LIBERTÉS PUBLIQUES ET LIBERTÉS INDIVIDUELLES

# Dalit Rights

▶ **To what extent is the Dalit situation changing in India?**

More on SPEAKEASY NEWS speakeasy-news.com

YOUR MISSION

MÉDIATION

## Write a report for the Dalit Lives Matter association

As a follower of the #DalitLivesMatter movement on social networks, you have decided to investigate the situation of Dalits in India today. Write a report on the evolution of the Dalit situation in India.

FOLLOW THE STEPS!

## 1 A Dalit reality

LANDMARKS p. 292-293

**Doc 1.**

VIDÉO

Political poster, *equalitylabs.org*, 2019 (Video: *Eyebeam*, 2019)

**Doc 2.**

In Indian villages and towns, everyone knows everyone else. Each caste has its own special roles and its own place to live. [...] The untouchables are not allowed to live in the village at all. In your own town or village, everyone already knows your caste: there is no escaping it. But how do people know your caste when you go elsewhere, to a place where no one knows you? There they will ask you: "What caste are you?" You cannot avoid the question. And you cannot refuse to answer. By tradition, everyone has the right to know.

If you are educated like me, if you don't seem like a typical untouchable, then you have a choice. You can tell the truth and be ostracized, ridiculed, harassed – even driven to suicide, as happens regularly in universities.

Or you can lie. If they don't believe you, they will try to find out your true caste some other way. They may ask you certain questions. [...] They may even seek[1] the opinion of someone from your region.

If you get them to believe your lie, then of course you cannot tell them your stories, your family's stories. You cannot tell them about your life. It would reveal your caste. Because your life is your caste, your caste is your life.

Sujatha GIDLA, *Ants Among Elephants*, 2017

1. look for

**a.** **Watch** the video and **find** information about Thenmozhi Soundararajan and the cause she fights for.

**b.** **Read** the text and **comment** on the former name given to Dalits. **Explain** what it implies to be a Dalit in today's India.

**c.** **Focus** on the poster and **analyse** the use of the expression *"caste apartheid"*.

CULTURE SPOT

**India's caste system** was legally abolished in 1950, but this old social hierarchy still exists in many aspects of life.

## Doc 3. Being an elite Dalit

https://feminisminindia.com/2019

*"You should write about your Dalit experience",* said my friend. *"Your elite Dalit experience".* [...] Yes, for a Dalit woman, I live a very privileged life but what does my privilege exactly include? As far as I know, I am just a regular working-class educated woman living an independent life. Apparently meeting the basic requirements[1] makes me elite [...]. However, when the same applied to a Savarna[2] woman, it qualifies her to be a 'normal' girl.

The point that I am trying to make here is that 'elite Dalit' is an oxymoron. It is intrinsically and fundamentally against the notion of being a Dalit in an Indian society. Yes, I accept that I am privileged when compared to other women from my community. Yes, my privilege has allowed me to enter spaces unimaginable to a Dalit, leave alone a Dalit woman. I learnt to talk like the Savarnas. I learnt to walk like the Savarnas. I learnt to eat like the Savarnas—but I couldn't learn to think like the Savarnas. From centuries of ostracization[3] and lack of access to knowledge systems, my struggles are of a very different kind, even with the badge of ' privilege'.

My privilege led me to Savarna social circles, and I ended up dating Savarna boys. One of them I almost got married to—almost, because [...] *"Even if your shoes are made of gold, you still wear them only on your feet".* According to Ambedkar[4], the only way caste could be eradicated from the Indian social fabric was through inter-caste marriages. It is 2019 and I am still not quite sure about this.

**a. Read** the text and **find out** why the author is said to be privileged.

**b. Explain** the author's statement: *"elite Dalit is an oxymoron".* What does it reveal about the Dalit condition today?

**c. Comment** on the conclusion that can be drawn from the author's testimony.

**STEP 1**

To start your report, **take** notes on the opposition between the legal situation of Dalits nowadays and their daily realities. Then **write** a paragraph insisting on the challenges the Dalits have to face and the means they use to improve the situation.

**1.** condition. **2.** Member of higher castes **3.** exclusion **4.** An Indian politician and social reformer

## 2 Dalit Art

Interview with Jithinlal NR, 2019

AUDIO

**a. Observe** the exhibition poster. **Imagine** how this work may echo the Dalit experience.

**b. Listen** to the interview and **say** what defines Dalit art.

**c. Explain** why the artist thinks it has become so visible.

**d. Discuss** the power of art and culture to fight oppression.

**STEP 2**

**Complete** your file: **write** a few lines on the role of art in raising awareness about the Dalit experience.

**BOOST YOUR SKILLS!**

**Sensibiliser à une situation**

- Expose la situation au présent simple : *It* ***determines*** *and* ***sentences*** *you to ... • Your caste* ***is*** *your life.*
- Souligne sa forme contraignante avec le modal *can/cannot* : *You* ***cannot*** *avoid the question. • You* ***can*** *tell the truth and be ostracized • Or you* ***can*** *lie.*
- Insiste sur son caractère subi avec la voie passive : *We* ***were oppressed*** *under Hindu scripture • You* ***are*** *basically* ***sentenced*** *into a caste.*

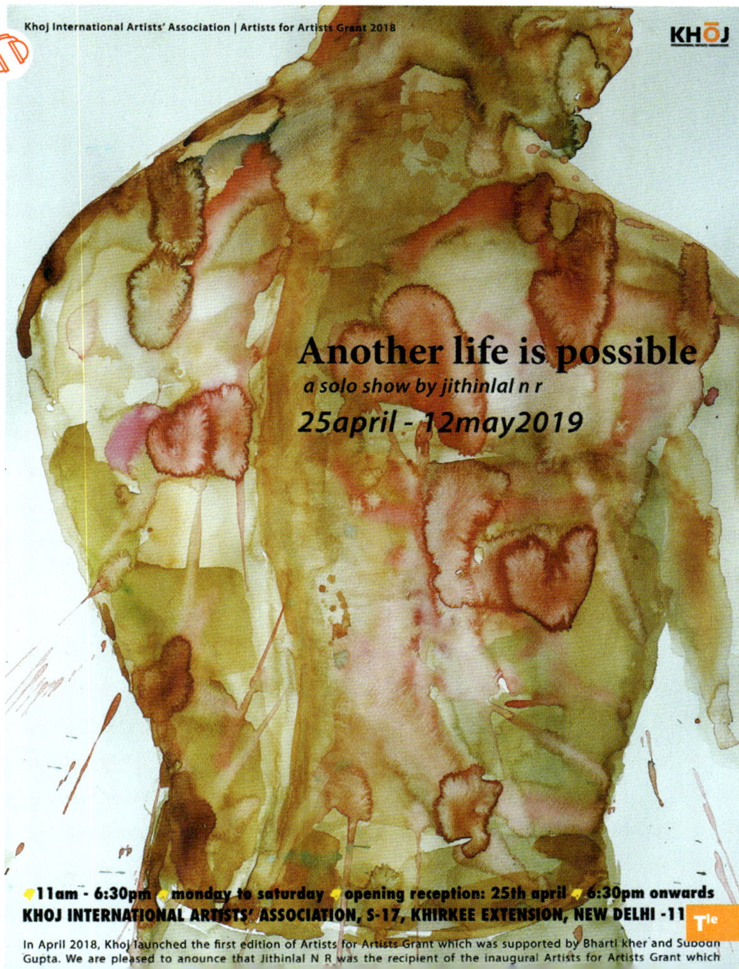


Jithinlal NR's art exhibition poster

# 3 The on-going fight

## Doc 1. Fighting caste violence

VIDÉO

TRTWorld, 2018

**a. Observe** the still and title of the document. **Imagine** who the people are and why they are gathering.

**b. Watch** the video and **take** notes on the forms of violence Dalits are victims of.

**c. Pick out** signs that *"Dalits are fighting back"*.

**d. Discuss** the journalist's conclusion that *"it's unlikely they will achieve equality any time soon"*.

## Doc 2.

### Undoing injustice against Dalits requires upper caste support

Even as Dalit politics takes centre stage, India's urban upper castes remain steadfastly indifferent to Dalit issues. [...] Unlike in the pre-1947 era, when eradicating casteism was an important strand of both the freedom struggle and many Hindu reform movements, most Savarnas today believe that there is little more that they need to do to redress three millennia of injustice against Dalits. Discrimination and violence against Scheduled Castes (SCs) are seen as an embarrassing relic of the past best left to the police and courts, while Dalit demands for economic justice are something for politicians and government to address.

Metropolitan liberals are more likely to embrace #MeToo and LGBT causes or even anti-racism than get involved in repairing the appalling legacy of caste. Combating casteism is neither cool nor a moral priority.

Many believe that with all the enabling conditions now in place it is simply up to the Dalit community to pull themselves up. [...] Most Dalit students are first-generation school-goers, their English is often weak and their mostly poor, rural origins ill prepares them for urban settings. In short, modern urban India does not give Dalits an equal shot at success. [...] Filling this black hole in our social consciousness cannot be the job of government—upper caste society needs to raise its own awareness and sensitivity to bias[1].

Heightened attention to "soft" discrimination must be underpinned[2] by owning up to our moral responsibility for the bequest[3] of caste bigotry[4].

Ramesh VENKATARAMAN, *indianexpress.com*, January 2019

**1.** favouritism **2.** established **3.** legacy **4.** sectarianism

**a. Read** the text and **find** the reasons why Dalit rights are still not a priority in India.

**b. Describe** the obstacles Dalits face when trying to escape the caste system.

**c. Conclude** on the conditions needed for the Dalits to achieve real progress.

### STEP 3

**Take** notes on the reasons why Dalit rights are still not secured in India's society and **complete** your file. **Explain** what would be necessary to achieve real progress for the community.

### BOOST YOUR SKILLS!

**Formuler des attentes**

- Souligne les besoins avec des infinitives : *Something **for** politicians **to address**. • It is up to the Dalits **to pull** themselves up • Society needs **to raise** its own awareness*
- Indique par des gérondifs les actions et les moyens possibles : ***Combating** casteism is... • **Filling** this black hole cannot be... • Discrimination must be underpinned **by owning** up to...*
- Précise avec des modaux ce qu'il faudrait faire : *Attention **must** be underpinned by... • They **should**...*

## 4 A global issue

# THE HINDU

## U.S. Black Lives Matter protests spur calls for India to wake up to Dalit discrimination

Spurred on by U.S. anti-racism protests, Dalit campaigners on June 10 called on India to acknowledge centuries of oppression they have endured and recognise that "every life matters".

Dalit campaigners said they supported the Black Lives Matter protests in response to the death of African-American George Floyd after he was knelt on by a white police officer, and hoped it would ignite[1] a similar conversation in India.

#AllLivesMatter demonstrations in 2020

"We extend our solidarity because we feel them and we have faced discrimination ourselves," said Omprakash Mahato, president of the Birsa Ambedkar Phule Students Association, a Dalit organisation at Jawaharlal Nehru University.

"In India, people need to admit their role in everyday discrimination faced by Dalits and only then can a dialogue for change be initiated. We hope what they are seeing unfolding globally will lead to soul searching," said Mr. Mahato. "People need to understand that every life matters."

Ruth Manorama, who works for rights of Dalit women, said, "Indian Dalits have historically learnt a lot from the struggle of African-Americans." She added: "This is a good moment to challenge the narrative in India also and talk about the age-old repression of Dalits, which is visible even during the COVID-19 pandemic with discrimination denying people aid."

Dalits were among the worst hit by India's strict lockdown[2], often having to wait longer for their turn to receive food or financial aid at local distribution points, and even being turned away, she said.

Over 300 people have signed a *Change.org* petition emphasising that the "lives of Dalits and minorities matter too" and urging Indian Prime Minister Narendra Modi to "admit that caste discrimination is included in racial discrimination".

"It is a good time for people in India to understand and to point out to the government that racial discrimination is not only what you see in America," said Henri Tiphagne of People's Watch, a charity backing the petition. "It is the same as how so-called 'untouchables' are treated in India."

*thehindu.com*, June 2020

**1.** start. **2.** *confinement*

**a. Observe** the photograph and **imagine** what the people are reacting to.

**b. Read** the text and **check** your hypotheses.
**Take** notes on the event which sparked this movement.

**c. Explain** why Dalit campaigners decided to join in the fight.

**d. Comment** on how globalising the fight for equality might increase their chances of success.

### STEP 4

**Take** notes on the impact of international struggles on the Dalit situation. **Write** a conclusion to your report explaining how globalising the fight could contribute to the improvement of Dalit lives in India.

### WORDS

- backing = support
- breakthrough = progress
- campaigner = activist
- inequity

- committed
- discriminated against

- hard-won
- joint

- cast out = ostracise
- demonstrate against/for
- endorse = side with
- gain momentum
- spark change

### FINAL STEP

MÉDIATION

Now you have completed your study, the time has come for you to **gather** your notes, **connect** the paragraphs you have written and **format** the final version of your report for the #DalitLivesMatter social movement.

**You've completed your mission. Well done!**

play **BAC** How to...

# WRITE A CONCEPT NOTE

OBJECTIF BAC ▸ p. 296

Le jour de l'**épreuve écrite**, tu devras **rédiger la synthèse** (en environ 500 mots) d'un dossier de 3 à 4 documents de natures diverses (texte de presse, texte littéraire, essai, document iconographique...) adossé à l'une des **thématiques au programme**. Cette synthèse pourra être guidée par deux ou trois consignes.

**Prenez connaissance des documents A, B, C et D et traitez le sujet suivant en anglais.**
[→ Doc 1 p. 130, Doc 2 p. 130, Doc 2 p. 132, Doc p. 133]

Say what the documents reveal about the way Dalits are considered in today's India and the methods they use to gain freedom and respect.

## 1 Analyse le sujet et identifie les documents

**a.** Lis bien la consigne et identifie la problématique du dossier.

*Is emancipation from casteism possible for Dalits?*

**b.** Détermine la nature, le sujet et le contexte de chaque document. Aide-toi des titres, des sources et de tes connaissances (inter)culturelles.

– Documents: *Political poster, literary or novel extract, newspaper article...*
– Sources: *famous author, first-hand testimony, well-established newspaper*, etc.
– Context: *BLM and Dalits protests in 2019, caste activism...*

- Repère les mots clés dans les titres : *caste, apartheid, injustice, Dalits, discrimination*
- Analyse la métaphore : *Ants among elephants*
- Identifie les champs lexicaux récurrents : *activism, civil rights denial, discrimination...*
- Repère les concepts clés : *soft discrimination, global fight*, etc.

## 2 Étudie les documents

**a.** Identifie la situation d'énonciation, dégage l'organisation logique de chaque document et repère les points de vue.

*Personal testimony, committed, subjective document* (docs 1 and 2) ; *Informative, objective article ; intercaste reflection, analysis of possible means of action, comparison between movements* (docs 3 and 4)

**b.** Mets en regard les documents pour faire émerger les thèmes ou les arguments qui se répondent ou se contredisent.

**c.** Trouve dans les documents des exemples ou citations.

*"Your life is your caste, your caste is your life."* (doc. 2) • *"Combating casteism is neither cool nor a moral priority."* (doc. 3)

- Lis attentivement les docs et relève les mots clés dans une carte mentale de ce type :

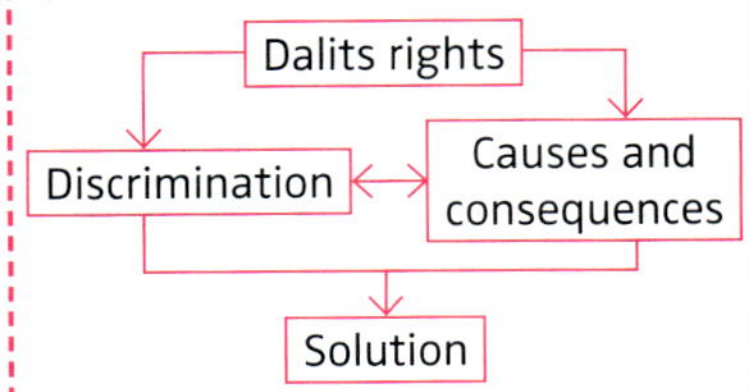


## 3 Fais un plan et rédige

**a.** À partir de tes notes et des thèmes ou arguments clés que tu as relevés, tu vas dégager la structure de ta synthèse en regroupant les documents par thèmes fédérateurs.

**b.** Au brouillon, contente-toi de rédiger les grandes lignes de ta synthèse sous forme de plan détaillé. Si tu en as le temps, rédige également ton introduction et ta conclusion.

**c.** Sur ta copie, rédige ta synthèse complète clairement structurée en paragraphes correspondant chacun à l'un des thèmes fédérateurs relevés.

- Annonce les grandes lignes de ta synthèse : *The file offers a perspective on...* • *The file addresses the issue(s) of ...* • *The topic under study here is ...*

- Apporte une réponse à la problématique : *To sum up ...* • *To conclude* • *By way of conclusion*

Vers le **BAC**

# BUILD YOUR PORTFOLIO

## Artwork

*Skyscape*, Rajyashri GOODY, 2017

“Viewers were invited to step into a room that held the installation and while the experiences were varied, the overall feeling of suffocation, gloom, of being made to feel unclean was common.”

- **Observe** this artwork and **discuss** its representation of Dalits' feelings.

## Book

*Caste Matters*, Suraj YENGDE, 2019

“Suraj Yengde challenges deep-seated beliefs about caste and unpacks its many layers. He describes his gut-wrenching experiences of growing up in a Dalit *basti*, the multiple humiliations suffered by Dalits on a daily basis, and their incredible resilience enabled by love and humour.”

- **Read** the book and **discover** concrete examples of Dalit living conditions in contemporary India and how they fight the caste system”

## Article

*"India's coronavirus pandemic shines a light on the curse of caste"*, *theconversation.com*, June 2, 2020

“The shunning of Dalits has not abated during this crisis. If anything, it has worsened, with some high-ranking members of the ruling Bharatiya Janata Party openly blaming the Dalits for spreading the coronavirus.”

- **Read** the article and **analyse** how the covid-19 pandemic has particularly affected the Dalit community in 2020.

ARTICLE

## Short film

*The Discreet Charm of the Savarnas*, Rajesh RAJAMANI, 2020

Three 'upper' caste friends are looking for a "Dalit-looking person" to act in their movie. Never could they have imagined that a Dalit could be so elegant, confident, beautiful or intelligent.

- **Watch** the short film and **take** notes on prejudice against Dalits among upper-caste members. **Comment** on their representation in this film.

VIDÉO

## Entraîne-toi à l'oral

ÉPREUVE ORALE

**Step 1** **Build up your speech!**

- Choose one of the issues presented in the mindmap p. 134.
- Pick out two documents from the file, add a personal one and pick out another one from this page to illustrate this issue. OBJECTIF BAC p. 305
- Prepare your presentation: make sure to explain how your documents relate to the topic you chose.

**Step 2** **Make your presentation in front of two classmates.**

- Show your documents to your classmates and explain your point in about 5 minutes. OBJECTIF BAC p. 306-307

**Step 3** **Answer your classmates' questions about your presentation.**

# Justice for all?

▶ **To what extent does the American system warrant equal rights?**

**FINAL TASK** Take part in a debate about the need for a reform of the American justice system.

More on SPEAKEASY NEWS
speakeasy-news.com

## 1 An unfair system?

VIDÉO

**AT HOME** **Watch** the video and **explain** what the adversarial system consists in. VIDEO

**Doc 1.**

### Review

Equally moving, informative, and infuriating, Netflix's *The Innocence Files* is one of the best true crime series ever made. Going well beyond the typically sensational whodunit[1] formula to paint a comprehensive portrait of our justice system's failures, it's a must-see for anyone interested in how innocent people end up going to jail. But we should all be enraged at a system that allows clearly innocent people to spend years on death row because it either relies on faulty evidence or encourages corruption. The best compliment I can pay *The Innocence Files* is that it reminded me of one of the best documentaries of all time, Errol Morris' *The Thin Blue Line*, another work about injustice that changed the way people looked at the entire system. Hopefully, this will have the same kind of effect.

Brian TALLERICO, *rogerebert.com*, April 2020

1. detective story

**a.** **Observe** and **analyse** the poster. What image of the American justice system does it give?

**b.** **Watch** the video and **find** information about the project (origin, motives).

**c.** **Explain** how the adversarial system relates to Peter Neufeld's statement.

**d.** RHETORIC **Identify** the stylistic device used by the speaker at the end of the video to share his emotion.

**e.** **Read** the review and **sum up** the author's opinion on the documentary.

**f.** **Identify** the common feeling expressed by both the speaker and the critic. What do they hope the documentary will achieve?

## Doc 2. Systemic inequality?

"How to get away with Murder", *ABC*, 2018

CULTURE SPOT

**The Sixth Amendment** ensures "the right to a speedy and public trial, by an impartial jury."

**a.** **Watch** the video and **pick out** information about the situation (place, type of speech, audience).

**b.** **Explain** what the speaker denounces and **give** the arguments she uses to do so.

**c.** **Comment** on the expected role of justice in this context.

**d.** RHETORIC How convincing is the speaker? **Use** precise elements to support your opinion.

## Doc 3.

**California Sen. Kamala Harris says she was bent toward a career fighting for civil rights almost since birth.**

The Democrat is the daughter of an Indian mother and a Jamaican father who met at the University of California, Berkeley, and were active in the movement during the 1960s.

"I was born realizing the flaws[1] in the criminal justice system," she told NPR's Steve Inskeep.

Inspired by Supreme Court Justice Thurgood Marshall, the first African-American to sit on the nation's highest court, she pursued a career in law to help right the wrongs she saw. That ambition would eventually take her from the San Francisco district attorney[2]'s office to the California attorney general's office to the Senate. Now she hopes it will take her to the White House. She's seeking to not only become the first woman to be president, but the first black woman.

Addressing inequality is a top priority for her. That includes her LIFT the Middle Class Act, a tax cut plan that would give families making less than $100,000 annually a credit of up to $500 a month, saying that "when we lift up the economic status of families, neighborhoods thrive, society thrives." [...]

She tells NPR that it's a "false choice" to suggest that someone is either tough on crime or soft on crime. Instead, she argues, people should be "smart on crime," pointing to public health as a model.

"If you want to deal with an epidemic—crime or health—the smartest and most effective and cheapest way to deal with it is prevention first," she says.

Jessica TAYLOR, *npr.org*, March 2019

Kamala Harris in presidential campaign, 2019 (She became vice-president of the US on November 3, 2020)

1. problems 2. *procureur*

**a.** **Read** the article and **pick out** information about Kamala Harris (origin, career).

**b.** **Analyse** her point of view on the criminal justice system.

**c.** **Discuss** her idea of being *"smart on crime"*. **Explain** how the LIFT the Middle Class Act can be linked to it.

MÉDIATION

**YOUR TASK** You start a podcast about the US justice system. **Record** the first episode entitled "An unfair system?" **Take stock** of the situation and **denounce** the flaws of the system.

**BOOST YOUR SKILLS!**

**Dénoncer une injustice**

- Souligne son caractère inacceptable : *We **won't even** give them that.* • *This promise has **never** been fulfilled.* • *They **don't** have **any** rights **at all**.*
- Utilise des adjectifs qui expriment l'émotion : *enraged* • *angry* • *hopeless* • *frustrated*
- Élargis la portée de ton propos avec des indéfinis : ***Something** I know I didn't do.* • ***Some** may claim that...* • *It's a "false choice" to suggest that **someone** is...* GRAMMAR p. 143

# 2 Justice for the haves and the have nots

## Doc 1.

AUDIO

(Audio: "You have the right to an attorney", *Last Week Tonight*, 2015)

**GOING FURTHER**
**Read** the extract from *Quarrels that have Shaped the Constitution*, and take the quiz. **Explain** how "public defendants" became a major principle of the American justice system.

EXO Quiz

**a. Observe** the poster and **analyse** its content (creators, cause, message).
**b. Listen** to the audio and **define** the mission of a "public defender".
**c. Explain** what makes this system so essential to the American justice system.
**d.** VOCABULARY **Find** two other expressions used to refer to a "public defender".
**e. Compare** the Supreme Court's decision to the reality of the situation today.

## Doc 2.

**WORDS**

- fee = cost
- ruling

- aggrieved = abused
- appointed
- collective
- low-income ≠ affluent

- band together = join forces
- file a complaint
- strike a deal

**a. Read** the article and **pick out** elements showing that it is an opinion piece.
**b. Say** what issue the author is dealing with and **explain** his point of view.
**c. Identify** the links between the two cases. **Explain** how the comparison helps the writer make his point.
**d. Comment** on the possible impact of such an article.
**e.** TRANSLATION **Translate** l. 13-14. **Pay** attention to the comparative forms.

### DO RICH PEOPLE GET AWAY WITH MORE CRIME?

On the evening of June 15th, 2013 in Texas, a person by the name of Ethan Couch stole alcohol from a Walmart. An hour after the stealing, Ethan was in his car with seven other passengers going 73mph and hit someone. The seven passengers survived, though one was paralyzed. I started with this because, instead of going to prison he got sent to ten years probation. Many people were asking why he got away with murder. Was it because he was 16? Or was it because his parents were rich with a median income of $250,000?

Many people assumed that it was because his parents were rich. During the time, people asked the question, do rich people get away with more crime than middle class or poor families? On the surface level, rich people do get away with more crimes because of bail[1]. It is most likely that the rich person has enough money to bail out of jail. We also can't forget that money buys you lawyers. The more money you have saved up to buy a lawyer, the better chance you have to get away with something like murder. The number one example of this is the O.J. Simpson case in the 90s. O.J. Simpson has gotten away with murder because he had enough money for successful lawyers. Not only that, but have you heard of affluenza? It's where someone's wealth status starts to influence their actions. In the Ethan Couch case, the judge decides to give Ethan a mental health check instead of going to prison because of affluenza. [...]

It's hard to accept that money buys everything, even the judicial system. I hope that in the future everyone gets equal consequences when they commit a crime. But from where we are now, it may be a long time until we get this.

Daniel GARCIA, *The Grizzly Express*, March 2020

1. *caution*

## Doc 3.

https://www.nbcnews.com

NBC NEWS — POLITICS | COVID-19 | U.S. NEWS | OPINION | BUSINESS | WORLD

### Michigan officials announce $600M settlement in Flint water crisis

The state of Michigan announced Thursday it has agreed to pay $600 million to Flint residents whose health was afflicted by lead-tainted drinking water in a crisis that spurred a class-action lawsuit and became emblematic of how poorer, majority-Black communities can suffer under government mismanagement.

The offices of Gov. Gretchen Whitmer and Attorney General Dana Nessel said they have been negotiating for more than 18 months with lawyers for thousands of Flint residents who have filed suits against the state in the wake of the scandal, which began in April 2014. [...]

Nessel, a Democrat, said the majority of the settlement would go toward resolving claims that benefit children, who were found through testing to have elevated lead levels in their blood. Exposure to lead can cause behavior problems and learning disabilities in young children, health officials warned. [...] "Ultimately, by reaching this agreement, I hope we can begin the process of closing one of the most difficult chapters in our State's history and writing a new one that starts with a government that works on behalf of all of its people."

Protest calls for governor to resign over Flint water crisis, January 2016

Trachelle Young, a former Flint city attorney and resident who filed a lawsuit in 2015 in response to the lead in the drinking water, told reporters that the settlement is "fair and reasonable," but stressed that it is partial because she believes "there is more to come and there is more of a price to pay." Other suits are pending against Flint, the Environmental Protection Agency and private consultants that advised the city on water issues.

"We were fighting a machine," Young said of the state's previous push back to the lawsuits. "They were standing their ground, and today is the day where there's actual accountability for Flint residents." [...]

Michael Pitt, a court-appointed interim co-lead counsel in the class-action lawsuit, said the legal team is endorsing the settlement deal and hopes that [U.S. District Judge Judy] Levy will approve it. [...] "Although it's not perfect overall, it's very good and it's a fair settlement and we believe wholeheartedly it's in the best interest of the Flint community," he told reporters.

Pitt said the claims from affected residents would be reviewed "without any discrimination, no favoritism" and with an "opt-out" measure, meaning residents do not have to be part of the compensation plan and can still pursue other legal options against the state if they so choose.

Erik ORTIZ, *NBC News*, August 2020

**CULTURE SPOT**

**A class action** lawsuit enables a group of people to be represented collectively by a member of that group. Thus, people who cannot afford a lawsuit on their own can unite with others to claim their cause.

**YOUR TASK** — MÉDIATION — DIFFÉRENCIATION

As the assistant of a US Representative, **write** a short report on "the situation of low-income Americans in the face of justice".

**WAY 1** **Highlight** the strengths and weaknesses of the system.

**WAY 2** **Complete** your report with suggestions to improve it.

**a.** **Read** the article and the culture spot. **Sum up** the case presented (plaintiff, defendant, accusation).

**b.** **Explain** why the class action lawsuit was the best option in this case.

**c.** VOCABULARY **Observe** these adjectives: *lead-tainted, court-appointed*. **Analyse** their structure and **translate** them.

**d.** **Focus** on the verdict: What does it show about this type of lawsuit?

**BOOST YOUR SKILLS!**

**Comparer des situations inégales**

- Utilise des structures comparatives : *Do rich people get away with **more** crime **than**... • **The more** money you have..., **the better** chance you have...*
- Souligne l'ampleur de l'inégalité : *Someone who is **too** poor to hire a lawyer • It's an idea **so** obvious that... • With caseloads **that** heavy... • That is **not** long **enough** to...*
- Sers-toi de métaphores frappantes : *We were fighting **a machine**. • It was **David** v. **Goliath**.* GRAMMAR p. 143

# 3 A delicate power balance

## Doc 1. The US court system

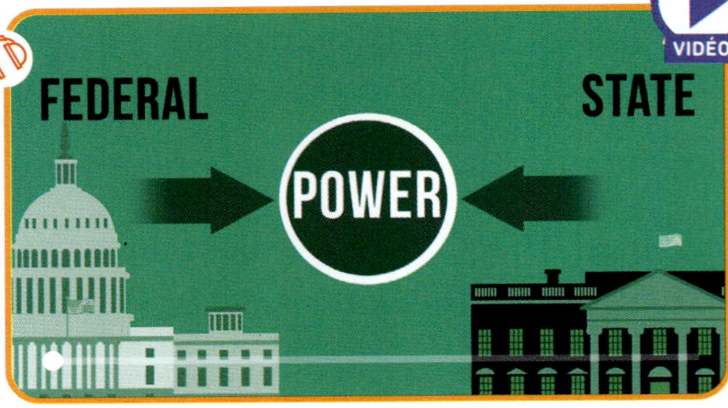


AJ+, 2015

**a. Watch** the video and **pick out** the names of the different courts. **Say** what their roles are.

**b. Explain** which courts have the "final call".

**c. Explain** the role of the federal US Supreme Court. Why is it considered the warrant of the US Constitution?

**d. Comment** on the role of the Supreme Court compared to the federal courts.

## Doc 2.

### Checks and Balances in a Trump-Era Supreme Court

Yesterday's Supreme Court rulings holding that the president is not immune from subpoenas[1] issued by Congress and local law enforcement were a relief to many. But even as the Court yesterday reaffirmed that the president is not above the law, we should not lose sight of another major decision from just last week suggesting a possible trend that could undercut[2] the ability of Congress to check abuses of presidential power over the long-term.

In *Seila Law v. Consumer Financial Protection Bureau*, the Court ruled that the president has absolute authority to remove the director of the Consumer Financial Protection Bureau (CFPB), striking down[3] a key provision of the law that created the agency in 2010. [...] For more than a century, Congress has created numerous executive branch positions insulated[4] either expressly or by implication from complete presidential control. [...]

Congress created the CFPB in 2010. It's one of several federal agencies charged with overseeing federal financial laws that protect consumers. Financial regulators are notoriously susceptible to pressure from politically influential corporations and industry; insulating agency leadership to some degree from presidential control has been a well-recognized way of helping them rebuff[5] pressure on behalf of industry from both Republican and Democratic White Houses. [...]

The Court doubled down on the principle [...] that it is unconstitutional to limit the president's ability to fire an executive branch official with authority as broad as the CFPB director's. As a result, the president can now remove the CFPB director without cause. [...]

In an era when so many other constraints on the abuse of presidential power are already buckling[6], this is an alarming prospect.

Daniel I. Weiner, Martha Kinsella, *Brennan Center for Justice*, July 2020

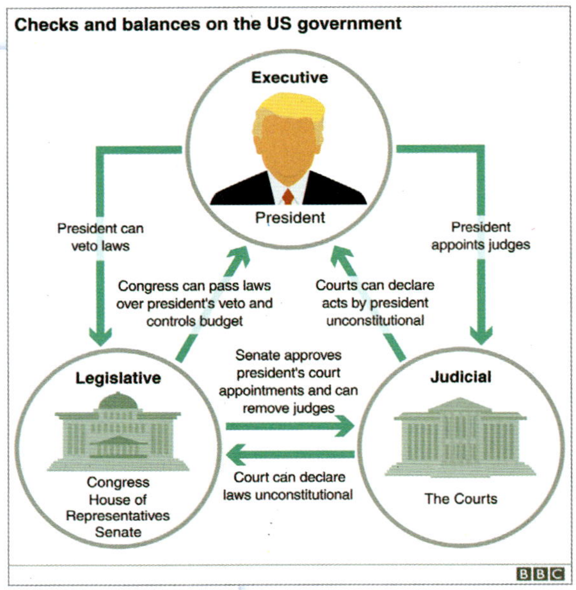


**CULTURE SPOT**

**Checks and balances** is a system for multiple branches of government where each has some control over the actions of the others.

1. /sə'pinə/ *citation à comparaitre* 2. weaken 3. invalidate 4. protect 5. refuse 6. collapse

**a. Read** the text and **identify** the decision of the Supreme Court.

**b. Say** what CFPB is and **explain** why its role is important.

**c. Read** the infographic and **explain** the role of Congress in the system of checks and balances.

**d.** VOCABULARY **Pick out** words and expressions showing that the decision of the Seila Law case could endanger the independence of justice.

AT HOME SITE **Go** online and **find out** more about the Seila Law case. Be ready to **explain** the main question raised by the case and **say** how it was answered to by the Supreme Court.

## Doc 3.

AUDIO

### What Bader Ginsburg's death means for the Supreme Court

The supreme court justice Ruth Bader Ginsburg passed away. [...] As messages of grief and gratitude for her life and career swept the country, here's a look at what the liberal icon's death means for the supreme court and what happens next. [...]

Donald Trump and Republicans in the Senate are determined to replace Ginsburg with a conservative justice. Their doing so could decisively tilt[1] the ideological balance of the court for a generation and would probably constitute the most lasting legacy of the Trump presidency.

Reproductive rights, voting rights, protections from discrimination, the future of criminal justice, the power of the presidency, the rights of immigrants, tax rules and laws, and healthcare for millions of vulnerable Americans, to name a few issues. Every big issue in American life is on the line.

Replacing Ginsburg with a young conservative justice would fundamentally shift the ideological balance of the court, creating a seemingly bulletproof conservative majority of five justices. [...] This new majority could usher in[2] a new legal landscape that could last at least 30 years.

Yes, Trump appointed justice Neil Gorsuch in 2017 and Brett Kavanaugh in 2018. But they replaced justices who were nominated by earlier Republican presidents. They have pulled the court right, but not as far right as replacing Ginsburg with a conservative would. Ginsburg was nominated by Bill Clinton in 1993.

Yes. An ideological tilt of this kind on the supreme court has not happened for 50 years. Since 1969, Republican presidents have appointed 14 out of 18 justices elevated to the court—but certain Republican appointments, such as Sandra Day O'Connor, Anthony Kennedy and David Souter turned out to occupy moderate ground or even drift liberal on some issues. In the recent hyper-partisan age, that middle ground on the court has mostly disappeared. [...]

Trump sees appointing conservative judges as a political winner with his base, and a third supreme court justice in his first term could help him win re-election.

Tom McCarthy, *The Guardian*, September 19, 2020

Ruth Bader Ginsburg mural in East Village, New York (Audio: *NPR*, Sept. 2020)

**"To those accustomed to privilege, equality feels like oppression."**
Ruth Bader Ginsburg

**WORDS**

- circuit (state courts)
- dissent = disagreement
- gender equality

- biased /'baɪəst/ = partial
- judicial
- moderate
- unconstitutional

- affirm = uphold a judgment
- appoint
- make a plea

1. cause to lean 2. lead to

**a.** **Listen** to the audio and **explain** who Justice Ginsburg was and what she specialised in.

**b.** **Describe** the role of federal laws in gender equality and **explain** how Justice Ginsburg managed to restore it.

**c.** **Read** the article and **say** how the judges at the Supreme Court are nominated.

**d.** RHETORIC **Pick out** the devices used by both journalists to highlight their positive point of view on Justice Ginsburg.

**e.** **Explain** what is at stake with the nomination of her replacement.

MÉDIATION

**YOUR TASK** As a law student, **write** an introduction to a study on the balance of the American legal system **raising awareness** on the fragility of this balance.

**BOOST YOUR SKILLS!**

**Mettre en garde contre d'éventuelles dérives**

- Envisage différentes hypothèses : *For all cases that **might** lead in court... • We **should** not lose... • A trend that **could** undercut...* PHONOLOGY p. 146
- Souligne ta logique argumentative : ***But even as** the Court reaffirmed that... • **Unless** a lawyer is provided... • **Yes**,... **but**... • **As a result**, the president can now...* GRAMMAR p. 143
- Utilise le lexique du pouvoir : *Absolute **authority** • Complete **control** • **Pressure** from politically **influential** people.*

EXPLORE

# 4 A landmark ruling

AUDIO

(Audio: "A major civil-rights decision", *ABC News*, June 2020)

**CULTURE SPOT**

The **Equality Act** is a bill in the United States Congress, based on the Supreme Court's ruling in *Bostock v. Clayton County*, that, if passed, would amend the **Civil Rights Act** of 1964 to prohibit discrimination on the basis of sexual orientation and gender identity in employment.

LANDMARKS p. 280

**a. Read** the extract of the Supreme Court decision and **explain** who Mr. Bostock is and why he sued his employer.

**b. Listen** to the audio and **say** what the decision of the Supreme Court was and what former decision it used.

**c. Comment** on Justice Gorsuch's lines: *"Only the written word is law and all persons are entitled to its benefit."* **Use** them to **explain** the role of the Supreme Court in the USA.

### *BOSTOCK V. CLAYTON COUNTY, GEORGIA*

A case argued before the Supreme Court of the United States on October 8, 2019, during the court's October 2019-2020 term.

"Clayton County, Georgia, fired Gerald Bostock for conduct "unbecoming[1]" a county employee shortly after he began participating in a gay recreational softball league."

In a 6-3 opinion, the court reversed the judgment of the United States Court of Appeals for the 11th Circuit, holding "a statutory violation occurs if an employer intentionally relies in part on an individual employee's sex when deciding to discharge the employee. An employer who fires an individual merely for being gay or transgender violates Title VII.", as a reference to 1964 Civil right act which outlawed discrimination based on race, color, religion, sex or national origin in public places, employment and education.

Abridged from Supreme Court decision

1. *inconvenant*

**CULTURE SPOT**

EXO Quiz

**Test your culture:** take the quiz to check what you understood about the American justice system.

## FINAL TASK

**Take part in a debate about the need for a reform of the American justice system.**

**As a law student, you participate in a roleplay in class to debate over Vice President Harris's criminal justice reform plan.**

1. **Choose** the role you would like to play (a congressman, a senator, a Justice at the Supreme Court, a citizen, a lawyer, a journalist).
2. **Define** the main position your character will defend in the debate (supporting, defending, explaining, reformulating, rejecting, criticising...).
3. **Browse** through the file to **gather** arguments to support your point of view. **Get ready** to illustrate your position with concrete examples of bills and cases of the American judicial system.
4. **Act out** the debate.

BOOST YOUR ENGLISH p. 143

# BOOST YOUR ENGLISH!

## Grammar — Prendre part à un débat juridique

- **Donne à ton propos une portée générale avec des pronoms indéfinis.**

*__Some__ may claim that slavery has ended.*
*The better chance you have to get away with __something__ like murder.*
*Have you heard of affluenza? It's where __someone__'s wealth...*

- **Veille à faire un usage précis des articles.**

*ø Seila Law v. Consumer Financial Protection Bureau*
*ø Racism is built into __the__ DNA of America.*
*ø Congress created __the__ CFPB.*
*__The__ Court doubled down on __the__ principle.*

- **Utilise des comparatifs ou des adverbes de degré pour défendre ton point de vue.**

*Do rich people get away with __more__ crime __than__...*
*__The more__ money you have..., __the better__ chance you have...*
*Someone who is __too__ poor to hire a lawyer...*

- **Expose tes idées en tissant des liens logiques (cause, conséquence, opposition, concession, etc.).**

*__Even as__ the Court yesterday reaffirmed that...* (concession)
*__Unless__ a lawyer is provided, they can't...* (condition)
*__Yes__,... __but__ they replaced justices who...* (opposition)
*__As a result__, the president can now...* (conséquence)

**1 Complète chaque phrase le connecteur logique qui convient.**

a. ... what most people think, American justice is still biased.
b. ... their differences, every American citizen should access justice.
c. ... he is represented by a public defender, he won't defend himself.
d. He was fired ... his sexual orientation.

**2 Traduis ces phrases en utilisant des comparaisons.**

a. Plus les plaignants sont nombreux, plus le recours collectif sera efficace.
b. Certains présidents ont nommé plus de juges à la Cour Suprême que d'autres.
c. Trop peu de cas sont portés devant la Cour Suprême.
d. Les gens plus riches s'en sortent-ils réellement mieux que les autres ?

## Vocabulary — The American justice system

**Accusations** AUDIO
- charges = accusations
- evidence = proof
- verdict
- warrant = court order
- witness
- arrest
- charge sb with
- enforce the law
- testify against

**Sentence** AUDIO
- fair ≠ unfair
- lenient /ˈliːniənt/ = indulgent
- merciful ≠ merciless
- convict
- jail = imprison
- release on bail

**Bias** AUDIO
- suspicion of guilt
- discrimination
- infringement = violation of rights
- be victimised
- suffer from

**Courts** AUDIO
- appeal court
- case law = jurisprudence
- ruling = decision
- be appointed
- legislate
- set a precedent

**Actors** AUDIO
- defendant ≠ plaintiff
- lawyer = attorney (US)
- prosecutor
- public defender = appointed lawyer

**Lawsuits** AUDIO
- appeal
- class action
- court case = trial /ˈtraɪəl/
- attend a trial
- make a ruling
- serve on a jury
- sue = attack

**Fight for equal rights** AUDIO
- constitutional ≠ unconstitutional
- lawful ≠ unlawful
- advocate for
- denounce
- plead for
- stand up against

OBJECTIF BAC p. 296-304

Grille d'auto-évaluation

# Sujet type bac

MÉDIATION

Durée : 3h30
Matériel autorisé : le dictionnaire unilingue (non encyclopédique) est autorisé.
Niveau attendu : C1

- **a. Prenez connaissance des documents A, B, C et D et traitez le sujet suivant en anglais (300 mots maximum).**

Taking into account their specificities, say how the documents show the tumultuous relationship between Native Americans and the US justice system. Pay particular attention to: the past treaties, the current situation and the reaction of Native Americans.

**b. En vous appuyant sur la citation de David Hill (Document C), expliquez en anglais et en 200 mots maximum pourquoi les décisions judiciaires sont des signes d'espoir pour la population amérindienne.**

- **Traduisez en français le passage suivant du document B.**

*"Still, he preaches caution in interpreting the ruling, pointing out that it centers on jurisdiction, not land ownership. 'The headlines are wrong,' says Gover in an emailed statement. 'The Court did not give eastern Oklahoma back to the Tribes. Nobody will lose their land or their home. The decision simply means that Indians in that part of the state are subject only to the criminal jurisdiction of the Tribes and the United States, as is true on Indian reservations in many other states.'"* (l. 31-41)

## Document A Broken Promises

For the Standing Rock Sioux Tribe, the controversial Dakota Access Pipeline perpetuates a long history of broken promises made by the U.S. government.

"We live with so many broken promises, there's no reason for it," Dave Archambault II, the chairman of the tribe, told ABC News.

"We understand what lands we own, and what lands were illegally taken from us," he added.

The nearly 1,200-mile-long, $3.7-billion Dakota Access pipeline plans to cross the Missouri River just north of the Standing Rock Reservation, prompting concerns for the safety of the tribe's drinking water and preservation of its sacred sites. [...]

The proposed route passes through land that was once set aside for the Sioux in the 1851 Treaty of Fort Laramie. That historic agreement ensured the Sioux could retain portions of five states, but ceded all of their land east of the Missouri River to the U.S. government in exchange for money, agricultural aid and strict rules about any access to Sioux territory by outsiders. However, the agreement was short-lived.

"Before the ink was dry, westerners were coming in," Archambault said.

The U.S. government did little to stop white settlers from infringing, according to the State Historical Society of North Dakota.

Things only got worse for the Sioux after gold was discovered at the headwaters of the Missouri River in 1861, prompting a flood of settlers. The tribes repeatedly objected to the intrusions and demanded government recognition of the 1851 Fort Laramie Treaty, but their complaints fell on deaf ears. [...]

[A]fter gold was discovered in the sacred Black Hills of South Dakota deep in Sioux territory, Congress passed the Act of 1877 which ceded the Black Hills to the United States without tribal approval in one of the most controversial land grabs in U.S. history.

More than a century later in 1980, the Sioux took the Black Hills case to the Supreme Court and won a decision that rewarded the tribe with more than $100 million. To this day, the Sioux have refused to accept the funds, hoping instead to get back the sacred land itself. [...]

"It's like a perpetrator committing a crime on an innocent individual," Archambault told ABC News. "If you do it once, you should be stopped; if you do it again, you should be stopped; if you're not, you become a serial perpetrator time and time and time again, and today we are saying, 'No, don't put this pipeline here, enough is enough,'" he said.

Evan SIMON, *ABC News*,
November 22, 2016

## Document B — What a New Supreme Court Decision Means for Native American Sovereignty

**The landmark ruling upholds[1] the sanctity of treaties between the United States and American Indians—to a certain point**

On Thursday, the Supreme Court of the United States ruled in the case *McGirt v. Oklahoma* that much of the eastern half of Oklahoma falls within Native American territory. The decision—which places criminal cases involving Native Americans on the Muscogee (Creek) Nation reservation under federal, rather than state, jurisdiction—is "one of the most consequential" legal wins for tribal rights in decades, report Jack Healy and Adam Liptak for the *New York Times*.

The case hinged on[2] a key question: Did the reservation, established by U.S. treaties during the 1830s, continue to exist after Oklahoma officially became a state in 1907?

In a 5-4 decision, the court declared that the land promised to the Creek remains a reservation for the purposes of legal jurisdiction. [...] "This is a historic day," Principal Chief David Hill tells the *Times*. "This is amazing. It's never too late to make things right." [...]

Kevin Gover, director of the Smithsonian's National Museum of the American Indian, acting under secretary for museum and culture, and a citizen of the Pawnee Tribe of Oklahoma, tells *Smithsonian* magazine that the court's decision is a "welcome" one because it upholds the principle that Native American treaties should be honored unless Congress explicitly revokes them. Still, he preaches caution in interpreting the ruling, pointing out that it centers on jurisdiction, not land ownership.

"The headlines are wrong," says Gover in an emailed statement. "The Court did not give eastern Oklahoma back to the Tribes. Nobody will lose their land or their home. The decision simply means that Indians in that part of the state are subject only to the criminal jurisdiction of the Tribes and the United States, as is true on Indian reservations in many other states."

Nora McGreevy, *smithsonianmag.com*, July 10, 2020

1. confirm
2. depend on

## Document D

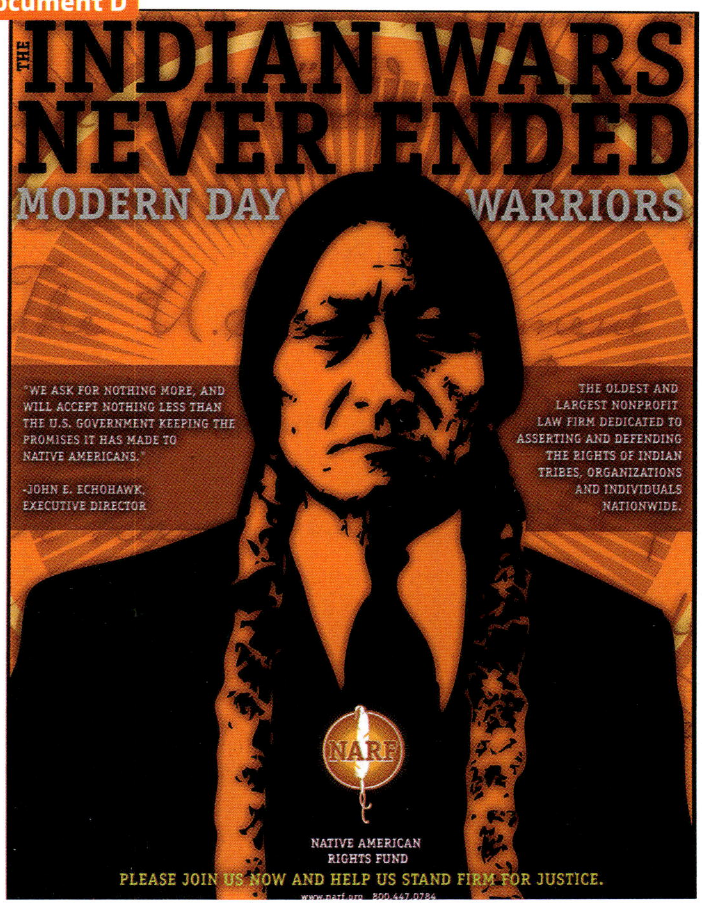


The Native American Rights Fund (NARF) provides legal assistance to Indian tribe organisations and individuals nationwide.

## Document C

"The Supreme Court decision was not merely a symbolic one that affirmed sovereignty in name only, it was a functional one and conversations about the future should start there and work within the framework of sovereignty, not seek to get around it."

Muscogee (Creek) Nation Principal Chief David Hill, interview with Allison Herrera, August 24, 2020

Vers le **BAC**

# LET'S BRAINSTORM!

OBJECTIF BAC p. 305-317

## Dealing with inequalities

- Racial or sexual discrimination

→ "How to get away with Murder", *ABC*, p. 137 • "Bostock *v.* Clayton County", Supreme Court decision, p. 142

- Social inequalities

→ "When money buys justice", *The Grizzly Bear*, p. 138 • "Flint water crisis", *NBC News*, p. 139

## A pillar of American democracy

- One part of the checks and balances system

→ "Checks and balances", infographic, *BBC*, p. 140 • "Checks and balances in a Trump-Era Supreme Court", *BCFJ*, p. 140

- Ensuring the 6th Amendment

→ "You have the right to an attorney", *Last Week Tonight*, p. 138

FAIRE SOCIÉTÉ **Axe 3**

**To what extent does the American system warrant equal rights?**

## The Supreme Court, guardian of the Constitution

- Federal *v.* state level courts

→ "The US court sytem", *AJ+*, p. 140 • "Checks and balances in a Trump-Era Supreme Court", *BCFJ*, p. 140

- Appointing Justices for life

→ "What Bader Ginsburg's death means for the Supreme Court", *The Guardian*, p. 141

## Advocating for a better system

- Investigating on previous cases

→ *The Innocence Files*, p. 136

- Ruth Bader Ginsberg, a committed Supreme Court Justice

→ "Crossover at the Supreme Court?", *NPR*, p. 141

- Reforming the whole system

→ "Fighting for civil rights", *NPR*, p. 137

## Phonology — L'accentuation des modaux

AUDIO

- Les **auxiliaires modaux** sont des mots grammaticaux. À l'oral, on utilise leur **forme réduite**, c'est-à-dire qu'ils ne sont pas accentués et que la voyelle se réduit à /ə/ : *can* /kən/, *should* /ʃəd/, *won't* /wənt/…
- Si l'on veut insister sur leur valeur modale, ils sont alors **accentués** et leur **forme pleine** est utilisée, notamment à la forme négative : *Any person who is too poor to hire a lawyer, **cannot** be assured a fair trial.*

**1** **Écoute puis entraîne-toi à prononcer les modaux dans leur forme pleine et réduite.**

a. ***Can*** *I attend the trial? Yes, you* ***can****.*
b. *The Supreme Court* ***could*** *announce their decision today, but they also* ***could*** *wait until tomorrow.*
c. *You absolutely* ***must*** *watch* The Innocence Files*. The filmmakers* ***must*** *be proud of their work.*

**2** **Accentue les modaux selon le message à transmettre. Écoute et vérifie.**

a. *These prisoners are victims of our system. We can't let them die in prison.*
b. *Would you like to join us in our class action lawsuit?*
c. *The US justice system can and must guarantee equal rights for all Americans.*
d. *I could talk about the justice system for hours.*

# BUILD YOUR PORTFOLIO

## Film

*Loving*, Jeff Nichols, 2016

*Loving* tells the true story of Richard and Mildred Loving, the plaintiffs in the 1967 U.S. Supreme Court decision *Loving* v. *Virginia*, which invalidated state laws prohibiting interracial marriage. A white construction worker in Virginia, falls in love with a local black woman. They decide to marry, but knowing that interracial marriage violates Virginia's anti-miscegenation laws.

- **Watch** the film and **explain** how this case was a breakthrough for American justice.

VIDÉO

## Article

"US criminal justice system fuels poverty cycle", *HRW*, 2018

"The United States government at all levels should act to prevent the criminal justice system from punishing poverty and further impoverishing the poor, the Criminal Justice Policy Program (CJPP) at Harvard Law School and Human Rights Watch said today. In particular, authorities should not rely on fines and fees to pay for government programs because they disproportionately hurt the poor."

- **Read** the article and **say** what Human Rights Watch reproaches the American judicial system with and why it should be reformed.

ARTICLE

## Chart

- **Observe** and **analyse** the chart. How does Florida local justice reflect the national judicial system?

## ÉPREUVE ORALE / GRAND ORAL — Entraîne-toi à l'oral

### Step 1 — Build up your speech!

**Épreuve orale**

- Choose one topic in the mindmap p. 146.
- Pick out two documents in the file and add one or two personal ones to illustrate this issue.
- Prepare your presentation: you must show how these documents relate to the issue you chose.

OBJECTIF BAC p. 305

**Grand oral**

OBJECTIF BAC p. 312-313

- Choose one topic in the mindmap p. 146.
- Find a key question about your topic and write it down. Think about links with other subjects (*DGEMC* for example).
- Gather arguments and examples from the file.
- Prepare an outline for your presentation and write your note sheet.

OBJECTIF BAC p. 308-309

### Step 2 — Make your oral presentation in front of two classmates.

**Épreuve orale**

- Show your documents to your classmates. Each of you makes their presentation to the others in about five minutes.

OBJECTIF BAC p. 306-307

**Grand oral**

- Give your note sheet to your classmates.
- Stand up and make a five-minute presentation to answer your key question.

OBJECTIF BAC p. 310-311

### Step 3 — Answer your classmates' questions about your presentation.

SNAPFILE 16

FAIRE SOCIÉTÉ

AXE 3 : ÉGALITÉS ET INÉGALITÉS

# Gender equality in NZ

▶ **How is New Zealand paving the way for gender equality?**

FINAL TASK — **Submit your project for an awareness campaign on gender equality.**

More on SPEAKEASY NEWS speakeasy-news.com

## 1 A unique model

LANDMARKS p. 286-287

**Doc 1.**

TRIO OF TRAILBLAZERS

**New Zealand's female Prime Ministers**

Current New Zealand Prime Minister, Jacinda Ardern, surrounded by former Prime Ministers Dame Jenny Shipley and Helen Clark.

It was the first time Dame Jenny Shipley, Helen Clark and Jacinda Ardern had been together since the latter took the top job. In the first country in the world to give women the vote, its three female leaders posed for an historic photoshoot at the *New Zealand Herald's* Auckland office. [...]

What message does this image send the world? "Girls can do it!" said Clark.

"I think that we're near normalising women in leadership," said Ardern. "In a role like Prime Minister, if you've got three, then you're pretty close to normalising it."

**Shipley**: "Each of us has made different life choices and, actually, that gives women everywhere role models. It's legitimate to choose. We don't have to be the same, we don't have to judge each other, we make our own choices. Whether you have children or not..."

**Ardern**: "Married, unmarried..."

**Shipley**: "We offer three really unique role model pathways for girls in New Zealand, but also women globally." [...]

They fought for these jobs, because: "Why wouldn't we?" said Shipley.

"Because we thought we could do the job," said Clark. "We thought we could do it better than anyone else who was doing it at the time."

*Otago Daily Times*, September 2018

**CULTURE SPOT**

As of 2019, the **proportion of women** in New Zealand's House of Representatives surpasses 40%. By comparison, women represent 34% of the members of the House of Commons in the UK and 23% of the House of Representatives in the USA.

**WORDS**

- equity = fairness
- milestone = landmark
- pioneer /paɪə'nɪə/ = trailblazer

- enfranchised = emancipated
- male-dominated
- progressive ≠ conservative
- underpaid

- achieve change
- ensure equality
- grant suffrage
- pass a bill

**a.** **Read** the article and **find out** why this photograph is emblematic of New Zealand's political world.

**b.** **Comment** on Shipley's statement (l. 19-21).

**c.** **Use** both the article and the culture spot to **account for** the greater representation of women in politics in New Zealand compared to other countries.

**d.** **Explain** how political representation can influence gender equality.

## Doc 2.

### The first country where women won the right to vote

125 years ago today, Aotearoa New Zealand became the first country in the world to grant all women the right to vote.

The event was part of an ongoing international movement for women to exit from an inferior position in society and to enjoy equal rights with men. But why did this global first happen in a small and isolated corner of the South Pacific?

In the late 19th century, Aotearoa New Zealand was a volatile and rapidly changing contact zone where British settlers confidently introduced systematic colonisation, often at the expense of the indigenous Māori population. Settlers were keen to create a new world society that adapted the best of Britain and left behind the negative aspects of the industrial revolution. [...]

Many supported universal male suffrage and a less rigid class structure, enlightened race relations and humanitarianism that also extended to improving women's lives. These liberal aspirations towards societal equality contributed to the 1893 women's suffrage victory. [...]

New Zealand was fortunate to have many effective women leaders. Most prominent among them was Kate Sheppard. In 1887, Sheppard became head of the WCTU[1]'s Christchurch branch and led the campaign for the vote. [...]

The Suffrage 125 celebratory slogan "whakatū wāhine – Women stand up!" captures the intention of continuing progressive and egalitarian traditions. Recognising diverse cultural backgrounds is now important. With hindsight, the feminist movement can be implicated as an agent of colonisation, but it did support votes for Māori women. Meri Te Tai Mangakāhia[2] presented a motion to the newly formed Māori parliament to allow women to vote and sit in it.

Katie PICKLES,
*theconversation.com*,
September 2018

Read the full article on ARTICLE

1. Women's Christian Temperance Union
2. A Māori woman suffrage activist (1868-1920)

**a. Read** the article and **explain** how the fight for gender equality is rooted in New Zealand history.

**b. Say** who Kate Sheppard was.

**c.** GRAMMAR *"It **did** support votes for Māori women"* (l. 45). **Comment** on the use of *"did"*.

**d. Analyse** the impact that the feminist movement had on the Māori population.

## Doc 3. Equal Pay Act

AUDIO

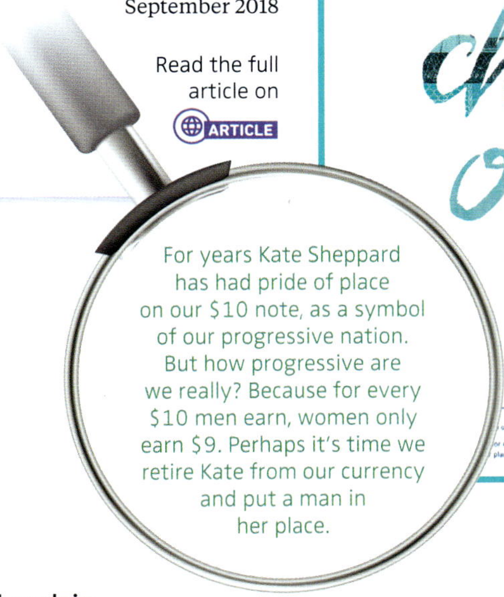


(Audio: *RNZ National*, August 2020)

**CULTURE SPOT**

**The Equal Pay Amendment Act** was voted in July 2020 and came into force on November 6th, 2020.

**a. Describe** the poster, **read** the caption and **explain** what issue it raises.

**b. Listen** to the audio and **describe** the legal situation regarding equal pay up until the act was amended.

**c. Explain** how this new Equal Pay law re-evaluates women's work.

**d.** RHETORIC **Focus** on the rhythm adopted by Tracey Martin. What does it say about her opinion on this law?

**YOUR TASK** **Create** an animated timeline to **praise** the different steps which have made New Zealand a unique model in gender equality.

**BOOST YOUR SKILLS!**

**Célébrer des avancées**

- Utilise des tournures emphatiques : *It **did** support votes for...* • ***Most** prominent among them was...* • ***That is that** women will finally...* • *This bill is **not just** about... **it's** about...*
- Varie les adjectifs mélioratifs : *fortunate* • *progressive* • *egalitarian* • *important*
- Souligne les conséquences bénéfiques : *A law that **makes** it easier **for** women **to be** paid* • *It **enables** lawmakers **to** compare...* • ***So that** women are supported.*

# 2 Gender equals?

## Doc 1.

Since the first Gender Attitudes Survey was carried out by the National Council of Women in 2017, the *#MeToo* and *#Time'sUp* movements have taken off globally.

Gender equality became a mainstay of newspaper front pages, Netflix documentaries and dinner-table conversations. It was enough to make president of the National Council of Women, Lisa Lawrence, hopeful that attitudes about gender would have started to progress.

So she was surprised to see from the results of the second Gender Attitudes Survey, published in 2019, that that hadn't really been the case.

One-fifth of New Zealanders do not agree that gender equality is a fundamental right: no change from 2017. But at the same time, significantly more Kiwis think gender equality has been achieved—42% in 2019 compared to 30% in 2017.

Lawrence said a lot of that likely had to do with Kiwi pride at having Prime Minister Jacinda Ardern do one of the most normal and extraordinary things as a woman—have a baby—while running the country.

"We've fallen into a level of inspiration that perhaps has brought comfort, so we're getting a bit complacent that the job is done," she said.

But complacency is risky, she said: "When you unpack the information underneath we still have a fair way to go".

Josephine FRANKS, *stuff.co.nz*, July 2020

**Gender Inequality**
Education

**GENDER EQUAL NZ**
MAKING EQUALITY REALITY

**The 2017 Gender Attitudes Survey tested attitudes around gender roles – at home, at school, at work and in the community. New Zealanders were most likely to say that women and gender diverse people are losing out. Let's take a look at what they said, in their own words:**

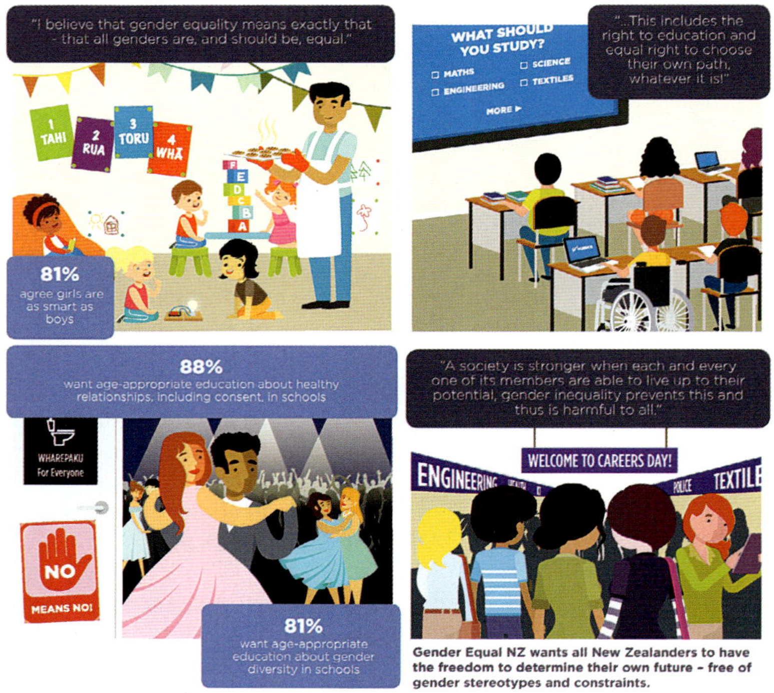


*Gender Equal NZ, NCWNZ, 2017*

**a. Read** the infographic and **say** where the data come from. **Sum up** New Zealanders' opinion on gender equality.

**b. Read** the article and **clarify** the data it relies on. **Explain** how it sheds light on the content of the infographic.

**c. Comment** on Lisa Lawrence's hopes and **explain** her disappointment.

**d. React** to this statement:*"complacency is risky."* (l. 29)

## Doc 2. Still striving for equality

VIDÉO

*NZ Human Rights Commission*, 2018

**a. Watch** the video and **explain** why the suffragettes are referred to. **Identify** the goal of this video.

**b. List** the elements that still need to be changed.

**YOUR TASK** MÉDIATION **Write** a series of tweets for the Gender Equal NZ account.

DIFFÉRENCIATION

**WAY 1 Take stock** of the situation and **clarify** what remains to be done.

**WAY 2 Acknowledge** the achievements but **raise awareness** on the risk of complacency by **emphasising** what remains to be done.

**BOOST YOUR SKILLS!**

**Relativiser des progrès sociétaux**

- Dresse le bilan de la situation au *present perfect* : *We* ***have*** *largely* ***achieved****....* • *It* ***hasn't*** *really* ***been*** *the case.*
- Utilise le conditionnel : *Suffragists* ***would*** *not want us to...*
  • *They* ***would*** *be horrified by...*
- Souligne par des adverbes ce qu'il reste à faire : *We* ***still*** *have a fair way to go.* • *We are* ***so*** *far from...*
  • *It's* ***even*** *worse for...*

## 3 "We too" can make it

### Doc 1. Men stand up

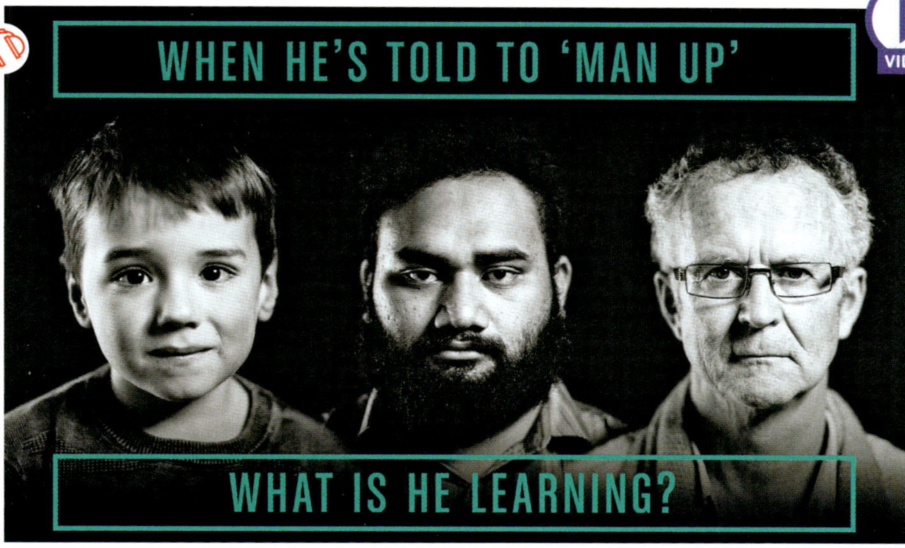


man up = be brave

*Gender Equal NZ, NCWNZ, 2017 (Video: White Ribbon, 2019)*

**WORDS**

- dispar**i**ty = inequ**a**lity
- emp**o**werment
- g**e**nder b**i**as /'baɪəs/

- egalit**a**rian
- g**e**nder-based
- well-b**a**lanced = fair

- ass**e**rt **o**neself
- c**a**rry on the l**e**gacy
- push for legisl**a**tion
- r**a**lly supp**o**rt
- stand up for = **a**dvocate (for)

**a. Focus** on the poster: How would you answer the question? **Imagine** the goal of this campaign.

**b. Watch** the video and **say** what these men are calling for. **Explain** what it means for them to be White Ribbon ambassadors.

**c. Say** what they admit on the way they consider women, and why.

**d.** RHETORIC **Focus** on the third comment and **say** how Mark Longley makes listeners feel concerned about his speech.

**e. Discuss** the possible impact of such a campaign.

**AT HOME** **Look up** more videos from the White Ribbon campaign. **Get ready** to **present** one that particularly strikes you and to **make** your classmates feel concerned.

*UNTV/Reuters, 2018*

### Doc 2. "We are all in this together"

**a. Watch** the video and **find** information about the speech (speaker, topic, place).

**b.** RHETORIC **Pick out** the expression repeated several times and **identify** the stressed word. **Comment** on the effect it produces.

**c. Explain** what *"Me too must become we too"* means.

**d. Discuss** the impact of such a speech in this context.

**YOUR TASK** On Women's Day (March 8th), **deliver** a short speech to convince an all-male assembly to commit to gender equality.

**BOOST YOUR SKILLS!**

**Captiver un auditoire**

- Implique directement ton auditoire : ***We** must redouble **our** efforts.* • ***We** have to recommit **ourselves**.*
- Intègre des questions rhétoriques : *You think we are... but, **are we?***
- Pense à l'emphase, aux répétitions et effets de rythme : *We still **do** have...* • *We **must**..., We **must**..., We **must**...* • *It's **really** essential that...*
- Trouve une formule accrocheuse : ***Me too** must become **we too**.*

**FINAL TASK**

As a publicist, you are in charge of a new campaign to promote gender equality in New Zealand. **Gather** ideas for your project (form, people involved, catchphrase...) and **submit** your project to a jury. **Make** it striking and powerful.

OBJECTIF BAC p. 307

Tu as présenté ton **dossier personnel** composé de 4 documents : **deux articles** ("Trio of trailblazers", p. 148 ; "The first country where women won the right to vote", p. 149) et **deux documents iconographiques** "Gender pay gap", p. 149 et "Gender inequality", p. 150.

Après avoir présenté ton dossier personnel, l'épreuve orale se poursuit par un entretien qui va durer 10 minutes. Les questions peuvent servir plusieurs objectifs :
– apporter des précisions sur un des aspects développés ;
– nuancer un des points de ta présentation ;
– élargir la réflexion menée ;
– expliquer le choix de document opéré.

Repère bien le type de question posée, cela t'aidera à aborder la réponse tout en nourrissant l'interaction.

## 1 Apporter des précisions

• *When you talked about the female Prime Ministers of New Zealand, you referred to Jacinda Ardern. Could you name another one?*

Écoute bien la question posée et repère les éléments sur lesquels t'appuyer : *Could you **name**...?*
*Could you give **another example**? Do you know **when**?*

• Utilise des marqueurs d'interaction pour rebondir sur la question posée : *Yes of course! Helen Clark for example* • *It's true, I could have mentioned them all.* • *I'm sorry, I am not sure I remember their names correctly.*

## 2 Nuancer des propos

• *When you presented the document "Gender pay gap", you said there was no equality between men and women in terms of salary. Do you mean that the law doesn't grant equal pay to New Zealand citizens?*

• Identifie bien à quelle partie de ta présentation le jury fait référence : *When you **said*** • *you presented the **article*** • *you commented on the **infographic**...*
• Repère bien les termes employés afin de mettre en évidence des nuances : *gender pay gap ≠ equal salary.*

• Pense à utiliser des connecteurs logiques pour préciser ta pensée : ***Indeed**, there is an essential difference that I need to introduce* • *It's true that I did not really explain this; **yet** it is essential to emphasise that...*

## 3 Élargir la réflexion

• *You presented a document about New Zealand's Prime Ministers. Using the information you gave, as well as your personal knowledge, can you comment on the place of New Zealand on the international stage?*

Ne t'inquiète pas si tu vois que le jury te propose d'élargir la conversation à un aspect que tu n'as pas évoqué. Cela ne veut rien dire quant à la qualité de ce que tu as déjà présenté.

• Reviens sur les documents déjà présentés en les abordant sous un nouvel angle : ***If we want to go further**, we can say that these heads of state play a major role internationally because...*
• Tu peux aussi évoquer de nouveaux documents en complément : ***It also reminds me of** an important speech delivered by Jacinda Arden to the United Nations.*

## 4 Expliquer ses choix

• *I'm sure you studied a multitude of documents in class, can you tell me which one you would choose if you had to keep only one to represent the issue?*

N'oublie pas qu'il n'y a pas forcément une bonne réponse aux questions posées. Il s'agit d'être capable de justifier tes choix et de montrer la réflexion personnelle que tu as menée dans la construction de ton dossier.

• Si tu as inclus un document personnel dans ton dossier, souligne-le : ***Outside of class**, I discovered this document which **really held my interest** because...* • *I **came across** this article...*

Vers le **BAC**

# BUILD YOUR PORTFOLIO

## Awareness campaign

"#demandequalpay", *YWCA Auckland*, 2014

This is of an awareness campaign by the Young Women's Christian Association (YWCA) advocating for equal pay. Activists used different strategies to denounce the gender pay gap.

VIDÉO

- **Watch** the video campaign and **say** how this banknote may question gender equality while seemingly putting a woman in the spotlight.

## Article

"The Kiwi women changing the face of Instagram", *thespinoff.co.nz*, May 8th, 2019

“Kiwi women with influence online are similarly embracing the trend towards body positivity and empowerment. It's a complicated movement, but one that feels a hell more nourishing than a Kardashian-endorsed appetite-suppressant lollipop.”

- **Read** the article and **explain** how Kiwi women are using social media as a form of activism to push for a more positive representation of women on screen.

ARTICLE

## Video

"Girl Boss Advantage Programme", Alexia Hilbertidou, November 2019

VIDÉO

“The GirlBoss Advantage programme connects industry and individual via interactive workshops, mentoring and rapid-fire internships. GirlBoss New Zealand works with corporate organisations who will help to mentor, grow and support high-school-aged young women to achieve their dreams.”

- **Watch** the video and **say** how her own experience pushed Alexia Hilbertidou into taking action in favour of women and **find out** more about the programme she created.

## Article

"New Zealand break new ground by paying women's team", *The Irish Times*, March 13th, 2018

“Twenty-three years after men's rugby union was made professional, New Zealand's national women's team—the Black Ferns—will be offered paid contracts for the first time […]. They will also have access to medical and life insurance, as well as maternity leave entitlements.”

- **Read** the article and **explain** how sports authorities are pushing for gender equality. **Identify** the source of the article and **say** how it shows the special place of New Zealand worldwide.

ARTICLE

## Entraîne-toi à l'oral — ÉPREUVE ORALE

**Step 1** **Build up your speech!**

- Choose one aspect of the issue you want to highlight: The special place of women in New Zealand throughout history, the country as a model for the world, the challenges that still remain….
- Pick out documents to build your portfolio: choose from the file, this page, or from your personal references.
- Prepare your presentation: show how these documents relate to the topic you chose. OBJECTIF BAC p. 305

**Step 2** **Make your presentation in front of two classmates.**

- Show the documents chosen to your friends and explain your point in about five minutes. Make sure you say how they illustrate the topic. OBJECTIF BAC p. 306-307

**Step 3** **Answer your classmates' questions about your presentation.**

FILE 17

ENVIRONNEMENTS EN MUTATION

AXE 1 : FRONTIÈRE ET ESPACE

# Border Line

▶ **How is Brexit reopening old wounds in Ireland?**

FINAL TASK **Record the trailer of a TV documentary on the issues related to the Irish border.**



## 1 The impossible border

LANDMARKS p. 280-281

Doc 1. VIDÉO

1. Democratic Unionist Party
2. J. Rees-Mogg: a British conservative politician

Cartoon by Bob MORAN, *The Telegraph*
(Video: "A real barrier to a Brexit deal", *WSJ*, 2019)

a. **Look** at the cartoon and **describe** it. **Guess** which problems and contradictions it refers to.

b. **Watch** the video and **pick out** information about the border between Ireland and Northern Ireland before Brexit.

c. VOCABULARY **Spot** all the words referring to the lexical field of the border. What idea of a frontier do they convey? ▶ p. 161

d. **Explain** how Brexit has questioned the status of the border.

e. **Find out** why setting up a physical border would be difficult.

**WORDS**

- proc**ee**dings: *procédure*
- t**ur**moil = agit**a**tion
- uph**ea**val /ʌp'hivəl/ = disr**u**ption
- **i**ntricate = c**o**mplicated
- unc**er**tain
- uns**o**lvable
- anti**ci**pate
- disr**u**pt = dist**ur**b
- dread /drɛd/ = fear

## Doc 2.

### Brexit renews discussions on sovereignty and identity around an unclear border

When the United Kingdom voted to withdraw from the European Union in June 2016, little attention was paid to the country's only land border with the EU This consequential border separates Northern Ireland, which is part of the UK, from the Republic of Ireland, which is an EU member state.

It was this border that repeatedly delayed Brexit, as negotiations over the failed "Irish backstop[1]" measure saw the demise of former Prime Minister Theresa May's government last year. [...]

Now, Brexit raises questions about whether this peace can stand by bringing those multidimensional, long-standing and difficult questions of identity in Northern Ireland to the fore: Catholic *vs.* Protestant, Irish *vs.* British, Nationalist *vs.* Unionist, Republican *vs.* Loyalist.

When Ireland and the UK were both part of the EU, the border between Ireland and Northern Ireland became little more than an afterthought[2] as peace flourished in the north in the past two decades.

But, now the prospect of that border becoming a meaningful delineation between the UK and Northern Ireland on one side and Ireland and the EU on the other, has forced the Northern Irish to consider: What does it mean to be Irish? To be British? To be European? And could one solution to these vexing[3] questions in the longer term be unifying Ireland? [...]

The outcome of the referendum did not reflect the sentiments of a majority in Northern Ireland—about 56% of Northern Ireland voted to remain in the EU.

Evan Collins, *USA Today*, July 2020

**CULTURE SPOT**

**Learn key words to understand Irish identities:**
- British
- Catholics
- Irish
- Loyalists
- Nationalists
- Protestants
- Republicans
- Unionists

Lexiquiz

LANDMARKS p. 271

1. protocol that was supposed to keep Northern Ireland and the Republic of Ireland from having a physical border
2. reconsideration
3. difficult

**a. Read** the text and **find out** why Northern Ireland was at the centre of Brexit negotiations.

**b.** RHETORIC **Explain** what the enumerations of issues and questions say about the situation in Northern Ireland.

**c. Find out** what Northern Ireland's opinion in the Brexit referendum was and **guess** why.

**d. Sum up** what concerns Brexit has revealed for Northern Irish society and people.

## Doc 3.

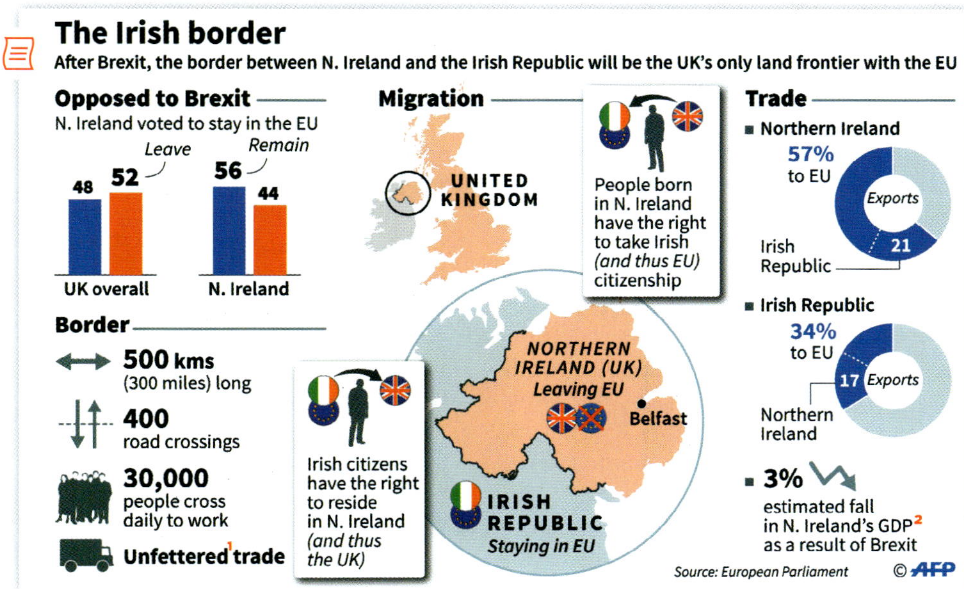


1. free 2. *PIB*

**a. Observe** the infographic and **explain** why Northern Ireland has a privileged relation with the EU.

**b. Imagine** why the Irish border will raise economic concerns.

**c. Guess** which other aspects of Northern Irish life will be impacted by the installation of a hard border.

**YOUR TASK** As a journalist, **write** the introduction to an article on the complexity of the Irish border in the context of Brexit.

**BOOST YOUR SKILLS!**

**Soulever un problème**
- Utilise du vocabulaire spécifique : *It is the major **sticking point**... • That's the **core of the issue** • Brexit **raises questions** about...*
- Souligne ses enjeux par des connecteurs : *That's **because**... • **While** the UK voted to leave... • **Unlike** many frontiers... • **But, now**...* GRAMMAR p. 161
- Invite à la réflexion par des questions rhétoriques : ***What does it mean** to be Irish? **Could** one solution **be** unifying Ireland?* PHONOLOGY p. 164

# 2 A never-ending story of division

## Doc 1.

Martin WOLTERINK, 2019 (Video: Brexit explained, *Channel 4 News*, 2018)

**WORDS**

- point = essence of a problem
- process
- unrest = trouble
- uprising: *soulèvement*

- divisive /dɪ'vaɪsɪv/
- reminiscent = evocative
- volatile /'vɒlətaɪl/ = unstable

- dismiss (an idea) = reject
- intimidate

**a. Watch** the video and **create** a timeline indicating the main events linked to the Irish border.

**b. Say** what the Good Friday Agreement is and what it allowed.

**c.** PHONOLOGY **Focus** on the rhetorical questions. **Say** how they are highlighted in the commentary. ▸ p. 164

**d. Focus** on the cartoon and **use** it to summarise the issue of the Irish border since 1970.

## Doc 2.

**The Guardian** **Border talk stirs up bad memories in Northern Ireland**

In Gortmullan—a patchwork of farms, bungalows and hedgerows[1]—there are no road markings to indicate the frontier. Jack McGann, 16, who works at a service station just inside the Irish border, hesitated when asked to identify where the UK began. [...] McGann has never known customs checks, army searches or terrorist attacks. "My parents told me stories about the hard border. I heard it was tough."

Eugene McAffrey, who worked at an adjacent service station just inside Northern Ireland, sighed at the mention of Brexit. "It's occupying the mind of everyone that walks in here. How could it not?"

In a pub at Derrylin, a few miles up the road, Shane McBrien, a painter, seethed[2] at the Democratic Unionist Party for endorsing[3] Boris Johnson's plan. "Any physical border will bring back bad memories. It's just going backwards." His brother, Eugene, said a hard border would compound the fact that Brexit ignored the will of most Northern Ireland voters. "The north voted to remain. We're being tossed out of the EU. We've no say." [...]

Dissident Republicans have hailed[4] Brexit—and specifically the prospect of a hard border—as a historic opportunity to revive an armed campaign. Public support for that seems negligible and attacks remain sporadic.

But even before Johnson unveiled his plan there was a sense of the police battening down the hatches[5]. Last Monday Irish police established a new armed support unit in Cavan, which borders Fermanagh, to combat a surge in criminality and to prepare for Brexit.

Rory CARROLL, *The Guardian*, October 2019

1. rows of bushes 2. furious 3. support 4. salute 5. (*fig.*) ready for an attack

**a. Read** the article and **pick out** elements showing the memory of the border is still very strong.

**b. Find out** what all the points of views expressed have in common.

**c. Explain** why the Irish border is associated with the notion of tension.

**d.** TRANSLATION **Translate** l. 31-39 focusing on how the author opposes the future with the idea of a haunting past.

## Doc 3.

An Ulster Unionist mural in North Belfast

### A return to violence?

BELFAST—As the countdown approached Friday for Britain to leave the European Union, the only sign it was being marked in Belfast was a small group of people celebrating outside the gates of Northern Ireland's regional parliament.

Around 50 people gathered at the national assembly building, known as Stormont, and waved Union Jacks. As the clock passed 11 p.m., a local politician led cheers of "Freedom" and shouts of "Who here is British?".

Since before the 2016 referendum, there have been fears that Brexit could destabilize Northern Ireland's complex peace, raising doubts about its place in the U.K. and stoking[1] talk that it could lead to unification with Ireland. [...]

For three years Northern Ireland had been the central obstacle to the UK's efforts to leave the EU, the result of the seemingly intractable problem produced by an apparently unavoidable consequence of Brexit—that the U.K. separating from Europe must inevitably mean putting a border between the two.

The prospect of a border between Northern Ireland and the Republic immediately triggered[2] fears that it could resurrect Northern Ireland's conflict between mostly Catholic Republicans who support unification with Ireland and the predominantly Protestant Unionists and Loyalists who support staying with the U.K. [...]

Rob McCartney, a Loyalist community organizer who was present at several meetings, told ABC News that paramilitary violence has been rejected by Loyalists, but that "civil disobedience" was raised at all the meetings.

"Does that mean masked men with guns marching back on the streets? No, it doesn't!" McCartney said in an interview at the East Belfast Constitutional Club, where one of the meetings was held. "But does it mean picketing[3] ports, protesting, marching? Yes it does," he said. [...]

Others, though, dismiss that Unionist opposition can be turned into large protests.

Peter Shirlow, a director at the University of Liverpool's Institute of Irish Studies and a veteran expert on Unionism, said changes in Northern Irish society have reduced the capacity of hardcore Unionist activists to mobilize.

"That section of Loyalism that wants to go back to conflict—it just doesn't have the capacity to bring people out anymore," Shirlow said.

After two decades of the peace process, most Northern Irish people have no appetite for a return to violence, he said.

Patrick REEVELL, *ABC News*, February 2020

1. inspiring 2. caused 3. blocking

**CULTURE SPOT**

**Learn key words to mention armed groups in Ireland**

- Paramilitary organisations
- IRA
- UFF
- UDA
- UVF

Lexiquiz

LANDMARKS p. 268

**a. Observe** the mural painted during the Troubles and **imagine** what the political situation must have been like in the area.

**b. Read** the article and **identify** the two opposing groups and their demands.

**c. Pick out** all the elements showing that Northern Ireland has a violent past.

**d.** GRAMMAR **Pick out** the modal auxiliary used to express probability. What does it say about the possible consequences of Brexit? p. 161

**e. Discuss:** is violence still likely to take place at the border after Brexit?

**YOUR TASK** As part of a podcast on Brexit issues in Ireland, **record** a short report on how and why Brexit has renewed fears on the Irish border.

**BOOST YOUR SKILLS!**

**Évoquer le poids du passé**

- Utilise des marqueurs temporels : *We need to go back almost **100 years**. • Between **1919** and **1921** • **In** the late **1960s** • Since **before the 2016** referendum • **After** two decades...*
- Souligner la peur d'un possible retour au passé : *It **could** resurrect Northern Ireland's conflict. • The border **would** become...* GRAMMAR p. 161
- Utilise le lexique de l'appréhension : *They are **worried about** how... • There are **fears** that... • A return of the violence of the past, **nobody wants that**. • The prospect of a border **triggered fears**.*

## Doc 1.

TEXTE LU

Tonight in a border pub, a young man and young woman get talking. They are no strangers, they grew up in the same area but, slowly, things are going to a new level. They have, in local lingo[1], "a notion" of each other. He has a notion of her. She has a notion of him. To have a notion of someone is to see potential in them, to see potential in the idea of you together. I'm talking about love.

Or perhaps that's old news, they became a couple months ago. They are not in a pub. They are at her kitchen table eating dinner with her parents. There is a polite intergenerational conversation. They all agree that reinstating border controls will be bad for business. He has just gotten a job with a wholesale supplier, delivering animal feed to farms both sides of the border. Her mother asks about this, she approves. It's all quite pleasant but there are sideways glances between the young couple. She lives with her parents and he lives with his, this is limiting, as you can imagine. Their toes tap soundlessly inside their shoes.

When they get a moment alone she says to him or perhaps he says to her, "Do you fancy a spin to Narrow Water?" Their pulses hop. "Yes", she replies. Or maybe, "Aye", or "Alright so," or "Go on then."

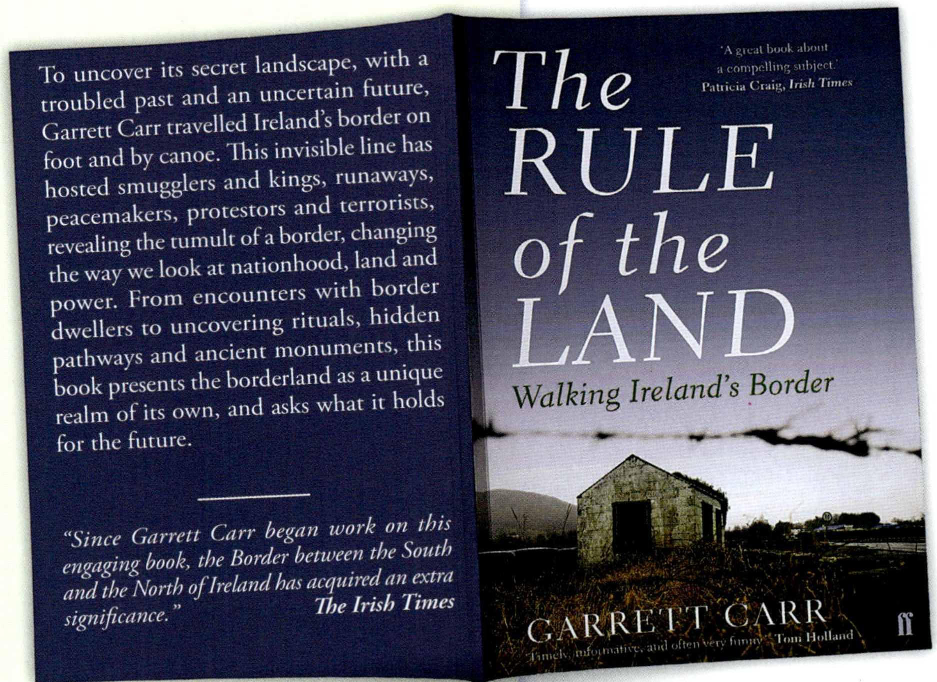


They get in his van and drive, following Carlingford Lough[2]'s southern shore. A stony lane leads off the road. It's after dark, most people would miss the turn-off[3], but the couple know the area. The lane leads through woods to the waterside and a slipway that is broken up and disused, no boat has tied up here in years. They park overlooking the canal. They can see Ireland's border slipping on the surface. He turns off the engine. The van has been unloaded and swept but there is still the odour of cattle feed. They turn to each other. They kiss. They kiss some more. They fumble at buttons. They begin to probe each other's boundaries.

This is obviously a spot for lovers, for "courting". It suits the role, secluded and quiet, with the breeze in the branches and darkening water sliding out to the lough. You can be sure of privacy here, nobody visits the border.

Garrett CARR, *The Rule Of The Land*, 2017

1. language 2. lake (*Irish*) 3. road exit

**WORDS**

- conjecture = supposition
- damage: *dégâts*
- dissent = disagreement
- partition = separation

- detrimental to = damaging
- frustrating

- advocate = suggest
- envision = imagine
- alter people's lives
- make things harder
- split up = divide

**a.** **Read** the back cover and the extract and **pick out** information about the place and the people mentioned.

**b.** **Describe** the importance of the border in these people's lives.

**c.** GRAMMAR **Explain** what impression the exclusive use of the present tense contributes to creating. ▸ p. 164

**d.** TRANSLATION **Translate** l. 6-16. **Try** and respect the tone of the extract.

**e.** **Comment** on how a sense of limitation pervades the whole text.

## Doc 2. The village on the border

*ITV News*, 2018

**a.** **Look** at the still and **comment** on the way Brexit and the border are perceived in the area.

**b.** **Watch** the video and **describe** life in Pettigo. **Say** what is special about this village.

**c.** **Clarify** how a hard border would concretely impact the life of the inhabitants.

**d.** GRAMMAR **Pick out** the modal equivalent most used by the woman interviewed. What does it say about her state of mind? ► p. 161

## Doc 3.

### The Harder the Brexit, the Harder the Impact on Northern Ireland

Very few analysts would have predicted three years ago that the question of the Irish border might be the rock upon which the Brexit dream would perish, in a debate obsessed by the narrow concerns of 'Little England'.

Three years on, the question of the Northern Ireland border has been front and centre throughout the tortuous negotiations between the UK and the EU. Those who dismissed this question during the referendum campaign can no longer pretend that such concerns are inconsequential. [...]

Northern Ireland is a beneficiary of significant E.U. funding[1] programmes, which is understood and felt by the people. The current E.U. budget from 2014-2020 will see the North receive 3.55 billion euro—of which 230 million euro has been set aside for peace projects. It goes without saying that future E.U. funding is under threat in the event of a U.K. departure.

The interdependence of the so-called 'All Island Economy'—the combined economies of Northern Ireland and the Republic of Ireland—is significant and growing. Cross-border trade in goods achieved a record high of six billion British pounds or seven billion euro in 2017, with average growth of four percent per annum achieved over the past 20 years.

The cross-border population, including the six counties[2] of Northern Ireland and the northerly counties of the Republic, is approximately 850,000 people and is predominantly rural. A Queen's University study of people living in this cross-border region showed that 73% believe Brexit will affect their community "to a great extent" and that the most important aspects of E.U. membership are citizenship rights and funding.

There is no doubt that the harder the Brexit, the harder the impact on Northern Ireland and the border counties in the Republic of Ireland. [...]

Those advocating in favour of a hard Brexit have no idea, or perhaps no concern, for the economic and political carnage this would cause in Northern Ireland.

Lucinda CREIGHTON[3], *Intereconomics.eu*, 2019

**1.** financing **2.** districts **3.** Ireland's former Minister for European Affairs

**a.** **Identify** the author of the text and **guess** what her opinion on Brexit might be.

**b.** **Read** the article and **describe** the current economic situation on the Irish border.

**c.** **Explain** what might happen in case of a hard Brexit, according to the author.

**d.** RHETORIC **Describe** the author's tone and **comment** on the passages revealing what she thinks of Brexit.

**AT HOME** **Visit** the following website and **take** notes on the current reality of the border crossings (crossings, people, goods, money). Get ready to **present** your findings to the class. SITE

**YOUR TASK** **Imagine** and **act out** a street interview of Irish border dwellers about the concrete consequences a hard Brexit would have for them.

### BOOST YOUR SKILLS!

**Exprimer une conviction personnelle**

- Énonce des assertions fortes : ***It goes without saying*** *that...* • ***There is no doubt*** *that...* • *They* ***have no idea,*** *or perhaps* ***no concern*** *for...* • ***Absolutely*** *not.*
- Donne une portée plus large à ton propos avec le présent de vérité générale : *This* ***is*** *obviously a spot for lovers.* • *It* ***suits*** *the role.* • *Nobody* ***visits*** *the border.*
- Affirme ta conviction avec des réponses courtes : *"Does that mean...?* ***No, it doesn't!****"* • *"Does it mean...?* ***Yes, it does!****"*

# 4 Prospects of a more united Ireland?

## The North must become an independent EU state

Are we really going to see Border crossings again with lines of trucks and cars? Are we really going to have a Border economy based on easy smuggling[1]? Are we going to blow up bridges in isolated Border places or block lonely Border roads? [...]

In this state of dark confusion, one option being suggested is the creation of a united Ireland. This seems to me to be the least likely option.

It is worthy of serious attention only as a way of making sure that it is not on the table at any time, that it remains where it has been for decades—a dream for some on the island, a nightmare for others, especially in the North [...].

Irish unity can only occur by agreement from a majority in Northern Ireland.

Even the loss of the sustaining cheque from the EU to Northern Irish farmers is unlikely to make farmers who treasure their British identity change their minds about what country they want to belong to.

“In this state of dark confusion, one option being suggested is the creation of a united Ireland. This seems to me to be the least likely option.”

Who then has a problem with Northern Ireland remaining a member of the European Union while also remaining a member of the Commonwealth, directly under the Crown? [...]

It would suit the Dublin government not to have hard borders within the island of Ireland.

It would console many in Northern Ireland to know that they were not losing their British identity, their flag, their drums, their right to a British passport and the many freedoms they associate with the sort of polity[2] that has evolved in Britain.

It would console others in the North, who feel more comfortable about the Republic of Ireland, that there would be no return to a hard and heavily policed border and further isolation.

Northern Ireland would then, effectively, be an independent state in the European Union, with three times the population of Luxembourg. It might start taking responsibility for itself. Since it could dictate its own taxation system, it could become an interesting place for outside investment. [...]

This is not about the breaking-up of Britain or the uniting of Ireland. It is about rescuing Northern Ireland and the Border counties in the South from further paralysis and estrangement[3].

Colm TÓIBÍN[4], *The Irish Times*, March 2017

**1.** *contrebande* **2.** *régime politique* **3.** isolation **4.** One of Ireland's most popular contemporary writers.

**a.** **Look** at the picture and **comment** on the way some Irish people reacted to Brexit.

**b.** **Read** the article and briefly **explain** what C. Tóibín's suggestion for Northern Ireland is.

**c.** **Find** out what the conditions to this solution would be and **name** all the problems that this idea would solve.

**d.** **Discuss** the statement *"This is not about the breaking-up of Britain or the uniting of Ireland."* (l. 55-56)

## FINAL TASK

**Record the trailer of a TV documentary on the issues related to the Irish border.**

**As a filmmaker, you have directed a documentary about the consequences of Brexit on the Irish border. Record the trailer of your documentary to draw attention to the issues the film deals with.**

1. A documentary aims at raising awareness on certain issues. **Browse** through the file and **choose** 2 or 3 issues related to the Irish border you would like to shed light on.
2. **Prepare** the pitch of your trailer focusing on the historical, geographical and political complexity of the Irish border in the context of Brexit.
3. **Choose** images of the Irish border (from the file or from personal research). **Imagine** a title for your documentary and **prepare** your storyboard.
4. **Compile** all the elements you have at your disposal (images, recordings, street interviews) and **record** your documentary trailer.

BOOST YOUR ENGLISH p. 161

# BOOST YOUR ENGLISH!

## Grammar — Analyser les enjeux d'un sujet d'actualité

- **Utilise la modalité à la forme interrogative pour évoquer un avenir incertain.**

*What **would** happen to the border dwellers in case of a hard Brexit?*
***Could** Ireland be reunited after all those challenges?*
*How **could** violence be avoided in the next few years?*

- **Souligne le lien entre le passé et le présent avec le *present perfect* et des marqueurs temporels.**

*This conflict dates **back to the 1970s**. Even **today**, tensions still exist.*
*The border **has been** invisible for more than **twenty years** and most people still don't see it **now**.*

- **Exprime la notion de contrainte par des verbes ou équivalents modaux.**

*Brexit **forces** us **to** reconsider many aspects of our everyday lives.*
*Customs officers **will not allow** people **to** cross the border so easily.*
*To go to my garden, I would **have to** go from Eire over to Northern Ireland.*
*Irish counties **will be compelled to** change their legislation.*

**1 Reformule les énoncés en utilisant *might*, *could* ou *would* à la forme interrogative.**

**a.** Brexit → change the course of Irish history?
**b.** Irish people → be happier if they were united?
**c.** What → future relations between the U.K. and the E.U.?
**d.** How → Companies → find ways to fill less paperwork?

**2 Choisis la forme verbale qui convient pour exprimer la contrainte.**

**a.** Because of the revived tensions, people [*force to – want to – have to*] deal with fear.
**b.** The 2016 referendum [*has made us – has told us to – has helped us to*] redefine the notion of border.
**c.** Ireland's troubled past [*needs – allows – compels*] historians to tackle this issue subtly.
**d.** Freight companies [*could – will be required to – will not*] pay heavy customs duty.

## Vocabulary — The Irish Border

Tensions and conflicts — Borders — Brexit

**Identity** (AUDIO)
- claim = demand
- disunity
- divide
- Loyalist ≠ Republican
- separatism ≠ unionism

**Violence** (AUDIO)
- armed struggle
- bombing
- guerrilla
- paramilitary
- terrorism

**Fear** (AUDIO)
- alarming
- concerned
- traumatised
- unsafe

- disrupt
- dread

**Administration** (AUDIO)
- application
- citizenship
- diplomacy
- foreign affairs
- paperwork
- passport
- taxes

**Controls** (AUDIO)
- checkpoint
- customs officer
- watchtower
- declare
- register

**Crossing** (AUDIO)
- border dwellers
- customs duty
- freight: *fret, marchandise*
- goods
- immigration

**Making a choice** (AUDIO)
- campaign
- referendum

- wrench

- cast a ballot = vote
- determine
- "leave" ≠ "stay"

**Consequences** (AUDIO)
- aftermath
- estrangement = alienation
- hardship
- uncertain
- upsetting

- disturb
- reshape
- split up

OBJECTIF BAC p. 296-304

Grille d'auto-évaluation

## Sujet type bac

MÉDIATION

Durée : 3h30
Matériel autorisé : le dictionnaire unilingue (non encyclopédique) est autorisé.
Niveau attendu : C1

- **Prenez connaissance des documents A, B et C et traitez le sujet suivant en anglais.**

Taking into account their specificities, show how these documents illustrate the issues raised by the Irish border in times of Brexit. You will pay particular attention to:
– the relationship between Britain and Ireland.
– the apprehension of Brexit in Britain and Ireland.
– Ireland's connexion to both the UK and the European Union.

- **Traduisez en français le passage suivant du document A.**

"We still don't have the full picture of the final terms of the UK's future relationship with the EU, but we know it will not be the same. What's clear to me, as it has been to successive Irish governments, is that Ireland's bilateral relationship with the UK is, and will remain, of vital importance. It is based on deep ties of friendship and family, our common European heritage and values—ties that are deeply cherished." (l. 15-24)

### Document A Ireland and UK's unique relationship

**The special bond between Ireland and the UK will not be undermined by Brexit**

*Simon Coveney is Ireland's Tánaiste (Deputy Prime Minister and Foreign Affairs Minister)*

Today marks an end and a beginning. Forty-seven years after both Ireland and the UK joined the European Economic Community, the latter has chosen to leave and to take a new path. It is a sombre day for some in the UK and a positive one for others. Whatever your perspective, it's clear that the decision to leave the EU will bring change. In Ireland, we will always regret that our closest neighbour and partner will no longer sit with us and the other member states around the EU table in Brussels.

We still don't have the full picture of the final terms of the UK's future relationship with the EU, but we know it will not be the same. What's clear to me, as it has been to successive Irish governments, is that Ireland's bilateral relationship with the UK is, and will remain, of vital importance. It is based on deep ties of friendship and family, our common European heritage and values—ties that are deeply cherished.

Our two nations are so deeply intertwined as a result of generations of personal contacts and interaction. Some 700,000 people from the island of Ireland live in towns and cities the length and breadth of Great Britain. Several million more are Irish citizens by descent. Tens of thousands travel back and forth between the UK and Ireland every single week, and the London-Dublin air corridor is the busiest in Europe, the second busiest in the world. The common travel area, which has long enabled profound connection between our countries, was last year protected through a memorandum of understanding[1] between both governments. British and Irish citizens will continue to move freely to live, to study, to work in any corner of these islands. British citizens resident in Ireland will be free to vote in our upcoming general election—a reciprocal privilege afforded to Irish citizens in the UK.

These deep networks and this freedom of movement drive an economic and trading relationship between Ireland and the UK worth £1.1bn per week. Our desire to continue to foster[2] such close ties will not change, although the level and intensity of this bilateral relationship will inevitably be shaped by future EU-UK arrangements. The closer the relationship between the EU and UK, the easier it will be to keep our two countries close.

Simon COVENEY, *The Guardian*, January 31, 2020

1. agreement protocol
2. cultivate

## Document B The sudden popularity of Irish citizenship after Brexit

**As Brexit looms closer, approximately 80,000 Irish passports were issued to UK residents so far in 2019**

It's a grand day to be Irish. At least, that's what many Britons appear to think.

Approximately 20,000 more first-time passports were issued to UK residents in the first six months of the year than were issued to Irish citizens, according to the Irish Passport Office. It said that 78.744 first-time passports were issued to residents of the UK during the first six months of 2019 compared to the 60,300 passports issued to Irish citizens. Based on those figures, the number of Irish passports being issued to UK residents has now likely exceeded 80,000.

There has been a spike in interest in Irish passports since the UK voted to exit the European Union three years ago. In 2015, there were approximately 46,000 applications from the U.K. There were more than twice as many (98,500) Irish passport applications from UK residents in 2018, two years after the country voted to exit the European Union. [...]

In the wake of the Brexit referendum, Ireland's Department of Foreign Affairs even published a guide to getting an Irish passport in the wake of the vote. In 2016, there were signs of a surge[1] in passport applications hours after the UK referendum result was known. Google UK searches for "getting an Irish passport" spiked 100% in the immediate aftermath of the UK vote to leave the EU, the first such country to do so since the formation of the political and economic union three decades ago. [...]

There are around 430,000 Irish-born people residing in Britain, according to the 2011 Census, but the Department of Foreign Affairs said estimates vary as to how many are second-generation and beyond Irish people. "However, one in four people in Britain have Irish heritage."

It's easier for some Britons than others to get an Irish passport. If you were born outside Ireland to an Irish citizen who was born outside Ireland, you are entitled to become an Irish citizen. [...]

Ireland's Prime Minister Leo Varadkar has been vocal in his defense of the open borders between the British province of Northern Ireland and the Republic of Ireland after the 1998 Good Friday Agreement, which ended three decades of sectarian violence between Protestants and Catholics in Northern Ireland known as The Troubles.

The popularity of Irish passports in the U.K. likely has little to do with its slower pace of life, green hills or friendly reputation—rather, It's a gateway to the rest of Europe.

Quentin FOTTRELL, *marketwatch.com*, September 14, 2019

1. rise

## Document C

Box installed by a group of artists in a street near the House of Parliament in London, in reaction to Brexit in March 2019.

# LET'S BRAINSTORM!

OBJECTIF BAC p. 305-317

## ENVIRONNEMENTS EN MUTATION — Axe 1

**How is Brexit reopening old wounds in Ireland?**

### Questioning Irish identity

- A people haunted by division and violence

→ "Border talk stirs up bad memories in Northern Ireland", *The Guardian*, p. 156 • A return to violence?, *ABC News*, p. 157

- An opportunity to re-define Irish identity

→ "Brexit renews discussions around an unclear border", *USA Today*, p. 155

### Making an invisible border reappear

- The border as a thing of the past

→ "Border talk stirs up bad memories in Northern Ireland", *The Guardian*, p. 156 • "The village on the border", *ITV News* p. 159

- Life prevails over the border

→ *The Rule of the Land*, Garrett CARR, p. 158 • "A real barrier to a Brexit deal", *Wall Street Journal*, p. 154

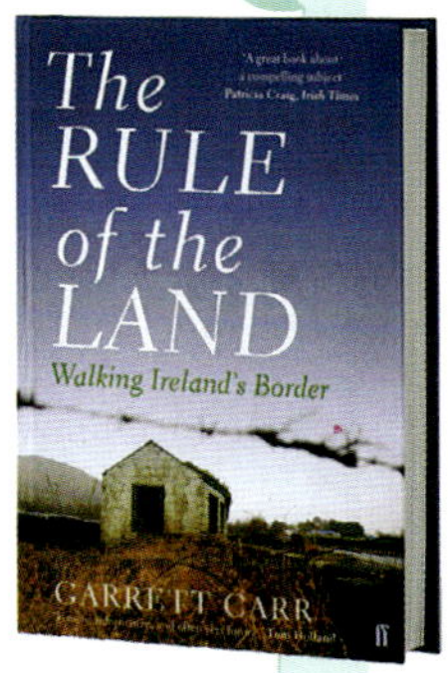


### A threat to the Irish economy

- Disrupting economic exchanges

→ "Brexit data on the Irish border", *AFP*, p. 155 • "Brexit explained", *Channel 4 News*, p. 156

- A threat to local prosperity

→ "The harder the Brexit…", *Intereconomics.eu*, p. 159 • *The Rule of the Land*, Garrett CARR, p. 158

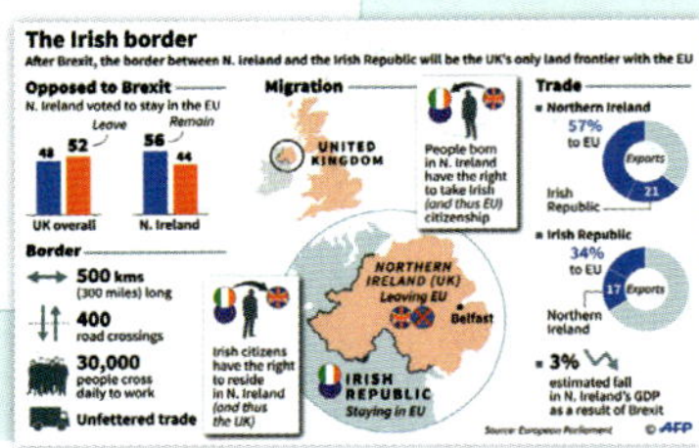


### Division over Brexit

- Northern Ireland's view of Brexit is different from the rest of the UK's

→ "The harder the Brexit…", *Intereconomics.eu*, p. 159 • "Brexit data on the Irish border", *AFP*, p. 155

- A path to independence?

→ "The North must become an independent EU state", *The Irish Times*, p. 160

## Phonology — Questions rhétoriques et accentuation

AUDIO

- Recourir à des **questions rhétoriques**, avec ou sans **réponse**, facilite la compréhension d'un sujet complexe. On marque alors l'importance de ces questions par **l'accentuation** forte du pronom interrogatif.
*But **why** is the Irish border question so important?*
*So **what** are the options?*

- Pour mettre en valeur certains aspects, le locuteur peut **faire une pause** avant d'avancer une conclusion ou un argument pivot (*the point* en anglais), et mettre l'accent sur le mot qui introduit cette conclusion.
*…[Pause] and **there** lies the big problem.*
*…[Pause] now **that's** really the core of the issue.*

**1 Distingue les questions rhétoriques des autres. Prononce chacune avec l'intonation qui convient. Écoute et vérifie.**

a. *But when will Brexit finally be effective?*
b. *Who is the Prime Minister of Great Britain?*
c. *So when are you coming back to Belfast?*
d. *So why is it such a big issue?*

**2 Recopie ces phrases et souligne le mot qui doit être mis en valeur. Prononce-les à voix haute, puis écoute et vérifie.**

a. *This is what it's all about.*
b. *And here lies the real issue.*
c. *So that's why the Irish border is a complex subject.*

Vers le **BAC**

# BUILD YOUR PORTFOLIO

## Painting

*The Raft Project*, Rita DUFFY, 2019

This large painting is based on a famous French classic and depicts the surreal and disastrous situation in which Northern Ireland is left in the aftermath of Brexit.

- **Look** at Rita Duffy's artwork, **read** her comments about it and **explain** how it sums up the overall vulnerability of Ireland in the process of Brexit.

SITE

## Artistic project

*The Border Interpretive Centre*, John BYRNE, 2000

The Border Interpretative Centre is a satirical art project by Irish visual artist John Byrne. In 2000, he decided to transform an old, tiny, decrepit house on the former border line into a museum 'twinned with the Korean Border'.

- **Check** the website of the contest for more information. **Explain** what this project showed about the way the border was perceived back in 2000, and **compare** this point of view to the situation in Ireland after Brexit.

SITE

## Song

*Give Ireland Back to the Irish*, Paul MCCARTNEY And Wings, 1972

“Give Ireland back to the Irish
Don't make them have to take it away
Give Ireland back to the Irish
Make Ireland Irish today.”

- **Listen** to the song and **explain** how the issue of national identity in Ireland is explored.

AUDIO

ÉPREUVE ORALE — GRAND ORAL — Entraîne-toi à l'oral

**Step 1** — **Build up your speech!**

ÉPREUVE ORALE:

- Choose one topic in the mindmap p. 164.
- Pick out two documents in the file and two personal ones to illustrate this issue.
- Prepare your presentation: you must show how these documents relate to the issue you chose.

OBJECTIF BAC p. 305

GRAND ORAL:

- Choose one topic in the mindmap p. 164.
- Find a key question about your topic and write it down. Think about links with other subjects (*HGGSP*).
- Gather arguments and examples from the file.
- Prepare an outline for your presentation and write your note sheet.

OBJECTIF BAC p. 308-309

**Step 2** — **Make your oral presentation in front of two classmates.**

ÉPREUVE ORALE:

- Show your documents to your classmates. Each of you makes their presentation to the others in about five minutes.

OBJECTIF BAC p. 306-307

GRAND ORAL:

- Give your note sheet to your classmates.
- Stand up and make a five-minute presentation to answer your key question.

OBJECTIF BAC p. 310-311

**Step 3** — **Answer your classmates' questions about your presentation.**

SNAPFILE 18

ENVIRONNEMENTS EN MUTATION
AXE 1 : FRONTIÈRE ET ESPACE

# Calexico chronicles

▶ **How do twin cities coexist in a cross-border relationship?**

More on SPEAKEASY NEWS
speakeasy-news.com

**YOUR MISSION**

**Create an animated map to explain the situation of sister cities.**

You are working for Calexico's City Hall and have been asked to create an animated map to introduce the specificities of this border town to newcomers.

FOLLOW THE STEPS!

## 1 The twin cities' unique bond

**Doc 1.**

AUDIO

(Audio: *"Where I come from*: Calexico", *PBS*, 2018)

TEXTE LU

We can all learn from Calexico. You may know where Calexico is on the map, located on the border with Mexico about a two-hour drive east of San Diego. But Calexico is more than a dot on the map; it is a city that draws into sharp focus the often blurred images of lives lived and ideas born where cultures meet, conflict, and merge. Calexico is a city filled with stories reflecting fundamental questions about who we are as Americans, what our values are, and how our democracy works.

Growing up in San Diego, I was introduced to Calexico by my mother, who took us on drives to that town and into northern Baja California. I remember sitting in the backseat of our 1968 Dodge Dart, poking my head out the window and being struck by the contrasts and poetry of the place: stretches of desert broken by long strips of agriculture and canals flowing next to the roads and highway near Calexico that people told me were filled with catfish the size of my little brother. I remember, also, whispering over and over the names Calexico and Mexicali, its sister city, and thinking that the people who came up with those names must have had a magical familiarity with the borderland where Mexico and California merge. A place, as one person interviewed in this book points out, that was not quite the United-States and not quite Mexico, but something else. The sister names well fit the meeting place of the two nation-families.

Peter LAUFER, *Calexico: True Lives of the Borderlands*, 2011

**a. Observe** the book cover and **read** the text. **Find** information about Calexico and **account** for the writer's fascination for this town.

**b. Listen** to the audio and **explain** what brings Calexico and Mexicali together.

**c. Use** both documents to **comment** on the names of Mexicali and Calexico and **explain** the expression *"sister cities"*.

**d. Compare** the two cities' relationship with other areas on the continent.

**e. Comment** on the statement *"A place [that is] not quite the United-States and not quite Mexico, but something else"*. (Text l. 20-22)

**STEP 1** **Start** the background research for your animated map. **Go** online to locate Calexico and **take** notes to **introduce** the city's unique identity.

## Doc 2. Crossing the border to go to school

CBBC, 2019

**a.** **Watch** the video and **sum up** the students' daily routine.

**b.** **Describe** their motivation to cross the border.

**c.** GRAMMAR *"It **might** be in the US, but 85% of the students live in Mexico."* **Comment** on the value of *might* here.

**d.** **Rephrase** the headteacher's viewpoint.

**e.** **Discuss**: *"America is the land of more opportunities."*

## Doc 3.

**a.** **Read** the article and **identify** people's purpose in the border city.

**b.** **Explain** why they have to be there so early.

**c.** GRAMMAR **Focus** on l. 13-18 and **spot** all the grammatical elements which help the journalist describe the people's routine.

**d.** **Comment** on the role of such a place in economic and agricultural sectors.

**AT HOME** **Read** the whole article online and **select** meaningful personal stories to be included in your animated map. ARTICLE

### 12 hours in a Calexico doughnut shop: After crossing the border, workers gather here before sunrise

For decades, thousands of people who live in Mexicali have entered the US legally through the port of entry[1] in the middle of the night and waited in downtown Calexico for rides to the fields in Southern California and Arizona. A shorter line at the point of entry means a longer wait on dark street corners or inside one of just a few all-hours restaurants in the border city, which is home to about 40,000 people.

For many, Donut Avenue has become a way station along this long commute from Mexicali to the Imperial, Palo Verde and Coachella valleys. […]

**It's 12:04 a.m.** and a worker slouches[2] forward in a booth[3] at Donut Avenue. He rests his head on the cool table, taking a quick nap before heading out to the fields.

People who commute from Mexicali to the fields of Southern California and Arizona are generally U.S. citizens or legal permanent residents. Most workers won't start until sunrise, but they cross the border in the middle of the night to avoid long lines at the Calexico port of entry. Sometimes, it takes them half an hour to cross; other times, it takes up to four hours.

The first workers to arrive at Donut Avenue tonight are those harvesting corn in Westmorland, 31 miles northwest of Calexico, and Calipatria, 33 miles north. Their shift begins at 2 a.m. Afterwards, they will cross the border and return to Mexicali to sleep, shower, eat and begin the cycle again. […]

**It's 3:02 a.m.** and the street corner outside Donut Avenue has become an unofficial work recruitment site.

Rebecca PLEVIN, *The Desert Sun*, August 2019

**1.** *douane* **2.** être avachi **3.** section of a diner

### STEP 2

**Complete** your map: **Add** an animation to symbolise the border and **include** one or two short vocal memos about students' and job seekers' situation at the border.

### BOOST YOUR SKILLS!

**Exprimer des liens**

- Précise par du lexique la nature de ces liens : *Where cultures **meet, conflict** and **merge**.* • *The **bond** is very strong.* • *Like **hand in hand*** • *The **meeting** place of…*
- Utilise des comparatifs : *Calexico is **more than**…* • *A small community **compared to**…* • *Mexicali and Calexico are **the same** thing.*
- Souligne avec des modaux la co-dépendance des lieux : *Calexico **couldn't** thrive without Mexicali* • *I don't think Calexico **would** have been here if…*

# 2 Calexico's big sister

## INDUSTRIAL CITIES ON THE BORDER

**This Mexican city was transformed by factories. Its people pay a heavy price.**

When Luz María Ortega Villa was growing up in Mexicali in the 1960s and '70s, she remembers seeing unspoiled vistas[1] of mountains in the distance. [...]

This majestic backdrop began to fade into a smoggy haze in the mid-1980s as factories proliferated and the city's population swelled[2]. Mexicali has kept expanding ever since.

**As the manufacturing industry grew, Mexicali's population surged. It dwarfs Calexico, just north of the border.**

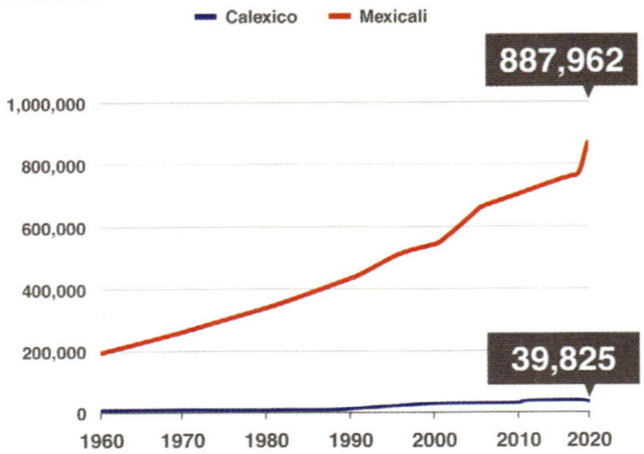


Source: Mexican National Institute of Statistics and Geography (INEGI): National Population and Housing Census; California Demographic Research Unit; U.S. Census Bureau decennial Census and American Community Surveys.

In her lifetime, maquiladoras have transformed what was once a farming town into an industrial city that is one of Mexico's main manufacturing hubs on the border. Mexicali's population has more than doubled since 1980 and is now about 750,000. Including other nearby towns and rural communities, the area is home to more than 1 million people. [...]

The factories in Mexicali vary from smoke-spewing behemoths[3] to assembly plants that appear to release little pollution. And while some residents say they are concerned about the environmental footprint, the maquiladoras are also widely seen as the city's vital economic engine.

In all, the city has about 180 maquiladoras. They employ more than 75,000 people and drive the rest of the border economy. [...]

Mexicali emerged as a major manufacturing center decades ago with the arrival of American companies that were looking to take advantage of cheap labor and government incentives. [...]

Since 1993, U.S. imports from Mexico have grown 687 percent. Mexico exported more than $400 billion worth of goods globally last year, and about three-fourths of those goods, $314 billion worth, were shipped to the United States.

Mexicali has fewer maquiladoras than Tijuana, which according to a business directory has a total of 476, but it's still one of the biggest industrial cities on the border.

A majority of Mexicali's factories are run by US companies, followed by Mexican companies and businesses from South Korea, Japan and Europe. [...]

On a typical hazy day in Mexicali, the soot from factories mixes with dust swirling from unpaved roads and columns of smoke rising from trash heaps[4].

The dirty air floats across the border fence and through the city of Calexico, where residents say it's frustrating living beside a city where pollution isn't effectively regulated.

Ian JAMES, *The Desert Sun*, December 2018

**CULTURE SPOT**

**Maquiladoras** are US factories built on the other side of the Mexican border in order to reduce production costs.

**WORDS**

- boundaries
- law enforcement
- tie = bond

- accountable
- intertwined
- one of a kind
- tenacious /tɪˈneɪʃəs/

- bridge a gap
- gather = bring together
- provide for

1. view 2. expand 3. giants 4. pile

**a. Observe** the graph and **find** elements in the article to **account** for the different evolution of the two cities.

**b. Describe** the maquiladoras phenomenon and **explain** its economic benefits. **Comment** on its impact on the region.

**c.** TRANSLATION **Translate** l. 34-40. **Pay** attention to tenses and time clauses.

**d. Comment** on the environmental issues mentioned in the article.

**STEP 3**

**Carry on** working on your map. **Include** a short video to **explain** maquiladoras' impact at the border.

**BOOST YOUR SKILLS!**

**Analyser l'impact d'un phénomène économique**

- Appuie-toi sur des données chiffrées : ***75,000*** *people* • *More than* ***$400 billion*** • *About* ***three-fourths*** *of...*
- Utilise le champ lexical de l'expansion : *Factories* ***proliferated*** • *Imports have* ***grown*** *687 percent* • *It has more than* ***doubled***.
- Dresse un bilan au *present perfect* : *Mexicali* ***has kept*** *expanding.* • *Maquiladoras* ***have transformed*** *a farming town into...*

# 3 A borderless community

## Doc 1.

Borderland communities reacting to President Trump's visit to Calexico to defend his wall project in April 2020

**Americans and Mexicans living at the border are more connected than divided**

During my travels, I started thinking of the space between the two countries as a kind of "third nation." I confess, I've never heard anyone in a border city refer to their turf[1] as a third nation.

I've often been told by people who live binational lives that they forget which side of the border they're on. But in my experience, the single most common expression of cross-border connection is when people assert that they have more in common with one another than with citizens of their countries. [...]

A 2016 survey of residents in the twin cities confirmed that the borderland is increasingly becoming "one giant economically integrated, bicultural society." An Arizona respondent emphasized the importance of maintaining connections across the line: "Our lifeline is across the border... Without Mexicans, we don't exist. Our life is sucked away." [...]

Interviews from the survey show that unlike many people in the U.S., border residents do not equate wall-building with national security. One man, originally from Mexico but now living in Texas, said that he was not opposed to more Border Patrol officers, nor the presence in Mexico of U.S. military helping in the drug war. But walls he resisted, because "A wall is a symbol of discrimination, racism, segregation, not a solution for security, or for reducing violence."

U.S. Rep. Beto O'Rourke, a Democrat from El Paso, captured a sentiment widely held by survey respondents: "It says something really beautiful that the border, two countries, two languages, two cultures, at this point become essentially one people."

Michael DEAR, *The Conversation*, March 2017

1. land

**a. Observe** the picture and **guess** what the demonstrators might be claiming.

**b. Read** the article and **define** the journalist's concept of a "third nation".

**c. Pick out** people's arguments about the wall.

**d. Comment** on the sociological specificities of the borderland.

## Doc 2. Erasing the border with art

VIDÉO

Volunteers painting the border fence between the USA and Mexico (Video: *LatiNation*, 2017)

**a. Observe** the picture and **guess** the volunteers' relationship to the border.

**b. Watch** the video and **describe** the artist's background. **Explain** how it influenced her connection to the border.

**c. Explain** the origins of her project and **comment** on its goals.

**d. Discuss**: Art can change our perception of borders.

STEP 4 **Prepare** new animations to **complete** your map, **focusing** on the sociological aspects of the borderland communities. You can **include** photographs and people's stories to illustrate their bond with the border.

FINAL STEP

**Gather** all the slides and animations you have created and **format** your animated map, adding titles and captions when necessary. **Play** the slideshow and **present** your map to **explain** the specificities of the sister cities.

**You've completed your mission. Well done!**

# PRÉPARER LA 1RE PARTIE DU GRAND ORAL

OBJECTIF BAC p. 308-311

Le jour du **Grand oral**, tu devras préparer une **question** pour chacune de tes deux spécialités et éventuellement **un support** à remettre au jury. Dans le cadre de la spécialité LLCER AMC, tu peux choisir de faire **une partie** de ta présentation **en anglais**. Ta question devra alors être formulée **dans les deux langues**.

Tu présenteras tes deux questions au jury, qui en choisira une. Tu auras alors **20 min** pour préparer ton oral, et un éventuel support. Ton oral comportera alors 3 parties :
– une présentation orale de ta question (5 min) ;
– un échange avec le jury pour approfondir la question (10 min) ;
– un échange sur ton projet d'orientation, en lien avec ta présentation (5 min).

Voici comment préparer la **première partie** de ton oral :

## 1 Choisir et formuler ta question

**a.** Si le thème de cette unité te plaît et te questionne, tu peux le choisir pour le Grand oral. Appuie-toi sur les documents vus en cours et sur d'autres issus de la p. 171 ou de tes recherches personnelles pour élaborer ta problématique.

**b.** Choisis également cette question en fonction de ton projet d'orientation : études de géographie, de sociologie, de sciences politiques etc.

Il s'agit de donner un point de vue nuancé à partir de ce que tu auras étudié dans l'année. Choisis des éléments qui te permettent de mettre ton idée principale en perspective pour en montrer les enjeux et formuler ta question : Calexico - Mexicali : atouts et défis *Calexico - Mexicali: assets and challenges*

- Appuie-toi sur les mots clés de question : *atouts* • *défis* (ici deux termes en tension).
- Note les idées, exemples, arguments, sources que tu peux mobiliser.
- Réfléchis à la façon dont tu pourras articuler cette question à ton projet d'orientation.

## 2 Préparer la présentation de ta question

**a.** Réfléchis aux réponses que tu peux apporter à ta question et organise-les en un plan de 2 ou 3 parties thématiques.

**b.** Prépare une introduction qui explique pourquoi tu as choisi de traiter cette question en lien avec la thématique « environnements en mutation ».

**c.** Développe ensuite chaque idée en l'illustrant d'exemples précis tirés de tes sources sur les villes frontières.

**d.** Conclus en suggérant des pistes, fais le lien avec ton orientation ou un autre point du programme ou de tes spécialités.

- *I've always been interested in...* • *I'm considering studying...* • *This is the reason why I've chosen to focus on...*
- *First, the twin-cities are linked by...* • *However, they face challenges such as...*
- *In fact...* • *It's quite possible to suggest that...*
- *To conclude, the complexity of the sister cities is deeply-rooted in/closely-linked to...* • *And therefore, it is likely to...*

## 3 Préparer ton support

**a.** Prépare en amont de l'examen un support visuel que tu pourras reproduire durant ta présentation, et qui servira à la fois de point d'appui, de fil directeur ou d'illustration de ta présentation.

**b.** Utilise des flèches ou tirets pour clarifier la structure.

**c.** Pense à mobiliser tes propres connaissances interculturelles pour aller plus loin dans ta réflexion.

- Ton support peut prendre diverses formes : dessin, carte mentale, plan détaillé, croquis, schéma, tableau...
- Si tu as choisi de faire ta présentation en anglais, pense à mobiliser les termes d'actualité en lien avec ton sujet : *Immigration policies* • *NAFTA* • *labor force* • *difference with the US-Canadian border?*

# BUILD YOUR PORTFOLIO

## Book

*Where we come from*, Oscar Cásares, 2019

The novel tells the story of Orly, a teenager spending the summer in Brownsville, a border town, with his Mexican family.

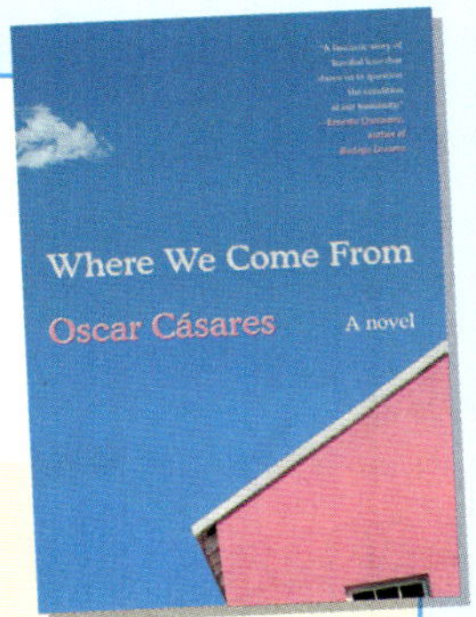


- **Read** the book and **explain** what it shows about people's unique relationship to the border.

## Poem

"Calexico", Karla Cordero, 2019

> My city is made of people
> Who know the taste of sun on their backs [...]
> How hard work speaks through fields of lettuce.

Karla Cordero is an American artist and activist, who grew up in Calexico.

- **Listen** to the poem and **explain** why life in Calexico can be a great source of inspiration. VIDÉO

## Art installation

"Why a Designer Turned the U.S.-Mexico Border into an Art Installation", *The New Yorker*, 2019

In 2019, Ronald Rael and Virginia San Fratello decided to use their architectural and artistic skills to convey a message on the uselessness of building borders.

- **Observe** the photograph and **explain** how art can be a committed act. **Watch** the report and **explain** the artist's goal with such an installation. VIDÉO

## Song

"Crystal Frontier", Calexico, 2008

Calexico is an American band from Arizona.

> Ramon tightens up his leather belt
> And slips through a hole in the fence
> He can get you anything you want
> Might cost you a life, might cost you
> The whole price of freedom here...
> On the Crystal Frontier

- **Watch** the video and **pay** attention to the lyrics. **Comment** on the message conveyed by Calexico in this song. VIDÉO

## Entraîne-toi à l'oral — ÉPREUVE ORALE

### Step 1 Build up your speech!

- Choose one aspect of the topic that you are particularly interested in: The unique bond of Calexico and Mexicali, life in a borderless community...
- Pick out documents to build your portfolio: choose from the file, this page, or from your personal references.
- Prepare your presentation: show how these documents relate to the topic you chose. OBJECTIF BAC p. 305

### Step 2 Make your presentation in front of two classmates.

- Show the chosen documents to your friends and explain your point in about five minutes. Make sure you say how they illustrate the topic. OBJECTIF BAC p. 306-307

### Step 3 Answer your classmates' questions about your presentation.

# Renewable USA

▶ **How are Americans facing the ecological transition challenge?**

**FINAL TASK** Take part in a podcast about the ecological situation and challenges in the USA.



## 1 A federal challenge

**Doc 1.**

AUDIO

(Audio: "The Green New Deal", *NPR*, 2019)

Democrat congresswoman Alexandria Ocasio-Cortez supporting the Green New Deal, February 2019

**a. Listen** to the audio and **pick out** information about the Green New Deal.

**b. Explain** to what extent this Deal is different from the previous plans.

**c. Comment** on the environmentalists' position.

**d. Discuss** the opposition this project may arouse.

**CULTURE SPOT**

In March 2019, U.S. Senate Republicans **defeated** the **"Green New Deal"** resolution that called to tackle climate change with 57 against the resolution in the 100-member chamber.

## Doc 2.

**Why is climate skepticism so successful in the United States?**

Despite massive worldwide demonstrations and increasing global awareness and anxiety, the December 2019 UN Climate Change Conference (a.k.a., COP25) in Madrid failed spectacularly.

The reason? A handful of countries blocked significant action, in particular the United States, Brazil, Australia and Saudi Arabia. A month before the COP25, President Trump formally confirmed the exit of the United States from the Paris climate agreement—just one policy change among more than 90 others aimed at rolling back environmental regulations. [...]

Even though Americans are less likely to be concerned about climate change than the rest of the world (by at least about 10 to 20 percentage points), a majority (59%) still see it as a serious threat—a 17-point increase in six years (Pew Research). But the devil is in the details. Only about 27% of Republicans say climate change is a major threat, compared with 83% of Democrats, a 56-percentage point difference!

**Republicans and Democrats are deeply divided on whether climate change should be a top priority**

*% of U.S. adults who say dealing with global climate change should be a top priority for the president and Congress*

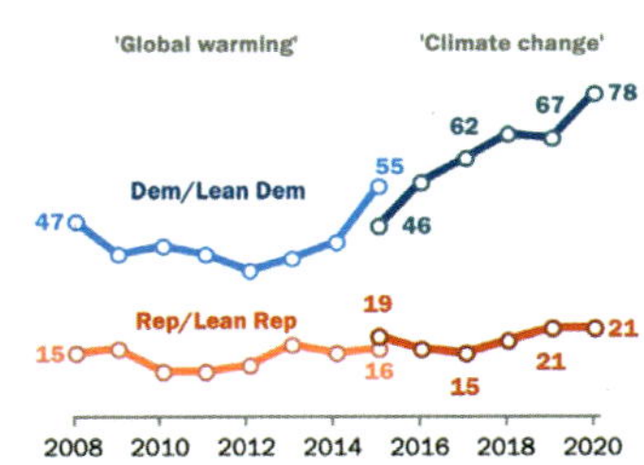


Note: In 2014 and earlier, respondents were asked about dealing with "global warming." In 2015, half the sample each was asked about "global warming" or "global climate change."
Source: Survey conducted Jan. 8-13, 2020.
PEW RESEARCH CENTER

This in turn raises another question: why are American Republicans more skeptical about climate change than right-wing voters in other countries? The first reason has to do with polarization[1] in politics and identity. [...]

The fact that progressive Democrats took on the issue of global warming early on—former vice president Al Gore was a leading voice on the issue—and that the solutions they offered had to do with statist measure such as carbon taxes, a cap-and-trade[2] system, or energy rationing resulted in further politicization of the issue. [...]

This is fertile ground for right-wing think-tanks and lobbyists to sow doubt in the minds of conservatives who have a cognitive bias against climate change. A recent study found that videos challenging the scientific consensus on climate change were outnumbered by those that supported it.

Confronted with the reality of natural disasters and rising temperatures, most Republicans no longer deny climate change, rather they deny that humans are responsible, and warn that it will affect the economy. [...]

This idea that nature offers vast untapped reserves that will yield[3] perpetual and painless growth is evocative of what historian Richard Slotkin called the Frontier's "bonanza economics". It is an old American story that goes back to the Puritans: that the wilderness had to be conquered and transformed, that the Anglo-Saxon race was defined by its ability to exploit it, which also justified the displacement of indigenous people who did not work the land.

J. VIALA, *The Conversation*, January 2020

### WORDS

- burning/topical issue
- environmental policy

- divisive = conflicting
- innovative = pioneering
- unconventional

- hinder
- wear out = exploit

### CULTURE SPOT

The **Paris Agreement**'s goal is to keep the increase in global temperature to 1.5°C on the long term. The 195 countries signing the agreement must set emissions targets to reach this goal. In 2017, former President Donald Trump withdrew the United States from the agreement. President elected Joe Biden reinstated the US into it in January 2021.

**1.** division into sharply contrasting groups of opinions
**2.** quotas
**3.** give

**a.** **Look** at the line graph and **comment** on Republicans' and Democrats' views on climate change.

**b.** **Read** the article. **Explain** the context of the COP25, its outcome and the reasons for it.

**c.** GRAMMAR **Find** elements in the article to account for the differences you noticed in the graph. ► p. 179

**d.** **Focus** on l. 58-74 and **explain** the reference to the "Frontier" in this context.

**e.** Using information from the article, **give** a possible answer to the question in the title.

**AT HOME** **Look** for information about Al Gore and **be** ready to **present** his involvement regarding the environmental issue. SITE

**YOUR TASK** As a citizen concerned about climate change, **post** a short video on your vlog to **explain** the polarisation of the issue in the USA.

### BOOST YOUR SKILLS!

**Présenter des avis divergents**

- Expose les points de vue au discours rapporté : *Backers* ***say*** *they want to... • Organisers* ***claimed****... • Republicans no longer* ***deny****...*
- Souligne les divergences avec des tournures emphatiques : *Americans are* ***deeply*** *divided on... • It* ***does*** *call for more...*
- Utilise des comparatifs : *One policy among* ***more than*** *90... • Americans are* ***less*** *likely to...* ***than****... • 27% of Republicans...,* ***compared with*** *83% of Democrats.*
GRAMMAR ► p. 179

## Doc 1.

**Clean energy firms lobby Congress as much as dirty firms do**

When lawmakers began a heated debate about climate change legislation in 2008, electric utilities Southern Co. and Pacific Gas and Electric Co. spent tens of millions on lobbying efforts.

Southern spent $14 million in lobbying related to climate change that year, while PG&E, which openly backed cap-and-trade legislation[1], spent $27 million and had a carbon footprint 40 times smaller than Southern. [...]

"Both dirty and clean firms are active in lobbying, suggesting that while dirty firms lobby to maintain the status quo, clean firms view environmental regulation as an opportunity to gain firm-level advantages," Magali Delmas, Jinghui Lim and Nicholas Nairn-Birch, researchers at UCLA, said in their report.

The authors analyzed lobbying records from 2006 and 2009 and greenhouse gas emissions data from 2004 and 2008. They concluded that companies with strong positions for or against climate legislation dole out[2] the most cash to sway[3] Congress. However, the motivation behind lobbying is different. [...]

"Although confirming the stereotype that dirtier firms are more politically active, our findings suggest that greener firms are also vying[4] for political influence," the report reads. Pro-environment companies are happy to accept the reputational benefits of sounding green without aggressively lobbying for climate action. The findings seem to contradict that assertion. [...]

The study did not examine political lobbying done through trade associations. While the law binds trade groups to disclose their lobbying expenses, it doesn't compel them to disclose what member companies contributed to their lobbying budgets.

The authors found that four industries—automobiles and parts, basic resources, oil and gas, and utilities—devote the majority of their lobbying dollars to climate change topics.

Benjamin HULAC, *Scientific American*, September 2016

1. quotas 2. give 3. influence 4. compete

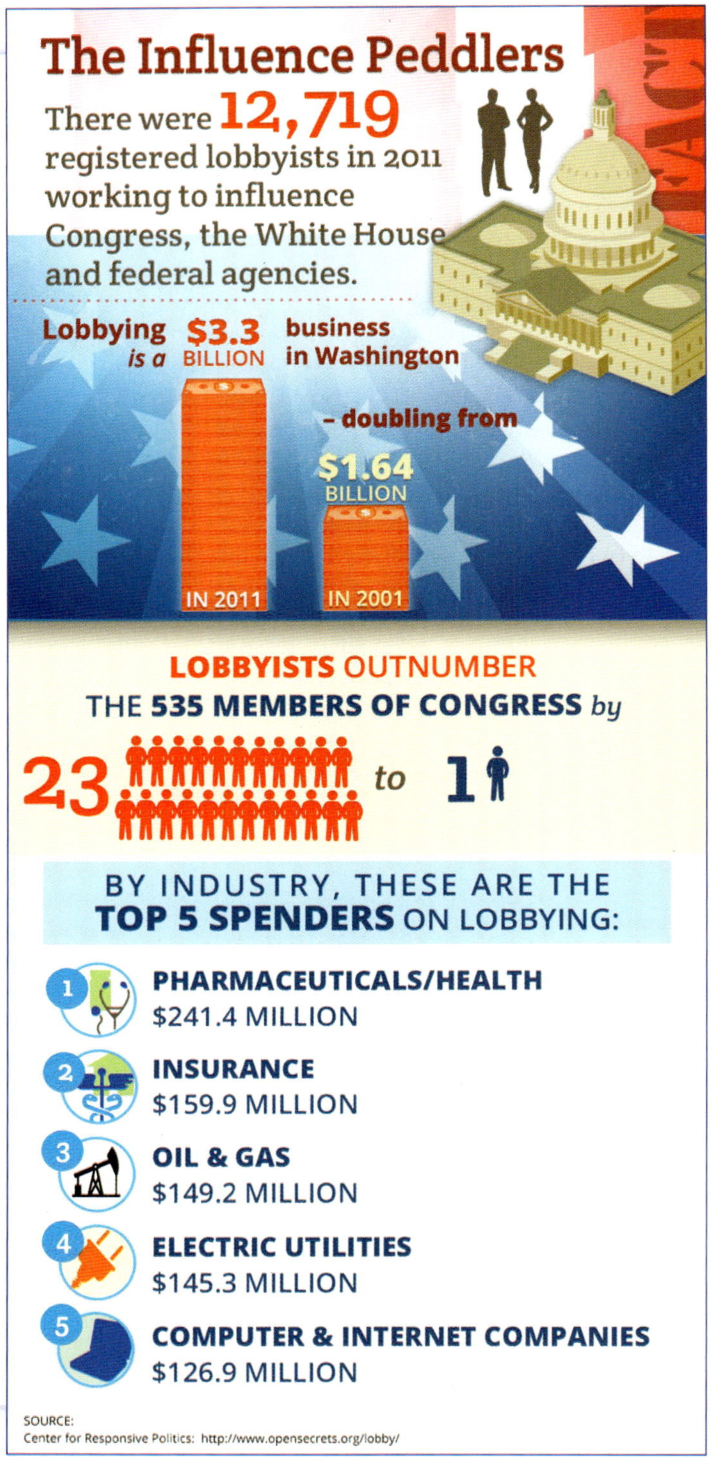


a. **Analyse** and **comment** on the content of the infographic.

b. **Read** the article and **find out** how active lobbyists are in both clean and dirty energy firms.

c. **Compare** the reasons why these firms resort to lobbying.

d. VOCABULARY *"Lobbyists **outnumber** the 535 members of Congress by 23 to 1."*. **Explain** the structure and meaning of the word in bold. What does it say about the influence of lobbying in the USA? ► p. 179

**CULTURE SPOT**

**Lobbying** consists in trying to convince governments to take policy actions that would give the lobbying company or corporation an advantage. It has a tremendous weight on American political life.

LANDMARKS ► p. 279

## Doc 2.

**Democrats' 'Green New Deal' is a Crazy New Deal that would be a disaster for us all**

The radical and impractical plan could suck trillions of dollars out of our economy, raise costs of much of what we buy, wipe out millions of jobs and plunge our country into a recession or perhaps even a depression. It would be a self-inflicted wound causing enormous harm to us all. [...]

The resolution aims to accomplish its ambitious goals by eliminating virtually all fossil fuels from U.S. electricity generation within 10 years. That would destroy at least 3.4 million jobs in the oil, natural gas and coal industries.

The radical plan would replace fossil fuels by building hundreds or even thousands of costly new renewable energy facilities across the country. It also calls for building high-speed rail and eliminating as many gasoline-powered vehicles "as is technologically feasible."

All this would hit American families and businesses hard in the wallet – not just with increased taxes to fund the Green New Deal but with dramatically higher prices of much of what we buy.

Renewable energy sources like wind and solar power are two to five times more expensive than existing conventional energy sources like natural gas. [...]

If manufacturers and all industries are forced to go "green," the cost of producing products in the United States will increase so substantially that it would be virtually impossible for American companies to beat their global competitors.

Justin HASKINS, *Fox News*, February 2019

**WORDS**

- defensive tactic
- political strategy
- wry/harsh criticism

- biased ≠ unbiased
- fallacious /fəˈleɪʃəs/
- hypocritical
- manipulative
- paradoxical

- disapprove of
- serve personal interests

## Doc 3.

Chappatte, *New York Times*, 2018

## Doc 4.

# THE NEW REPUBLIC

### Corporate America Is Terrified of the Green New Deal

There is a "major shift" afoot in corporate America on climate change, according to Axios. On Monday, energy reporter Amy Harder reported that major companies "across virtually all sectors of the economy, including big oil producers, are beginning to lobby Washington, D.C., to put a price on carbon dioxide emissions." These companies, in other words, are asking the government to make them pay more in taxes in an effort to solve global warming. [...] They want a carbon tax because it doesn't threaten the industry's very existence and allows them to keep polluting—so long as they pay for it. [...]

A carbon tax does not appear in the Green New Deal—at least, not the version popularized by Congresswoman Alexandria Ocasio-Cortez and Senator Ed Markey. [...] Even Washington Governor Jay Inslee—who is running for president explicitly on climate change—doesn't include a carbon tax in his $9 trillion climate jobs plan.

There are many reasons for the absence of a tax in these plans, but the main one appears to be that it doesn't guarantee emissions reductions. Instead, the main strategy must be to convert the economy to clean energy and—eventually—to wipe out fossil fuels.

Emily ATKIN, *The New Republic*, May 2019

**a.** **Focus** on both the title and source of **doc. 2**. What can you infer from this information?

**b.** **Read** and **pick out** the problems related to a Green policy according to the author. **Comment** on this viewpoint.

**c.** **Read doc. 4** and **explain** the paradoxical questions raised by carbon taxes.

**d.** TRANSLATION **Translate** l. 31-38. **Pay** attention to the translation of the adverbs.

**e.** **Describe** the cartoon (**doc. 3**) and **explain** how it sheds light on the issues raised in the article (**doc. 4**).

**BOOST YOUR SKILLS!**

**Souligner des incohérences**

- Reformule les arguments avancés : ***According** to Axios.* • ***In other words...***
- Utilise des marqueurs d'opposition : ***Instead*** • ***Rather than...***

**YOUR TASK** As a Green activist, **react** to the Fox News article. **Write** a tweet to question their position.

EXPLORE

# 3 States' and cities' commitment

## Doc 1. Beyond federal decisions

**a.** **Watch** the video and **pick out** information about the reason for the demonstration.

**b.** **Explain** the governors' and mayors' reactions to Donald Trump's decision regarding the Paris Agreement.

**c.** TRANSLATION *"**By** up to 28%", "**by** 2045".* How would you translate each "by"?

**d.** **Discuss**: To what extent can states' environmental policies balance federal ones?

VIDÉO

Video: *France 24 English*, 2017

## Doc 2.

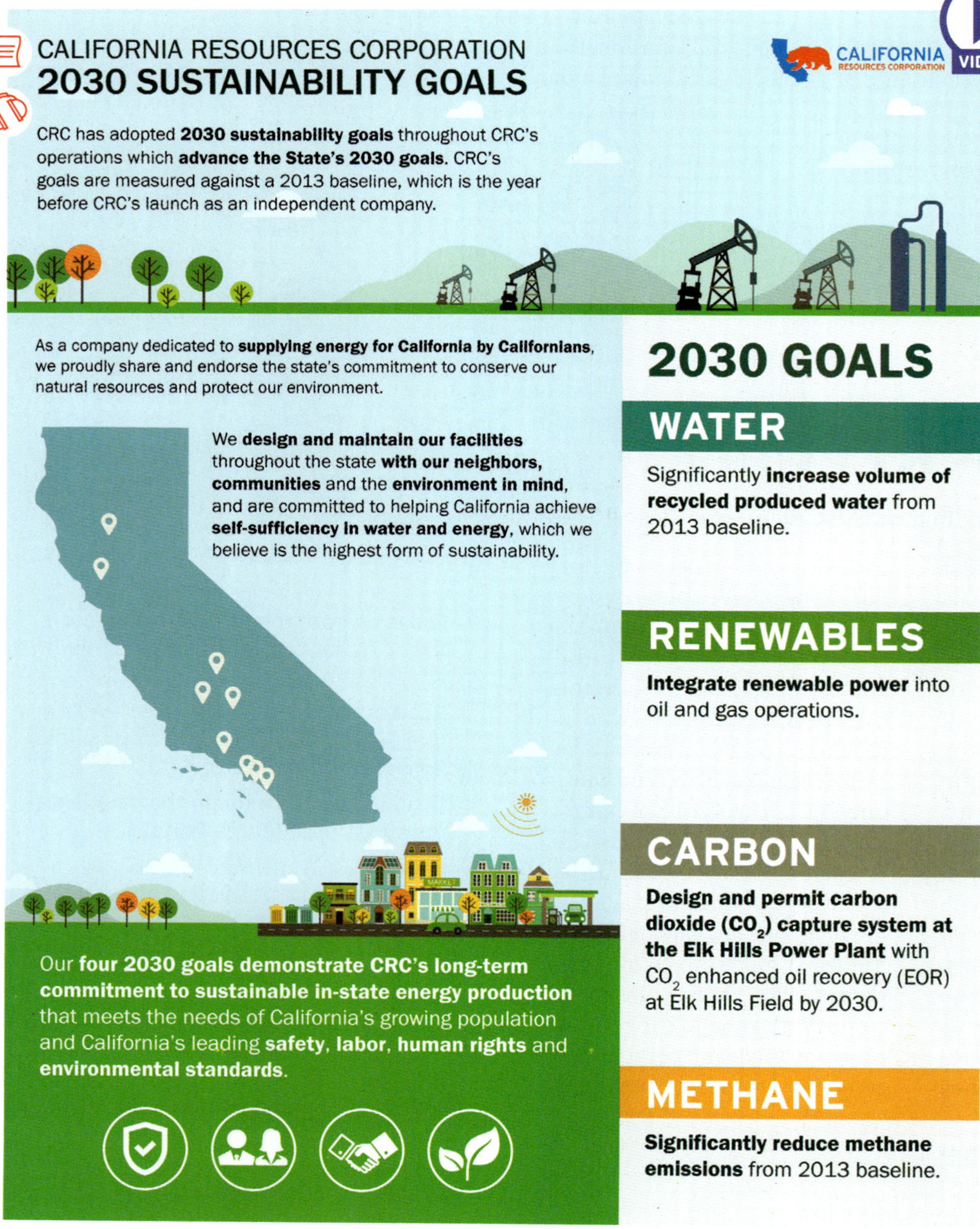


Infographic: *California Resources Corporation* (Video: "Sustainable California", *CalMatters*, 2018)

**a.** **Watch** the video and **pick out** California's green actions since the 1960s. How would you define the state's position regarding ecology?

**b.** **Read** the infographic and **take** notes about the "sustainability goals" presented.

**c.** **Explain** how these goals are in keeping with the resolutions mentioned in the video.

**d.** RHETORIC **Focus** on the tone of the video. How does it tend to make the Californian model an example to follow?

### WORDS

- commitment = dedication
- inception = beginning
- mandate = mission

- adamant = uncompromising
- ambitious = aspirational
- tough-minded = determined

- curb = limit
- improve
- set high standards
- up the ante /'ænti/ = raise the stakes

## Doc 3.

# WHY 1.5°?

The Paris Climate Agreement (Paris Agreement), signed by nearly every country, commits signatories to limit global temperature rise to well below 2 degrees Celsius (3.6°F) and to aspire to limit global temperature rise to 1.5 degrees Celsius (2.7°F). New York City's Executive Order 26, signed by Mayor de Blasio on June 2, 2017, commits the City to develop a pathway to achieve the greenhouse gas emissions reductions necessary to align with the principles of the Paris Agreement and a 1.5 degree Celsius outcome.

The difference between current global warming trends and a 1.5 degree Celsius outcome may seem inconsequential, but the difference in impacts would be dramatic. If the world collectively limits warming to 1.5 degrees, we will see reduced impacts from climate change relative to the risks we face in a warmer world. For example, current climate projections from the NYC Panel on Climate Change show that:

- NYC faces increased sea level rise, flooding, precipitation, and a greater frequency of more intense storms from climate change. This will result in heightened risks for residents, buildings, and public infrastructure. By the 2050s, high-end projections show sea levels may rise by up to 30 inches. [...]
- If climate change goes unabated, NYC can expect an increase in average temperatures and frequency of heat-waves that would change the livability of the city and put vulnerable populations further at risk. On the high-end for the 2050s, average temperatures are projected to rise by up to 6.6°F (3.7°C) in the NYC metropolitan region. [...]

Aligning with a 1.5 degree Celsius outcome is about preventing the worst projected climate impacts, both locally and globally. The actions necessary to ensure a 1.5 degree Celsius outcome will mean a future where New Yorkers can breathe cleaner air, live in more comfortable homes, enjoy access to safe and diverse modes of sustainable transportation, and reside in a city resilient to severe weather effects. This is the NYC we are building today. [...]

Achieving the City's climate objectives is no easy task and will require active participation by New Yorkers to transform the buildings we live in, the places we work, the ways we travel, and the goods we consume. The City must prioritize resources, policies, and programs that facilitate this transition.

*NYC Mayor's Office of Sustainability*, 2020

**a. Read** the text and **find out** what the "1.5°C" refers to.

**b. Explain** the consequences if the 1.5°C outcome was not achieved by 2050.

**c.** PHONOLOGY **Pronounce** the words *"increased"* and *"increase"* (l. 18 and 25). **Identify** their nature and **comment** on the stress fall. ► p. 182

**d. Focus** on l. 29-38 and **give** details about NYC's plan (actions, actors, scale, impact...).

**e. Discuss:** How can local initiatives make a difference?

**YOUR TASK** As a NYC environmentalist, you are given the opportunity to speak for a minute on the local radio news.

DIFFÉRENCIATION

**WAY 1** **Explain** the goals the city has set and what is likely to happen in a near future.

**WAY 2** **Explain** the city's goals and **praise** what locals and officials are determined to achieve.

### BOOST YOUR SKILLS!

**Saluer un engagement**

- Envisage les conséquences de l'inaction : *The difference **would** be dramatic* • *That **would** change the livability of the city.* GRAMMAR p. 179
- Souligne les actions engagées avec le gérondif : ***Achieving** the City's objectives is...* • ***Aligning** with a 1.5° outcome is about **preventing**...*
- Mets en avant les objectifs : *It **aims to** continue...* • *The US **goal of** reducing emissions* • *The Plan **seeks to** reduce...*
- Souligne ton adhésion par des tournures assertives : *I can **assure** you that we will...* • ***No one ever** accused us of...*

# 4 A rising individual concern

## Doc 1.

**Americans really want the US to adopt renewable energy like wind and solar power, while rejecting fossil fuels like coal**

A new *Insider* poll found that a large majority of Americans strongly favor cleaner sources of energy over fossil fuels—and it's a belief that transcends party lines.

The data shows that both self-identified Democrats and Republicans support the idea of the nation transitioning towards renewable sources of energy.

Solar and wind power were the top two preferred alternative energy sources among both groups of respondents, while coal was ranked dead last. [...]

The use of renewable energy sources like wind and solar power has doubled in the last decade, according to the US Energy Information Administration, and federal and state policies combined with the declining cost of production drove much of the growth.

Natural gas, which is a cleaner-burning fossil fuel, overtook coal as the nation's top source of electricity in 2016, highlighting the energy transition currently underway in the United States.

However, the Trump administration has loosened environmental regulations and sought to open up more public lands to drilling, and in June it threw a lifeline to the struggling coal industry by easing restrictions on coal-burning power plants. [...]

Yet as the federal government pulls back from combating climate change under the Trump administration, states and cities are increasingly filling the void, setting the US in the direction the public favors on reducing emissions and developing cleaner sources of energy.

Joseph ZEBALLOS-ROIG, Angela WANG, *Business Insider*, October 2019

**WORDS**

- consumer society
- wind/solar/ wave power

- eye-opening
- groundbreaking

- be eager to = willing to
- be involved in
- raise awareness

**a. Read** the article and **take** notes on the American population's position regarding renewable energies.

**b. Compare** their position to the 2019 government's one. **Comment** on the paradox.

**c. Explain** how the election of Joe Biden may be a glimmer of hope regarding this issue.

## Doc 2. Personal commitment

**a. Watch** the video and **pick out** information about Rob Greenfield's goals on his bike trip. **Explain** the reasons for it.

**b. Comment** on the average American's daily waste. How does Greenfield account for it?

**c. Give** your opinion on this statement: "*I don't expect anybody at home to do just this.*" Would that be impossible?

Rob GREENFIELD, *Zero Waste*, 2016

## FINAL TASK

**Take part in a podcast about the ecological situation and challenges in the USA.**

**You host a podcast on National Public Radio. Today, you invited members of Congress, NYC Mayor, and members of an environmental association to talk about ecological issues and challenges in the USA.**

1. **Choose** your role (host, member of Congress NYC Mayor, member of the association) and **browse** through the file to **write** down the points you want to focus on.
2. As the host: **Introduce** your guests and **present** the current situation in the USA regarding ecological plans and challenges.
3. As a guest, **prepare** your arguments according to your role (position towards green deals; Congress's polarisation; lobbying's influence; local initiatives; challenges for the future). **Express** your position by emphasising the contradictions of your opponents or praising individual initiatives.
4. **Organise** your notes and **practise** your intervention. **Record** the podcast all together, trying to sound as natural as possible. **Be careful** with the pronunciation of homograph words.

BOOST YOUR ENGLISH p. 179 PHONOLOGY p. 182

# BOOST YOUR ENGLISH!

## Grammar — Présenter les enjeux d'une situation

- **Utilise le gérondif pour présenter la situation.**

*Despite **increasing** global awareness and anxiety...*
*Among 90 policies aimed at **rolling** back environmental regulations...*
*Confronted with **rising** temperatures...*

- **Varie les expressions de la cause pour expliquer la situation.**

*They want a carbon tax **because** it doesn't threaten their very existence...*
*There are many **reasons for** the absence of a tax.*
*Yet, **as** the federal government pulls back from combating climate change...*
*Some have criticised the activists **for** not understanding...*

- **Utilise des structures comparatives pour confronter les positions.**

*Just **one** policy change among **more than** 90 others aimed at...*
*Americans are **less likely to** be concerned about climate change **than**...*
*27% of Republicans say..., **compared with** 83% of Democrats...*
*These goals keep getting **more** and **more** strict, **higher** and **higher**...*

- **Sers-toi des modaux *will* ou *would* pour évoquer les conséquences possibles ou probables de cette situation.**

*We **will** follow the guidelines of the Paris Agreement.*
*We **will** see reduced impacts from climate change.*
*The Green New Deal **would** also transform the US economy.*
*The difference in impacts **would** be dramatic.*

**1 Complète ces phrases en exprimant la cause.**

a. Trump decided to withdraw from the Paris Agreement because...
b. Some companies were blamed for...
c. Oil companies lobby and pressure Congress since...
d. Every little action impacts our environment as...

**2 Traduis les phrases suivantes en utilisant *will* et *would*.**

a. De nouvelles mesures seront bientôt appliquées.
b. Nos actions seraient plus efficaces avec l'aide du gouvernement.
c. Les initiatives individuelles auraient également plus de poids.
d. Les entreprises agiront davantage pour l'environnement dans quelques années.

## Vocabulary — Climate issues in the US

Political forces — Sustainability — Commitments

**The Green New Deal** AUDIO
- backers
- cap-and-trade programs
- carbon taxes
- energy rationing
- environmental regulations

**Polarisation** AUDIO
- congressional Democrats/Republicans
- environmental groups
- progressive ≠ conservative
- deny climate change

**Lobbying** AUDIO
- influence = pressure
- gain firm-level advantages
- have a cognitive bias
- sow doubt in sb's mind

**Concerns** AUDIO
- floods
- heatwaves
- natural disasters
- rising temperatures
- storms
- use up resources

**Renewable energies** AUDIO
- biomass
- geothermal energy
- hydro-electric power
- solar panels
- wind turbines

**Goals** AUDIO
- cap greenhouse gas emissions
- phase out power plants
- reduce one's carbon footprint
- tackle the oil industry

**Activism** AUDIO
- campaign for/against
- curb = limit
- demonstrate = protest
- raise awareness

**Initiatives** AUDIO
- pioneering = groundbreaking
- achieve
- meet a challenge
- seek a solution
- support a resolution
- take the lead

OBJECTIF BAC p. 296-304

Grille d'auto-évaluation

## Sujet type bac

Durée : 3h30
Matériel autorisé : le dictionnaire unilingue (non encyclopédique) est autorisé.
Niveau attendu : C1

- **Prenez connaissance des documents A, B, C et traitez le sujet suivant en anglais (≃ 500 mots).**

Taking into account their specificities, show how these documents illustrate some of the tensions in American society regarding environmental policies and the polarisation of the issue. Make sure to address:
– the positive impact of fracking on the economy;
– the controversy about fracking;
– what is implied about the "dark side" of fracking.

- **Traduisez en français le passage suivant du document B.**

*"Concerns over the environment and climate change have also driven a push to move away from fracking and fossil fuels. Carbon dioxide emissions from burning fossil fuel are a major contributor to global warming, and environmental activists have long warned that fracking also damages local resources, polluting the air and contaminating drinking water in some cases."* (l. 46-54)

### Document A — How Has Fracking Changed Our Future?

The use of hydraulic fracturing to extract oil and gas from the earth dates back to the 1940s, but only in the past few years has "fracking" become an energy buzzword, alluding primarily to the shale[1] gas boom in the United States and all of the controversy that has accompanied it. Fracking—the high-pressure injection of water, chemicals and sand into shale deposits to release the gas and oil trapped within the rock—in recent years has been combined with horizontal drilling and other improvements in technology to harvest stores of gas and oil that previously were thought commercially unfeasible to access. [...]

Debate rages on about whether these worldwide reserves can be tapped safely, and whether environmental damage from fracking natural gas will outweigh the gains from using a fuel that is cleaner than oil or coal, but remains a fossil fuel nonetheless. A few viewpoints on both sides of the issue follow. [...]

**Positive impacts of fracking**

"Today, the industry supports 1.7m jobs—a considerable accomplishment given the relative newness of the technology. That number could rise to 3 million by 2020. In 2012, this revolution added $62 billion to federal and state government revenues, a number that we project could rise to about $113 billion by 2020. It is helping to stimulate a manufacturing renaissance in the United States, improving the competitive position of the United States in the global economy, and beginning to affect global geopolitics." – Daniel Yergin, vice chair of global consulting firm IHS. [...]

**Negative impacts of fracking**

"According to a number of studies and publications GAO reviewed, shale oil and gas development poses risks to air quality, generally as the result of engine exhaust[2] from increased truck traffic, emissions from diesel-powered pumps used to power equipment, gas that is flared (burned) or vented (released directly into the atmosphere) for operational reasons, and unintentional emissions of pollutants from faulty equipment or impoundment-temporary storage areas. Similarly, a number of studies and publications GAO reviewed indicate that shale oil and gas development poses risks to water quality from contamination of surface water and groundwater as a result of erosion from ground disturbances, spills and releases of chemicals and other fluids, or underground migration of gases and chemicals." – General Accounting Office report on shale development.

Christina NUNEZ,
*National Geographic*,
September 1rst, 2015

1. *schiste*
2. *gaz d'échappement*

## Document B Trump's final pitch to Pennsylvania: I love fracking

President Donald Trump crisscrossed Pennsylvania on Monday in a frenzied attempt to pull out a critical victory with a singular message: fracking, fracking, fracking.

A strategy the Trump campaign has turbocharged in recent days. It took off after Thursday night's presidential debate, when Democratic presidential nominee Joe Biden said he would transition away from the oil industry in the coming decades. [...]

"Biden confirmed his plan to abolish the entire U.S. oil industry," Trump said Monday, speaking to supporters in Allentown, Pa., incorrectly describing Biden's stance, which is actually focused on ending federal subsidies[1] for fossil fuel companies, barring new fossil fuel permits on public lands and transitioning to renewable energy sources over three decades to combat climate change.

"That means no fracking, no jobs, no energy for Pennsylvania families," Trump added, misleadingly. "He wants to go wind." [...]

Over the past decade, fracking boomed along the Marcellus Shale that stretches through Appalachia and Pennsylvania, becoming part of the state's economic lifeblood. It fuelled local investments from shale operators, pipeline companies and service companies that now employ thousands of Pennsylvanians with, on average, well-paying jobs.

Trump's Pennsylvania pitch has focused largely on the economy, a complicated subject for him in the state.

On the campaign trail in 2016, Trump made bold proclamations about revitalizing the state's manufacturing sector. While the state added manufacturing jobs in 2017 and early 2018, it has been shedding them since October 2018. And with the pandemic-driven economic decline, the state has 600,000 fewer jobs overall than when Trump took office.

More specifically, fracking supports from 20,000 to 50,000 jobs in the state, according to the Pennsylvania Department of Labor and Industry. [...]

Concerns over the environment and climate change have also driven a push to move away from fracking and fossil fuels. Carbon dioxide emissions from burning fossil fuel are a major contributor to global warming, and environmental activists have long warned that fracking also damages local resources, polluting the air and contaminating drinking water in some cases.

Still, Trump's allies say it's a winning issue for the president. They point to Trump's deregulation of the energy industry as a way to create more industry jobs. And they say Trump will push to expand oil and gas drilling into new domestic locations.

Meredith McGraw, *Politico*, October 2020

1. financial help

## Document C

"The Optimist", John Cole, *The Times Tribune*, 2013

Vers le **BAC**

# LET'S BRAINSTORM!

OBJECTIF BAC p. 305-317

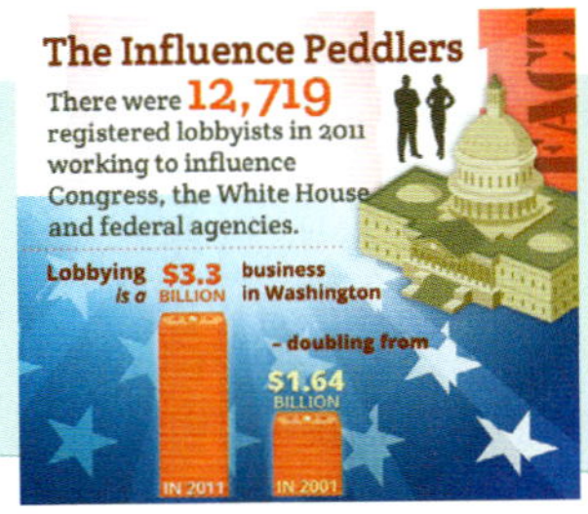


**ENVIRONNEMENTS EN MUTATION**
**Axe 2**
**How are Americans facing the ecological transition challenge?**

## Federal disagreements

- Failed measures

→ "Green New Deal", *NPR*, p. 172

- Presidents' rivalry?

→ "How Has Fracking Changed Our Future?", *National Geographic*, p. 180 • "Trump's final pitch to Pennsylvania: I love fracking", *Politico*, p. 181

## Opposing political forces

- Polarisation of climate change issues

→ "Why is climate skepticism so successful in the US", *The Conversation*, p. 173 • "Democrats' 'Green New Deal' is a Crazy New Deal that would be a disaster for us all", *Fox News*, p. 175 • Cartoon, Chapatte, p. 175

- The power of lobbying

→ "Clean energy firms lobby congress as much as dirty ones", *Scientific American*, p. 174 • "Corporate America is Terrified of the Green New Deal", *The New Republic*, p. 175

## Governors and mayors take the lead

- Pioneering States

→ "Beyond federal decisions", *France 24 English*, 2017, p. 176 • "Sustainable California", *CalMatters*, p. 176

- Cities commitments

→ "Why 1.5°?", *NYC Mayor's Office of Sustainability*, p. 177

## Citizens' growing commitment

- Growing awareness

→ "Americans really want to adopt renewable sources of energy", *Businees Insider*, p. 178

- Individual commitment

→ "Sutainable living series", Rob Greenfield, p. 178

## Phonology — Noms et verbes homographes

AUDIO

- En anglais, il arrive souvent que **le verbe et le nom** soient **homographes** (aient la même orthographe). Mais à l'oral, l'accentuation peut différer.
- Le nom est généralement accentué sur la **première syllabe** alors que le verbe est accentué sur la deuxième ou dernière syllabe, comme dans ***in**crease* (N) / *in**crease*** (V). Il existe néanmoins des exceptions.
- Parfois, la différence se note à la réalisation du [s] **intervocalique** comme dans *use* /ju:s/ (N) / *use* /ju:z/ (V).

**1 Écoute et repère la syllabe accentuée dans chacun des mots de ces paires.**

a. *decrease (N) – decrease (V)*
b. *transport (N) – transport (V)*
c. *extract (N) – extract (V)*
d. *abuse (N) – abuse (V)*

**2 Lis et anticipe l'accentuation des mots en gras. Écoute et vérifie.**

a. *The **use** of hydraulic fracturing to **extract** oil and gas from the earth dates back to the 1940s.*

b. *Shale oil and gas development poses risks to air quality, generally as the **result** of engine exhaust from **increased** truck **traffic**, emissions from diesel-powered pumps **used** to **power** equipment.*

# BUILD YOUR PORTFOLIO

## Website

C40 Cities, Website

C40 is a network of the world's megacities committed to addressing climate change. C40 supports cities to collaborate effectively, share knowledge and drive meaningful, measurable and sustainable action on climate change.

- **Visit** the website and **find out** how these 40 cities take action and help build a greener future.

SITE

## Documentary

*Ice on Fire*, OCS City, 2019

Produced by Leonardo DiCaprio *Ice on Fire* is an eye-opening documentary that focuses on many never-before-seen solutions designed to slow down our escalating environmental crisis.

- **Watch** the trailer and **comment** on the future situation that is described. **Explain** the solutions mentioned.

VIDÉO

## Campaign

Joe Biden's presidential campaign 2020

- **Watch** the video and **explain** Biden's plans for a greener future. Note down the benefits they would have for both the planet and the American economy.

VIDÉO

## Chart

2020 Elections survey, *Data for progress*, July 2020

- **Have** a look at the chart and **explain** the polarisation regarding the renewable energies issue.

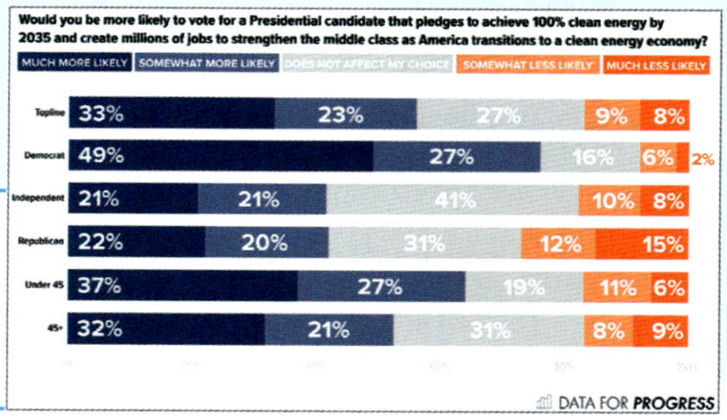


ÉPREUVE ORALE | GRAND ORAL — Entraîne-toi à l'oral

## Step 1 — Build up your speech!

OBJECTIF BAC p. 314-315

**Épreuve orale**

- Choose one topic in the mindmap p. 182.
- Pick out one document in the file and two personal ones to illustrate this issue.
- Prepare your presentation: you must show how these documents relate to the issue you chose.

OBJECTIF BAC p. 305

**Grand oral**

- Choose one topic in the mindmap p. 182.
- Find a key question about your topic.
- Gather arguments and examples from the documents in the file to support your point.
- Prepare an outline for your presentation and write your note sheet.

OBJECTIF BAC p. 308-309

## Step 2 — Make your oral presentation in front of two classmates.

**Épreuve orale**

- Show your documents to your classmates. Each of you makes their presentation to the others in about five minutes.

OBJECTIF BAC p. 306-307

**Grand oral**

- Give your note sheet to your classmates.
- Stand up and make a five-minute presentation to answer your key question.

OBJECTIF BAC p. 310-311

## Step 3 — Answer your classmates' questions about your presentation.

SNAPFILE 20

ENVIRONNEMENTS EN MUTATION

AXE 2 : DE LA PROTECTION DE LA NATURE À LA TRANSITION ÉCOLOGIQUE

# The bush is burning

▶ **Can the great fires lead to a shift in Australia's environmental policies?**

More on SPEAKEASY NEWS
speakeasy-news.com

**YOUR MISSION**

**Write an open letter to the Australian Prime Minister to demand climate action.**

You are a WWF volunteer in Australia, aware of the emergency to act against climate change. Question the Australian Prime Minister in an open letter to prompt climate change action.

FOLLOW THE STEPS!

## 1 Australia's climate emergency

LANDMARKS p. 286

**Doc 1.**

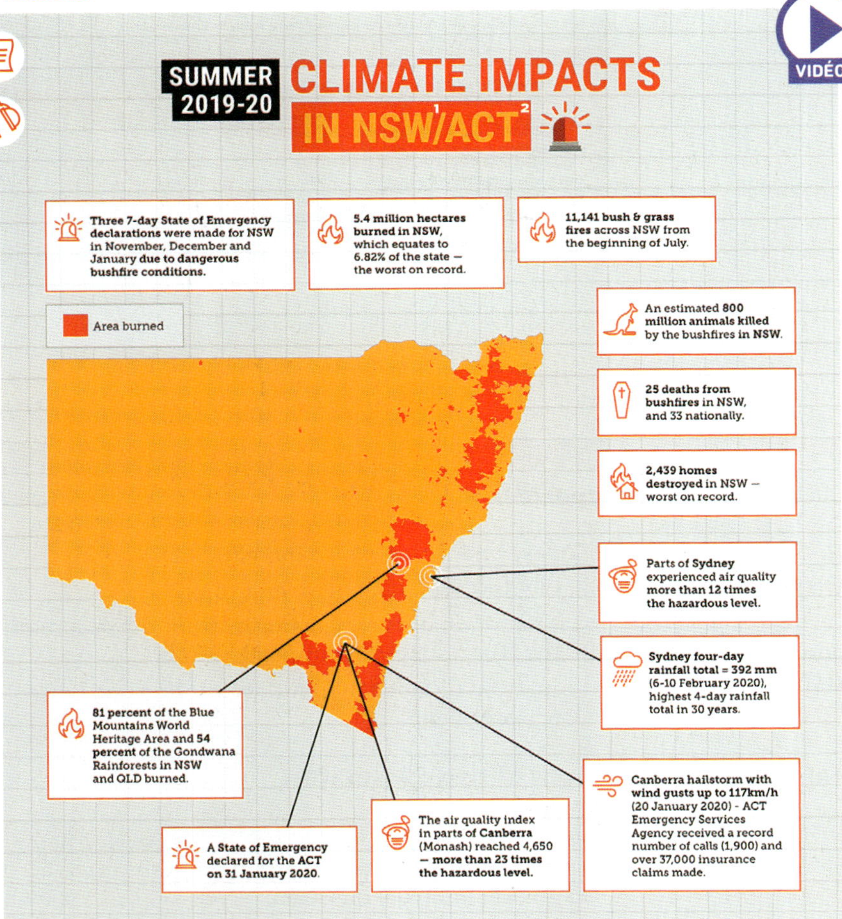


VIDÉO

1. New South Wales
2. Australian Capital Territory

*Climatecouncil.org.au*, 2020
(Video: "An apocalyptic summer", *Global News*, 2019)

**a. Study** the infographic and **describe** the consequences of bushfires.

**b. Watch** the video and **pick out** the figures. **Explain** what they correspond to.

**c. Explain** why bushfires have been multiplying.

**d.** GRAMMAR *"One mayor wants leaders to embrace the science."* **Account for** the infinitive form here and **translate** the sentence.

**e. Say** how the news report contributes to calling for action.

**WORDS**

- aftermath /'ɑːftəmæθ/
- casualty /'kæʒuəlti/
- data /'deɪtə/
- disaster
- endangered species /'spiːʃiːz/

---

- apocalyptic
- hazardous /'hæzədəs/ = dangerous

---

- obliterate = destroy
- scorch = burn
- take a toll: damage

## Doc 2.

AUSTRALIA'S 2019-2020 BUSHFIRES: THE WILDLIFE TOLL

WWF REPORT AUS 2020

In January, as fires still burned, WWF helped inform the world that 1.25 billion animals – mammals, birds and reptiles – were impacted by Australia's bushfire disaster. This early estimate, led by Professor Chris Dickman working with WWF scientists, generated headlines across the globe and helped people grasp the magnitude of the crisis. WWF, a science-based organisation, felt it was crucial to update this figure. By February, we had commissioned scientists to complete a more detailed and final estimate. Their interim findings, released in this report, are shocking. Nearly three billion animals were in the path of the flames.

© ADAM DEDERER

VIDÉO

(Video: "The worst wildlife disaster", *WWF Australia*, 2020)

**a. Look** at the picture and **read** the report. **Comment** on the impact of bushfires on wildlife.

**b. Watch** the video and **identify** the type of document, the speakers and the purpose of the video.

**c.** RHETORIC *"It felt like Armageddon." "It felt like there was nothing there." "The trees look like burnt matchsticks."* **Identify** the figure of speech used in these sentences and **explain** what it conveys. **Translate** the sentences into French.

**d. Explain** how donations will be used.

## Doc 3.

### Right fire for right future

Indigenous fire practitioners have warned that Australia's bush will regenerate as a "time bomb" prone to[1] catastrophic blazes, and issued a plea[2] to put to use traditional knowledge which is already working across the Top End[3] to reduce bushfires and greenhouse gas emissions.

"This is a time bomb ticking now because all that canopy[4] has been wiped out," says Oliver Costello of the national Indigenous Firesticks Alliance. [...]

As Australia comes to terms with this season's catastrophic fires, Indigenous practitioners like Costello are advocating a return to "cultural burning".

### What is cultural burning?

Small-scale burns at the right times of year and in the right places can minimise the risk of big wildfires in drier times, and are important for the health and regeneration of particular plants and animals.

Different species relate to fire in different ways, Costello explains. Wombats[5], for example, dig burrows[6] to escape, while koalas climb into the canopy.

"When you understand the fire relationships they have, their own fire culture, then you are really applying the right fire for that culture so that you're supporting the identity of that place.

"When you do that, you get more productive landscapes, you get healthier plants and animals, you get regeneration, you discourage invasive elements, which are sometimes native species that might belong in the system next door."

Lorena ALLAM, *The Guardian*, January 2020

**1.** *sujet à* **2.** legal appeal **3.** northern part of the Northern Territory **4.** branches at the top of trees **5.** Australian marsupials **6.** animal tunnels

**a. Read** the text and **explain** what "cultural burning" consists in.

**b.** GRAMMAR *"...all that canopy has been wiped out..."* (l. 10-11) **Explain** the use of the present perfect here.

**c. Comment** on the advantages of "cultural burning".

**AT HOME Watch** the report on cultural burning and **reflect** on the role of traditional practices in conserving the environment. VIDEO

**STEP 1**

**Take** notes on the devastating impacts of Australia's bushfires for your open letter.

**BOOST YOUR SKILLS!**

**Décrire une situation qui se dégrade**

- Utilise des indications temporelles précises : ***In the last*** *72 hours* • ***Over the last*** *one hundred years*
- Choisis des verbes ou expressions qui montrent une évolution : *multiplying* • *declined* • *climbed*
- Utilise le *present perfect* pour faire un bilan : *Temperatures* ***have climbed****...* et le présent en *be* + V-*ing* pour commenter la gravité de la situation : *The fires* ***are multiplying*** *in the last 72 hours.*

# 2 Tackling the issue of coal

## Doc 1.

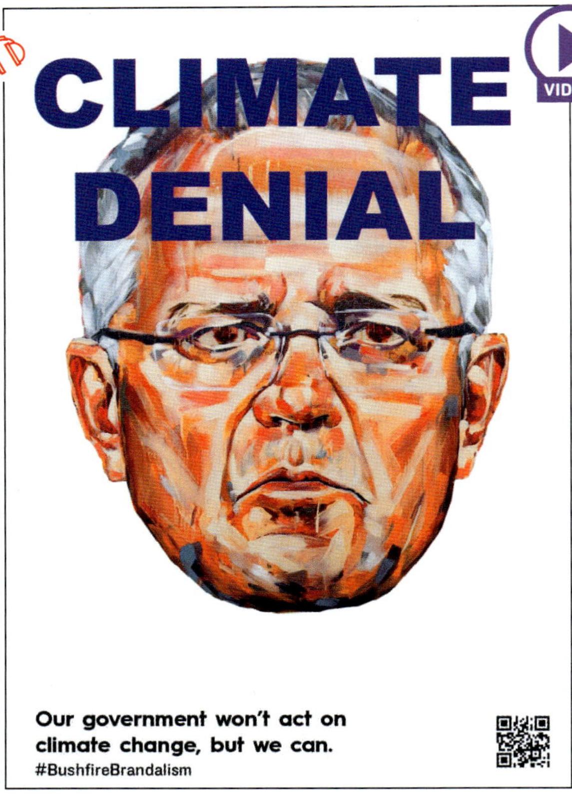


Scott MARSH, *Climate Denial*, 2020
(Video: "Acknowledging the impact of climate change", *Sky News*, 2019)

VIDÉO

**a.** **Look** at the poster and **imagine** what the video may be about.

**b.** **Watch** the video and **find out** about Australian politicians' attitudes toward climate change.

**c.** **Explain** Australia's tactics to do less to tackle greenhouse gas emissions.

**d.** **Say** how the news report contributes to denouncing Australian politicians' decisions.

AT HOME **Read** Darcy Prendergast's poem entitled "Tomorrow's on fire" and **explain** its message. POEM

### CULTURE SPOT

**Scott Marsh** is part of the "Bushfire Brandalism" collective, a group of Australian artists who have created posters and have installed them at local bus stops in order to draw attention to the bushfire crisis.

**a.** **Read** the article and **explain** what coal is mainly used for in Australia. **Comment** on the consequences.

**b.** **Explain** why the government supports coal power.

**c.** **Find out** about the decisions of Australia's customers of coal regarding this sector.

**d.** **Comment** on the gradual transition to renewable energy around the world.

STEP 2 **Take** notes on the main causes of Australian bushfires: the Australian government's energy policy and its attitude towards climate change.

### BOOST YOUR SKILLS!

**Alerter l'opinion publique**

- Utilise des adjectifs péjoratifs pour critiquer : *The government's **intransigent** defence* • ***Obsolete** thermal coal*
- Exprime la nécessité d'agir avec des infinitives : *...**force** politicians **to wake up** to their responsibilities.*
- Cite des défenseurs de ta cause : *Australia's climate protesters **say**... • Buckley **argues that**...*

## Doc 2.

**The world has made the link between Australian coal, fires and climate**

Tim Buckley, the director of Energy Finance Studies at the Institute for Energy Economics and Financial Analysis, says his frustration at the government's intransigent defence of increasingly technologically obsolete thermal coal (coal burnt for energy rather than steel manufacturing) at the cost of effective climate-change policy and international reputation is compounded[1] by his view that the industry has commenced its drawn-out death throes[2], sustained by political muscle rather than economic reality.

Coal power's defenders point to a recent uptick[3] in imports to China and India and the long-term potential of customers such as Bangladesh, Pakistan and Vietnam. Buckley concedes China and India will continue to buy Australian coal in the short term as they seek to maintain economic growth at up to 6 or 7 per cent annually.

But both have made clear their intention to first transition to domestic coal as fast as they can build the necessary infrastructure, while concurrently decarbonising their economies in line with the rest of the world. [...]

Both South Korea and Japan, he says, are already showing signs that they want to abandon the sector. Buckley argues that the thermal-coal industry's tipping point has already passed, missed by its champions in Morrison's government but already factored in by global money markets.

US coal stocks[4] dropped an average 50 per cent in 2019 while Exxon remained flat in a US equity market that rose 28 per cent overall, meanwhile the share[5] price of the world's largest investor in renewables, the US utility Nextera Energy, leapt by 42 per cent.

Nick O'MALLEY, *The Sydney Morning Herald*, January 2020

**1.** made worse **2.** agony **3.** increase **4.** *actions (en bourse)* **5.** *action*

# 3 A shift in environmental policy?

## Doc 1.

Paul DORIN, 2019 (Audio: *PBS NewsHour*, January 2020)

AUDIO

**a. Explain** the cartoon.

**b. Listen** to the audio and **find** elements showing that climate change is a reality.

**c. Account for** the different opinions expressed.

**d.** GRAMMAR *"It **might** be exactly right", "opinions **may** in fact be changing", "that **would** be a disaster", "that **might** mean..."* **Comment** on the use of the modals and what they reveal about the issue.

**WORDS**

- ackn**o**wledge = re**c**ognize
- cr**i**ticise/blame sb for d**o**ing sth
- halt /hɔːlt/ cl**i**mate change
- t**a**ckle the **i**ssue

## Doc 2.

**PM Scott Morrison admits failings in response to crisis as he proposes review**

The Australian Prime Minister has admitted to not dealing with parts of the nation's ongoing wildfire crisis very well, as well as proposing a review into the country's response. Scott Morrison, who has had some tense exchanges with residents while visiting affected areas, said: "There are things I could have handled on the ground much better." [...]

Mr Morrison has been criticised for not doing more to combat climate change, even as Australia battles its worst wildfire season on record [...].

In the interview, he suggested the country should have a "national review" into the response to the wildfires. However, the PM rejected criticism that his government had not done enough before the bushfire season started. Talking about the response co-ordinated and supported by the state, he said: "I think we have to acknowledge how exemplary it has been in response to what has been the scale of fire."

The PM has so far been defiant in rejecting any links between his government's conservative climate policies and the bushfires – for example, defending his country's reliance[1] on its coal industry – but said his government will look into improving its performance on curbing[2] emissions.

Zoe TIDMAN, *The Independent*, January 2020

1. dependence 2. limiting

**a. Read** the article and **pick out** elements showing that Scott Morrison admits his mistakes.

**b.** GRAMMAR *"He suggested the country should have a 'national review'."* (l. 11-12) **Explain** the use of *should* here.

**c. Explain** Scott Morrison's new measures.

**d. Focus** on the last sentence. **Comment** on the limits of the Prime Minister's acknowledgement.

**STEP 3**

**Take** notes on the solutions and **ask** the government to change their opinion on climate change.

**FINAL STEP**

**Gather** your notes and **write** your open letter to the Australian Prime Minister to demand climate action. **Provide** details about the impacts of the bushfires, the Australian government's energy policy and its failings in responding to the bushfire crisis. **Suggest** solutions and **be** convincing.

**You've completed your mission. Well done!**

# WRITE AN ESSAY

OBJECTIF BAC p. 296

Le jour de l'**épreuve écrite** en Terminale, tu devras analyser et faire la synthèse d'un dossier documentaire. Il pourra t'être demandé de rédiger un **écrit complémentaire argumentatif**. En voici un exemple :

**Documents du dossier :**
Document A: "The world has made the link between Australian coal, fires and climate", Nick O'Malley, *The Sydney Morning Herald*, January 2020 (Doc 2 p. 186)
Document B: *Cartoon* by Paul Dorin, 2019 (Doc 1 p. 187)
Document C: "PM Scott Morrison admits failings in response to crisis as he proposes review", Zoe Tidman, *The Independent*, January 2020 (Doc 2 p. 187)

**Sujet d'écrit complémentaire :**
*"Mr Morrison has been criticised for not doing more to combat climate change, even as Australia battles its worst wildfire season on record."* (*Document C, l. 8-10*). À la lumière des documents A et B, expliquez en anglais et en 200 mots maximum dans quelle mesure la politique environnementale de l'Australie a contribué aux feux de brousse en Australie.

## 1 Analyser la consigne et la citation

**a. Identifie** les mots-clés et mets-les en relation pour comprendre les enjeux.

**b. Étudie** les documents du dossier à l'aune de cette question. Prends des notes sur chaque document la concernant.

Il s'agit de donner un point de vue nuancé à partir d'une citation. Identifie les éléments de la question qui précisent l'objet de ta réflexion : dans quelle mesure (qui correspond à *To what extent* en anglais).

- Repère les mots-clés de la citation : *Mr Morrison • criticised • combat • climate change • Australia • battles • wildfire* et de la consigne : politique gouvernementale • contribué aux feux de brousse.
- Quels liens les différents documents ont-ils avec la citation proposée ?
***Document A:*** *In this article, Tim Buckley criticises Australia's reliance on coal which contributes to climate change.*
***Document B:*** *The cartoonist blames the Australian government for the bushfire crisis.*
***Document C:*** *The PM himself admits he could have handled bushfires "much better".*

## 2 Réfléchir et s'organiser

**a. Prépare** tes idées en les classant selon qu'elles s'opposent ou se complètent pour faire émerger un plan.

**b. Choisis** comme point de départ une idée qui soutient celle avancée dans la citation ou qui s'en rapproche.

**c. Développe** ensuite une idée en contrepoint, ou qui nuance le point de vue exposé.

**d. Illustre** ces idées grâce à des exemples extraits des documents.

- Pour soutenir le point de vue de la citation, utilise : *There are many points in support of this view... • We must acknowledge... • We may agree that...*
- Pour contredire le point de vue de la citation, utilise: *However... • Some objections can be raised against... • It is hard to agree with... • I find it impossible to accept/agree...*
- Pour nuancer le point de vue de la citation, utilise : *Nevertheless, it may be that... • It is possible that... • It is likely that...*
- Souviens-toi : **1 argument = 1 paragraphe** !

## 3 Prendre position

**a. Prépare** une conclusion qui ne se contente pas de résumer ce que tu as expliqué mais qui synthétise la confrontation de tes arguments.

**b. Conclus** en donnant un point de vue personnel sur le sujet.

Fais appel à tes connaissances interculturelles personnelles pour aller plus loin dans ta réflexion. Tu peux évoquer ici le climato-scepticisme qui caractérise d'autres dirigeants anglo-saxons comme Donald Trump, l'ancien président des États-Unis (2017-2021).

- La conclusion doit apporter une réponse à la problématique posée au départ. *To conclude, ... • In conclusion, ... • Finally...*

# BUILD YOUR PORTFOLIO

## Campaign

"Change the Future", *350.org.au*, 2019

"Change The Future" is a campaign created by 350.org. It uses illustrations to show what will happen if the government does not take action on climate change: "We believe that a global grassroots movement can hold our leaders accountable to the realities of science and the principles of justice."

- **Describe** the poster and **explain** its message. **Give** your opinion about 350.org's statement.

SITE

## Cartoon

Paul Dorin, September 2019

- **Describe** the cartoon and **comment** on the Prime Minister's stance on climate change.

## Article

"'Australia's largest unsanctioned art show': guerrilla bushfire campaign hijacks bus shelters", Jenny Valentish, *The Guardian*, February 2020

"On Thursday 30 January, pedestrians in some suburbs of Melbourne, Sydney and Brisbane would have walked straight past activist artists (vandals, some critics might call them) removing advertising from bus shelters and inserting artwork protesting the Morrison government and its handling of Australia's bushfire crisis. "Bushfire Brandalism", the action is being called."

- **Read** the article and **explain** how street art can be used to fight for the protection of nature.

ARTICLE

## Poem

"My Country", John 'Polly' Farmer, 2020

John 'Polly' Farmer, a cartoonist, took inspiration from the famous poem "My Country" written by Dorothea Mackellar in order to write his own poem about the Australian bushfires.
Dorothea Mackellar's original poem expresses her passion and love for Australia.

- **Read** the poem and **explain** its message. **Compare** it with the original poem by Dorothea Mackellar.

POEM

## Entraîne-toi à l'oral

ÉPREUVE ORALE

**Step 1** **Build up your speech!**

- Choose one of the issues presented in the file.
- Pick out one document from the file, add a personal one and pick out another one in this page to illustrate the topic. OBJECTIF BAC p. 305
- Prepare your presentation: you must show how these documents relate to the topic.

**Step 2** **Make your presentation in front of two classmates.**

- Show your documents to your classmates and explain your point in about five minutes. OBJECTIF BAC p. 306-307

**Step 3** **Answer your classmates' questions about your presentation.**

# A tale of British cities

► How are post-industrial cities in the UK reinventing themselves?

**FINAL TASK** Take part in a roundtable at the city council of a post-industrial British town.

More on SPEAKEASY NEWS
speakeasy-news.com

## 1 Post-industrial cityscapes

Doc 1.

(Video: "Death of Industry", *timelinesTV*, 2013)

**a.** **Observe** the photographs of these contemporary British towns and **say** what signs of the past are displayed in their architecture.

**b.** **Watch** the video and **find out** what major shift in British history is presented here.

**c.** RHETORIC **Pick out** the expression repeated four times by the speaker. What does it refer to and what effect does it produce?

**d.** **Contrast** the past function of Lister's Mill with what it has become today. **Say** what it reveals about today's society.

**e.** **Pick out** the expressions used by the speaker to describe this shift. **Imagine** why he chose such strong words.

LANDMARKS p. 262

## Doc 2. Post-industrial life

"Manchester's Industrial Decline", *CitiesX*, 2018 AUDIO

**a. Listen** to the audio and find out what the speaker refers to when talking about a *"period of great depression"* (dates, places, and event).

**b. Take notes** on the various consequences of this period on the area.

**c. Pick out** some adjectives used to describe this period. **Comment** on the atmosphere created by this testimony.

### CULTURE SPOT

First elected in 1979, Prime Minister **Margaret Thatcher** introduced the privatisation of many British industrial sectors, leading to major **miners strikes** in 1984-85.

LANDMARKS p. 268-269

## Doc 3. Hard times to overcome

TEXTE LU

### "Then"

Back to the studio. And in other news: the countryside cattle pyres[1] still burning. The privatised transport infrastructures dangerous and inoperable. A health service that needed a health warning, an education system no one seemed to learn anything from. Twenty-first century Britain. The legacy.

More ghosts to exorcise. More work to do. [...]

### "Now"

It was the first time he had been back to the town since he had started working on the book. The first time away from libraries, documents, dry facts. The first time in the present and not the past. Larkin didn't recognise the place.

He had driven in, parked the Saab in the car park of the new shopping mall. It held the kind of stores that appeared only in poor areas; retailers[2] selling furniture and electrical items on the never-never[3], stores offering under a pound tat, supermarkets with harsh, guttural names selling discount goods, unfamiliar brands of dubious quality. Staffed by part-timers on short-term, no-benefits contracts, women with families to support, ex-colliers[4] retained to push trolleys together, beep barcodes on food packaging.

Sadness clung to the small, adjacent bus station. It seemed the buses never managed to take people far enough away, always brought them mournfully back. On the low wall outside the toilets was a gathering of career alcoholics, crack-and smack-heads[5], a meeting place for the dispossessed.

The only thing Larkin recognised was the old church, but even that had changed. Its doors looked as if they were hardly opened, its graveyard now a home to weeds, lichen and discarded hypos. The hope of any salvation long since gone.

The town was now a patched-up thing, dead, just not lying down yet. A town with no industry or future. Post-strike. Post-industrial. Post everything.

Martyn WAITES, *Born Under Punches*, 2004

1. large fire. 2. *détaillants* 3. *à crédit* 4. coal miners 5. *(fam.) camés*

Newcastle in the 1970's

**YOUR TASK** As a history student, **make** a 3-minute presentation on the difficulties faced by some post-industrial cities at the turn of the 20th century.

**a. Read** the extracts and **describe** the type of atmosphere created by the author's description.

**b. Pick out** elements in this depiction that illustrate the speaker's declarations in **doc 2**.

**c.** RHETORIC **Identify** the nominal sentences. **Deduce** how they serve the author's purpose.

**d. Comment** on the final repetition *"Post-strike. Post-industrial. Post everything."*

### BOOST YOUR SKILLS!

**Décrire une transformation**

- Décris l'évolution de la situation avec des formes en *be* + V-*ing* : *All the mills* ***were closing*** *down.* • *Unemployment* ***was*** *go**ing*** *up.* • *Lister's* ***is being converted*** *into designer appartements.*
- Souligne l'ampleur de la transformation avec des quantifieurs : ***So much*** *has changed.* • ***So many*** *profound transformations.* • *There was* ***no*** *money in the community.* GRAMMAR p. 197

# 2 An economic renewal

## THE MANCHESTER MIRACLE

*Salford Quays in Manchester*

**How did a city in decline become the poster child for urban regeneration?**

Manchester was the first of western Europe's industrial boomtowns—but the city underwent a catastrophic process of deindustrialisation following the Second World War. Between 1971 and 1981, Manchester lost almost 50,000 full-time jobs and 17.5 per cent of its population.

Whole areas were described as "emptied", characterised by social exclusion, crime and deteriorating living conditions. The world's first industrial city seemed to be in terminal decline by the 1980s. [...]

Manchester's city leaders have since employed new economic strategies to re-define its role and improve its position in the global market. The turnaround witnessed in recent years has been so successful that it's sometimes termed the "Manchester miracle".

To prosper in the competitive global economy, cities need to harness[1] their "monopolies of place"—those distinctive qualities granted by location and local assets that cannot be easily imitated elsewhere.

Improving regional and international connectivity via transport infrastructure upgrades is one economic strategy being employed to exploit Manchester's position within the northern English conurbation, and at the tip of the European "blue banana"[2].

Specific changes include the Northern Hub, a project to improve the rail connections between Manchester and other cities in the north, and the development of its airport's international flight connections. The recent announcement of direct flights from Manchester to Beijing by Chinese President Xi Jinping, underlines the importance of this strategy. [...]

Another set of assets contributing to Manchester's growth are its universities, which draw highly-skilled future employees from across the globe to the city and produce innovative research which has major economic benefits when commercialised. A 2003 report from Manchester Council termed the city's universities its "knowledge factories". The term makes clear that they aren't merely sites for scholarly learning but play a role in economic growth.

Fred PAXTON, *citymetric.com*, September 2016

1. learn how to use 2. corridor of urbanisation spreading over Europe

### WORDS

- growth = expansion
- network
- rebirth

- affiliated to/with
- prominent = outstanding

- breathe new life into
- prosper = thrive
- revitalise

**a. Read** the text and **focus** on the first three paragraphs. **Explain** the use of the expression *"Manchester miracle"*.

**b. Read on** and **find out** what contributed to Manchester's regeneration. **Pick out** specifics and figures to support your answer.

**c. Define** what *"monopolies of place"* (l. 27) are in this context. **Say** why they may be considered key here.

**d.** TRANSLATION **Translate** l. 51-55. **Pay** special attention to the translation of *"knowledge factories"*.

**e. Give** at least two examples showing that Manchester is now connected to global markets. **Imagine** why this might be necessary in today's world.

### CULTURE SPOT

EXO **Quiz**

**Check what you know about Manchester's...**
- geographical situation
- industrial past
- modern assets

# 3 Turning ruins into riches

## Doc 1. Reviving the past

**Why is the film industry hooked on industrial cityscapes?**

We're wandering around Liverpool's Georgian Quarter, along with Kevin Bell, [from] the Liverpool Film Office [...]. The first of its kind in the UK, their department was set up in 1989 to facilitate film and television productions in Liverpool. Now, they say, their phone is ringing off the hook. In the last few years, the city has already been featured in *Peaky Blinders, Utopia, Foyle's War* and many more. "On average," Saunders says, "it works out to about three productions a day."

Britain's post-industrial cities are enjoying their first major boom in years—on the screen. [...] At the heart of this devolved production are the old powerhouses of UK industry—the buildings, the landscapes and the can-do attitude. Indeed, there remain plenty of disused factories and warehouses[1] awaiting regeneration, but they're not quite there yet. In their dormant periods, they can double as ideal (if draughty[2]) spaces for filming. They're also often cavernous enough to build multi-storey sets. [...].

Unlike many cities in North America, Britain's post-industrial cities also boast a range of architectural styles, which makes them good doubles for other places. "We can do New York, we can do Birmingham, we can do London, we can do the 1920s," says Bell of Liverpool.

The filming of *Peaky Blinders* in Rodney Street, Liverpool

Ellie Violet BRAMLEY,
*The Guardian*, July 2020

1. *entrepôt* 2. *ouvert à tous les vents*

**a.** **Read** the text and and **pick out** information about the economic activity at stake (location, services, origins).

**b.** **Find out** elements showing Liverpool's growing success in this activity.

**c.** **Explain** why industrial cities represent a unique opportunity for this industry.

**d.** **Imagine** how it can help regenerate the city's economy.

## Doc 2. Challenging regeneration

The Three Graces on Liverpool waterfront (Video: *ITV News*, 2017)

**a.** **Watch** the video and **find out** the connection between Liverpool and UNESCO.

**b.** **Sum up** the recent controversy.

**c.** GRAMMAR **Focus** on the use of *would* in the video. **Say** who uses it and to what purpose. ▸ p. 197

**d.** **Compare** both sides of the argument.

**e.** **Conclude** on what this debate reveals about modern-day challenges for post-industrial cities.

**YOUR TASK** The city of Liverpool is holding a debate for its citizens to discuss the project of building a modern hotel in the place of a disused warehouse regularly used as a movie set. **Take part** in the debate.

**STUDENT 1** You think plans for the future and modernisation of the city must come first.

**STUDENT 2** You believe protecting the city's heritage is more important.

**BOOST YOUR SKILLS!**

**Exprimer des avis contraires**

- Exprime au conditionnel la façon dont tu envisages les choses : *That **would** drive away tourists.* • *It **would** compromise the authenticity of...* GRAMMAR p. 197
- Réagis en citant les avis contraires : *The project's **supporters say**...* • ***To some**, it would...* • ***Critics** of the new development say...*
- Exprime ton accord ou ton désaccord : *People **don't** like change, **but**...* • *UNESCO are **not** our enemies...* • *Many Liverpudlians take **a different** view...*

# CITU CLIMATE INNOVATION DISTRICT

Developed by CITU, the Climate Innovation District in Leeds is a zero-carbon development that puts sustainability at its heart.

Rather than drab[1] apartment blocks packed into the urban landscape, CITU are creating a community focused around parks and shared gardens all along a river where otters, herons and kingfishers live. The new homes are the first family homes to be built in Leeds City Centre in over 90 years and will bring open, communal spaces to allow children to play in a car-free environment, whilst the short walk into the city centre makes it ideal for those who work in the city. […]

CITU Managing Director Chris Thompson said: "From a city-wide context, the development forms part of the South Bank which is the biggest regeneration site in the region and its ambition is to double the size of Leeds City Centre. [We] will be delivering around 520 homes, between one and four bedrooms, plus some commercial space, leisure space and there are plans in place for a primary school, with the emphasis being on delivering the highest possible sustainable communities. […]

"I hope the development brings a new typology to the city," said Chris." It is an ambitious standard of place making and I hope that creates a ripple effect[2] through other neighbouring developments and raises the ambitions of other sites. I think its immediate impact will be a lot of connectivity from other areas of the city. The bridge is a fundamental piece of the structure and will improve the connectivity of the city and different communities. The change in demographic will also bring a whole different category of life to the city. […]

> **SOLAR AVENUE IS THE HEART OF THE CLIMATE INNOVATION DISTRICT**

"As a business we want to tackle climate change by accelerating the transition to zero carbon cities, so we want to be making an impact with the developments that we do. This project has the opportunity to make a lasting impact on the South Bank and the wider city, so it is hugely important."

Roma Publications, *premierconstructionnews.com*, 2018

**WORDS**

- gentrific**a**tion
- L**oi**ner = c**i**tizen from Leeds
- f**a**mily-friendly
- tr**e**ndsetting
- **u**pscale
- w**e**ll-off
- build up = exp**a**nd
- ent**i**ce = **a**ttract

**a.** **Read** the text and **say** why the urban project at stake is perfect for families.

**b.** **Explain** how sustainability has been put at the heart of the new district.

**c.** GRAMMAR **Focus** on l. 5-9 and **rephrase** the sentence by replacing "rather than…". ▸ p. 197

**d.** **Identify** the double impact the plan is expected to have.

**e.** **Comment** on the new image of the city the plan wants to give.

**f.** **Discuss** the potential limits to this plan.

1. not colourful 2. *effet d'entraînement*

# 5 Cultural revival

## Doc 1.

### A beacon[1] of urban renewal: how post-industrial Dundee transformed itself

In recent years there has been a growing realisation of the value of the arts as an economic driver. Cities have woken up to the fact that a vibrant cultural offering makes people want to live there, and the numbers back this up. [...] In Dundee, a small city on the east coast of Scotland, the creative industries produce a total annual turnover of £190m and provide employment for 3,000 people. When you consider that the population of the city is just 150,000, you get some indication of the importance of the cultural sector to its economic well-being.

Dundee is a dynamic city with a strong cultural identity and a history of innovation and creativity. But by the late 1980s, profound post-industrial decline had turned a once proud and world-facing city into a fragmented shadow of its former self.

Now the city [...] has become home to a thriving digital media industry, internationally respected universities, world-renowned drug discovery and medical advancements, not to mention a vibrant design and creative sector.

The fact that the V&A will soon open its first building outside of London coupled with its elite UNESCO City of Design status, means that Dundee is finally being recognised as a design hothouse[2]. Both of these initiatives are the result of dogged[3] determination by groups of passionate people within the city, who believe in the city and wouldn't live anywhere else. Why move when you can help build? [...]

This and Dundee's transformation is not lost on the growing audience for cultural tourism. A thriving cultural scene can drive exponential growth in both tourism and inward investment. It makes a place not just attractive to visit, but also to live, study and work in.

Paul HARRIS, *theconversation.com*, October 2017

1. symbol 2. place of creativity 3. resolute

**WORDS**

- expectancy
- trade = business
- multifaceted
- thrilling = stimulating
- embolden
- exhibit
- make familiar

## Doc 2.

VIDÉO

V&A Museum in Dundee (Video: *V&A Dundee*, 2016)

### Focus on doc 1 or 2

**a. Read** the article or **watch** the video and **identify** why the V&A chose to open a new building in Dundee.

**b. Explain** the potential impact of such a project on some areas or industries of the city.

**c. Take** notes on how the museum project has been received by the citizens.

**d. Conclude** on how culture can empower other industries in a city or region.

**CULTURE SPOT**

The original **Victoria and Albert Museum**, also known as V&A, was founded in 1852 in London. To this day, it is the world's largest museum dedicated to decorative art and design.

**YOUR TASK** As a member of the V&A staff in Dundee, **share** your experience of the new museum in a radio podcast. **Present** the project and **say** how it could help regenerate the city.

**BOOST YOUR SKILLS!**

**Exposer des enjeux**

- Mets en avant les objectifs : *Spaces **to allow** children **to** play.* • *The investment is **set to**...* • *We're **working on**...* • *I **look forward to**...*
- Souligne leur importance avec des superlatifs : *The **biggest** site* • *The **highest** sustainable community.* • *The **first** designer to...* GRAMMAR p. 197
- Valorise les réalisations avec des adjectifs en *-ing* : *A **thriving** industry* • *A **growing** realisation* • *An **exciting** development*

# 6 An unequal success

Animation interactive

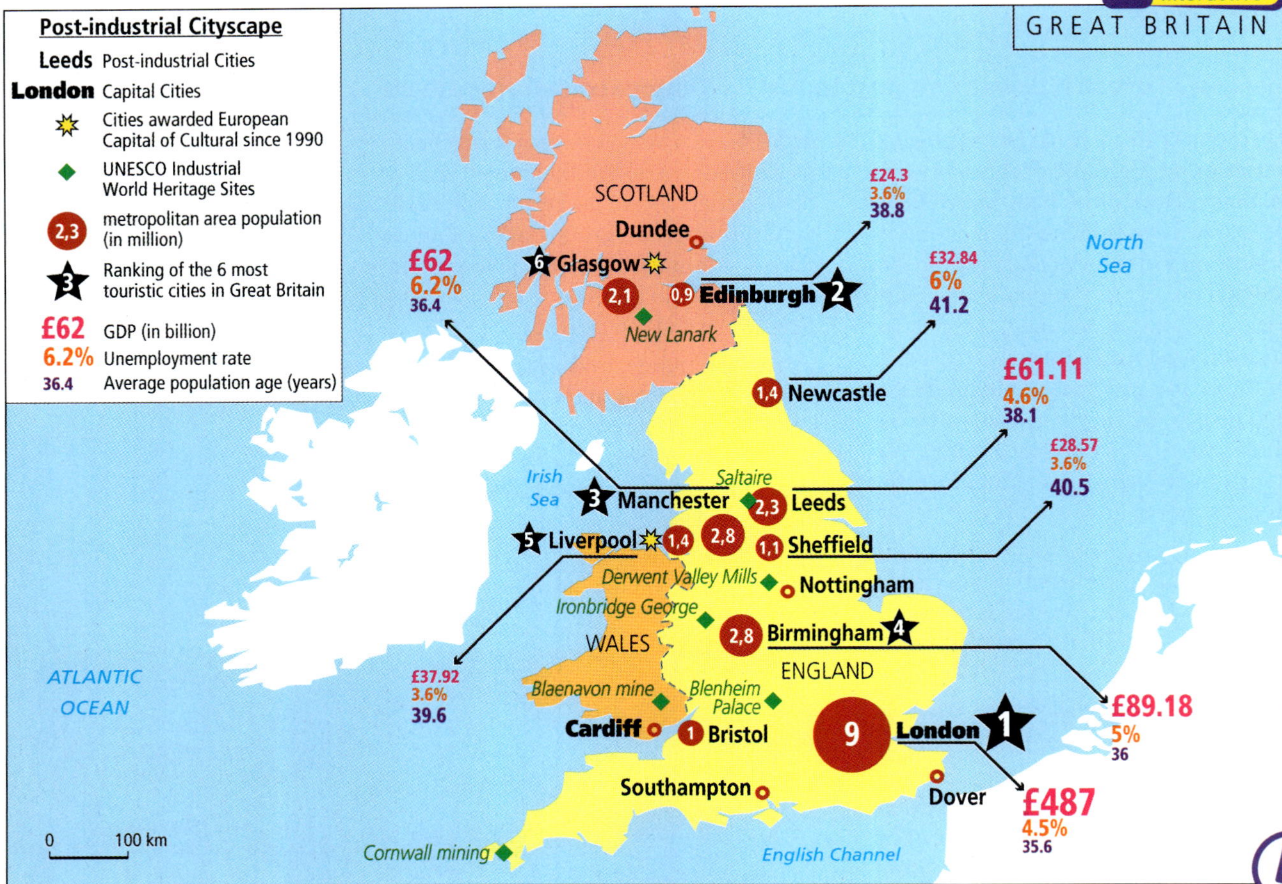


(Audio: "Regional planning in post-industrial Great Britain", *CitiesX*, 2018)

**a.** **Observe** the map and **take notes** on the variety of situations for post-industrial cities today.

**b.** **Say** what data you find most revealing about post-industrial recovery. **Justify** your answer.

**c.** **Listen** to the audio and **complete** your notes on the heterogeneity of post-industrial realities.

**d.** **Explain** what the speaker thinks is necessary for urban regeneration policies to be successful.

**e.** **Recap** the various documents studied in this file and **conclude** on the varied performances achieved by post-industrial cities to reinvent themselves.

## FINAL TASK

**Take part in a roundtable at the city council of a British post-industrial town.**

**As a citizen of a British post-industrial town, you are invited to the city council to discuss the best policies to regenerate the area.**

1. **Join** your team and **choose** your role: the mayor (moderator of the debate); the cultural advisor, or curator of a local museum; a UNESCO representative; an industry worker; a student, a social worker, a teacher, a parent, etc.
2. Together, **decide** the British post-industrial city you would like the debate to focus on.
3. **Browse** through the file. **Gather** arguments, examples and figures to support your point. **Be prepared** also to respond to some of your challengers' ideas with counter-arguments or examples.
4. **Take** part in the round-table discussion: **Give** your viewpoint and **react** to your partners' statements.

BOOST YOUR ENGLISH p. 197

# BOOST YOUR ENGLISH!

## Grammar — Échanger des points de vue

- **Exprime au conditionnel ce que tes idées ou celles des autres peuvent induire.**

*That **would** be an international embarrassment.*
*That **would** drive away tourists.*
*It **would** compromise the authenticity of this historic waterfront.*

- **Utilise des structures comparatives ou superlatives pour confronter les idées.**

***Rather than**..., the developers are creating...*
***Fewer** investors are willing to...*
*It is **the biggest** regeneration site **in** the region.*
*One of the world's **most** important heritage sites.*

- **Donne de l'ampleur à tes arguments avec des quantifieurs.**

*There remain **plenty of** disused factories.*
*This was true **all** the way across the region.*
*There was **no** money in the community.*

- **Souligne les enjeux de la discussion par des relations de cause et conséquence.**

*And this is because a vibrant cultural offering **makes** people **want** to live there.*
*The city has **such a** creative impact **that**...*
*The cultural scene can **drive** huge growth in...*

**1** **Traduis ces phrases en faisant attention aux éléments en gras.**

a. **Rather than** implementing the same policies in all cities, each one **should** choose whatever project is **most appropriate** for their situation.
b. Deindustrialisation **has led to** a higher unemployment rate in some cities, **so that** some post-industrialised areas have often been impoverished.
c. **Extending** transport networks **would** boost exchanges within post-industrialised areas.

**2** **Utilise le conditionnel pour décrire ce que pourrait apporter la transformation de ce quartier de Manchester.**

## Vocabulary — British post-industrial cities

**Business areas** (AUDIO)
- education
- health service
- manufacturing
- transport
- tourism

**Housing** (AUDIO)
- accommodation
- connectivity
- leisure park
- mall
- communal
- upscale

**Challenges** (AUDIO)
- bankruptcy
- depression
- pollution
- shortage of
- turmoil
- unemployment

**Economy** (AUDIO)
- development policy
- exchange rate
- expansion ≠ decrease
- growth ≠ recession
- job market

**Places** (AUDIO)
- coal mine
- factory = mill
- warehouse
- workshop

**Renewal** (AUDIO)
- sustainable
- competitive
- innovative
- extend
- implement a plan
- upgrade = improve

**Workers** (AUDIO)
- labourer (UK)
- trade unionist
- full-time ≠ part-time
- low ≠ high-skilled
- demonstrate
- go on strike

**Feelings** (AUDIO)
- hardship
- struggle
- trauma
- depressed
- disheartened
- downtrodden

OBJECTIF BAC p. 296-304

Grille d'auto-évaluation

## Sujet type bac

MÉDIATION

Durée : 3h30
Matériel autorisé : le dictionnaire unilingue (non encyclopédique) est autorisé.
Niveau attendu : C1

- **Prenez connaissance des documents A, B et C et traitez le sujet suivant en anglais (500 mots maximum).**

Taking into account their specificities, show how these documents illustrate the issue of urban regeneration and gentrification in Manchester's Northern Quarter. Compare and contrast the positions on this question presented in each document.

- **Rendez compte en français des principales idées exprimées dans le document B. Veillez à ne pas simplement en dresser la liste mais à les expliciter lorsque cela vous paraît pertinent.**

### Document A

http://joeblakey.com/geography/greater-manchester-gentrification/

Joe Blakey

#### Greater Manchester gentrification

The cotton industry helped to foster economic activity in the Northern Quarter into the 20th century. [...] Following the First World War, the high cost of British cotton, and the increase in production elsewhere in the world, led to a slow decline of the British cotton industry. In the 1960s and 1970s, mills were closing in Greater Manchester at a rate of almost one a week, and by the 1980s only specialised textile production remained, although clothing manufacture and the wholesale[1] trade continue to form a strong part of Manchester's economy.

Following the Second World War, attention focused away from the Northern Quarter as Manchester began to build itself a modern city centre in the ruins left by German bombers. As a commercial area, Oldham Street became quieter, particularly as nearby Market Street and the Arndale Centre grew in importance. Over time certain types of business were attracted to the area, which offered low rents and an alternative feel to the typical British high street. This became the main strength of the Northern Quarter—today it is known for hip, independent stores, cafes and bars, and for offering a distinct alternative to the shopping experiences to be found elsewhere in Manchester city centre.

In 1988 the Central Manchester Development Corporation (CMDC) was created to formulate a regeneration policy for nearly 187ha of central Manchester (approximately 40% of the city centre), which included Castlefield, and to pump-prime private sector development using Government grants. CMDC's proposals were based on the City Centre Local Plan, and its mixed-use approach to Castlefield's revitalisation included several key aims—strengthening the tourism base, consolidating and supporting business activity and establishing a vibrant residential community were to accompany the imaginative and sensitive conservation and enhancement of listed buildings, canals, viaducts and spaces, and all was to be achieved with high standards of urban design. [...] Many of the key projects proposed by the CMDC during its eight years' existence, including hotel, housing and leisure developments, an interpretation and information centre, environmental works and improved parking facilities have now been realised. Visitors soon flowed in, attracted by the industrial heritage elements, but also by tours of Granada Television Studios.

*joeblakey.com*, October 2020

1. *commerce de gros*

## Document B How Manchester's Northern Quarter lost its soul

Dominic Sagar [...] has been a key player in the regeneration of Manchester's Northern Quarter, with his architectural practice helping to restore nearly 150 historic buildings in the neighbourhood.

But rather than become a zone for experimentation and an incubator for small businesses as he had envisioned, Dominic felt the Northern Quarter was en route to full blown gentrification—and he worried that he'd unwittingly been part of that process.

"I'm fuming[1] about what's happening to my city," he says, "Where are the new places to play—the cheap creative places to establish independent businesses? We were a group of caring people who had real love for the area—but, like many other places, the Northern Quarter became a victim of its own success."

The Northern Quarter, which lies in the north east of the city centre, is classified by Google as Manchester's 'indie' heartland. It's home to artist studios, alternative music venues, record stores, and vintage clothing shops.

But in recent years, the area has become increasingly overrun with bars and restaurants, many of which appear to be independent but are actually owned by a small handful of 'mini empires'. It has also become a party zone and hotspot for short-term lets[2], characterised by out-of-towners throwing all-night parties and failing to follow waste management rules.

Now big property developers have moved in, signaling what academics have identified as the final stage of gentrification. The 'luxury' flats being built don't provide mixed-income housing, with one developer telling me openly the scheme won't be marketed to locals because they won't be able to afford it. With property prices pushed up further, the area will become a 'ghetto for the well-off'. [...]

Within the past 18 months this has ramped up[3], with small arts and community organisations pushed out when rents were put up 30-40 per cent. Big property developers are now hungrily moving into the area, building 'luxury' flats for sale to overseas investors.

The Northern Quarter has become a tourist magnet, Airbnb hotspot, and party district. At the same time, due to austerity and financialisation of the housing market, the condition of the area is miserable. Bins overflow, remaining derelict buildings crumble, while anti-social behaviour and drug use often take place in broad daylight.

The Council has left the area to develop organically, which was a prudent approach at a time when there were individuals and groups who genuinely cared for the neighbourhood and were given some resources. But these groups are now mostly gone, either priced out or fled from an area that developed into something they didn't want it to become.

Andrea SANDOR, *huckmag.com*, 19 October 2020

1. very upset about
2. *location*
3. increase

## Document C

Tibb Street in Manchester's vibrant Northern Quarter, UK, 2019

Vers le **BAC**

# LET'S BRAINSTORM!

OBJECTIF BAC ▸ p. 305-317

**ENVIRONNEMENTS EN MUTATION** Axe 3

**How are post-industrial cities in the UK reinventing themselves?**

## Hard times to overcome

- The end of an era
  → "Manchester's Industrial Decline", *CitiesX*, p. 191 • *Born Under Punches*, M. Waites, p. 191
- Post-industrial landscapes
  → Death of Industry, *timelinesTV*, p. 190

## Economic renewals

- The Manchester miracle
  → "How did a city in decline become the poster child for urban regeneration?", *citymetric.com*, p. 192
- Heterogeneity of post-industrial cities today
  → "Regional planning in Post-industrial Great Britain", *CitiesX*, p. 196

## Betting on cultural assets

- Industrial landscapes for the film industry
  → "Why the film industry is hooked on industrial landscapes", *The Guardian*, p. 193
- UNESCO World Heritage Site status
  → "Why Liverpool could lose its UNESCO status", *ITVNews*, p. 193
- Museum, design and tourism
  → "A beacon of urban renewal", *theconversation*, p. 195 • V&A Museum in Dundee, *V&A Dundee*, p. 195

## Focusing on sustainability

- New sustainable housing plans
  → "CITU Climate Innovation district, *premierconstructionnews.com*, p. 194

## Phonology — Relancer la conversation : *tags* et réponses courtes

AUDIO

En anglais, pour relancer la conversation, on peut utiliser les ***question tags*** ou les **réponses courtes**. L'intonation varie alors en fonction de l'intention.

- Lorsque l'on attend une confirmation, l'intonation descend :
  *I think they'd find that remarkable about our modern world? Don't you?* ↘
  *Sure they **would**.* ↘ • *I sup**pose** **so**.* ↘
- Lorsqu'il s'agit d'une véritable question, l'intonation monte :
  *Do you know what I think would surprise them most?* ↗
  *Frankly, I **don't**.* ↘ • *Absolutely **not**.* ↘
- Lorsqu'une réponse courte contient un **auxiliaire**, c'est lui qui est accentué. Sinon, c'est le verbe qui est accentué, ainsi que ***so*** et ***not***. Dans tous les cas, l'intonation est **descendante**.

**1** **Écoute et note les intonations montantes. Déduis-en l'intention du locuteur.**

**a.** *It was never the same once the mills closed, was it?*
**b.** *But we can't decide on a strategy on our own, can we?*
**c.** *This plan is a real success, isn't it?*

**2** **Recopie et note les mots sur lesquels l'intonation monte ou descend. Écoute et vérifie.**

**a.** *Would you say the V&A had a real impact on the city's image? Yes, absolutely, I would.*
**b.** *But then, it was the first initiative of this kind, wasn't it? Yes, it was. You're right.*

# BUILD YOUR PORTFOLIO

## Website

Liverpool museums website

“From the beginning The Beatles were closely associated with Liverpool. As fascination with The Beatles and their home city spread, Beatles fans from around the world began to visit Liverpool to see for themselves the birthplace of The Beatles, the place where it all began.”

- **Read** the page and **explain** how The Beatles tourism industry reinvented Liverpool.

SITE

## Article

“Aestheticising the Post-Industrial Debris”, *openedition.org*, 2019

This article concentrates on contemporary British artistic photography and on how it has represented industrial and post-industrial sites in the period of de-industrialisation.

- **Read** the article and **observe** the photographs to find out to what extent post-industrial ruins have been turned into artistic objects.

ARTICLE

## Photography

“Reinventing urbanisation”, Neale Smith, 2020

Neale Smith is a Scottish photographer who takes pride in showing the best of his city's architecture throughout the years.

- **Browse** the website to **observe** Neale Smith's photographs and **analyse** the image he shows of Glasgow as a post-industrial city.

SITE

## Book

*The Cotton Harvest*, AK Nawaz, 2013

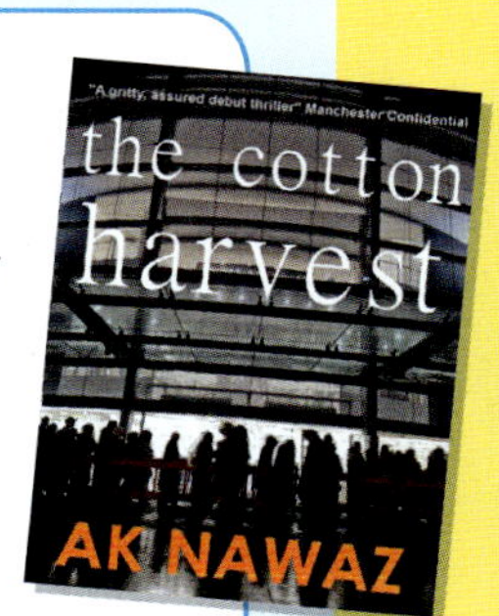


Disillusioned police officer Khorum Choudry was ready to quit when a Czech girl went missing. After a body is found, a brutal trafficker is the prime suspect. But Khorum isn't so sure that a strange secret in the housing estates of Manchester isn't at the heart of the matter.

- **Read** the novel and **study** the way post-industrial Manchester is used as a setting for crime novels.

## ÉPREUVE ORALE / GRAND ORAL — Entraîne-toi à l'oral

### Step 1 — Build up your speech!

**Épreuve orale**

- Choose one topic in the mindmap p. 200.
- Pick out two documents in the file and one or two personal ones to illustrate this issue.
- Prepare your presentation: you must show how these documents relate to the issue you chose.

OBJECTIF BAC p. 305

**Grand oral**

- Choose one topic in the mindmap p. 200.
- Find a key question about the topic and write it down. Think about links with other subjects (*SES* for example).
- Gather arguments and examples from the file.
- Prepare an outline for your presentation and write your note sheet.

OBJECTIF BAC p. 308-309

### Step 2 — Make your oral presentation in front of two classmates.

**Épreuve orale**

- Show your documents to your classmates. Each of you makes their presentation to the others in about five minutes.

OBJECTIF BAC p. 306-307

**Grand oral**

- Give your note sheet to your classmates.
- Stand up and make a five-minute presentation to answer your key question.

OBJECTIF BAC p. 310-311

### Step 3 — Answer your classmates' questions about your presentation.

# Nairobi megacity

▶ **How can Nairobi face the challenges generated by its urban sprawl?**

**YOUR MISSION**

MÉDIATION

**Make a report with French subtitles about the impact of urban sprawl in Nairobi.**

You are an urban-planning expert and you have just visited Nairobi. Make a report in English with French subtitles for your colleagues in France focusing on the impact of urban sprawl in the Kenyan city.

FOLLOW THE STEPS!

## 1 A city of contrasts

LANDMARKS p. 290

### Doc 1. A sprawling city

VIDÉO

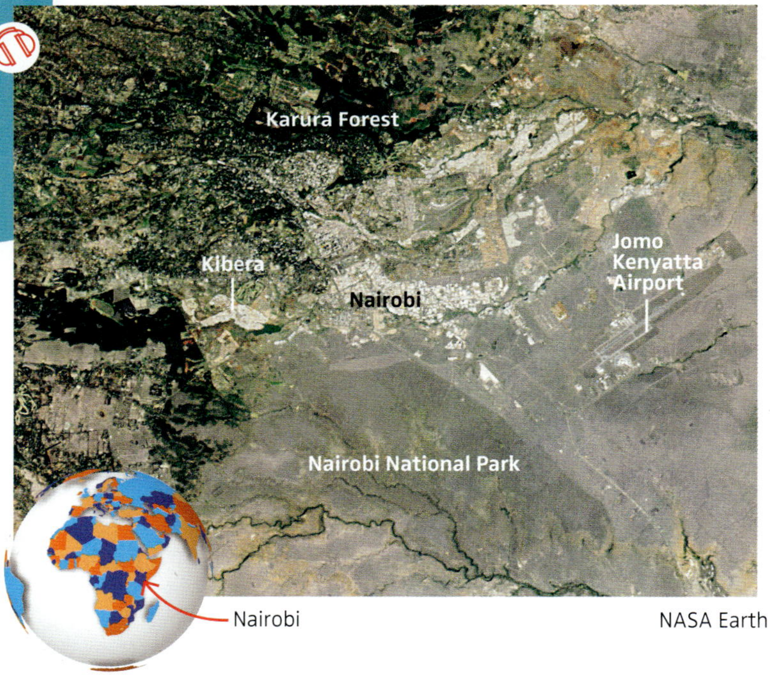


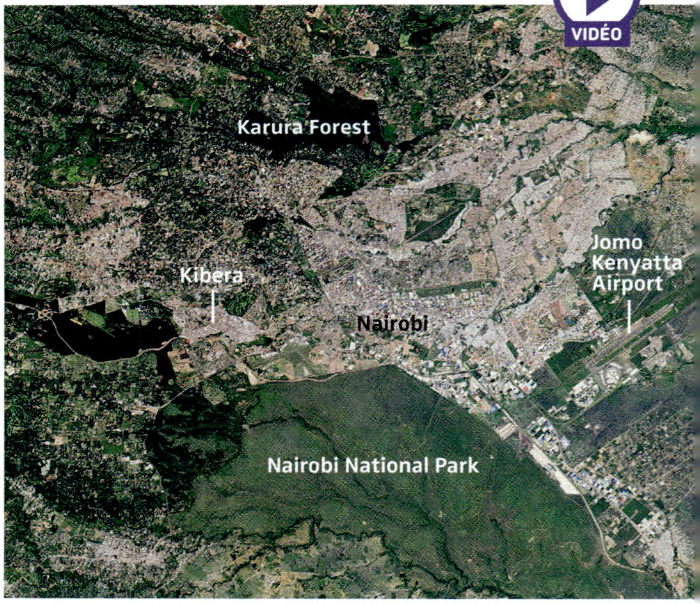


Nairobi

NASA Earth Observatory images of Nairobi, Kenya, 1986 (left) and 2016 (right)
(Video: *CGTN Africa*, 2019)

**a. Observe** both images and **identify** the major changes in Nairobi city.

**b. Watch** the video and **explain** what "urban sprawl" consists in. **Translate** the expression into French.

**c. Explain** what challenges Nairobi and other similar African cities are facing.

**d. Comment** on the role played by urban planners and architects regarding the city's development.

**WORDS**

- sk**y**scraper = h**i**gh-rise
- s**o**cio-econ**o**mic inequ**a**lities
- urbanis**a**tion = **u**rban dev**e**lopment
- w**a**steland
- dil**a**pidated = in disrep**ai**r
- insal**u**brious = unh**ea**lthy
- left on the s**i**delines
- grow = spread
- rehab**i**litate /ˌriːhəˈbɪlɪteɪt/

## Doc 2. A vertical city on the rise

VIDÉO

Downtown Nairobi (Video: *K24 TV*, 2017)

**a. Watch** the video and **find out** what gives Nairobi a *"modern personality"*.

**b. Pick out** expressions used to describe the development of the city. **Comment** on the impression it creates.

**c.** PHONOLOGY **Observe** the stress on *"majestically"*, *"predominantly"* and *"especially"*. Does the suffix "-ly" change the stress placement?

**d. Explain** why the Pinnacle is the perfect example of a flourishing economy.

**e. Discuss** the possible impacts of such changes.

## Doc 3. The other side of the tracks

TEXTE LU

As we walk, the big skyscrapers of downtown Nairobi, several miles to the northeast of us, melt into the distance. We weave[1] through markets with everything from chickens to chairs displayed for sale. Abruptly the paved road stops, and the buildings seem to shrink and huddle[2] closer together. We continue on a dirt path. There are people everywhere. I have to push my way through the dense crowd, trying my best not to fall in the mud. There are so many people I can hardly make out individuals—people are going every which way, with determined strides[3].

Before us sprawls Kibera, one of Africa's largest slums. Separated by a set of train tracks from the nearby lower-middle-class areas that enjoy formal provision of electricity and water, Kibera gives new meaning to the saying: *the other side of the tracks*. In Kibera, hundreds of thousands of houses made from sheets of corrugated[4] metal and other recycled materials are piled nearly on top of one another. Garbage-lined paths thread the neighborhood instead of roads, and the terrain consists of hilly slopes and steep inclines that without paving are uneven, making it difficult to maintain balance. With its own markets and shops, Kibera is almost a city unto itself, except that inside of the slum there are no government schools or health services, running water or legal power services. No one knows how many people live inside the slum—estimates range up to one million people in a space about the size of Central Park, entirely marginalized.

Kennedy ODEDE and Jessica POSNER, *Find Me Unafraid: Love, Loss, and Hope in an African Slum*, 2016

1. move in zigzag 2. *se blottir* 3. long steps 4. *ondulé*

Kibera slum, Nairobi

**a. Read** the text. **Focus** on the first paragraph and **quote** the visual elements used to draw the transition between the two parts of the city.

**b.** RHETORIC **Observe** the repetition of the word *"people"* (l. 7-10) and **comment** on its effect.

**c. Explain** the reference to *"the other side of the tracks"* and **say** how the narrator manages to convey the image of an abandoned part of the city.

**d. Discuss:** *"Kibera is almost a city unto itself."* (l. 21)

STEP 1 **Take** notes on the urbanisation of Nairobi and on the contrasts between the different parts of the city. **Illustrate** your notes with images from the web.

### BOOST YOUR SKILLS!

**Faire le point sur une situation existante**

- Utiliser le présent en *be* + V-*ing* pour décrire ce qui se passe actuellement : *What**'s happening** now on the continent...* • *Some of the challenges the cities **are facing**...*
- Utilise des superlatifs pour caractériser les éléments présentés : *The continent is **the least urbanised** in the world, globally, but has **the highest** rate of urbanisation.* • *One of Africa's **largest** slums...*
- Mets en avant des exemples : ***A good example is** Kenya....* • ***One example is** the five billion shillings UAP Old Mutual Tower...*

# 2 Water: the #1 challenge

## Doc 1.

**NATION** **Kenya's broken sewerage system**

Murky[1] water gushes[2] from the bottom of a cliff facing the densely populated Katwekera area in Kibera, an informal settlement in Nairobi. It is an open sewer[3] flowing through several villages including Kisumu Ndogo, Lindi and Siranga, Soweto, Makina, Kianda, Mashimoni and Laini Saba. The waste drains into Nairobi River, and ends up in the Nairobi Dam[4]. [...] Water that used to be clean is now mixed with sewage and of no use to residents.

Along the open sewer are jumbled[5] clean drinking-water pipes which supply adjacent houses. [Resident Joshua] Mungai is not sure about the safety of the drinking water given the proximity of the pipes to the open sewer, but he knows where the sewage generated in the settlement goes. This is the story of part of the one half of Nairobi, where only 50 per cent of residents are covered by a sewerage system. For those that are not covered, but rely on exhausters[6] to empty their septic tanks, the destination of their waste might not be so clear. [...]

Kenya had set a target of 40 per cent sewerage collection, treatment and disposal in urban centres and 10 per cent in rural areas by 2015, but four years later, it is way below target. This, according to WASREB, is because of high investment and maintenance costs for sewerage systems. Moreover, the agency adds in its impact report, in places where settlements are unplanned and water consumption is low, sewerage systems cannot be built and operated.

[There] are also places where the sewerage system exists but a large proportion of households are not connected due to the costs of maintaining a connection or due to the poor functioning of the system, and in many places (such as medium towns) where residents can afford to pay for the services, they are not existent.

Bernardine Mutanu, *Nation*, June 2019

**1.** muddy **2.** flows **3.** *égout* **4.** reservoir **5.** mixed up. **6.** *extracteurs*

**a. Read** the text and **pick out** information about the state of the sewerage system in Kibera.

**b. Focus** on figures and **say** what they reveal about Kibera's situation.

**c. Explain** the consequences for Kibera's residents. **Use** both the article and the photo.

**WORDS**

- faci**l**ities: *installations*
- pipes = drains
- sanit**a**tion
- aff**o**rdable
- dr**i**nkable
- equ**i**pped with

## Doc 2. Dealing with the water cartels

Kennedy Odede in Kibera, Nairobi (Video: *DW*, 2020)

**a. Watch** the video and **pick out** elements related to the water situation in the slum.

**b. Explain** what experiences led Kennedy Odede to become committed to the community.

**c.** TRANSLATION **Translate** *"Having grown up in Kibera, and experienced the effects of unsafe water first hand, Kennedy Odede founded the NGO SHOFCO but he would soon face fierce opposition from the so-called water cartels."* **Pay attention** to the verb forms.

**d. Comment** on the role of the "cartels" in Kibera and on Kennedy Odede's courage and determination.

**STEP 2** **Take** notes about the issue of water, its access and the way it is distributed by the "cartels" in Kibera. **Add** an example from the solutions raised by Kennedy Odede.

**BOOST YOUR SKILLS!**

**Faire prendre conscience des défis à relever**

- Emploie des expressions présentatives : ***This is*** *the story of part of the one half of Nairobi...* • ***There are*** *also places where...*
- Cite des propos avec des expressions appropriées : ***According to*** *WASREB...* • ***She said that*** *the government...*
- Utilise la voix passive : *Sewerage systems* ***cannot be built*** *and* ***operated***.

# 3 Bringing natural resources

## Doc 1.

VIDÉO

Kiroko Enterprises, an urban farm in Nairobi (Video: "Urban farming", *East Africa Institute of the Aga Khan University*, 2016)

**WORDS**

- bare minimum
- compliance /kəm'plaɪəns/: following a law or rule
- staple: basic food

- supportive of (sb/sth)

- contribute to + V-ing
- empower
- promote = foster

## Doc 2.

HUNTER COLLEGE NEW YORK CITY FOOD POLICY CENTER

**Policy Name:**
Urban Agriculture Promotion and Regulation Act, Nairobi

**Overview:**
The Urban Agriculture Promotion and Regulation Act establishes a regulatory framework under which urban agriculture in Nairobi may be practiced and creates the Nairobi City County Urban Agriculture Promotion Advisory Board to oversee compliance with the law. [...]

**Program goals:**
The objectives of the Act are to:

- Contribute to food security through the development of agriculture in the county by empowering the people and institutions through allowing and facilitating agricultural activities for subsistence and commercial purposes.
- Promote increased access to agricultural extension services and promote the development of people's capacity in food production, value addition, value chain development and employment creation.
- Promote, support, and guide the development of urban agriculture.

Regulate access to land and water for use in urban agriculture.

**Why it is important:**
Food insecurity is a significant problem throughout Kenya. According to a report by the Kenya National Bureau of Statistics and the University of Nairobi African Women's Studies Centre, 14.5% of Nairobians suffer from low food security, and 11.7% are chronically food insecure. Furthermore, a study from the African Population Health Research Center shows that in Nairobi's poorest neighborhoods, only one in five households is food secure. Urban agriculture has the potential to provide healthy food to the city's most vulnerable communities.

*nycfoodpolicy.org*, 2018

**a. Watch** the video (**Doc 1**) and **explain** the different challenges evoked.

**b. Read** the text (**Doc 2**) and **give** details on the goals of the Urban Agriculture Promotion and Regulation Act.

**c. Pick out** the figures and **comment** on the issue of food insecurity in the two documents.

**d. Explain** how urban farming can contribute to improving the situation.

### STEP 3 (MÉDIATION)

French homologues would like to know about the Urban Agriculture Promotion and Regulation Act.
**Translate** the first objective of the Act (l. 11-14) to help them understand this ambitious political programme.

### FINAL STEP (MÉDIATION)

**Gather** your notes and **select** images to prepare your report about the impact of urban sprawl in Nairobi.
**Record** the voice-over narration and **translate** it to add French subtitles to your report.

**You've completed your mission. Well done!**

play BAC How to... **TRANSLATE INTO FRENCH**

MÉDIATION

OBJECTIF BAC p. 302-303

L'**épreuve écrite** en Terminale comprend deux parties. Suite à la synthèse de documents et éventuellement de l'essai argumentatif (partie 1), tu devras procéder à la transposition en français d'un document du dossier ou bien à la **traduction en français d'un court passage** de l'un des documents (partie 2).
Voici un exemple de texte, extrait du Doc 3 p. 203, qui pourrait t'être donné pour l'exercice de traduction :

**Traduisez en français le passage suivant de l'extrait de *Find me unafraid: Love, Loss, and Hope in an African Slum* (2016) de Kennedy Odede et Jessica Posner.**

As we walk, the big skyscrapers of downtown Nairobi, several miles to the northeast of us, melt into the distance. We weave through markets with everything from chickens to chairs displayed for sale. Abruptly the paved road stops, and the buildings seem to shrink and huddle closer together. We continue on a dirt path. There are people everywhere. I have to push my way through the dense crowd, trying my best not to fall in the mud. There are so many people I can hardly make out individuals—people are going every which way, with determined strides.

## 1 Analyse l'extrait

**a. Identifie** les pronoms personnels utilisés.

**b. Observe** le temps des verbes. Quel est l'effet produit par le choix de ce temps ?

**c. Repère** où se passe l'action. **Visualise** l'itinéraire de la narratrice.

• Pour conserver l'effet de « travelling », respecte le présent et la longueur des phrases.

## 2 Utilise des procédés de traduction : la transposition grammaticale, le chassé-croisé

OBJECTIF BAC p. 303

**a.** Lorsque la traduction littérale (mot-à-mot) n'est pas possible ou pas souhaitable, on a recours à la modulation, ou à la transposition grammaticale. Cette dernière consiste à changer de catégorie grammaticale quand on passe de l'anglais au français.
**Observe** et **commente** cette traduction : *abruptly* → de façon soudaine.

**b. Observe** cette phrase et sa traduction. Que deviennent la préposition *through* et le verbe *weave*?

*We **weave through** markets...*
Nous traversons les marchés en zigzaguant...

Cette double transposition grammaticale s'appelle un chassé-croisé.

**c. Traduis** cette phrase en utilisant le procédé du chassé-croisé.

*I have to **push my way through** the dense crowd...*

• Les verbes à préposition se traduisent très souvent en utilisant le chassé-croisé : la préposition devient un verbe et le verbe une locution adverbiale.

• Certains verbes prépositionnels peuvent se traduire par des expressions idiomatiques.

## 3 Traduis l'extrait

OBJECTIF BAC p. 302

**Traduis** le passage en veillant aux points suivants :

• L'agencement syntaxique, c'est-à-dire l'ordre des mots : il diffère souvent entre l'anglais et le français. Par exemple, où vas-tu placer la traduction de l'adverbe *abruptly* en français ?

• La ponctuation : elle n'est pas la même en anglais et en français. Par exemple, comment vas-tu ponctuer la traduction française des incises qui sont entre virgules en anglais ?

• La personnification des bâtiments dans la phrase *the buildings seem to shrink and huddle closer together* : il faudra la conserver dans la traduction française.

• Utilise un dictionnaire unilingue pour vérifier le sens des termes que tu ne comprends pas. Attention notamment à *dirt* qui a plusieurs sens ou à *hardly* qui n'a rien à voir avec *hard*.

Vers le **BAC**

# BUILD YOUR PORTFOLIO

## Article

"Development in action: Expansion of Nairobi's Outer Ring Road reduces traffic congestion and public commute times", *African Development Bank Group*, July 2018

“The expansion of a 13-kilometre outer ring road in the Kenyan capital has significantly reduced travel times and road congestion demonstrating the power of road infrastructure in development, says African Development Bank President, Akinwumi Adesina.”

- **Read** the article and **explain** the benefits of the road project. **Pay attention** to the source of the document and **say** how it may influence the tone of the report.

ARTICLE

## Photograph

"Ballerina Elsie", Brian Otieno, 2018

Documentary photographer Brian Otieno was raised in Kibera. His photographic project entitled "Kibera Stories" presents life in the slum from a socio-economic, cultural, political and environmental point of view.

- **Observe** the photograph and **explain** how it is showing that in the slum there is more to life than hunger and misery.

VIDÉO

## Chart

Nairobi National Park Threat Assessment, in "Nairobi National Park Situation Analysis", Shane Feyers (Yale University), December 2015

Located in a highly economically active and densely populated area, Nairobi National Park faces a growing number of threats. This university report aims at informing the management of the park and helping decision-makers to implement actions and strategies for its protection.

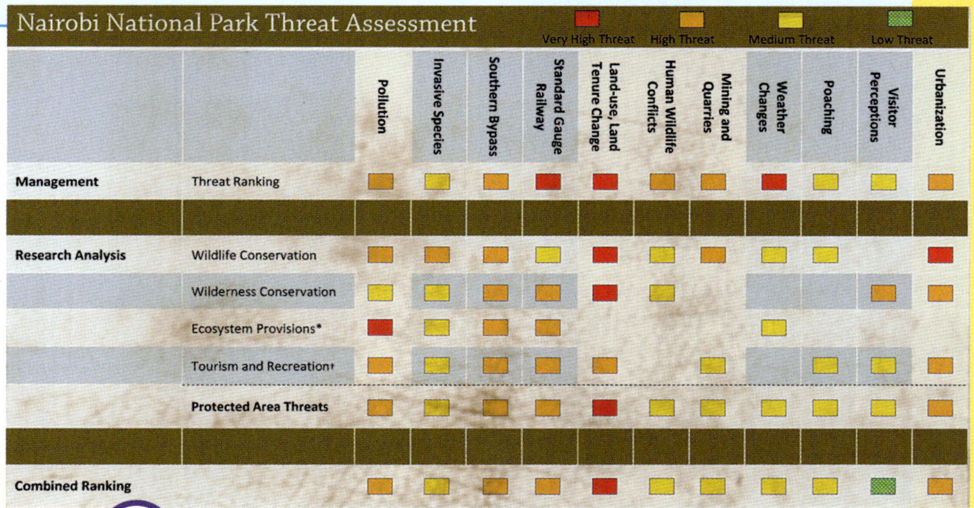


- **Analyse** the major threats to the protected area of the national park and to its ecosystem.

REPORT

## Report

"Sh28bn grand plan to transform Nairobi", *The Star*, October 2019

“Traffic congestion, lack of affordable housing and water supply problems within Nairobi could be a thing of the past following plans to expand the central business district and develop a new railway station to link all city suburbs.”

- **Watch** the video and **read** the article. **Explain** how the proposed plan will transform Nairobi.

VIDÉO ARTICLE

## Entraîne-toi à l'oral

ÉPREUVE ORALE

**Step 1** **Build up your speech!**

- Focus on how Nairobi is changing to become a megacity.
- Pick out documents from the file, add a personal one and pick out another one in this page to illustrate the topic. OBJECTIF BAC p. 305
- Prepare your presentation. You must show how these documents relate to the topic.

**Step 2** **Make your presentation in front of two classmates.**

- Show the documents to your classmates and explain your point in about five minutes. OBJECTIF BAC p. 306-307

**Step 3** **Answer your classmates' questions about your presentation.**

FILE 23

RELATION AU MONDE
AXE 1 : PUISSANCE ET INFLUENCE

# Tech Giants

▶ **Is the power of Big Tech unlimited?**

FINAL TASK — **Write an opinion piece entitled "Tech Giants: power and influence".**

More on SPEAKEASY NEWS speakeasy-news.com

## 1 The Big Five's superpower

**Doc 1.** VIDÉO

Christopher WEYANT, *The Boston Globe* (Video: "Life without Big Tech", *Gizmodo*, 2019)

**CULTURE SPOT**

**Big Tech**, also known as the **Tech Giants** or **Big Five**, are the most dominant companies in the American technology industry: Google, Apple, Facebook, Amazon, and Microsoft (GAFAM).

LANDMARKS ▶ p. 281

**a. Look at** the cartoon and **say** what issue it raises.

**b. Watch** the video. **Find** information about Kashmir Hill's project and the challenges she had to face.

**c.** GRAMMAR ▶ *"It's changed our lives in ways that we regret".* **Identify** the verb forms and **explain** what they convey. ▶ p. 215

**d. Discuss** the statement *"We don't feel that [life with big tech] is healthy, but we don't know how to step back."*

**WORDS**

- d**o**minance = supr**e**macy
- ubi**q**uitous = omnipr**e**sent
- break up a mon**o**poly
- comp**e**te with
- exp**a**nd
- g**o**bble up = eat up
- have a mon**o**poly on

## Doc 2. Running the world?

**a.** **Look** at the chart and **account for** the evolution of tech companies from 2005 to 2020.

**b.** **Listen to** the audio. **Pick out** the names of companies mentioned and **explain** their evolution through time.

**c.** **Define** what Tim Wu calls America's curse and **explain** its consequences.

**d.** **Comment** on the speakers' tone.

**e.** PHONOLOGY **Listen** to the words *"antitrust"* and *"privacy"*, focusing on <i>. What is the American pronunciation? **Compare** it to the British one.

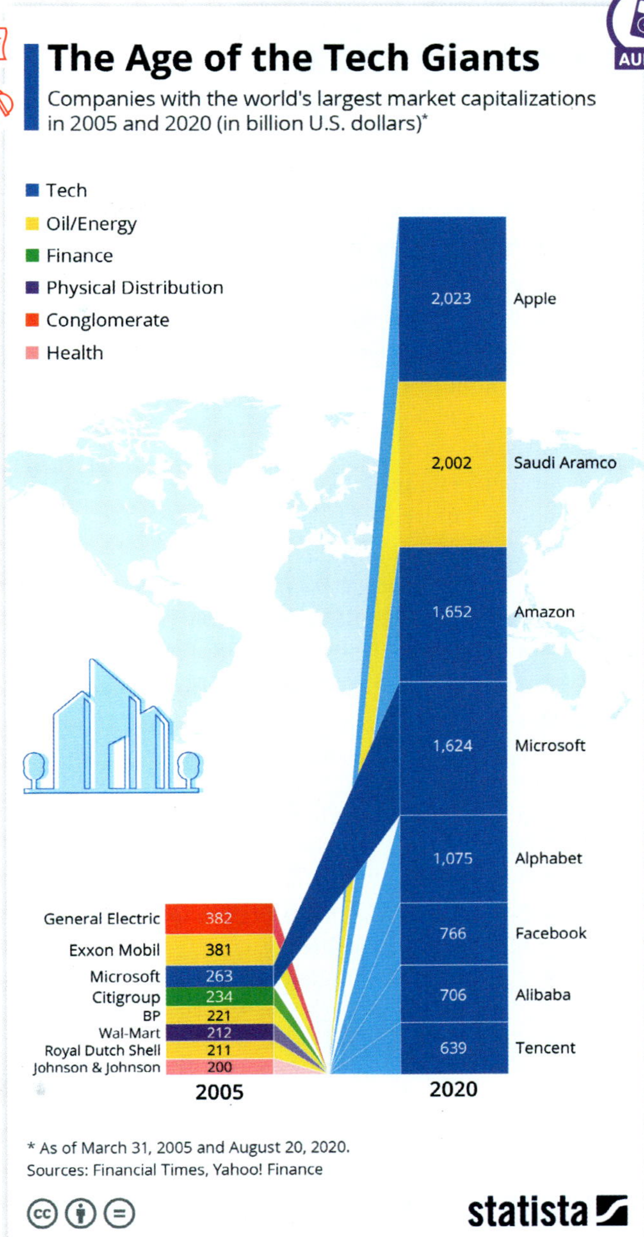


(Audio: "Curse of bigness", *PBS NewsHour*, 2019)

## Doc 3.

### The trouble with charitable billionaires

In February 2017, Facebook's founder and CEO Mark Zuckerberg was in the headlines for his charitable activities. The Chan Zuckerberg Initiative, founded by the tech billionaire and his wife, Priscilla Chan, handed out over $3m in grants to aid the housing crisis in the Silicon Valley area. [...]

Mark Zuckerberg was by no means the first contemporary CEO to promise and initiate large-scale donations of wealth to self-nominated good causes. In the CEO society it is positively a badge of honour for the world's most wealthy businesspeople to create vehicles to give away their wealth. This has been institutionalised in what is known as The Giving Pledge[1], a philanthropy campaign initiated by Warren Buffett and Bill Gates in 2010. The campaign targets billionaires around the world, encouraging them to give away the majority of their wealth. There is nothing in the pledge that specifies what exactly the donations will be used for [...].

Essentially, what we are witnessing is the transfer of responsibility for public goods and services from democratic institutions to the wealthy, to be administered by an executive class. In the CEO society, the exercise of social responsibilities is no longer debated in terms of whether corporations should or shouldn't be responsible for more than their own business interests. Instead, it is about how philanthropy can be used to reinforce a politico-economic system that enables such a small number of people to accumulate obscene amounts of wealth.

Carl RHODES and Peter BLOOM, *The Guardian*, May 2018

1. promise

**a.** **Read** the text and **explain** why Mark Zuckerberg hit the headlines.

**b.** **Describe** what makes philanthropy a "badge of honour".

**c.** RHETORIC **Focus** on this quote: *"A politico-economic system that enables **such a small number of** people to accumulate **obscene amounts of wealth**"*. (l. 26-28) **Identify** the rhetorical device and account for the authors' opinion on the issue.

**BOOST YOUR SKILLS!**

**Présenter un monopole**

- Souligne son expansion avec des verbes prépositionnels : *Tech giants have steadily **bought up** companies.* • *Facebook **gobbled up** Instagram.* GRAMMAR p. 215
- Sers-toi de quantifieurs: ***All of** its competitors...* • *Just a **few firms**...* • ***Amounts of** wealth...*
- Utilise le *present perfect* pour faire le bilan : *Google **has extinguished** many industries.* • *Amazon **has made** it easier to get a lot of products.*

**YOUR TASK** **Record** the introduction to a podcast about Big Tech. **Present** its evolution and monopoly.

# 2 Big Tech ubiquity

## Doc 1.

TEXTE LU

*The Circle*, film by James Ponsoldt, 2017

*Eamon Bailey is the CEO of the Circle, a technology company. Every Friday he speaks to his employees.*

Now the page was refreshed, and the coastline was full-screen, and the resolution was perfect. There were sounds of awe[1] throughout the room.

"Yes, this is live video of Stinson Beach. This is Stinson right at this moment. Looks pretty good, right? [...]

Annie leaned into Mae. "The next part's incredible. Just wait."

"Now, many of you still aren't so impressed. [...] But there are a couple new aspects to all this. The first part is how we're getting this image. Would it surprise you to know that this isn't coming from a big camera, but actually just one of these?"

He was holding a small device in his hand, the shape and size of a lollipop. [...]

"Okay, so I set up that camera this morning. I taped it to a stake, stuck that stake in the sand, in the dunes, with no permit, nothing. In fact, no one knows it's there. So this morning I turned it on, then I drove back to the office, accessed Camera One, Stinson Beach, and I got this image. Not bad. But that's not the half of it. Actually, I was pretty busy this morning. I drove around, and set up one at Rodeo Beach, too."

And now the original image, of Stinson Beach, shrunk and moved to a corner of the screen. Another box emerged, showing the waves at Rodeo Beach, a few miles down the Pacific coast. "And now Montara. And Ocean Beach. Fort Point." With each beach Bailey mentioned, another live image appeared. There were now six beaches in a grid, each of them live, visible with perfect clarity and brilliant color.

"Now remember: no one sees these cameras. I've hidden them pretty well. To the average person they look like weeds, or some kind of stick. Anything. They're unnoticed."

A smattering[2] of applause.

Dave EGGERS, *The Circle*, 2013

1. *stupéfaction* 2. small quantity

**a. Read** the text and **find** information about the situation (people, place, activity).

**b. Comment** on the audience's reactions to the presentation.

**c.** RHETORIC *"No permit, nothing. In fact, no one knows it's there."* (l. 15), *"They're unnoticed."* (l. 29). **Say** what these expressions have in common. What does it imply about The Circle's goal?

**d. Discuss** the potential advantages and dangers of this new technology.

**e.** A critic described the novel *The Circle* as a *"Google fantasy dystopia"*. Do you agree?

## Doc 2. Invading our privacy?

VIDÉO

*Your Morning*, 2018

**a. Watch** the video and **define** what Daniel Bader calls an ad company.

**b. Compare** and **contrast** Google and Facebook concerning data collection.

**c.** GRAMMAR **Focus** on *"Google keeps it inside the company so that you'll spend more time on Google services."* **Explain** the use of *"so that"* and **translate** the sentence.

**d. Discuss** Daniel Bader's statement: *"We are the products."*

## Doc 3.

### Facebook's controversial cryptocurrency gets a new name: Diem

Libra, the cryptocurrency spearheaded[1] by Facebook, got a new name on Tuesday, a move designed to reinforce "its organizational independence" as the ever-shrinking project seeks regulatory approval.

The cryptocurrency will likely be backed one-for-one by the US dollar, *The Financial Times* reported, rather than proposed multiple single-currency stablecoins backed by major currencies. A stablecoin is a cryptocurrency that links its market value to an external source like the dollar.

Here's what you need to know.

**Why does Facebook want a cryptocurrency?**

This isn't actually Facebook's cryptocurrency. It's a project of the Diem Association, which Facebook originally co-founded as the Libra Association. The association, which will serve as a monetary authority for the cryptocurrency, says its purpose is to "empower billions of people," citing 1.7 billion adults without bank accounts who could use the currency.

But Facebook has its own interest in digital cash that predates[2] Diem. The social network ran a virtual currency, called Credits, for about four years as a way to make payments on games played within Facebook. Mark Zuckerberg, Facebook's CEO, has said that sending money online should be as simple as sending photos. Diem is designed to make it easier and cheaper for people to transfer money online, which might also attract new users to the social network. But Zuckerberg acknowledged that having people use cryptocurrency would likely benefit Facebook by making advertising on the social network more desirable and, therefore, more expensive.

Facebook may also have other plans for the cryptocurrency. A new subsidiary[3] will run a wallet for holding and using the digital currency.

**Is this just a ploy[4] so Facebook can get my financial data and send more targeted ads?**

We hear you. Facebook doesn't have a great reputation for privacy protection.

The social network says don't worry—not that you expected it to say anything else. When the plans were first unveiled, Facebook took pains to point out its wallet was housed in a subsidiary of the social network. The arrangement was designed to allow the wallet company to be regulated by authorities and prevent money laundering[5] and other financial crimes. The company also said it would keep financial data separate from Facebook's social data.

Andrew MORSE, *cnet.com*, December 2020

1. initiated. 2. dates back earlier. 3. company 4. strategy 5. *blanchiment d'argent*

**WORDS**

- browser
- distrust = suspicion
- oligopoly
- search engine

---

- intrusive

---

- be wary of = be cautious about
- have a hold on
- keep track of = monitor
- target

**a. Read** the text. **Say** what Diem consists of and how it works.

**b. Comment** on the possible risks of using Diem.

**c.** VOCABULARY **Pick out** the expressions of probability. What do they mean about the issue?

**d. Explain** the role and interests of Facebook in this project. Would you be ready to use Diem?

**YOUR TASK** After reading the article, **post** a comment online to **react** to the hold Big Tech companies have on our lives.

**BOOST YOUR SKILLS!**

**Souligner la mainmise de grands groupes**

- Personnifie ces entreprises en position sujet : ***Google*** *doesn't share your information.* • ***Google*** *scans your email...* • ***Facebook*** *may have other plans...*
- Précise leurs intentions : *Diem* ***is designed to*** *make it easier...* • ***Its purpose is to*** *empower...* • *Google keeps it inside the company* ***so that*** *you'll spend...* GRAMMAR p. 215
- Souligne leur emprise par l'usage des pronoms : ***You*** *are the product.* • ***You*** *are the people* ***they*** *want to show ads to...*

EXPLORE

# 3 Too big to regulate?

## Doc 1.

### Big Tech companies want to act like governments

For years, big technology companies have acted as though they were above the law. More people use Microsoft, Facebook or Amazon than the populations of most countries. Their profits exceed the budgets of many states.

Tech and social media companies have become powerful global actors and their corporate governance decisions already affect the rights and freedoms of billions of people. But, tech companies are now going a step further, by positioning themselves as governments. [...]

"The New Titans", David PARKINS for *The Economist*

At the annual security conference in Munich, presidents, prime ministers and politicians usually share the sought-after stage to engage in conversations about conflict in the Middle East, the future of the EU, or transatlantic relations. This year, executives of Alphabet, Facebook and Microsoft were added to the speakers list.

Facebook boss Mark Zuckerberg went on from Munich to Brussels to meet with EU commissioners about a package of regulatory initiatives on artificial intelligence, data and digital services. Commissioner Thierry Breton provided the apt reminder that companies must follow EU regulations — not the other way around. But making sure EU lawmakers stay in the driver's seat will require significant catching up.

Tech executives who initially resisted regulation now call it desirable. As long as regulations serve their interests, companies support them. [...]

If tech executives want change, there is no need to wait for government regulation to guide them in the right direction. They can start in their own "republics" today. As regulators of the domains they govern, nothing stops them proactively aligning their terms of use with human rights, democratic principles and the rule of law. When they deploy authoritarian models of governing, they should be called out. Instead of playing government, they should take responsibility for their own territories. This means anchoring terms of use and standards in the rule of law and democratic principles and allowing independent scrutiny from researchers, regulators and democratic representatives alike. Credible accountability is always independent. It is time to ensure such oversight is proportionate to the power of tech giants.

Companies seeking to democratise would also have to give their employees and customers more of a say, as prime "constituents". If leaders are serious about their state-like powers, they must walk the walk and treat consumers as citizens. Until then, calls for regulations will be seen as opportunistic, and corporations unfit to lead.

Marietje SCHAAKE, The *Financial Times*, February 2020

**a. Observe** the illustration and **share** your impressions.

**b. Pick out** elements showing that Big Tech behaves as though it were a government.

**c.** RHETORIC *"They can start in their own "republics" today."* **Identify** the figure of speech and **justify** its use.

**d. Explain** and **comment** on the need for regulation.

**WORDS**

- competitor = opponent
- unhampered freedom = free rein /reɪn/

---

- entangled = enmeshed
- intricate

- paradoxical

---

- curb = curtail = limit
- keep up with ≠ get left behind
- thrive = expand = prosper

## Doc 2. Towards policy changes?

How will tech policy change in the Biden White House?, *NPR*, Nov. 2020 AUDIO

**a.** VOCABULARY **Before** listening, **match** each word with its translation:
– techlash • in the crosshairs • shield
– *dans la ligne de mire • retour de bâton • protection*

**b. Listen** to the audio and **explain** the changes expected from the Biden White House.

**c. Define** what Section 230 is and **comment** on the issue it raises.

## Doc 3.

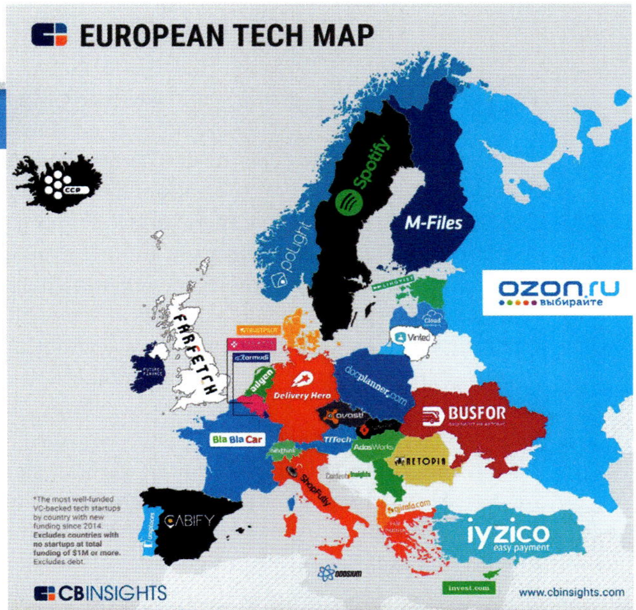


**DSX HUB** THE ULTIMATE TECH BLOG

### EU unveils plan to compete with GAFAM on AI and Big Data

The European Union intends to catch up with the United States and China in the field of Big Data and Artificial Intelligence. In order to enable European GAFAMs to emerge, the European Commission today unveils its strategic plan for the next ten years. […]

The EU has decided to say "stop." At a press conference on Wednesday 19 February 2020, the President of the European Commission, Ursula von der Leyen, unveiled Brussels' ambitious plan to finally bring the old continent into the digital age. Several measures aimed at enabling the bloc to gain technological sovereignty have therefore been unveiled.

**The EU wants a European data market so that our tech giants can compete with GAFAMs**

In the field of Big Data, the Commission would firstly like to create a "single European data market" by 2030. To this end, it intends to promote the free movement of data within the Union.

This way, European companies in turn will be able to exploit the vast volumes of data which has allowed American giants such as Google and Amazon to surpass 1 trillion in market capitalization. […] In order to stimulate innovation, public-sector data will also be made available via the opening of "high-value data sets" that can be reused. To this end, the EU will also invest in Cloud infrastructures

**The European Union wants to attract 20 billion euros per year to AI, while ensuring its ethics.**

As far as artificial intelligence is concerned, the Commission intends to stimulate the development of this technology of the future in Europe. To achieve this, it aims to attract more than 20 billion euros of investment per year over the next ten years. […] The EU therefore wishes to encourage the development of AI, while taking care to guard against the potential risks associated with this revolutionary technology.

*dsxhub.org*, Oct 2020

**YOUR TASK** MÉDIATION

DIFFÉRENCIATION

As a member of the EU Commission, **write** a note to **inform** your staff about the Big Data development plans.

**WAY 1 Explain** the different measures and their aim.

**WAY 2 Insist** on the importance of such measures and **stress** how they will be implemented and what for.

**a. Look** at the European Tech Map and react, having in mind your use of American Big Tech.

**b. Read** the article and **find** information about the "ambitious plan".

**c. Explain** the reasons for setting up such a plan.

**d.** VOCABULARY **Focus** on *"in order to"*, *"aims to"*, and *"wishes to"*. **Explain** what the preposition *"to"* means.

**e. Compare** Europe's and America's strategies regarding the regulation of Big Tech companies.

**BOOST YOUR SKILLS!**

**Exposer une stratégie**

- Présente les objectifs avec des connecteurs logiques : ***In order to*** *stimulate innovation.* • *The EU* ***therefore*** *wishes to encourage…*
GRAMMAR p. 215
- Utilise le lexique de l'intention : *The EU therefore* ***wishes to*** *encourage…* • *The Commission* ***intends*** *to stimulate…* • *It* ***aims to*** *attract…* • *The European Union* ***wants*** *to…*
- Utilise le modal *will* pour évoquer les résultats escomptés : *European companies in turn* ***will*** *be able to…* • *Public sector data* ***will*** *also be made…*

# 4 Redeeming themselves?

Columbia Journalism Review The voice of journalism JOIN US

## For Big Tech, what follows 'free expression'?

**For Big Tech,** free expression was always part of the business plan.
Since the goal of any social media company is to have as much user-generated stuff as possible, and since monitoring content and deciding what to take down is both expensive and controversial, embracing free speech was always good for the bottom line[1]. It also allowed the companies to stay out of the political fray[2] by making the case that their hands-off approach aligned with an essential American value.
But free expression is no longer the guiding principle at Big Tech, as the hearings before the Senate Commerce Committee last month demonstrated. In those hearings, Twitter's Jack Dorsey, Facebook's Mark Zuckerberg, and Google's Sundar Pichai were compelled[3] in the most politicized and polarized environment to explain their companies' content-moderation policies [...].
Because of its decentralized structure and the libertarian ethos[4] of its founders, "the First Amendment is hardwired[5] into the Internet," Danny O'Brien, now director of strategy at the Electronic Frontier Foundation, explained to me several years ago when I was researching a book on new forms of censorship. [...] But as the Internet became a unitary global system, the companies found that the First Amendment was not always so popular in the rest of the world. While Internet utopians believed a free and unfettered[6] Internet could liberate the world from tyranny, governments around the world had other ideas. [...]
The first step for Big Tech is articulating a framework that accurately describes their new model. For the companies to continue to say they are guided by free-expression principles does not cut it[7], given how much control they are exercising over content. Perhaps the new goal should be to create an online information environment that serves the public interest. The companies should welcome a political and public debate as to how the public interest is defined.

Joel SIMON, *cjr.org*, November 2020

1. profit 2. battle 3. forced 4. spirit 5. permanent part of 6. free 7. not limited

**a.** **Read** the article and **describe** Big Tech's initial *"hands-off"* approach.
**b.** **Explain** why and how things are evolving.
**c.** **Discuss** the two viewpoints presented in l. 14-15.
**d.** TRANSLATION **Translate** l. 16-18. **Pay** particular attention to the compound word.

**CULTURE SPOT**

**Libertarianism** is a political philosophy that values liberties and argues for minimal state intervention in the free market and lives of citizens.

## FINAL TASK

**Write an opinion piece entitled "Tech Giants: power and influence" for the tech magazine *Wired*.**

**As an independent journalist, write an article about the Tech Giants' influence today for a special issue of the magazine.**

1. **Browse** the documents to get an overview of the Tech Giants (economic growth, monopoly, invasion of privacy, regulations, influence, changes to come etc.).
2. **Define** your position as a journalist (supportive, critical, or both).
3. **Gather** arguments to support your point of view. **Illustrate** it with examples, figures, and a few quotes.
4. **Write** your article. Remember to **write** a catchy headline to grab your readers' attention.

# BOOST YOUR ENGLISH!

## Grammar — Rédiger un article d'opinion

- **Dresse un bilan de la situation au *present perfect*.**

*It's **taken** us closer to this structure that we had in the Gilded Age.*
*The tech industry **has enjoyed** decades free of major regulation.*
*The EU **has decided** to say "stop".*

- **Utilise l'expression du but pour souligner les enjeux du sujet.**

***In order** to stimulate innovation, public sector data will also be made available.*
*Google keeps it inside the company **so that** you'll spend more time on Google services.*
*Is this just a ploy **so** Facebook can get my financial data?*

- **Confronte les arguments avec des subordonnées d'opposition et de concession.**

***While** Internet utopians believed..., governments around the world had **other** ideas.*
*Biden's people sound like they're ready to..., **though** executives from Amazon [...] are part of Biden's transition team.*

- **Utilise les modaux *should* et *must* pour formuler des conseils ou fortes recommandations.**

*Perhaps the new goal **should** be to create an online information environment that...*
*He said Section 230 **should** be revoked immediately.*
*As net states expand their powers beyond the digital world, we **must** pay attention.*

**1** **Conjugue les verbes au *present perfect* ou au prétérit.**

**a.** Amazon (start) in 1994 and (grow) into a multinational tech company since then.
**b.** It's the first time the journalist (try) to cut out the Big Five from her life.
**c.** She (never/have) a Facebook account but she is changing her mind.
**d.** Antitrust laws (be) stricter in the Gilded Age.

**2** **Traduis les phrases suivantes.**

**a.** L'UE a dévoilé un plan ambitieux pour réguler les GAFAM.
**b.** L'UE veut un marché des données pour que ses entreprises puissent concurrencer les GAFAM.
**c.** Pour y arriver, l'UE projette d'attirer 20 milliards d'euros.
**d.** Les GAFAM ont l'intention d'exploiter une grande quantité de données.

## Vocabulary — Tech Giants

Technology — Power — Challenges

### Developments (AUDIO)
- AI = artificial intelligence
- big data
- cryptocurrency
- digital wallet

### Tools (AUDIO)
- algorithm
- browser: *navigateur*
- data tracking
- search engine: *moteur de recherche*

### Economic (AUDIO)
- capitalism
- dominion over
- free enterprise = liberal economics
- investment
- oligarchy

### Philanthropy (AUDIO)
- altruism
- charitable giving
- charity
- foundation
- patronage
- sponsorship

### Supremacy (AUDIO)
- dominance
- expansion
- monopoly
- surveillance
- ubiquity = omnipresence
- ubiquitous
- unavoidable

### Threats to the public (AUDIO)
- data theft
- ethical/moral (dilemma)
- insidious
- pervasive
- eavesdrop = monitor
- invade privacy

### Regulation (AUDIO)
- jurisdiction
- lawsuit
- public policy
- curtail = restrain
- limit ≠ give free rein
- pass/implement a law

OBJECTIF BAC p. 296-304

Grille d'auto-évaluation

## Sujet type bac

MÉDIATION

Durée : 3h30
Matériel autorisé : l'usage du dictionnaire unilingue non encyclopédique est autorisé.
Niveau attendu : C1

- **Prenez connaissance des documents A, B, C et traitez le sujet suivant en anglais (500 mots maximum).**

Taking into account their specificities, say how the documents show the role given to Big Tech in the environmental crisis.

- **Traduisez en français le passage suivant du document C.**

*"There are a lot of days at Cloud I remember, but the one I remember most fondly is the first day.*
*I remember it because it was the hardest. Every day after that was a little easier.*
*People thought I was nuts to start this company. A lot of people probably don't even remember, back in the day, there was another company that did some of the same stuff we do now, except on a much smaller scale.*
*Problem was, their interests were too earthbound."* (l. 1-6)

### Document A — Silicon Valley is fuelling the climate crisis

***Big Tech isn't interested in a better world, just a more profitable one***

Silicon Valley, California

The climate crimes of big tech are legion. This summer the Amazon burned. Why? In part because of the policies of the new anti-environmental, anti-human-rights president, Jair Bolsonaro.

How did Bolsonaro rise to prominence and then the presidency? YouTube, and certain of its algorithms that push people toward more extreme content, played a large part. As the *New York Times* reported in August, not long ago Bolsonaro was "a marginal figure in national politics—but a star in YouTube's far-right community in Brazil, where the platform has become more widely watched than all but one TV channel". Members of the nation's newly empowered far right—from grassroots organisers to federal lawmakers—say their movement would not have risen so far, so fast, without YouTube's recommendation engine. [...]

What the climate emergency demands of us and what capitalism does to us are at war with each other, and big tech is a ruthless new version of robber-baron[1] capitalism, with new tools and powers for the same old agenda of consolidating power at the top. While Silicon Valley's remake of so many parts of our lives could have been elegantly environmental and empowering for ordinary people, mostly it's been profit-driven.

Rebecca SOLNIT, *The Guardian*, October 10, 2019

1. derogatory term for powerful businessmen

Document B

**Big Tech all have a lot to learn from the Green New Deal**

For many years, the biggest technology companies have made pioneering commitments to reducing their energy footprint. Google and Apple claim to be completely carbon neutral: Apple says all its facilities are powered entirely by renewable energy, while Google has become the world's largest buyer of renewable energy to offset its energy costs. In 2018, Apple said it had reduced carbon emissions by 58% since 2011. Microsoft is on track to reach 60% renewable energy across its data centers by the end of 2019, while Facebook's goal is to reach 100% renewable energy by 2020. In 2019, Amazon announced that it is aiming to make half of its shipments carbon neutral by 2030, and the company says it has eliminated 244,000 tons of packaging materials, avoided 500 million shipping boxes, and continues to invest in electric vehicles, aviation bio fuels, and renewable energy.

Given that many corporations aren't as focused on sustainability, the tech companies' efforts to reduce emissions appear at first to be a good track record. But as the fight against climate change heats up, the big tech companies' claims and commitments still are not enough to make an impact on a widening emissions gap—in 2018, global emissions levels rose 2.7% after years of not growing at all. The UN says that these levels must drop 55% by 2030 to avoid the most catastrophic effects of climate change.

And while much of that growth in emissions can be attributed to a range of corporate bad actors, some leaders in the climate community think tech companies are not doing enough to use their clout[1] and tech prowess[2] to make real change.

"Let's get over this notion that [tech companies] are some kind of heroes. They're not," says Richard Wiles, the director of the Center for Climate Integrity. "They're doing the least they can do to get the most greenwashing benefit out of it," he says

Katharine SCHWAB, *fastcompany.com*, June 27, 2019

1. influence 2. expertise

Document C **The Warehouse**

*In this novel, Gibson, the narrator, is the founder of Cloud, the giant tech company that's eaten much of the American economy in the near future.*

There are a lot of days at Cloud I remember, but the one I remember most fondly is the first day. I remember it because it was the hardest. Every day after that was a little easier.

People thought I was nuts to start this company. A lot of people probably don't even remember, back in the day, there was another company that did some of the same stuff we do now, except on a much smaller scale. Problem was, their interests were too earthbound.

Ever since I was a kid, I was obsessed with the sky. The broadness of it. Like we had this giant resource over us every day and we weren't really using it. Sure, we had planes flying this way and that, but there seemed to be so much more potential.

At a pretty young age I knew the future was in drone technology. The air and the roads had been all gummed up[1] by these giant trucks, taking up space, spitting out poison. If we could solve the truck problem, we could solve a lot of other problems. Traffic, pollution, crash fatalities.

Do you know what traffic costs? About ten years ago, when it reached epidemic proportions, you're talking about something like $305 billion in direct and indirect losses in a single year. This was according to the Institute for Economics and Business Research.

Now, what does that mean? Losses include time wasted while sitting in traffic, the cost of fuel, impact on the environment, road maintenance, traffic fatalities. Mass transit helps, but only so much. Even way back when I was young, a lot of our mass-transit infrastructure was already falling apart, and the cost to fix it was astronomical. We all remember when the New York City subway system finally fell apart. That city has never been the same since.

The key was getting drones into the sky for more than just fun and games.

Rob HART, *The Warehouse*, 2019

1. obstructed

Vers le **BAC**

# LET'S BRAINSTORM!

OBJECTIF BAC p. 305-317

## A monopoly power

- Big Tech is unavoidable

→ "Life without Big Tech", *Gizmodo*, p. 208

- Lack of antitrust regulations leads to monopolies

→ "Curse of bigness", *PBS*, p. 209

- Philanthropy allows Big Tech to reinforce its power

→ "The trouble with charitable billionaires", *The Guardian*, p. 209

## Invading every inch of our lives

- Tech companies collect private data

→ "Invading our privacy?", *Your Morning*, p. 210 • *The Circle*, D. EGGERS, p. 210

- Financial privacy concerns

→ "Facebook's controversial cryptocurrency", *cnet.com*, p. 211

RELATION AU MONDE **Axe 1**

**Is the power of Big Tech unlimited?**

## Companies challenging entire nations

- Can't Big Tech be regulated?

→ "Big Tech companies want to act like governments", *The Financial Times*, p. 212

- What governments can do

→ "Towards policy changes?", *NPR*, p. 213 • "EU unveils plan to compete with GAFAM", *dsxhub.org*, p. 213

## Big Tech *v.* freedom?

- Free speech under question

→ "For Big Tech, what follows 'free expression'?", *cjr.org*, p. 214

- When lack of control leads to loss of freedom

→ "Big Tech companies want to act like governments", *The Financial Times*, p. 212 • "Invading our privacy?", *Your Morning*, p. 210

## Phonology — L'accentuation des adjectifs composés

AUDIO

En anglais, les **adjectifs composés**, reconnaissables par le trait d'union entre les deux (parfois trois) éléments qui les composent, peuvent être accentués **sur le premier ou sur le deuxième** élément selon **la nature** de chaque mot. L'accent porte le plus souvent sur l'élément nominal.

- Accent sur le **premier élément** :
  Nom + forme en *V-ing* : *l**o**ss-making, pr**o**fit-making*
  Nom + participe passé : *st**a**te-led, regul**a**tion-proofed*
- Accent sur le **second élément** :
  Adjectif + nom : *single-c**u**rrency, high-t**e**ch*
- Si les **deux éléments sont des adjectifs**, c'est le **1er élément** qui est accentué : *f**a**st-growing*

**Lis l'extrait suivant. Anticipe l'accentuation des mots composés, écoute et vérifie.**

*Mark Zuckerberg, the world-famous billionaire, was by no means the first contemporary CEO to initiate large-scale donations of wealth to self-nominated good causes. Instead, it is about how so-called philanthropy can be used to reinforce a politico-economic system that enables such a small number of virtue-signalling people to accumulate obscene amounts of wealth.*

# BUILD YOUR PORTFOLIO

## Book

*Break'Em Up*, Zephyr Teachout, 2020

This essay not only explores how big tech companies have taken control of our lives — whether it is on an economic, social or even political level — but it also shows a possible way out.

- **Read** the foreword and introduction and **explain** to what extent these monopolies can be a threat to democracy.

## Film

*The Social Dilemma*, Jeff Orlowski, 2020

This Netflix documentary investigates the seamy side of social networks and big tech companies to reveal how they have managed to enter our minds and even control us, somehow affecting our mental health.

- **Watch** the trailer and **list** the side effects of Facebook on its users.

VIDÉO

## Book

*The Warehouse*, Rob Hart, 2019

"A thrilling story of corporate espionage at the highest level... and a powerful cautionary tale about technology, runaway capitalism, and the nightmare world we are making for ourselves." — Blake Crouch, *New York Times* bestselling author

- **Read** the book and **explain** how far fiction is from reality.

## Article

"America's New Antitrust Trend Is So European", *Bloomberg*, October 13, 2020

Are American and European governments responding the same way to big tech companies? By comparing their approaches, this article gives an insight into the jurisdictions—both in the US and in the EU—and how they have evolved over the last decade.

- **Read** the article in order to **explain** and **compare** the strategies and legislation adopted by the US and the EU regarding Big Tech companies.

ARTICLE

## ÉPREUVE ORALE | GRAND ORAL — Entraîne-toi à l'oral

### Step 1 — Build up your speech!

OBJECTIF BAC p. 316-317

**Épreuve orale**

- Choose one topic in the mindmap p. 218.
- Pick out two documents in the file and one or two personal ones to illustrate this issue.
- Prepare your presentation: you must show how these documents relate to the issue you chose.

OBJECTIF BAC p. 305

**Grand oral**

- Choose one topic in the mindmap p. 218.
- Find a key question about the topic and write it down. Think about links with other subjects (*SES, DGEMC* for example).
- Gather arguments and examples from the file.
- Prepare an outline for your presentation and write your note sheet.

OBJECTIF BAC p. 308-309

### Step 2 — Make your oral presentation in front of two classmates.

**Épreuve orale**

- Show your documents to your classmates. Each of you makes their presentation to the others in about five minutes.

OBJECTIF BAC p. 306-307

**Grand oral**

- Give your note sheet to your classmates.
- Stand up and make a five-minute presentation to answer your key question.

OBJECTIF BAC p. 310-311

### Step 3 — Answer your classmates' questions about your presentation

# Five Eyes, one power

► **How does the Five Eyes intelligence alliance strengthen the international power of English-speaking countries?**

More on SPEAKEASY NEWS
speakeasy-news.com

YOUR MISSION

MÉDIATION

**Enquire about the Five Eyes alliance for an investigation newspaper.**

At the end of your internship for a big investigation newspaper, you are given a practical task to test your capacities. Enquire about the Five Eyes alliance and present your findings to the editorial board.

FOLLOW THE STEPS!

## 1 The secret alliance of the Anglosphere

**Doc 1.**

AUDIO

"Five Eyes alliance and key events", *Graphic News*, 2019
(Audio: "The secret alliance", *NPR*, 2013)

**WORDS**

- agreement = treaty
- alliance /əˈlaɪəns/ = partnership
- analyst
- data flow
- joint forces = cooperation

- comprehensive: covering a wide range of sth

- eavesdrop /ˈiːvzdrɒp/ = listen secretly
- keep a close eye on sb/sth
- spy on sb/sth
- wiretap = spy on sb's phone

**a. Observe** the infographic and **give** information about Five Eyes.

**b. Listen** to the interview of Ambassador John Negroponte and **pick out** the events which shaped the history of Five Eyes.

**c.** PHONOLOGY **Focus** on the three dates mentioned and **comment** on the way they are said and stressed.

**d. Explain** what the five members have pledged to do and why.

**e. Give details** about their activities.

## Doc 2. A complex role

https://ukdefencejournal.org.uk/the-five-eyes-the-intelligence-alliance-of-the-anglosphere/

**ukdj.** HOME LAND SEA AIR SPACE CYBER INDUSTRY INTERNATIONAL ANALYSIS ABOUT US

### The Five Eyes – The Intelligence Alliance of the Anglosphere

The current role of the Five Eyes has many ramifications, such as the 'maritime domain' where the alliance monitors shipping[1] traffic passing through strategic maritime areas and the 'aerospace domain' which covers ballistic missile tests, foreign satellite deployments and the military activities of relevant air forces.

Terrorist organisations and weapons business deals made by 'problematic regimes' are also within the scope[2] of the Five Eyes; these two, in particular, are growing source of worries for all the five members and the intelligence co-operation between them is essential to keep their governments updated with the most recent information. This aids the process of policy-making, for the data collected and analysed by the alliance may turn out to be vital for more than a time of crises but also for the daily basis of government; notably, these daily efforts consist in tracking and identifying possible sources of terrorism and other non-conventional threats.

Such complex agreement would never exist if not for the convergent aspects of all the five members. They share common principles, such as the liberal democratic values, similar or complementary national interests and cultures. Beyond that, since the Second World War Britain, Canada, Australia, New Zealand and the United States share the same threats to their national security be they conventional or not. […]

In addition, the Five Eyes works with various 'Third Party' countries, the co-operation with Denmark, France, Norway and the Netherlands receives the name of 'Nine Eyes', and there is the 'Fourteen Eyes' which consists of the previously mentioned 'Nine Eyes' plus Belgium, Germany, Italy, Spain and Sweden.

J. Vitor Tossini, *ukdefencejournal.org.uk*, April 2020

1. transporting goods on ships 2. field of competence

**a. Read** the text and **identify** the missions carried out by Five Eyes.

**b. Comment** on the importance of collaboration within Five Eyes and **identify** their new partners.

**c. Explain** what makes such a cooperation possible.

**d.** VOCABULARY *"…these efforts **consist in** tracking and identifying possible sources…"* (l. 10-11) *"…which **consists of** the previously mentioned…"* (l. 20) **Explain** the different meanings of the verb *"consist"* and **translate** the sentences.

## Doc 3. Common objectives

This book is dedicated to the men and women of the Five Eyes intelligence community who since World War II have composed the bedrock[1] intelligence agencies and departments for sustaining freedom and democracy in our fragile world. The trust and relationships built between the individuals of each member nation has been the single most important factor for the continuing success of the "Special Relationship" in the provision of timely[2], accurate, and unvarnished actionable intelligence to their individual national leaderships, and the collective good of the five nations. Those relationships, built so successfully over the decades since World War II, will endure because of the quality, commitment, and loyalty of each serving individual. We all have reason to be grateful for their service. They are the continuity that in an age of global political uncertainty provides the bedrock foundations for modern society's security. May intelligence cooperation between the United States, the United Kingdom, Canada, Australia, and New Zealand continue onwards and upwards, and provide the bedrock security for future society.

Anthony R. Wells, *Between Five Eyes: 50 Years of Intelligence Sharing*, 2020

1. solid foundation 2. in good time

**CULTURE SPOT**

**Anthony R. Wells** worked for British Intelligence as a British citizen and US Intelligence as an American citizen.

**a. Read** the text and **identify** which part of the book it is from.

**b. Focus** on the point of view of the author and **pick out** elements to describe the tone of the passage.

**c. Explain** what Five Eyes draws its strength from according to Anthony Wells.

**STEP 1** **Start** a mindmap that you will use to present your findings to the editorial board. **Fill** it **in** with information about the history of Five Eyes.

# 2 Facing criticism

## Doc 1. Top-secret leaks

LANDMARKS p. 294

**Edward Snowden discloses[1] U.S. government operations**

On June 6, 2013, Americans learned that their government was spying broadly on its own people.

That's when *The Guardian* and *The Washington Post* published the first of a series of reports put together from documents leaked[2] by an anonymous source. The material exposed a government-run surveillance program that monitored the communications records of not just criminals or potential terrorists, but law-abiding citizens as well.

Three days later the source unmasked himself as Edward Snowden, a National Security Agency contractor. But the question remained: Was he a whistleblower or a traitor?

In the wake of the 9/11 attacks and the perceived need for heightened national security, the US government relaxed its rules around surveillance. The first story published in *The Guardian* revealed that the NSA was collecting and monitoring the telephone records and the texts of citizens. Days later, *The Washington Post* and *The Guardian* reported that the US government was tapping into[3] the servers of nine Internet companies, including Apple, Facebook and Google, to spy on people's audio and video chats, photographs, emails, documents and connection logs, as part of a surveillance program called PRISM. Later articles revealed that the government was even spying on leaders of other countries, including Germany's Angela Merkel.

In the same month, Snowden was charged with theft of government property, unauthorized communication of national defense information and willful communication of classified communications intelligence. Facing up to 30 years in prison, Snowden left the country, originally traveling to Hong Kong and then to Russia, to avoid being extradited to the US.

*History.com*, 2013

Dan WASSERMAN, "NSA in court", *The Boston Globe*, December 2013

**a. Read** the text and **explain** what PRISM is.

**b. Explain** and **discuss** what happened to Edward Snowden.

**c.** VOCABULARY **Pick out** all the synonyms of the verb *"reveal"* and **translate** them.

**d. Look** at the cartoon and **explain** why it is ironical.

**e. Explain** why it could be used to illustrate the text.

1. exposes
2. revealed
3. using the data of

## Doc 2. A presidential response

*CBS Evening News*, 2014

**a. Watch** the video and **identify** the context of President Obama's speech.

**b. Explain** his position regarding surveillance.

**c. Discuss:** Does President Obama go far enough to protect civil liberties?

STEP 2 **Fill in** your mindmap with new elements. **Focus** on the controversial aspects of secret intelligence agencies.

BOOST YOUR SKILLS!

**Montrer les limites d'une organisation**

- Utilise le modal *can* pour en montrer le pouvoir : *It* ***can*** *search its massive trove of telephone and internet data.* • *The US* ***can*** *still spy on friendly foreign governments...*
- Mets en avant les excès d'un système : *A surveillance program* ***that*** *monitored the communications records of* ***not just*** *criminals or potential terrorists,* ***but*** *law-abiding citizens* ***as well.***
- Utilise le modal *will* pour insister sur les décisions prises et leurs limites : *There* ***will*** *be more scrutiny and higher-level approval required.* • *Our intelligence agencies* ***will*** *continue to gather information about the intentions of governments.*

# 3 More challenges to come

**CIPS** Centre for **International Policy Studies**

## Huawei or Our Way?: Fissures in the Five Eyes Alliance in the Face of a Rising China

In January this year, the UK Government broke ranks with its Five Eyes allies, confirming that Huawei would be involved in building part of its 5G network.

The condemnation of allies and growing domestic political pressure has since provoked a reversal in the UK position on Huawei. In mid-July, British Secretary of State for Digital, Culture, Media and Sport, Oliver Dowden, announced that buying new Huawei equipment would be banned after December 2020 and that all existing Huawei technology would be removed from 5G networks by the end of 2027. Many consider the timeframe too long, and also note that Britain's earlier position was made virtually untenable after the US banned semiconductors that rely on US chip technology from provisioning Huawei without US government permission. Nonetheless, there is relief among the Five Eyes community that a consistent[1] position on the use of Huawei for critical infrastructure has ultimately emerged. (For its part, Canada has not yet officially prohibited Huawei technology in its 5G build, but many observers consider it inevitable following Britain's change of heart.)

The Huawei episode illustrates the challenges of keeping the alliance together in the face of growing pressure from China.

In a post-COVID world the difficulty of keeping all Five Eyes allies on the same strategic page is only going to increase. Small, export-reliant, and now heavily indebted countries like NZ cannot afford to jeopardize[2] trade with China. Indeed, New Zealand need only look across the Tasman Sea to know that taking a tougher stance[3] towards Beijing can have immediate economic repercussions. Similarly, the Victorian Labor government's MOU[4] with Beijing suggests a change in partisan government at the national level could well see Australia split from the US and adopt a more accommodating position toward China. Canada too, may not be so unflinching[5] the next time China slaps a ban on Canadian canola[6] or sentences Canadian citizens to death on dubious charges. In sum, it seems very unlikely that the Five Eyes alliance will hang together as naturally and seamlessly as it did during the unipolar period of the immediate post-Cold War era.

Helen Baxendale, "Understanding the Five Eyes: Twitter Conference", *University of Ottawa*, October 2020

**1.** common and agreed **2.** endanger **3.** posture **4.** Memorandum of Understanding: *protocole d'accord* **5.** determined **6.** *colza*

### WORDS

- hegemony
- secrecy /'si:krəsi/
- video monitoring

---

- cautious = prudent
- defying
- diplomatic

---

- challenge
- induce = cause
- monitor = observe
- process = treat, convert
- provoke
- query /'kwɪəri/ = doubt /daʊt/
- stake out = keep under surveillance

LANDMARKS p. 281

**a. Read** the text and **describe** the situation the UK had to face with its allies in January 2020.

**b. Say** what the UK's answer was and **imagine** why.

**c. Comment** on the interdependence of the Five Eyes countries with China.

**d.** TRANSLATION **Translate** the last sentence of the text. (l. 29-31)

**STEP 3** **Complete** your mindmap with new elements from the page. **Focus** on the economic challenge that might divide the alliance in the future.

**FINAL STEP** MÉDIATION

**Use** your mindmap to **organise** your oral presentation of the Five Eyes alliance. **Present** your findings to the editorial board, using your mindmap as a personal reminder and a visual presentation to show your audience.

**You've completed your mission. Well done!**

play BAC How to... TRANSPOSE A TEXT INTO FRENCH

MÉDIATION

OBJECTIF BAC p. 304

L'**épreuve écrite** en Terminale comprend deux parties. Suite à la synthèse de documents (partie 1), tu devras procéder à la **transposition en français d'un document du dossier** ou bien à la traduction en français d'un court passage de l'un des documents (partie 2).
Voici un exemple de transposition, basée sur le Doc p. 223, qui pourrait t'être demandée le jour de l'épreuve.

Rendez compte en français des principales idées exprimées par l'extrait de "Huawei or Our Way?: Fissures in the Five Eyes Alliance in the Face of a Rising China" (*Centre for International Policy Studies, University of Ottawa*, October 2020) de Helen Baxendale. Veillez à ne pas simplement en dresser la liste, mais à les expliciter lorsque cela vous paraît pertinent.

## 1 Analyse l'extrait

**a. Repère** le type de texte et sa tonalité.

**b. Identifie** la problématique du texte.

Dans un article, la problématique est souvent sous-entendue dans le titre, le sous-titre ou le premier paragraphe.
*Fissures in the Five Eyes Alliance in the Face of a Rising China*

**c. Résume** les arguments principaux qui répondent à cette problématique.

**d. Explique** comment la crise avec Huawei illustre la fragilité du pacte de confiance de Five Eyes.

• La transposition consiste à rendre compte des idées principales d'un document sans en reprendre tous les détails, donc sans le traduire mot pour mot. Pour réussir cet exercice, une bonne compréhension du texte est nécessaire.

## 2 Découvre comment faire une transposition

**a. Lis** le texte en entier une ou deux fois. **Repère** les idées principales et **surligne**-les.

*In January this year, the UK Government broke ranks with its Five Eyes allies, confirming that Huawei would be involved in building part of its 5G network.*

**b. Repère** les articulations du texte pour avoir en tête le cheminement logique et le faire apparaître dans ta transposition.

**c. Fais** le tri pour **distinguer** ce qui tient de l'argument, de l'idée et ce qui tient de l'exemple, de l'illustration. Ne **retiens** que les arguments, les idées.

**d. Numérote** toutes les idées soulignées afin d'éviter tout oubli.

• Souligne les connecteurs logiques pour mettre en évidence le raisonnement présent dans le texte.

## 3 Rédige la transposition

**Rends compte** du texte, en veillant aux points suivants :

• **Utilise** des connecteurs logiques.

**Néanmoins**, l'alliance a exprimé son soulagement d'être arrivée à un consensus sur l'utilisation de Huawei.

• **Rédige** dans un français de qualité et adapte la ponctuation.

Le Royaume Uni a revu sa position sur Huawei, suite à la condamnation unanime de ses alliés.

• **Relis** l'ensemble de ta transposition pour vérifier qu'elle est équilibrée et que toutes les idées sont exprimées.

• Il ne faut pas confondre traduction et transposition. Veille à ne pas traduire quelques phrases tirées du texte à transposer, mais bien à rendre compte des idées principales qu'il dégage : il faut donc reformuler.

# Vers le BAC

## BUILD YOUR PORTFOLIO

### Documentary

*I Spy (with My Five Eyes)*, Justin Pemberton, 2016

“It was going in this direction anyway, but 9/11 incredibly accelerated it. Once you got the terrorist attack here, we became very unforgiving in not grabbing communications, and so we accelerated our ability, our, for want of a better word, invasiveness into communications networks, in which legitimate targets co-existed with legitimately protected communications.”
– Former NSA director
General Michael Hayden

- **Watch** the online documentary and **explain** how the alliance managed to change its activities after World War II.

VIDÉO

### Official document

United Kingdom – United States of America Agreement, 5 March 1946

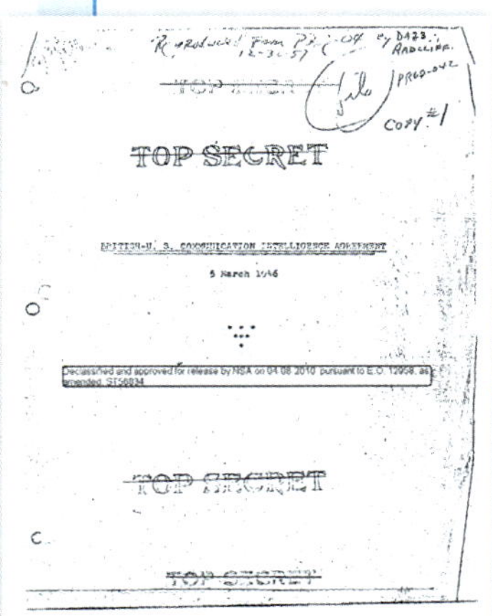
TOP SECRET

5 March 1946

TOP SECRET

- **Read** the document, **focus** on page 3 and **explain** what the operations mentioned in the extract consist in.

TEXT

### Article

“Five Eyes alliance could expand in scope to counteract China”, *The Guardian*, July 2020

“The Five Eyes intelligence alliance could be expanded to include Japan and broadened into a strategic economic relationship that pools key strategic reserves such as critical minerals and medical supplies, according to centre-right MPs working internationally to decouple the west from China.”

- **Read** the article and **explain** the context that requires Five Eyes to expand its alliances.

ARTICLE

### Cartoon

“Five go mad in Queenstown”, Toby Morris, 2017

A meeting of intelligence leaders from the United States, the United Kingdom, Canada, Australia and New Zealand was held in Queenstown in April 2017.
**Toby Morris**, a New Zealand cartoonist, comics artist, illustrator and writer, gave his point of view on what the secretive club was getting up to.

- **Look** at the cartoon and **analyse** the way the New Zealand cartoonist portrays the Five Eyes alliance.

### Film

*Snowden*, Oliver Stone, 2016

- **Watch** the trailer and **explain** what issue director Oliver Stone wanted to denounce and how he chose to portray the character of Edward Snowden.

VIDÉO

## Entraîne-toi à l'oral

ÉPREUVE ORALE

**Step 1** **Build up your speech!**

- Focus on the way the Five Eyes alliance has managed to strengthen the international power of English-speaking countries.
- Pick out documents to build your portfolio: choose from this file, this page, or from your personal references.
- Prepare your presentation: show how these documents relate to the topic. OBJECTIF BAC p. 305

**Step 2** **Make your presentation in front of two classmates.**

- Show your documents to your classmates and explain your point in about five minutes. OBJECTIF BAC p. 306-307

**Step 3** **Answer your classmates' questions about your presentation.**

FILE 25

RELATION AU MONDE
AXE 2 : RIVALITÉS ET INTERDÉPENDANCES

# The new Cold War?

▶ **What is at stake between the USA and China?**

FINAL TASK **Take part in a talk on US-China relations.**

More on SPEAKEASY NEWS speakeasy-news.com

## 1 A new world balance

LANDMARKS p. 278

Doc 1.

VIDÉO

Illustration by Martin WOLF, *The Financial Times* (Video: "China: a challenger", *The Economist*, 2019)

**a.** **Observe** the illustration, **describe** and **comment** on how this new "Cold War" is presented.

**b.** **Watch** the video and **explain** what the two superpowers are fighting over.

**c.** RHETORIC **Find out** how the solutions that could help America in its competition with China are presented. What effect does it produce?

**d.** **Discuss** what these solutions reveal about the situation.

WORDS

- adversary
- ally /'ælaɪ/ = partner
- geopolitics
- hegemonic = predominant
- threatening
- challenge = defy
- perceive sb as
- trade with = do business with

## Doc 2.

### What does it mean to be a superpower?

The staggering[1] rise of China has become one of the most prominent stories of the 21st century.

Since the fall of the Soviet Union in 1991, the United States has generally been considered the world's only real superpower, while China is still generally referred to as an emerging superpower.

Some analysts are certain that the Asian giant is well on its way to leaving its developing status behind and will pass the US as a global power in coming decades, while others maintain the US will stay in front for years to come.

Those who argue against the US's unrivalled status suggest the very concept of a superpower is losing its relevance in an increasingly "multi-power" world while maintaining that the Western giant no longer meets all the required criteria.

For example, while the US continues to wield[2] the most superior military capabilities on Earth, it is losing its dominant role in world affairs and calling the shots on the global economic stage.

But what does it mean to be a "superpower" in 2019? How will we know if or when China has rivalled or passed the US? And are recent phenomena like the rise of US President Donald Trump to blame or are we witnessing the transformative stages of a future inevitability?

Perhaps surprisingly, there is no official definition of what constitutes a superpower—but according to a range of definitions, a superpower is typically characterised by a state's ability to exert influence and project itself as a dominating power anywhere in the world.

There are several measurements of power which include military and economic strength, as well as diplomatic and cultural influence—a superpower should be a leader in all of these areas.

International-relations and US-policy expert Gordon Adams told the ABC that if power were solely measured in military terms, there is no question the US is the only military superpower. [...]

However, when other dimensions of powers are considered, Dr Adams said the US's leading status becomes a little murkier[3].

Christina ZHOU, *ABC*, June 2019

**1.** impressive **2.** possess **3.** less clear

**Many see U.S. as their country's top ally**

*% who say their country can most rely on __ as a dependable ally in the future*

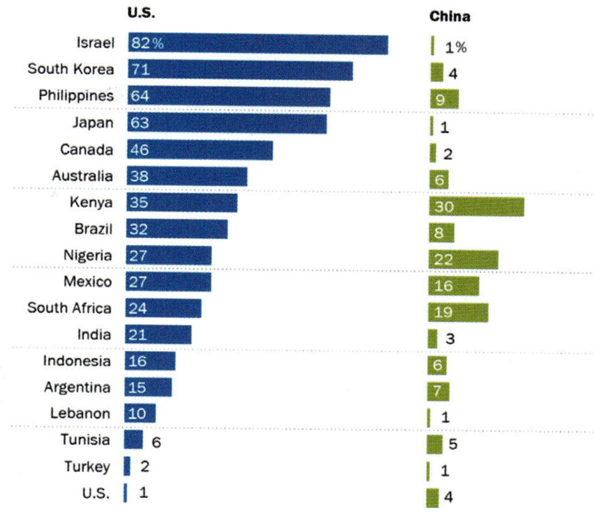


**Accross different countries, both the U.S. and China emerge as key threats**

*% who say __ is the country or group that poses the greatest threat to their country in the future*

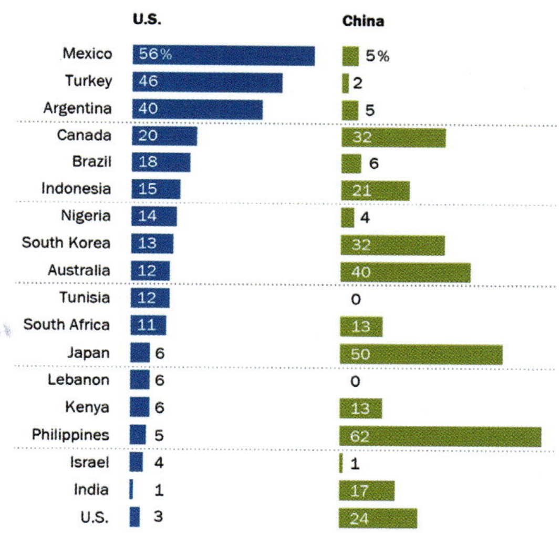


Note: Figures represent results of an open-ended question, where interviewers selected from a precoded list. Other countries named not shown.

Source: Spring 2019, Global Attitudes Survey. Q22 & Q23

PEW RESEARCH CENTER

**a. Observe** the charts and **compare** how the United States' and China's influences are perceived in other countries.

**b. Focus** on Mexico and Japan and try to **explain** why those influences are seen differently.

**c.** GRAMMAR **Read** the article. Find which subordinating conjunction is repeatedly used in the text. What does it highlight? ▸ p. 233

**d. Compare** and **contrast** the evolution of American and Chinese positions on the world stage.

**e. Name** all the criteria that must be considered to define a country as a superpower.

**YOUR TASK** Two diplomats **discuss** the following question: "Is America the only superpower in the world?" **Act** out the conversation.

**BOOST YOUR SKILLS!**

**Interroger un statut**

- Utilise le discours indirect pour rapporter les propos d'experts : ***Those*** *who* ***argue*** *against the status of the US* ***suggest that***... • ***Some analysts*** *are certain that..., while* ***others maintain***...
- Varie les expressions permettant de définir ce statut : *They don't meet* ***all the required criteria***. • *According to a* ***range of definitions***... • *There are* ***several measurements of***...
- Utilise des structures comparatives : *It* ***seems like*** *the beginnings of...* • *It is about* ***much more than*** *trade.* • *Well it's* ***a bit more complicated than*** *that.*

## Doc 1.

# FINANCIAL TIMES

## A New Cold War: Trump, Xi and the escalating US-China confrontation

"From Stettin in the Baltic to Trieste in the Adriatic, an 'iron curtain' has descended across the continent." Winston Churchill's speech in Fulton, Missouri, in March 1946 is remembered as a key moment in the outbreak of the Cold War.

If future historians are ever looking for a speech that marked the beginning of a second cold war—this time between America and China—they may point to an address by Mike Pence delivered at Washington's Hudson Institute in October 2018. "China wants nothing less than to push the United States of America from the western Pacific... But they will fail. We will not be intimidated and we will not stand down." Pointing to China's political system, Mr Pence argued: "A country that oppresses its own people rarely stops there." For students of the first cold war between the US and the USSR, some of this sounded eerily and worryingly familiar. Once again, the US is facing off against a rival superpower. Once again, a military rivalry is taking shape—although this time, the main theatre is the western Pacific rather than central Europe. And once again, the conflict is being framed as one between the free world and a dictatorship. To add to the sense of symmetry, the People's Republic of China, like the Soviet Union, is run by a Communist party. [...]

But while the parallels between the current US-China rivalry and the start of the Cold War are striking, there are also some important differences. The most obvious is that the economies of the US and China are deeply integrated with each other. Trade between China and the US amounts to more than half a trillion dollars a year. China owns more than $1tn[1] of US debt. Important American companies rely on making and selling their products in China. [...] There are more Kentucky Fried Chicken restaurants in the PRC than in the US. This economic intertwining[2] has also created a degree of social convergence. China may be run by a Communist party, but its major cities are throbbing[3] with commercial life, private enterprise and Western brands, and could never be mistaken for the grey uniformity of Soviet Russia. "Chinese society is more similar to American society than Soviet society ever was," Yale University historian Odd Arne Westad noted in *Foreign Affairs* magazine. There are also strong scientific and educational ties between China and the US. Mr Xi's daughter was educated at Harvard. Stalin's daughter was not sent to Yale.

Gideon RACHMAN, *The Financial Times*, October 2020

**1.** trillion **2.** *enchevêtrement* **3.** vibrating

**a.** **Look** at the cartoon and **identify** the protagonist. **Imagine** what *"upgrade"* he is talking about.

**b.** **Read** the first two paragraphs and **explain** why the tensions between the USA and China *"sounded eerily and worryingly familiar"* (l. 24).

**c.** **Read** the last paragraph and **find out** in what ways both countries are *"deeply integrated with each other."* (l. 41)

**d.** RHETORIC **Focus** on the last two sentences and comment on their structure. **Say** what effect is produced by this parallel.

**e.** **Give** a title to each paragraph and **analyse** the argumentative structure of this article.

### WORDS

- escal**a**tion of t**e**nsions
- trade b**a**lance

- ideol**o**gical
- inter-rel**a**ted = intertw**i**ned

- degenerate = det**e**riorate
- d**e**monise: *diaboliser*
- det**e**r from V-ing: *dissuader*
- incr**i**minate
- **j**eopardise = thr**ea**ten
- v**i**lify = def**a**me

LANDMARKS p. 281

## Doc 2.

(Audio: "A trade war against China", *NPR*, 2020)

**a. Look** at the infographic and **comment** on the balance of commercial power between the USA and China.

**b. Listen** to the audio and **identify** the different people speaking. **Sum up** their points of view on China's foreign policies.

**c. Explain** how Trump's presidency started a new era of tension between China and the USA.

**d.** PHONOLOGY **Focus** on Joe Biden's speech and Zarroli's reaction. **Pick out** the two negative forms. **Say** which one is stressed and why. ▸ p. 236

**e. Say** whether a change can be expected from Joe Biden's presidency and why.

## Doc 3.

### Where the US and China Could Clash

Perhaps nowhere do the US and Chinese militaries come closer to each other than in the South China Sea. Fears have grown that a miscalculation between warships could spark a wider military confrontation. [...]

President Donald Trump's administration increased the number of "freedom of navigation operations"—known as FONOPs—in the South China Sea to challenge China's sovereignty claims. Biden looks set to maintain or even expand the number of FONOPs.

China claims more than 80% of the South China Sea, one of the world's busiest shipping routes. [...] The US estimates that more than 30% of the global maritime crude-oil[1] trade passes through the waters. [...]

Under the waters, lots of fishing and energy resources are at stake. The U.S. Energy Information Administration estimates the South China Sea holds about 190 trillion cubic feet of natural gas (about 30% of total proved reserves in the Asia-Pacific region) and 11 billion barrels of oil reserves (about 25% of the region's total proved reserves), with more possibly awaiting discovery. The US says those unexploited hydrocarbons could be worth $2.5 trillion.

While the interdependence between the U.S. and China gives a strong disincentive[2] for either side to escalate any incident, that calculation changes the further they grow apart, said Andrew Chubb, a specialist on Chinese nationalism and territorial claims at Lancaster University. "The probability of US-China clashes has probably increased," he said.

Karen LEIGH, Peter MARTIN and Adrian LEUNG, *Bloomberg*, December 2020

An American assault ship in the Pacific Ocean, Feb. 2020

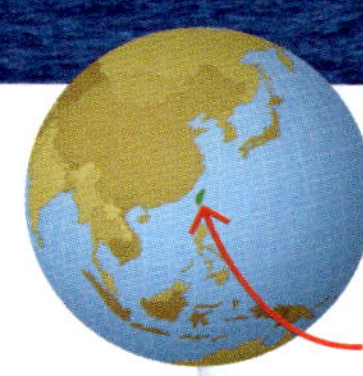


1. *pétrole brut* 2. dissuasion

**AT HOME Visit** this website and **find** the origins of the US-China military tensions in the South China Sea. SITE

**a. Read** the text and **pick out** the claims China has on the South China Sea.

**b. Find** elements from the text to **explain** the reasons why that place is so strategical.

**c. Explain** why the situation could evolve into a military conflict. **Comment** on Andrew Chubb's viewpoint.

**YOUR TASK** As a member of a "Young Diplomats" club, you are worried about the possibility of a military conflict between the USA and China. **Discuss** with other members of the club who are less pessimistic.

**BOOST YOUR SKILLS!**

**Nuancer ses propos**

- Exprime la probabilité avec *may* : *They **may** point to...* • *Biden's approach **may** be **more** about style than substance.*
- Utilise des adverbes d'atténuation : *A country that... **rarely** stops there.* • *China is still **generally** referred to as...*
- Formule des concessions : *Once again,... **although** this time...* • ***But while** the parallels between... , there are **also** some...* • *China **may** be run by a Communist party, **but**...*

# 3 A technological challenge

WIRED

## The AI Cold War That Threatens Us All

At the dawn of a new stage in the digital revolution, the world's two most powerful nations are rapidly retreating into positions of competitive isolation, like players across a Go[1] board. And what's at stake is not just the technological dominance of the United States. [...]

More than any other country, China has shown that, with a few adjustments, autocracy is quite compatible with the Internet age. But those adjustments have caused the Internet itself to start to break apart, like two continents cracking along a shelf. There's the freewheeling[2], lightly regulated Internet, dominated by the geeks of Silicon Valley. And then there's China's authoritarian alternative, powered by massive, home-grown[3] tech giants as innovative as their Western counterparts.

"Two Giant Tech Nations", illustration by Georgia PERRY

In the beginning, the communications revolution made computers affordable to the masses. It wired devices together in a giant global network and shrank them down to the size of your hand. It was a revolution that empowered the individual—the lone programmer with the power to create in her pocket, the academic with infinite research at his fingertips, the dissident with a new and powerful way of organizing resistance.

Today's stage of the digital revolution is different. [...] In today's digital world, in China and the West alike, power comes from controlling data, making sense of it, and using it to influence how people behave. That power will only grow as the next generation of mobile networks goes live.

China has two fundamental advantages over the US in building a robust AI infrastructure, and they're both, generally, advantages that authoritarian states have over democratic ones. The first is the sheer scope[4] of the data generated by Chinese tech giants. [...] China has a second big advantage as we move into the era of AI, and that's the relationship between its largest companies and the state. In China, the private-sector companies at the cutting edge of AI innovation feel obliged to keep President Xi's priorities in mind. [...]

But for now, at least, conflicting goals, mutual suspicion, and a growing conviction that AI and other advanced technologies are a winner-take-all game are pushing the two countries' tech sectors further apart.

Nicholas THOMSON and Ian BREMMER, *Wired*, October 2018

**1.** traditional Asian game **2.** independent **3.** national **4.** *étendue*

**a. Observe** the illustration and **describe** the way new technologies and power are connected for each country.

**b. Comment** on the illustrator's message.

**c. Read** the article and **identify** the sources of power referred to. **Describe** and **explain** the evolution mentioned.

**d.** VOCABULARY **Find** out which adjective is used twice to describe China's strategy and government. **Say** what it shows of the authors' point of view. ▸ p. 233

**e. Sum up** the reasons why the USA should consider China a serious rival in the race for tech power.

### WORDS

- predicament = awkward situation
- privacy
- surveillance /sər'veɪləns/ = monitoring

- concerning = worrying
- confrontational = conflicting

- dependent on
- intrusive
- over-indebted

- compile data
- cooperate
- polarise = divide

# 4 Global investors

## Doc 1. The Belt and Road Initiative

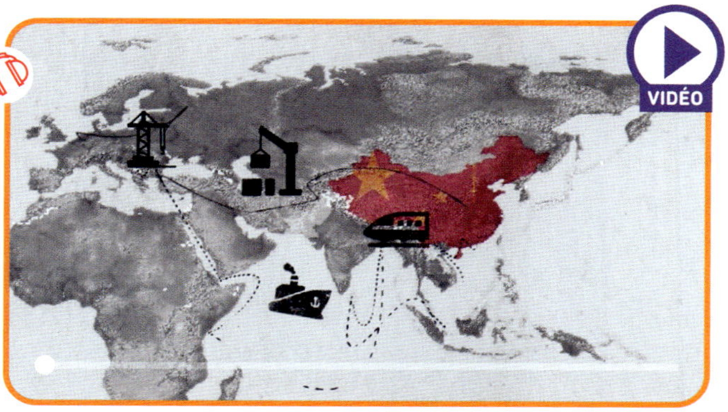


*Wall Street Journal*, 2018

**a. Watch** the video and **say** what China's Belt and Road Initiative consists of.

**b. Say** how the US responded to this programme and **pick out** the differences between the Chinese and American strategies.

**c.** PHONOLOGY *"We will **not** be intimidated and we will **not** stand down"*. **Explain** the effect produced by *"will not"* as opposed to *"won't"* ▸ p. 236

**d. Explain** why the USA feels challenged by China's programme and what is at stake for the US.

## Doc 2.

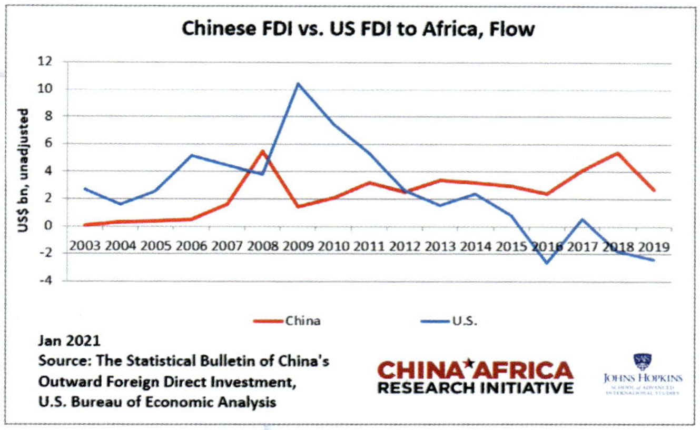


### US-China War Poses Threat to Africa

In recent years, Washington has heightened tension with Beijing in trade, the South China Sea, telecoms, Hong Kong, Taiwan and a host of other areas of development such as the Belt and Road Initiative.

Although Africa has no bone in this fight, the conflict has the potential to derail its development. Why is this the case? Where are the fault lines of this emerging Cold War and how will they affect Africa? [...]

First, Africa has good and flourishing trade relations with both the US and China. The bulk[1] of the continent's trade is with China and other Asian nations. The South China Sea, therefore, becomes Africa's major trading route in this increasing trade with Asian nations.

The skirmishes[2] between Washington and Beijing in these waters pose a grave danger to Africa's prosperity.

Second, the trade war between Washington and Beijing has a huge negative impact on the world economy. [...]

Third, the escalating tension between the US and China will result in a polarised global economy.

Likewise, African companies will find themselves in a predicament as the tension accelerates, particularly in the digital economy. Recently, Huawei and TikTok came under enormous pressure in the US and some Western countries. If unresolved, it could bring two separate tech ecosystems into the world, making it difficult to do business. To prosper, Africa needs a stable global environment, free of endless obstacles placed on trade, trading routes, digital co-operation and multilateral co-operation. [...] As the African proverb goes: "When elephants fight, it is the grass that suffers."

David MONYAE, *IOL news*, September 2020

1. main part 2. quarrel

MÉDIATION

**YOUR TASK**

As an intern at the French Development Agency, **record** a memo on the issues and impact of the Belt and Road initiative.

**a. Look** at the graph and **say** what it shows about the USA's and China's strategies in Africa.

**b. Read** the article and **find** information about the impact of the US-China rivalry on Africa according to the author.

**c.** TRANSLATION *"Africa has no bone in this fight"* (l. 7). **Find** what image that idiomatic expression evokes and **give** an equivalent expression in French.

**d. Comment** on the choice of the proverb as a conclusion (l. 45-46).

**e. Find** information about the source of the article and **comment** on the author's point of view.

**BOOST YOUR SKILLS!**

**Faire une étude d'impact**

- Envisage les conséquences au conditionnel ou au futur : ***If** unresolved, it **could** bring two separate tech eco-systems.* • *The escalating tension **will** result in...*
- Utilise le lexique du danger : *A **grave danger**.* • *A **huge negative impact**.*
- Souligne par des causatives le rapport de cause à effet : *Adjustments **have caused** the Internet itself **to start** to break apart.* • *It **made** computers **affordable to** the masses.* • *...**making** it difficult **to do** business...*

## Doc 1.

### FBI Releases Movie to Alert Americans of Foreign Spy Threats

US national intelligence agencies released a movie Wednesday to raise awareness of how foreign intelligence entities use social media to target Americans.

The film, called "The Nevernight Connection," tells the fictional account of a former US intelligence official who went to spy for the Chinese. [...]

The production is the US intelligence community's latest effort to combat espionage and cyber-attack threats from foreign adversaries. Foreign intelligence services and other hostile actors often pose online as headhunters, interested employees, someone with a shared interest or use other guises to connect and develop relationships with people who have access to valuable information, the NCSC said in a statement.

"Through this movie, we hope to raise awareness among Americans so they can guard against online approaches from unknown parties that could put them, their organization and even national security at risk," said NCSC Director William Evanina.

Jacqueline DAVALOS, *Bloomberg*, Septembrer 2020

## Doc 2.

VIDÉO

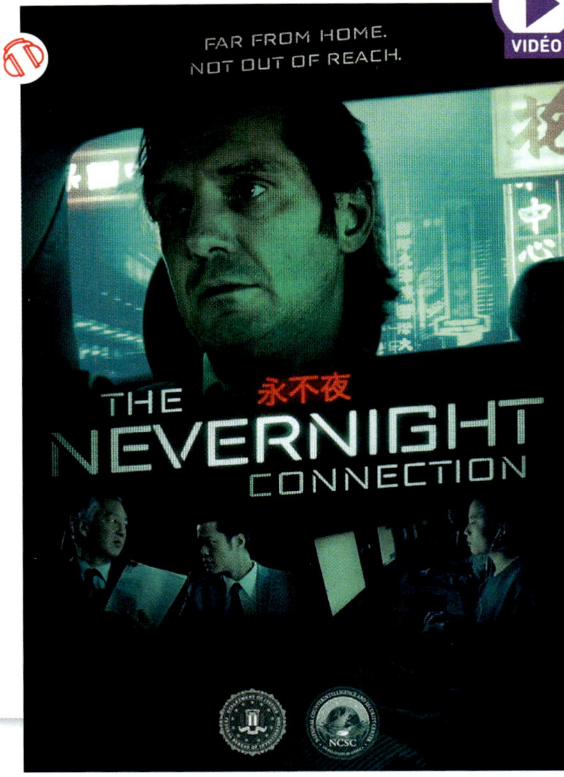


*The Nevernight Connection*, FBI, Sept 2020

## Doc 3.

### FBI new film smears China on espionage, poisons bilateral relations

A film released by the FBI and National Counterintelligence and Security Center (NCSC), allegedly based on a real case, fabricates a *Global Times* website article and smears[1] China for recruiting former US intelligence officials to have access to classified information.

It reveals the US government's intense efforts to further poison China-US relations [...] The US, which is well known for conducting the world's widest range of espionage activities, has accused China of hacking and spying without providing any substantive investigations or evidence, experts said.

The US has abused its legal system against a number of Chinese firms and individuals in the past years to create political issues, but did not conduct any actual investigations and almost never provided evidence of misdeeds[2] to Chinese side, the experts noted.

Zhang HUI, *Globaltimes.cn*, October 2020

1. . hurt the reputation 2. crime

**a.** **Read** the article (**doc. 1**) and **identify** the producers and the target audience of the film. **Explain** its goals.

**b.** **Focus** on the poster (**doc. 2**) and **comment** on the impression it gives.

**c.** **Watch** the trailer and **explain** how it portrays the methods of Chinese intelligence.

**d.** **Read** the other article (**doc. 3**), **identify** its source and **say** whose point of view is expressed.

**e.** **Compare** the three documents and **explain** how the film is at the same time efficient and problematic.

## FINAL TASK

### Take part in a talk on US-China relations.

**As members of your country's association of "Young Diplomats", you attend the annual Washington Seminar on US-China relations. Take part in a talk entitled "New challenges".**

1. **Browse** through the issues raised in the file (diplomacy, trade or technology in the context of American-Chinese relations) and **choose** a role. **Make sure** each group member picks a different subject.
2. **Make** notes about the challenges raised by that issue and **prepare** arguments explaining why it contributes to the increase of tensions between the two countries (problems faced, consequences).
3. **Get** ready to **discuss** the risks associated with these tensions and **share** the possible solutions to improve the global situation.
4. **Act out** the discussion with your partners.

BOOST YOUR ENGLISH p. 233

# BOOST YOUR ENGLISH!

## Grammar — Évoquer une situation géopolitique à risque

• **Souligne les points de convergence ou de divergence.**

***Both*** *sides see rules as something to break.*
***Neither*** *of them is ready to make concessions.*
***Unlike*** *the USA, China relies on state-owned social media for its communication.*

• **Utilise des structures hypothétiques pour envisager les risques.**

***If*** *Europe* ***does not consolidate*** *its influence, we* ***will*** *end up in a bipolar world.*
***If*** *unresolved, it* ***could*** *bring two separate tech economic systems.*
***Unless*** *the USA leaves the area, tensions* ***may*** *well grow.*

• **Nuance tes propos avec des formes concessives.**

***Although*** *the situation is tense, a diplomatic solution is to be expected.*
***While*** *the parallels with the Cold War are striking, there are* ***also*** *important differences.*
***However****, when other dimensions of powers are considered...*

• **Utilise des adverbes d'intensification et d'atténuation.**

*President Joe Biden* ***probably*** *won't use the same threatening tone.* (atténuation)
*This sounded* ***eerily*** *and* ***worryingly*** *familiar.* (intensification)
*The USA and China are* ***deeply*** *integrated with each other.* (intensification)

**1 Formule des hypothèses à partir des éléments suivants en utilisant les modaux *may, could, would* ou *will*.**

a. The USA / discover a spying system / provoke diplomatic crisis.
b. China / buy African public infrastructures / control over the continent.
c. China / refuse to comply with US rules / raise tariffs.

**2 Traduis cet extrait en prêtant attention à l'emploi des modaux et aux liens logiques.**

*There's an interesting phenomenon in which thriving Chinese tech firms assure the world's consumers that they do not and would not comply with unreasonable demands from the Beijing dictatorship. Meanwhile U.S. tech firms can't operate freely in China because of the regime's unreasonable demands. Whom should consumers believe?*

## Vocabulary — The US-China relationship

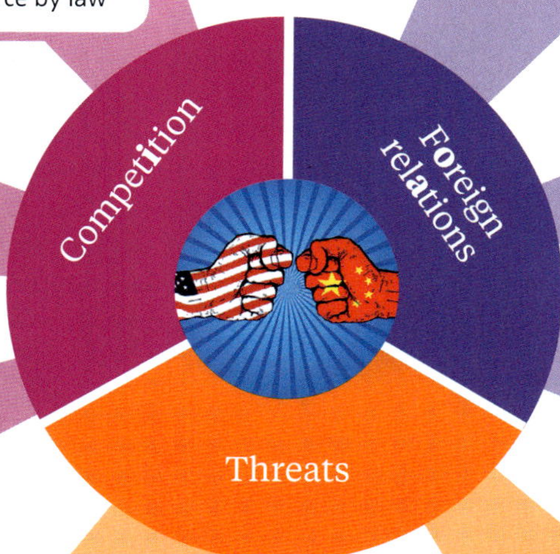


**Economic development** (AUDIO)
- Gross Domestic Product (GDP): *PIB*
- Investments

- ambitious

- fast-growing

- expand
- impose = enforce by law

**Trade** (AUDIO)
- deficit ≠ profit
- prosperity ≠ recession
- transaction

- acquire
- export ≠ import
- supply = provide

**Influence** (AUDIO)
- ally
- leadership
- sovereignty
- superpower

- monopolise = dominate
- rule over

**Diplomacy** (AUDIO)
- bargaining = negotiation
- bilateral treaties
- coexistence
- conciliation
- trade agreements

**Policies** (AUDIO)
- appeasement
- blockade: *blocus*
- deadlock

- restrain = limit
- simplify

**Ideologies** (AUDIO)
- authoritarian rule
- Communism
- free-market economy ≠ isolationism
- Imperialism
- liberalism

**Military** (AUDIO)
- arbitration
- friction
- withdrawal
- antagonistic = hostile
- coercive = intimidating

**Intelligence** (AUDIO)
- classified information
- data theft
- spying
- surveillance
- treason

OBJECTIF BAC p. 296-304

Grille d'auto-évaluation

## Sujet type bac

MÉDIATION

Durée : 3h30
Matériel autorisé : l'usage du dictionnaire unilingue non encyclopédique est autorisé.
Niveau attendu : C1

- **Prenez connaissance des documents A, B et C et traitez le sujet suivant en anglais (environ 500 mots).**

Taking into account their specificities, show how these documents illustrate the relations between the United States and China. You will pay particular attention to:
– the possible connections between the two governments and tech companies,
– how social networks can be seen as strategic threats.

- **Traduisez en français le passage suivant du document A.**

*"TikTok is just another app in the string of social-media-platform reform that needs to occur to ensure a clear understanding of privacy control, transparency around data collection, sharing and use, education associated with the risk of oversharing and the link between users' rights and responsibilities and national security. The main issue policymakers have with TikTok is its alleged connections to the Chinese government."* (l. 40-49)

### Document A — A foreign social network collecting data

TikTok has generated a great deal of controversy and re-ignited[1] the debate over social media and privacy in corporate America and across the nation. As employers consider whether the app should be deleted from employees' phones, it's unclear as to whether the concern is in response to TikTok's massive popularity, over-reach associated with collection of user data, finding of bugs that allowed attackers to access personal data, or its historical connection with the Chinese government. The app is currently under national security review by the Committee on Foreign Investment in the United States (CFIUS) after being accused of censoring videos to satisfy the Chinese government. [...]

Recently, TikTok has distanced itself from the Chinese government. The company has said that the app is not available in China, and they recently hired an American CEO. However, in their privacy policy, they state: "We may disclose your information to respond to subpoenas[2], court orders, legal process, law enforcement requests, legal claims, or government inquiries." [...]

Besides user data, the main purpose of TikTok is the creation and sharing of videos. If employees are creating these at work, they might reveal information about their location, nature of operations, security provisions, etc. Most of the time this is done inadvertently, but because of location tracing, high-resolution video, and the tie to identity, users might provide sensitive information. Rather insignificant data from different users could be pieced together to provide sensitive information in aggregate. For example, the fitness app Strava gave away the location of secret Army bases.

TikTok is just another app in the string of social-media-platform reform that needs to occur to ensure a clear understanding of privacy control, transparency around data collection, sharing and use, education associated with the risk of oversharing and the link between users' rights and responsibilities and national security. The main issue policymakers have with TikTok is its alleged connection to the Chinese government. Other countries like India have already banned the app, citing privacy concerns that it posed a threat to India's sovereignty and security.

Ari LIGHTMAN, *the hill.com*, July 19, 2020

1. re-start.
2. *citation à comparaître*

Document B

THE WALL STREET JOURNAL

## Facebook, TikTok and China

**What does the regime demand of technology companies?**

There's an interesting phenomenon in which thriving Chinese tech firms assure the world's consumers that they do not and would not comply with unreasonable demands from the Beijing dictatorship. Meanwhile U.S. tech firms can't operate freely in China because of the regime's unreasonable demands. Whom should consumers believe?

Banned in China since 2009, Facebook is now aggressively defending its U.S. home turf[1] against a China-based competitor. And the Silicon Valley giant is not just competing in the marketplace. Facebook is also employing a significant Washington lobbying campaign. Georgia Wells, Jeff Horwitz and Aruna Viswanatha report in the *Journal*:

*"When Facebook Inc. Chief Executive Mark Zuckerberg delivered a speech about freedom of expression in Washington, D.C., last fall, there was also another agenda: to raise the alarm about the threat from Chinese tech companies and, more specifically, the popular video-sharing app TikTok.*

*Tucked into the speech was a line pointing to Facebook's rising rival: Mr. Zuckerberg told Georgetown students that TikTok doesn't share Facebook's commitment to freedom of expression, and represents a risk to American values and technological supremacy.*

*That was a message Mr. Zuckerberg hammered[2] behind the scenes in meetings with officials and lawmakers during the October trip and a separate visit to Washington weeks earlier, according to people familiar with the matter."*

The message was self-interested. But was it wrong? As the *Journal* reporters note, the Facebook CEO spent years trying to get back into the Chinese market. And his experience there provides ample reason to wonder whether any social-media platform can avoid serving the interests of the surveillance state.

Alyssa Abkowitz, Deepa Seetharaman and Eva Dou reported in the *Journal* in 2017 on "Facebook's running tale of woe in China, where it has been trying to set the stage for a return." The *Journal* reporters noted that eight years earlier Chinese regulators had "blocked Facebook and Twitter in an information lockdown after riots in China's Muslim Xinjiang region. State media said riot leaders used social media to stir unrest." The *Journal* report added that Beijing "remains uneasy with Facebook's ability to be a dissident's megaphone" and reported:

*"Facebook has already agreed to take down, in some countries, content that is illegal there, including pro-Nazi material in Germany. Chinese law would demand more, and censorship is a price that has led Western internet companies such as Alphabet Inc.'s Google to abandon the market."*

James FREEMAN, *Wall Street Journal*, August 24, 2020

**1.** territory **2.** repeat constantly

Document C

Arcadio ESQUIVEL, (a Costa Rican cartoonist who collaborates with several newspapers all over the world), August 7, 2020

# LET'S BRAINSTORM!

OBJECTIF BAC p. 305-317

**RELATION AU MONDE Axe 2**

**What is at stake between the USA and China?**

## Fighting for influence

- International superpowers

→ "What does it mean to be a superpower?", *ABC*, p. 227 • "Allies or enemies", chart, *Pew Research*, p. 227 • "China: a challenger?", video *The Economist*, p. 226

- The technological competition

→ "The AI Cold War That Threatens Us All", *Wired* p. 230

## Complicated trade relations

- Two connected economies

→ "The escalating US-China confrontation", *The Financial Times*, p. 228 • "US trade deficit with China", *The Balance*, p. 229

- Investing worldwide

→ "US-China War Poses Threat to Africa", *IOL News*, p. 231 • "Chinese FDI *vs.* US FDI to Africa, Flow", chart, *Johns Hopkins*, p. 231

## The shadow of conflict

- Tense diplomatic relations

→ "The escalating US-China confrontation", *The Financial Times*, p. 228 • "The Nevernight Connection", *FBI*, p. 232 • "FBI new film poisons bilateral relations", *Global Times*, p. 232

- Real threats?

→ "Where the US and China Could Clash", *Bloomberg*, p. 229 • "FBI Releases Movie to Alert Americans of Foreign Spy Threats", *Bloomberg*, p. 232

## Two very different nations

- Opposing political systems

→ "The escalating US-China confrontation", *The Financial Times, p. 228* • "The AI Cold War That Threatens Us All", *Wired* p. 230

- Diverging lifestyles and points of view

→ "Two giant tech-nations", Georgia Perry, p. 230 • "FBI Releases Movie to Alert Americans of Foreign Spy Threats", *Bloomberg*, p. 232 • "FBI new film poisons bilateral relations", *Global Times*, p. 232

## Phonology | La négation à l'oral

AUDIO

- En anglais, **à l'oral**, le marqueur de **négation *not*** est la plupart du temps **contracté** avec l'auxiliaire qui le précède : *isn't, aren't, don't, couldn't, won't*. La réalisation de la **forme pleine** marque l'insistance ou la détermination : *We do **not** trust China and we will **not** stand down.*
- Dans les phrases **interro-négatives**, l'emphase sur la négation exprime l'étonnement :
***Aren't*** *you surprised at their reaction?* (véritable question avec intonation montante : on demande à l'interlocuteur s'il est surpris).
*Are you **not** surprised at their reaction?* (intonation descendante : on s'étonne que l'interlocuteur n'ait pas l'air surpris).

**1 Lis ces phrases à voix haute puis écoute et explique en quoi l'accentuation ou non de la forme négative change le message.**

a. *Chinese tech firms assure that they will not comply with unreasonable demands. / Chinese tech firms assure that they won't comply with unreasonable demands.*

b. *It's not a social network, Rob! / It isn't a social network, Rob.*

c. *Aren't you aware of how serious the situation is? / Are you not aware of how serious the situation is?*

d. *She isn't a friend of yours. / She is no friend of yours.*

Vers le **BAC**

# BUILD YOUR PORTFOLIO

## Cartoon

Cartoon by SUMMERS, *Tribune Media Services*, 2020

- **Observe** the cartoon and **identify** the issue tackled. **Explain** why this question is highly sensitive between the USA and China.

VIDÉO

## Article

"United States and China enter a new cold war", *Reuters*, July 2020

> The superpowers have articulated a lengthening list of grievances and almost no significant interests in common. Both are attempting to push third countries into an alliance system that would see the world carved into two decoupled blocs. Red versus Blue. With us or against us. Total confrontation. Basically the definition of cold war.

- **Read** the article and **show** how the relations between the United States and China have degraded and evolved into a serious threat for one another and for the rest of the world.

ARTICLE

## Short film

*The Nevernight Connection*, FBI and NCSC, September 2020

The film tells the fictional account of a former US intelligence official who went to spy for the Chinese. ► p. 232

- **Watch** the whole film and **get** ready to **discuss** it with your classmates. **Focus** on the message and the tone, and **say** whether you find it realistic and efficient and why.

VIDÉO

## Infographic

"A Tale Of Two Economies", *visualcapitalist.com*, 2015

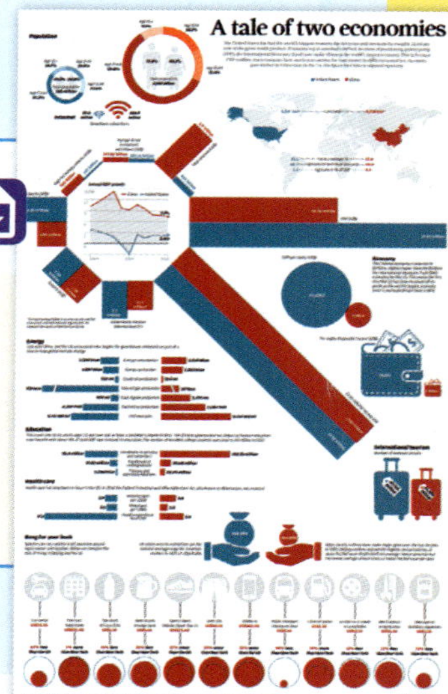


- **Download** the whole infographic and **analyse** it. **Comment** on the major common points and differences between American and Chinese economies.

ÉPREUVE ORALE | GRAND ORAL — Entraîne-toi à l'oral

## Step 1 — Build up your speech!

**Épreuve orale**

- Choose one topic in the mindmap p. 236.
- Pick out two documents in the file and one or two personal ones to illustrate this issue.
- Prepare your presentation: you must show how these documents relate to the issue you chose.

OBJECTIF BAC ► p. 305

**Grand oral**

- Choose one topic in the mindmap p. 236.
- Find a key question about the topic and write it down. Think about links with other subjects (*SES, HGGSP* for example).
- Gather arguments and examples from the file.
- Prepare an outline for your presentation and write your note sheet.

OBJECTIF BAC ► p. 308-309

## Step 2 — Make your oral presentation in front of two classmates.

**Épreuve orale**

- Show your documents to your classmates. Each of you makes their presentation to the others in about five minutes.

OBJECTIF BAC ► p. 306-307

**Grand oral**

- Give your note sheet to your classmates.
- Stand up and make a five-minute presentation to answer your key question.

OBJECTIF BAC ► p. 310-311

## Step 3 — Answer your classmates' questions about your presentation

SNAPFILE 26

RELATION AU MONDE
AXE 2 : RIVALITÉS ET INTERDÉPENDANCES

# The world's drugstore

▶ **How is the Indian pharmaceutical industry intertwined with the rest of the world?**



**YOUR MISSION**

**Write an editorial on the global weight of the Indian pharmaceutical industry.**

As a pharmacy student, write an editorial for a special youth issue of *The Economist*. Give your opinion on the growing influence of the Indian pharmaceutical industry in the world.

FOLLOW THE STEPS!

## 1 Indian medicines needed

**Doc 1.**

VIDÉO

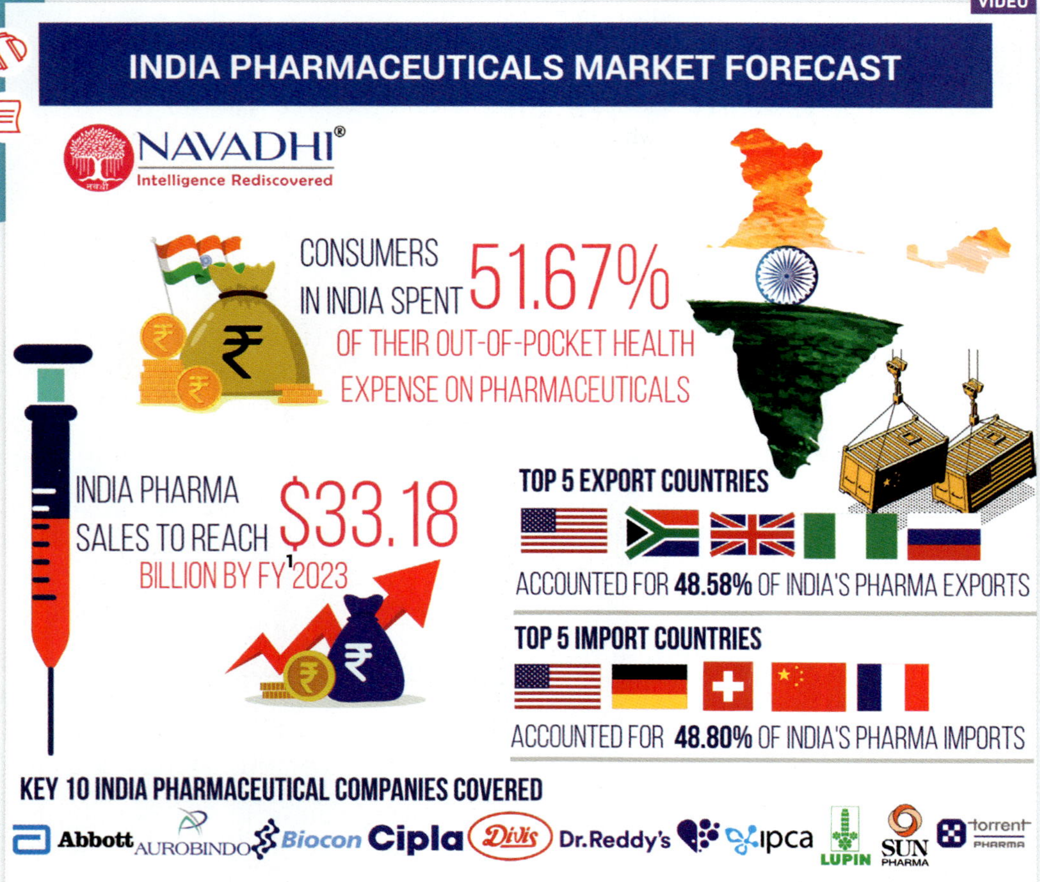


1. Financial Year

*Navadhi*, 2019 (Video: "A pharmaceutical powerhouse", *Make in India*, 2017)

**a.** **Read** the infographic and **explain** what the pharmaceutical industry draws its power from.

**b.** **Watch** the video and **find out** how productive the Indian pharmaceutical industry is.

**c.** **Explain** the reasons for its productivity and success.

**d.** **Identify** the target market and **comment** on the benefits for the patients.

**STEP 1**

As an introduction to your editorial, **write** a short paragraph to **emphasise** the modernity and productivity of the Indian pharmaceutical industry and **underline** its potential on the global stage.

Audio:

1. Janahushadi = Public Health
2. FDI = Foreign Direct Investment

## Doc 2.

### Reasons Why India Is the 'Pharmacy' of the Developing World

Developing countries across the world face several challenges, key among which is providing their people with affordable medicines of high-quality. [...]

Before 2005, India did not grant product patents[1] on medicines. This allowed for the production of low-cost, generic versions of medicines that were patented in other countries. Robust competition among generic producers in India has resulted in a price reduction of more than 99 percent for medicines.

Today, India is the world's primary source of affordable HIV medicines as it is one of the few countries with the capacity to quickly produce newer HIV drugs as generics. These drugs are not only affordable but are also of high quality.

India is a main supplier of vaccines to UNICEF and to the Ministries of Health in numerous countries.

In 2005, India adopted a strict medicines patent law that, while allowing patent protection for new pharmaceutical compounds, makes it tougher to get a patent on new forms of existing medicines. [...]

The prices of medicines in the United States are one of the highest in the world because US laws and policies blindly favour pharmaceutical companies over generic competition, allowing multiple and extended monopolies on the same medicine, leading to exorbitant prices for lengthy periods of time. On the other hand, India's policy and lawmakers have identified generic competition as the strongest and most effective force to reduce drug prices.

In contrast to India's stricter patentability criteria, the US allows the practice of 'evergreening' that helps delay generic competition and keeps prices high. It is a common tactic by which the pharmaceutical industry extends their monopoly on drugs beyond the original patent's 20 years. Long monopoly of a single company in the US keeps prices high because generic competition is blocked.

Doctors Without Borders,
*The Better India*, 2016

1. *brevets*

"Hands off Our Medicine" campaign by Doctors Without Borders, to defend affordable, generic life-saving medicines, 2016

1. *brevet*

**WORDS**

- hegemony /hɪˈgɛməni/
- patented drugs
- regulatory body

- generic (medicine)
- low-cost
- profitable

- extend
- overcome
- supply sb with sthg

**a. Read** the article and **identify** the needs of developing countries regarding medicines.

**b.** TRANSLATION **Translate** l. 5-12. **Pay** attention to the tenses.

**c. Explain** the challenges India had to face and the assets of its pharmaceutical industry.

**d. Describe** what evergreening consists in and **comment** on Indian policies regarding this practice.

**e. Discuss** the choices of India and the USA regarding patent laws.

STEP 2 **Write** a paragraph for your editorial about the large range of propositions offered by Indian pharmaceuticals and their advantages.

**BOOST YOUR SKILLS!**

**Mettre en valeur des atouts**

- Fais valoir leur importance avec des superlatifs : *One of the* ***fastest*** *growing markets.* • *The* ***largest*** *provider of...* • *The* ***strongest*** *and* ***most*** *effective force*
- Utilise des adjectifs positifs : *India is a* ***main*** *supplier of...* • ***Affordable*** *but also of* ***high*** *quality.*
- Souligne les bénéfices par des structures causatives : *It* ***makes*** *affordable generics possible.* • *A practice that* ***helps*** *delay...*

# 2 Facing new challenges

## Doc 1. The race for online pharmacy space

Amazon announced last week it's launching its online drugstore in India. The Amazon Pharmacy service offers prescription medicines, over-the-counter drugs for common ailments[1] like cough and colds, and some traditional medicine. [...] Amazon's pilot in India follows its recent efforts to penetrate the US market, after it acquired an online pharmacy. [...]

Within a few days of Amazon's announcement to pilot in India, the All India Organization of Chemists & Druggists, an industry group that claims to represent hundreds of thousands of retail pharmacies and distributors, drafted a letter to Amazon CEO Jeff Bezos and Amit Agarwal, an Amazon executive based in India.

"We are writing to you as we came to know that *www.amazon.com* has decided to enter 'Online Pharmacy' space, probably oblivious to[2] the fact that the e-Pharmacies are illegal and not recognized by the laws under Drug & Cosmetic Act & Rules there under." [...]

In light of its concerns about online pharmacies, the All India Organization of Chemists & Druggists' Yash Aggarwal told CNBC that his group will do everything in its power to resist Amazon.

The organization has said it will talk with government officials to make its case that Amazon's move is illegal.

Christina Farr, *CNBC*, August 2020

1. illness 2. not knowing that

**a. Read** the article and **explain** what Amazon Pharmacy's services are.

**b. Describe** the reaction of Indian pharmacy groups.

**c.** What does the reaction of these groups say about the global pharmaceutical market?

## Doc 2. A cumbersome dependence

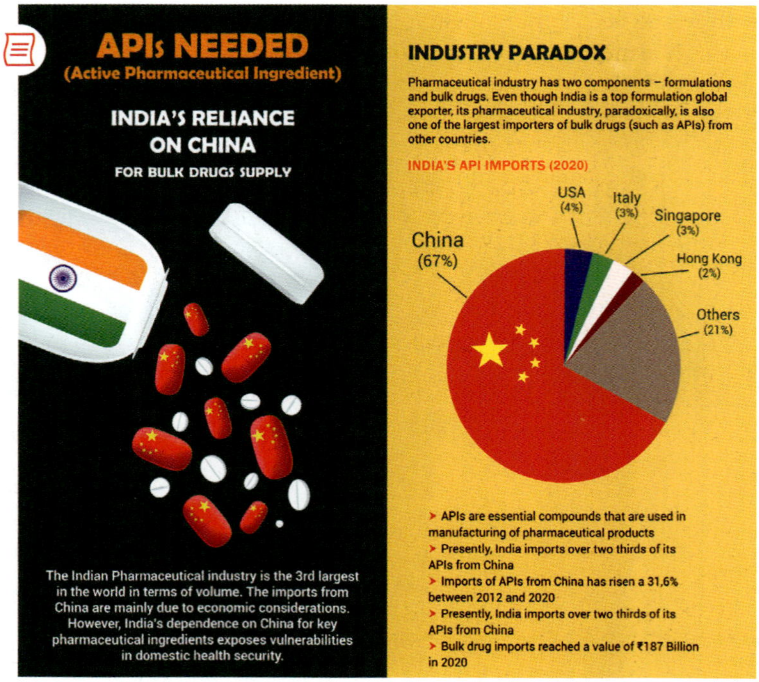


**a. Read** the infographic and **explain** what APIs consist of and how essential they are.

**b. Define** what India's "Industry paradox" consists in.

**c. Comment** on the relationship between China and India.

**d. Discuss**: To what extent does this relationship illustrate the idea of "rivalry and interdependence?"

STEP 3 **Write** a new paragraph to **qualify** the argument of your editorial. **Set out** the risks of India's dependence on China and **underline** the remaining challenges for the country to **assert** its role on a global pharmaceutical scale.

### BOOST YOUR SKILLS!

**Évoquer des défis à relever**

- Souligne par des adverbes les obstacles à surmonter : *We are **totally** dependent on...* • *This is **really** a question of national priority.*
- Exprime la combativité par des idiomatismes : ***In light of** its concerns about...* • *The group will do **everything in its power** to resist.*
- Précise les objectifs à atteindre : *Recent efforts **to penetrate** the market.* • *The group will do everything **to resist**.* • *...and talk with officials **to make its case**.*

# 3 Towards international cooperation

### India's medical diplomacy during COVID-19 through South-South Cooperation

Since the WHO[1] declared COVID-19 as a pandemic, it has become a defining crisis of our time. Indian Prime Minister Narendra Modi, on 12 May 2020, stated that while India believes in self-reliance, it does not agree with self-centric arrangements [...]

In the wake of this pandemic, India has advocated availability of medicines across the globe through international cooperation and development partnerships. India's recent efforts to export Hydroxychloroquine (HCQ) to affected countries around the world is based on India's history of medical diplomacy. [...]

In addition to extending support to the global South, India has also reached medical supplies to developed Northern countries such as the USA, Spain, Bahrain, Germany and the United Kingdom under commercial agreements signed with Indian pharmaceutical companies. Given the predicament, India's medical diplomacy is enabling India to emerge as a responsible and reliable player during a time when many established international actors have failed to do so.

In a post COVID-19 world, India has a comparative advantage in becoming a reliable provider of global public goods and services in healthcare. India's pharma industry is the third largest in the world. According to the Government of India, 18% of the world's generic drugs are supplied by India. It is also a leading producer of vaccines in the world and contributes to about 50% of global vaccine demands. This high demand is due to lower pricing. [...]

With Union Health Minister Dr Harsh Vardhan appointed as chairman of the WHO Executive Board, India is expected to play a pivotal role in strengthening WHO to deal with future pandemics by promoting international cooperation.

As the pandemic rages through the world, transcending geographical boundaries, it has taught humankind the need for *Atma Nirbharata* (Self-reliance), as the Prime Minister underlined in his national address last week. Self-reliance which is not self-centric, but looking inwards to explore and delve into[2] the strength within so that the fruits of your labour can be a boon[3] to the world.

Kaustuv CHAKRABARTI, *Orfonline.org*, July 2020

1. World Health Organisation: *OMS* 2. dig into 3. great opportunity

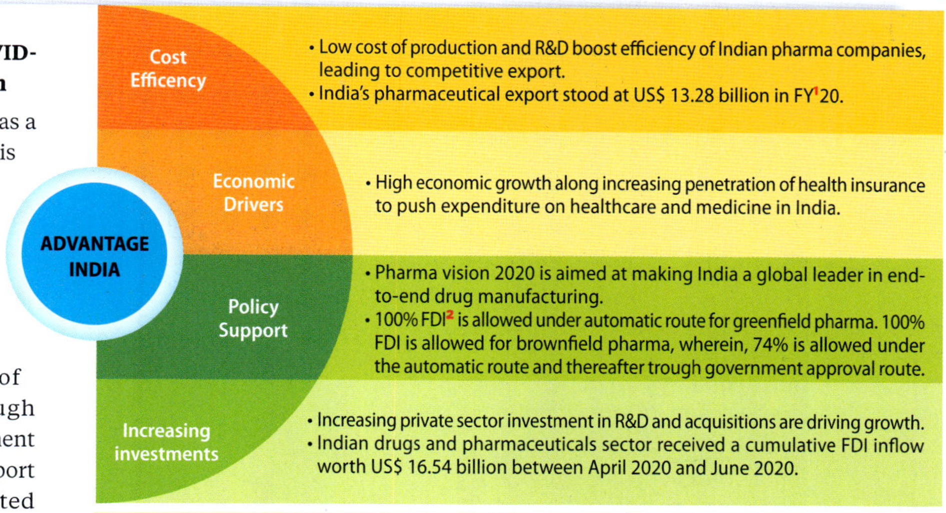


Note: Top 10 companies as per research by HDFC Securites, R&D – Research & Development.

1. Financial Year
2. Foreign Direct Investment

*India Brand Equity Foundation*, December 2020

**a. Read** the article and **comment** on the role played by India during the pandemic regarding medicines.

**b. Explain** what medical diplomacy is.

**c. Explain** how India could play a major part in a post-pandemic world.

**d. Read** the infographic and **focus** on the last sentence of the article. **Comment** on India's stance regarding international partnership.

**STEP 4**

As a conclusion to your editorial, **assess** the situation and **discuss** the importance for India to have partnerships with other countries.

**BOOST YOUR SKILLS!**

**Evaluer des liens d'interdépendance**

- Appuie-toi sur des données chiffrées : *The **third** largest industry.* • ***18%** of the world's generic drugs.* • *Contributes to **about 50%** of...* • *Exports stood at **US$ 13.28 billion**.*
- Précise le rôle de chacun: *A **responsible** and **reliable** player.* • *A **leading** producer.* • *A **pivotal** role.*
- Détermine l'étendue de ces liens avec des prépositions : ***Across** the globe.* • ***Through** international cooperation.* • *Countries **around** the world.*

**FINAL STEP**

**Connect** the paragraphs you have written to format your editorial. **Add** a headline, a subheading and a photograph to make it more attractive.

**You've completed your mission. Well done!**

play BAC

# INTERARGIR AVEC LE JURY DU GRAND ORAL

OBJECTIF BAC p. 310-311

Le jour du **Grand oral**, tu présenteras pendant 5 minutes une question que tu auras choisie et préparée pendant l'année. Tu auras ensuite une **discussion** de 10' avec le jury, puis 5' pour présenter ton projet d'orientation.

Voici un exemple de question de Grand oral sur l'axe « Rivalités et interdépendances » dans la thématique « Relation au monde » :

***Dans quelle mesure le développement de l'industrie pharmaceutique indienne fait-il du pays un acteur majeur sur la scène internationale ?***

Écoute cet exemple d'une présentation de la question au Grand oral par un(e) élève, puis mets-toi à sa place pour t'entraîner à l'interaction.

AUDIO

Tina présentant sa question au Grand oral

• Ceci est un exemple de question traitée. En écoutant la présentation, note les arguments, objections ou questions qui te viennent à l'esprit comme si tu étais le jury.

## 1 Préparer la discussion avec le jury

OBJECTIF BAC p. 308-309

Les questions des examinateurs sur ta présentation viseront le plus souvent à :
– te faire apporter des précisions sur un des aspects développés (a) ;
– nuancer un point (b) ;
– élargir ta réflexion dans le cadre global de ton enseignement de spécialité (c).
Repère bien le type de question posée, cela t'aidera à aborder la réponse tout en nourrissant l'interaction.

Voici trois questions que le jury pourrait poser à Tina après sa présentation orale :

**a.** Vous avez parlé de l'influence mondiale de l'industrie pharmaceutique indienne, dans quelle mesure la crise de la Covid a-t-elle contribué à accélérer cette influence ?

**b.** En quoi les relations de l'industrie pharmaceutique indienne avec la Chine sont-elles susceptibles de limiter cette influence ?

**c.** Dans quelle mesure la question que vous avez traitée interroge-t-elle également l'axe d'étude « Égalités et inégalités » de la thématique « Faire société » ?

• Identifie bien à quelle partie de ta présentation le jury fait référence : **Quand vous dites**, est-ce bien... ?
• Utilise des marqueurs d'interaction pour rebondir : **En effet**, on pourrait... • **Il est vrai** que j'aurais pu...

• Apprends bien le lexique en français et en anglais pour pouvoir nuancer : rivalité ≠ antagonisme • interdépendance ≠ partenariat • *rivalry ≠ antogonism* • *mutual dependence ≠ partnership*

## 2 Echanger sur ton projet d'orientation

OBJECTIF BAC p. 309

Voici ce que le jury pourrait demander à Tina suite à leurs échanges :
En quoi la question de « L'Industrie pharmaceutique indienne » éclaire-t-elle vos choix d'orientation, ou votre projet professionnel ?

Mets-toi à la place de Tina, pour présenter son projet d'orientation.
– Donne l'intitulé exact de la formation qu'elle vise (PASS, LMD sciences, technologies, santé) et précise le mode d'accès (concours, dossier...)
– Précise comment elle s'est informée sur cette formation, et fais le lien entre la spécialité LLCER Anglais, Monde Contemporain, la question choisie et les attendus de sa formation.
– Utilise des exemples de centres d'intérêts personnels, d'activités ou de stages pour mettre en avant son intérêt pour le sujet et la pertinence de son choix d'orientation.

• Assure-toi de connaître l'intitulé exact de la formation que tu vises et les voies d'accès. Précise en quoi ta question sera approfondie dans tes études supérieures.

Vers le **BAC**

# BUILD YOUR PORTFOLIO

## Campaign

"Evergreening", *MSF access Campaign*, 2018

The Campaign for Access to Essential Medicines is an international campaign started by Doctors Without Borders to increase the availability of essential medicines in developing countries.

- **Read** the infographic and **watch** the video. **Recap** what *Evergreening* consists of and **explain** the importance of fighting such a practice.

VIDÉO

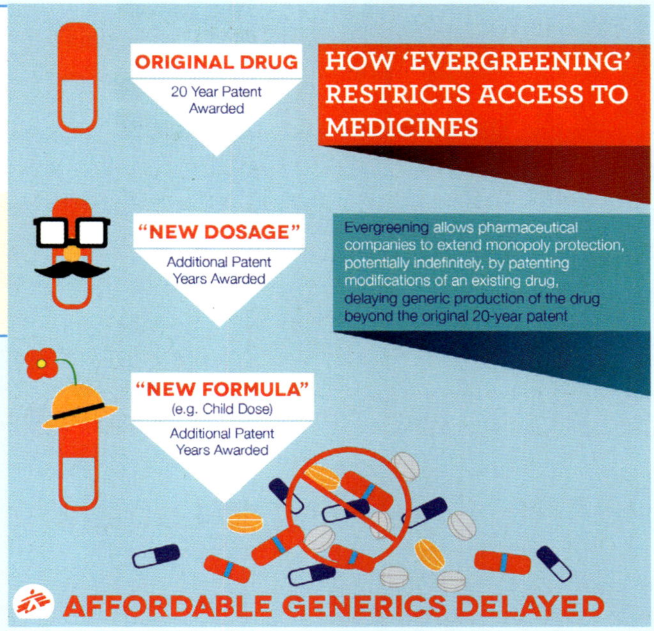


## Article

"Indian pharma is being squeezed", *The Conversation*, October 2020

"India's pharmaceutical industry is renowned for selling medicines to the world at reasonable prices. Now, the advantages that have enabled India to play this role are in danger of being eroded, and it could make it harder for developing countries to access the medicines they need—threatening the UN Sustainable Development Goals in the process."

- **Read** the article and **explain** the challenges India's pharmaceutical industry is facing. **Comment** on what the COVID-19 crisis has shed light on.

ARTICLE

## Article

"The menace of counterfeit drugs that India must fight", *Mint*, 2020

How to make sure that the drugs available on the market are reliable and safe? This is a big issue recently raised by worldwide organisations.

- **Read** the text and **explain** what is at stake regarding counterfeit drugs.

ARTICLE

## Film

*Fire in the blood*, Dylan Mohan Gray, 2013

The movie tells the story of how Western pharmaceutical companies and governments aggressively blocked access to low-cost AIDS drugs for the countries of Africa and the global South in the years after 1996—causing ten million or more unnecessary deaths—and the improbable group of people who decided to fight back.

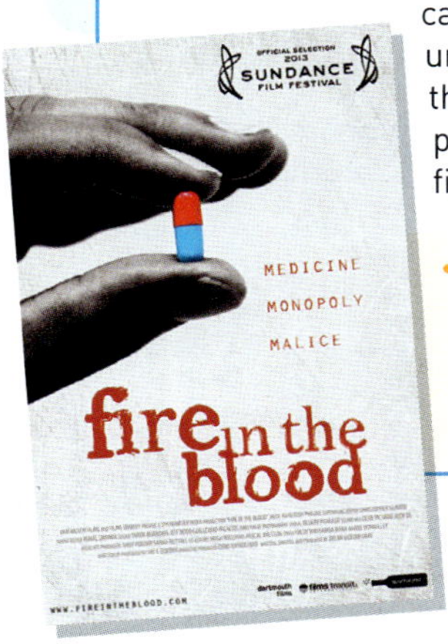


- **Watch** the trailer and **comment** on the devices used to highlight the dramatic event.

VIDÉO

## Entraîne-toi à l'oral

ÉPREUVE ORALE

**Step 1** **Build up your speech!**

- Choose one aspect of the issue you want to highlight: the importance of medicine production in developing countries, the role of India on the global industrial scale, the need for international cooperation regarding health care...
- Pick out up to 6 documents to build your portfolio: choose from the file or from your personal references.
- Prepare your presentation: show how these documents relate to the topic you chose. OBJECTIF BAC p. 305

**Step 2** **Make your presentation in front of two classmates.**

- Show the documents chosen to your friend and explain your point in about five minutes. Make sure you say how they illustrate the topic. OBJECTIF BAC p. 306-307

**Step 3** **Answer your classmates' questions about your presentation.**

FILE 27

RELATION AU MONDE

AXE 3 : HÉRITAGE COMMUN ET DIVERSITÉ

# Colours of Louisiana

▶ **How does Louisiana rely on its cultural diversity to stand out?**

**FINAL TASK** **Make a TED Talk to praise Louisiana's heritage and cultural diversity.**

## 1 The free spirit of Louisiana

### Doc 1. The cradle of jazz

(Video: *Visit the USA*, 2019)

VIDÉO

Jazz was born in New Orleans. Congo Square, to be precise. This public square was one of the only places in America where slaves were allowed to gather and play drums. They did so on "free Sundays," where the sharing of African rhythms and dance kept their ancestral tradition alive until, as it happened, it would become the very rhythm of American popular culture. Jazz is the music that erupted when African (and Afro-Caribbean) and European traditions converged in America, and nowhere was that mix more potent than in New Orleans.

*louisianatravel.com*, 2020

**a.** **Watch** the video and **focus** on the images and sounds: what impression of New Orleans do they convey?

**b.** **Comment** on the multicultural dimension of New Orleans.

**c.** **Look** at the poster and **read** the text. **Pick out** information about the origin of jazz.

**d.** Use the three documents to **define** the free spirit of New Orleans.

**WORDS**

- perf**o**rmer
- r**i**tuals = pr**a**ctices

- ensl**a**ved ≠ free
- entert**ai**ning

- sp**i**rited = l**i**vely

- be r**oo**ted in
- live on = pers**i**st
- w**o**rship = rev**e**re

## Doc 2. The free people of colour

*Edmond Dédé Piano Recital*, by Andrew LaMar Hopkins, revisiting the lively creole culture of New Orleans, 2019.

Free people of color, or *gens de couleur libres*, lived in Louisiana from its very founding. [...] The first free people of color were typically the illegitimate children of white slave owners who freed them. But the group also included slaves who had escaped. When Spain took over the territory, slaves were allowed to buy their freedom and the freedom of other slaves. [...]

By 1803, when Louisiana became part of the United States, about 1,300 free people of color lived in New Orleans. Several free people of color emigrated to Louisiana from Haiti after the Haitian Revolution, and by the time of the first U.S. Census in 1810 there were 7,585 free persons of color out of a total population of 76,556 people in the Orleans Territory.

The free persons of color distinguished themselves in art and business as the population of free persons of color grew to about 25,000 by 1840. Most of the free men of color were employed as doctors, clerks, teachers and in skilled trades. Before, during and after the Civil War—in which 1,500 free men of color fought for the Confederacy—the liberal and tolerant attitude toward the free persons of color changed.

Some free people of color moved away rather than be treated poorly alongside newly freed slaves. But the influence of *gens de couleur libres* lives on in the city's art, music and architecture.

*Nola.com*, October 2017

**a. Read** the text and **explain** who the free people of colour were.

**b. Account** for the evolution of their status.

**c. Say** how they have influenced today's Louisiana.

**CULTURE SPOT** EXO Quiz

**Check what you know about...**

- The abolition of slavery
- The Confederacy
- The Civil War
- The Union

LANDMARKS p. 273

## Doc 3. Louisiana Voodoo

*Facts Base*, 2018

**a. Watch** the video and **find** information about the origins of voodoo.

**b. Say** what its original goal was and **pick out** the items people needed to express their belief.

**c. Find out** why voodoo developed in Louisiana.

**d. Explain** how voodoo culture is still closely associated with Louisiana and **comment** on its evolution.

**YOUR TASK** You work for a tour operator. For the company's catalogue, **write** the introduction for a trip in Louisiana and **praise** the state's cultural diversity.

**AT HOME Watch** this James Bond scene of *Live and let die* VIDEO or an extract from the cartoon *The Princess and the Frog* VIDEO. Be ready to **comment** on how voodoo culture is represented on screen.

**BOOST YOUR SKILLS!**

**Célébrer la diversité**

- Utilise des formules accrocheuses : ***Celebration*** *of life* • ***Full of*** *life* • ***Full of*** *culture* • *The* ***spirit of*** *New Orleans*
- Emploie des marqueurs d'intensité : *We have* ***so*** *many genres of influence* • *The magical ethics are* ***anything but*** *evil.* • *Their population drew* ***drastically***. GRAMMAR p. 251
- Souligne l'héritage d'un passé riche : *New Orleans* ***continues to*** *be...* • *Their influence* ***lives on***...

# EXPLORE 2 A rich legacy to preserve

## Doc 1.

### Cajun culture thriving and evolving 250 years after Acadians arrived

Mural depicting the Acadian settlement, Windsor, Canada

Cajun filmmaker Pat Mire recalls an epiphany[1] of sorts he had at the age of 5 while watching the 1950s sitcom "Ozzie and Harriet" in the farmhouse where he grew up outside of Eunice[2]. He wondered aloud, "Why don't they speak French?" His mom laughed.

"The rest of the world is not like us," she said.

Five decades later, despite all the modern forces that eat away at tradition and regional distinctiveness, south Louisiana is still different, thanks in large part to a group of Acadian exiles who arrived on the banks of Bayou Teche in 1765—250 years ago this year.

The food alone sets the region apart, the product of two centuries of cross-cultural borrowing and innovation that has created a culinary world filled with gumbo, étouffée, fricassée, maque choux, boudin, chaudin, andouille and boiled crawfish.

People still know how to dance, which is unusual enough but even more so because the dancing is done to music often played on an instrument—the button accordion—that has long since fallen out of favor in mainstream American culture.

And the songs are still sung in French, a language that is no longer widespread in the region but has somehow managed to hang on 250 years after the arrival of French-speaking Acadians and more than a century after any other significant French immigration to the state.

The people who would come to be known as Cajuns arrived in what is now Canada in the 1600s, part of a wave of early New World settlers from Europe. They came as families, focused on learning how to survive and create a society in a strange new environment rather than on fighting, building new trade routes or expanding the boundaries of an empire.

A cohesive and independent culture flourished in the New World before the Acadians—a name derived from the French colony of Acadia where they settled—found themselves under the authority of a hostile British government, which gained control of that section of eastern Canada in the early 1700s. [...] "We sought[3] Louisiana as a refuge to continue the culture we had in Canada. We didn't come here to assimilate," said Warren Perrin, a Lafayette lawyer and cultural activist.

They planned to re-create the life they had lost. Over the next two decades, more than 2,000 Acadians from France and the Atlantic seaboard made their way to Louisiana.

*The Acadiana Advocate*, December 2015

**1.** *révélation* **2.** a small town in Louisiana **3.** seek < sought

**a. Read** the beginning of the text (l. 1-9). **Explain** what Pat Mire discovered at the age of 5.

**b. Read** the whole text and **pick out** information about who the Acadians are (origins, arrival in Louisiana).

**c.** TRANSLATION **Focus** on l. 24 and l. 31. How you would translate "*still*" in each occurrence? **Explain** what it shows about the Acadian culture.

**d.** GRAMMAR "*They planned to re-create the life they had lost*" (l. 62-63). **Identify** the tenses and **say** what time period they each refer to. ▸ p. 251

**e. Focus** on the last three paragraphs to explain what sets Louisiana apart from the rest of the USA.

Acadian lighthouse, New Brunswick, Canada

## Doc 2. The Louisiana Purchase

VIDÉO

*Linopa Films*, 2016

**a. Look** at the map and **say** what made the Louisiana territory so special at that time.

**b.** PHONOLOGY **Watch** the video and **focus** on the first sentence. **Say** which word is stressed and why.

**c. Pick out** the reason why the map of the USA evolved.

**d. Identify** the benefits of this deal for the Americans and for the French.

**e.** *"The world could be a very different place today"*. **Imagine** what the world would have been like if this had not happened.

**CULTURE SPOT** — EXO **Quiz**

Take the quiz: check what you know about Louisiana.

## Doc 3. Modernising Louisiana French

AUDIO

*Sweet Crude* on singing in Louisiana French, NPR, 2020

**a. Listen** to the document and **say** what makes Sweet Crude unique.

**b. Pick out** historic elements about Louisiana French.

**c. Comment** on the purpose of the band today.

**YOUR TASK** **Make** a short speech for the opening of the History of Louisiana museum.

DIFFÉRENCIATION

**WAY 1** **Present** the impact of the past on today's culture.

**WAY 2** **Explain** how the past still influences today's Louisiana and **emphasise** the importance of keeping traditions alive.

**BOOST YOUR SKILLS!**

**Évoquer l'influence du passé**

- Évoque le passé plus ou moins lointain au prétérit ou au *past perfect* : *They* ***planned*** *to re-create the life they* ***had lost***. GRAMMAR p. 251
- Souligne l'influence sur le présent au *present perfect* : *Cross-cultural borrowing* ***has created*** *a culinary world* • *A language that* ***has*** *somehow* ***managed*** *to hang on.*
- Utilise des marqueurs de temps et de durée : *250 years* ***ago*** *this year.* • ***In the*** *early 1700s.* • *A dialect spoken* ***for*** *generations.* • ***After*** *300 years.*

**WORDS**

- crossover = mix
- inheritance = legacy
- landmark = milestone

---

- enriched
- exiled
- infused with
- uprooted = displaced

---

- assimilate = acculturate
- forbid sb to do sthg
- prohibit = ban
- update = modernise

The group *Sweet Crude*, June 2020

# 3 Authenticity at risk

## Doc 1. The "new" New Orleans

10 years after Katrina, *AJ+*, 2015

**a. Watch** the video and **read** the culture spot. **Find** information about the new face of New Orleans.

**b. Say** how the evolution of the city has impacted the people who originally come from New Orleans.

**c.** PHONOLOGY *"Kevin grew up in housing projects here before the city tore them down after Katrina."* **Focus** on the stressed words. What idea do they insist on?

**d. Focus** on the end of the video and **explain** how Neal Morris's project contributes to preserving the authenticity of the city.

**CULTURE SPOT**

**Katrina** was a devastating hurricane that affected Louisiana and particularly the city of New Orleans in 2005. It caused over 1,800 deaths and the entire city was almost torn apart.

## Doc 2. Does NOLA[1] sound different?

15 years after flood waters forced people out of the city or onto rooftops, some believe the city doesn't just look different. It sounds different, too.

"With people, you know they're from New Orleans just by the way they talk," said Terry Baquet, who grew up in the city's historic Treme neighborhood. "There's a level of comfort when you meet someone from New Orleans and they sound just like you.

"Since Katrina, that's changed a lot."

New Orleans' traditional dialects are as distinctive and colorful as the city's architecture, drawing from French, Creole, African American, Irish, Italian and Jewish influences.

"The great irony is if you walk around in the famous historic neighborhoods, you're less likely to hear traditional New Orleans accents," said Richard Campanella, a Tulane University geographer who has studied the post-Katrina shift in demographics. "And if you go out to the working-class suburbs, those places are actually treasure troves[2] of local culture, which includes those accents and dialects."

New Orleans has shown signs of defending its authenticity and by extension, its way of speaking.

"We've gotten to the point where we look on it with affection," said Brennan, [a dialect coach,] who said she now feels like something of a preservationist. "We look at it as this precious thing that has to be protected and we don't want it to go away."

At apparel shops[3], more merchandise is targeting pre-Katrina nostalgia with logos from K&B and Schwegman's, local chains that closed long before Katrina. Some t-shirts demonstrate how to pronounce street names (it's Cal-ee-ope not Calliope).

*US News*, September 2020

**a. Read** the article and **explain** what it means for New Orleans to *"sound different"* (l. 5-6).

**b.** GRAMMAR *"Since Katrina, that's changed a lot."* (l. 16) **Focus** on the verbal group and **say** why this tense was used. ▸ p. 251

**c. Explain** why Katrina can be seen as a catalyst for change.

**d. Comment** on the people's attachment to their way of speaking and **say** how they try to preserve it.

1. **N**ew **O**rleans, **L**ouisian**A** 2. *trésor* 3. clothes shops

## Doc 3.

# A LOUISIANA TRIBE FIGHTS TO STAY PUT

Ten years ago, as news of the BP oil disaster reached Louisiana's Grand Bayou Indian Village, Rosina Philippe dispatched her brother Maurice Phillips on a reconnaissance mission. [...] He returned with a passenger: a brown pelican, alive but slathered in petroleum.

As they scrambled to save the pelican, Phillips told his sister that he saw other oiled birds but could wrangle only that one onto his boat. Nearly two months after the April 2010 disaster, then governor Bobby Jindal visited the same bay and declared that BP's oil was "killing the marsh[1]."

The Deepwater Horizon explosion and resulting 87-day oil spill proved catastrophic for Grand Bayou. The community had just rebuilt after Hurricane Katrina, which devastated the area in 2005, and residents had returned in time for the 2010 commercial shrimping season. "A lot of guys, what little bit of cash they had, they invested into making repairs on their boats because they envisioned the seafood to come," says Philippe, a tribal elder. The springtime waters brimmed with[2] shrimp. "So, it was almost like the anticipation of Christmas morning." Except that Christmas never came. The oil spewing from BP's open well about 5,000 feet below the Gulf's surface shut down the nearby fisheries for months. [...]

Now, with the 10th anniversary of the explosion approaching next week, the tribe is clear on two points. First, the BP disaster cannot be viewed in a vacuum. It is part of a litany of stresses that Grand Bayou has survived for decades, including the loss of more than 5,000 acres of fertile Delta land. And, second: they have no plans to leave.

"We're resilient," says Carmalita Sylve, who grew up in Grand Bayou, moved to Colorado after Hurricane Katrina, and returned to a rebuilt home in 2009. From the tribe's mainland headquarters, she gestures outside toward a grass-lined bank where boats dock and neighbors come to fish. "It's like this grass out here. You smoosh it down, but you know what? It will come right back. And that's how we are. You think that you're going to just overcome us with the different ways. But we'll adapt."

Barry YEOMAN, *nrdc.org*, April 2020

**1.** *marécage* **2.** be full of

## Doc 4. Losing land

*PBSNewsHour*, 2016

### WORDS

- gentrification
- inner city = downtown

- citizen-led (project)
- endangered
- environmental

- overcome (obstacles)
- relocate
- revitalise /riˈvaɪtəlaɪz/

**a. Read** the text (**doc. 3**) and **say** what problem threatens Indigenous land.

**b. Watch** the video (**doc. 4**) and **explain** how climate change is affecting Native Americans in Louisiana.

**c. Use** both documents to **comment on** the changing way of life of Native people.

**d. Explain** the concept of resilience and **say** what it means for Native Americans.

**YOUR TASK** **Take** part in a talk show on a statewide TV channel. **Discuss** the threats that Louisiana's unique culture is facing today.

### BOOST YOUR SKILLS!

**Exprimer des craintes**

- Évoque tes inquiétudes face à l'avenir : *Not everybody* ***is going to*** *be a home-owner.* • *We****'re not gonna have*** *anything for our children.* • *The sea* ***is coming*** *for his ancestral home.* • *It* ***will*** *come right back.* GRAMMAR p. 251
- Formule des hypothèses : ***If*** *it keeps on washing away...* • ***If*** *they don't try to stop in some kind of way...*
- Souligne ton attachement à l'existant : *We try* ***to keep*** *them in neighborhoods...* • *We* ***don't want*** *it to go away...*

EXPLORE

# 4 Where culture means business

## Doc 1.

### Louisiana's Cultural Economy

Louisiana has an economic asset that other states can only dream of: a multifaceted, deeply-rooted, authentic, and unique culture. Its cultural continuum spans[1] history and peoples, geography, and art forms. As a state that has long relied on oil, gas, and timber[2] to fuel its economy, Louisiana is now realizing that, in culture, it may have a new source of largely untapped[3] economic energy.

But if culture—abundant, renewable, and clean—is Louisiana's metaphorical new oil then it requires the industrial equivalent of the skilled workers, refineries, pipelines, and business entities to bring it to the global marketplace. That connection between a healthy culture and a healthy economy is now beginning to be made. [...]

Tourism is one of Louisiana's largest industries. In 2003, the state hosted 25.1 million visits, 76 percent of which were from outside of the state. African-American travelers represented 14 percent of all travel in the state. According to the most recent estimates, the tourism industry provides employment to about 116,000 workers, has a payroll of close to $2 billion, and returns about $635 million back to state and local governments in the form of tax revenues. In Louisiana it is very difficult to separate out what is cultural tourism, from the all of tourism.

Yes, there are people who come to Louisiana for business or to visit family and friends. And, yes, people come to gamble[4], to fish and hunt, and to experience the state's natural environment. Yet, whatever the reason for coming, few would dispute that it is the state's cultural environment that is the greatest draw[5].

*Report: Louisiana*, by Mt. Auburn Associates, State of Louisiana, July 2005

**1.** concern **2.** wood **3.** not used **4.** play in casinos **5.** asset

**a. Read** the report and **explain** how Louisiana's culture and its economy are intertwined.

**b. Comment** on the metaphor *"Louisiana's new oil"* (l. 8).

**c. Explain** the idea that culture means business and **illustrate** it with precise figures.

## Doc 2. The soul of opportunity

Video: *NOMTN*, 2019

**a. Watch** the video and **pick out** information about the place of tourism in New Orleans.

**b. Define** the concept of "intentional spending". **Explain** how it can boost the city's economy.

**c. Analyse** the link between cultural diversity and the local economy.

YOUR TASK **Convince** Louisiana Economic Development to finance an ad campaign for the state cultural attractions. **Highlight** the economic repercussions.

## FINAL TASK

### Make a TED Talk to praise Louisiana's heritage and cultural diversity.

**You work for the Department of Culture and Tourism of Louisiana. Make a TED Talk to help the audience understand the richness of Louisiana's culture.**

1. **Browse** through the file and **gather** elements about Louisiana's cultural diversity and the way it lives on today.
2. **Organise** your ideas focusing on: **presenting** the special past of Louisiana and how it shaped the state; **emphasising** the way multiculturalism enriches it; **including** some threats facing Louisiana's cultural heritage today.
3. **Watch** an example of a TED Talk to make sure you know how it is usually staged: a black background, one speaker, no lectern, no notes, etc.
4. **Record** your TED Talk.

BOOST YOUR ENGLISH p. 251

# BOOST YOUR ENGLISH!

## Grammar — Présenter les spécificités d'un lieu

• **Utilise les temps appropriés pour rapporter des faits passés plus ou moins éloignés ou souligner leur influence présente.**

*They **planned** to re-create the life they **had lost**.*
*The group also **included** slaves who **had escaped**.*
*Voodoo **has** similarly **become** a part of popular culture.*

• **Mets en avant les enjeux à venir.**

*Not everybody **is going to** be a homeowner.*
*We'**re not gonna have** anything for our children.*
*The sea **is coming** for its ancestral home.*
*I think possibly some of it **will** rub off on our grandchildren.*

• **Souligne les articulations de ta présentation.**

***While** voodoo may be a well-known practice, **not everyone is aware of**...*
***What's more**, it's designed to support...*
***On the one hand**..., and then **on the other hand**, we **also** believe that we can do...*

• **Utilise des procédés d'intensification pour capter l'attention de l'auditoire.**

*New Orleans is **such a** rich and diverse city.*
*We have **so** many genres of influence.*
***Nowhere** was that mix **more** potent **than** in New Orleans.*

**1 Conjugue les verbes entre parenthèses au temps qui convient.**

a. Napoleon (*buy*) the Louisiana territory from Spain and three years later (*sell*) it to Jefferson.
b. Today, Mardi Gras (*become*) the perfect example of New Orleans' spirit.
c. The Acadians (*flee*) Canada where they (*be*) persecuted.

**2 Reformule ces phrases avec des intensifieurs pour mettre en valeur certains points.**

a. Here is the French Quarter. It is a lively neighborhood.
b. Native Americans have a lot to teach about land management.
c. Tourism represents an economic opportunity for Louisiana.
d. New Orleanians can have diverse accents.

## Vocabulary — Colours of Louisiana

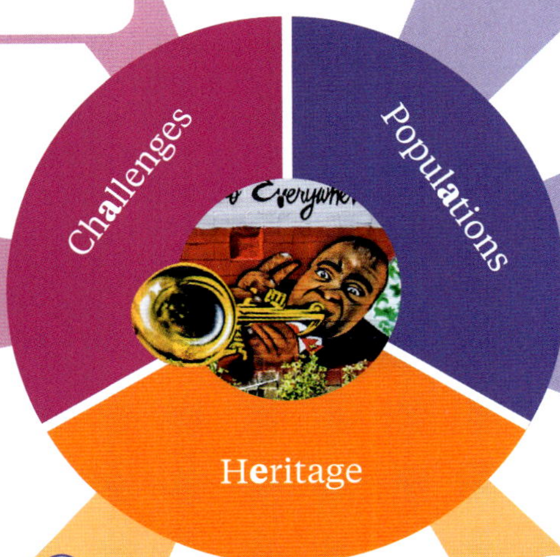


### Challenges

**Nature** (AUDIO)
- (natural) disaster
- hurricane
- refuge
- rising sea level
- species /'spi:ʃiz/
- destroy > damage
- rehabilitate
- shrink = narrow
- sink

**Business** (AUDIO)
- capital
- opportunity
- revenue = profits
- wealth
- boost
- take advantage of

### Populations

**Acadians** (AUDIO)
- Cajun /'keɪdʒən/
- customs = traditions
- descent = lineage
- exile
- sense of community
- settlement

**Native Americans** (AUDIO)
- endangered = at risk
- resilient
- uprooted = displaced
- preserve
- relocate

**Free slaves** (AUDIO)
- disenfranchised
- emancipated ≠ enslaved
- mixed-race

### Heritage

**Legacy** (AUDIO)
- (musical) genre
- inherit from
- keep alive
- modernise
- pass on
- recall = recollect

**Multiculturalism** (AUDIO)
- blend = mixture
- crossroads
- melting pot
- hearty = warm
- inviting = appealing
- intermingle = mix

OBJECTIF BAC p. 296-304

Grille d'auto-évaluation

## Sujet type bac

MÉDIATION

Durée : 3h30
Matériel autorisé : le dictionnaire unilingue (non encyclopédique) est autorisé.
Niveau attendu : C1

- **a. Prenez connaissance des documents A, B et C et traitez le sujet suivant en anglais (300 mots maximum).**

Taking into account their specificities, say what the documents reveal about the place of Louisiana French today.

**b. Vous rédigerez, au choix, l'un des deux écrits complémentaires demandés ci-dessous.**

– Expliquez en anglais et en 200 mots maximum en quoi le document C illustre l'état d'esprit actuel présenté dans les documents A et B.

**ou**

– *"'My French is bad,' is the first thing most Creole or Cajun French-speaking people will say to a foreigner's bonjour."* (Document B, l. 19-21). À la lumière des documents A et B, expliquez en anglais et en 200 mots maximum, en quoi cette citation reflète l'histoire de la Louisiane.

- **Traduisez en français le passage suivant, extrait du Document A.**

*"Sue Vasseur, known as Tante Sue de Mamou, worries about the survival of the Louisiana French culture. The current generation, she said, isn't picking up the French language, which is part of the soul of the Acadian people who settled in Louisiana in the mid-1700s, when they were expelled from the present-day Canadian province of Nova Scotia after refusing to swear their allegiance to the British crown."* (l. 1-10)

### Document A — Louisiana French: L'heritage at risk

MAMOU, La. — Sue Vasseur, known as Tante Sue de Mamou, worries about the survival of the Louisiana French culture. The current generation, she said, isn't picking up the French language, which is part of the soul of the Acadian people who settled in Louisiana in the mid-1700s, when they were expelled from the present-day Canadian province of Nova Scotia after refusing to swear their allegiance to the British crown.

"I'm hoping it's going to continue. They are teaching French in our schools here now in Mamou and Evangeline Parish. So I think possibly some of it will rub off on our grandchildren, our great-grandchildren," said Vasseur, 81. [...]

There's a major effort in Louisiana, a state named for French King Louis XIV, to restore the French language. It's part of a resurgence in cultural pride, and there are signs the decline in French speakers has slowed.

Among the last hopes is the nation's largest French-immersion program, in which every subject except English is being taught in French to kindergartners through eighth-graders[1]. Just under 4,000 students in nine parishes are in the program, typically with teachers imported from France, Belgium, Quebec and French-speaking African nations.

Bureaucrats and schoolteachers long sought to stamp out Louisiana French in the name of Americanization. They almost succeeded. Cajuns and others who spoke the language were told it was shameful and a sign of ignorance. Students were punished for speaking it after the state board of education decided in 1915 to suppress French, a move strengthened six years later when the Louisiana Constitution forbade the use of any language other than English in the public-school system.

It was estimated that there were a million French speakers in Louisiana in 1968. Today the number is pegged at 150,000 to 200,000. Those who speak French as their first language tend to be older than 70, and their children often never picked it up. [...]

Efforts to sustain Louisiana French are particularly strong in the oil and university

1. *équivalent de la 4e*

town of Lafayette, a regional hub where old-timers and young professionals alike speak French in cafes.

Lafayette is a city of festivals and music. Popular young French-speaking bands such as the Lost Bayou Ramblers and the Pine Leaf Boys perform around town and around the world. Members of the band Feufollet, who sing only in French, learned the language in Lafayette Parish schools.

The popularity of the Lafayette program is growing and there are waiting lists to get in, said Nicole LeBlanc, who leads a parents' group, Les Amis de L'Immersion, that provides support for the program.

LeBlanc, who has three French-speaking children, said older people have stopped her children in the grocery store, eyes lighting up on hearing them speaking in French.

Sean COCKERHAM, *The Seattle Times*, July 2012

## Document B French-friendly America

In Louisiana, a [...] branding project is now underway, led by the Council for the Development of French in Louisiana, or CODOFIL.

The organization hopes to have its first Zagat[1]-like "FrancoResponsable" ("French-friendly") stickers in the windows of restaurants, shops and hotels in New Orleans and Acadia within a month. [...]

The goal is to bump up the already sizable population of francophone tourists who visit Louisiana, and to validate the French language in a public way.

Promoters of the campaign and others like it say they recognize that inviting outsiders to experience Louisiana's French dialects may sometimes put locals in awkward positions. In Louisiana, French has been stigmatized and repressed; "My French is bad," is the first thing most Creole or Cajun French-speaking people will say to a foreigner's bonjour.

However, according to a spokesperson from CODOFIL, French businesses are already excited about the FrancoResponsable program, which may one day be extended to doctor's offices and other non-tourist locales. What's more, it's designed to support all forms of French in the state—regional, Haitian, European, or African. It's also hoped that young Louisianans will see that French is connected to the job market, so they'll have an incentive to master the language. In the 1960s, about a million people spoke French in the state. Today there are about 175,000 native speakers.

Whether tying the language to the whims of the tourist market is a good idea is not yet clear. "French isn't alive and well like it used to be, so I feel that it is like everything—there are good and bad points," says Emilie Urbain, a Belgian-born adjunct professor at the University of Moncton who has conducted linguistic research in Louisiana. Economically, though, it may deliver, says Joseph Dunn, a former CODOFIL director. Already, francophone visitors bring $250,000 in revenue per year to just one site, the Laura Plantation, Dunn's current marketing client.

Lila MACLELLAN, *qz.com*, March 27, 2015

1. a guide rating restaurants

## Document C

Signage at Mamou Elementary School in Mamou, La. often appears in both English and French, William WIDMER, *The New York Times*, 2019

Vers le **BAC**

# LET'S BRAINSTORM!

OBJECTIF BAC p. 305-317

RELATION AU MONDE Axe 3

**How does Louisiana rely on its cultural diversity to stand out?**

## A special history

- Becoming American
  → "The Louisiana Purchase", *Linopa films*, p. 247
- A unique melting pot
  → "A thriving Cajun culture", *The Advocate*, p. 246 • "The free people of colour", *Nola.com*, p. 245

## A rich culture

- The legacy of slavery
  → "The cradle of jazz", *Visit the USA*, p. 244 • "Louisiana voodoo", *Facts Base*, p. 245
- Native American traditions
  → "Losing land", *PBSNewsHour*, p. 249
- Speaking Louisianan languages
  → "A thriving Cajun culture", *The Advocate*, p. 246 • "Does NOLA sound different?", *US News*, p. 248

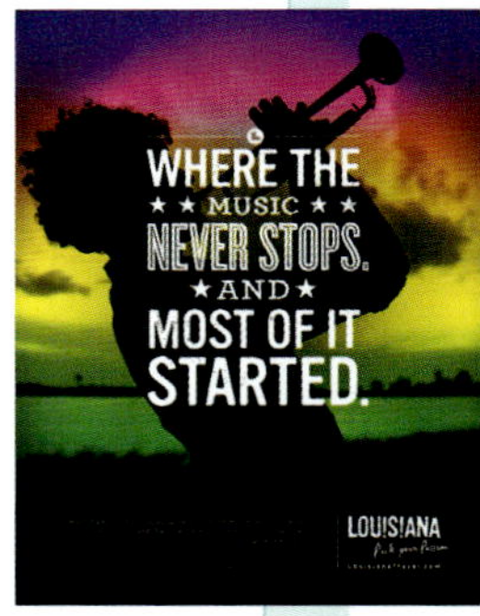


## Preserving a common heritage

- Overcoming natural catastrophes
  → "The "new" New Orleans", *AJ+*, p. 248 • "Losing land", *PBSNewsHour*, p. 249 • "A Louisiana tribe fights to stay put", *nrdc.org*, p. 249
- A generational issue
  → "Modernising Louisiana French, *NPR*, 247 • "The cradle of jazz", *Visit the USA*, p. 244

## Taking advantage of diversity

- Creating business opportunities
  → "The soul of opportunity", *NONTM*, p. 250 • "Louisiana's cultural economy", *State of Louisiana*, p. 250 • "Louisiana voodoo", *Facts Base*, p. 245
- Reinventing New Orleans
  → "The "new" New Orleans", *AJ+*, p. 248

## Phonology — Rythme et accentuation dans les énoncés

AUDIO

- Dans un énoncé, on **accentue** les **mots lexicaux**, c'est-à-dire les mots **porteurs de sens** : noms, verbes, adjectifs.
- Les **mots grammaticaux** sont généralement non accentués : déterminants, propositions, etc.
Cependant, certains mots grammaticaux peuvent être accentués : mots interrogatifs, auxiliaires en début de phrase.
- À l'oral, les mots **non accentués** semblent « disparaître » car on utilise leur **forme réduite**.
- L'alternance de mots accentués ou non accentués donne du **rythme** et permet d'attirer **l'attention** sur les points clés du discours.

**1** **Écoute et repère les mots accentués. Pourquoi ceux-ci ?**

*Voodoo is an incredibly diverse culture whose name may be misunderstood.*

**2** **Lis cet énoncé et anticipe les mots accentués. Écoute et vérifie.**

*There are multiple causes for the continuing land-loss, including decades of oil and gas canals, speeding up erosion and the sinking of the land by three feet in the past century.*

# BUILD YOUR PORTFOLIO

## Series

"Treme", *HBO series*, 2010-2013

The series is named after a neighbourhood of New Orleans. The show follows musicians, chefs, Mardi Gras Indians and ordinary New Orleanians as they try to rebuild their lives, their homes and their unique culture in the aftermath of the 2005 Hurricane Katrina.

- **Watch** the series and **explain** how it illustrates the motto *"Won't bow, don't know how"*.

VIDÉO

## Poem

"I am Louisiana", Paul Ott, 2006

“I'm Spanish moss on a live oak tree
Cajun fried shrimp and a cypress knee.
I'm Bienville, Captain Shreve, Beauregard, Zack
Taylor and Jean Lafitte.
I'm New Orleans, the land of dreams Creole cookin'
and a Mardi Gras king. [...]”

(Adopted as the official state poem in 2006)

- **Read** the whole poem and **identify** the references to Louisiana's cultural heritage. **Say** what the decision to make it the official poem of Louisiana shows about it.

SITE

## Mural

"Jazz funeral", mural in New Orleans

The mural next to the historic Ashé Cultural Arts Center reflects musicians influenced by NOLA.

- **Observe** the mural and **comment** on the way it depicts New Orleans' rich cultural heritage.

## Book

*The Awakening*, Kate Chopin, 1899

Kate Chopin (1850-1904) was an American author of short stories and novels based in Louisiana. *The Awakening* is set in Grand Isle and shows the ethnic and cultural diversity of the area.

- **Read** the novel and **describe** 19th century Louisiana's society. **Draw** links between the past and today's cultural diversity.

ÉPREUVE ORALE | GRAND ORAL | Entraîne-toi à l'oral

## Step 1

**Build up your speech!**

ÉPREUVE ORALE:

- Choose one topic in the mindmap p. 254.
- Pick out two documents in the file and add one or two personal ones to illustrate this issue.
- Prepare your presentation: you must show how these documents relate to the issue you chose.

OBJECTIF BAC p. 305

GRAND ORAL:

- Choose one topic in the mindmap p. 254.
- Find a key question about your topic.
- Gather arguments and examples from the documents in the file to support your point.
- Prepare an outline for your presentation and write your note sheet.

OBJECTIF BAC p. 308-309

## Step 2

**Make your oral presentation in front of two classmates.**

ÉPREUVE ORALE:

- Show your documents to your classmates. Each of you makes their presentation to the others in about five minutes.

OBJECTIF BAC p. 306-307

GRAND ORAL:

- Give your note sheet to your classmates.
- Stand up and make a five-minute presentation to answer your key question.

OBJECTIF BAC p. 310-311

## Step 3

**Answer your classmates' questions about your presentation and give some feedback.**

RELATION AU MONDE
AXE 3 : HÉRITAGE COMMUN ET DIVERSITÉ

# Captain Pacific

▶ **To what extent is Captain Cook a national hero?**



**YOUR MISSION**

**Write an op-ed on the controversy regarding Cook's voyages.**

As a descendant of an Indigenous people of Oceania, write an op-ed for *Oz Magazine* on the controversy linked to the commemoration of Cook's voyages on the anniversary of the expedition.

FOLLOW THE STEPS!

## 1 A controversial legacy

### Doc 1. The end of a national figure?

VIDÉO

Statue of James Cook in Gisborne, New Zealand, 2019
(Video: *9 News Australia*, 2020)

a. **Watch** the video and **explain** who James Cook was.
b. **Give** details about the different commemorations of Cook's voyages.
c. **Observe** the graffiti in the picture and **draw** a parallel with the video.
d. **Discuss** Prime Minister Scott Morrison's quote *"the landing is nationally significant"*.

LANDMARKS p. 286

**WORDS**

- icon /'aɪkɒn/
- ownership
- skull and crossbones = death's head
- vandalism

- appropriate
- subjective = biased /'baɪəst/
- unlawful

- mock official history
- step onto a territory

## Doc 2. Repainting history

Emanuel Phillips Fox, *Landing of Captain Cook at Botany Bay, 1770*, 1902

Daniel Boyd, *We Call them Pirates Out Here*, 2006

**a.** **Observe** Emanuel Phillips Fox's painting and **describe** the situation.

**b.** **Compare** it with Daniel Boyd's painting and **comment** on the differences.

**c.** **Contrast** both artworks' titles and **imagine** Daniel Boyd's goal when painting his.

**d.** **Discuss** the impact of Daniel Boyd's artwork on Cook's legacy.

**CULTURE SPOT**

**Daniel Boyd** is an indigenous artist whose work focuses on colonial and post-colonial history. He challenges the subjective history of discovery and settlement.

## Doc 3. The real aims of Cook's voyage

The military nature of the *Endeavour*'s[1] voyage – as part of an aggressive reconnaissance and defence against Indigenous resistance – has historically been overlooked or downplayed[2]. But musket[3] fire was used many times to teach lessons of British military superiority.

Violence underscored[4] almost all of Cook's Pacific encounters with Indigenous peoples. In the broader strategic sense – as all 18th and early 19th century scientific voyages were – Cook's voyages were part of a European drive to conquer. The aim was to claim resources and trade in support of the British Empire's expansion. At its heart, Cook's first voyage was first a Royal Navy expedition and he was chosen as a military commander who had a background in mathematics and cartography. During the "great age" of Pacific voyaging, expeditions always had several goals at once. Cook's first voyage in 1769 occurred during the perennial cold war of Anglo-French rivalry after what has been regarded as the first global conflict, the Seven Years War (1756-1763). This was also at the height of the promotion of "imperial science" – the idea that scientific advancement and colonial expansion were twin goals. As industrialisation drove upheaval in Europe, scientific "discovery" was seen as a critical part of establishing, developing and controlling an empire.

Stephen Gapps, "Make no mistake: Cook's voyages were part of a military mission to conquer and expand", *The Conversation*, April 2020

1. British Royal Navy vessel that Lieutenant Cook commanded on his first voyage (1768-1771)
2. minimised
3. old type of gun
4. underlined

**STEP 1**

**Take** notes on the debate surrounding Cook's status as a national hero.

**a.** **Read** the text and **pick out** information about the different purposes of Cook's first voyage.

**b.** **Comment** on the link between conquest and scientific progress.

**c.** TRANSLATION *"...he was chosen as a military commander..."* (l. 16-17) Why is the passive form used here? **Translate** the whole sentence (l. 15-18).

**BOOST YOUR SKILLS!**

**Attirer l'attention sur des faits**

- Emploie le passif pour mettre en avant une personne ou un fait : *But musket fire **was used** many times... • He **was chosen** as a military commander...*
- Utilise des quantifieurs pour montrer l'importance des faits : ***Many** times • **Almost all of** Cook's voyages • **Several** goals*

## 2 Restoring the missing part of history

### Doc 1. A two-sided figure

Vincent Namatjira, *Close Contact*, 2018

Video : *ABC News*, 2019

**a. Focus** on the work of art (left) and **imagine** what its title refers to.

**b. Comment** on the way the colonisation of Australia is represented.

**c. Watch** the video and **pick out** information about the artist and his project.

**d.** RHETORIC **Focus** on the structure *"these two sides of our history, these two sides of our story"* and **explain** the effect of this rhetorical device.

**e. Comment** on the statement *"He sees Cook as part of that history."*

**WORDS**

- **a**nchorage /'æŋkərɪdʒ/
- **la**nding
- po**ss**ession /pə'zeʃən/

- Abo**ri**ginal
- contro**ver**sial = in dis**pu**te

- **e**thnic
- indi**g**enous = **na**tive

- chart = map /tʃɑːt/
- claim a **con**tinent
- de**mand**
- **wi**den = ex**pand**

### Doc 2. Who was behind Cook?

Exhibition at Auckland War Memorial Museum, New Zealand, 2019
(Video: *The Voyage*, 2020)

**a. Watch** the video and **pick out** information on Tupaia and his role.

**b. Look** at the poster and **imagine** the goal of the exhibition.

**c.** GRAMMAR *"**What** this exhibit **is** great at **is** explaining..."* **Describe** the structure of the sentence and **comment** on its effect.

**d. Comment** on Tupaia's rehabilitation as a master navigator.

**CULTURE SPOT**

***Aotearoa*** /aʊˌterə'rəʊə/ is the Māori name for New Zealand, usually translated as "the land of the long white cloud".

## Doc 3.

### Renaming the Cook Islands would be a vital step towards true independence

Fifty-four years after independence, the Cook Islands is considering a name change. Named after Captain Cook, the Pacific islands, located between New Zealand and Hawaii, comprise 15 Polynesian islands, each with their own pre-colonial names and histories and complicated dynamics in the present. [...] If you thought decolonisation in the Pacific was a mid-20th-century moment that ended with political independence, you would be wrong. Decolonisation is a continuing undoing of the legacies of colonialism. It involves re-examining names and categories, but it is not always about going back to the past to claim some authentic identity. Hence, Danny Mataroa, chair of the Cook Islands name change committee, has suggested a name that encompasses[1] Christian faith (which arrived after colonialism) and Māori heritage (which predates colonialism).

But what does decolonisation have to do with place names? Place names are the meeting points of history and geography that shape part of our identities. Under colonialism, Eurocentric naming practices were commonplace. For example, New Zealand – the country to which the Cook Islands chose to be in association with after independence in 1965 – was named after a province in the Netherlands. [...] It makes perfect sense then that the Polynesian citizens of the Cook Islands would see the current name as a rupture of their own indigenous geographies, a colonially inherited map that erases the long and remarkable history of Polynesian ocean navigation in favour of the name of a single British explorer.

Some might argue that to rename a place is to destroy history at the stroke of a pen. This is the argument of some who oppose the renaming of streets named after wealthy slave-owners in Glasgow. [...]

Renaming can also restore history and give back a sense of place and culture. [...] A new place name for the Cook Islands (such Avaiki Nui, a local term and a frequently suggested new name) offers the possibility to reclaim ancestral legacies and envision[2] new futures – futures that do not belong to the limited choices laid out by colonialism that foreclose[3] true independence, but a more hopeful map for the next generation that opens up the spirit of liberation.

Nalini MOHABIR,
*The Guardian*,
March 2019

1. includes 2. conceive 3. prevent

**a. Read** the article and **pick out** information about the Cook Islands.

**b. Account for** the context of the article.

**c.** RHETORIC **Focus** on *"But what does decolonisation have to do with place names?"* (l. 17-18) **Explain** the effect of this rhetorical device.

**d. Explain** the controversy sparked today regarding the legacy of Eurocentric naming practices.

**e. Discuss** Danny Mataora's suggestion regarding the renaming.

### BOOST YOUR SKILLS!

**Capter l'attention du lecteur pour convaincre**

- Introduis des relatives pour mettre des informations en relief : *Māori heritage (**which** predates colonialism)...* • *The country **to which** the Cook Islands chose to be in association with...*
- Emploie des tournures stylistiques de mise en relief : *These two sides of our **history**, these two sides of our **story**...*

### STEP 2

**Take** notes on the Indigenous peoples' role during Cook's voyages and on the consequences of these voyages for them today. **Give** your opinion on the initiatives aiming at reconciliation.

### FINAL STEP

**Gather** your notes and **prepare** the outline of your op-ed on the controversy regarding the commemoration of Cook's voyages. **Start** writing: **explain** the issue and **mention** both sides' visions. **Elaborate** arguments and **give** your opinion on the matter. **Try** to captivate and convince your readers.

**You've completed your mission. Well done!**

play BAC How to... **PRESENT A PORTFOLIO**

OBJECTIF BAC p. 305-306

Concentre-toi sur les tableaux de Daniel Boyd *We Call them Pirates Out Here* et de Emanuel Phillips Fox *Landing of Captain Cook at Botany Bay, 1770* (Doc 2 p. 257) ainsi que sur les articles "The real aims of Cook's voyages" (Doc 3 p. 257) et "Renaming the Cook Islands would be a vital step towards true independence" (Doc 3 p. 259). **Entraîne-toi** à présenter ce dossier comme s'il s'agissait de **ton dossier personnel** pour l'épreuve.

• C'est un exemple de dossier de 4 documents qui pourrait constituer un dossier personnel d'élève. Pour rappel, à l'épreuve orale de Terminale, tu dois présenter 4 à 6 documents textuels et/ou iconographiques, dont au moins un article de presse et pas plus de deux textes d'une autre nature ni plus de deux documents iconographiques. Tu peux choisir des documents que tu as étudiés en classe ou non.

## 1 Analyse le dossier

OBJECTIF BAC p. 305

**a. Identifie** la nature des documents proposés, le sujet, le contexte mais aussi les dates.

**b. Prends** des notes sur les points communs ou les différences entre chaque document.

**c. Formule** une problématique en suivant un fil conducteur qui sera celui de ton dossier.

**d. Trouve** deux ou trois axes qui deviendront les grandes parties de ta présentation.

• Quels points de vue sont exprimés dans les documents ?
• Quelles sont les perspectives envisagées (nationale et officielle, historique et interculturelle) ?
• Organise ton brouillon en utilisant un schéma qui reprend les différences ou similitudes de points de vue.

## 2 Présente ton dossier à l'oral

OBJECTIF BAC p. 306

**a. Entraîne**-toi avec deux autres camarades. Pendant que tu présentes ton dossier à l'oral, tes camarades prennent des notes et préparent des questions.

**b. Structure** ton propos et présente le thème dans l'introduction, la problématique, puis les axes.

**c. Marque** une pause dans ta présentation lorsque tu passes d'une partie à l'autre et **sois** logique dans ta présentation.

**d. Appuie**-toi sur les documents choisis pour présenter la logique de ton dossier.

**e. Conclus** ta présentation en exprimant ton opinion sur ce dossier et, en imaginant que les choix soient les tiens, **explique** et **justifie**-les.

• Ta problématique (*key question*), ancrée dans une des thématiques du programme, doit permettre une analyse croisée des documents. *The documents under study shed light on...*

• *Document X enhances the importance of... Document Y focuses on another perspective...*
• *This enables me to speak about... which is at the core of...*

## 3 Interagis

**Réponds** aux questions préparées par tes camarades. Cet entretien doit te permettre de reprendre des éléments du dossier, de les développer ou d'apporter des précisions.

• Mobilise tes connaissances culturelles et personnelles pendant l'entretien. *Actually, your question reminded me of...* • *Well, this idea is related to...* • *I suppose it is connected to...*

Vers le BAC

# BUILD YOUR PORTFOLIO

## Article

"The stories of Tupaia and Omai and their vital role as Captain Cook's unsung shipmates", Kate Fullagar, *MENAFN – The Conversation*, April 2020

> "Shining a light on the islanders who travelled with Cook is necessary to put his achievements in proper context. Cook was more reliant on their assistance for his empire-expanding project than is often acknowledged."

- **Read** the article and **focus** on the role of the forgotten islanders during Cook's voyages.

ARTICLE

## Map

James Cook's three Pacific voyages, *Encyclopædia Britannica, Inc.*, 2020

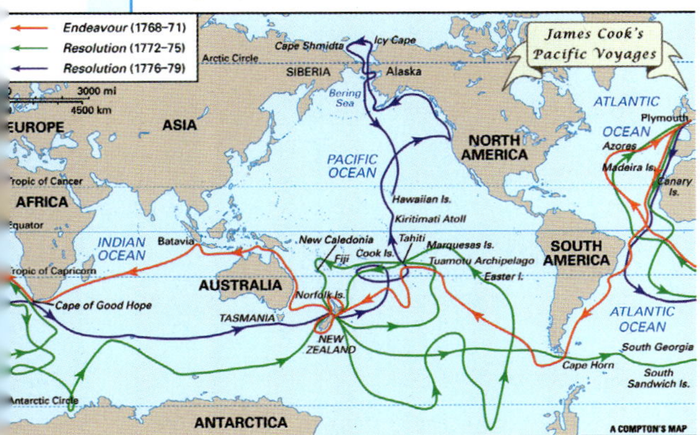


- **Look** at the map and **observe** the three expeditions led by Cook to extend the power of the British Empire. **Explain** the legacy of these discoveries today.

## Book

*The Journals of Captain Cook*, James Cook, 1999

The journals of Captain Cook were published after the recent discovery of the originals; only accounts could be found before that. These journals tell the story of his voyages as Cook wanted it to be told, enhancing the ambition, courage and skills that enabled him to carry out this series of expeditions in dangerous waters.

- **Select** a passage of your choice that illustrates the nature of Cook's voyages.

## Painting

*Cookie in the Cook Islands*, Michel Tuffery, 2008

- **Observe** the way the painter reimagines Cook and **say** to what extent this vision differs from his traditional image.

## Documentary

*The Pacific: In The Wake of Captain Cook with Sam Neill*, 2018

This documentary series follows Cook's footsteps for the 250th anniversary year of Cook's first voyage. The Pacific is being charted and its people known: it is a navigation through different cultures shaping history.

- **Watch** an extract and **comment** on the new perspectives presented by the documentary series.

VIDÉO

## Entraîne-toi à l'oral — ÉPREUVE ORALE

**Step 1** **Build up your speech!**

- Focus on the impact of Cook's voyages and their historical interpretation through time with the commemorations.
- Pick out two documents from the file, add a personal one and choose another one in this page to illustrate the topic. OBJECTIF BAC p. 305
- Prepare your presentation: you must show how these documents relate to the topic.

**Step 2** **Make your presentation in front of two classmates.**

- Show the documents to your classmates and explain your point in about five minutes. OBJECTIF BAC p. 306-307

**Step 3** **Answer your classmates' questions about your presentation.**

# The U.K. in the 19th Century

## The Industrial Revolution

- The Industrial Revolution began in Great Britain around 1760, and many of the technological innovations, such as the **steam engine** invented by Scottish engineer James Watt or the Bessemer process were British.
- The **textile** industry led the way. **Manchester**, the world's first industrial city, was nicknamed "'Cottonopolis".
- **Mechanised agriculture** and agronomy transformed food production; the **factory system** led to **urbanisation** and affordable consumer goods. Canals, railways, steamboats changed **transportation**, while the telegraph and later telephone systems transformed **communication**.
- In 1850, Britain produced 40% of the world's manufactured goods. And by 1900, it controlled 60% of the world traffic of goods thanks to its **merchant navy**.
- In 1846 the **Corn Laws**, which taxed imported food highly, were repealed. Britain led the world into a new era of **free trade** which announced globalisation.
- The Industrial Revolution witnessed the triumph of a middle class of industrialists and businessmen. But **Victorian society** remained very hierarchical, with a **rigid class system**.
- There were major scientific advances such as the theory of evolution proposed by Charles Darwin, which questioned religious certainties.

London c.1887: *St Paul's and Ludgate Hill*, William Logsdail.

REIGN OF GEORGE III (1760-1820) | REIGN OF GEORGE IV | REIGN OF WILLIAM IV

- **1798** – *Essays on the Principle of Population* Thomas Malthus
- **1801** – **Act of Union** England, Wales, Scotland and Ireland become the United Kingdom.
- **1802** – **Treaty of Amiens** Temporary peace between Britain and Napoleonic Empire
- **1805** – **Battle of Trafalgar** The British Navy defeats the French and Spanish.
- **1811** – **Luddite movement** Textile workers destroy machinery that they believe is threatening their jobs. (1811-1816)
- **1813** – *Pride and Prejudice* (novel) Jane Austen
- **1815** – **Battle of Waterloo** Napoleon defeated.
- **1818** – *Frankenstein, A Modern Prometheus* (gothic novel) Mary Wollstonecraft Shelley
- **1820**
- **1825** – **The world's first passenger railway line** opens in the north of England.
- **1825** – **Combination of Workmen Act** suppresses the right to strike.
- **1830**
- **1832** – **The Reform Act** extends the right to vote in Britain (though not to women, nor poor men).
- **1833** – **Slavery abolished** in the British Empire.
- **1834** – **New Poor Law**
- **1837** – *Oliver Twist* (novel) Charles Dickens
- **1838** – **Chartist movement** for electoral reform begins.
- **1844** – *The Condition of the Working Class in England* (political essay) Friedrich Engels
- **1847** – *Jane Eyre* (novel) Charlotte Brontë; *Wuthering Heights* (novel) Emily Brontë
- **1848** – *The Communist Manifesto* (political essay) published in London. Friedrich Engels and Karl Marx

The Great Exhibition, 1851. Charlotte Brontë, wrote "It is a wonderful place – vast, strange, new and impossible to describe."

## London in the 19th Century

- The **most populated city** in the world grew from 2 million inhabitants in 1801 to 6 million in 1897.
- London gave the new middle class access to culture and entertainment.
- Its wealth and modernity attracted visitors from across the world for the **Great Exhibition** held at the Crystal Palace in 1851, or to the **first public national museum** in the world (the British Museum, founded in 1753).
- London's growth was so quick, its infrastructure could not keep pace. It lacked **sanitation** and **epidemics** were common in the slums, where people lived in crowded conditions. In the summer of 1858, the smell of human waste became intolerable. This "Great Stink" convinced the MPs to invest in an extensive **sewerage** system.
- Burning cheap coal and industry were responsible for the city's notorious thick **fog** which, in addition to being a health hazard, also provided a cover for thieves.
- A new network of **metropolitan railways** allowed the development of **suburbs** from which middle-class and wealthy people could commute to the centre. London was also the first city to adopt gas street lighting, to build an underground transit system, and adopt traffic lights.

→ File 21 p. 191

## Working-class Britain

- People flocked to cities to work in the new factories and a new **urban working class** developed. Their living and working conditions were very difficult.
- Dozens of Acts were passed to improve the workers' labour and living conditions, but they were piecemeal and most of the time non-binding for employers.
- Inspired by the ideas of Thomas Malthus, who thought that population growth should be checked before it outstripped food supplies, the New Poor Law (1834) decided that able-bodied persons would only be granted relief in **workhouses**, where conditions were made as bad as possible to deter paupers from entering them.
- Charles Dickens used his novels and the magazines he edited to promote reform and criticise overcrowded **slums**, cruelty and injustice. He opposed **child labour**, particularly in *Oliver Twist* and the semi-autobiographical *David Copperfield* (1850).
- **Socialist** ideas developed. Germans Friedrich Engels and Karl Marx believed that a "class struggle" opposed the **bourgeoisie** to the **"proletariat"** (working class) and that a proletarian revolution was necessary to achieve equality and build a Communist world.
- Other movements, such as **Chartism** aimed at gaining political rights for the working classes.

Charles Dickens denounced child labour in novels like *Oliver Twist*. Here, a scene from the 2005 film version.

### REIGN OF QUEEN VICTORIA (1837-1901)

- **1851** The Great Exhibition, London. Urban population reaches 50% in Britain, first society in human history to do so.
- **1856** Bessemer process allows the mass production of cheap steel.
- **1857** The Matrimonial Causes Act legalises divorce but it is extremely limited.
- **1859** *On the Origin of Species* (scientific essay) Charles Darwin
- **1863** First Underground line opens in London.
- **1866** Last cholera epidemic in London
- **1867** National Society for Women's Suffrage founded.
- **1869** Suez Canal built.
- **1870** Education Act sets the frame for elementary schooling but does not make it free nor compulsory.
- **1871** Trade Union Act legalises trade unions.
- **1876** Victoria crowned Empress of India.
- **1880** First Boer War in South Africa (to 1881)
- **1880** The Married Women's Property Act gives married women the right to their own property and money.
- **1886** *Dr Jekyll and Mr Hyde* (gothic novel) Robert Louis Stevenson
- **1890** First electric underground railway opened in London.
- **1893** The Labour Party founded (socialist)
- **1899** Second Boer War in South Africa (to 1902)

## The British Empire

- By the end of Victoria's reign in 1901, the British Empire included one-fifth of the world's surface, spanning four continents and a quarter of its population.
- Despite the **abolition of slavery**, colonised populations were exploited and disenfranchised. Resistance to the British Empire never ceased. The largest **rebellion** against British rule took place in **India** in 1857-58.
- Faith in **moral and religious superiority**, the quest for **national prestige** and the need to provide industries with **raw materials** and **new markets** in which to sell Britain's manufactured goods explain imperial expansion.
- European powers competed in a "**scramble for Africa**" of which only 10% was colonised in 1870 (90% by 1914). This created considerable rivalry between them. In 1898 Britain almost went to war with France over Sudan, and a succession of international crises involving Germany, Britain and France partly explain the outbreak of WWI.

The Colonial and Indian exhibition in London, 1886.

Now test your culture!

EXO Quiz

# The U.K. from 1900 to 1945

British propaganda posters urged Britons to join the war effort, playing on the guilt of those who did not enlist. (1915)

## The Horrors of World War I

- In 1914, public opinion was generally enthusiastic about the war and 2 million men enlisted to join the largest **all-volunteer army** in history.
- In 1916 though, **conscription** was introduced for the first time in Britain. It became compulsory to join for men aged 18 to 40.
- For many in Britain, the **Battle of the Somme** is the most painful and infamous episode of WWI. Its first day was the bloodiest in the British Army's history. Over 120,000 **Allied** troops—including those from Australia, India, South Africa, New Zealand, Newfoundland and Canada—launched the initial attack. Nearly 20,000 were killed, most of them in the first hour, and another 37,000 were wounded.
- **Siegfried Sassoon** described the battle as a "sunlit picture of hell." Sassoon and other war poets directly involved in trench warfare such as **Wilfred Owen** and **Roland Leighton**, protested against the absurdity, the waste and the horror of war.
- In an era when news reporting from the front was generally censored, the poems gave a more realistic sense of life for the soldiers and medical personnel.

### Timeline

REIGN OF EDWARD VII (EDWARDIAN PERIOD) — REIGN OF GEORGE V

- **1901** — End of the Second Boer War. Britain takes control of all of South Africa.
- **1901** — *The Hound of the Baskervilles* (Sherlock Holmes novel) Sir Arthur Conan Doyle
- **1903** — Women's Social and Political Union founded by Emmeline Pankhurst. Members known as Suffragettes.
- **1904** — 'Entente Cordiale' is signed between Britain and France.
- **1908** — London Olympic Games
- **1910**
- **1912** — *Titanic* sinks with the loss of 1,503 lives.
- **1914** — Irish Home Rule Bill passed but implementation suspended for the duration of WWI.
- **1914–1918** — First World War
- **1916** — Battle of the Somme 1 July-18 Nov. 420,000 British casualties in 4 months
- **1917** — Bolshevik Revolution in Russia
- **1918** — Suffrage extended to all men, and women over 30 with property.
- **1918** — "The Send-Off" (WWI poetry) Wilfred Owen
- **1919** — Treaty of Versailles
- **1921** — Partition of Ireland: Northern Ireland stays part of the UK while the south becomes independent.
- **1922** — Mussolini's Fascist Italy established.

## Home Front and Blitz Spirit

Sir Winston Churchill giving his famous "V for victory" sign.

- In May 1940, **Winston Churchill** (1874-1965) became Prime Minister of a war coalition government. He was famous for his memorable **speeches**, broadcast on BBC radio. He promised '"blood, toil, tears and sweat" in order to win "victory at all costs", and the country followed him.
- On the Home Front, Britons got organised. Children were **evacuated** to the countryside during Operation Pied Piper. A total **blackout** prevented enemy aircraft from spotting populated areas. **Rationing** was introduced for food, clothes and petrol. Women were encouraged to "make-do and mend" by propaganda. In 1941 for the first time in history, they were drafted into war work.
- The biggest danger came from **air raids**. Authorities celebrated the stoicism and courage of the population in face of the bombings. This attitude became known as the **"Blitz spirit"**, though historians now think it was more of a myth, well captured by the famous slogan "Keep calm and carry on" though it was never in fact released for public display during the war.
- Today reference to the Blitz is often used whenever Britain is in a crisis, such as in 2020 when the government evoked wartime Blitz spirit for fight against Covid 19.

## 1930s: Social and Moral Concerns

- Though Britain's world trade fell by half during the **Great Depression**, the downturn was less severe than in many other countries.
- Particularly hard hit were the industrial and mining areas where **unemployment** could reach 70%. This economic misery raised awareness of the need for social change.
- The rise of **dictators** in Italy, the U.S.S.R., Germany and Spain, also worried the nation.
- Through the story of a group of animals rebelling against their farmer, George Orwell's *Animal Farm* echoes events leading up to the Russian Revolution and into the **Stalinist** era, while his 1949 dystopia *Nineteen-Eighty-Four* reflects on the consequences of totalitarianism. Orwell also volunteered to fight with Franco's Republican opponents in the Spanish Civil War and wrote about it in 1938 in *Homage to Catalonia*.

Prime Minister Neville Chamberlain, left, and Adolf Hitler sealing the Munich pact in September 1938.

- But vivid memories of the horrors of WWI made most Britons strongly inclined to **pacifism** in the interwar era. The country decided to not interfere in the Spanish Civil War. **Appeasement** of Germany—giving in to its demands—was Prime Minister Chamberlain's policy, notably when he signed the **Munich agreement** with Hitler, which Churchill called "A Total and Unmitigated Defeat" in a famous speech.

REIGN OF GEORGE VI (1936-52)

Spanish Civil War (1936–1939) — Second World War (1939–1945)

- **1924** Stalin comes to power in the U.S.S.R. — *A Passage to India* (novel) E.M. Forster
- **1925** *Mrs Dalloway* (Modernist novel) Virginia Woolf
- **1928** Women get full rights to vote at age 21, like men.
- **1929** Wall Street Stock Exchange Crash
- **1932** National Hunger March
- **1933** Hitler's Nazi Germany established — Unemployment reaches 25% as a result of the Great Depression. — *Brave New World* (dystopian novel) Aldous Huxley
- **1934** *Death on the Nile* Agatha Christie
- **1936** *The General Theory of Employment, Interest, and Money* John Maynard Keynes
- **1938** Munich Agreement — *The Lady Vanishes* (film) Alfred Hitchcock
- **1939** Operation Pied Piper: Children evacuated from cities to the country
- **1940** Winston Churchill becomes Prime Minister for the duration of the war. — The Blitz (from German "lightning"): German bombing raids over Britain till 1941
- **1942** Beveridge report proposes a social welfare system.
- **1945** United Nations created — *Animal Farm* (dystopian novel) George Orwell

## The Bloomsbury Group

- From 1905 to about 1940, an influential group of intellectuals, writers and artists used to meet, work or study together near Bloomsbury, London.
- John Maynard Keynes spearheaded a revolution in economic thinking during the 1930s. His policy recommendations were adopted by almost all **Capitalist** countries by the time of his death in 1946.
- Virginia Woolf (as well as Irish author James Joyce) was famous for developing a narrative technique called stream-of-consciousness, using interior monologue.
- In 1917, Woolf and her writer husband Leonard created a publishing company, the Hogarth Press. It published some of the most influential writing of the period: poet T.S. Eliot, short-story specialist Katherine Mansfield, novelist E.M. Forster and many works of psychoanalysis, including Sigmund Freud's.

*Life in Squares*, a 2015 BBC series. Its title comes from American critic Dorothy Parker's witticism that the Bloomsbury Group, whose lives it portrays, had, "lived in squares, painted in circles and loved in triangles."

Now test your culture!

EXO Quiz

# From 1946 to 1979

## Post-War British society

- After WWII, Britain was deep in **debt**. The damage was huge. More than 70,000 buildings had been completely demolished in London. **Rationing** of food and petrol continued until 1954.
- Inspired by Keynes's ideas, the post-war Labour government led by Clement Attlee committed itself to building a better world.
- In response to the 1942 Beveridge report, the government introduced the **Welfare State** system, designed to care for British citizens "from the cradle to the grave" with old-age **pensions**, **unemploymen**t benefits and free healthcare with the **National Health Service**. The economy was reformed: many industries were **nationalised**, and the **tax** system became more redistributive. Reform of the **education** system opened new opportunities for working-class children, though it remained divisive.
- When the Conservatives came back to power in 1951, they did not go back on the reforms. This period when Labour and Conservatives supported the same policies is known as **the post-war consensus**. It lasted until the late 1970s.

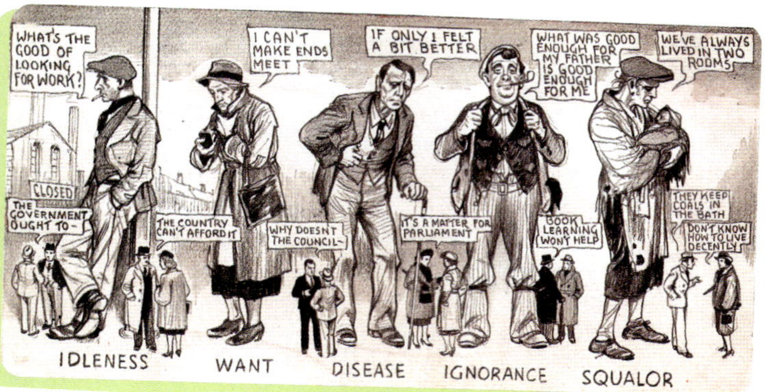


Tackling the "five giants" identified in the 1942 Beveridge report was a primary focus of the 1945 government's social programme and remained important throughout the second half of the 20th century.

**REIGN OF GEORGE VI (1936-52)**

**Labour Government (Attlee)** — **Conservative Governments (Churchill, Eden, Macmillan, Douglas-Home)**

- **1945**
- **1947** – Indian independence
- **1947** – The British coal industry is nationalised (transferred into governement ownership.)
- **1948** – Windrush: beginning of post-war immigration from the Commonwealth
- **1948** – Creation of the National Health Service
- **1949** – *The Third Man* (film) Carol Reed
- **1949** – *Kind Hearts and Coronets* (film) Robert Hamer
- **1951**
- **1952**
- **1953** – Scientists James Watson and Francis Crick discover the structure of DNA.
- **1954** – *Lord of the Flies* (dystopian novel) William Golding
- **1954** – *The Lord of the Rings* (fantasy novel) JRR Tolkien
- **1956** – Suez Crisis: Franco-British invasion of Egypt proves to be a complete disaster.
- **1957** – Independence of Ghana
- **1960** – PM Macmillan's "Wind of Change" speech in South Africa acknowledges the necessity for decolonisation.
- **1960** – Penguin Books obscenity trial
- **1961** – The contraceptive pill is introduced.
- **1962** – *Dr No*, the first James Bond film

## From the Empire to the Commonwealth

- By 1945, there were **independence** movements building in several **colonies** and Britain didn't have the money or the military capacity to maintain its colonies by force.
- In India, Mohandas Gandhi's pacific civil-disobedience campaigns had been very successful. India was therefore the first major colony to become independent, in 1947. It was divided into two separate countries: **India** and **Pakistan**.
- Decolonisation continued in **Africa** and the **Caribbean**. Most of the former colonies decided to keep links with the UK as members of the **Commonwealth**.
- From 1948, there were a series of recruitment campaigns encouraging citizens from the Empire and Commonwealth to work in Britain to help reconstruct the country and staff the NHS. Many people from the Caribbean and South Asia arrived in the UK in this way. The first group travelled from Jamaica on a ship called the *Empire Windrush* in 1948, and so these migrants are referred to as the **Windrush Generation**.

Prize-winning student nurses, 1954. The government encouraged young Caribbeans to migrate to the U.K. as 30% more medical workers were needed with the creation of the NHS.

Media, Culture & Arts
Social & Economic change
International Relations
National politics

## Changing Social Conventions

- The period was a time of ground-breaking social reforms. For some, the changes brought a more "civilised society", when others saw it negatively as more "permissive".
- **Church** attendance fell and the **death penalty** was abolished.
- There was a shift in attitudes to sex and the family. The **contraceptive pill** was launched in 1961, **abortion** legalised and **homosexuality** decriminalised. In 1969, it became easier for women to seek a **divorce**.
- The **Equal Pay Act** aimed at abolishing wage disparities. Female participation expanded in new areas: in 1968 women won the right to be ordained ministers in the Church of Scotland.
- Before the 1960s, **censorship** was applied to films, the theatre and literature regarding sex and violence. When publisher Penguin Books was prosecuted under the Obscene Publications Act for having printed D.H. Lawrence's novel *Lady Chatterley's Lover*, it won the case and the book became a bestseller. The **Theatre Act** later abolished censorship on the stage. On the very same day, American musical *Hair*, depicting drug-taking, anti-war protests and nudity, revolutionised the London scene.

On 27 September 1968, the show *Hair, the Musical* premiered in London.

**REIGN OF ELIZABETH II**

Labour Government (Wilson) · Conservative Government (Heath) · Labour Government (Wilson, Callaghan)

- 1963: De Gaulle vetoes the U.K.'s application to the European Economic Community.
- 1964
- 1965: Abolition of death penalty
- 1967: De Gaulle's 2nd veto
- 1967: Abortion and homosexuality legalised.
- 1967: *Sgt. Pepper's Lonely Hearts Club Band* (album) The Beatles. Considered one of the most influential records of all time.
- 1968: Theatre Act abolishes censorship on the stage.
- 1969: British troops deployed in Northern Ireland.
- 1969: Creation of the Booker Prize for Fiction
- 1970: Equal Pay Act for women
- 1970: Creation of Women's Liberation Movement
- 1972: Bloody Sunday massacre in Northern Ireland
- 1973: Britain joins the EEC.
- 1974
- 1976: Britain is forced to borrow money from the International Monetary Fund.
- 1977: *God Save the Queen* (punk music) Sex Pistols
- 1978: World's first test-tube baby is born in England.
- 1978: Winter of Discontent: strikes and disputes bring the country to a standstill (1978-79).
- 1979: Margaret Thatcher is elected Prime Minister.

## Youth Culture

- The 1960s, known as the **Swinging Sixties**, was a golden decade in the U.K., where young people enjoying more holidays and higher wages led the world in fashion and music.
- **Carnaby Street** in London became the place to buy the most fashionable clothes. Fashion designer Mary Quant invented the mini-skirt, which became an international sensation. Models like Twiggy became icons around the world.
- Influenced by the arrival of American rock 'n' roll in the 1950s, British **pop music** spread around the world in its turn with bands like The Beatles and The Rolling Stones.

The Sex Pistols, formed in London in 1975, lasted only two and a half years but are regarded as one of the most ground-breaking acts in the history of popular music.

- The Hippy movement developed in the late 1960s. Beatle John Lennon and wife Yoko Ono organised Bed-ins for Peace to protest against American involvement in Vietnam.
- As unemployment and economic hardships grew, more aggressive subcultures such as Skinheads and Punk appeared among working-class youths. The Sex Pistol's "God Save the Queen" song was an attack on the treatment of the working class in England in the 1970s by the government. Their loud and aggressive music and their lyrics were very controversial but proved very influential.

Now test your culture!

EXO Quiz

# From 1980 to 2000

## Thatcher and Thatcherism

- Conservative Margaret Thatcher was Britain's first female Prime Minister. She won three consecutive elections: the longest unbroken period for any PM in the 20th century. Very few political leaders are influential enough to have an 'ism' after their name.
- Like American President Reagan, she was part of a **"New Right"** movement. She broke with consensus politics and Keynesian economics by encouraging the **free market** and rolling back state intervention to a minimum.

Margaret Thatcher remains a very divisive figure in Britain, as could be seen on the front pages on newspapers after her death in 2013.

- Thatcher's governments **privatised** 50 industries such as telecommunications, gas, buses and trains, which had been nationalised in the post-war era. She **deregulated the City**: with much less control on financial operations, the London Stock Exchange outpaced all its European competitors, but this also led to unethical behaviour, like corruption. Health services were reformed, and hospitals were to be managed like businesses.
- **Unemployment** doubled in the first two years after Thatcher's election, reaching a high of almost 12% of the working population. The 1984-85 **miners' strike** ended with the closure of many mines and devastation of towns in mining areas. Thatcher had wanted to limit the powers of **trade unions** and had succeeded.
- She believed in Victorian family values and thought that conventional marriage and family were the building blocks of society.

→ File 21 p. 191

REIGN OF ELIZA

Conservative Governments (Margaret Thatcher)

- **1981** — Hunger strike by IRA prisoners ends after ten die.
- **1981** — Race riots in Brixton, London, and other areas.
- **1981** — *Midnight's Children* (post-colonial novel) Salman Rushdie
- **1981** — Wedding of Prince Charles and Lady Diana Spencer reaches a global TV audience of 750 million people.
- **1982** — Unemployment reaches 3 million out of a population of 56 million.
- **1982** — Falklands War: Argentina invades the British islands. Victory leads to Thatcher's re-election.
- **1984** — IRA terrorist attack kills 5 at the Conservative conference in Brighton.
- **1984–1985** — Miners' strike over pit closures
- **1985** — Live Aid benefit concert against famine in Africa.
- **1985** — *My Beautiful Laundrette* (film) Stephen Frears
- **1986** — British Gas privatised, first in a series of national industries.
- **1988** — Pan Am Flight explosion over Lockerbie, Scotland kills 259 in deadliest terrorist attack in history of the U.K.
- **1988** — *Matilda* (novel) Roald Dahl
- **1989** — The Berlin Wall comes down
- **1989** — *Remains of the Day* (class novel) Kazuo Ishiguro
- **1989** — Hillsborough disaster: 96 football fans die in a stampede at a match in Sheffield.
- **1990** — First Gulf War in Kuwait (to 1991)

## "The Troubles"

- Also known as the Northern Ireland conflict, "The Troubles" began in the late 1960s. It opposed **Unionists**, who were mostly **Protestants** and wanted Northern Ireland to remain within the U.K., to Northern Irish **Nationalists**, who were mostly **Catholics** and wanted it to join the **Republic of Ireland**.
- British troops were brought in to restore order. The conflict intensified as the **IRA** (Irish Republican Army) and Protestant paramilitary groups carried out **bombings** and other acts of terrorism.
- In 1972 during a march by Northern Irish Catholics protesting against imprisonment without trial, the British army opened fire, killing 13. The world was outraged. The Irish rock band U2 commemorated the incident in their 1983 protest song **"Sunday Bloody Sunday"**.
- Despite efforts to bring about a resolution to the conflict, terrorist violence continued into the early 90s, and British troops remained in full force.
- The **Good Friday Agreement** in 1998 put an end to the effective civil war in Northern Ireland. It set up a power-sharing government in Northern Ireland but accepts that one day the people of Northern Ireland may choose to join the Republic of Ireland.

→ File 17 p. 154

Two Northern Irish boys stare at British soldiers on the other side of the wire which enforces the divide between Catholic and Protestant homes in Belfast in 1969.

Media, Culture & Arts
Social & Economic change
International Relations
National politics

## Multicultural Britain

At the 1987 election, four ethnic-minority MPs were the first of the modern era. From left to right: Paul Boateng, Bernie Grant, Keith Vaz and Diane Abbott.

- Since 1945, **immigration** to the United Kingdom has been significant, in particular from the Republic of **Ireland**, from the **former British Empire** especially India, Bangladesh, Pakistan, the Caribbean, South Africa, Nigeria, Ghana and Kenya, and more recently from member states of the **European Union**.
- Cultural integration brought literature, art, food, fashion and music from different parts of the world, such as **ska** and **reggae** from the Caribbean. Over 250 languages are spoken in London, making the capital the most linguistically diverse city in the world.
- Contrary to France, where immigrants are expected to take on the cultural behaviour and values of their new home, the U.K.'s approach to multiculturalism tended to expect migrants to continue practising their own **cultural traditions**.
- However, tolerant multicultural Britain has had its opponents. As early as 1958, white mobs attacked black men in **the Notting Hill race riots**. In 1968, Conservative MP Enoch Powell promised "Rivers of Blood" if immigration was left unchecked.
- Since 1962, more and more restrictive quota systems have been introduced and today the U.K. still has the tightest migration policy in Europe.
- In recent years, there has been a noticeable increase in nationalistic sentiment in the U.K. A 2018 poll found that 4 in 10 thought British culture was undermined by multiculturalism.

EGAN 1952)

Conservative Governments (John Major) — Labour Government (Tony Blair)

- **1991** — World Wide Web invented by Tim Berners-Lee.
- **1992** — **The Maastricht Treaty:** the European Community becomes the European Union.
- **1992** — Channel Tunnel opens, linking London and Paris by rail.
- **1994** — First women priests are ordained by the Church of England.
- **1994** — *Four Weddings and a Funeral* (film) Mike Newell
- **1995** — "Wonderwall" (pop song) Oasis
- **1995** — *The Golden Compass* (novel) Philip Pullman
- **1996** — The world's first mammal cloning: Dolly the sheep.
- **1997** — Britain hands Hong Kong back to China, after more than 150 years of British rule.
- **1997** — Referendums decide devolved parliaments for Scotland and Wales.
- **1997** — Diana, Princess of Wales, dies in a car crash in Paris.
- **1997** — *The Full Monty* (film) Peter Cattaneo
- **1998** — The Good Friday Agreement finally brings peace in Northern Ireland and establishes a devolved Northern Irish assembly.
- **1999** — Creation of the London Eye.
- **2000** — *White Teeth* (novel) Zadie Smith

## British Literature's Global Reach

Sarah Ozeke and Christopher Simpson in the TV adaptation of Zadie Smith's novel *White Teeth*.

- The 1980s saw the beginning of a literary trend of authors from diverse ethnic backgrounds reaching large audiences.
- British Indian Salman Rushdie's debut novel *Midnight's Children* won the Booker Prize in 1981 and was deemed to be "the best novel of all winners" in 2008.
- Zadie Smith started out exploring the lives of characters from English-Jamaican heritage like herself. Her first novel *White Teeth* immediately became a bestseller.
- In recent years Britain's imaginative literature has also become one of the country's chief cultural exports.
- Roald Dahl's extraordinary imagination produced many classic children's books. He also wrote chilling short stories for adults. J.K. Rowling revived book sales worldwide with her *Harry Potter* books (1997-2007).
- Like Rowling, Philip Pullman's *His Dark Materials* trilogy (1995-2000) has been enjoyed by millions of children and adults alike.

**Now test your culture!**

EXO Quiz

# From 2001 to 2020

## The U.K. and the European Union

Newspaper headlines on 1 February 2020, the day when Brexit went into effect.

- The U.K. did not sign the **1957 Treaty of Rome**, which joined Germany, France, Italy, the Netherlands, Belgium, and Luxembourg — in the **European Economic Community**.
- The British government soon grew alarmed at the rapid economic advances made by the E.E.C. members and sought to join the union. French President **Charles de Gaulle** vetoed Britain's application in 1963 and 1967. He doubted Britain's motivation and feared its allegiance would first go to the U.S. rather than the E.E.C. **Georges Pompidou**, who succeeded de Gaulle, finally relented and Britain joined in 1973.
- Successive governments felt Britain was unfairly treated and contributed too much to the E.U. budget. **Margaret Thatcher** even negotiated a rebate in 1984.
- Britain consistently resisted supranational policies and negotiated "opt-outs". It refused to adopt the **Euro** (1999) or join the **Schengen** Area (1985) which abolished internal border control.
- **Euroscepticism** continued growing and in June 2016, Conservative Prime Minister **David Cameron** gave in to demands from his own party for a referendum on leaving the European Union. Voters chose **Brexit** by 52% overall. Since then the "Brexit" debate has been tearing British politics apart.

→ File 17 p. 154

REIGN OF ELIZ

Labour Government (Tony Blair) — Labour government (Gordon Brown)

**2001**
- September 11 terrorist attacks
- Afghanistan War: The U.K. joins the U.S. led coalition against the Islamic Taliban regime.

**2002**
- Last coal mine in Scotland closes.
- *Bend it Like Beckham* (film) Gurinder Chadha

**2003**
- Iraq War: The U.K. joins the U.S.-led coalition despite significant opposition.

**2005**
- London Bombings of 7/7: Suicide bombers kill 52 people on London's transport system.

**2006**
- Animal Welfare Act

**2007**
- *Harry Potter and the Deathly Hallows*: J.K. Rowling 7th and final book in the series
- *The Tudors* (historical TV series) 2007-2010

**2008**
- Global financial crisis plunges the U.K. into recession and weakens Labour's image.

**2010**
- British forces withdraw from Iraq.
- *Downton Abbey* (series) 2010-2015 a chronicle of the lives of a British aristocratic family and their servants in the early twentieth century

## A Nation of Animal Lovers

Queen Elizabeth II has owned more than 30 corgi dogs during her reign.

- Since the 19th century, the U.K. has led the way in **animal welfare**. It was the first country to recognise animals as capable of experiencing pain and suffering.
- The Royal Society for the Prevention of Cruelty to Animals, or **RSPCA**, founded in 1824, was the first welfare animal charity in the world. The **WWF** (World Wide Fund for Nature) was also created in Britain.
- The U.K.'s **animal-protection-legislation** is widely regarded as the strictest in the world. In 2006, a welfare offence was introduced: an owner who does not provide appropriate care (food and water, veterinary treatment, etc.) to their pet may be fined and even sent to prison.
- In 1976, cosmetic company The Body Shop was one of the first to build its business using **cruelty-free** ingredients. Others followed, such as Lush (specialised in soaps and shampoos).
- At the beginning of the 19th century, one of the major English Romantic poets, Percy Bysshe Shelley already advocated **vegetarianism**. It is also an Englishman who coined the term "vegan" in 1944. Interest in **veganism** increased in the 2010s.
- Animal-protection activists sometimes engage in **controversial actions**. Critics of the Animal Liberation Front have labelled them as ecoterrorists.

Media, Culture & Arts | Social & Economic change | International Relations | National politics

## From Devolution to Disunited Kingdom

2019: protests in Scotland in favour of independence and staying in the E.U.

- The U.K. is a **parliamentary democracy** under a **constitutional monarchy** in which the monarch is the **head of state** while the Prime Minister is the **head of government.**
- **Legislative power** is held by the two chambers of Parliament: The House of **Commons** and the House of **Lords**, as well as the Scottish and Welsh parliaments and the Northern Ireland Assembly.
- The level of **independence** of each part of the U.K. has changed over time. At one point, each country was completely independent before they each became entirely under the control of London. Now, they are again trying to assert some form of independence.
- In 1997, Scotland and Wales gained a degree of self-government – called **devolution**. Northern Ireland began a process towards devolution after the **Good Friday Agreement** in 1998.
- Unlike the **U.S.A.**, the U.K. is not a federation and remains a unitary state: legislation creating devolved parliaments or assemblies can be repealed or amended by central government.
- In 2014, the Scottish government went further and demanded a **referendum** on independence, which it lost 45% to 55. Unlike English and Welsh voters, Scotland and Northern Ireland voted strongly to remain in the European Union, and the Scottish government has called for a new independence referendum.

→ SnapFile 6 p. 60

EGAN 1952)

oalition Conservative-Liberal Democrat government (David Cameron) — Conservative government (David Cameron) — Conservative government (Theresa May) — Conservative government (Boris Johnson)

- **2011** — edding of Prince illiam and ate Middleton
- **2012** — London Olympic and Paralympic Games
- **2014** — Scottish independence referendum
- **2014** — Support surges for UKIP (the U.K. Independence Party) in local and European elections.
- **2014** — Same-sex marriage becomes legal in England, Wales and Scotland.
- **2016** — Brexit referendum
- **2016** — *I, Daniel Blake* (film) Ken Loach. Denounces social injustice and the unfairness of the welfare system.
- **2017** — *Why I'm No Longer Talking to White People About Race* (political and social essay) Reni Eddo-Lodge
- **2017** — Elections lead to a "hung parliament" No party has an absolute majority which results in political instability and difficulties to agree on Brexit.
- **2017** — Three Islamist terrorist attacks kill 36.
- **2017** — Grenfell Tower Fire 71 people die in badly maintained London council flats.
- **2018** — Windrush Scandal People from former British colonies denied citizenship.
- **2018** — Cambridge Analytica firm is exposed for gathering data from more than 50 million Facebook profiles without people's consent.
- **2019**
- **2020** — Brexit goes into effect.
- **2020** — Global coronavirus pandemic

## Labour and Conservatives

Rival supporters of the two parties campaigning in 2017.

- Two dominant parties occupy the British political scene: The **Conservative Party** and the **Labour Party**. Before Labour rose in British politics in the 1920s, the **Liberal** Party was the other major political party, along with the Conservatives.
- The Conservative Party, also known colloquially as the **Tories**, was founded in 1834 from the Tory Party. It sits on the **centre-right** of the British political spectrum.
- Conservative Prime Ministers, most notably Winston Churchill and Margaret Thatcher, led governments for 57 years of the 20th century. The Conservatives have been in government since 2010.
- The Labour Party is a **centre-left** political party. It was founded in 1900, having grown out of the **trade-union movement** and **socialist** parties of the 19th century.
- In the 1990s, Tony Blair took Labour to the centre as part of his **New Labour** project which governed from 1997 to 2010.

→ SnapFile 6 p. 60

Now test your culture!

EXO Quiz

LANDMARKS

# From 1775 to 1900

*Declaration of Independence*, John Trumbull, 1818. The painting shows the five-man drafting committee presenting their draft of the Declaration to Congress.

## The War of Independence

- People living in the 13 British colonies in America had no representation in British Parliament but were under its rule.
- In the 1760s Britain was deep in debt, so the British Parliament imposed a series of taxes on the colonists, who were frustrated and angry at Britain for imposing **"taxation without representation"**.
- Protests steadily escalated: in 1773 American colonists dumped a whole cargo of highly taxed tea, imported by the British East India Company into the Atlantic (the **Boston Tea Party**). In 1774, the **Continental Congress**, an unofficial parliament, began meeting.
- Armed conflict began in 1775. The Revolutionaries received support from France, Spain and the Netherlands.
- On July 4, 1776, Congress adopted the **Declaration of Independence** written by Thomas Jefferson.
- George Washington led the Revolutionary Army to victory in 1781 and the war officially ended with the **Treaty of Paris** in 1783.

- 1775–1783: War of Independence
- 1776: The Declaration of Independence
- 1776: *Common Sense* (political pamphlet) Thomas Paine
- 1783: Treaty of Paris — Britain accepts loss of colonies
- 1787: American Constitution
- 1789–1797: First President: George Washington
- 1794: Invention of the Cotton Gin — Cotton becomes the main cash crop in the South.
- 1800: Library of Congress founded.
- 1803: France sells Louisiana territories: the U.S.A. doubles in size.
- 1805: The Lewis and Clark Expedition reaches the Pacific Ocean.
- 1808: Atlantic slave trade abolished.
- 1823: Monroe Doctrine — U.S. President sets the doctrine for American isolationism.
- 1826: *The Last of the Mohicans* (novel) James Fenimore Cooper
- 1830: The Indian Removal Act — Native Americans moved to reservations.
- 1836: Samuel Colt patents his revolver — Leads to widespread use of this firearm.

## Contrasting Views

### Transcendentalism

- An extremely influential **philosophical movement** which stated that people and nature are good by essence, and that society has corrupted the purity of the individual. It encouraged ideas such as **nonconformity, free thought** and **self-reliance**.
- Ralph Waldo Emerson (1803-1882) urged Americans to stop looking to Europe for inspiration and be themselves.
- Henry David Thoreau's (1817-1862) philosophy of civil disobedience later greatly influenced figures such as Mahatma Gandhi and Martin Luther King, Jr.

### Non-white perspectives

- Contrasting with the dominant white European-American perspective, Black and Native Americans produced important narratives that document their lives in the U.S.A. in the 19th century.
- A number of **former slaves** published accounts of their enslavement and their escapes to freedom. Particularly influential were Sojourner Truth, Frederick Douglass and Harriet Jacobs.
- There are fewer documents recording the experiences of **Native Americans** displaced by the settlers. Sarah Winnemucca's autobiography (1883) documents the life of her Paiute tribe and its displacement to reservations.

This 1864 portrait of Sojourner Truth was sold to help raise money for her speaking tours.

Media, Culture & Arts
Social & Economic change
International Relations
National politics

## The Civil War and Abolition

- The Civil War of 1861-1865 resolved two fundamental questions: should the U.S.A. be a **confederation** of sovereign states or an indivisible **nation** with a sovereign national government? Should this nation continue to exist as the largest **slaveholding** country in the world?
- In 1860, Republican and abolitionist Abraham Lincoln was elected President. Seven Southern slave-holding states declared themselves an independent country, **"The Confederacy"**. The resulting Civil War caused the death of more than 600,000 people.
- In 1863, Lincoln signed the **Proclamation of Emancipation**, freeing all slaves.
- Confederate states were readmitted to the Union during the **Reconstruction era**, after each ratified the **13th Amendment to the U.S. Constitution**, which outlawed slavery.

→ File 27 p. 245

## Philanthropy

Andrew Carnegie's philanthropy. *Puck* magazine cartoon by Louis Dalrymple, 1903.

- At the end of the 18th century, the new nation had weak national, state and local governments.
- Associations and newly rich American businessmen initiated philanthropic work. In the 1830s, French observer Alexis de Tocqueville described it as a distinguishing feature of being American.
- Andrew Carnegie sold his giant steel company in the 1890s and gave away almost 90% of his fortune. He focused on local **libraries, world peace, education**, and **scientific research**.
- In the 1890s John D. Rockefeller spent the last 40 years of his life creating **foundations** that had a major effect on **medicine**, education, and scientific research.

→ File 23 p. 209

- 1844 — Samuel Morse's telegraph. A new era in communication
- 1845 — *Essays* (transcendentalism) Ralph Waldo Emerson
- 1846–1848 — Mexican War. US acquires California and New Mexico.
- 1848 — The California Gold Rush
- 1850 — *The Narrative of Sojourner Truth* (slave autobiography) Sojourner Truth
- 1851 — Treaty of Fort Laramie
- 1854 — Republican Party set up by opponents of slavery, or abolitionists.
- 1855
- 1861–1865 — Civil War
- 1865 — Abolition of slavery. 13th amendment to the Constitution
- 1865 — Lincoln is assassinated.
- 1865–1877 — Reconstruction era
- 1867 — Alaska purchase from Russia
- 1870 — Standard Oil Company founded by John D. Rockefeller.
- 1870 — JP Morgan Bank founded
- 1872 — Creation of Yellowstone National Park, first National Park
- 1876 — *Adventures of Tom Sawyer* (abolitionist novel) Mark Twain
- 1876 — Alexander Graham Bell patents the telephone.
- 1877
- 1885 — *Life Among the Piutes: their Wrongs and Claims* (Native American autobiography) Sarah Winnemucca Hopkins
- 1890 — End of the Frontier
- 1892 — General Electric founded by Thomas Edison.
- 1895 — *The Red Badge of Courage* (Civil War novel) Stephen Crane
- 1896 — Plessy v. Ferguson. The Supreme Court rules that segregation is legal
- 1898 — Spanish-American War. US takes control of Puerto Rico, Guam, the Philippines, Cuba and Hawaii

## Manifest Destiny and the Frontier

*American Progress*, John Gast, 1872. Columbia, the "Spirit of the Frontier", carries telegraph lines across the western frontier to fulfill Manifest Destiny.

- **Manifest Destiny**, a phrase coined in 1845, is the idea that the U.S.A. is destined by God to expand its dominion and spread democracy and capitalism across the entire North American continent.
- White settlers moving westwards used it to justify territorial expansion and the **forced removal of Native Americans** from their homes.
- The 1890 census showed the West was effectively settled and declared the **frontier officially closed**.
- Images of life in the wilderness of frontier country remained emblematic of the U.S.A.: cowboys, "Indians", rifles, horses and buffaloes.
- Up to the present day, the idea of a **frontier-induced American character** and of Manifest Destiny are the justifications for many Americans suggesting that the U.S.A. should assume a role as a world-leading power.

→ File 15 p. 144

Now test your culture!

EXO Quiz

# From 1900 to 1945

## The Roaring Twenties

### The Jazz Age

- The 1920s were a period of **prosperity** often called the **Roaring Twenties** or the Jazz Age, in reference to the new, free, improvisational **music** that was taking the country by storm.
- The experience of **WWI** and the **Spanish flu epidemic** inspired in young people a feeling that life could end at any moment. Everything seemed to be feasible through modern **technology**.
- Many young women, "the **flappers**", broke with tradition and abandoned their corsets, wore short skirts and bobbed hair, smoked and drove automobiles.

The Cotton Club in Harlem, New York, featured black performers but black clients were almost never allowed inside.

- F. Scott Fitzgerald's characters in novels such as *The Great Gatsby* are typical of this Jazz Age: glamorous and dissipated.

### A prejudiced society

- Black people were excluded from the prosperity experienced by many white Americans. They were **segregated** and even **lynched** by the Ku Klux Klan in the South. As African-American musicians migrated north looking for a better life, Harlem, New York, became a jazz centre, famous for its clubs.
- The **Harlem Renaissance** describes an intensely creative period for African-Americans in all the arts. W.E.B. du Bois, a philosopher, activist and author, was one of its main thinkers.
- Racial prejudice and the "Red Scare" of Communism also led to strict immigration quotas.

→ File 5 p. 50

## Timeline

- **1903** – *The Souls of Black Folks* (essays) W.E.B Du Bois
- **1906** – *The Jungle* (socialist novel) Upton Sinclair
- **1907** – Peak immigration year: 1.2 million migrants enter the U.S.A.
- **1908** – Henry Ford's first Model T car: beginning of assembly-line production. General Motors founded.
- **1909** – The NAACP founded: National Association for the Advancement of Colored People
- **1911** – IBM founded
- **1914–1918** – First World War
- **1917** – U.S.A. declares war on Germany.
- **1918** – The Fourteen Points: President Woodrow Wilson's statement of principles for peace.
- **1919–1920** – Paris Peace Conference: Creation of the League of Nations.
- **1920** – Women gain the right to vote. 19th amendment to the Constitution
- **1921** – 1921 & 1924 Immigration Acts impose quotas to limit immigration mostly of Asians, Southern Europeans, and Eastern European Jews.

## The Golden Age of Hollywood

- Around 1910, Hollywood, Los Angeles, became the film capital of the world. The constant Californian sun was perfect for making movies on an industrial scale.
- The Golden Age of Hollywood was a time between the 1920s and 1960s when the "**Big Five studios**" controlled the film industry: actors and directors had long-term contracts with a specific studio and often made several films a year. Stars had to follow very strict studio rules regarding their diet, clothing, dating or even maternity.
- Hollywood was first famous for **silent films**, like the comedies by Charlie Chaplin or Buster Keaton. By the 1930s films had sound and colour. They adhered closely to a genre: western, comedy, drama, musical, thriller, or animated cartoon.
- Victor Fleming's *Gone with the Wind* (1939) is viewed as an all-time classic. It set a record by receiving 10 Academy Awards. Hattie McDaniel became the first African American to win an Oscar but sat at a segregated place during the ceremony. In the 21st century, criticism of the film's depiction of race and women grew. In 2020, amid the Black Lives Matter protests, HBO Max even removed the film from its streaming platform. → File 5 p. 50

Vivien Leigh and Hattie McDaniel in *Gone with the Wind* (1939)

## Prohibition

Prohibitionists succeeded in having alcohol banned nationwide (1920-1933) for moral and health reasons. But it proved impossible to eliminate **"speakeasies"** (illegal bars) and **"bootleggers"** (manufacturers of illegal liquor), and gang violence became part of the American scene, especially in Chicago where Al Capone made himself a fortune.

## The Great Depression and the New Deal

- The **1929 Wall Street stock-market crash** caused the U.S.A. to plunge into an economic crisis which quickly spread to most of the industrialised world.
- By 1933, 25% of U.S. workers were **unemployed**. Adding to that, a **drought** in the midwest States which became known as the **"Dust Bowl"**, caused millions of people to abandon their farms and to migrate to the west or north.
- Democrat Franklin D. Roosevelt was elected President in 1932. He broke with the classical liberal approach of his Republican predecessors who advocated very little state intervention. Inspired by the ideas of British economist Keynes, he took action to bring about immediate economic relief and greatly expanded the size and role of the federal government through his **New Deal** social programmes.
- The situation improved slowly though the Depression continued until World War Two. War industry and the draft solved the unemployment issue.
- President Roosevelt was reelected 4 times! He died in office in April 1945.

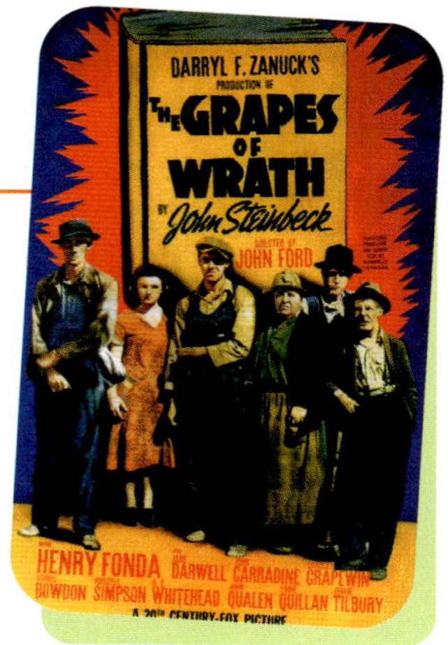


John Steinbeck's 1939 novel *The Grapes of Wrath*, and the 1940 film adaptation, told the tragic story of an Oklahoma family migrating after losing their farm.

**Prohibition period** Alcohol made illegal

**Harlem Renaissance**

**Second World War**

- **1927** – *The Jazz Singer* First sound film. Marks the end of the silent film era.
- **1928** – First Mickey Mouse animation by Walt Disney
- **1929** – Wall Street Crash Leads to world Depression years.
- **1933** – Roosevelt elected President: The New Deal to combat the Depression.
- **1936** – *Migrant Mother* (Depression photograph) Dorothea Lange; *Gone with the Wind* (novel) Margaret Mitchell
- **1937** – *Their Eyes Were Watching God* (Harlem Renaissance novel) Zora Neale Hurston
- **1939** – *The Grapes of Wrath* (Depression novel) John Steinbeck; *The Wizard of Oz* (film) Victor Fleming
- **1941** – Pearl Harbor Japanese attack on U.S. naval bases. The U.S.A. enters the war.; *Citizen Kane* (Considered by many to be the best film ever made.) Orson Welles
- **1942** – *Casablanca* (film) Michael Curtiz
- **1944** – D-Day Allied landings in Normandy
- **1945** – Hiroshima and Nagasaki atomic bombs dropped by the U.S.A.; *Black Boy* (Harlem Renaissance autobiography) Richard Wright

## From Isolationism to World Power

- In 1823, President Monroe had set the principles of the U.S.A.'s **isolationist foreign policy** (Monroe Doctrine). Though the U.S.A. was meant to be a great economic power it was to remain isolated from other countries and not intervene in their affairs.
- In 1917, Democrat President Wilson caused a major shift by convincing Congress to enter **WWI**. His **"Fourteen Points"** (1918) initiated a new diplomacy in which the **League of Nations** was meant to prevent wars through **international cooperation**.
- The U.S. Congress rejected the League of Nations and in 1920 Americans elected Republican and isolationist Warren G. Harding.
- In the 1930s, the rise of fascism in Europe worried President Roosevelt but he had promised to keep the Americans out of any war. He eventually prevailed over the isolationists. The U.S. started supporting the Allies though it was not before **Pearl Harbor** on 7 December 1941 that Congress voted to enter the war.
- By 1945 the U.S.A. had become a **superpower**. It joined the **United Nations**. The beginning of the **Cold War** prevented it from going back to isolationism. It wholly assumed its role as the "leader of the free world".

→ File 25 p. 226

Now test your culture!

EXO Quiz

# From 1946 to 1979

## The Triumph of Television

- After WWII, television quickly emerged as the main source of **entertainment** and **information**. Attendance dropped at movies and sporting events and TV replaced radio. In 1953, about 50% of U.S. households had television sets. It was **94%** in 1965.
- President Kennedy's assassination in 1962 brought television into a new age. People no longer relied on their newspapers; instead, they turned to television for information in a crisis.
- By the beginning of 1967, all three networks had expanded their evening newscasts from 15 to 30 minutes to cover the **Vietnam War**, dubbed "the living room war", as TV brought images of the reality of armed conflict into homes for the first time. President Johnson was very concerned that TV reporting was undermining popular support for his Vietnam policy.
- **Anti-war demonstrations** and the **civil-rights movement** also gained wide exposure on television. Added to TV **advertising** – which encouraged massive expansion of consumerism – TV was a key component in creating **disillusionment** for some younger people and the development of rebellious countercultures.

The first televised debate between presidential candidates, in 1960. John F. Kennedy (photo) debated with Richard Nixon.

Media, Culture & Arts | Social & Economic change | International Relations | National politics

- **1946** – Creation of the Indian Claims Commission by Congress to hear Indian claims against the U.S.A.
- **1947** – Creation of the CIA (Central Intelligence Agency)
- **1947** – Truman Doctrine of containment. Beginning of the Cold War
- **1948** – The Marshall Plan. The U.S.A. provides financial aid to Western Europe in wake of WWII.
- **1949** – Formation of NATO
- **1950** – McCarthyism anti-communist crusade begins.
- **1950–1953** – Korean War. First Cold War proxy war
- **1951** – *A Change of World* (feminist poetry) Adrienne Rich
- **1951** – *The Catcher in the Rye* (coming-of-age novel) J.D. Salinger
- **1953** – *The Crucible* (play) Arthur Miller
- **1954** – *Brown v. Board of Education ruling*
- **1954** – First commercially viable solar panels
- **1954** – *The Doors of Perception* (counterculture novel) Aldous Huxley
- **1955–1956** – Montgomery bus boycott
- **1957** – The Little Rock Nine arrive at Central High School, Little Rock, Arkansas.
- **1957** – *On the Road* (Beat novel) Jack Kerouac
- **1960** – John F. Kennedy elected president. First Catholic president
- **1960** – *To Kill a Mockingbird* (novel) Harper Lee
- *Silent Spring* (environmental science book) Rachel Carson
- **196[2]** – The Cuban missile crisis

## The Cold War

Stanley Kubrick's 1963 film about Cold War tensions.

- The rivalry between the **U.S.A.** and the **U.S.S.R.** and their allies developed quickly after WWII.
- In a dramatic speech to Congress in March 1947, President Harry Truman established his **containment of Communism** doctrine.
- In the 1950s, Republican Senator Joseph McCarthy led a campaign to find and neutralise Communist supporters, in particular in Hollywood and the theatre world. People denounced as Communists were blacklisted and couldn't get work.
- Arthur Miller's *The Crucible* seems to be about the Salem witch trials of 1692. But it drew clear parallels between the historic **witch-hunt** and the contemporary McCarthyist search for Communist infiltrators.
- The U.S. went to war to contain or roll-back Communism in **Korea** and **Vietnam**. The Korean War led to a military stalemate. In Vietnam, 58,000 U.S. soldiers died, and the army withdrew without having reached its objective. Communist forces were victorious.
- In 1962, the U.S. and the U.S.S.R. came close to firing their **nuclear weapons** when the U.S. discovered Soviet missiles in Cuba. A period of "détente" followed.
- The two superpowers continued to compete in other sectors such as Olympic sports, economy or the space race.

→ File 25 p. 220

## The Civil-Rights Movement

- Although **slavery** had been abolished in 1863, **segregation** remained legal as long as citizens had "separate but equal" facilities.
- In 1954, the Supreme Court outlawed segregation in schools (Brown v. Board of Education). But when nine black students tried to begin classes in a formerly segregated school in **Little Rock**, Arkansas, in 1957, they had to be escorted by federal troops.
- **Students** in dozens of cities drew international attention by multiplying peaceful sit-ins and demonstrations.
- In 1955 Rosa Parks refused to give up her seat to a white man in a Montgomery, Alabama, bus and sparked a year-long bus boycott. Dr Martin Luther King, Jr led the Montgomery black community to victory in 1956.
- In 1963, 250,000 people marched to Washington, D.C. to hear King deliver his **"I Have a Dream"** speech. In 1964, the **Civil Rights Act** made racial segregation illegal. In 1965, all African Americans got the right to vote.
- Some Black activists disagreed with King's peaceful methods. **The Black Power** movement inspired by Malcom X, advocated self-defence and the liberation of African Americans "by any means necessary." Malcom X eventually accepted to join Dr King but was murdered in 1965 by members of the organisation he was formerly part of.
- In 1968, Dr King was assassinated by a white racist. Riots broke out in over 100 American cities.

→ File 5 p. 50

African-American students escorted by federal troops, Little Rock Central High School, 1957.

**Cold War** (1947–)

**Vietnam War** (1964–1973)

- 1963: Kennedy assassinated. Civil Rights March on Washington. *The Feminine Mystique* (feminist theory), Betty Friedan
- 1964: Martin Luther King is awarded the Nobel Peace Prize. The Civil Rights Act outlaws discrimination.
- 1965: Immigration Act ends 1920s quotas that limited immigration for non-north-western Europeans.
- 1966: National Organization for Women founded. *In Cold Blood* (novel), Truman Capote
- 1968: Dr King assassinated. American Indian Movement founded. Black Panther salute at the Mexico Olympics.
- 1969: First landing on the moon. Woodstock Festival. *I Know Why the Caged Bird Sings* (memoir), Maya Angelou
- 1971: The Pentagon Papers. Voting age lowered to 18.
- 1972–1974: Watergate Scandal. President Nixon resigns in 1974.
- 1973: *Roe v. Wade* The Supreme Court confirms abortion is legal.
- 1975: Microsoft founded.
- 1976: Apple founded.
- 1977: Trans-Alaska Pipeline System. *Star Wars* (film), George Lucas
- 1979: The U.S.A. officially recognises the People's Republic of China. Islamist Revolution in Iran: 52 American citizens held hostage for 444 days in Tehran. The U.S.S.R. invades Afghanistan. The Cold War resumes

## Challenging countercultures

- The **Beat Generation** was a literary movement in the 1950s that rebelled against capitalism, consumer society and Cold War politics. In their search for interior truth, any means was acceptable: sex, hallucinogens, but also meditation and religious mysticism.
- In the 1960s, counterculture movements gained momentum with the **civil-rights struggle** and the opposition to the U.S.A.'s growing involvement in **Vietnam**. The **Hippies** rejected conventional values, worshipped nature, and embraced radical political causes.
- **Environmentalism** grew in the 1960s and 1970s. Rachel Carson documented the adverse effects of pesticides. She played a key role in raising awareness of the fragility of our planet; while the Cuban crisis fuelled **anti-nuclear** activism.
- Whereas first-wave **feminism** focused mainly on suffrage, in the 1960s a second wave led by activists such as Betty Friedan broadened the debate to include a wider range of issues: patriarchy, sexuality, family, and the workplace.

→ File 19 p. 172

The Woodstock Festival, which took place from August 15th to 17th 1969 in Bethel, New York, was one of the most monumental events for the Hippie movement in the Sixties.

Now test your culture!

EXO Quiz

# From 1980 to 2000

## The Internet Revolution

Microsoft's first ever home page (1994).

- Initially the system that would evolve into the Internet was developed by the **U.S. military** in the 1970s, primarily for government use. By the 1980s it had spread to U.S research and academic organisations. If the Internet initially arose from research in the U.S, it involved international collaboration.
- Americans Vint Cerf and Bob Khan are credited with the invention of the **Internet Protocol** (IP). Cerf launched the first commercial email service in 1982.
- In 1991, the first **web page** was created by British engineer Tim Berners-Lee and, much like the first email explained what email was, its purpose was to explain what the World Wide Web was.
- Internet was not accessible to the general public before the mid-1990s. Furthermore, smartphones and laptops were nascent, and most households did not have computers. Social media in the modern sense had not yet come to existence. Data rates were also very slow.
- In 1993 the Internet communicated only 1% of **information flows**. In 2000 it was 50%, and 97% in 2007.
- Today half the world's population still lives without a reliable Internet connection, whether because of poverty or because of intentional governmental cuts or total blackouts.

→ File 23 p. 208

Republican Ronald Reagan's presidency

Cold War

- **1981**
- **1982** — Highest rate of unemployment recorded since 1940 — *The Color Purple* (African-American novel) Alice Walker
- **1983** — Motorola launches first mobile phone.
- **1984** — *The House on Mango Street* (Latino novel) Sandra Cisneros
- **1986** — Martin Luther King Day is first observed as a federal holiday. — Heidelberg Project created in Detroit: outdoor urban restoration art project.
- **1987** — *Beloved* (African-American novel) Toni Morrison
- **1989** — The Berlin Wall comes down. — *The Mambo Kings Play Songs of Love* (Latino novel) Oscar Hijuelos
- **19[…]** — First Gulf War coalition (to 1991) — First commercial Internet provider

## From the End of the Cold War to a "New World Order"

- The 1980s saw a flare-up, and later the end, of the Cold War. President Reagan took a hard-line stance against the U.S.S.R. that he dubbed "the Evil Empire". By 1991, the U.S.S.R. had ceased to exist.
- With the end of the Cold War, the U.S.A. appeared as the sole leader of a world reunited around the United Nations. President Bush promised a "New World Order" based on the **rule of law** and **multilateral action**. American political scientist Fukuyama even argued that the world was witnessing "the universalisation of Western liberal democracy".
- In the 1990s, the U.S. took the lead in several U.N or NATO coalitions to intervene in conflicts such as Kuwait, Haiti, the Balkans and Somalia.
- But the U.S. was overwhelmed by conflicts and often accused of acting to safeguard American interests. They were also criticised for not ratifying the Kyoto Protocol. The 1998 U.S. embassy bombings in East Africa, showed that the U.S.'s actions could create resentment, even hatred.
- Political scientist Samuel Huntington responded to Fukuyama's thesis by arguing that people's cultural and religious identities would be the primary source of conflict in the post-Cold War world.

→ File 25 p.226

Ridley Scott's 2001 film was inspired by the botched 1993 U.S. intervention in Somalia.

Media, Culture & Arts
Social & Economic change
International Relations
National politics

## Finding a Voice

- As U.S. society became more diverse, book awards, the music industry and the arts started featuring more varied experiences and voices.

### Literature

- In 1969, N. Scott Momaday won the Pulitzer Prize for *The House Made of Dawn*, the story of a young Native American man torn between the reservation and the city.
- African American writer Toni Morrison won the Nobel Prize for Literature in 1993. Maya Angelou used her own extraordinary life as her subject matter in her series of memoirs.
- Latino authors have in common the experience of bilingualism and often a dual culture. Oscar Hijuelos won the 1984 Pulitzer Prize for the story of Cuban musicians adapting to life in New York.

### Music

- Hip-hop was developed by Black and Latino Americans in New York City in the 1970s. It includes music, breakdancing and graffiti art.
- Hip-hop music was not officially recorded for play on radio or TV until 1979. It then spread quickly across the world. Subgenres such as Gangsta rap, that focuses on the violent lifestyles and impoverished conditions of inner-city African American youth, gained popularity in the 1980s.

Breakdancers in front of a graffitied wall in Brooklyn, NYC, 1984.

### Visual Arts

- Graffiti artists tagged trains, walls and subways. Jean-Michel Basquiat started as a street artist in lower Manhattan but quickly became a gallery artist.
- Tyree Guyton started his outdoor art project to transform his hard-core inner Detroit neighbourhood into a place in which residents took pride.

Republican George H.W. Bush's presidency — Democrat Bill Clinton's presidency **(to 2001)**

- **1991** The U.S.S.R. is dissolved. Creation of Green Party U.S.A.: first national environmental party. First Web page created. MP3 created as a standard.
- **1992** *The End of History and the Last Man* (political essay) Francis Fukuyama
- **1993** The World Trade Center, New York, bombed. Operation Black Hawk in Somalia. First Internet web browser accessible to non-geeks
- **1994** Operation "Uphold democracy" in Haiti. Foundation of Amazon
- **1995** North American Free Trade Agreement (NAFTA) between Canada, the U.S.A and Mexico. American-led NATO bombing of Sarajevo, Bosnia. Oklahoma City bomb kills 168.
- **1996** *The Clash of Civilization and the Remaking of World Order* (political essay) Samuel Huntington. First online issue of *The New York Times*
- **1997** Kyoto Protocol to reduce climate change
- **1998** Foundation of Google. Bill Clinton/Monica Lewinsky scandal is first major news story to be broken online.
- Columbine High School shooting in Colorado leaves 15 dead.
- **2000**

## Party Polarisation

- The U.S. electoral system is designed with **checks and balances** between the three main parts: The **Presidency**, the two houses of **Congress** and the **Supreme Court**.
- The House of Representatives is entirely renewed and the Senate partly renewed every two years at the Presidential election, and halfway through the Presidential term. This often leads to Presidents having difficulty enacting their policies, if one, or both houses are held by the opposing party.
- After the **New Deal** in 1932, there was a general consensus in both major political parties that it was the government's role to provide welfare services for citizens, paid for by taxes. Ronald Reagan opposed this, cutting taxes, and services.
- Since the 1980s, the polarisation between the two parties has become wider. Generally, **Republicans** want low taxation, little government intervention, oppose immigration and gun control, and prefer the status quo in terms of diversity. **Democrats** tend to support raising taxes to provide welfare services. They are generally anti-guns and pro-diversity, whether that is ethnic, cultural or sexual.

→ File 19 p. 172

The Democratic Party is represented by a donkey and the Republican Party by an elephant.

Now test your culture!

EXO Quiz

# From 2001 to 2020

## War on Terror

- In 2001, the **9/11 terrorist attacks** by the Islamist terrorist group **Al-Qaeda**, which killed 3,000 people, changed American foreign policy. President George W. Bush declared that the U.S. had the right to protect itself against countries that promote terrorism. This "war on terror" justified **unilateralism** (taking action without regard to the interests of other states or without their support) and **pre-emptive war** (striking first to avoid an imminent attack).
- In 2001, the U.S. invaded **Afghanistan,** from which Al-Qaeda operated, leading a coalition of more than 60 NATO and UN countries. But the 2003 invasion of **Iraq** was much more controversial and countries such as France or Germany refused to join.
- The U.S. was also criticised for the treatment of prisoners in **Guantanamo Bay** detention camp.
- President Obama's election announced a new era. He reached out to Muslim leaders,calling for a "new beginning" in foreign relations. He scheduled a withdrawal from Iraq, but the rise of the so-called Islamic State (ISIS) in the region stopped the process.
- President Trump's focus was on security, by fighting terrorists abroad and strengthening immigration controls. Decisions such as introducing a travel ban for certain Muslim-majority countries were perceived by many as provocations. → File 24 p. 220

The twin towers of the World Trade Center after the 9/11 terrorist attack in 2001.

**Republican George W. Bush's presidency**

- **2001** — **9/11 terrorist attacks** / **Afghanistan War** (until 2014). — **U.S. v. Microsoft** monopoly court case
- **2002** — **Guantanamo Detention Camp opens.** / **The International Criminal Court enters into force.** The U.S.A refuses to participate.
- **2003** — **Iraq War** (until 2011) — **Wikipedia founded.**
- **2004** — **Facebook founded** (at first open to college students only). — *Gilead* (novel) Marilynne Robinson
- **2005** — **Hurricane Katrina** kills 1,800 and leaves more than a quarter of the New Orleans population homeless. — **YouTube launched.**
- **2006** — **Twitter launched.** — **Phrase "MeToo"** used for the first time. — *The Road*, (novel) Cormac McCarthy
- **2007** — **First iPhone released.** — *The Absolutely True Diary of a Part-Time Indian* (novel) Alexie Sherman
- **2008** — **Lehman Brothers bank collapse** signals the start of an international financial crisis.
- **2009** — *The River Runs North* (novel) Graciela Limón
- **2010** — **China overtakes Japan** as the world's second-largest economy. — *Freedom* (novel) Jonathan Franzen

## Raising their Voices

- Minorities' and women's battles for equality and respect have entered a new phase in the 21st century.
- The **Black Lives Matter** movement began in 2013 after the acquittal of a man in the shooting of a black 17-year-old high school student. It became one of the largest in U.S. history and gained further attention during the protests following the 2020 killing of George Floyd by a police officer.
- Whereas public opinion on BLM was negative in 2018, a poll found that 67% of Americans supported it in 2020 and recognised that unfair treatment of black people in the U.S. has contributed a great deal to the protests.

Demonstrators in favour of legislation protecting LGBT workers from discrimination, in front of the Supreme Court in 2019.

- In 2017 film producer Harvey Weinstein was exposed for widespread sexual abuse. The **hashtag #MeToo** began to spread virally after American actress Alyssa Milano posted a Tweet asking to "give people a sense of the magnitude of the problem". The movement soon turned international.
- LGBT Americans, or women seeking an abortion still face some legal and social challenges, particularly in states with large conservative populations, such as in the "Bible Belt" in the Deep South and the Midwest.

→ File 15 p. 142

## The U.S. in a Multipolar World

- With the end of the Cold War, the world went from **bipolar** (U.S.S.R. and U.S.A. dominated) to **unipolar** (U.S.A. only). It is now **multipolar**. **China** rivals the U.S. for the world's largest economy. **Japan** and supranational entities, such as the **European Union**, or **emerging countries** such as India, Brazil, South Korea, South Africa, Russia... also challenge the U.S.'s leadership.
- The ongoing China–U.S. **trade war** has impacted the globalised economies of many countries. President Trump began imposing trade barriers on China with the goal of forcing it to change "unfair trade practices", including alleged theft of intellectual property. In response, China imposed tariffs on many American goods it imports.
- Despite an agreement in 2020, tensions persist.
- **U.S.- Russian** relations, warm in the aftermath of the Cold War, are now strained again. Russian interference (using social media and Internet trolls) in the 2016 U.S. presidential election, with the goal of boosting the candidacy of Donald Trump, has led observers to speak of a "new Cold War".

President Obama at a 2014 G7 meeting with the leaders of France, the U.K., Germany, Japan and the European Union.

- In 2015, 196 states negotiated the Paris Agreement on Climate Change.
- The U.S. withdrew from the accord as Donald Trump argued that it undermined the American economy. Joe Biden rejoined the Agreement in 2021.

→ File 25 p. 226

Democrat Barack Obama's presidency
First African-American President.

Republican Donald Trump's presidency
(2017-2021)

- **2011** – **Bin Laden killed** by U.S. troops in Pakistan. / **Occupy Wall Street** protests opposing economic inequality and the power of big finance / **Homosexual people allowed to serve** openly in the military.
- **2013** – **Black Lives Matter movement starts** to oppose police brutality to African Americans.
- **2014** – **U.S. air strikes against ISIS in Syria** / **"Obamacare"** begins to be implemented. / ***Serial*, most downloaded podcast of all time** launched by the *New York Times*.
- **2015** – ***Obergefell v. Hodges***: same-sex marriage legalised nationwide. / **Paris agreement on climate change**
- **2016** – **Hillary Clinton** first female candidate for the Presidency.
- **2017** – ***The Hate U Give*** (African-American novel) Angie Thomas
- **2018** – **California wildfires** Deadliest wildfire season in California's history / **Beginning of China-U.S. trade war** / President Trump signs an order to keep **Guantanamo prison open indefinitely.**
- **2019** – **Preventing Animal Cruelty and Torture (PACT) Act**
- **2020** – **Democrat Joe Biden elected President.** / **U.S. v. Google** monopoly court case

## Big Tech

- The 1890 and 1914 U.S. **anti-trust laws** were passed to promote competition and make sure big companies didn't create **monopolies** and abuse their power. In 1911, for instance, Rockefeller's Standard Oil was broken up into 34 different companies.
- In 2001, **Microsoft** was sued for illegally maintaining its monopoly position in the PC market, but it won the case.
- In 2020, Congress reported that **Google**, **Amazon**, **Facebook** and **Apple** abused their power and had turned into "the kinds of monopolies we last saw in the era of oil barons and railroad tycoons." The lawmakers accused them of often dictating prices and rules for commerce, advertising, social networking and publishing.

The "big five" tech companies are collectively called GAFAM.

- The subsequent suit filed against Google is the government's most significant challenge to a tech giant's power in a generation and one that could reshape the way consumers use the Internet.

→ File 23 p. 208

**Now test your culture!**

EXO Quiz

## Ireland Before the 20th Century

- The **Celts** arrived in Ireland before 500 B.C., bringing with them their culture and language, which became known as Irish or **Gaelic** culture.
- In the 12th century, **England invaded Ireland** and claimed sovereignty, which set off more than seven centuries of Anglo-Irish struggle marked by **fierce rebellions and harsh repressions**.
- In the 1690s, a system of Protestant English rule was designed to materially disadvantage the Catholic majority. With the **Act of Union in** 1801, Ireland became a part of the United Kingdom.
- By the 1840s, about half of Ireland's population were **tenant farmers:** they had to pay rent to British landlords who had been given the land confiscated from the Irish. Therefore, most were extremely poor.

## Irish Demographics

A family being evicted from their home when they couldn't pay the rent. (Illustration 1881.)

- In the 18th and early 19th centuries, Ireland experienced a major **population boom** as a result of the Agricultural and Industrial Revolutions, notably thanks to the introduction of the **potato crop**, which grew well in Irish conditions. The population reached a peak of 8.5 million in the 1840s.
- From 1845 to 1849, the potato crop was affected by **blight** (a disease). A terrible **famine** ensued.
- About one million people died from **starvation** or famine-related diseases. Up to two million were forced to **emigrate**. The poorest went to Great Britain, especially Liverpool; those who could afford it went farther, including almost five million to the United States.
- Emigration continued for decades. By independence in 1921, the population was four million, only half that of the 1840s. In 1960, it was down to three million.
- At the end of the 20th century, the country entered a period of rapid economic growth as a result of the **Celtic Tiger** Irish economic boom. People from around the world began to move back to their ancestral roots in Ireland for employment and it became an attractive destination for immigrants, such as those from Central Europe.

---

- **1845–1849** Irish Potato Famine
- **1870** The Home Rule League founded. It becomes a party and sends 56 MPs to Westminster in 1874.
- **1879** Irish National Land League founded.
- **1884** Gaelic Athletic Association founded to promote specifically Irish sports.
- **1886** Irish Home Rule Bill fails to pass in Westminster.
- **1890** *"The Lake Isle of Innisfree"* (poetry) WB Yeats; *The History of Ireland* (history) Standish O'Grady
- **1893** The Gaelic League founded to promote the Irish language. Irish Home Rule Bill rejected by the House of Lords.
- **1894** *Arms and the Man* (play) George Bernard Shaw; *Dracula* (novel) Bram Stoker
- **1895** *The Importance of Being Earnest* (play) Oscar Wilde
- **1905** A nationalist party, Sinn Féin ("We Ourselves"), founded.
- **1913** Paramilitary organisations established: Ulster Volunteer Force (UVF) to oppose Home Rule and the Irish Volunteers to support it.
- **1914** Irish Home Rule Bill passed.
- **1914–1918** First World War (1914-1918)
- **1916** Easter Rising
- **1918** Sinn Féin wins a majority of seats in election.
- **1919** Creation of the Irish Republican Army (IRA)
- **1919–1921** War of Independence
- **1921** Creation of the Irish Free State. Ulster (Northern Ireland) remains in the UK.
- **1922** *Ulysses* (novel) James Joyce
- Civil war (1922-1923)

---

## The Celtic Tiger

This area of Dublin was nicknamed Silicon Docks because of the concentration of European headquarters of American high-tech companies.

- Ireland experienced an economic boom in the years 1995-2007 and was dubbed the "Celtic Tiger." It moved from being one of the poorest countries in Europe to one of the richest in only a matter of years.
- This growth came to an abrupt end in 2008 with the meltdown of the Irish banking system and the country fell into **recession** for the first time since the 1980s.
- The government took draconian **austerity measures** and had to accept E.U. and I.M.F. bailouts. The economy picked up in 2014, and Ireland was again the fastest growing economy in the E.U.
- To help attract investors, Ireland has chosen to become a **tax haven** by setting very low corporate tax rates. It also boasts a talented pool of **high-tech workers**. Hence, more than a thousand big, mostly American **global companies** have operations in Ireland, among them: Google, Apple, Facebook, PayPal, Microsoft, Yahoo, eBay, AOL, Twitter and Intel. Foreign multinationals employ one quarter of the Irish private sector workforce and Apple is Ireland's largest employer.
- However, the U.S. and the E.U. are becoming more resolute in curbing what they see as excessive **tax avoidance** by U.S. multinationals in Ireland.

→ File 23 pp. 208

Media, Culture & Arts
Social & Economic change
International Relations
National politics

# Ireland

Ken Loach's 2006 film *The Wind that Shakes the Barley* depicts the War of Independence and the Civil War.

## The Struggle for Independence

- Irish demands for independence had been growing through the 19th century. Two **Home Rule** bills, which would allow self-government of domestic affairs, failed in 1886 and 1893. In 1914, a third bill passed but was not put into effect because of WWI.
- On **Easter Monday, 1916**, a small group of nationalists proclaimed a provisional Irish government and occupied government buildings. The **Rising** only lasted a week, and its leaders were executed.
- In the General elections in 1918, Sinn Féin won a majority of the Irish seats. It declared a **Republic** under Eamon de Valera. This began a **War of Independence** which ended with the 1921 **Anglo-Irish Treaty**. The U.K. agreed to the creation of the **Irish Free State** (a self-ruling Dominion like Canada), but partitioned the island. Six northern counties with Unionist majorities stayed in the U.K. as Northern Ireland.
- A **civil war** broke out between the Irish who supported the treaty and the anti-treaty Irish Republican Army (IRA) who saw it as a betrayal of the Irish Republic.
- In 1937, a new Constitution re-established the state as Ireland, and in 1949 it declared itself a Republic and cut the final ties with Britain by leaving the Commonwealth.

→ File 17 p. 154

**Timeline**

- **1937** – **New Constitution.** The country is renamed Ireland (Éire). — *At Swim-Two-Birds* (novel) Flann O'Brien
- **1939–1945** – **Second World War** Ireland remains neutral.
- **1949** – **Ireland becomes a Republic** and leaves the Commonwealth.
- **1952** – *Waiting for Godot* (play) Samuel Beckett
- **1969** – **"The Troubles" begin in Northern Ireland.**
- **1973** – **Ireland joins the European Economic Community.**
- **1993** – **A period of economic prosperity till 2001:** Ireland dubbed "the Celtic tiger".
- **1995** – **Divorce legalised.**
- **1996** – *Angela's Ashes* (memoir) Frank McCourt
- **1998** – **The Good Friday Agreement** finally brings peace in Northern Ireland. Ireland no longer claims Northern Ireland as part of its territory.
- **2002** – **Ireland joins the Euro Zone.**
- **2007** – **World financial crisis. Ireland falls into recession** for the first time since the 1980s.
- **2009** – *Brooklyn* (novel) Colm Tóibín
- **2011** – **Ireland requests financial support** from the E.U. and the International Monetary Fund (2011-2013).
- **2014** – **Irish economy begins to recover** and experiences a 4.8% economic growth.
- **2015** – Ireland is the first country in the world to establish **same-sex marriage.**
- **2016** – **Brexit referendum in the UK:** the Irish border is a sticking point in negotiations.
- **2021** – **Brexit comes into effect.** As an exception the border with Northern Ireland remains open.

## A Specific Culture with a Global Reach

A production of Samuel Beckett's *Waiting for Godot* at the Abbey Theatre, Dublin, 2017.

- At the end of the 19th and beginning of the 20th century, Irish literature flourished alongside the nationalist movement to define an **Irish identity**, separate from Britain, and based on the Irish language, poetry, music and myth.
- The major figure of the revival was William Butler Yeats, poet and playwright who was the first Irish writer to win the Nobel Prize for Literature. In 1899, he co-founded the Abbey Theatre (the first national theatre in the world) in Dublin to stage plays about Ireland by Irish writers.
- Ireland is the only nation to have a musical instrument as a national emblem, the **harp**, and music is an important part of Irish life.
- Irish culture has had a significant influence on other cultures, especially in the field of literature, with authors such as Oscar Wilde, George Bernard Shaw, James Joyce or Samuel Beckett.
- Irish pop and rock musicians are also known around the world whether it's U2's rock anthems like "Sunday Bloody Sunday" or The Cranberries' relentless "Zombie" both referring to the Troubles in Northern Ireland.

**Now test your culture!**

EXO Quiz

# Canada

## Aboriginal Canadians

- Canada' s first inhabitants were there long before Europeans arrived. Today, Aboriginal people make up **5%** of the population.
- The **First Nations** live south of the Arctic circle. The **Inuit** people live in the Arctic, and have had an autonomous territory, Nunavut, since 1999. The **Métis** are a distinct people of mixed Aboriginal and European ancestry.
- In the early days of European contact, Aboriginal populations were decimated by European **diseases**. They signed many **treaties** with the colonists, which were often disregarded by the Europeans.
- In 1876, the Indian Act aimed to **eradicate First Nations culture** in favour of **assimilation** into Euro-Canadian society. The **Residential School** system, created in the 1880s, separated Aboriginal children from their communities. The mortality rate of students was as high as 25%. When a report revealed the horrors of Residential Schools, the government removed children to live with white families.
- It wasn't until 2007 that Aboriginal people started receiving official recognition and compensation. In 2015, the **Truth and Reconciliation Commission's** report recognised assimilation as a cultural genocide.

→ File 11 p. 101

The Residential Schools for Aboriginal children were generally run by religious orders.

- **1867** — Canada becomes a self-governing British Dominion.
- **1876** — The Indian Act defines how the Government should interact with the First Nations.
- **1885** — The Canadian Pacific Railroad is completed, crossing the country.
- **1887** — Creation of the first National Park
- **1898** — Klondike Gold Rush. 100,000 prospectors migrate to north-western Canada.
- **1908** — *Anne of Green Gables* (novel) Lucy Montgomery
- **1914–1918** — First World War
- **1918** — Women obtain the right to vote in Federal elections.
- **1929** — New York Stock Exchange Crash followed by Depression.
- **1931** — Canada and other British Dominions have complete autonomy.
- **1939–1945** — Second World War
- **1941** — *As for Me and My House* (novel) Sinclair Ross
- **1947** — Oil discovered in Alberta.

## British and French Legacy

- From the 15th to the 17th century, France and Britain successively **explored**, claimed and settled in Canada at the expense of the **First Nations**. In 1763 France sold its settlement of Quebec to Britain. However, the **1774 Quebec Act** recognised the French language and Catholic religion and established the bilingual, bicultural country that continues today.
- In 1867, Canada became a self-ruling **Dominion**, while retaining ties to the British crown. The 1982 Constitution Act achieved full **independence** for Canada by allowing the country to change its constitution without approval from Britain.
- Canada has two main linguistic groups. There are 18 million **Anglophones** and 7 million **Francophones**. Most Francophones live in the province of Quebec, but about a million live in the other provinces.
- Parti Québécois governments held two unsuccessful sovereignty referendums. In 2006, Parliament passed a symbolic motion recognising "the Quebecois as a nation within a united Canada".

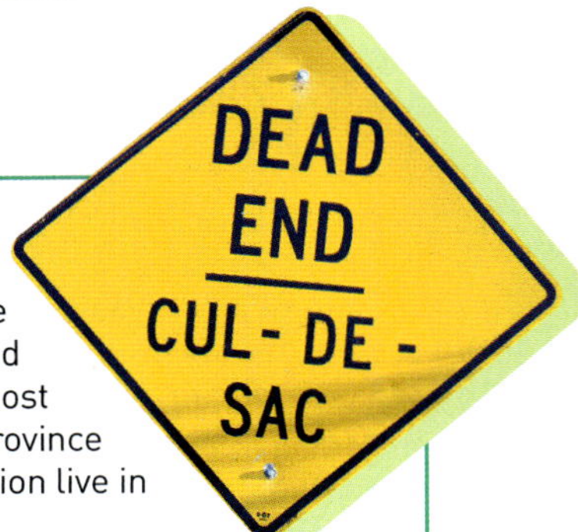


Many signs in Canada are bilingual.

→ File 11 p. 102

## Wilderness

- The history and identity of Canada is inseparable from its immensity and wilderness. It is the world's second **largest country by area** but home to only **38 million** people. The vast majority of the country is sparsely inhabited, more than half of Canadians live in just two provinces: Ontario and Quebec.
- Critic Northrop Frye said that Canadian literature is haunted by the question, "Where is here?" as writers struggle with the immensity of the country, the harsh climate, infertile soil and isolated towns.
- Canada's geography is also a major asset. Canada boasts 39 National Parks spanning plains and prairies to frozen peaks. The country's abundant **natural resources** include gas and oil, minerals but also renewable resources such as timber, fresh water and fish. Canada is home to about 20% of the world's fresh water.
- These resources are essential to the country's economy. Finding a balance between nature conservation and the exploitation of these resources is difficult and has led to protests, political movements and legal cases.

Canada boasts 39 national parks.

- **1960** First Nations people win the right to vote in Federal elections without having to give up their status and treaty rights.
- **1965** The Canadian flag is adopted.
- **1968** Pierre Trudeau (Liberal) becomes Prime Minister until 1984. Parti Québecois is formed to demand independence.
- **1969** *I Am an Indian* (anthology)
- **1970** A campaign by Quebec separatists culminates in two kidnappings, a killing and the suspension of civil liberties.
- **1978** *Who Do You Think You Are?* (short stories) Alice Munro
- **1980** Referendum on separation of Quebec defeated 60% to 40%.
- **1985** *The Handmaid's Tale* (dystopian novel) Margaret Atwood
- **1988** Canadian Multiculturalism Act
- **1992** The North American Free Trade Agreement (NAFTA)
- **1994** National Sports Act recognises hockey and lacrosse as the winter and summer national sports of Canada.
- **1995** Referendum on separation of Quebec defeated by just 1%.
- **1999** The Inuit territory of Nunavut created
- **2001** *Life of Pi* (novel) Yann Martel
- **2003** Canada says "no" to joining the U.S. in war in Iraq.
- **2005** Same-sex marriage is legalised.
- **2008** Truth and Reconciliation Commission created.
- **2012** *Indian Horse* (novel) Richard Wagamese
- **2015** Justin Trudeau becomes Prime Minister.
- **2016** Canada signs a free-trade agreement with the E.U.
- **2018** Canada becomes the second country to legalise recreational use of cannabis.

## An Attractive Country

- Canada, one of the most developed countries in the world, enjoys a high standard of living. Its highly subsidised educational and health facilities rank among the best.
- Canada is the world's seventh-largest oil producer, has a highly skilled labour force and a very diversified economy. The 1994 **North American Free Trade Agreement** (which includes Mexico) dramatically increased trade and economic integration between the U.S. and Canada. Over 75% of Canada's merchandise exports are destined for the U.S. each year. NAFTA was replaced by USMCA in 2018.
- In recent years, Canadian writers have made a big impact on the world scene. Alice Munro was awarded the Nobel Prize for literature in 2013. Margaret Atwood suddenly became an international star with the 2016 TV adaptation of her dystopian novel *The Handmaid's Tale*. Yann Martel's *Life of Pi* has sold more than ten million copies worldwide.
- Canada is one of the world's most ethnically diverse nations. It has instigated **multiculturalism** as an ideology and a policy since the 1970s and 1980s and emphasises the social and economic importance of **immigration**, especially of skilled workers.

The University of Toronto ranks 1st in Canada and 18th globally. 1 in 5 students is international.

Now test your culture!

EXO Quiz

# Australia and New Zealand

## Australian History

Aboriginal protests on 26 May, Sorry Day.

- Archaeologists say **Aboriginal people** have been living in Australia for more than 50,000 years. They are one of the oldest surviving human civilisations.
- In 1770 British explorer James Cook "discovered" part of the east coast of Australia. He declared it was British and named it **New South Wales**. In 1788, the British government started a colony for prisoners there. Other colonies followed. The **penal-colony** system ended in 1868.
- The **Aboriginal** population was decimated by brutal treatment and by European diseases. Estimated at about 750,000 at Cook's arrival, by 1901, there were less than 95,000. Today there are 650,000 Aboriginal and Torres Strait Islander people, **2.8%** of the population.
- Policies of "assimilating" indigenous children became systematic from 1910 till the 1970s. Children were sent to boarding schools or placed with white families as foster children or servants. Many never saw their families again. Indigenous languages were banned. Today the children who were taken away are called the **Stolen Generations**.
- **"Sorry Day"** has been commemorated since 2008. Since 2021, the national **anthem** no longer refers to Australia as "young and free" in an attempt to reflect the country's long indigenous history. → File 28 p.257

- 1840 – Treaty of Waitangi (NZ)
- 1845–1872 – The New Zealand Wars
- 1850 – A series of gold rushes attracts immigrants. Population triples in 10 years. (AU)
- 1860
- 1861 – The first of a series of Gold Rushes. (NZ)
- 1868 – End of the penal colony system. (AU)
- 1869 – The first Māori MPs are elected to Parliament. (NZ)
- 1872
- 1880 – Execution of outlaw and folk hero Ned Kelly. (AU)
- 1893 – NZ is the first country in the world where women can vote.
- 1901 – The six colonies unite as the Commonwealth of Australia. The Immigration Restriction Act puts a brake on non-white immigration. (AU)
- 1902 – The national flag is adopted in NZ.
- 1903 – "Waltzing Matilda", Banjo Paterson's bush ballad, becomes unofficial anthem. (AU)
- 1907 – NZ becomes a self-ruling Dominion within the British Empire.
- 1911 – Canberra is founded and designated the capital. (AU)
- 1914–1918 – First World War
- 1915 – The Gallipoli Campaign
- 1922 – *The Garden Party and Other Stories*, Katherine Mansfield (NZ)
- 1929 – New York Stock Exchange Crash followed by Depression
- 1939–1945 – Second World War
- 194[8] – Australia encourages immigration from Europe. Two million people immigrate in the next 30 years.

## Australasia

- Australia, NZ and some neighbouring islands form the region Australasia. Its **geographic isolation** has influenced its **biodiversity**. Kangaroos, koalas, Tasmanian devils and dingoes, or kiwis in New Zealand, exist nowhere else in the world.
- New Zealand's mountainous and narrow islands stretch 1,600 km. Its outstanding scenery makes it an excellent movie location. Australia's size gives it a wide variety of landscapes, from deserts to tropical rainforests and alpine mountain ranges.
- Australia's **natural reserves** of coal, iron, copper, gold, natural gas, and uranium makes it a significant exporter. Both countries have among the largest marine exclusive economic zones, thanks to their long coastlines and numerous islands.
- But Australia is the **driest inhabited continent** on earth, making it particularly vulnerable to the challenges of **climate change**. The 2019-2020 bushfire season was particularly intense. An estimated 1 billion animals were killed. New Zealand's **geology** makes it prone to volcanism and earthquakes.

→ File 20 p. 184

Peter Jackson's film adaptations of Tolkien's *The Lord of the Rings* starred New Zealand landscapes.

## "Populate or Perish"

Greek Australians parade for Australia Day in Melbourne in 2014. Australia is home to one of the largest Greek communities in the world.

- In the years after World War II, Australia stepped up its **white immigration policy** with the catchphrase 'Populate or perish!' It encouraged immigration from Europe.
- In the 1970s it repealed its 1901 policy which forbade the entrance into Australia of people of non-European ethnic origins.
- Asia became the largest source of immigrants. The Vietnamese "boat people" arrived in the 1970s. They were followed by a second wave from Cambodia and southern China.
- In 1992, Australia adopted a mandatory detention policy with no time limit for anyone entering the country without a valid visa. From 2001 to 2007 vessels were intercepted and migrants sent to detention centres in Pacific islands such as Nauru or Papua New Guinea, while their refugee status was determined. Today the question of how to deal with **undocumented asylum seekers** remains one of the most polarising debates in contemporary Australia.
- Immigrants account for 30% of the population, the highest proportion in any country with a population over 10 million. A majority of Australians agree that multiculturalism and immigration have a positive impact on the country. **Legal migration** is still encouraged, though working visas are most commonly granted to highly skilled workers or students.

## New Zealand History

- The **Māori** arrived from **Polynesia** in canoes about 1,000 years ago.
- In 1769, Captain James Cook declared New Zealand was British.
- In 1840, the British signed a treaty with 500 Māori chiefs. The **Waitangi Treaty** is the basis of New Zealand government. But many years of internal wars followed as the Māori resisted colonial rule.
- The Māori population is estimated to have been about 100,000 at Cook's arrival. It reached a low of about 42,000 in 1896. In 2018, Māori comprised approximately 16.5% of the population (775,836 people).

→ Snapfile 16 p. 148 pp. → File 28 p. 257

- **1949** NZ becomes formally independent.
- **1950** Australia and NZ commit troops to the U.N. forces in the Korean war.
- **1953** Everest conquered by Sir Edmund Hillary (NZ) and Sherpa Tenzing Norgay.
- **1964** *We Are Going*, Oodgeroo Noonuccal (Aboriginal poetry, AU)
- **1965** Australia and NZ commit troops to the U.S. war effort in Vietnam.
- **1967** Referendum on changes to the Constitution (AU). Aboriginal people no longer excluded from census. (AU)
- **1977** A plebiscite chooses "Advance Australia Fair" as the national anthem
- **1982** *To the Is-Land*, Janet Frame (autobiography, NZ)
- **1985** Greenpeace ship *Rainbow Warrior* is blown up by the French secret service in NZ.
- **1993** The Native Title Act establishes Aboriginal land rights. (AU)
- **1993** Jane Campion (NZ) first and only female director to receive a Palme d'Or, for *The Piano*.
- **1997** First woman Prime Minister: Jenny Shipley. (NZ)
- **1999** Referendum on making Australia a republic defeated.
- **1999** Filming of *The Lord of the Rings* starts in NZ.
- **2010** First woman Prime Minister: Julia Gillard. (AU)
- **2011** A severe earthquake devastates Christchurch, NZ.
- **2013** NZ becomes the first country in the Asia-Pacific region to legalise same-sex marriage.
- **2017** Jacinda Ardern becomes Prime Minister. (NZ)
- **2018** Scott Morrison becomes Prime Minister. (AU)

## The ANZACs and Gallipoli

- At the outbreak of WWI, many citizens of the British Empire volunteered to fight. A joint **Australian and New Zealand Army Corps** was formed. They were first sent into action at **Gallipoli** (Ottoman Empire) in 1915.
- The Gallipoli Campaign was ordered by British Navy Minister Winston Churchill. It was disastrous from the outset. The Turkish forces were well prepared and the Allied forces landing in small boats were decimated. They held out for eight months before being quietly evacuated. More than **10,000 ANZAC troops died**.
- The Gallipoli Campaign has become enshrined in both countries as a **founding moment**, an example of courage and resilience, and a type of fraternity and solidarity called **"mateship"**, considered a major feature of the Australian character. April 25, ANZAC Day, is a public holiday similar to 11 November in other countries.

A New Zealand artist, Alan Somerville, sculpted the Australian soldier featured at the west end of the ANZAC bridge in Sydney.

Now test your culture!

EXO Quiz

## The English Language: a Colonial Heritage

- In 1492, Italian navigator **Christopher Columbus**, working for the Spanish crown, thought he had arrived in India. For this reason the Caribbean islands are also called the **West Indies**.
- In the 16th century, **Spanish** colonisation in the Caribbean and Latin America wiped out the **native Arawak and Carib peoples**.
- Between 1625 and 1814, **Britain** either colonised directly or supplanted Spanish, French or Dutch colonists in 18 Caribbean territories.
- In the 1930s, a series of strikes and riots began as the Great Depression wore on. The unrest spurred the development of indigenous political parties and movements that led to **self-government** and **independence** in the postwar period.
- The territories became independent sovereign states between 1962 and 1983, except for five which remain **British Overseas Territories.**

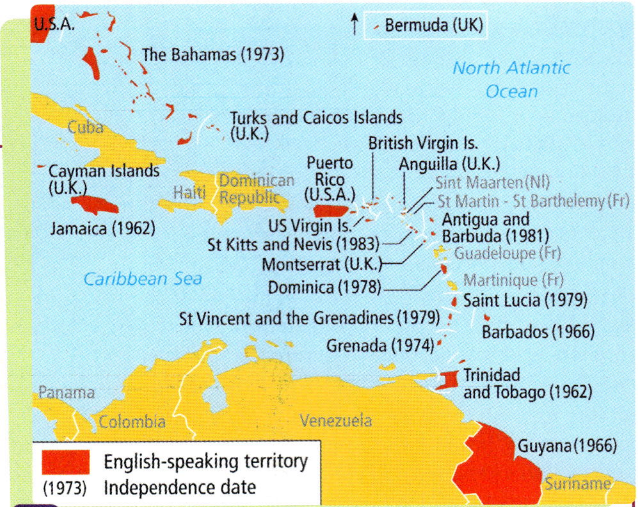


Carte animée

Most English-speaking Caribbean islands are independent (see date) while a few are still British Overseas Territories.

- **English** is now the official language of 6 million people in the Caribbean, though their vernacular language is more often an English-based **creole**.

**1736** – A slave revolt in Antigua, the first of many on British islands (1736-1832).

**1739** – The colonial authorities in Jamaica sign treaties with the Maroons.

**1804** – Haiti becomes the world's first free, black republic after 9 years of slave rebellion against French forces.

**1831** – Slave revolt in Jamaica: more than 20,000 rebels set planters' houses on fire.

**1834** – Slavery abolished in the British Empire.

**1848** – Slavery abolished in the French Empire.

**1912** – *Songs of Jamaica* (poetry) Claude McKay

**1914–1918** – First World War

**1929** – New York Stock Exchange Crash

**1930** – Beginning of the Great Depression in the Caribbean. Development of Rastafari religion in Jamaica in the 1930s.

**1933** – *The Case for West-Indian Self Government* (political pamphlet) C.L.R. James

**1934** – British West Indian labour unrest: a series of strikes and riots till 1939.

**1938** – People's National Party, first to be founded in Jamaica.

**1939–1945** – Second World War

**1944** – Universal adult suffrage introduced in Jamaica, then Trinidad and Tobago.

**1948** – Windrush: beginning of post war immigration to Britain from the Commonwealth

## Music, Literature and Caribbean Identity

- Music played a vital role in shaping national identity leading up and following independence.
- In **Trinidad**, slaves used **Calypso** songs as a way to communicate, and to criticise their slave masters in a mocking style.
- **Reggae** emerged in Jamaica at the end of the 1960s as rebel music: the songs were protests about the injustice of slavery and colonisation. There are many reggae artists but Bob Marley (1945-1981) was the one whose music inspired people around the world.
- Intellectuals such as Jamaican Claude McKay, Dominican Jean Rhys, and Trinidadian C.L.R. James created a distinctly Caribbean and national literature. It celebrates the islands and often reflects the Caribbean's mixed culture and estrangement, addressing questions of Caribbean identity. Saint Lucian Nobel laureate Derek Walcott identified himself as "absolutely a Caribbean writer", a pioneer, helping to make sense of the legacy of deep colonial damage.
- McKay emigrated to the U.S.A. and became a leading light of the **Harlem Renaissance**. Trinidadian Nobel laureate V.S. Naipaul, like Rhys and many other West Indians, migrated to the UK.

In Jamaica, athletics are part of the nation's identity. Two-time Olympic Champion and four-time World Champion in the 100m, Jamaican Shelly-Ann Fraser-Pryce (1986-) is widely regarded as one of the greatest sprinters of all time.

# The English-speaking Caribbean

## Slaves and Maroons

- Initially colonists grew **tobacco** but most plantations switched to **sugar cane** when it became very popular in Europe. **Slave labour** produced this very labour-intensive crop along with cocoa and coffee.
- The use of African slaves became fundamental to growing colonial cash crops and the **Atlantic slave trade** developed in the 17th century. A third of the slaves died within three years.
- As the population of enslaved Africans grew, there were more rebellions. Some slaves called **Maroons** managed to escape, hide in isolated country and survive independently.
- **Jamaica** had the most developed Maroon community. The British couldn't defeat them and in 1739 and 1740 they signed **treaties** with two Maroon groups leaving them their land and autonomy. In return, they would help capture rebel slaves and runaways from the plantations and return them to their owners.

Nanny of the Maroons was a legendary Maroon leader. She is commemorated as a National Hero in Jamaica and is represented on the $500 note.

- There are still four autonomous Maroon communities in Jamaica today. In 2003, UNESCO added one of their settlements to the List of the Intangible Cultural Heritage of Humanity for its traditional ceremonies and music.

- **1951** Universal adult suffrage introduced in Barbados.
- **1953** First Prime Minister elected in Barbados.
- **1956** People's National Movement, first political party founded in Trinidad and Tobago.
- **1958–1962** West Indies Federation attempts to federate around 24 British islands.
- **1961** *A House for Mr Biswas* (novel) VS Naipaul
- **1962** Jamaica and Trinidad and Tobago become independent. The Cuban Missile Crisis almost provokes nuclear war.
- **1966** Barbados becomes independent. *Wide Sargasso Sea* (novel) Jean Rhys
- **1973** 15 states create the Caribbean Community (CARICOM) to promote economic integration and cooperation.
- **1974** Grenada becomes independent.
- **1977** *Exodus* (reggae album) Bob Marley and the Wailers
- **1978** Dominica becomes independent, followed by St Lucia (1979).
- **1979** Nobel Prize for Economics: Sir Arthur Lewis from St Lucia
- **1981** Antigua and Barbuda become independent, followed by Saint Kitts and Nevis (1983).
- **1988** Hurricane Gilbert. 2nd most intense ever recorded in the region kills 45 in Jamaica.
- **1992** Nobel Prize for Literature: Derek Walcott, poet from St Lucia.
- **2001** Nobel Prize for Literature: VS Naipaul, Trinidadian novelist.
- **2005** Hurricane Wilma. Most intense tropical cyclone ever recorded in the region. $USD100 million damage in the Bahamas, $93 million in Jamaica.
- **2009** Jamaican athlete Usain Bolt sets the world record for 100m at 9.58 seconds, still unchallenged.
- **2015** *A Brief History of Seven Killings* (novel) Marlon James.
- **2017** Hurricanes Maria and Irma devastate the region

## Promising but Struggling Economies

- With its stunning scenery and vibrant cultures, the Caribbean is one of the world's top **tourist** destinations. Its economy is heavily tourism-dependent. In Jamaica, it accounts for 20% of GDP (Gross Domestic Product).
- **Jamaica** is the largest island in the English-speaking Caribbean, and the most populated with 3 million people. Like its neighbours, it is vulnerable to natural disasters and the effects of climate change. Hurricanes and flooding, or crises such as the Covid pandemic, stall the economy.
- Some islands such as the **Bahamas** or the **British Virgin islands** are **tax havens:** very low tax and bank secrecy attract companies and individuals who seek tax evasion and money laundering.
- Caribbean families rely a lot on remittances – money sent back home by migrants – to make ends meet.
- **Crime and violence** levels remain high, emphasizing the need to address the issues of corruption, youth unemployment and education.

The British Virgin Islands.

Now test your culture!

EXO Quiz

# English-speaking Africa

Livingstone preaching the gospel. (Magic lantern slide c. 1900). Like other missionaries of the mid-19th century he had a low success rate and is credited with a single conversion.

## The Scramble for Africa

- By 1870, **Europe's imperial powers** had colonised large parts of the world but only 10% of Africa, mostly coastal regions.
- In 1884, they met for a three-month conference in Berlin meant to organise "the scramble for Africa."
- European motives included rivalry and the quest for national prestige, as well as the desire to control **valuable natural resources** and find **new markets** for their growing industries.
- Explorer and missionary David Livingstone was one of the most popular British heroes of the Victorian era. In 1853-56 he became the first European to cross the African continent. His travels filled huge gaps in western knowledge of central and southern Africa.
- Like many imperialists, Livingstone justified Africa's conquest as a mission of **civilisation** and a necessity to introduce Africans to **Christianity**.
- By 1914, 90% of Africa was under European control, mainly by Britain, France, Germany, Belgium, Spain and Portugal. Only Ethiopia and Liberia remained independent.

**Timeline**

- 1850 – Diamonds, and later gold are discovered in South Africa.
- 1853 – David Livingstone explores central Africa (to 1856)
- 1879 – Britain wins the Zulu War against the Zulu nation in South Africa.
- 80 – The first Boer War (1880-81) opposes Dutch and British settlers in South Africa.
- 1884 – Berlin Conference (1884-85) organises and regulates European colonisation and trade in Africa.
- 1899 – Second Boer War (to 1901). Britain takes control of all of South Africa.
- 1912 – Foundation of the South African Native Congress (later the ANC)
- 1914–1918 – First World War
- 1922 – Egypt becomes independent.
- 1930 – *Mhudi* (novel) Thekiso Plaatje (SA)
- 1934 – South Africa becomes independent.
- 1939–1945 – Second World War
- 1948 – Apartheid introduced in South Africa.
- 1948 – *Cry, the Beloved Country* (novel) Alan Paton (SA)
- 1952 – The Mau Mau uprising in Kenya (to 1956) is savagely repressed by the British.
- 1955 – Peter Magubane begins taking photos of the anti-Apartheid struggle.
- 1956 – Sudan becomes independent.
- 1957 – Ghana becomes independent.
- 1958 – *Things Fall Apart* (novel) Chinua Achebe (Nigeria)

## Apartheid in South Africa

- From 1948 through the 1990s, **apartheid** (Afrikaans for "apartness") kept the country's black majority population under the thumb of a small white minority, descending from Dutch and British settlers.
- The system legally classified every South African as white, black, coloured, or Asian, and gave them different rights. Black people were forced to live in "homelands" where the agricultural land was poor, or in "**townships**" – ghettos outside the big cities or industrial sites where black people worked. They couldn't vote and had limited access to education.
- Though they were disempowered, black South Africans protested against their treatment. The **African National Congress** (ANC) promoted demonstrations, mass action, boycotts, strikes and acts of **civil disobedience**.
- Tired of what they saw as ineffective nonviolent protests, some activists embraced **armed resistance**. Among them was Nelson Mandela who was arrested and sentenced to life imprisonment in 1964.
- Elected in 1989, President de Klerk and his government dismantled apartheid and introduced universal suffrage, which led to Nelson Mandela being elected as the first black president in 1994. They were jointly awarded the Nobel Peace Prize in 1993.

Nelson Mandela campaigning for the 1994 election, in which he voted for the first time, and was elected the country's first black president.

→ File 10 pp. 94

## The "Wind of Change"

Boxing champion Muhammad Ali greeted by President Nkrumah in 1964. Newly independent Ghana attracted many African Americans who saw there an opportunity to return to their roots.

- After WWII, European powers were no longer able to afford the resources needed to maintain control of their African colonies. This allowed for **African nationalists** to negotiate decolonisation.
- In 1957 independence leader Kwame Nkrumah led Ghana to independence. He showed the way for many others.
- In 1960, British Prime Minister Harold McMillan made a momentous speech to the South African parliament in which he spoke of the "**wind of change**" blowing through the continent of Africa. He urgently wanted to avoid the same kind of **colonial war** that France was fighting in Algeria. Under his premiership **decolonisation** proceeded rapidly.
- By the end of the 1960s, all but two of the 18 British African colonies had become independent.
- British withdrawal was not always a peaceful process. Kenyan independence was preceded by the eight-year **Mau Mau Uprising**. In Rhodesia (Zimbabwe), the white minority wanted to remain British and it resulted in a civil war that held up independence until 1980.

## Decolonising the Mind

- Africa is culturally very diverse and home to about 2,000 indigenous languages. When English is chosen, it is to facilitate linguistic unity at the national level. Kenyan Ngugi wa Thiong'o called English "a cultural bomb in the African mind" that would slowly destroy what remains of African culture.
- In his 2006 ironic essay, Kenyan Binyavanga Wainaina criticised foreigners for writing picturesque or tragic stories treating, "Africa as if it were one country."
- Some authors use fiction as a way to explore their country's history and identity. Nigerian author Chinua Achebe's *Things Fall Apart* was one of the first novels to show an international audience the effects of colonisation and evangelisation on African populations.
- In *Americanah*, Chimamanda Ngozi Adichie examines how blackness is different for African Americans and Nigerians living in America. Her character Ifemelu didn't realise she was black in her native country — she fit that description only after she landed in America.

→ File 12 p. 112

Harold McMillan's "Wind of Change" speech

Somalia and Nigeria become independent.

Soweto Uprising in South Africa: 600 schoolchildren killed.

Daniel arap Moi becomes president of Kenya until 2002.

The E.E.C. and the U.S.A. impose economic sanctions against South Africa.

First Liberian Civil War (to 1997)

Nelson Mandela is freed and the ANC legal again.

First multi-party elections in Kenya

Sierra Leone Civil War (to 2002)

Egyptian Boutros Boutros-Ghali: first African to lead the United Nations (1992-1997).

Kenyan ecologist Wangari Maathai receives the Nobel Peace Prize.

Liberian Ellen Johnson Sirleaf is Africa's first elected female head of state.

*Americanah* (novel) Chimamanda Ngozi Adichie (Nigeria)

Boko Haram Islamic group abducts 276 schoolgirls in northern Nigeria.

1960 1964 1968 1989 90 91 92 2004 2006 2013 2014

1964 1967 1978 1981 1986 1994 1999 2000 2021

Malawi, Tanzania and Zambia become independent.

Biafra: Three years of civil war in Nigeria and a million dead.

*July's People* (novel) Nadine Gordimer (SA)

*Decolonising the Mind, The Politics of Language in African Literature* Ngugi wa Thiong'o (Kenya)

Wole Soyinka (Nigeria): the first African to win a Nobel Prize in Literature.

Nelson Mandela is elected president.

Second Liberian Civil War (to 2003).

Civilian rule in Nigeria after 3 decades of military control.

The AIDS epidemic is the leading cause of death in Sub-Saharan Africa.

*How to Write About Africa* (essay) Binyavanga Wainaina (Kenya)

Dr Nkozi Okonjo-Iweala (Nigeria) is first African and woman to lead the WTO.

## Fast-growing Economies

- As of 2020, Nigeria, South Africa and Kenya were the 1st, 2nd and 3rd largest economies in sub-Saharan Africa.
- Kenya is the economic, financial, and transport hub of East Africa. **Agriculture** remains the backbone of its economy, a strong **tourism** industry coming second.
- Nigeria is the largest **oil and gas producer** in Africa. The Nigerian film industry is known as **Nollywood** (a blend of Nigeria and Hollywood) and is now the 2nd-largest producer of movies in the world.
- Both countries have a growing entrepreneurial middle class, but their economic development has been impaired by weak governance, corruption, terrorism, inadequate power supply and lack of infrastructure.
- South Africa is an emerging country with a more diversified economy and abundant **natural resources**. Its **stock exchange** is Africa's largest and among the top 20 in the world.
- **Unemployment, poverty** and **inequality** remain a challenge in all sub-Saharan countries. Over 62% of Nigeria's 200 million people still live in extreme poverty. Even in South Africa, unemployment is roughly 27% of the workforce.
- Their growing and youthful populations are assets but also pose many challenges to governments in terms of food, education, employment and housing

→ File 22 p. 202

The exportation of fruit and vegetables to Europe is an important sector of the Kenyan economy, the climate allowing continuous supply.

Now test your culture!

EXO Quiz

# India and Pakistan

## "The Jewel in the Crown"

- The **Indus Valley civilisation** is one of the world's oldest. It dates back at least 5,000 years, and spread over much of what is now Pakistan, Bangladesh and India. The area underwent successive invasions from the Persians, Greeks, Scythians, Arabs (who brought Islam), Afghans, and Turks.
- From the 16th century, Portuguese, French, Dutch and British colonists invaded and set up coastal **trading posts**.
- By 1818, the **British East India Company** effectively ruled most of India. Less than 100,000 British employees, and a number of Indian princes, dominated a country of 120 million multicultural people: a Hindu majority, a large Muslim minority, Sikhs, Buddhists and Christians.
- In 1857, soldiers in Bengal mutinied and caused a rebellion. Britain responded by making India a **colony** and governed officially, making Queen Victoria Empress of India, "the Jewel in the Crown" of the British Empire.

Independence talks in 1947 with, from left to right, Jawaharlal Nehru, Lord Mountbatten and Mohammed Ali Jinnah

- Mohandas Gandhi and Jawaharlal Nehru led years of nonviolent resistance to British rule. They believed in a multi-faith India. Ali Jinnah, leader of the Muslim League demanded a two-state solution. He thought the **Hindu** majority could not be trusted to treat the **Muslims** fairly.
- Their struggle resulted in Indian **independence** in 1947 and the **partition** of India.

**1857** Soldiers mutiny in Bengal. First war of independence to 1859.

**1858** The British government takes control in the place of the East India Company.

**1885** The Indian National Congress is founded to push for independence.

**1906** The All-India Muslim League is founded.

**1913** Bengali poet Rabindranath Tagore wins the Nobel Prize for Literature.

**1914–1918** First World War

**1920** Gandhi launches campaign of civil disobedience (to 1922).

**1925** *My Experiments with Truth* (autobiography) Mohandas Gandhi

**1930** The Muslim League embraces the two-nation theory in favour of an Indian-Muslim nation-state.

**1930** Gandhi's salt march.

**1931** Round Table conference in London on Independence.

**1933** The name "Pakistan" for a separate Muslim homeland is first used.

**1935** Government of India Act. Britain grants a large measure of autonomy to India

**1935** *Untouchable* (novel) Mulk Raj Anand

**1939–1945** Second World War

**1942** Congress leaders imprisoned after rejecting a proposal for more autonomy (to 1944).

**1943** Famine in Bengal claims 3 million lives.

**1946** *The Discovery of India* (philosophy) Jawaharlal Nehru

**1947** Independence and Partition into two countries: India and Pakistan.

**1947** First Indo-Pakistani war over Kashmir.

**1948** Gandhi assassinated. Ali-Jinnah dies.

**1965** Second Indo-Pakistani war

**1966** Nehru's daughter Indira Gandhi becomes Indian Prime Minister.

The migration of the population at Partition in 1947 is the biggest in world history.

## Tense relations

- The 1947 **Indian Independence Act** partitioned British India into the two new independent countries of largely Hindu India and Muslim Pakistan (with West and East sections).
- Communal violence and **partition** triggered mass **migrations**. Millions of people moved to what they hoped would be safer territory, with Muslims heading towards Pakistan, and Hindus and Sikhs in the direction of India. Historians believe a million people died.
- Since 1947, the two countries have fought three major wars over the border Kashmir region, the last in 1971. It was combined with an Indian-supported war of Independence in East-Pakistan, which led to the birth of **Bangladesh**.
- In the context of the **Cold War**, Pakistan allied with the U.S.A., which led India to seek ties with the U.S.S.R. Suspicious of each other, both countries developed a **nuclear-weapons** programme and conducted tests in 1998.
- Though relations are still tense, India and Pakistan have maintained a **cease-fire** in Kashmir since 2003.
- In 2008, Islamic terrorists originating from Pakistan conducted a series of coordinated attacks in Mumbai, India's financial capital.

## Gandhi

Gandhi spinning cotton in 1925. He encouraged Indians to make their own traditional clothes, which explains why the Indian flag has a spinning-wheel symbol.

- Mohandas Gandhi (1869-1948) was a lawyer from Bombay. He trained in London and spent 23 years in **South Africa** opposing racial discrimination against Indians. He refined his philosophy of **non-violent resistance** there.
- From 1916 on, he devoted himself to the idea of an independent India which would embrace all its **religions**.
- He encouraged people to refuse to buy British products, or pay taxes, but always be **pacifist**. In 1931, he led a national **"salt march"** to the sea to protest at taxes on salt. He was **imprisoned** several times.
- In January 1948, Gandhi was **assassinated** by a Hindu extremist who thought Gandhi was too accommodating to Muslims.

## Militant writers and scholars

- **Postcolonialism** is the critical academic study of the cultural and social legacy of colonialism. Indian scholars are among its most influential theorists.
- Postcolonial intellectuals such as Homi K. Bhabha and Gayatri Spivak develop "subaltern studies" which is the study of social groups excluded from dominant power structures: colonised people, racial minorities, lower castes, women, etc.
- Arundhati Roy's 1997 masterpiece *The God of Small Things* addresses the fate of the Untouchable class against the background of Communist uprisings in 1969.
- Mohammed Hanif writes irreverently of the plane crash that killed Pakistan's General Zia, whereas Aravind Adiga condemns corruption in modern India.

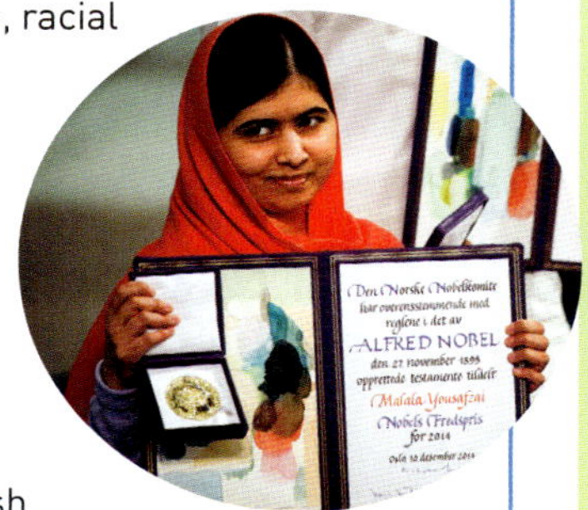

Malala Yousafzai is a Pakistani activist for female education and empowerment. In 2014 she was awarded the Nobel Peace Prize at 17, the youngest laureate.

→ SnapFile 14 p. 130

- **1967** – *The Murder of Aziz Khan* (novel) Zulfikar Ghose (PK)
- **1971** – War between West and East Pakistan results in Bangladesh declaring independence.
- **1973** – Zulfikar Bhutto becomes Prime Minister of Pakistan.
- **1976** – *The Painter of Signs* (novel) RK Narayan (IN)
- **1977** – Military coup in Pakistan by General Mohammad Zia-ul-Haq. Zulfikar Bhutto is executed.
- **1981** – *Midnight's Children* (novel) Salman Rushdie (IN)
- **1984** – Indira Gandhi assassinated. Her son Rajiv becomes PM. An explosion at a U.S. chemical plant in Bhopal, India, kills 20,000.
- **1988** – General Zia is killed in an air crash. Bhutto's daughter Benazir is elected PM.
- **1990** – Benazir Bhutto is dismissed for corruption.
- **1991** – Rajiv Gandhi is assassinated.
- **1993** – *A Suitable Boy* (novel) Vikram Seth (IN)
- **1994** – *The Location of Culture* (postcolonial studies) Homi K. Bhabha (IN)
- **1996** – Hindu nationalist BJP party wins Indian elections.
- **1997** – *The God of Small Things* (novel) Arundhati Roy
- **1990** – Military coup in Pakistan by General Pervez Musharraf.
- **2005** – Deadliest earthquake to hit South Asia kills 87,000 in Pakistan.
- **2007** – Benazir Bhutto assassinated.
- **2008** – *The White Tiger* (novel) Aravind Adiga (IN); *A Case of Exploding Mangoes* (novel) Mohammed Hanif (PK); "Can the Subaltern Speak?" (postcolonial studies) Gayatri Spivak (IN)
- **2011** – Osama bin Laden is killed by U.S. forces in Pakistan.
- **2014** – BJP leader Narendra Modi becomes India's Prime Minister.
- **2018** – Imran Khan becomes Pakistan's Prime Minister.

## South-Asian giants

- **India** is the world's most populous **democracy**: 1.3 billion people. It has capitalised on its large, educated, English-speaking population to become a major exporter of **information-technology** and **business outsourcing** services, though 47% of the workforce is still in **agriculture**.
- **Pakistan** is an Islamic Republic. It has known periods of military rule and has been involved **for decades in conflict** with Taliban terrorist groups whose aim is to overthrow the government. More than 40 political leaders have been assassinated since 1947. This explains low levels of foreign investment. **Textiles and apparel** account for more than half of exports and Pakistan lags behind India in development.
- Though India has five major megacities and Pakistan two, their population remains overwhelmingly **rural**. 2.4 million people live in Orangi Town (Karachi), the world's largest **slum**, while Dharavi slum (Mumbai) is home to 1 million people and is used as the backdrop for movies, like such as Danny Boyle's *Slumdog Millionaire* in 2008.
- Both countries face pressing problems such as a still too fast-growing population, extensive **poverty, gender inequality** and widespread **corruption**. **Pollution** is a major issue: New Delhi's air quality is the worst of any major city in the world.

→ File 26 p. 235

*Bahubali 2*: The Conclusion (2017). Bollywood, the Indian cinema industry, produces more films annually than any other country.

**Now test your culture!**

EXO Quiz

# News media in the English-speaking world

## Newspapers

- Until the 1870s, major papers such as the London *Times*, and the *New York Tribune*, were expensive and directed to an elite. Most papers were political, interested in shaping party positions.
- Thanks to technical advances, the price of newspapers fell, and the rapid expansion of elementary education meant a vast increase in the number of readers. Famous for costing one cent, **penny press** papers were revolutionary in making the news accessible to middle-class citizens for a reasonable price in the U.S.
- By 1900, advertising was well-established and had become the main source of revenue for newspaper owners. Entrepreneurs interested in profit developed a more popular press: **yellow journalism** (U.S.) or **tabloid journalism** (U.K.) focusing on sensational news.
- The advent of broadcast media, and later the Internet caused newspaper circulation to fall. But **newspapers of record**, or **broadsheets**, whose editorial and news-gathering functions are considered authoritative, are still seen as essential to the functioning of democracy.

→ Snapfile 8 p. 78

| Centre Left | Centre | Centre Right |
|---|---|---|
| *The Guardian* | *The Economist* (weekly) | *The Daily Telegraph* |
| *The Washington Post* | *Time* (weekly) | *The Financial Times* |
| *The New York Times* | *USA Today* | *The Times* |
| | | *The Wall Street Journal* |

**GOLDEN AGE OF NEWSPAPERS** — **GOLDEN AGE OF RADIO**

- **1695** Government-granted licenses are no longer needed for publishing, de facto establishing the Freedom of the Press in the U.K.
- **1791** First amendment of the Constitution guarantees the freedom of the press.
- **1890s** Competition between press barons W. Hearst and J. Pulitzer leads to the development of "yellow journalism".
- **1896** *The Daily Mail* first paper designed to make most of its revenue from advertising.
- **1900s** Beginning of "Muckraking" or Investigative journalism
- **1914–1918** First World War: Governments impose censorship on the press for the duration of the war.
- **1917** Pulitzer Prize established as an award for achievements in journalism.
- **1920** First radio news programme broadcast in Detroit. First commercial radio station established in Pittsburgh.
- **1922** Creation of the BBC
- **1923** *Time*, first news magazine
- **1927** The BBC becomes a non-commercial public service.
- **1930** Half the homes in Britain have a radio.
- **1933** President Roosevelt addresses Americans through "fireside chats" on the radio (to 1944).
- **1936** BBC TV is first in the world to offer regular broadcasts.
- **1937** First live outside TV broadcast for George VI's coronation
- **1939** First TV broadcast in the U.S.
- **1939–1945** Second World War
- **1941** The first of the "Big Three" television networks founded: NBC, CBS. (ABC in 1948.) The BBC plays a starring role in WWII as informant, morale-booster and propaganda weapon.
- **1950** First commercial cable television system
- **1952** First TV ads for a U.S. presidential campaign
- **1955** End of the BBC monopoly on TV

## Investigative Journalism and Whistleblowers

- Investigative journalism, in which reporters deeply investigate a single topic of interest, has traditionally been conducted by newspapers.
- In 1971, **the Pentagon Papers** revealed by *The New York Times* contributed to the erosion of public support for the Vietnam War.
- In 1972, Journalists from *The Washington Post* exposed the political **Watergate scandal** which led to President Nixon's resignation in 1974. They were provided information by an anonymous informant – or **whistleblower** – whose pseudonym was "Deep Throat".
- The decline in income through advertising has caused many traditional news services to stop investigative journalism. With the Internet, some whistleblowers have decided to publish news leaks themselves.
- The whistleblowing website **Wikileaks** has exposed government secrets worldwide, notably leaking U.S. military and diplomatic files.
- In 2013, American Edward Snowden released classified material on top-secret U.S intelligence programmes. He is charged with espionage in the U.S. and has sought refuge in Russia.

→ File 13 p. 120

A 2016 news conference launching a campaign for a presidential pardon for Edward Snowden.

U.K. · U.S. · World

## News Agencies

- News agencies (or wire services) provide newspapers and broadcasters with information about a wide variety of news events happening around the world. Most media rely on news agencies to obtain information they could not afford otherwise.
- The two biggest news agencies in the world are **Associated Press (U.S., founded 1848)** and **Reuters (U.K., founded 1852)**.
- AP is a non-profit news agency. The news reports it distributes to its subscribers are produced in English, Spanish and Arabic. AP has earned 54 Pulitzer Prizes, including 32 for photography, since the award was established in 1917.
- **Reuters** employs some 2,500 journalists and 600 photojournalists in about 200 locations worldwide.

## Radio and Television

- The **British Broadcasting Corporation** founded in the 1920s is publicly financed, which allows it to work without advertising.
- The BBC is the largest broadcaster in the world, with a staff of more than **23,000 people, 10 U.K. channels, 59 radio stations** and a strong presence on the Internet. In Britain, more than 30% of all TV viewing is on the BBC. The BBC broadcasts in 27 languages and 188 million listen each week.
- Unlike in the U.K., where the BBC held a monopoly for decades, the American broadcast media were privately operated from the start and public TV and radio has a more limited scope. **"The Big Three" (CBS, NBC and ABC)** have been the most watched networks since the 1930s. Their challengers are **Fox**, and the cable all-news channels **Fox News, MSNBC** and **CNN**.

→ File 7 pp. 63-75

In 1968, CBS anchor Walter Cronkite, "the most trusted man in America" declared the Vietnam War "unwinnable" on TV.

**GOLDEN AGE OF TV**

- 1960 – First televised presidential debate (Kennedy-Nixon)
- 1962 – Walter Cronkite serves as anchor for the *CBS Evening News* (until 1981).
- 1964–1973 – Vietnam War
- 1965 – 94% of U.S. households with a TV set
- 1967 – U.S. TV newscasts expanded to 30 min to cover the Vietnam War.
- 1969 – First step on the Moon broadcast on TV.
- 1973–1986 – End of the BBC monopoly on radio services
- 1980 – First online newspaper *Columbus Dispatch*; CNN: first 24-hour TV news channel
- 1986 – Fox Broadcasting company founded and challenges the "Big Three".
- 1991 – First Web page created.
- 1993 – 1% of information flows communicated via the Internet.
- 1996 – The *New York Times* first online edition
- 1997 – Funeral of Princess Diana most-watched broadcast of all time.

**GOLDEN AGE OF THE INTERNET**

- 2000
- 2005 – YouTube launched.
- 2006 – Wikileaks founded.
- 2006 – Twitter launched.
- 2007 – 97% of information flows communicated via the Internet.
- 2010 – Instagram launched.
- 2013 – Edward Snowden reveals NSA global surveillance programmes.

## Citizen Journalism

- The Internet brought "free" news to audiences that no longer cared for paid subscriptions, which undercut the business model of many newspapers.
- Meanwhile, **citizen journalism** was made more feasible by the development of social media platforms such as blogs, YouTube, and Twitter. Collecting, reporting, analysing, and disseminating news is no longer restricted to professionals.
- Many citizens are the first to report on breaking stories, with eye-witness videos. In countries affected by political upheaval or where media are controlled by the government, they play a pivotal role in documenting events.
- But critics are concerned over whether citizen journalists are as reliable as trained professionals who conduct background research and fact-checking. Furthermore, while professional journalists are supposed to seek objectivity and make no secret of their political affiliation when it exists, a non-professional and sometimes heavily opinionated and subjective approach can be misleading.

Citizens with smartphones are often the first cameras on the scene of accidents and natural disasters. Here, New York, 2018.

**Now test your culture!**

EXO Quiz

Objectif **BAC** ÉCRIT

# Élaborer une synthèse

**La première partie de l'épreuve écrite consiste en une synthèse, c'est-à-dire une mise en lien de documents sous forme d'une expression écrite structurée contenant les idées directrices de ces documents organisées de manière logique.**

## A
## ANALYSER LE SUJET

La **consigne** t'apporte des éléments qui te guideront dans la **rédaction** et l'**organisation** de ta synthèse. Il est important de bien l'analyser et d'en faire ressortir la **problématique** et les éléments clés qui devront apparaître dans ta synthèse. Dans un premier temps, lis la consigne, surligne les **mots-clés** et note les idées qui te viennent en tête.

*conflict, tension, no agreement*

*U.S. E.P.A. (Environmental Protection Agency), getting out of the Paris Agreement, Green New Deal?*

*How dependent on politics is the management of ecological issues in the U.S.A.?*

**Thématique :** Environnements en mutation
**Axe :** De la protection de la nature à la transition écologique
Taking into account their specificities and viewpoints, say what the documents show about the contentious relationship between ecology and politics in the USA. You will pay particular attention to partisan conflicts and opposing actions at the different levels (federal, state, industry, local, etc.).
**Documents:**
- "Why is climate scepticism so successful in the United States?", J. VIALA, *The Conversation*, 2020 (p.173)
- Line graph: "Republicans and Democrats are deeply divided…", 2020 (p.173)
- "Corporate America is terrified of the Green New Deal", E. ATKIN, *The New Republic*, 2019 (p.175)
- "Americans really want the U.S. to adopt renewable energy…", J. ZEBALLOS-ROIG, A. WANG, *Business Insider*, 2019 Doc 1 (p.178)

**TIPS**

Tu n'auras sans doute pas étudié en profondeur le sujet présenté lors de l'examen. C'est pourquoi un travail de veille de l'actualité du monde anglophone contemporain est nécessaire, tout au long de l'année.

## B
## IDENTIFIER LES DOCUMENTS À SYNTHÉTISER

Lors de ta première lecture, repère dans les documents du dossier :
– leur **nature**,
– leur **source** (auteur, date, moyen de publication, etc.),
– leur **lien** avec tes notes et la problématique mise en avant.

**TIPS**

- Ta première lecture devra être **rapide** : lis les titres, les sous-titres, les sources, regarde rapidement le sujet d'un graphique, etc.
- Les documents peuvent être de **natures diverses** : article de presse, éditorial, statistiques d'un organisme public ou privé, discours, etc.
- Les **sources** sont-elles américaines, britanniques, australiennes, etc. ? Ainsi, tu pourras t'interroger sur le point de vue adopté.

## C
## ÉTUDIER LES DOCUMENTS

- Repère les éléments de **contexte** et **analyse** les documents :
– À quel **sujet d'actualité** fait référence le document ?
– Quel est le **point de vue** adopté par l'auteur ? Quel lien peut être fait entre la **source** et le contenu du document ?
– À quels **éléments extérieurs** fait référence l'auteur pour éclairer son propos ?
– Comment est **organisé** le document ?
- Mets en regard les documents pour faire émerger les **arguments** qui vont dans le même sens ou qui exposent des opinions contraires, ou complémentaires.
- Mobilise tes **connaissances (inter)culturelles** pour enrichir ton analyse (connaissances de la thématique et du sujet). Attention toutefois à ne pas substituer tes connaissances personnelles au contenu du dossier.

**TIPS**

Tu peux choisir une couleur par élément de guidage dans la consigne (ou par ligne directrice et **surligner** les extraits qui te permettent d'y répondre dans les documents.

## D
## FAIRE UN PLAN ET REDIGER

- A partir de tes notes, dégage **la structure de ta synthèse** : il ne s'agit pas d'analyser les documents les uns après les autres, mais bien de **traiter les thèmes fédérateurs communs** en **mettant en exergue les convergences et les divergences**.
- Ta synthèse doit être organisée et comporter les trois parties suivantes :
– une introduction dans laquelle tu identifies les documents et annonces leur lien à la problématique et les thèmes communs traités dans les documents ;
– un développement en 2-3 paragraphes traitant chacun d'un thème fédérateur ;
– une conclusion qui doit faire le lien avec la thématique et éventuellement ouvrir sur de nouvelles perspectives.

**TIPS**

L'exercice de la synthèse signifie que tu devras faire des **choix**. Il est en effet important de **ne pas dépasser le nombre de mots attendus**. (500 mots maximum, voire moins si un écrit argumentatif est demandé.) Même si certaines idées dans un document te semblent intéressantes, assure-toi qu'elles soient bien en lien avec les autres documents et la problématique du dossier.

# Comprendre un document iconographique

**L'analyse d'un document iconographique est une compétence attendue pour les épreuves écrites et orales du baccalauréat.**

## A
## IDENTIFIER ET RÉAGIR

- **Relève des informations relatives à l'image :** sa nature, le titre, le nom de l'auteur, sa date de publication ou de création, sa source.
- **Appuie-toi sur ton ressenti pour comprendre le document :** quelle émotion cette image suscite-t-elle ? Quelle atmosphere crée-t-elle ?

*This photograph was taken on June 19, 2020 in New York City at a Black Lives Matter demonstration against police brutality following the recent murder of George Floyd. An atmosphere of gravity mixed with emotions prevails in this scene.*

## B
## OBSERVER ET ANALYSER

- **Concentre-toi sur ce que tu vois** et note des **mots-clés** pour décrire l'image.
- **Explique ce que l'on peut apprendre des personnages** en décrivant leurs gestes, leurs attitudes, leur regard, leur expression.
- **Identifie la structure** qui compose l'image, repère les éléments situés au centre de l'image, au premier plan, à l'arrière-plan et essaie d'en dégager du sens. Repère également les lignes et les couleurs, les éléments **de contraste et/ou de similitude** qui s'en dégagent.

*Protesters are holding signs with a painted portrait of George Floyd with the Pan-African colours of red, black and green while other protesters are holding signs that say, "Celebrate Black Lives Everyday" and "Indigenous People for Black Power". George Floyd's portrait appears in the middle of the picture, with colours strongly contrasting with the dull brown of the other signs. This contributes to highlighting his central figure as the key element that prompted this citizens' demonstration.*

in the top left-hand corner
at the top
on the right-hand side
in the background
in the middle
in the foreground
at the bottom

A Black Lives Matter protest over the death of George Floyd in Manhattan, New York, on 19 June 2020.

## C
## INTERPRÉTER L'IMAGE

- **Place le document dans son contexte** culturel, historique ou artistique et détermine l'intention de l'artiste ou du photographe. Explicite le titre et/ou la référence.
- **Partage ton opinion** sur le message de l'auteur, l'efficacité des techniques utilisées ou encore de la valeur du document aujourd'hui.

*The protesters are attempting to **give a voice** to the need for human rights for African Americans and to stop police brutality against people of colour. They are also **protesting** deep-seated racism in America, all the while respectfully wearing their masks due to the coronavirus pandemic.*

***By placing** the portrait of George Floyd in the centre, the photographer **gives a human face** to the demonstration. It **contrasts** with the protesters' faces, which are obscured by their masks. The **second focus** the photographer has chosen in the only face we can see entirely (despite the mask), the man on the right in the foreground holding the Indigenous people sign. With his closed eyes, **he looks almost as if** he is having a spiritual experience, as if he were at a funeral.*

***Personally**, I find it very effective **in that**…*

### BOOST YOUR VOCABULARY!

- Exprimer son ressenti : ***What strikes me the most** about this picture is (that)… • **It arouses a feeling of** joy ≠ sadness / empathy ≠ disgust • **It makes me** want to laugh ≠ cry, etc.*
- Parler de ses impressions : *The picture **reminds me of**… • We are **under the impression that**…*
- Commenter la prise de vue : *a close-up ≠ a wide-angle view • The subject **is seen from** above/below.*
- Décrire le regard : ***stare at*** (fixer) • ***gaze at*** (contempler) • ***glance at*** (regarder furtivement) • ***glare at*** (lancer un regard furieux).
- Mettre en relief : *The author wants to **highlight/emphasise**… • It **draws the viewer's attention to**… • It **points out**…*
- Évoquer l'atmosphère : *The author **manages to convey/create** a lighthearted ≠ oppressive / peaceful ≠ threatening / warm ≠ cold / idyllic ≠ nightmarish / pleasant ≠ desolate atmosphere.*
- Le but recherché : ***The author intends to** show/demonstrate/prove/denounce/suggest/encourage/motivate…*

# Objectif BAC ÉCRIT Analyser un graphique

## A LES STATISTIQUES, C'EST QUOI ?

Les statistiques sont un **recueil de données chiffrées** complexes et nombreuses qui, une fois analysées, permettent **d'établir des prévisions et comprendre des phénomènes**. Elles sont en général obtenues via des sondages, des enquêtes et des recensements :

- Un sondage d'opinion (*opinion poll*) est le recueil des réponses d'un groupe de personnes à qui l'on a demandé leur opinion sur un sujet précis.
- Une enquête (*survey*) est une étude réalisée sur un échantillon de la population.
- Un recensement (*census*) est un décompte officiel de la population effectué pour le compte du gouvernement.

## B SAVOIR IDENTIFIER LES GRAPHIQUES ET LES STATISTIQUES

- Une visualisation d'un ensemble de données sous forme de tableau (*table*), de diagramme (*chart* ou *diagram*) ou de graphique (*graph*).

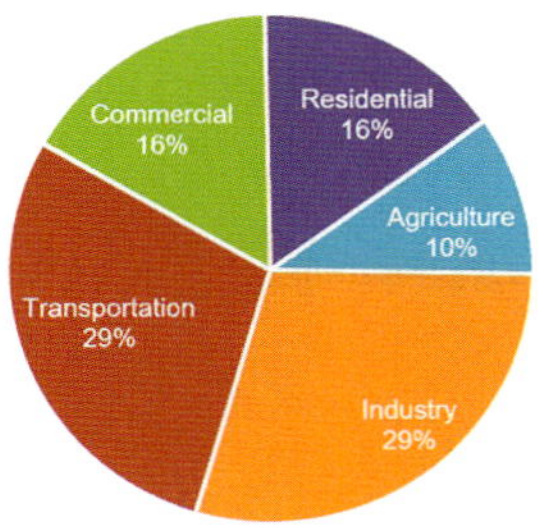


- *A pie chart* (un diagramme circulaire ou « camembert ») *is a circle divided into several segments. The whole "pie" represents 100% and a segment represents a percentage.*

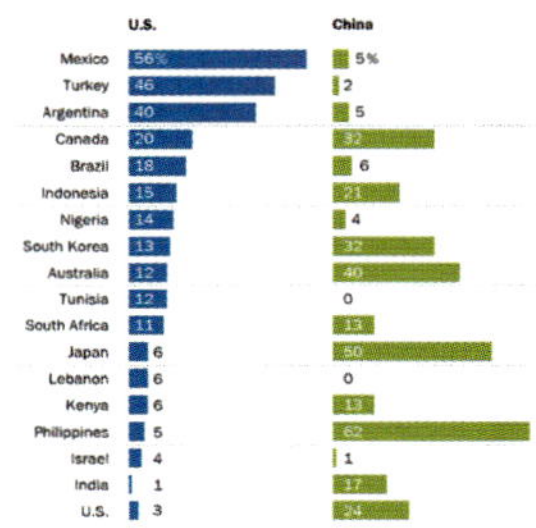


- *A bar chart* (un histogramme) *uses rectangular shapes side by side horizontally or vertically.*

- *A diagram* (un diagramme) *is a drawing, a graphic representation used to explain a process, an action or a result.*

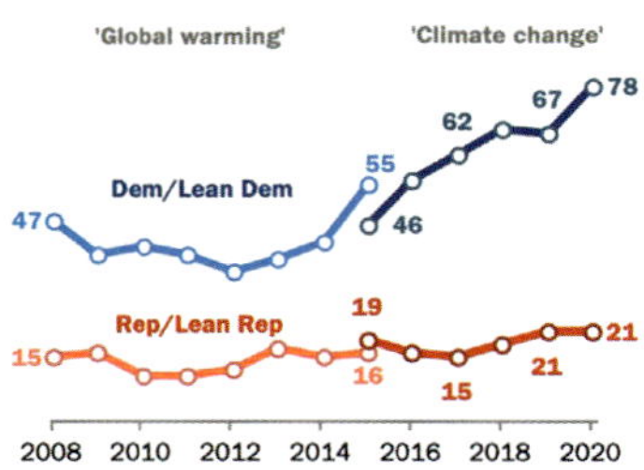


- *A graph* (un graphique) *is usually is a line or a curve which shows the relation between two variable quantities, each measured along one of a pair of axes at right angles.*

**PERCENTAGE OF U.S. UNIVERSITY STUDENTS ENROLLED IN DISTANCE EDUCATION**

| | 2016-2017 | 2017-2018 | 2018-2019 |
|---|---|---|---|
| Enrolled only in distance-education courses | 14.7% | 15.4% | 16.3% |
| Enrolled in some distance-education courses | 16.5% | 17.6% | 18.4% |
| **Total** | 31.2% | 33% | **34.7%** |

- *A table* (un tableau) *presents information in columns.*

## BOOST YOUR VOCABULARY!

- **Pour indiquer un mouvement ascendant :**
*The figures/the graph are/is increasing/rising/going up/climbing/soaring/sky-rocketing by x percent/millions • There's an increase/a rise/a growth in... • to exceed • to take off • to recover • to catch up with • to overtake • to take the lead • to rise to • to peak/a peak year • reach/hit its highest point*
- **Pour indiquer un mouvement descendant :**
*The figures/The curve are/is decreasing/falling/going down/dropping/collapsing • There's a decrease/a drop in... • The curve is falling • fall to a low of • fall behind • be caught up by • bottom out • reach/hit its lowest point*
- **Pour indiquer une stagnation :**
*remain steady/stable • stagnate • stabilise • stand at • stop*
- **Indiquer le degré du changement :**
*The solid/broken line shows the increase/decrease of... from... • Swing from x% above/below average to y% below/above average.*
*+++ dramatically • steeply • hugely • vastly • enormously*
*++ substantially • significantly • considerably • greatly*
*+ moderately • slightly*
- **Indiquer la vitesse du changement :**
*+++ sharply • rapidly • quickly • fast • swiftly • at a fast pace*
*++ gently • gradually • smoothly*
*+ slowly • at a slow pace*
- **Exprimer les quantités :**
*a small fraction • a small number • a significant majority • almost 12% • more than half • approximately a quarter • over a third*

# Lire et comprendre un texte

## A
## CHERCHER DES INDICES ET ANTICIPER

Commence par **repérer le paratexte** pour déterminer la **nature** du texte que tu vas lire (titre, auteur, source, date de publication, illustration ou photographie etc. ) et faire des **hypothèses** sur le contenu.

**Nature du texte ?**

**Texte de fiction**
- **Qui :** les différents personnages, le narrateur
- **Quoi :** les éléments principaux de l'intrigue
- **Quand et où :** le lieu et le moment de l'action, la date de publication, le contexte d'écriture

**Texte de presse**
- **Qui :** l'auteur de l'article (journaliste ? auteur ?, etc.)
- **Quoi :** le sujet abordé, la thèse défendue, le point de vue du journaliste
- **Quand et où :** la source, la date de publication, le contexte d'écriture

## B
## CONSTRUIRE LE SENS DU DOCUMENT

Pour bien comprendre le document, tu peux prendre en compte **trois critères** qui visent une compréhension de **l'implicite (niveaux B2-C1 visés)**.

**Networks cut Trump speech as some Republicans Chastise President over Election Lies**

Donald Trump addressed Americans from the White House on Thursday evening, illegitimately declaring victory in the presidential election for the second time this week. Several US news networks cut their feeds of the 16-minute speech, and numerous Republicans condemned the many falsehoods proclaimed in it.

MSNBC halted its live stream of the speech just a few minutes in, with host Brian Williams saying: "Here we are again in the unusual position of not only interrupting the President of the United States but correcting the President of the United States. "It was not rooted in reality – and at this point, where our country is, it's dangerous." [...]

Will Hurd, the Republican Congressman of Texas, said: "A sitting president undermining our political process and questioning the legality of the voices of countless Americans without evidence is not only dangerous and wrong, it undermines the very foundation this nation was built upon. Every American should have his or her vote counted."

Meanwhile, CNN's Anderson Cooper had perhaps the most bruising words of the night: "That is the most powerful person in the world and we see him like an obese turtle on his back, flailing in the hot sun, realizing his time is over."

Maanvi SINGH and Max BENWELL, *The Guardian*, Fri 6 Nov 2020

**Critère 1 > Comprendre la situation d'énonciation et le contexte**
- Repère les informations sur le contexte: les **lieux**, les **personnes**, les événements et les **enjeux**.
- Identifie **qui parle**, **d'où** et à qui, l'**implicite** de la situation. Dans un article de presse, la source est un élément essentiel à analyser.

*Maanvi Singh and Max Benwell are journalists from "The Guardian", a centre-left media. It is a British point of view on an American issue. The article was published just after Donald Trump illegitimately declared victory in the presidential election. It reports American criticisms against Donald Trump's attitude.*

**Critère 2 > Construire les réseaux de sens**
- Identifie la **logique** du document (relations de cause à effet) ou la **chronologie** des faits. Appuie-toi sur les **connecteurs logiques** et les **temps**.

*American networks cut Donald Trump's speech as he declared victory in the presidential election for the second time that week. His attitude was strongly criticized, even by Republican politicians.*

**Critère 3 > Comprendre la stratégie de communication**
- Identifie l'**intention** et la **visée** du document (relater, informer, critiquer, dénoncer, divertir, amuser etc.). **Explicite-les** en t'appuyant sur les **figures de style** ou les **procédés d'écriture**.

*The journalists inform the readers about the political situation in the USA. They also indirectly criticize Donald Trump's attitude as they quote people who find it dangerous for democracy.*

Objectif **BAC** ÉCRIT

# Comprendre le monde de la presse anglophone

**La presse anglophone possède ses codes qu'il est important de connaître pour bien comprendre les documents que tu vas rencontrer dans ton enseignement de spécialité LLCER AMC.**

## A IDENTIFIER LE TYPE DE JOURNAL

Un rapide coup d'œil te permet **d'identifier le type de journal**. La presse anglophone est divisée en **deux grands types de presse** : **la presse dite 'sérieuse', et la presse tabloïde**. Le traitement du sujet sera forcément très différent. Regarde bien la source de l'article qui t'est également d'une aide précieuse.

### The quality press (broadsheets)

**Definition:** The type of newspaper that covers **serious matters**.

**Format:** broadsheet (the largest newspaper format, although today many "broadsheet" papers publish in compact format)

**Colours:** neutral, pastel

**Type:** mainly neutral

**Tone:** sober writing

**Coverage:** in-depth

**Examples:** *The Sunday Times, The Daily Telegraph, The Guardian*... (UK)
*The New York Times, The Wall-Street Journal, The Washington Post*... (USA)

### The tabloid press (the gutter press/the yellow press)

**Definition:** the type of newspapers that pays more attention to **shocking sensational stories** than to serious matters.

**Format :** tabloid (half the page size of an ordinary newspaper)

**Colours:** flashy, vivid, mastheads printed in red ink

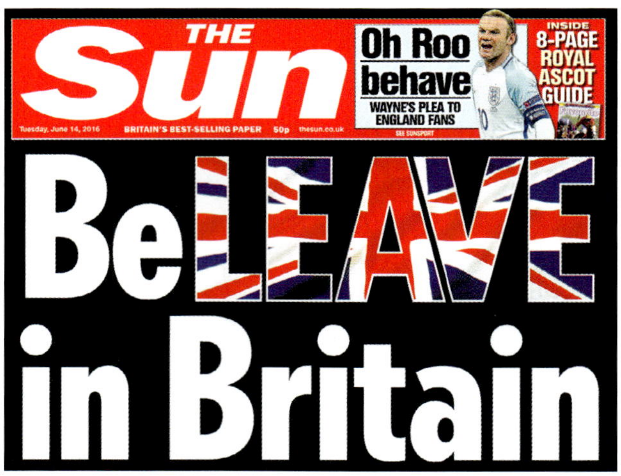


**Tone:** irreverent, presence of puns (play-on-words)

**Type:** bold and neutral

**Coverage:** superficial

**Examples:** *The Sun, the Daily Star, The Daily Mail, The Daily Mirror, The Daily Express*... (UK)
*The Chicago-Sun Times, The New York Post, The New York Daily News*... (USA)

p. 78

LANDMARKS p. 294-295

## B ÉTUDIER LA CONSTRUCTION DE L'ARTICLE (*the layout*)

La mise en page d'un article te donne de nombreux renseignements sur le contenu. C'est déjà un accès au sens. Observe la une du *Sun* et réponds aux consignes en anglais pour mieux te familiariser avec la structure d'un article.

***The headline:*** *it needs to grab the readers' attention and tries to create an emotion.*

**2** *Analyse the size and the colours of the headline. Comment on the pun.*

***The subheading:*** *it sums up the contents of the article.*

**1** *Explain the goal of the article.*

***The contents:*** *it develops the topic. Each paragraph corresponds to an idea.*

***The photograph:*** *it illustrates the article but it is not neutral. It already gives a viewpoint on the topic.*

**3** *Comment on the fact that the photograph is replaced by the Union Jack in the word 'LEAVE'.*

### BOOST YOUR SKILLS!

Comment on the following headlines. What may the articles be about?

- NEW YEAR'S LEAVE
- Flu York City
- OTTER DEVASTATION
- Kate Expectations

## C REPÉRER LE MESSAGE DU/DE LA JOURNALISTE

- **Quand tu es confronté(e) à un article de presse, identifie :**

– **l'article d'information sans commentaire** (*informative article*) : c'est un article qui se veut objectif, dont le but est d'informer les lecteurs ;

– **l'entretien** (*interview*) ;

– **le reportage** (*report*) ou **enquête** (*investigative article*) : il s'agit d'un article de fond avec chiffres ou témoignages directs à l'appui. L'enquête s'attachera à l'explication les faits à partir de plusieurs sources et de témoignages.

– **les articles d'opinion** :
• **l'éditorial** (*editorial*) : texte rédigé par le rédacteur en chef ou un autre rédacteur, qui reflète la ligne du journal) ;
• **la chronique** (*column*) : réflexion menée par un journaliste spécialisé ou une **personne extérieure au journal, qui apparaît régulièrement** ;
• **la tribune libre** (*opinion article / opinion piece / OpEd*) : article d'opinion rédigé et signé par une personne identifiée, membre de la rédaction ou extérieure au journal.

- **Repère les indices de l'objectivité ou de subjectivité du journaliste et du journal :** un(e) journaliste peut **donner son opinion** ou **émettre des jugements de valeur** en accord avec la ligne éditoriale du journal. Certains mots appréciatifs comme des adjectifs ou des adverbes sont des indices.

- **Identifie la place accordée au lecteur :** le/la journaliste peut essayer d'obtenir la complicité du lecteur en l'interpellant plus ou moins directement. L'interpellation directe peut comprendre l'impératif, l'utilisation de pronoms 'you', 'we'. Le ton peut également jouer sur l'émotion du lecteur (empathie, ironie, etc.). De manière plus subtile, le journaliste peut utiliser des références communes ou des valeurs partagées.

Relis l'article du *Sun* p. 78 et réponds aux questions en anglais :
*Identify the nature of the article. Find the adjectives and the adverbs which show the journalist's opinion. Comment on the journalist's tone and goal.*

**AT HOME** Pour connaître la ligne éditoriale d'une média anglophone, il y a une excellente infographie en ligne, mise régulièrement à jour. Tu peux cliquer sur le titre d'une média pour avoir plus d'informations. SITE

### BOOST YOUR VOCABULARY!

- advert (*publicité*) • caption • censorship • circulation (*tirage*) • review (*une critique*) • current events (*actualité*) • front page • lead (U.S.), standfirst (U.K.) (*chapeau*) • headline (*titre*) • investigative press • layout (*maquette*) • leading article (U.S. : *article principal* • U.K. : *éditorial*) • libel = defamation • news in brief (*faits divers*) • print press • scoop • small ads (*petites annonces*)
- accurate • biased • bold (print) (*caractères gras*) • daily • weekly • monthly • quarterly • misleading • reliable • slanderous • trustworthy • unbiased = impartial.
- by hearsay • censor • cover (*faire un reportage sur*) • cover up = hush up • dig out • disclose = reveal • gag • inform • make the news = hit the headlines • make sb aware of/conscious of • pry into • run • sensitise

Objectif **BAC** ÉCRIT

# Traduire de l'anglais vers le français

**Pour bien traduire un texte, il faut respecter certaines étapes et apprendre à manipuler les différents procédés de traduction.**

## A ANALYSER ET COMPRENDRE LE TEXTE

Avant de te lancer dans la traduction de l'extrait, **relis plusieurs fois** le texte entier et **analyse** les éléments suivants.

**Texte**

1. Le titre, la source, le nom de l'auteur, la date de publication
2. Le sens global du texte : *Who? Where? When? What? Why?*
3. L'organisation du texte (structure chronologique, logique, etc.)
4. Le ou les temps utilisés, les aspects (aspect *-ing*…)
5. Le point de vue : celui d'un journaliste ? d'un narrateur qui écrit à la première personne ? d'un narrateur extérieur et omniscient ?
6. Le ton (factuel, humoristique, ironique, revendicatif, etc.) et le registre de langue (familier, soutenu)
7. Les images et l'imagerie dominante : y a-t-il un champ sémantique particulier, une métaphore filée à travers le texte ? Va-t-on pouvoir garder ces images en français ?
8. Les éventuels effets stylistiques

**TIPS**

- Surligne les connecteurs pour t'aider à repérer la structure du texte.
- Repère les temps verbaux avec des crayons de couleurs différentes pour faire ressortir la structure temporelle.
- S'il y a des mots ou expressions que tu ne connais pas dans le texte, essaie d'en déduire le sens à partir de la racine ou de la formation du mot ou du contexte. En dernier recours, sers-toi d'un dictionnaire unilingue.

## B TRADUIRE

L'objectif de la traduction est de fournir une « photocopie » du texte en français : on garde exactement le même sens et on restitue le plus possible les images et les effets de sens que l'auteur a créés.

- **Fais un premier brouillon** de ta traduction en essayant d'éviter les écueils suivants :

– Le « mot à mot », qui aboutit souvent à une phrase incompréhensible. La traduction implique parfois de changer l'ordre des mots ou d'avoir recours à des expressions de même sens mais formulées différemment.

– Le non-respect du texte, c'est-à-dire une traduction qui « réécrit » le texte de départ.

Utilise les procédés présentés à la page suivante pour t'entraîner.

- **Relis ensuite attentivement ton brouillon** en prenant garde à :

– L'orthographe et la ponctuation ;

– La qualité du français : cohérence des temps, accords, respect des règles de grammaire, etc.

**TIP**

Attention aux faux-amis dont la forme est proche ou semblable à celle de mots français mais dont le sens est différent. Quand tu as un doute, appuie-toi sur le contexte.

**BOOST YOUR TRANSLATION!**

**La ponctuation :**

- Les signes de ponctuation sont les mêmes en anglais et en français, sauf :
  – les guillemets : "..." ou '...' (anglais) ≠ « ... » (français) ;
  – le tiret à valeur d'incise : — (anglais) ≠ – (français).
- Dans les dialogues en anglais, la virgule ou le point se placent avant la fermeture des guillemets pour marquer une incise. Chaque passage à la ligne marque l'intervention d'un nouvel interlocuteur.

# Les procédés de traduction

**Pour bien traduire, il faut combiner les différents procédés ci-dessous en fonction du texte. Tu peux commencer par essayer la traduction littérale, puis, si ça ne fonctionne pas, la modulation, et enfin, la transposition.**

**TEXTE À TRADUIRE**

## LA TRADUCTION LITTÉRALE

Traduction **mot à mot**, possible lorsque l'image de départ reste la même en français.
*That's the cherry on the cake!*
➜ C'est la cerise sur le gâteau !

L'emprunt est une forme de traduction littérale dans laquelle le mot étranger est utilisé tel quel afin de garder la couleur locale.

- Les noms et prénoms ; les titres anglais : *Mr • Mrs • Miss • Lady • Sir...*
- Certains noms de lieux et termes géographiques : ***Trafalgar Square*** ➜ Trafalgar Square • ***New York*** ➜ New York • They went to the **pub**. ➜ Ils se rendirent au **pub**.
- Les unités de mesure : *The tavern was five **miles** away.* ➜ La taverne était à cinq **miles** de là.

## LA MODULATION

Changement de point de vue, soit à cause d'une différence culturelle ou bien en passant de la voix active à la forme passive. La modulation est souvent nécessaire pour des raisons syntaxiques.
*the <u>Lost Property</u> **Desk***
➜ le **bureau** des <u>objets trouvés</u>
• *You **will be missed**.*
➜ *Vous* **allez nous manquer**.

**L'équivalence** consiste en la recherche d'une expression équivalente au message entier (procédé notamment utilisé pour les expressions idiomatiques).
*Do not count your chickens before they are hatched.* ➜ Il ne faut pas vendre la peau de l'ours avant de l'avoir tué. • *Hold your peace!* ➜ Restez calmes ! • *What's up?* ➜ *Ça va ?* • *What a kick!* ➜ Quel pied !
On peut aussi avoir recours à des équivalences culturelles (lorsqu'un emprunt ne serait pas compris par un lecteur français) :
*I'm in **year 13**.* ➜ Je suis en **Terminale**.

Il est parfois nécessaire de rajouter des mots (sans changer le sens) pour que la phrase soit correcte ou garde le même sens en anglais : cela s'appelle l'**étoffement**.
***Off the motorway**, they took the second on the left.* ➜ **En sortant de l'autoroute**, ils prirent la deuxième à droite.
*Don't hesitate to **call on me!*** ➜ *N'hésite pas à* **me demander de l'aide**.

## LA TRANSPOSITION GRAMMATICALE

Changement de catégorie grammaticale lorsqu'on passe dans une autre langue :
*He **shivered**.* ➜ Il **eut des frissons**.

Le **chassé-croisé** est utilisé notamment pour traduire les verbes à préposition : on traduit la préposition par un verbe et le verbe par une locution adverbiale.
*He **ran** <u>down</u> the hill.*
➜ Il <u>descendit</u> la montagne **en courant**.
*She **rowed** <u>across</u> **the river**.*
➜ Elle <u>traversa</u> la rivière **en barque**.

Le **contraire négativé** consiste à reproduire le sens d'une expression ou d'une phrase en utilisant son contraire (quand il est impossible de garder la syntaxe de départ).
*Quite **clever**!* ➜ Pas **idiot** !
***With small** hope* ➜ ***Sans grand*** espoir

**Objectif BAC** ÉCRIT

# Transposer un texte de l'anglais vers le français

**Pour réussir la transposition, il te faut dégager les idées essentielles d'un texte pour les retranscrire en français.**

## A ANALYSER ET COMPRENDRE LE TEXTE

1. Commence par analyser le **paratexte** pour déterminer la **nature** du texte et le **contexte d'écriture** (titre, auteur, source, date de publication).
2. Procède à une première lecture globale pour identifier **les mots-clés** et dégager le **thème** du texte.
3. • Lors de relectures suivantes, surligne d'une couleur **les idées-clés du texte**. Pour cela, il faut faire la distinction entre les **arguments** que tu vas conserver et les exemples et les détails que tu vas écarter.
   • Surligne d'une autre couleur les **connecteurs logiques** pour faire émerger la **structure** du texte. Aide-toi de la structuration en **paragraphes**. En général il y a une idée par paragraphe.
4. Pose-toi les questions suivantes pour t'assurer de bien comprendre les enjeux du texte : **qui** parle ? dans quel **contexte** ? à qui ? quel est le **sujet principal** ? quel **ton** ? quelle **stratégie communicative** ?

## B RÉDIGER LE COMPTE RENDU EN FRANÇAIS

La transposition n'est pas la traduction mot-à-mot du texte. Il s'agit d'une **synthèse**.

1. Restitue **l'idée essentielle de chaque paragraphe**. Rédige directement en français sans passer par l'anglais.
2. Respecte **l'ordre d'argumentation du texte**. Il faut que tu montres que tu en as compris son cheminement logique.
3. Respecte les proportions du texte de départ. Il faut que la transposition respecte **l'équilibre argumentatif**.

**Renaming the Cook Islands would be a vital step towards true independence**

Fifty-four years after independence, the Cook Islands is considering a name change. Named after Captain Cook, the Pacific islands, located between New Zealand and Hawaii, comprise 15 Polynesian islands, each with their own pre-colonial names and histories and complicated dynamics in the present. [...] If you thought decolonisation in the Pacific was a mid-20th-century moment that ended with political independence, you would be wrong. Decolonisation is a continuing undoing of the legacies of colonialism. It involves re-examining names and categories, but it is not always about going back to the past to claim some authentic identity. Hence, Danny Mataroa, chair of the Cook Islands name change committee, has suggested a name that encompasses[1] Christian faith (which arrived after colonialism) and Māori heritage (which predates colonialism).

But what does decolonisation have to do with place names? Place names are the meeting points of history and geography that shape part of our identities. Under colonialism, Eurocentric naming practices were commonplace. For example, New Zealand – the country to which the Cook Islands chose to be in association with after independence in 1965 – was named after a province in the Netherlands. [...] It makes perfect sense then that the Polynesian citizens of the Cook Islands would see the current name as a rupture of their own indigenous geographies, a colonially inherited map that erases the long and remarkable history of Polynesian ocean navigation in favour of the name of a single British explorer.

Some might argue that to rename a place is to destroy history at the stroke of a pen. This is the argument of some who oppose the renaming of streets named after wealthy slave-owners in Glasgow. [...]

Renaming can also restore history and give back a sense of place and culture. [...] A new place name for the Cook Islands (such Avaiki Nui, a local term and a frequently suggested new name) offers the possibility to reclaim ancestral legacies and envision[2] new futures – futures that do not belong to the limited choices laid out by colonialism that foreclose[3] true independence, but a more hopeful map for the next generation that opens up the spirit of liberation.

Nalini MOHABIR,
*The Guardian*,
March 2019



## C RELIRE SA PRODUCTION

1. Relis une première fois en te concentrant sur le contenu pour éviter les contre-sens.
2. Relis une deuxième en te concentrant sur la forme (orthographe, conjugaison, accords, ponctuation).

## D EXEMPLE TRAITÉ

1. Fais la transposition du texte *"Renaming the Cook Islands"* p. 259 en appliquant la méthode donnée.
2. Compare ta production avec le texte ci-dessous :

*Cinquante-quatre ans après leur indépendance, les îles Cook, nommées ainsi en hommage au Capitaine Cook, envisagent de changer de nom. La décolonisation est un processus qui est loin d'être terminé et un nom rassembleur qui fait à la fois référence au christianisme et à l'héritage maori est proposé. Les noms de lieux sont sensibles du fait qu'ils réfèrent à l'histoire et à la géographie, toutes deux constitutives de l'identité d'un pays. Pendant la colonisation, les noms géographiques étaient eurocentrés. Les habitants des îles Cook perçoivent le nom actuel de leur pays comme une négation de leur propre histoire maritime. Certains sont opposés au changement de nom car ils trouvent que cela équivaut à une destruction de l'histoire d'un coup de crayon. D'autres au contraire pensent que renommer un lieu permet de restaurer son histoire, de revendiquer la culture passée et de se tourner vers un avenir plus libre et indépendant.*

# Construire ton dossier personnel

**Dès la Première, tu dois commencer à penser à la constitution de ton dossier personnel, que tu devras présenter et mettre en valeur à l'oral en fin de Première ou en Terminale.**

## A DÉFINIR LES CONTOURS DU DOSSIER

• Le dossier *(the set of documents)* que tu vas présenter doit être **construit en lien avec une ou plusieurs des thématiques des programmes de Première et de Terminale**. Il ne s'agit pas simplement de présenter les documents les uns après les autres : il faut les **relier par une problématique** *(a key question)*.

• Pour définir cette **problématique**, appuie-toi sur ce que tu as étudié en cours comme une séquence que tu as particulièrement appréciée.

Thématique "Savoirs, création, innovation" ➜ *How has Wikipedia become a trusted source of information?*

Thématique "Faire société" ➜ *How central is the notion of freedom to American society?*

Thématiques "Relation au monde" et "Faire société" ➜ *To what extent is the U.S.A.'s particular vision of freedom influencing the world?*

**TIPS**

- Une bonne problématique :
  - correspond à **un questionnement sur l'ensemble du dossier** qui te semble important ;
  - est **une question ouverte** qui peut mettre en jeu des **arguments contradictoires** ;
  - doit être **ancrée dans une réalité culturelle du monde anglophone**.
- Ta problématique évoluera peut-être en fonction de tes choix de documents et de tes découvertes sur la question.

## B BIEN SÉLECTIONNER TES DOCUMENTS

• En **Première**, ton dossier doit comprendre **3 à 5 documents** que tu as soit étudiés en classe, soit découverts par toi-même (à l'occasion par exemple d'une exposition, une sortie au théâtre, un article que tu as lu ou un reportage que tu as vu). Dans ces 3 à 5 documents, il faut que tu intègres :
– **au moins un article de presse** ;
– **un texte d'une autre nature** ;
– **un document iconographique**.

• En **Terminale**, ton dossier doit comprendre **4 à 6 documents** que tu as soit étudiés en classe, soit découverts par toi-même (à l'occasion par exemple d'une exposition, une sortie au théâtre, un article que tu as lu ou un reportage que tu as vu). Dans ces 4 à 6 documents, il faut que tu intègres :
– **au moins un article de presse** ;
– **au plus deux textes d'une autre nature** ;
– **au plus deux documents iconographiques**.

• Fais attention à ce que tes documents ne se répètent pas : ils doivent **dialoguer**, c'est-à-dire **se compléter, proposer des points de vue différents voire s'opposer**.

• Pour chaque document choisi, prends des notes pour **expliquer comment il répond à la problématique**. Elles te serviront pour mettre en forme ton dossier et également pour préparer ta présentation orale.

• Pour articuler les documents dans ton dossier, tu peux choisir **une approche chronologique, diachronique (qui suit l'évolution d'un fait à travers le temps) ou thématique**.

**TIPS**

- **Fais-toi un classeur ou un carnet à part** pour les documents que tu choisis et pour tes notes avec tes impressions, les éléments qu'il te semble important de donner, les exemples percutants. N'attends pas et complète au fur et à mesure de tes découvertes.
- Commence à sélectionner des documents **le plus tôt possible** : mieux vaut en avoir trop que pas assez pour pouvoir ensuite choisir les plus pertinents.
- En découvrant d'autres documents ou d'autres approches, tu pourras **amender ou compléter tes notes**.

## C METTRE EN FORME SON DOSSIER

• Sur la première page (page de titre), indique clairement **la ou les thématiques du programme** que tu as choisies et **la problématique** de ton dossier.

• Sur les pages suivantes, présente tes documents en utilisant une typographie bien lisible pour les textes. N'oublie pas d'indiquer les sources précises (auteur, titre, date de publication, etc.).

Objectif **BAC** ORAL

# Présenter ton dossier à l'oral

**Le jour de l'épreuve, tu auras 10 minutes pour présenter ton dossier et justifier tes choix à la lumière de ta problématique. Ensuite, tu disposeras de 10 minutes maximum pour interagir avec le jury.**

## Étape 1 - PRÉPARER DES FICHES SYNTHÉTIQUES

**FICHE 1**

- Introduction de ta présentation.
- Plan succinct de ton intervention, en indiquant à quel moment tu évoques chacun de tes documents, des mots-clés et des exemples pour soutenir ton argumentation.
- Conclusion dans laquelle tu pourras davantage t'engager personnellement.

**FICHE 2**

- Liste le vocabulaire que tu seras amené(e) à mobiliser dans ta présentation.
Note des noms, des adjectifs mais aussi des verbes.

**TIPS**

- Le jour de l'épreuve, tu n'auras **pas de temps de préparation** et tu n'auras **pas de notes** sur lesquelles t'appuyer : il faut donc **bien te préparer et t'entraîner en amont**.
- Un même document peut intervenir à différentes étapes de ton développement. Il ne s'agit pas de présenter les documents les uns après les autres mais bien de montrer **comment ils dialoguent**.

**TIP**

**10 minutes de présentation = 1600 mots environ.**
Entraîne-toi avec une montre pour vérifier que tu es dans le timing !

## Étape 2 - S'ENTRAÎNER SEUL(E)

- Appuie-toi sur tes fiches pour t'entraîner à présenter à l'oral : **tu peux t'enregistrer afin de pouvoir te réécouter** et modifier ce qui ne convient pas.
- Pendant ta présentation, fais attention à bien **naviguer entre tes documents** et à **parler avec naturel** : n'apprends pas par cœur pour ne pas donner l'impression de réciter mais bien d'expliquer, de justifier.
- **Auto-évalue ensuite ta prestation** à l'aide de la fiche téléchargeable, puis entraîne-toi à nouveau en modifiant les critères sur lesquels tu n'as pas encore atteint le niveau (B2 en 1re et C1 en Terminale). Fiche d'auto-évaluation
- **Vérifie aussi que ta présentation n'est ni trop longue, ni trop courte** et que tes sous-parties sont équilibrées en termes de longueur.

**TIPS**

- Lors de l'interaction, **écoute bien la question** et prends le temps de réfléchir à ta réponse pour ne pas te limiter à un oui ou à un non.
- Pour anticiper les questions du jury, prépare une fiche qui présente d'autres documents et articles pour pouvoir donner des exemples supplémentaires pertinents. Les pages *Landmarks* te permettront d'approfondir le contexte culturel de tes supports.

LANDMARKS p. 262-265

## Étape 3 - S'ENTRAÎNER AVEC QUELQU'UN

- Quand tu es suffisamment en maîtrise du contenu, **entraîne-toi à nouveau avec un camarade**, cette fois-ci **sans tes fiches** et en t'appuyant uniquement sur le dossier.
- Au terme de ta présentation, ton camarade te posera des questions, soit pour te faire préciser quelque chose qui n'était pas clair ou erroné, soit pour approfondir ou élargir d'autres points.

## Étape 4 - LE JOUR DE L'ÉPREUVE

- Traite ton sujet de manière **fluide** et **convaincante** en étayant ta présentation par des éléments culturels pertinents.
- Développe ton propos en n'oubliant pas d'**illustrer tes arguments** à l'aide des documents de ton dossier.
- Utilise un **répertoire lexical vaste et nuancé** pour montrer ta maîtrise de la langue.
- Exprime-toi de manière **intelligible**, en prenant garde à la prononciation.
- Au terme de ta présentation, reste concentré(e) pour aborder la seconde partie de l'épreuve : l'échange avec le jury est aussi **important** que la présentation. Il s'agira pour toi de montrer ta capacité à écouter et répondre de manière pertinente et argumentée d'une part ; et à nourrir l'échange en proposant d'autres perspectives d'autre part.

**TIPS**

- Le jour de l'épreuve, n'oublie pas :
  – ton dossier personnel en deux exemplaires ;
  – ta montre.
- Pense à bien respirer, à te tenir droit(e) et à ne pas parler trop vite. Tu t'es entraîné(e), tu seras convaincant(e) !
- Rappelle-toi qu'on a le droit d'hésiter (*Err... Well...*) ou de revenir sur ce qu'on a dit dans un entretien, ce n'est pas un problème !
- N'hésite pas à faire répéter une question (*Could you repeat please* ?) ou à demander des précisions (*I'm not sure I understand, do you mean...?*).

# Interagir avec l'examinateur

**La partie d'interaction orale de l'épreuve nécessite de comprendre ton interlocuteur(trice) et de t'exprimer, mais également d'être prêt(e) à gérer l'imprévu, de réagir et de t'adapter à ses propos.**

## A
## ÉCOUTER ET COMPRENDRE LES QUESTIONS

- Sois attentif(ve) à la **formulation des questions** et repère bien les **mots-clés employés**.
- Si le débit de ton interlocuteur est trop rapide ou si son élocution te pose un problème, n'hésite pas à lui demander de **répéter** ou de **reformuler** ses propos.
- Sois proactif(ve) et montre ton intérêt.

**PROMPTS**

*• I'm sorry, I didn't hear/catch what you said. • I didn't get your point. • Sorry but I didn't understand what you said. • Could you say that again please? • Can you repeat what you said, please? • Does that mean...? • Could you speak more slowly, please? • Excuse me, what do you mean by...? • I'm sorry, but I am not sure I have understood the question.*

*• Oh I see...• Really? • That's an interesting point: if I undestand it right...*

**TIP**

Mets-toi dans une posture d'écoute active en regardant ton interlocuteur et en réagissant à ce qu'il te dit.

## B
## RÉPONDRE DE MANIÈRE ÉLABORÉE

- La réponse aux questions doit être **élaborée** et **ne peut se limiter à des mots isolés**. Il faut que tu montres **ta capacité à argumenter en anglais** et **ta maîtrise des attendus du programme** de l'enseignement de spécialité.
- N'hésite pas à **réutiliser les termes de la question** ou **à les reformuler** pour commencer ta réponse : cela te laisse le temps de réfléchir à ce qui suit.

  *• To be perfectly clear on the issue of... • When you say that..., it makes me think/wonder... • The question of... in the curriculum is indeed crucial.*

- **Ta réponse ne doit pas être un long monologue**. Assure-toi que ton interlocuteur te comprend. Dialogue avec lui.

  *• Do you know what I mean? • Do I make myself clear? • To answer your question, I'm going to give you an example...*

- Sois **assuré(e)** et **convaincant(e)** et **donne ton avis clairement** sur ce que dit ton interlocuteur(trice) en justifiant.

  *• Yes, I think so because... / No, I don't think so because... • I (dis)agree with you about... because... • You may be right, but I wonder whether... • I suppose it's true, however...*

- Reprends-toi si nécessaire en **t'auto-corrigeant** ou en **nuançant tes propos**.

  *• In other words... • That is to say... • Excuse me, let me rephrase... • Let me correct myself/put it differently...*

- Dans le cas où la question porte sur un élément de ton dossier abordé dans ta présentation, veille à **reformuler tes idées afin de montrer ta capacité à clarifier et à te faire comprendre**.

  *• Indeed, to complete what I said earlier... • Yes, maybe I wasn't clear, what I meant is... • What I intended to show with this example is that...*

- Veille à **mobiliser tes connaissances** pour t'impliquer dans l'entretien et défendre ton point de vue.

  *• What you have just said makes me think of... • Sure, this idea may be related to... • There is also another film I have not mentioned yet, it is... • You may be referring to this painting by...*

**TIP**

Utilise des *gap fillers* pour éviter les moments de silence et te donner le temps de réfléchir.

*Actually... • You see... • You know... • Let me think...*

# Réussir le Grand oral : se préparer

**En fin d'année de Terminale, tu vas passer l'épreuve du Grand oral.**
**Cette épreuve ne doit pas te stresser car :**
**– c'est toi qui choisis des questions qui t'intéressent ;**
**– tu vas préparer les réponses, pas de surprise ;**
**– tu as l'appui de tes professeurs, des autres élèves, du CDI... ;**
**– tu pourras compter sur la bienveillance du jury qui est là pour t'écouter, t'encourager et échanger avec toi.**

## A CHOISIR ET FORMULER SES QUESTIONS

**Les deux questions doivent t'intéresser : c'est la clé de ta réussite !**
**Pour rappel, ces questions doivent « mettre en lumière un des grands enjeux du programme » et « sont adossées à tout ou partie du programme de Première et de Terminale ».**

- Les questions choisies doivent **t'inspirer** des idées, des arguments, des exemples, des sources... qui rendront ta présentation attractive et convaincante.
- Établis **des liens entre les questions et ton projet d'orientation**. Par exemple, si tu te destines à des études de sciences politiques, choisis plutôt une question en lien avec ce sujet.
- Demande-toi aussi s'il est réaliste d'y répondre en 5 minutes : **ne choisis pas un sujet trop vaste, ni trop pointu**. Et n'oublie pas que plus tes questions seront personnelles, plus tu seras à l'aise.

**TIPS**

- **Quelques types de questions :** *Comment ? Pourquoi ? Depuis quand ? Peut-on ? Doit-on ? Dans quelle mesure ? Et si ? Est-il souhaitable ? Est-il vrai que ? Faut-il ? Pour quelles raisons ? Quelles sont ? Quelles seraient les conséquences ? ...*
- Consulte les exemples de questions traitées p. 312 à 317 de ton manuel : elles peuvent t'aider à définir et préparer ta question.

## B PRÉPARER SON INTERVENTION ORALE

**Tu n'es pas seul(e)pour préparer ton oral. Interroge tes professeurs, ils sont là pour t'aider !**

- **Se documenter**

– **Élargis et varie tes sources d'information :** ouvrages documentaires (manuels scolaires, revues, essais, etc.), personnes (ton professeur de spécialité, le ou la professeur(e) documentaliste, tes camarades...), ressources numériques (Internet, ressources numériques du manuel, etc.).

– **Sélectionne tes sources** en fonction de leur fiabilité et de leur pertinence par rapport à ta question.

– **Conserve** et **classe tes sources** (par type, par date...) afin de les citer lors du Grand oral.

- **Organiser ta réponse**

**En introduction :**

– explique pourquoi tu as choisi cette question ;

– éveille la curiosité du jury par une accroche bien choisie.

**Tu es libre du choix de ton plan :**

– dégage deux ou trois idées qui éclairent ta question. Chaque idée est soutenue par plusieurs arguments, illustrés par un exemple ou un fait ;

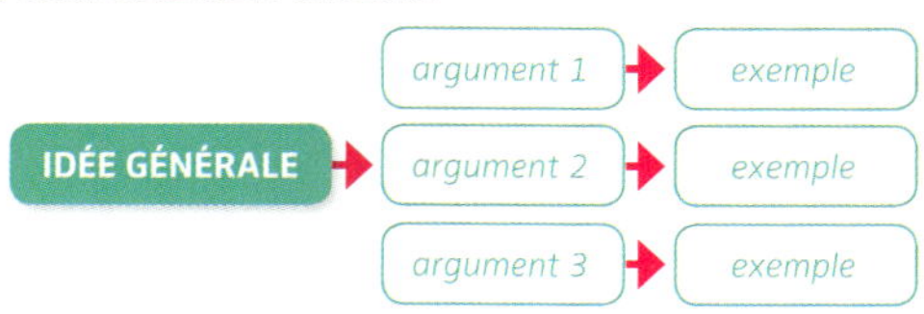


– recherche des exemples, des liens qui te concernent personnellement, avec l'actualité...

**En conclusion :**

– suggère des idées, fais le lien avec l'actualité, ton orientation ou un autre point de programme d'une de tes spécialités ;

– montre que la question posée reste ouverte.

**TIP**

**Appuie-toi sur l'actualité :** crée un dossier dans lequel tu regrouperas toutes les actualités entendues au cours de l'année et qui se rapportent à ton sujet.

**TIPS**

- **Tu n'as que 5 min :** inutile d'annoncer ton plan, surtout si le jury dispose de ton support sur lequel tu l'auras indiqué.
- Tu peux choisir entre **plusieurs types de plan** : thématique, analytique, chronologique, dialectique...

Les différents types de plan

**TIP**

Tu peux profiter de la conclusion pour « tendre une perche au jury », en posant une autre question par exemple.

## C PRÉPARER LE SUPPORT À REMETTRE AU JURY

20'

**Même s'il n'est ni obligatoire ni évalué, prends le temps de remettre un support au jury. Il prouvera la qualité de ta préparation.**

- Tu dois **préparer ce support manuscrit à l'avance** et le **reproduire durant le temps de préparation**. Cela clarifiera tes idées avant la présentation.
- Fais apparaître ton **plan**, les **mots-clés**, tes **arguments**, tes **exemples**, tes **sources les plus originales**, tes **choix d'orientation**, etc.
- Écris, dessine, souligne proprement, relis et évite les fautes d'orthographe.
- Si une ressource t'a été particulièrement précieuse pour préparer ta question, tu peux la porter à la connaissance du jury en l'indiquant sur le support (titre, auteur, source, nature, année).

**TIP**

Toutes les formes sont possibles : plan détaillé, fiche mémo, carte mentale, organigramme, tableau, schéma...

Des exemples de support

## D PRÉSENTER LA RÉPONSE À LA QUESTION DEVANT LE JURY

5'

- Si la question choisie par le jury concerne l'enseignement de spécialité LLCER AMC, « chacun des deux premiers temps de l'épreuve orale terminale peut se dérouler, en partie, dans la langue vivante concernée par l'enseignement de spécialité, selon le choix du candidat. (BO spécial n°2 du 13 février 2020). Avant de commencer, annonce ton choix au jury.
- Le jour J, tu devras parler debout, sans note, pendant 5 min. Ce n'est pas un exercice facile, mais avec un peu d'entraînement, tu vas rapidement progresser. Rendez-vous pp. 310-311 pour des conseils détaillés sur cette étape importante.

**TIP**

Si ta présentation est en français, ta question est également en français. Si tu choisis de t'exprimer en partie en anglais, ta question est libellée dans les deux langues.
Si tu choisis de faire une partie de ta présentation en anglais, ne monte pas la voix en fin de phrase : l'anglais utilise plutôt l'intonation descendante. Mets en relief les mots-clés en les accentuant.

## E PRÉPARER LA DISCUSSION AVEC LE JURY

10'

**Contrairement à ce que tu pourrais croire, il est possible d'anticiper une partie des questions du jury et de s'y préparer. Ici encore, tout est une question d'entraînement ! Multiplie les séances de travail à plusieurs et alternez les rôles : candidat, jury...**

- Lors de tes entraînements en public : note les questions, contre-arguments, objections, discussions, demandes de précisions qui reviennent le plus souvent... et prépare-toi à y répondre !
- Apprends bien **le lexique dans les deux langues** et méfie-toi des faux-amis (ex. : *liberal* et libéral n'ont pas le même sens).
- Si tu ne sais pas quoi répondre à une question, ne reste pas muet(te) : essaie de faire le lien avec ce que tu sais, demande des indications au jury, voire la réponse qui t'aidera certainement à rebondir.

*Actually what I meant was...*

*I'd like to make myself clear...*

*Do you mean... ?*

**TIP**

N'oublie pas de réviser le programme de tes deux spécialités !

## F ÉCHANGER SUR SON PROJET D'ORIENTATION

5'

**Tu sais que le jury te demandera : « En quoi la question que vous avez choisie éclaire vos choix d'orientation, voire votre projet professionnel ? ». Sois prêt(e) à répondre à cette question.**

- Au moment du Grand oral, en juin, tu connaîtras tes choix d'orientation. **Entraîne-toi à les exprimer précisément** : intitulé exact de la formation, lieu, mode d'accès (non sélectif, sélectif, concours...).
- Le jury ne te demandera pas de savoir quel métier tu veux faire, mais quelle voie tu emprunteras après le bac.
- Rappelle **comment tu t'es informé(e)** (Parcoursup, ONISEP, salons, rencontres, Portes ouvertes, sites étudiants...), fais le lien entre la spécialité et les attendus de la formation.
- Enfin, utilise tes activités associatives, sportives, artistiques, engagements, jobs, stages pour mettre en avant certaines de tes qualités en phase avec tes choix d'orientation, voire avec ton projet professionnel.

**TIP**

Exprime ta motivation en t'appuyant sur ton projet de formation motivé.

**TIP**

Tu dois connaître le contenu des formations visées : consulte les plaquettes, sites Internet ; vas aux journées portes ouvertes...
Tu pourras ainsi montrer en quoi la question que tu viens de traiter sera approfondie lors de tes études supérieures.

Grilles d'auto-évaluation

Objectif **BAC** GRAND ORAL

# Réussir le Grand oral : prendre la parole en public

## A ENTRAÎNE-TOI !

**Prendre la parole, ça s'apprend ! Ta préparation et tes entrainements te permettront d'améliorer ton travail et de te mettre en confiance. La réussite de ton Grand oral vient d'abord de ta maîtrise du contenu et d'un entraînement régulier à la prise de parole.**

- **Entraîne-toi régulièrement :**

– à **la réponse aux questions**, en te chronométrant : il est fondamental d'en maîtriser la durée. Tu as 5 minutes, pas plus, pas moins !

– **en classe avec tes professeurs, avec tes amis, ta famille**, devant un miroir, avec un smartphone, une montre… ;

– à **la discussion avec le jury** et à **présenter tes choix d'orientation**.

- Joue la scène comme au Grand oral : le « jury » s'assoit derrière une table, règle le volume de ta voix et ta position dans la salle.
- Travaille également ton oral dans toutes tes situations quotidiennes.

**TIP**

Soyez bienveillant(e)s les un(e)s envers les autres ! Utilisez-la grille d'évaluation pour être objectifs.

Grilles d'auto-évaluation

## B DÉDRAMATISE !

**Le Grand oral n'est pas un concours d'éloquence, ni une performance. Le jury sait la difficulté qu'il y a à passer un oral, tu peux donc compter sur sa bienveillance.**

*J'ai le trac…*

- Le trac est normal, il te permet de te concentrer et de bien démarrer. Il disparaitra vite car tu maîtrises le contenu.

*Je ne suis pas à l'aise à l'oral…*

- Ton entraînement t'apportera plus d'aisance. En spécialité LLCER AMC, tu as l'habitude de prendre la parole souvent. Appuie-toi sur ton épreuve orale d'anglais qui a lieu plus tôt dans l'année pour te préparer au Grand oral.

*Je ne sais pas quoi faire de mes jambes et de mes mains…*

- Ne surestime pas l'importance du « non verbal » ou des gestes parasites (ni même des tics verbaux). Concentre-toi sur le contenu et le jury.

*Dois-je apprendre mes réponses par cœur ou les rédiger intégralement…*

- Ne change pas tes habitudes mais tu ne devras pas donner l'impression de réciter.

**TIPS**

- On estime qu'une durée de 5 minutes correspond à environ 800 mots, soit environ 1 copie double à grands carreaux rédigée.
- Choisis une tenue soignée (chaussures de ville), pas trop décontractée (pas de survêtement ni de T-shirt), tout en étant à l'aise.

## C ADOPTE UNE POSTURE SEREINE ET DES GESTES EXPRESSIFS

**Fais simple : reste le plus naturel possible.**

- Une fois dans la salle, **place-toi au centre de la pièce**, à environ **deux mètres du jury.**
- **Ancre-toi dans le sol**, les pieds bien droits et légèrement écartés, la tête haute tournée vers le jury. Puis, conserve cette posture , comme référence, même si tu bouges un peu pour te tourner vers les membres du jury en parlant.
- **Ce sont tes mains qui vont parler pour toi.** Assure-toi qu'elles soient propres.
- Sois naturel avec tes mains, tu n'es ni une personnalité politique en campagne ni un mime ! Évite de croiser les bras, ne garde pas tes mains jointes : utilise-les plutôt **pour appuyer ce que tu dis.**

**TIP**

Si, comme tu en as la possibilité, tu choisis de t'asseoir après ta réponse de cinq minutes, de même, sur la chaise, ancre-toi au sol avec la tête et le dos droits.

RENDEZ-VOUS SUR LE SITE NATHAN.FR/GRAND-ORAL

## D
## PRÊTE ATTENTION À TA VOIX

**La voix est le premier instrument de l'orateur. Ses différentes composantes sont mêlées mais tu peux en travailler les différents éléments.**

- **Le volume sonore**

Entraîne-toi à parler de manière **suffisamment audible**, puis **varie les volumes** (plus bas / plus fort) et les distances en restant audible, sans jamais crier. Travaille ton élocution, exagérément parfois.

- **Le débit (vitesse / rythme)**

– Le rythme de ta prise de parole influera sur la qualité de sa réception.

– Tu attireras et garderas l'attention en **variant ton débit** en fonction de tes propos. Par exemple, en parlant plus vite quand tu racontes une anecdote, moins vite quand tu arrives en fin d'une sous-partie ou que tu veux insister sur un point.

– Si tu as l'habitude de parler vite, ce sera difficile à modifier. Dans ce cas, évite les phrases trop longues et surtout, fais des pauses !

- **L'intonation**

C'est le ton que tu prendras pour t'adresser au jury en accord avec le texte. Entraîne-toi à bien l'adapter à différents contenus et surtout à varier pour **éviter la monotonie**. Si tu choisis de présenter ta question en anglais, prête une attention particulière à la prononciation et au rythme de la langue.

TIP

**La prise de parole, c'est aussi des pauses !**
Ne commence pas à parler dès qu'on te donne la parole. Silence, d'abord.
Tu attireras l'attention et tu en profiteras pour respirer un grand coup.
Les pauses te permettront de marquer le début ou la fin d'une sous-partie, de réfléchir avant de répondre, et d'attirer l'attention sur ce que tu vas dire ensuite.

## E
## SOIGNE TON VOCABULAIRE

**Même si tu n'en n'as pas toujours conscience, il se peut que tu utilises un langage trop familier, trop quotidien. N'oublie jamais que tu t'adresses à un jury.**

- Élimine tous les termes qui te paraissent relever d'un langage trop familier. Même si ce n'est pas toujours facile, essaye de **bannir tes tics de langage** (en français : *ben, comment, euh, de base, trop, carrément, en mode, bof, je kiffe, au jour d'aujourd'hui...*/ en anglais : *like, whatever*). Si tu optes pour une présentation en anglais, prête une attention particulière à la forme et au choix des mots.
- Emploie des **termes précis** : tu dois connaître les définitions de toutes les notions que tu emploies. Tu peux nuancer ta réponse en utilisant des modalisateurs (*« Il m'a semblé... » / « J'ai trouvé... » / « J'ai apprécié... » / « En revanche... »*).

TIP

Entraînez-vous à plusieurs : un élève présente son exposé, les autres relèvent les mots issus d'un langage trop familier. Cherchez ensemble des synonymes ou des expressions plus adaptés.

## F
## REGARDE ET SOURIS

**Crée un lien visuel avec les membres du jury dès ton entrée.**

- Comme tu ne liras pas tes notes, tu n'as que les membres du jury à regarder ! Regarde-les alternativement et en fonction de leurs actions (regarde le membre du jury qui t'interroge, débute ta réponse en le regardant, puis regarde le second).
- Souris régulièrement, c'est un ingrédient important d'un oral réussi.

TIP

Pense à saluer le jury en arrivant et à le remercier en concluant.

## G
## INSPIRE-TOI !

**Crée un lien visuel avec les membres du jury dès ton entrée.**

- Visionne les vidéos proposées via le lien ci-contre ou sur le site **nathan.fr/grand-oral**.
- Tu peux aussi regarder des vidéos type conférences TED ou « Ma thèse en 180 s » ; des discours politiques, même en langue étrangère pour n'étudier que les postures et les gestes.

Nathan GRAND ORAL

**Objectif BAC** GRAND ORAL

# Question traitée 1 : exemple en français uniquement

## A BIEN CHOISIR SA QUESTION

**Ne choisis pas ta question au hasard. Elle doit émaner d'un centre d'intérêt personnel.**

**TIP**

La question peut être libellée sous diverses formes (interrogative, infinitive, nominale). La formulation interrogative peut être rassurante pour garantir un questionnement personnel.

**Dans quelle mesure la Cour Suprême américaine est-elle garante d'égalité ?**

**Une question qui t'intéresse**
Si tu es intéressé(e) par les questions de société, le domaine de la justice, la culture américaine.

**Une question faisable**
Choisis une question ni trop pointue ni trop large. Tu dois y répondre en 5 minutes !

**Une formulation problématisée**
Une question qui permet d'opposer des arguments et de montrer ta capacité d'analyse et de réflexion.

**En lien avec le programme LLCER AMC**
**Faire société / axe 3 :** Egalités et inégalités – l'ancrage dans le monde anglophone est fondamental : ici les États-Unis

**En lien avec un choix d'orientation**
Des études de droit, de LEA, de sciences politiques, etc.

**Qui peut croiser d'autres disciplines**
DGEMC : Liberté, égalité, fraternité
Philosophie : la justice
SES : inégalités et justice sociale

**TIP**

Il est essentiel de bien connaître les institutions américaines pour répondre à la question.

## B FAIRE DES RECHERCHES

**Bien définir les mots-clés du sujet :**

**La Cour Suprême :** article 3 de la Constitution des Etats-Unis.
- Sommet du pouvoir judiciaire
- Elle décide si les lois des États-Unis ou celles des différents États, sont conformes à la Constitution, dont elle est l'interprète ultime.
- Devise : *'Equal Justice Under Law'* : « Justice égale selon la loi ».
- Siège à Washington D.C.
- 9 juges nommés à vie par le président et approuvés par le Sénat.

**Égalité :**
- **Relation** d'identité entre **deux termes** référés à une **norme**.
- Trois grands types d'égalité peuvent être retenus : l'égalité de nature, l'égalité de droit, l'égalité économique. Ici focale sur **l'égalité de droit**. Article premier de la Déclaration universelle des droits de l'homme (1948).

**Ressources utiles :**

***File 15 Justice for all***
- **Doc 1** p. 140 "*The US system*" (vidéo informative)
- **Doc 2** p. 140 "*Checks and Balances in a Trump-Era Supreme Court*" (article)
- **Doc 3** p. 141 "*What does Bader Ginsburg's death mean for the Supreme Court?*" (article)
- **Doc 1** p. 142 "*A major civil-rights decision*" (audio ABC news)
- **Doc B et C** p. 145 "*What a New Supreme Court Decision Means for Native American Sovereignty*"
- Film *Loving*, James Nichols, 2016 (article et citation)

**Convoquer ses autres connaissances :**
- Arrêt *Dred Scott v. John F. A. Sandford* de 1857 qui déclare que les descendants d'esclaves ne sont pas citoyens américains.
- Arrêt *Plessy v. Ferguson* du 18 mai 1896 qui légalise la ségrégation au nom de «égaux, mais séparés».
- Arrêt *Brown v. Board of Education* du 17 mai 1954 qui déclare la ségrégation raciale inconstitutionnelle dans les écoles publiques.

## C
## ORGANISER SES IDÉES ET PRÉPARER SON SUPPORT

**Exemple de plan**

**1. La Cour Suprême garante de la Constitution**
**a.** La hiérarchie des tribunaux : système constitué de 3 niveaux : les tribunaux de district des Etats-Unis, la Cour d'appel de premier niveau, et la Cour Suprême. Les poursuites fédérales commencent au niveau du district dans une cour fédérale.
**b.** Question du litige concernant les états fédérés : très peu de cas, choisis en fonction des implications pour les Américains ou pour un groupe en particulier, sont traités par la Cour Suprême. Pouvoir de contrôle de la constitutionnalité (dès 1803 *Marbury v Madison*). Une garantie de l'égalité du droit au niveau fédéral.

**2. L'institution des inégalités ?**
**a.** La rédaction de la Constitution américaine et la question des minorités : question de l'esclavage, statut des amérindiens. Des inégalités de fait. Rédaction des amendements (garante des libertés).
**b.** Rôle de la Cour Suprême quant à la doctrine 'séparés mais égaux' (*Plessy v Ferguson*). Institution d'inégalités dans différents domaines (scolarité, transports publics, culture, logement, etc.)

**3. La Cour Suprême et la lutte contre les discriminations**
**a.** Une longue bataille pour l'acquisition des droits civiques. *Brown v. Board of Education*
**b.** Une bataille qui se poursuit (*Bostock v. Clayton County, Georgia*). La lutte contre la discrimination d'orientation sexuelle.

**TIP**

Le choix de la langue :
Tu peux choisir de faire ta présentation en français. Dans ce cas, ta question sera rédigée en français seulement. Veille à bien utiliser les termes français appropriés : *The Bill of Rights* est la Déclaration des droits en français par exemple.
→ OBJECTIF BAC p. 309

**TIP**

Le support n'est pas obligatoire ni évalué, mais il prouve la qualité de ta préparation.

**Exemple de support**

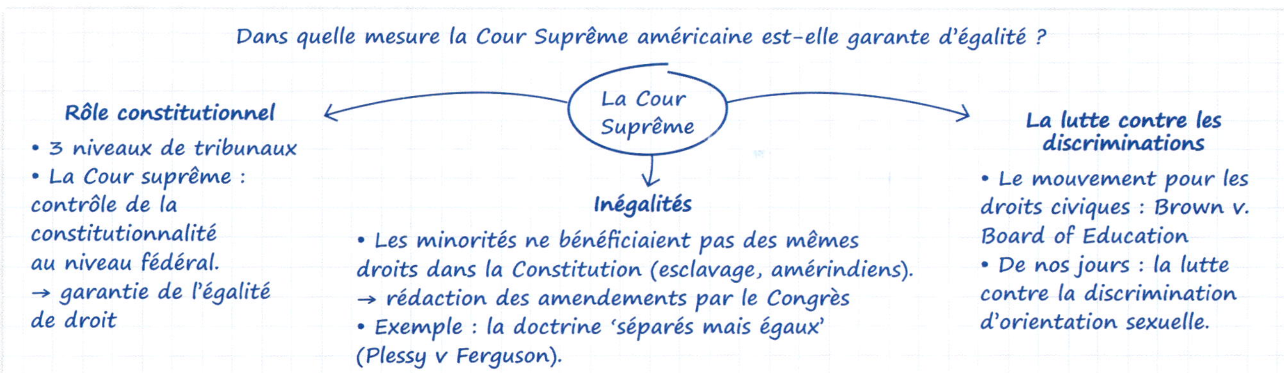


## D
## ANTICIPER LES QUESTIONS DU JURY

### Préciser une définition

Le jury pourra te demander de préciser les **trois grandes institutions** américaines : le président, le Congrès et la Cour Suprême.

- Le **Président** exerce la fonction de chef de l'Etat. Il est **l'exécutif**.
- Le **Congrès** est composé de la Chambre des représentants et du Sénat. Il est la branche **législative**.
- La **Cour Suprême** est le sommet du pouvoir **judiciaire**.
- Il y a une séparation stricte des pouvoirs.

### Faire le lien avec d'autres chapitres

Le jury pourra te demander de **faire le lien avec « libertés publiques et libertés individuelles »**. Le principe d'égalité entre-t-il en tension avec le principe de liberté ?

- La liberté est inscrite dans la Déclaration des droits – *the Bill of Rights* - 10 premiers amendements de la Constitution, parmi lesquels le 1er amendement (liberté de parole) ou le 2e amendement (le droit du port d'arme).
- La Cour Suprême garantit le respect de ces libertés qui peuvent entrer en tension ou non avec le principe même d'égalité.

### Évoquer ton avenir professionnel

- Ce type de question laisse imaginer que tu te destines à des études de droit ou de sciences politiques.
- Pense à prévoir tes arguments pour mettre en lien la question avec ton projet d'orientation.

**Objectif BAC GRAND ORAL**

# Question traitée 2 :
## exemple de question qui porte sur 2 enseignements de spécialité

### A BIEN CHOISIR SA QUESTION

**Tu peux choisir une question te permettant de croiser tes deux enseignements de spécialité. Par exemple, ici avec l'HGGSP.**

**Une question qui t'intéresse**
Si tu es intéressé(e) par les questions de société, la préservation de l'environnement, le développement durable, les enjeux économiques internationaux.

**Une question faisable**
Choisis une question ni trop pointue ni trop large. Tu dois y répondre en 5 minutes !

**Une formulation problématisée**
Une question qui permet d'opposer des arguments et de montrer ta capacité d'analyse et de réflexion.

**TIP** La question peut être libellée sous diverses formes (interrogative, infinitive, nominale). La formulation interrogative peut être rassurante pour garantir un questionnement personnel.

**Dans quelle mesure la politique environnementale américaine est-elle compatible avec une économie prospère ?**

**En lien avec le programme LLCER AMC**
**Environnements en mutation / axe 2 :** De la protection de la nature à la transition écologique L'ancrage dans le monde anglophone est fondamental : ici les États-Unis.

**En lien avec un choix d'orientation**
Des études de génie biologique, de génie de l'environnement, de sciences politiques, etc.

**Croisement avec l'enseignement de spécialité HGGSP**
**Thème 5 :** L'environnement, entre exploitation et protection : un enjeu planétaire.
**Objectif de travail conclusif :** Les États-Unis et la question environnementale : tensions et contrastes.

**TIP** Il est essentiel de bien connaître la politique américaine en matière d'écologie pour répondre à la question.

### B FAIRE DES RECHERCHES

**Bien définir les mots-clés du sujet :**

**Politique environnementale :**
- Faire la distinction entre l'ère **Trump** et l'ère **Biden**.
- Connaître en quoi consistent **les accords de Paris** ainsi que le ***Green New Deal***.
- Savoir expliquer les **motivations** derrière ces politiques environnementales ainsi que les **freins** à celles-ci.
- **Mettre en perspective** avec d'autres pays, notamment européens.

**Economie prospère :**
- Création d'emplois
- Consommation
- Poids des grandes entreprises

**Compatible :**
- Qui peut s'accorder avec quelque chose et / ou exister en même temps.
- Qui va de pair.

**Ressources utiles :**

***File 19 Renewable USA***
- **Doc 1** p. 172 *"The Green New Deal"* (audio)
- **Doc 2** p. 175 *What is at stake with these Green New Deals?* (article)
- **Doc 3** p. 177 *"Why 1.5°?"* (article)
- **Doc 2** p 178 *"A personal commitment"* (vidéo)
- **Doc 4** p. 180 *"How Has Fracking Changed our Future?"* (article)
- **Doc B** p. 181 *"Trump's final pitch to Pennsylvania: I love fracking"* (article)
- Vidéo : *"Joe Biden's Presidential campaign, 2020"* (Portfolio p. 183)

***Snap File 20 The bush is burning***

***HGGSP Terminale,*** Cote, Godeau, Janin, Le Quintrec, Nathan 2020. p.354-373

**Convoquer ses autres connaissances :**
- *The Paris Agreement* SITE
- Les types d'énergie renouvelable SITE

## C ORGANISER SES IDÉES ET PRÉPARER SON SUPPORT

**Exemple de plan**

**1. Croissance économique et déclin environnemental ?**
**a.** Économie des États-Unis basée sur l'énergie fossile qui est abordable et génère de nombreux emplois. Aussi, sa suppression au profit d'énergies renouvelables aurait des conséquences désastreuses sur l'économie.
**b.** La fracturation hydraulique soutenue par Donald Trump car génératrice d'emplois et fait vivre certaines régions américaines mais impact hautement négatif sur l'environnement.

**2. Une révolution verte plutôt que des mesures environnementales**
**a.** *Green New Deal* qui n'est pas aisé à mettre en place et peu suivi ➔ une vraie révolution, et non juste une nouvelle loi. Besoin d'un changement de mentalités
**b.** Recycler, réparer au lieu de racheter. Pour l'instant, seulement à l'échelle individuelle ou locale, pas nationale : besoin d'une prise de conscience et d'un investissement à plus grande échelle ➔ besoin d'un soutien de l'état.

**3. Une question hautement politique**
**a.** le débat semble plutôt mettre en exergue des désaccords politiques : les Républicains minorent le réchauffement climatique, les Démocrates en font un sujet de préoccupation.
**b.** Poids des groupes de pression au sein même du gouvernement vs poids de la population qui est désireuse de changements, donc prête à s'engager par des actions quotidiennes. Nouveau président = nouvelle ère ?

**TIP**
Le choix de la langue : Tu peux choisir de faire ta présentation en français. Dans ce cas, ta question sera rédigée en français seulement. Veille à bien utiliser les termes français appropriés : *an environmentalist* est un écologiste en français par exemple.
➔ OBJECTIF BAC p. 309

**TIP**
Le support n'est pas obligatoire ni évalué, mais il prouve la qualité de ta préparation.

**Exemple de support**

*Dans quelle mesure la politique environnementale américaine est-elle compatible avec une économie prospère ?*

***1. Croissance économique et déclin environnemental ?***
*– Économie des États-Unis basée sur la consommation d'énergie fossiles qui sont abordables flèche leur suppression au profit d'énergies renouvelables aurait des conséquences désastreuses sur l'économie*
*– La fracturation hydraulique soutenue par Donald Trump car génératrice d'emplois mais impact hautement négatif sur l'environnement.*

***2. Une révolution verte plutôt que des mesures environnementales***
*– Green New Deal pas aisé à mettre en place → une vraie révolution. Besoin d'un changement de mentalités*
*– Recycler, réparer au lieu de racheter : pour l'instant, seulement à l'échelle individuelle ou locale, pas nationale → besoin d'un soutien de l'état.*

***3. Une question hautement politique***
*– le débat met en exergue des désaccords politiques bipartisans entre les et les Démocrates (cf campagne de Biden).*
*– Poids des groupes de pression au sein du gouvernement vs poids de la population prête à s'engager par des actions quotidiennes. Nouveau président = nouvelle ère ?*

## D ANTICIPER LES QUESTIONS DU JURY

**Préciser une définition**
Le jury pourra te demander de préciser en quoi consiste le ***Green New Deal*** ou bien t'interroger sur l'exploitation des ressources et la transformation des milieux depuis le XIXe siècle.

**Faire le lien avec d'autres chapitres**
Le jury pourra te demander de faire le lien avec les autres axes de la thématique : « **Repenser la ville** » ou bien « **Puissance et influences** ».
- Une réorganisation de la ville peut-elle favoriser un développement économique responsable ?
- Dans un jeu de puissance et d'influences à l'échelle mondiale, les États-Unis peuvent-ils gagner à s'inspirer de modèles européens ?

**Évoquer ton avenir professionnel**
- Ce type de question laisse imaginer que tu te destines à des études de géographie, de sciences de la terre, de risques en environnement ou de sciences politiques.
- Pense à prévoir tes arguments pour mettre en lien la question avec ton projet d'orientation.

Objectif BAC GRAND ORAL

# Question traitée 3 : exemple dans les 2 langues

## A BIEN CHOISIR SA QUESTION

**Ne choisis pas ta question au hasard. Elle doit émaner d'un centre d'intérêt personnel.**

**TIP**

La question peut être libellée sous diverses formes (interrogative, infinitive, nominale). Si tu t'exprimes aussi en anglais, ta question sera rédigée en français et en anglais.

**Le pouvoir des GAFAM aux États-Unis et en Europe.**
***The power of Big Tech companies in the USA and Europe.***

**Une question qui t'intéresse**
Si tu es intéressé(e) par les domaines des technologies ou de la politique publique.

**Une question faisable**
Choisis une question ni trop pointue ni trop large. Tu dois y répondre en 5 minutes !

**Une formulation problématisée**
Une question qui permet d'opposer des arguments et de montrer ta capacité d'analyse et de réflexion.

**En lien avec le programme LLCER AMC**
**Relation au monde / axe 1 :** Puissance et influence – l'ancrage dans le monde anglophone est fondamental : des entreprises américaines et leur pouvoir dans le monde.

**En lien avec un choix d'orientation**
Des études d'économie, de LEA, de sciences politiques, d'ingénieur, etc.

**Qui peut croiser d'autres disciplines**
SES : Comment les marchés imparfaitement concurrentiels fonctionnent-ils ?
HGGSP : Thème 2 de première : Analyser les dynamiques des puissances internationales (axe 2 : Formes indirectes de la puissance : une approche géopolitique)

## B FAIRE DES RECHERCHES

| Bien définir les mots-clés du sujet : | Ressources utiles : |
|---|---|
| **GAFAM :**<br>• Il s'agit de l'acronyme employé en français pour désigner **cinq grandes entreprises américaines :** Google, Apple, Facebook, Amazon et Microsoft. Si tu choisis de répondre à la question en anglais, on parlera de *Big Tech* ou des *tech giants*. | **File 23 Tech giants**<br>• **Doc 1** p 208 "*Life without Big Tech*" (vidéo)<br>• **Doc 3** p 209 "*Saving the world?*" (article)<br>• **Doc 2** p 210 "*Invading our privacy?*" (entretien filmé)<br>• **Doc 3** p 211 "*Entering our wallets*" (article) |
| **Pouvoir :**<br>• Les pratiques de ces entreprises sont monopolistiques (*monopolistic practices*) selon certains : elles contrôlent entièrement leur marché.<br>• On peut comparer cette situation à celle de l'oligopole (*oligopoly*), quand quelques acteurs dominants contrôlent un marché.<br>• Les lobbies, ou groupes d'influence, ont un rôle crucial dans les institutions politiques, particulièrement aux États-Unis : ils promeuvent des intérêts en exerçant leur influence sur les pouvoirs publiques. Les GAFAM ont développé leur influence à Bruxelles en espérant avoir un effet sur les décisions de la Commission européenne. | **File 23 Tech giants**<br>• **Doc 2** p 209 "*Running the world*" (graphique et entretien filmé)<br>• **Doc 1** p 212 "*Taking over?*" (article)<br>• **Doc 2** p 212 "*Towards policy changes?*" (émission de radio) |
| **Les États-Unis et l'Europe :**<br>• Aux États-Unis, le Congrès a tenté d'agir. Définis son rôle. Le parti démocrate devient de plus en plus critique vis-à-vis des GAFAM.<br>• La Commission européenne prépare des propositions de règlements sur les services numériques (DSA) et sur les marchés numériques (DMA).<br>• Ces institutions tentent de limiter le pouvoir des GAFAM avec des lois antitrust, des lois visant à protéger les données privées, ou encore des lois sur la liberté d'expression et les *fake news*. | **File 13 The land of the free**<br>• **Doc 3** p 119 "*Liberties in the U.S. Constitution*" (articles de la Constitution)<br>• **Doc 1** p 120 "*Should every speech be protected?*" (émission de radio)<br>**File 23 Tech giants**<br>• **Doc 3** p 213 "*Challenging Big Tech?*" (article)<br>• **Doc 1** p 214 "*Fighting online disinformation*" (article) |
| **Convoquer ses autres connaissances :** Lire la presse pour se renseigner sur l'actualité des GAFAM face au Congrès, à la Commission européenne et suivre l'influence des lobbyistes. | |

RELATION AU MONDE

AXE 1 : PUISSANCE ET INFLUENCE

## C ORGANISER SES IDÉES ET PRÉPARER SON SUPPORT

**Exemple de plan**

**1. Unlimited power?**
**a.** The question of freedom is inherent to Big Tech (free enterprise, and free speech for Facebook); (statistics showing the power of these companies; impossible not to use these services.
**b.** Companies which are both in positions of monopoly and oligopoly as they often dominate specific markets, and are in stiff competition with each other.

**2. Nations and their institutions vs. this monopoly**
**a.** Congress: antitrust laws; evolution in the Democratic Party's position: the Tech Giants at first seen as symbols of modernity, now perceived as dangerous for the economy (monopoly, working conditions at Amazon) and politics (hate speech, etc.)
**b.** The European Commission: regulating data protection and preventing monopolies by helping smaller companies, through two sets of proposed regulations on digital services (DSA) and digital markets (DMA).

**3. The future of the Tech Giants: Invincible?**
**a.** The influence of lobbies in Washington and now Brussels.
**b.** Government-style power: according to some analysts, the Tech Giants, sometimes called the Frightful Five, have similar powers to national governments (economic, political).
Issue of Big Tech's involvement in politics, philanthropy, etc.

**TIP**

Le choix de la langue :
Si tu choisis de t'exprimer dans les deux langues, préfère une approche par blocs pour ne pas déstabiliser le jury.
Tu peux faire ton introduction en français et poursuivre en anglais.
→ OBJECTIF BAC p. 309

**TIP**

Le support n'est pas obligatoire ni évalué, mais il prouve la qualité de ta préparation.

**Exemple de support**

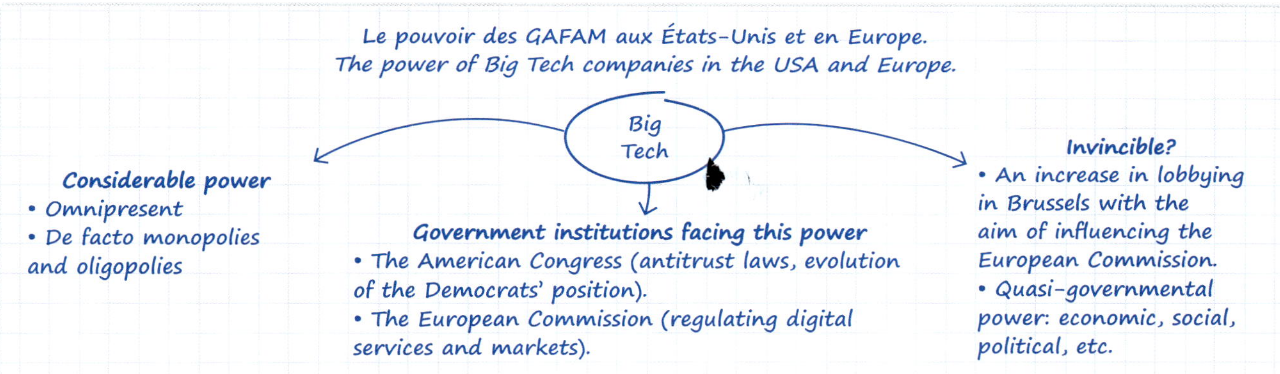


## D ANTICIPER LES QUESTIONS DU JURY

### Préciser une définition

Le jury pourra te demander de préciser le rôle du **Congrès américain** et de la Commission européenne.

• Le **Congrès** est composé de la Chambre des représentants et du Sénat. Il est la branche **législative**, qui vote les lois. (Les autres branches sont la branche **exécutive**, le Président, et la branche **judiciaire**, qui interprète la loi.)

• La **Commission européenne** élabore et met en œuvre la politique de l'Union européenne. Son statut est particulier puisqu'elle réunit vingt-sept Etats membres ; ses décisions ont donc un réel poids international.

### Faire le lien avec d'autres chapitres

Le jury pourra te demander de **faire le lien avec l'axe « libertés publiques et libertés individuelles »**. Quelles libertés fondamentales sont liées à la problématique des GAFAM ?

• La liberté d'entreprendre : l'économie de marché, la compétition entre les acteurs/

• La liberté d'expression (Premier amendement de la Constitution américaine) : particulièrement pour Facebook et les réseaux sociaux plus généralement.

• Le droit au respect de la vie privée (lié au Quatrième amendement de la Constitution) : les GAFAM sont critiqués pour leur non-respect des données privées des usagers.

### Evoquer ton avenir professionnel

• Ce type de question laisse imaginer que tu te destines à des études de sciences politiques, d'économie, de droit, ou même d'ingénieur.

• Pense à prévoir tes arguments pour mettre en lien la question avec ton projet d'orientation.

## Crédits photographiques

**Couverture g** GETTY IMAGES/Corbis/Ira L. Black ; **hd** ISTOCK/Hadynyah ; **md, 10** REA/Redux/The New-York Times/Matthew Abbott ; **bd** GETTY IMAGES/In Pictures/Mike Kemp ; **16** Soizic Le Gouguec (création)/National Center for Education Statistic (source) ; **17** © The Open University/DR ; **18** © Satish Acharya/India ; **19 h, 24 hd** PHOTO12.COM/Alamy/Bill Bachman ; **19 b, 23, 24 bd** © DR/IBM ; **21, 24 bg, 6** ADOBE STOCK/As-artmedia ; **25 g** Atingi DR ; **d** © WASHINGTON POST/Signe Wilkinson , 19 may 2020 ; **26** © CAGLE CARTOONS, INC/Jeff Korerba ; **27** CBS NEWS DR ; **28** Kiyomi Taguchi/University of Washington ; **29 g** AFP/Getty Images Europe/Nadine Rupp ; **29 d, 6** ISTOCK/Zmeel ; **31 g** Reagle, Joseph, and Jackie Koerner, eds., Wikipedia @ 20, excerpt, © 2020 Massachusetts Institute of Technology, by permission of The MIT Press. ; **d** WIKIMEDIA Statistics ; **32, 40 hg** Soizic Le Gouguec (creation)/How Nanotechnology Could Reengineer Us - Keithley Instruments (source) **33 h** AFP/Getty Images North America/Kevork Djansezian ; **b** Discovery Digital Networks/DR ; **34 g, 40 bg** © Roger Moore ; **34 d, 40 hd** © Lisa Memmel ; **35, 6** ADOBE STOCK/Dmytro Tolokonov ; **36** © PENGUIN RANDOM HOUSE LLC ; **37** ITV/DR ; **41 g** © CARTOON STOCK LTD/Jon Carter ; **41 d** CHRISTOPHE L COLLECTION/© Alcon Entertainment/DMG Entertainment/Straight Up Films ; **42** © DAVID HOCKNEY INC, „The Arrival of Spring in Woldgate, East Yorkshire in 2011, 2 January", 2011 ; **43 h** Google/DR ; **m** Maria Takeuchi ; **44 d** Alphr.org DR ; **44 g** © Paula Aguilera ; **47 g, 6** © Created by artist Matthew Mohr and fabricated by Design Communications Limited ; **b** Matthew Mohr/DCL DR ; **49** The Daily Mail DR ; **50 h, 6** GETTY IMAGES/LightRocket/Erik McGregor ; **50 b, 57 b, 58 hg** AFP/Daniel Leal-Olivas ; **51 h** AFP/Getty Images/Thearon W. Henderson ; **b** Newsy/DR ; **52** Basic Books/Hachette DR ; **53, 58 hd** AFP/Kerem Yucel/© Greta McClain, Xena Goldman, Cadex Herrera ; **54** © USA TODAY NETWORK/Jarrad Henderson ; **55, 58 bg** © Voting Squad/DR ; **56** AFP/Getty Images/Thearon W. Henderson ; **57 h** PHOTO12.COM/Alamy Live News/UPI/Jonathan Ernst ; **59 d** ADOBE STOCK/Snaptitude ; **59 g** © Harper Collins Publishers ; **60 g, 7** AFP/Getty Images/Chris Jackson Collection/Chris Jackson ; **60 bd** AFP/Getty Images Europe/WPA Pool ; **60 hd** AFP/Getty Images Europe/WPA Pool ; **61** © KRAUZE Andrzej ; **62 h** © Copyright Guardian News & Media Ltd 2019/Sebastien Thibault ; **b** Channel 4 News ; **63** Channel 4/ITN ; **65 hg** CHRISTOPHE L COLLECTION/© Netflix - Left Bank Pictures - Sony Pictures Television Production UK ; **hd** Contains Parliamentary information licensed under the Open Parliament Licence v3.0 ; 66 Soizic Le Gouguec (creation)/ © Pew Research Center ; **67, 73, 74 hg** AURIMAGES/REX/Kobal/Apple TV+/Media Res ; **68, 74 hd** © HarperCollins DR ; **69, 74 bd, 7** © 2017 David Horsey All rights reserved. Distributed by TRIBUNE CONTENT AGENCY LONDON ; **70** CNBC DR ; **71, 74 bg** AURIMAGES/BBQ_DFY/HBO ; **72** AURIMAGES/Courtesy Everett Collection/HBO ; **75 hg** GCP/Hachette Group DR ; **hd** AURIMAGES/BBQ_DFY/Bold Films ; **bd** © Pew Reseach Center ; **76** © Play Bac Presse ; **77** SIPA PRESS/Shutterstock/Alastair Muir ; **78 h** The Sun/©News Licensing ; **b** The Times/ ©News Licensing ; **79** FORA.tv/DR ; **81 g** AFP/Léon Nael ; **d** © Atlantic Books ; **82** © THE SLOW JOURNALISM COMPANY ; **83 g, 90 hg** CHRISTOPHE L COLLECTION/© Kudos Film/BBC ; **83 d** AURIMAGES/Courtesy Everett Collection/Lionsgate ; **84 h, 90 bg** AURIMAGES/The Kobal Collection/Rex/Kobal/Universal/Photo by Working Title ; **84 b, 90 hd** AURIMAGES/The Kobal Collection/Rex/Kobal/Netflix/photo by Sophie Mutevelian ; **85 h** CHRISTOPHE L COLLECTION/© Danjaq/MGM/Universal/Eon ; **85 b, 90 bd** © Legally Black ; **86 h** AURIMAGES/The Kobal Collection/Rex/kobal/Focus/Photo by Jaap Buitendijk ; **86 bd, 88** PHOTONONSTOP/Picture Alliance/Geisler-Fotopress ; **86 bg** AURIMAGES/BBQ_DFY/Sixteen Films/Les Films du Fleuve/Why Not Productions ; **87, 89; 7** CHRISTOPHE L COLLECTION/© BBC - Red Production Company/DR ; **91 g** AURIMAGES/The Kobal Picture/Rex/Kobal/Universal/Photo by Focus Features ; **91 bd** AURIMAGES/courtesy Everett Collection/IFC Films ; **91 hd** © CARTOON STOCK LTD/Chaff ; **92, 7** © MILLER Johnny/Unequal Scenes ; **93 h** © MARIAN GOODMAN GALLERY/Jabulani Dhlamini ; **b** Design Indaba/DR ; **94 h** Photo © MAGUBANE Peter ; **94 b** © Courtesy The David Goldblatt Legacy Trust ; **95 b** © Zanele Muholi. Courtesy of Stevenson, Amsterdam/Cape Town/Johannesburg and Yancey Richardson, New York : **hg** Ntozakhe II, Parktown, 2016 ; **mg** MaID X, Durban 2015 ; **bg** Kodwa 1, Amsterdam, 2017. **d** Bester 1, Mayotte, 2015 ; **95 h** Image © 2019, Kamohelo Mahlatsi courtesy of MAHLATSI GALLERY ; **97 hg** Santu Mokofeng, June 16 Commemoration, Regina Mundi (Soweto 1986) © Santu Mofokeng Foundation/Images courtesy Lunetta Bartz, MAKER, Johannesburg ; **97 d** © Sam Nzima Foundation ; **97 bg** MAGNUM Photos/Mikhael Subotzky ; **99** Statista/Felix Richter ; **100, 110 hg, 8** REUTERS/Chris Waitte ; **101** © Ministère de la Justice Canada ; **102 h, 110 hd** ADOBE STOCK/Salman ; **102 b, 110 bd** Soizic Le Gouguec (création)/ © Mapsofworld (source) ; **103 h** © The Globe and Mail DR ; **b** Air Canada ; **105 h** CBC News DR ; **m** Global News DR ; **b** SHUTTERSTOCK/Susan G. Enberg ; **107** AFP/Chris Roussakis ; **109** Government of Canada DR ; **111 g** © Naomi Harris ; **hd** © 2016 Cover from Wenjack by Joseph Boyden, published by Hamish Hamilton, reprinted by permission of The Random House Group Limited ; **bd** Soizic Le Gouguec (création)/Statistics Canada (source) ; **112** © CARTOON STOCK LTD/David Donar ; **113** © Cambridge University Press ; **114 h** © 2018 Cover from The Prodigal Tongue by Lynne Murphy, published by Penguin USA, reprinted by permission of The Random House Group Limited ; **b** © FoneArena ; **115** © Statista ; **117 hg** © Ryan Lash ; **d** South China Morning Post Publishers Ltd/Alberto Lucas Lopez ; **bg** © 2009 Cover from Mother Tongue by Bill Bryson, published by Hamish Hamilton, reprinted by permission of The Random House Group Limited ; **118** © For Freedoms (Hank Willis Thomas and Emily Shur, in collaboration with Eric Gottesman and Wyatt Gallery of For Freedoms), 2018 ; **119** ADOBE STOCK/Eyetronic ; **120 g, 128 hd** AURIMAGES/BBQ_DFY/Dreamsworks Pictures ; **120 d** AURIMAGES/BBQ_DFY/Dreamsworks Pictures ; **121 g, 128 bd** BRIDGEMAN IMAGES/Everett ; **121 d** The Heritage Foundation DR ; **122 h** Tom Cole DR ; **bg** Java Films ; **bd** CNBC ; **123, 128 bg** AFP/Getty Images North America/Zach Gibson ; **124 g** © Courtesy of Lucie Hutchins ; **d** © Co Nguyen ; **125, 128 hg, 8** ADOBE STOCK/Rawpixel.com ; **127** © IES/NCES ; **129 hg** © MARGULIES Jimmy ; **hd** © Aziloth Books/Cathedral Classics ; **bg** Robert Reich/Lionsgate DR ; **bd** © Center Survey ; **130, 8** © Equality Labs ; **131 b** © Images from Jithinlal NR's solo show Another life is possible as part of Artists for Artists Grant 2018 at Khoj International Artists' Association, New Delhi ; **131 h** © Priyanca Ambalvi ; **132 h** TRT World/DR ; **b** PHOTO12.COM/Alamy/Roger Parkes ; **133** © https://cjp.org.in/; **135 h** © Courtesy of Rajyashri Goody ; **m** © 2019 Cover from Caste Matters by Suraj Yengde, published by India Viking, reprinted by permission of The Random House Group Limited ; **b** Rajesh Rajamani DR ; **136, 146 bd** CHRISTOPHE L COLLECTION/© Netflix ; **137 h** ABC DR ; **b,143** AFP/Noah Berger ; **138** The Legal Aid Society DR ; **139** HEMIS/Alamy/Jim West ; **140 h** AJ+/DR ; **b** BBC ; **141** @JLovallo on Instagram ; **142, 146 hg, 9** AFP/Getty Images North America/Chip Somodevilla ; **145** © Native American Rights Fund ; **147 g** AURIMAGES/Zumpapress.com/Entertainment Pictures/Focus Feature ; **d** © ACLUFL ; **148** © New Zealand Herald/Babiche Martens ; **149** © DDB New Zealand and the YWCA Auckland ; **150, 151 h** © The National Council of Women of New Zealand, Te Kaunihera Wahine o Aotearoa/White Ribbon ; **151 b** AFP/Getty Images North America/John Moore/UNTV ; **153 hd, 9** PRESSE-SPORTS/INPHO/Billy Stickland ; **153 bg** © GirlBoss NZ and Alexia Hilbertidou ; **153 hg** © DDB New Zealand and the YWCA Auckland ; **154** © TELEGRAPH MEDIA GROUP LIMITED 2021/Bob ; **155, 164 bg** AFP/Sophie Ramis, Gillian Handyside, Robin Millard ; **156** © MAARTEN WOLTERINK ; **157, 164 hg** PHOTO12.COM/Alamy/DMC Photography ; **158** Faber & Faber DR ; **159, 164 bd** AFP/Getty Images/Charles Mc Quillan ; **160, 9** AFP/Paul Faith ; **161** HEMIS/Alamy Live News/Kevin J. Frost ; **163** AFP/NurPhoto/Alberto Pezzali ; **165 g** © John Byrne ; **165 d** © Rita Duffy ; **166** University of Arizona Press ; **167 h** GETTY IMAGES/Los Angeles Times/Genaro Molina/; **167 b** GETTY IMAGES/Los Angeles Times/Irfan Khan ; **168** Soizic Le Gouguec (création)/INEGI/CDRU (source) ; **169 h** © Photo courtesy of The Desert Review ; **169 b, 9** REUTERS/Sandy Huffaker ; **171 h** Penguin Random House LLC ; **m** © Rael San Fratello ; **b** City Slang/Universal ; **172 h, 182 hg** © gp.org/Xavier_Ascanio/Istock ; **172 b, 179, 10** REA/The New York Times-REDUX/Pete Marovich ; **173** © Pew Research Center ; **174, 182 hd** Face the Facts USA ; **175** © Chappatte, The New York Times www.chappatte.com ; **176 h** REUTERS/Mike Theiler ; **b** California Resources Corporation ; **177, 182 bg** © NYC Mayor's Office of Sustainability ; **178, 182 bd** Rob Greenfield ; **181** © CAGLE CARTOONS, INC/John Cole ; **183 g** AURIMAGES/Courtesy Everett Collection/HBO ; **hd** League of Conservation Voters (LCV) ; **184** © Climate Council (2020) Summer of Crisis. Lesley Hughes, Will Steffen, Greg Mullins, Annika Dean, Ella Weisbrot and Martin Rice. Accessed at https://www.climatecouncil.org.au/resources/summer-of-crisis/; **185 h** © 2020 WWF, https://www.wwf.org.au ; **b** © Copyright Guardian News & Media Ltd 2020 **186** © Scott Marsh ; **187** © Paul Dorin ; **189 h** 350.org Ltd ; **d** ; **bg** © Paul Dorin ; **190 g** HEMIS/Andrea Pistolesi ; **190 bd** HEMIS/Alamy/Graham Hardy ; **190 hd** ADOBE STOCK/SakhanPhotography ; **191, 200 hg** GAMMA RAPHO/Camerapress/Reg Wilkins ; **192 h, 193 h, 194 h, 195 h,** ADOBE STOCK/Okili77 ; **192 b, 200 hd, 10** HEMIS/Jon Arnold Images ; **193 d** © REACH PUBLISHING SERVICE LIMITED/Mirror Pix ; **193 b** SHUTTERSTOCK/Graeme Lamb ; **194, 200 bd** © Roma Publications; **195, 200 bg** HEMIS/Alamy/Iain Masterton ; **197 h** HEMIS/Alamy/Joe Dunckley ; **197 b** ISTOCK/George-Standen ; **199** SHUTTERSTOCK/Lachlan1 ; **201 hd** © John Kippin ; **g** © Neale Smith ; **bd** © AK Nawaz ; **202 h** © NASA/NASA Earth Observatory/Jesse Allen ; **202 b** ADOBE STOCK/Pyty ; **203 h** ADOBE STOCK/Eunikas ; **203 b, 10** HEMIS/John Warburton Lee ; **204 h** PHOTONONSTOP/DPA/Li Baishun ; **b** DW ; **205** © Kiroko urban farmers ; **207 h** © 2021 OTIENO Brian ; **207 b** © Shane Feyers ; **208, 218 hg** copyright @ Christopher Weyant/Boston Globe ; **209** Statista/Martin Armstrong **; 210 h, 218 hd** AURIMAGES/courtesy Everett Collection/EuropaCorp USA/Frank Masi ; **b** CTV News/DR ; **211** GETTY IMAGES/Photothek/Thomas Trutschel ; **212, 215, 218 bg, 11** © David Parkins/The Economist ; **213** © CBInsights/DR ; **216** ADOBE STOCK/Yuval Helfman ; **219 hg** © 2020 Extract from Break'em Up by Zephyr Teachout, published by Macmillan, reproduced with permission of the Licensor through PLSClear. ; **hd** CHRISTOPHE L COLLECTION © Exposure labs/Netflix ; **bg** © 2019 Cover from The Warehouse by Rob Hart, published by Ballantine Books, reprinted by permission of The Random House Group Limited ; **220** © Graphic News Ltd ; **221** © Casemate Publishers – Casemate has granted permission for the use of the cover image of *Between Five Eyes* in this publication. The inclusion of this image does not indicate Casemate's approval of, or contribution to, any other content in this book. ; **222 h** © 2013 Dan Wasserman All rights reserved. Distributed by TRIBUNE CONTENT AGENCY LONDON ; **b** GETTY IMAGES/Bloomberg/Pete Marovich ; **223** ADOBE STOCK/Spainter_vfx ; **225 hd, 11** © Toby Morris ; **225 bd** AURIMAGES/Courtesy Everett Collection/Open Road Films ; **226** © Used under licence from THE FINANCIAL TIMES Limited. All Rights Reserved ; **227** © Pew Research Center ; **228** © CARLOS LATUFF ; **229 h** Soizic Le Gouguec (création)/United States Census Bureau (source) ; **md** © Mass Communication Specialist 3rd Class Nicholas V. Huynh ; **b** ADOBE STOCK/Gagarych ; **230 © Wired/Conde Nast** ; **231 h** Wall Street Journal/DR ; **d** © sais-cari.org ; **232, 237 b** CHRISTOPHE L COLLECTION/© The Nevernight Connection @ Mis en ligne par le FBI ; **233, 236 hg, 11** ADOBE STOCK/Anson_adobe ; **235** © CARTOON MOVEMENT/Arcadio Esquivel ; **237 h** © 2013 Dana Summers All rights reserved. Distributed by TRIBUNE CONTENT AGENCY LONDON ; **bd** South China Morning Post Publishers Ltd ; **238** © Mr. Ambarish Kumar Verma, Founder and President, Market Research Reports, Inc.https://www.marketresearchreports.com/navadhi/india-pharmaceuticals-industry-analysis-and-trends-2023 ; **239, 11** © Médecins Sans Frontières/Hands off ; **240 h** SHUTTERSTOCK/Sm.Shakhov ; **b** Soizic Le Gouguec (création)/CII/KPMG (source) **242** ISTOCK/SDI Productions ; **243 h** Médecins Sans Frontières ; **b** AURIMAGES/Courtesy Everett Collection/International Film Circuit ; **244, 254 hd** © www.LouisianaTravel.com ; **245 h** © Andrew LaMar Hopkins ; **b** Facts Base ; **246 h** © Zeqirja Rexhepi ; **b** HEMIS/Alamy/Gunter Marx ; **247 h, 254 hg** Linopa Films DR ; **247 b** © Augusta Sagnelli ; **248 h** REA/Redux/William Widmer ; **b** New Orleans Saints ; **249 h** PBS Newshour ; **249 b, 251** The Advocate/Scott Threlkeld ; **250 g** Mt. Auburn Associates/State of Louisiana ; **d** NOMTN/DR ; **253** REA/Redux/The New-York Times/William Widmer ; **255 h** PHOTO12.COM/Alamy/AF Archive/HBO ; **255 m** © Shakor ; **b** Herbert S. Stone & Co. DR ; **256** © Courtesy Gisborne Herald ; **257 g** BRIDGEMAN IMAGES/Gilbee Bequest ; **257 d, 12** © Courtesy of the artist and Roslyn Oxley9 Gallery, Sydney/

Daniel Boyd ; **258 h** © ART GALLERY OF SOUTH AUSTRALIA, Adelaïde © Vincent Namatjira/© Adagp, Paris 2021 ; **hd** ABC Australia ; **b** © 2019 Mat Tait, Auckland War Memorial Museum ; **259** HEMIS/Gil Giuglio ; **261 h** © Michel Tuffery/DR ; **mg** © Encyclopaedia Britannica ; **b** © PENGUIN RANDOM HOUSE LLC ; **262 h** BRIDGEMAN IMAGES/Christie's Images ; **262 b** PHOTO12.COM/Alamy/IanDagnall Computing ; **263 h** AURIMAGES/Courtesy Everett Collection/Columbia ; **263 b** BRIDGEMAN IMAGES/MEPL ; **264 h** BRIDGEMAN IMAGES/Liss Fine Art ; **264 b** BRIDGEMAN IMAGES/MEPL ; **265 h** BRIDGEMAN IMAGES/UIG ; **265 b** CHRISTOPHE L COLLECTION/BBC ; **266 h** Cadbury/Mondelezinternational.com/DR ; **266 b** GETTY IMAGES/Hulton Archive/Fox Photos/Meager ; **267 h** GETTY IMAGES/ Michael Ochs Archives ; **267 b** GETTY IMAGES/Popperfoto/Rolls Press ; **268 h** PHOTO12.COM/Ann Ronan Picture Library ; **268 b** GETTY IMAGES/Popperfoto/ Rolls Press ; **269 h** ABACA PRESS/PA Images/PA Archives ; **269 b** AURIMAGES/ Everett Collection ; **270 h** AFP/Getty Images Europe/Leon Neal ; **270 b** REUTERS/ Andy Clark ; **271 h** AFP/Andy Buchanan ; **271 b** REUTERS/Toby Melville ; **272 h** BRIDGEMAN IMAGES ; **272 b** LIBRARY OF CONGRESS, Prints and Photographs Division, Alfred Bendiner Memorial Collection, LC-DIG-ppmsca-08978 ; **273 h** PHOTO12.COM/Archives Snark ; **273 b** AKG-Images/LOC/Science Source ; **274 h** BRIDGEMAN IMAGES/Lebrecht ; **274 b** AURIMAGES/Everett Collection/MGM/ Selznick ; **275 g** BRIDGEMAN IMAGES/Prismatic Pictures ; **275 d** AURIMAGES/ The Advertising Archive ; **276 b** AURIMAGES/The Kobal Collection/Columbia/ Hawk Films Prod ; **276 h** GETTY IMAGES/Time Life Pictures/National Archives ; **277 h** AKG-Images/TT News Agency/TT Nyhetsbyran ; **277 b** GETTY IMAGES/ Redferns/Elliot Landy ; **278 h** DR/Microsoft ; **278 b** AURIMAGES/Everett Collection/ Revolution Studios/Columbia ; **279 h** GETTY IMAGES/Michael Ochs Archives ; **279 b** ISTOCK/WildLivingArts ; **280 h** SIPA PRESS/Rex features ; **280 b** REUTERS/ Jonathan Ernst ; **281 b** SHUTTERSTOCK/Koshiro K ; **281 h** REA/HH/Pool/Jerry Lampen ; **282 h** AURIMAGES/Mary Evans ; **282 b** HEMIS/Alamy/Darren McLoughlin ; **283 h** AKG-Images/Album/Prisma ; **283 b** Matthew Thompson ; **284 h** Bibliothèque et Archives Canada/Fonds du ministère des Affaires indiennes et du Nord canadien/e011080274 ; **284 b** HEMIS/Alamy/P. Spiro ; **285 h** ANDIA/ ImageBROKER/Moritz Wolf ; **285 b** HEMIS/Philippe Renault ; **286 b** AURIMAGESThe Kobal Collection/New Line Cinema ; **286 h** PHOTO12.COM/Alamy/Richard Milnes ; **287 h** Chris Phutully from Australia CC BY2.0 ; **287 b** AFP/Greg Wood ; **288 h** GETTY IMAGES/De Agostini ; **288 b** AFP/Karim Jaafar ; **289 b** ADOBE STOCK/ Napa74 ; **290 h** PHOTO12.COM/Alamy/Art Collection 3 ; **290 b** AFP/Alexander Joe ; **291 h** AFP ; **291 b** GETTY IMAGES/Photothek/Thomas Imo ; **292 h** AKG-Images/GandhiServe India ; **292 b** GETTY IMAGES/The LIFE Picture Collection/ Margaret Bourke-White ; **293 hg** AKG-Images/GandhiServe India ; **293 hd** AFP/ Odd Andersen ; **293 b** AURIMAGES/Everett Collection/Great India Films ; **294 h** Soizic Le Gouguec (création) ; **b** AFP/Getty Images North America/Spencer Platt ; **295 h** GETTY IMAGES/CBS Photo Archive ; **295 b** AFP/Getty Images North America/Drew Angerer

## Crédits textes

**17** *sales-academy.net* ; **18** India Today DR ; **19** ©Bizcommunity ; **20 h** The Irish Times DR ; **b** The Blockchain University DR ; **21** *bestcollegesonline.org* ; **27** © 2021 The Slate Group LLC. All rights reserved. ; **28** Reagle, Joseph, and Jackie Koerner, eds., *Wikipedia @ 20, excerpt, © 2020 Massachusetts Institute of Technology, by permission of The MIT Press.* ; **29** © Wired/Conde Nast ; **33** © Dezeen Limited 2006-2021 ; **35** © Newsweek DR ; **36** © *2019 Extract from Machines Like Me* by Ian McEwan, published by Jonathan Cape, reprinted by permission of The Random House Group Limited ; **37** © 2016 World Economic Forum ; **42** © Marie Chatel, Digital Art Weekly, on *medium.com* ; **43** © Essilor International DR ; **44** *alphr.com* DR ; **45 g** *bregman.dartmouth.edu* ; **d** Ivy T. Schweitzer ; **48** Government Office for Science (UK) DR ; **49** Computer World DR ; **51** © *2020 CNN, article from* https://edition.cnn.com/2020/08/24/sport/ nfl-roger-goodell-colin-kaepernick-spt-intl/index.html ; **52** © Basic Books/ Hachette DR ; **53** © 2020 VICE MEDIA LLC ; **54** © *2021* Verizon Media. All rights reserved ; **55** © Barack Obama, on *medium.com* ; **61** © 2019 POLITICO LLC ; **62** © Copyright Guardian News & Media Ltd 2019 ; **63** © Josh Westerling, *British Future*, London 2019 ; **66** © *All Rights Reserved Poynter Institute 2021* ; **67 h** This article is republished from The Conversation under a Creative Commons license. Original article: "The origins of the all-powerful news anchor" by Mike Conway on February 2015 ; **b** Lauren Sointu/Daily Collegian DR ; **68** HarperCollins DR ; **69** Social Media HQ DR ; **70** © Copyright Guardian News & Media Ltd 2020 ; **71** HBO DR ; **77** SBS News DR ; **78 h** The Sun/©News Licensing ; **b** The Times/ ©News Licensing ; **79 h** Press Gazette/ New Statesman Media Group ; **b** © Copyright Guardian News & Media Ltd 2020 ; **83** © Copyright Guardian News & Media Ltd 2016 ; **84** © *2021 Prospect Publishing Limited* ; **85** Cinemablend DR ; **86** ©2016 ITHAKA. All Rights Reserved. ; **87** © 2019 National Public Radio, Inc. Excerpts from news report titled "Imagining A Dismal Future, 'Years And Years' Says Plenty About The Present" by John Powers were originally published on npr.org on June 24, 2019, and were used with the permission of NPR. Any unauthorized duplication is strictly prohibited. ; **92** © © MILLER Johnny/Unequal Scenes ; **93** © *2021 - 1854 MEDIA LTD* ; **94** © Copyright Guardian News & Media Ltd 2018 ; **98, 99 h** Cheddar.com DR ; **99 b** CBS News DR ; **102** © *2021* Canora Courier, Glacier Media Group. All Rights Reserved ; **103** The Globe and Mail DR ; **104** © Copyright Guardian News & Media Ltd 2020 ; **106** © Dace McKay ; **108** © Copyright Guardian News & Media Ltd 2017 ; **109 h** CBC News DR ; **b** © Justin Trudeau, 2017 ; **113** © Copyright Guardian News & Media Ltd 2018 ; **114** © 2018 National Public Radio, Inc. Excerpts from news report titled "Opinion: U.S. And U.K. Remain United, Not Divided, By Their Common Language" by Geoff Nunberg were originally published on npr.org on July 18, 2018, and were used with the permission of NPR. Any unauthorized duplication is strictly prohibited. ; **115** © *2021 ASIA TIMES* ; **119 h** Rob Mitchel/Murfreesboro Voice ; **121** DK DR ; **122** Tom Cole DR ; **123** The Trace DR ; **124** © WBUR 2020 ; **126** The excerpt comes from a news article published by the Harvard Graduate School of Education (HGSE) online on July 13, 1995 and refers to research that was eventually published in several articles by Bruce Fuller. Eventually, the research was published in a book, Who Chooses? Who Loses? Culture, Institutions, and the Unequal Effects of School Choice (Sociology of Education Series Vol 2), Bruce Fuller, Richard F. Elmore, Gary Orfield, published 1996 by Teachers College Press (ISBN-13: 978-0-8077-3537-4, ISBN: 0-8077-3537-X). ; **127** © *2020* The Detroit News, a Digital First Media Newspaper ; **130** Faber & Faber DR **; 131** © *2019* Feminism in India, https://feminisminindia.com/2019/04/02/elite-dalit-woman-experience/ ; **132** © 2021 The Indian Express Ltd. All Rights Reserved ; **133** The Hindu DR ; **136** © Ebert Digital LLC ; **137** © 2019 National Public Radio, Inc. Excerpts from news report titled "In Pitch For President, Sen. Kamala Harris Focuses On Criminal Justice, Inequality" by Jessica Taylor were originally published on npr.org on March 14, 2019, and were used with the permission of NPR. Any unauthorized duplication is strictly prohibited. ; **138** The Grizzly Express DR ; **139** NBC News DR ; **140** © Brennan Center for Justice ; **141** © Copyright Guardian News & Media Ltd 2020 ; **142** Supreme Court ; **144** ABC News DR ; **145** © 2020 Smithsonian Magazine ; **148** Otago Daily Times DR ; **149** This article is republished from The Conversation under a Creative Commons license. Original article: "The first country where women won the right to vote" by Katie Pickles on September 2018 ; **150** © 2020 Stuff Limited ; **155** USA TODAY NETWORK/Evan Collis ; **156** © Copyright Guardian News & Media Ltd 2019 ; **157** ABC News DR ; **158** Faber & Faber DR ; **159** Intereconomics DR ; **160** The Irish Times DR **; 162** © Copyright Guardian News & Media Ltd 2020 ; **163** © *2021* MarketWatch, Inc. All rights reserved. ; **166** © University of Arizona Press ; **167, 168** The Desert Sun DR ; **169** This article is republished from The Conversation under a Creative Commons license. Original article: "Americans and Mexicans living at the border are more connected than divided" by Michael Dear on March 2017 ; **173** This article is republished from The Conversation under a Creative Commons license. Original article: "Why is climate skepticism so successful in the United States?" by Jérôme Viala-Gaudefroy on January 2020 ; **174** © *2016* Scientific American, a division of Springer Nature America, Inc. ; **175 h** © 2019 – Fox News DR ; **b** © The New Republic ; **177** © NYC Mayor's Office of Sustainability ; **178** © 2019 Business Insider Inc. ; **180** © *2015* National Geographic Society ; **181** © 2020 POLITICO LLC ; **185 h** © 2020 WWF, https://www.wwf.org.au ; **b** © Copyright Guardian News & Media Ltd 2020 ; **186** © Nick O'Malley, in The Sydney Morning Herald ; **187** The Independent DR ; **191** From BORN UNDER PUNCHES by Martyn Waites. Copyright © 2004 by Simon & Schuster. Reprinted with the permission of Simon & Schuster Books. All rights reserved. ; **192** © New Statesman Media Group Ltd. ; **193** © Copyright Guardian News & Media Ltd 2020 ; **194** © Roma Publications ; **195** This article is republished from The Conversation under a Creative Commons license. Original article: "A beacon of urban renewal: how post-indsutrial Dundee transformed itself" by Paul Harris on October 2017 ; **198** Courtesy of Joe Blakey ; **199** © Huckmag ; **203** © 2016 by Kennedy Odede and Jessica Posner. Used by permission of HarperCollins Publishers. ; **204** © 2019 The Nation Company LLC ; **205** © 2018 NYC Food Policy ; **209** © Copyright Guardian News & Media Ltd 2018 ; **210** © 2013 Extract from The Circle by Dave Eggers, published by Knopf, reprinted by permission of The Random House Group Limited ; **211** © 2020 CNET, A Red Venture Company. All rights reserved. ; **212** © The Financial Times – Source : Marietje Schaake, 2020: "Big Tech companies want to act like governments", The Financial Times. Used under licence from The Financial Times. All rights reserved. ; **213** DSX Hub DR ; **214** © 2020 Columbia Journalism Review ; **216** © Copyright Guardian News & Media Ltd 2019 ; **217 h** Fast Company & Inc © 2019 Mansueto Ventures, LLC ; **b** © 2019 Extract from The Warehouse by Rob Hart, published by Ballantine Books, reprinted by permission of The Random House Group Limited ; **221 h** © 2020 UK Defence Journal, all rights reserved. ; **b** Casemate Publishers DR ; **222** © 2013 A&E Television Networks, LLC. All Rights Reserved. ; **223** CIPS-CEPI/Helen Baxendale ; **227** ABC DR ; **228** Used under licence from THE FINANCIAL TIMES Limited. All Rights Reserved **; 229** ©2020 Bloomberg L.P. All Rights Reserved/the YGS Group ; **230** © Wired/Conde Nast ; **231** © *2020* Independent Online and affiliated companies. All rights reserved ; **232 h** ©*2020* Bloomberg L.P. All Rights Reserved/the YGS Group ; **b** © *2020 Global Times All Right Reserved* ; **234** ©*2020* Capitol Hill Publishing Corp., a subsidiary of News Communications, Inc. ; **235** Wall Street Journal/DR ; **239** © Médecins Sans Frontières/The Better India ; **240** CNBC ; **241** Observer Research Foundation DR ; **244** Louisiana Travel ; **245** © © *2017 NOLA.com* ; **246** © 2015 The Advocate ; **248** US News DR ; **249** © *Natural* Resources Defense Council 2020 ; **250** Mt. Auburn Associates/State of Louisiana **; 252** © Sean Cockerham ; **253** © 2015 Lila MacLellan, "A new way to attract tourists: fake accents and dying languages", published by Quartz, reproduced with permission of the Licensor through Copyright Clearance Center ; **257** This article is republished from The Conversation under a Creative Commons license. Original article: "Make no mistake: Cook's voyages were part of a military mission to conquer and expand" by Stephen Gapps on April 2020 ; **259** © Copyright Guardian News & Media Ltd 2019.

---

*L'éditeur et les auteurs remercient Catherine Baudry, professeure d'anglais à Saint-Denis (93) pour sa relecture pédagogique.*

**Direction éditoriale :** Marie Lucas

**Édition :** Perrine Dutertre, Pauline Gaberel, Seonaid Cruickshank assistées de Soizic Le Gouguec

**Relecture :** Seonaid Cruickshank

**Iconographie :** Geoffroy Mauzé

**Conception de la couverture :** Massimo Miola, Elise Launay

**Conception de la maquette :** Massimo Miola, Elise Launay

**Cartographie :** AFDEC

**Mise en pages :** Anne-Danielle Naname, Laure Gros, Typo-Virgule (malle avant), Thomas Winock (pages Landmarks)

# The English-speaking world

Animation interactive

Dépôt légal : Avril 2021 - N° de projet : 10277046
Imprimé en Italie en Août 2021 par Rotolito S.p.A.